C. S. Lewis Sele

Clive Staples Lewis (1898–1963)
giants of the twentieth century and
tial writer of his day. He was a Fellow and Tutor in English literature at Oxford University until 1954 when he was unanimously elected to the Chair of Medieval and Renaissance English at Cambridge University, a position he held until his retirement. He wrote more than 30 books, allowing him to reach a vast audience, and his works continue to attract thousands of new readers every year. His most distinguished and popular accomplishments include *The Chronicles of Narnia*, *The Cosmic Trilogy*, *The Four Loves*, *The Screwtape Letters* and *Mere Christianity*.

Also available:

C. S. Lewis Signature Classics:

The Four Loves
The Great Divorce
Mere Christianity
Miracles
The Problem of Pain
The Screwtape Letters
Surprised by Joy

C. S. Lewis Collections:

Essay Collection – Literature, Philosophy and Short Stories
Essay Collection – Faith, Christianity and the Church
Collected Letters Volume I
C. S. Lewis: A Companion and Guide
edited by Walter Hooper

C.S. Lewis

SELECTED BOOKS

The Pilgrim's Regress
Prayer: Letters to Malcolm
Reflections on the Psalms
The Abolition of Man
Till We Have Faces

HarperCollins*Publishers*

HarperCollins*Publishers*
1 London Bridge Street
London SE1 9GF
www.harpercollins.co.uk

This edition first published 2002

The Pilgrim's Regress first published in Great Britain
by J.M. Dent 1933
Copyright © C. S. Lewis Pte Ltd 1933, 1943

Prayer: Letters to Malcolm first published in Great Britain
by Geoffrey Bles 1964
Copyright © C. S. Lewis Pte Ltd 1963, 1964

Reflections on the Psalms first published in Great Britain
by Geoffrey Bles 1958
Copyright © C. S. Lewis Pte Ltd 1958

The Abolition of Man first published in Great Britain
by Oxford University Press 1943
Copyright © C. S. Lewis Pte Ltd 1943, 1946, 1978

Till We Have Faces first published in Great Britain
by Geoffrey Bles 1956
Copyright © C. S. Lewis Pte Ltd 1956

A catalogue record for this book is
available from the British Library

ISBN 978-0-00-713744-2

MIX
Paper from
responsible sources
FSC C007454

CONDITIONS OF SALE
This book is sold subject to the condition that it shall not,
by way of trade or otherwise, be lent, re-sold, hired out or
otherwise circulated without the publisher's prior consent
in any form of binding or cover other than that in which it
is published and without a similar condition including this
condition being imposed on the subsequent purchaser.

All rights reserved. No part of this publication may be
reproduced, stored in a retrieval system, or transmitted,
in any form or by any means, electronic, mechanical,
photocopying, recording or otherwise, without the prior
permission of the publishers.

Printed by CPI Group (UK) Ltd, Croydon CR0 4YY

Contents

THE PILGRIM'S REGRESS	1
PRAYER: LETTERS TO MALCOLM	223
REFLECTIONS ON THE PSALMS	305
THE ABOLITION OF MAN	395
TILL WE HAVE FACES	443

THE PILGRIM'S REGRESS

An allegorical apology
for Christianity,
Reason and Romanticism

*As cold waters to a thirsty soul,
so is good news from a far country.*
PROVERBS

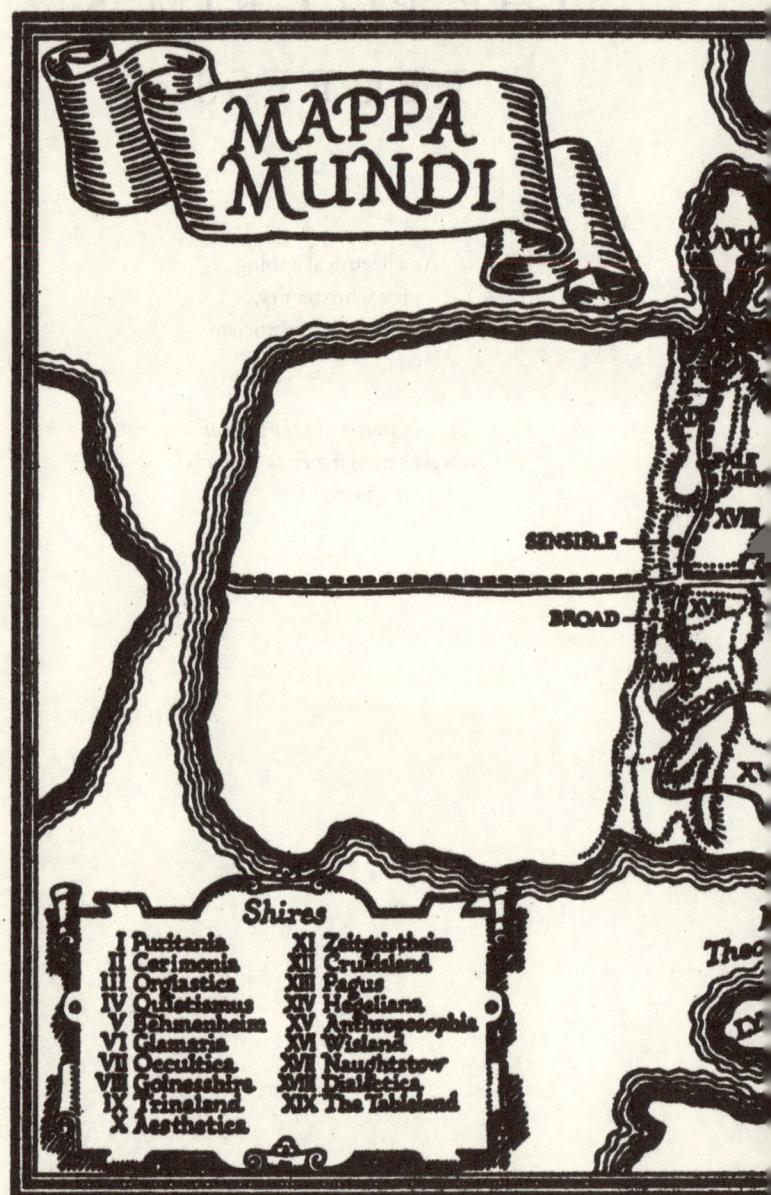

To Arthur Greeves

PREFACE TO THE THIRD EDITION

On re-reading this book ten years after I wrote it, I find its chief faults to be those two which I myself least easily forgive in the books of other men: needless obscurity, and an uncharitable temper.

There were two causes, I now realise, for the obscurity. On the intellectual side my own progress had been from 'popular realism' to Philosophical Idealism; from Idealism to Pantheism; from Pantheism to Theism; and from Theism to Christianity. I still think this a very natural road, but I now know that it is a road very rarely trodden. In the early thirties I did not know this. If I had had any notion of my own isolation, I should either have kept silent about my journey or else endeavoured to describe it with more consideration for the reader's difficulties. As things were, I committed the same sort of blunder as one who should narrate his travels through the Gobi Desert on the assumption that this route was as familiar to the British public as the line from Euston to Crewe. And this original blunder was soon aggravated by a profound change in the philosophical thought of our age. Idealism itself went out of fashion. The dynasty of Green, Bradley, and Bosanquet fell, and the world inhabited by philosophical students of my own generation became as alien to our successors as if not years but centuries had intervened.

The second cause of obscurity was the (unintentionally) 'private' meaning I then gave to the word 'Romanticism'. I would not now use this word to describe the experience which is central in this book. I would not, indeed, use it to describe anything, for I now believe it to be a word of such varying senses that it has become useless and should be banished from our vocabulary. Even if we exclude the vulgar sense in which a 'romance' means simply 'a love affair' (Peer and Film Star Romance) I think we can distinguish at least seven kinds of things which are called 'romantic'.

1. Stories about dangerous adventure – particularly, dangerous adventure in the past or in remote places – are 'romantic'. In this sense Dumas is a typically 'romantic' author, and stories about sailing ships, the Foreign Legion, and the rebellion of 1745, are usually 'romantic'.

2. The marvellous is 'romantic', provided it does not make part of the believed religion. Thus magicians, ghosts, fairies, witches, dragons, nymphs, and dwarfs are 'romantic'; angels, less so. Greek gods are 'romantic' in Mr James Stephens or Mr Maurice Hewlett; not so in Homer and Sophocles. In this sense Malory, Boiardo, Ariosto, Spenser, Tasso, Mrs Radcliffe, Shelley, Coleridge, William Morris, and Mr E. R. Eddison are 'romantic' authors.

3. The art dealing with 'Titanic' characters, emotions strained beyond the common pitch, and high-flown sentiments or codes of honour is 'romantic'. (I welcome the growing use of the word 'Romanesque' to describe this type.) In this sense Rostand and Sidney are 'romantic', and so (though unsuccessfully) are Dryden's Heroic Dramas, and there is a good deal of 'romanticism' in Corneille. I take it that Michelangelo is, in this sense, a 'romantic' artist.

4. 'Romanticism' can also mean the indulgence in abnormal, and finally in anti-natural, moods. The macabre is 'romantic', and so is an interest in torture, and a love of death. This, if I understand them, is what M. Mario Praz and M. D. de Rougemont would mean by the word. In this sense *Tristan* is Wagner's most 'romantic' opera; Poe, Baudelaire, and Flaubert, are 'romantic' authors; Surrealism is 'romantic'.

5. Egoism and Subjectivism are 'romantic'. In this sense the typically 'romantic' books are *Werther* and Rousseau's *Confessions*, and the works of Byron and Proust.

6. Every revolt against existing civilisation and conventions whether it looks forward to revolution, or backward to the 'primitive' is called 'romantic' by some people. Thus pseudo-Ossian, Epstein, D. H. Lawrence, Walt Whitman, and Wagner are 'romantic'.

7. Sensibility to natural objects, when solemn and enthusiastic, is 'romantic'. In this sense *The Prelude* is the most 'romantic' poem in the world: and there is much 'romanticism' in Keats, Shelley, de Vigny, de Musset, and Goethe.

It will be seen, of course, that many writers are 'romantic' on more than one account. Thus Morris comes in my first class as well as my second, Mr Eddison in my second as well as my third, Rousseau in my sixth as well as my fifth, Shelley in my sixth and fifth, and so on. This may suggest some common root, whether historical or psychological, for all seven: but the real qualitative difference between them is shown by the fact that a liking for any one does not imply liking for the others. Though people who are 'romantic' in different senses may turn to the same books, they turn to them for different reasons and one half of William Morris's readers do not know how the other half live. It makes all the difference in the world whether you like Shelley because he provides a mythology or because he promises a revolution. Thus I myself always loved the second kind of

Romanticism and detested the fourth and fifth kinds; I liked the first very little and the third only after I was grown-up – as an acquired taste.

But what I meant by 'Romanticism' when I wrote *The Pilgrim's Regress* – and what I would still be taken to mean on the title page of this book – was not exactly any one of these seven things. What I meant was a particular recurrent experience which dominated my childhood and adolescence and which I hastily called 'Romantic' because inanimate nature and marvellous literature were among the things that evoked it. I still believe that the experience is common, commonly misunderstood, and of immense importance: but I know now that in other minds it arises under other *stimuli* and is entangled with other irrelevancies and that to bring it into the forefront of consciousness is not so easy as I once supposed. I will now try to describe it sufficiently to make the following pages intelligible.

The experience is one of intense longing. It is distinguished from other longings by two things. In the first place, though the sense of want is acute and even painful, yet the mere wanting is felt to be somehow a delight. Other desires are felt as pleasures only if satisfaction is expected in the near future: hunger is pleasant only while we know (or believe) that we are soon going to eat. But this desire, even when there is no hope of possible satisfaction, continues to be prized, and even to be preferred to anything else in the world, by those who have once felt it. This hunger is better than any other fullness; this poverty better than all other wealth. And thus it comes about, that if the desire is long absent, it may itself be desired, and that new desiring becomes a new instance of the original desire, though the subject may not at once recognise the fact and thus cries out for his lost youth of soul at the very moment in which he is being rejuvenated. This sounds complicated, but it is simple when we live it. 'Oh to feel as I did then!' we cry; not noticing that even while we say the words the very feeling whose loss we lament is rising again in all its old bitter-sweetness. For this sweet Desire cuts across our ordinary distinctions between wanting and having. To have it is, by definition, a want: to want it, we find, is to have it.

In the second place, there is a peculiar mystery about the *object* of this Desire. Inexperienced people (and inattention leaves some inexperienced all their lives) suppose, when they feel it, that they know what they are desiring. Thus if it comes to a child while he is looking at a far off hillside he at once thinks 'if only I were there'; if it comes when he is remembering some event in the past, he thinks 'if only I could go back to those days'. If it comes (a little later) while he is reading a 'romantic' tale or poem of 'perilous seas and faerie lands forlorn', he thinks he is wishing that such places really existed and that he could reach them. If it comes (later still) in a context with erotic suggestions he believes he is desiring the perfect beloved. If he falls upon literature (like Maeterlinck or the early Yeats) which treats of spirits and the like with some show of serious belief, he may think that he is hankering for real magic and occultism. When it darts out upon him from his studies in history or science, he may confuse it with the intellectual craving for knowledge.

But every one of these impressions is wrong. The sole merit I claim for this book is that it is written by one who has proved them all to be wrong. There is no room for vanity in the claim: I know them to be wrong not by intelligence but by experience, such experience as would not have come my way if my youth had been wiser, more virtuous, and less self-centred than it was. For I have myself been deluded by every one of these false answers in turn, and have contemplated each of them earnestly enough to discover the cheat. To have embraced so many false Florimels is no matter for boasting: it is fools, they say, who learn by experience. But since they do at last learn, let a fool bring his experience into the common stock that wiser men may profit by it.

Every one of these supposed *objects* for the Desire is inadequate to it. An easy experiment will show that by going to the far hillside you will get either nothing, or else a recurrence of the same desire which sent you thither. A rather more difficult, but still possible, study of your own memories, will prove that by returning to the past you could not find, as a possession, that ecstasy which some sudden reminder of the past now moves you to desire. Those remembered moments were either quite commonplace at the time (and owe all their enchantment to memory) or else were themselves moments of desiring. The same is true of the things described in the poets and marvellous romancers. The moment we endeavour to think out seriously what it would be like if they were actual, we discover this. When Sir Arthur Conan Doyle claimed to have photographed a fairy, I did not, in fact, believe it: but the mere making of the claim – the approach of the fairy to within even that hailing distance of actuality – revealed to me at once that if the claim had succeeded it would have chilled rather than satisfied the desire which fairy literature had hitherto aroused. Once grant your fairy, your enchanted forest, your satyr, faun, wood-nymph and well of immortality *real*, and amidst all the scientific, social and practical interest which the discovery would awake, the Sweet Desire would have disappeared, would have shifted its ground, like the cuckoo's voice or the rainbow's end, and be now calling us from beyond a *further* hill. With Magic in the darker sense (as it has been and is actually practised) we should fare even worse. How if one had gone that way – had actually called for something and it had come? What would one feel? Terror, pride, guilt, tingling excitement ... but what would all that have to do with our Sweet Desire? It is not at Black Mass or seance that the Blue Flower grows. As for the sexual answer, that I suppose to be the most obviously false Florimel of all. On whatever plane you take it, it is not what we were looking for. Lust can be gratified. Another personality can become to us 'our America, our New-found-land'. A happy marriage can be achieved. But what has any of the three, or any mixture of the three, to do with that unnameable something, desire for which pierces us like a rapier at the smell of a bonfire, the sound of wild ducks flying overhead, the title of *The Well at the World's End*, the opening lines of *Kubla Khan*, the morning cobwebs in late summer, or the noise of falling waves?

It appeared to me therefore that if a man diligently followed this desire, pursuing the false objects until their falsity appeared and then resolutely abandoning them, he must come out at last into the clear knowledge that the human soul was made to enjoy some object that is never fully given – nay, cannot even be imagined as given – in our present mode of subjective and spatio-temporal experience. This Desire was, in the soul, as the Siege Perilous in Arthur's castle – the chair in which only one could sit. And if nature makes nothing in vain, the One who can sit in this chair must exist. I knew only too well how easily the longing accepts false objects and through what dark ways the pursuit of them leads us: but I also saw that the Desire itself contains the corrective of all these errors. The only fatal error was to pretend that you had passed from desire to fruition, when, in reality, you had found either nothing, or desire itself, or the satisfaction of some different desire. The dialectic of Desire, faithfully followed, would retrieve all mistakes, head you off from all false paths, and force you not to propound, but to live through, a sort of ontological proof. This lived dialectic, and the merely argued dialectic of my philosophical progress, seemed to have converged on one goal; accordingly I tried to put them both into my allegory which thus became a defence of Romanticism (in my peculiar sense) as well as of Reason and Christianity.

After this explanation the reader will more easily understand (I do not ask him to condone) the bitterness of certain pages in this book. He will realise how the Post-War period must have looked to one who had followed such a road as mine. The different intellectual movements of that time were hostile to one another; but the one thing that seemed to unite them all was their common enmity to 'immortal longings'. The direct attack carried out on them from below by those who followed Freud or D. H. Lawrence, I think I could have borne with some temper; what put me out of patience was the scorn which claimed to be from above, and which was voiced by the American 'Humanists', the Neo-Scholastics, and some who wrote for *The Criterion*. These people seemed to me to be condemning what they did not understand. When they called Romanticism 'nostalgia' I, who had rejected long ago the illusion that the desired object was in the past, felt that they had not even crossed the *Pons Asinorum*. In the end I lost my temper.

If I were now writing a book I could bring the question between those thinkers and myself to a much finer point. One of them described Romanticism as 'spilled religion'. I accept the description. And I agree that he who has religion ought not to spill it. But does it follow that he who finds it spilled should avert his eyes? How if there is a man to whom those bright drops on the floor are the beginning of a trail which, duly followed, will lead him in the end to taste the cup itself? How if no other trail, humanly speaking, were possible? Seen in this light my ten-years-old quarrel both with the counter-Romantics on the one hand and with the sub-Romantics on the other (the apostles of instinct and even of gibberish) assumes, I trust, a certain permanent interest. Out of this double quarrel came the dominant image of my allegory – the barren, aching rocks of its 'North', the foetid swamps of its 'South', and between them the Road on which alone mankind can safely walk.

The things I have symbolised by North and South, which are to me equal and opposite evils, each continually strengthened and made plausible by its critique of the other, enter our experience on many different levels. In agriculture we have to fear both the barren soil and the soil which is irresistibly fertile. In the animal kingdom, the crustacean and the jellyfish represent two low solutions of the problem of existence. In our eating, the palate revolts both from excessive bitter and excessive sweet. In art, we find on the one hand, purists and doctrinaires, who would rather (like Scaliger) lose a hundred beauties than admit a single fault, and who cannot believe anything to be good if the unlearned spontaneously enjoy it: on the other hand, we find the uncritical and slovenly artists who will spoil the whole work rather than deny themselves any indulgence of sentiment or humour or sensationalism. Everyone can pick out among his own acquaintance the Northern and Southern types – the high noses, compressed lips, pale complexions, dryness and taciturnity of the one, the open mouths, the facile laughter and tears, the garrulity and (so to speak) general greasiness of the others. The Northerners are the men of rigid systems whether sceptical or dogmatic, Aristocrats, Stoics, Pharisees, Rigorists, signed and sealed members of highly organised 'Parties'. The Southerners are by their very nature less definable; boneless souls whose doors stand open day and night to almost every visitant, but always with readiest welcome for those, whether Maenad or Mystagogue, who offer some sort of intoxication. The delicious tang of the forbidden and the unknown draws them on with fatal attraction; the smudging of all frontiers, the relaxation of all resistances, dream, opium, darkness, death, and the return to the womb. Every feeling is justified by the mere fact that it is felt: for a Northerner, every feeling on the same ground is suspect. An arrogant and hasty selectiveness on some narrow *a priori* basis cuts him off from the sources of life. In Theology also there is a North and South. The one cries 'Drive out the bondmaid's son', and the other 'Quench not the smoking flax'. The one exaggerates the distinctness between Grace and Nature into a sheer opposition and by vilifying the higher levels of Nature (the real *praeparatio evangelica* inherent in certain immediately sub-Christian experiences) makes the way hard for those who are at the point of coming in. The other blurs the distinction altogether, flatters mere kindliness into thinking it is charity and vague optimisms or pantheisms into thinking that they are Faith, and makes the way out fatally easy and imperceptible for the budding apostate. The two extremes do not coincide with Romanism (to the North) and Protestantism (to the South). Barth might well have been placed among my Pale Men, and Erasmus might have found himself at home with Mr Broad.

I take our own age to be predominantly Northern – it is two great 'Northern' powers that are tearing each other to pieces on the Don while I write. But the matter is complicated, for the rigid and ruthless system of the Nazis has 'Southern' and swamp-like elements at its centre: and when our age is 'Southern' at all, it is excessively so. D. H. Lawrence and the Surrealists have perhaps reached a point further 'South' than humanity ever reached before. And this is what one would expect. Opposite evils, far from balancing, aggravate each other. 'The heresies that men leave are hated most'; widespread drunkenness is the father of Prohibition and Prohibition of widespread drunkenness. Nature, outraged by one extreme, avenges herself by flying to the other. One can even meet adult males who are not ashamed to attribute their own philosophy to 'Reaction' and do not think the philosophy thereby discredited.

With both the 'North' and the 'South' a man has, I take it, only one concern – to avoid them and hold the Main Road. We must not 'hearken to the over-wise or to the over-foolish giant'. We were made to be neither cerebral men nor visceral men, but Men. Not beasts nor angels but Men – things at once rational and animal.

The fact that, if I say anything in explanation of my North and South, I have to say so much, serves to underline a rather important truth about symbols. In the present edition I have tried to make the book easier by a running headline. But I do so with great reluctance. To supply a 'key' to an allegory may encourage that particular misunderstanding of allegory which, as a literary critic, I have elsewhere denounced. It may encourage people to suppose that allegory is a disguise, a way of saying obscurely what could have been said more clearly. But in fact all good allegory exists not to hide but to reveal; to make the inner world more palpable by giving it an (imagined) concrete embodiment. My headline is there only because my allegory failed – partly through my own fault (I am now heartily ashamed of the preposterous allegorical filigree on p.199), and partly because modern readers are unfamiliar with the method. But it remains true that wherever the symbols are best, the key is least adequate. For when allegory is at its best, it approaches myth, which must be grasped with the imagination, not with the intellect. If, as I still sometimes hope, my North and South and my Mr Sensible have some touch of mythical life, then no amount of 'explanation' will quite catch up with their meaning. It is the sort of thing you cannot learn from definition: you must rather get to know it as you get to know a smell or a taste, the 'atmosphere' of a family or a country town, or the personality of an individual.

Three other cautions remain to be given. 1. The map on the end leaves has puzzled some readers because, as they say, 'it marks all sorts of places not mentioned in the text'. But so do all maps in travel books. John's route is marked with a dotted line: those who are not interested in the places off that route need not bother about them. They are a half whimsical attempt to fill in the 'Northern' and 'Southern' halves of the world with the spiritual phenomena appropriate to them. Most of the names explain themselves. *Wanhope* is Middle English for Despair; *Woodey* and *Lyssanesos* mean 'Isle of Insanity'; *Behmenheim* is named, unfairly, after Jakob Boehme or Behmen; *Golnesshire* (Anglo-Saxon *Gál*) is the county of Lechery; in *Trine*land one feels 'in tune with the infinite'; and *Zeitgeistheim*, of course, is the habitat of the *Zeitgeist* or Spirit of the Age. *Naughtstow* is 'a place that is no good at all'. The two military railways were meant to symbolise the double attack from Hell on the two sides of our nature. It was hoped that the roads spreading out from each of the enemy railheads would look rather like claws or tentacles reaching out into the country of Man's Soul. If you like to put little black arrows pointing South on the seven Northern roads (in the fashion of the newspaper war maps) and others pointing North on the six southern roads, you would get a clear picture of the Holy War as I see it. You might amuse yourself by deciding where to put them – a question that admits different answers. On the Northern front, for example, I should represent the enemy in occupation of Cruelsland and Superbia, and thus threatening the Pale Men with a pincer movement. But I don't claim to know; and doubtless the position shifts every day. 2. The name *Mother Kirk* was chosen because 'Christianity' is not a very convincing name. Its defect was that it not unnaturally led the reader to attribute to me a much more definite *Ecclesiastical* position than I could really boast of. The book is concerned solely with Christianity as against unbelief. 'Denominational' questions do not come in. 3. In this preface the autobiographical element in John has had to be stressed because the source of the obscurities lay there. But you must not assume that everything in the book is autobiographical. I was attempting to generalise, not to tell people about my own life.

C. S. LEWIS

Contents

BOOK 1 – THE DATA

1	The Rules	19
2	The Island	22
3	The Eastern Mountains	24
4	Leah for Rachel	27
5	Ichabod	29
6	Quem Quaeritis in Sepulchro? Non Est Hic	30

BOOK 2 – THRILL

1	Dixit Insipiens	35
2	The Hill	39
3	A Little Southward	41
4	Soft Going	43
5	Leah for Rachel	44
6	Ichabod	46
7	Non Est Hic	47
8	Great Promises	48

BOOK 3 – THROUGH DARKEST ZEITGEISTHEIM

1	Eschropolis	53
2	A South Wind	55
3	Freedom of Thought	57
4	The Man Behind the Gun	59

5	Under Arrest	61
6	Poisoning the Wells	63
7	Facing the Facts	65
8	Parrot Disease	66
9	The Giant Slayer	68

BOOK 4 – BACK TO THE ROAD

1	Let Grill Be Grill	73
2	Archetype and Ectype	74
3	Esse *is* Percipi	76
4	Escape	79

BOOK 5 – THE GRAND CANYON

1	The Grand Canyon	85
2	Mother Kirk's Story	88
3	The Self-Sufficiency of Vertue	91
4	Mr Sensible	93
5	Table Talk	98
6	Drudge	100
7	The Gaucherie of Vertue	103

BOOK 6 – NORTHWARD ALONG THE CANYON

1	First Steps to the North	107
2	Three Pale Men	109
3	Neo-Angular	112
4	Humanist	114

5	Food from the North	115
6	Furthest North	116
7	Fool's Paradise	120

BOOK 7 – SOUTHWARD ALONG THE CANYON

1	Vertue is Sick	123
2	John Leading	126
3	The Main Road Again	127
4	Going South	128
5	Tea on the Lawn	130
6	The House of Wisdom	133
7	Across the Canyon by Moonlight	135
8	This Side by Sunlight	136
9	Wisdom – Exoteric	139
10	Wisdom – Esoteric	143
11	Mum's the Word	145
12	More Wisdom	146

BOOK 8 – AT BAY

1	Two Kinds of Monist	151
2	John Led	154
3	John Forgets Himself	156
4	John Finds his Voice	158
5	Food at a Cost	160
6	Caught	162
7	The Hermit	164
8	History's Words	167

| 9 | Matter of Fact | 172 |
| 10 | Archetype and Ectype | 176 |

BOOK 9 – ACROSS THE CANYON

1	Across the Canyon by the Inner Light	181
2	This Side by Lightning	183
3	This Side by the Darkness	185
4	Securus Te Projice	187
5	Across the Canyon	190
6	Nella Sua Voluntade	192

BOOK 10 – THE REGRESS

1	The Same Yet Different	197
2	The Synthetic Man	199
3	Limbo	200
4	The Black Hole	202
5	Superbia	204
6	Ignorantia	207
7	Luxuria	209
8	The Northern Dragon	213
9	The Southern Dragon	216
10	The Brook	218

BOOK I

THE DATA

This every soul seeketh and for the sake of this doth all her actions, having an inkling that it is; but what it is she cannot sufficiently discern, and she knoweth not her way, and concerning this she hath no constant assurance as she hath of other things.

PLATO

Whose souls, albeit in a cloudy memory, yet seek back their good, but, like drunk men, know not the road home.

BOETHIUS

Somewhat it seeketh, and what that is directly it knoweth not, yet very intentive desire thereof doth so incite it, that all other known delights and pleasures are laid aside, they give place to the search of this but only suspected desire.

HOOKER

I

THE RULES

*Knowledge of broken law precedes all other
religious experiences – John receives his first
religious instruction –
Did the instructors really mean it?*

I dreamed of a boy who was born in the land of Puritania and his name was John. And I dreamed that when John was able to walk he ran out of his parents' garden on a fine morning on to the road. And on the other side of the road there was a deep wood, but not thick, full of primroses and soft green moss. When John set eyes on this he thought he had never seen anything so beautiful: and he ran across the road and into the wood, and was just about to go down on his hands and knees and to pull up the primroses by handfuls, when his mother came running out of the garden gate, and she also ran across the road, and caught John up, and smacked him soundly and told him he must never go into the wood again. And John cried, but he asked no questions, for he was not yet at the age for asking questions. Then a year went past. And then, another fine morning, John had a little sling and he went out into the garden and he saw a bird sitting on a branch. And John got his sling ready and was going to have a shot at the bird, when the cook came running out of the garden and caught John up and smacked him soundly and told him he must never kill any of the birds in the garden.

'Why?' said John.

'Because the Steward would be very angry,' said cook.

'Who is the Steward?' said John.

'He is the man who makes rules for all the country round here,' said cook.

'Why?' said John.

'Because the Landlord set him to do it.'

'Who is the Landlord?' said John.

'He owns all the country,' said the cook.

'Why?' said John.

And when he asked this, the cook went and told his mother. And his mother sat down and talked to John about the Landlord all afternoon: but John took none of it in, for he was not yet at the age for taking it in. Then a year went past, and one dark, cold, wet morning John was made to put on new clothes. They were the ugliest clothes that had ever been put upon him, which John did not mind at all, but they also caught him under the chin, and were tight under the arms, which he minded a great deal, and they made him itch all over. And his father and mother took him out along the road, one holding him by each hand (which was uncomfortable, too, and very unnecessary), and told him they were taking him to see the Steward. The Steward lived in a big dark house of stone on the side of the road. The father and mother went in to talk to the Steward first, and John was left sitting in the hall on a chair so high that his feet did not reach the floor. There were other chairs in the hall where he could have sat in comfort, but his father had told him that the Steward would be very angry if he did not sit absolutely still and be very good: and John was beginning to be afraid, so he sat still in the high chair with his feet dangling, and his clothes itching all over him, and his eyes starting out of his head. After a very long time his parents came back again, looking as if they had been with the doctor, very grave. Then they said that John must go in and see the Steward too. And when John came into the room, there was an old man with a red, round face, who was very kind and full of jokes, so that John quite got over his fears, and they had a good talk about fishing tackle and bicycles. But just when the talk was at its best, the Steward got up and cleared his throat. He then took down a mask from the wall with a long white beard attached to it and suddenly clapped it on his face, so that his appearance was awful. And he said, 'Now I am going to talk to you about the Landlord. The Landlord owns all the country, and it is *very, very* kind of him to allow us to live on it at all – very, very kind.' He went on repeating 'very kind' in a queer singsong voice so long that John would have laughed, but that now he was beginning to be frightened again. The Steward then took down from a peg a big card with small print all over it, and said, 'Here is a list of all the things the Landlord says you must not do. You'd better look at it.' So John took the card: but half the rules seemed to forbid things he had never heard of, and the other half forbade things he was doing every day and could not imagine not doing: and the number of the rules was so enormous that he felt he could never remember them all. 'I hope,' said the Steward, 'that you have not already broken any of the rules?' John's heart began to thump, and his eyes bulged more and more, and he was at his wit's end when the Steward took the mask off and looked at John with his real face and said, 'Better tell a lie, old chap, better tell a lie. Easiest for all concerned,' and popped the mask on his face all in a flash. John gulped and said quickly, 'Oh, no, sir.' 'That is just as well,' said the steward through the mask. 'Because, you know, if you did break any of them and the Landlord got to know of it, do you know what he'd do to you?' 'No, sir,' said John: and the Steward's eyes seemed to be twinkling dreadfully through the holes of the mask. 'He'd take you and shut you up for ever and ever in a black hole full of snakes and scorpions as large as lobsters – for ever and ever. And besides that, he is such a kind, good man, so very, very kind, that I am sure you would never *want* to displease him.' 'No, sir,' said John. 'But, please, sir ...' 'Well,' said the Steward. 'Please, sir, supposing I did break one, one little one, just by accident, you know. Could nothing stop the snakes and lobsters?' 'Ah!...' said the Steward; and then he sat down and talked for a long time, but John could not understand a single syllable. However, it all ended with pointing out that the Landlord was quite extraordinarily kind and good to his tenants, and would certainly torture most of them to death the moment he had the slightest pretext. 'And you can't blame him,' said the Steward. 'For after all, it *is* his land, and it is so very good of him to let us live here at all – people like us, you know.' Then the Steward took off the mask and had a nice, sensible chat with John again, and gave him a cake and brought him out to his father and mother. But just as they were going he bent down and whispered in John's ear, 'I shouldn't bother about it all too much if I were you.' At the same time he slipped the card of the rules into John's hand and told him he could keep it for his own use.

2

THE ISLAND

He is more serious than the instructors: and
discovers the other Law in his members – He
awakes to Sweet Desire; and almost at once
mixes his own fantasies with it

Now the days and the weeks went on again, and I dreamed that John had little peace either by day or night for thinking of the rules and the black hole full of snakes. At first he tried very hard to keep them all, but when it came to bedtime he always found that he had broken far more than he had kept: and the thought of the horrible tortures to which the good, kind Landlord would put him became such a burden that next day he would become quite reckless and break as many as he possibly could; for oddly enough this eased his mind for the moment. But then after a few days the fear would return and this time it would be worse than before because of the dreadful number of rules that he had broken during the interval. But what puzzled him most at this time was a discovery which he made after the rules had been hanging in his bedroom for two or three nights: namely, that on the other side of the card, on the back, there was quite a different set of rules. There were so many that he never read them all through and he was always finding new ones. Some of them were very like the rules on the front of the card, but most of them were just the opposite. Thus whereas the front of the card said that you must be always examining yourself to see how many rules you had broken, the back of the card began like this:

Rule 1
  Put the whole thing out of your head
  The moment you get into bed.

Or again, whereas the front said that you must always go and ask your elders what the rule about a certain thing was, if you were in the least doubt, the back said:

Rule 2
  Unless they saw you do it,
  Keep quiet or else you'll rue it.

And so on. And now I dreamed that John went out one morning and tried to play in the road and to forget his troubles; but the rules kept coming back into his head so that he did not make much of it. However, he went on always a few yards further till suddenly he looked up and saw that he was so far away from home that he was in a part of the road he had never seen before. Then came the sound of a musical instrument, from behind it seemed, very sweet and very short, as if it were one plucking of a string or one note of a bell, and after it a full, clear voice – and it sounded so high and strange that he thought it was very far away, further than a star. The voice said, Come. Then John saw that there was a stone wall beside the road in that part: but it had (what he had never seen in a garden wall before) a window. There was no glass in the window and no bars; it was just a square hole in the wall. Through it he saw a green wood full of primroses: and he remembered suddenly how he had gone into another wood to pull primroses, as a child, very long ago – so long that even in the moment of remembering the memory seemed still out of reach. While he strained to grasp it, there came to him from beyond the wood a sweetness and a pang so piercing that instantly he forgot his father's house, and his mother, and the fear of the Landlord, and the burden of the rules. All the furniture of his mind was taken away. A moment later he found that he was sobbing, and the sun had gone in: and what it was that had happened to him he could not quite remember, nor whether it had happened in this wood, or in the other wood when he was a child. It seemed to him that a mist which hung at the far end of the wood had parted for a moment, and through the rift he had seen a calm sea, and in the sea an island, where the smooth turf sloped down unbroken to the bays, and out of the thickets peeped the pale, small-breasted Oreads, wise like gods, unconscious of themselves like beasts, and tall enchanters, bearded to their feet, sat in green chairs among the forests. But even while he pictured these things he knew, with one part of his mind, that they were not like the things he had seen – nay, that what had befallen him was not seeing at all. But he was too young to heed the distinction: and too empty, now that the unbounded sweetness passed away, not to seize greedily whatever it had left behind. He had no inclination yet to go into the wood: and presently he went home, with a sad excitement upon him, repeating to himself a thousand times, 'I know now what I want'. The first time that he said it, he was aware that it was not entirely true: but before he went to bed he was believing it.

3

THE EASTERN MOUNTAINS

*He hears of Death and what his elders
pretend to believe about it – An
uncomfortable funeral, lacking both Pagan
fortitude and Christian hope – Everyone
except John cheers up on the way home*

John had a disreputable old uncle who was the tenant of a poor little farm beside his father's. One day when John came in from the garden, he found a great hubbub in the house. His uncle was sitting there with his cheeks the colour of ashes. His mother was crying. His father was sitting very still with a solemn face. And there, in the midst of them, was the Steward with his mask on. John crept round to his mother and asked her what the matter was.

'Poor Uncle George has had notice to quit,' she said.

'Why?' said John.

'His lease is up. The Landlord has sent him notice to quit.'

'But didn't you know how long the lease was for?'

'Oh, no, indeed we did not. We thought it was for years and years more. I am sure the Landlord never gave us any idea he was going to turn him out at a moment's notice like this.'

'Ah, but it doesn't need any notice,' broke in the Steward. 'You know he always retains the right to turn anyone out whenever he chooses. It is very good of him to let any of us stay here at all.'

'To be sure, to be sure,' said the mother.

'That goes without saying,' said the father.

'I'm not complaining,' said Uncle George. 'But it seems cruelly hard.'

'Not at all,' said the Steward. 'You've only got to go to the Castle and knock at the gate and see the Landlord himself. You know that he's only turning you out of here to make you much more comfortable somewhere else. Don't you?'

Uncle George nodded. He did not seem able to get his voice.

Suddenly the father looked at his watch. Then he looked up at the Steward and said:

'Well?'

'Yes,' said the Steward.

Then John was sent up to his bedroom and told to put on the ugly and uncomfortable clothes; and when he came downstairs, itching all over, and tight under the arms, he was given a little mask to put on, and his parents put masks on too. Then I thought in my dream that they wanted to put a mask on Uncle George, but he was trembling so that it would not stay on. So they had to see his face as it was; and his face became so dreadful that everyone looked in a different direction and pretended not to see it. They got Uncle George to his feet with much difficulty, and then they all came out on to the road. The sun was just setting at one end of the road, for the road ran east and west. They turned their backs on the dazzling western sky and there John saw ahead of them the night coming down over the eastern mountains. The country sloped down and eastward to a brook, and all this side of the brook was green and cultivated: on the other side of the brook a great black moor sloped upward, and beyond that were the crags and chasms of the lower mountains, and high above them again the bigger mountains: and on top of the whole waste was one mountain so big and black that John was afraid of it. He was told that the Landlord had his castle up there.

He trudged on eastward, a long time, always descending, till they came to the brook. They were so slow now that the sunset behind them was out of sight. Before them, all was growing darker every minute, and the cold east wind was blowing out of the darkness, right from the mountain tops. When they had stood for a little, Uncle George looked round on them all once or twice, and said, 'Oh, dear! Oh, dear!' in a funny small voice like a child's. Then he stepped over the brook and began to walk away up the moor. It was now so dark and there were so many ups and downs in the moorland that they lost sight of him almost at once. Nobody ever saw him again.

'Well,' said the Steward, untying his mask as they turned homeward. 'We've all got to go when our time comes.'

'That's true,' said the father, who was lighting his pipe. When it was lit he turned to the Steward and said: 'Some of those pigs of George's have won prizes.'

'I'd keep 'em if I were you,' said the Steward. 'It's no time for selling now.'

'Perhaps you're right,' said the father.

John walked behind with his mother.

'Mother.'

'Well, dear?'

'Could any of us be turned out without notice like that any day?'

'Well, yes. But it is very unlikely.'

'But we *might* be?'

'You oughtn't to be thinking of that sort of thing at your age.'

'Why oughtn't I?'

'It's not healthy. A boy like you.'

'Mother.'

'Yes?'

'Can *we* break off the lease without notice too?'

'How do you mean?'

'Well, the Landlord can turn us out of the farm whenever he likes. Can we leave the farm whenever we like?'

'No, certainly not.'

'Why not?'

'That's in the lease. We must go when he likes, and stay as long as he likes.'

'Why?'

'I suppose because he makes the leases.'

'What would happen if we did leave?'

'He would be very angry.'

'Would he put us in the black hole?'

'Perhaps.'

'Mother.'

'Well, dear?'

'Will the Landlord put Uncle George in the black hole?'

'How dare you say such a thing about your poor uncle? Of course he won't.'

'But hasn't Uncle George broken all the rules?'

'Broken all the rules? Your Uncle George was a very good man.'

'You never told me that before,' said John.

4

LEAH FOR RACHEL

*Greed to recover Desire hides the real offer
of its return – John tries to force himself to
feel it, but finds (and accepts) Lust instead*

Then I turned over in my sleep and began to dream deeper still: and I dreamed that I saw John growing tall and lank till he ceased to be a child and became a boy. The chief pleasure of his life in these days was to go down the road and look through the window in the wall in the hope of seeing the beautiful Island. Some days he saw it well enough, especially at first, and heard the music and the voice. At first he would not look through the window into the wood unless he had heard the music. But after a time both the sight of the Island, and the sounds, became very rare. He would stand looking through the window for hours, and seeing the wood, but no sea or Island beyond it, and straining his ears but hearing nothing except the wind in the leaves. And the yearning for that sight of the Island and the sweet wind blowing over the water from it, though indeed these themselves had given him only yearning, became so terrible that John thought he would die if he did not have them again soon. He even said to himself, 'I would break every rule on the card for them if I could only get them. I would go down into the black hole for ever if it had a window from which I could see the Island.' Then it came into his head that perhaps he ought to explore the wood and thus he might find his way down to the sea beyond it: so he determined that the next day, whatever he saw or heard at the window, he would go through and spend the whole day in the wood. When the morning came, it had been raining all night and a south wind had blown the clouds away at sunrise, and all was fresh and shining. As soon as he had had his breakfast John was out on the road. With the wind and the birds, and country carts passing, there were many noises about that morning, so that when John heard a strain of music long before he had reached the wall and the window – a strain like that which he desired, but coming from an unexpected quarter – he could not be absolutely certain that he had not imagined it. It made him stand still in the road for a minute, and in my dream I could hear him thinking – like this: 'If I go after that sound – away off the road, up yonder – it is all luck whether I shall find anything at all. But if I go on to the window, there I *know* I shall reach the wood, and there I can have a good hunt for the shore and the Island. In fact, I shall *insist* on finding it. I am determined to. But if I go a new way I shall not be able to insist: I shall just have to take what comes.' So he went on to the place he knew and climbed through the window into the wood. Up and down and to and fro among the trees he walked, looking this way and that: but he found no sea and no shore, and indeed no end to the wood in any direction. When it came to the middle of the day he was so hot that he sat down and fanned himself. Often, of late, when the sight of the Island had been withheld, he had felt sad and despairing: but what he felt now was more like anger. 'I must have it,' he kept on saying to himself, and then, 'I must have something.' Then it occurred to him that at least he had the wood, which he would once have loved, and that he had not given it a thought all morning. Very well, thought John, I will enjoy the wood: I *will* enjoy it. He set his teeth and wrinkled his forehead and sat still until the sweat rolled off him in an effort to enjoy the wood. But the more he tried the more he felt that there was nothing to enjoy. There was the grass and there were the trees: 'But what am I to *do* with them?' said John. Next it came into his head that he might perhaps get the old feeling – for what, he thought, had the Island ever given him but a *feeling*? – by imagining. He shut his eyes and set his teeth again and made a picture of the Island in his mind: but he could not keep his attention on the picture because he wanted all the time to watch some other part of his mind to see if the *feeling* were beginning. But no feeling began: and then, just as he was opening his eyes he heard a voice speaking to him. It was quite close at hand, and very sweet, and not at all like the old voice of the wood. When he looked round he saw what he had never expected, yet he was not surprised. There in the grass beside him sat a laughing brown girl of about his own age, and she had no clothes on.

'It was me you wanted,' said the brown girl. 'I am better than your silly Islands.'

And John rose and caught her, all in haste, and committed fornication with her in the wood.

5

ICHABOD

The deception does not last: but it leaves a
habit of sin behind it

After that John was always going to the wood. He did not always have his pleasure of her in the body, though it often ended that way: sometimes he would talk to her about himself, telling her lies about his courage and his cleverness. All that he told her she remembered, so that on other days she could tell it over to him again. Sometimes, even, he would go with her through the wood looking for the sea and the Island, but not often. Meanwhile the year went on and the leaves began to fall in the wood and the skies were more often grey: until now, as I dreamed, John had slept in the wood, and he woke up in the wood. The sun was low and a blustering wind was stripping the leaves from the branches. The girl was still there and the appearance of her was hateful to John: and he saw that she knew this, and the more she knew it the more she stared at him, smiling. He looked round and saw how small the wood was after all – a beggarly strip of trees between the road and a field that he knew well. Nowhere in sight was there anything that he liked at all.

'I shall not come back here,' said John. 'What I wanted is not here. It wasn't you I wanted, you know.'

'Wasn't it?' said the brown girl. 'Then be off. But you must take your family with you.'

With that she put up her hands to her mouth and called. Instantly from behind every tree there slipped out a brown girl: each of them was just like herself: the little wood was full of them.

'What are these?'

'Our daughters,' said she. 'Did you not know you were a father? Did you think I was barren, you fool? And now, children,' she added, turning to the mob, 'go with your father.'

Suddenly John became very much afraid and leaped over the wall into the road. There he ran home as fast as he could.

6

QUEM QUAERITIS IN SEPULCHRO? NON EST HIC

Sin and the Law torment John, each aggravating the other – Sweet Desire returns and he resolves to make it the object of his life

From that day forth until he left his home John was not happy. First of all the weight of all the rules that he had broken descended upon him: for while he was going daily to the wood he had almost forgotten the Landlord, and now suddenly the whole reckoning was to pay. In the second place, his last sight of the Island was now so long ago that he had forgotten how to wish for it even, and almost how to set about looking for it. At first he feared to go back to the window in the wall, lest he should meet the brown girl: but he soon found that her family were so constantly with him that place made no difference. Wherever he sat down to rest on a walk, there sooner or later, would be a little brown girl beside him. When he sat of an evening with his father and mother, a brown girl, visible only to him, would sidle in and sit at his feet: and sometimes his mother would fix her eyes on him and even ask him what he was staring at. But most of all they plagued him whenever he had a fit of fright about the Landlord and the black hole. It was always the same. He would wake one morning full of fear, and take down his card and read it – the front of it – and determine that today he would really begin to keep the rules. And for that day he would, but the strain was intolerable. He used to comfort himself by saying, It will get more easy as I go on. Tomorrow it will be easier. But tomorrow was always harder, and on the third day it was worst of all. And on that third day when he crept away to bed, tired to death and raw in his soul, always he would be sure to find a brown girl waiting for him there: and on such a night he had no spirit to resist her blandishments.

But when he perceived that no place was more, or less, haunted than another, then he came sidling back to the window in the wall. He had little hopes of it. He visited it more as a man visits a grave. It was full winter now, and the grove was naked and dark, the trees dripped in it, and the stream – he saw now that it was little more than a gutter – was full of dead leaves and mud. The wall, too, was broken where he had jumped over it. Yet John stood there a long time, many a winter evening, looking in. And he seemed to himself to have reached the bottom of misery.

One night he was trudging home from it, when he began to weep. He thought of that first day when he had heard the music and seen the Island: and the longing, not now for the Island itself, but for that moment when he had so sweetly longed for it, began to swell up in a warm wave, sweeter, sweeter, till he thought he could bear no more, and then yet sweeter again, till on the top of it, unmistakably, there came the short sound of music, as if a string had been plucked or a bell struck once. At the same moment a coach had gone past him. He turned and looked after it, in time to see a head even then being withdrawn from the window: and he thought he heard a voice say, Come. And far beyond the coach, among the hills of the western horizon, he thought that he saw a shining sea, and a faint shape of an Island, not much more than a cloud. It was nothing compared with what he had seen the first time: it was so much further away. But his mind was made up. That night he waited till his parents were asleep, and then, putting some few needments together, he stole out by the back door and set his face to the West to seek for the Island.

BOOK 2

THRILL

Thou shalt not make to thyself any graven image, nor the likeness of anything that is in the heaven above.
EXODUS

The soul of man, therefore, desiring to learn what manner of things these are, casteth her eyes upon objects akin to herself, whereof none sufficeth. And then it is that she saith, 'With the Lord and with the things whereof I spoke, there is nothing in that likeness; what then is it like?' This is the question, oh son of Dionysius, that is the cause of all evils – or rather the travail wherein the soul travaileth about it.
PLATO[1]

Following false copies of the good, that no Sincere fulfilment of their promise make.
DANTE

*In hand she boldly took
To make another like the former dame,
Another Florimell in shape and look
So lively and so like that many it mistook.*
SPENSER

---

[1] Some think it wrongly attributed to him.

I

DIXIT INSIPIENS

*John begins to think for himself and meets
Nineteenth Century Rationalism, which can
explain away religion by any number of
methods – 'Evolution' and 'Comparative
Religion', and all the guess-work which
masquerades as 'Science'*

Still I lay dreaming in bed, and looked, and I saw John go plodding along the road westward in the bitter black of a frosty night. He walked so long that the morning broke. Then presently John saw a little inn by the side of the road and a woman with a broom who had opened the door and was sweeping out the rubbish. So he turned in there and called for a breakfast, and while it was cooking he sat down in a hard chair by the newly-lit fire and fell asleep. When he woke the sun was shining in through the window and there was his breakfast laid. Another traveller was already eating: he was a big man with red hair and a red stubble on all his three chins, buttoned up very tight. When they had both finished the traveller rose and cleared his throat and stood with his back to the fire. Then he cleared his throat again and said:

'A fine morning, young sir.'

'Yes, sir,' said John.

'You are going West, perhaps, young man?'

'I – I think so.'

'It is possible that you don't know me.'

'I am a stranger here.'

'No offence,' said the stranger. 'My name is Mr Enlightenment, and I believe it is pretty generally known. I shall be happy to give you my assistance and protection as far as our ways lie together.'

John thanked him very much for this and when they went out from the inn there was a neat little trap waiting, with a fat little pony between the shafts: and its eyes were so bright and its harness was so well polished that it was difficult to say which was twinkling the keener in the morning sunshine. They both got into the trap and Mr Enlightenment whipped up the fat little pony and they went bowling along the road as if nobody had a care in the world. Presently they began to talk.

'And where might you come from, my fine lad?' said Mr Enlightenment.

'From Puritania, sir,' said John.

'A good place to leave, eh?'

'I am so glad you think that,' cried John. 'I was afraid –'

'I hope I am a man of the world,' said Mr Enlightenment. 'Any young fellow who is anxious to better himself may depend on finding sympathy and support in me. Puritania! Why, I suppose you have been brought up to be afraid of the Landlord.'

'Well, I must admit I sometimes *do* feel rather nervous.'

'You may make your mind easy, my boy. There is no such person.'

'There is no Landlord?'

'There is absolutely no such thing – I might even say no such *entity* – in existence. There never has been and never will be.'

'And this is absolutely certain?' cried John; for a great hope was rising in his heart.

'Absolutely certain. Look at me, young man. I ask you – do I look as if I was easily taken in?'

'Oh, no,' said John hastily. 'I was just wondering, though. I mean – how did they all come to think there was such a person?'

'The Landlord is an invention of those Stewards. All made up to keep the rest of us under their thumb: and of course the Stewards are hand in glove with the police. They are a shrewd lot, those Stewards. They know which side their bread is buttered on, all right. Clever fellows. Damn me, I can't help admiring them.'

'But do you mean that the Stewards don't believe it themselves?'

'I dare say they do. It is just the sort of cock and bull story they would believe. They are simple old souls most of them – just like children. They have no knowledge of modern science and they would believe anything they were told.'

John was silent for a few minutes. Then he began again:

'But how do you *know* there is no Landlord?'

'Christopher Columbus, Galileo, the earth is round, invention of printing, gunpowder!!' exclaimed Mr Enlightenment in such a loud voice that the pony shied.

'I beg your pardon,' said John.

'Eh?' said Mr Enlightenment.

'I didn't quite understand,' said John.

'Why, it's as plain as a pikestaff,' said the other. 'Your people in Puritania believe in the Landlord because they have not had the benefits of a scientific training. For example, now, I dare say it would be news to you to hear that the earth was round – round as an orange, my lad!'

'Well, I don't know that it would,' said John, feeling a little disappointed. 'My father always said it was round.'

'No, no, my dear boy,' said Mr Enlightenment, 'you must have misunderstood him. It is well known that everyone in Puritania thinks the earth flat. It is not likely that I should be mistaken on such a point. Indeed, it is out of the question. Then again, there is the palaeontological evidence.'

'What's that?'

'Why, they tell you in Puritania that the Landlord made all these roads. But that is quite impossible for old people can remember the time when the roads were not nearly so good as they are now. And what is more, scientists have found all over the country the traces of *old* roads running in quite different directions. The inference is obvious.'

John said nothing.

'I said,' repeated Mr Enlightenment, 'that the inference was obvious.'

'Oh, yes, yes, of course,' said John hastily, turning a little red.

'Then again, there is anthropology.'

'I'm afraid I don't know –'

'Bless me, of course you don't. They don't mean you to know. An anthropologist is a man who goes round your backward villages in these parts, collecting the odd stories that the country people tell about the Landlord. Why, there is one village where they think he has a trunk like an elephant. Now anyone can see that that couldn't be true.'

'It is very unlikely.'

'And what is better still, we know how the villagers came to think so. It all began by an elephant escaping from the local zoo; and then some old villager – he was probably drunk – saw it wandering about on the mountain one night, and so the story grew up that the Landlord had a trunk.'

'Did they catch the elephant again?'

'Did who?'

'The anthropologists.'

'Oh, my dear boy, you are misunderstanding. This happened long before there were any anthropologists.'

'Then how do they know?'

'Well, as to that ... I see that you have a very crude notion of how science actually works. To put it simply – for, of course, you could not understand the *technical* explanation – to put it simply, they know that the escaped elephant must have been the source of the trunk story because they know that an escaped snake must have been the source of the snake story in the next village – and so on. This is called the inductive method. Hypothesis, my dear young friend, establishes itself by a cumulative process: or, to use popular language, if you make the same guess often enough it ceases to be a guess and becomes a Scientific Fact.'

After he had thought for a while, John said:

'I think I see. Most of the stories about the Landlord are probably untrue; therefore the rest are probably untrue.'

'Well, that is as near as a beginner can get to it, perhaps. But when you have had a scientific training you will find that you can be quite certain about all sorts of things which now seem to you only probable.'

By this time the fat little pony had carried them several miles, and they had come to a place where a by-road went off to the right. 'If you are going West, we must part here,' said Mr Enlightenment, drawing up. 'Unless perhaps you would care to come home with me. You see that magnificent city?' John looked down by the by-road and saw in a flat plain without any trees a huge collection of corrugated iron huts, most of which seemed rather old and rusty.

'That,' said Mr Enlightenment, 'is the city of Claptrap. You will hardly believe me when I say that I can remember it as a miserable village. When I first came here it had only forty inhabitants: it now boasts a population of twelve million, four hundred thousand, three hundred and sixty-one souls, who include, I may add, the majority of our most influential publicists and scientific popularisers. In this unprecedented development I am proud to say that I have borne no small part: but it is no mock modesty to add that the invention of the printing press has been more important than any merely personal agency. If you would care to join us –'

'Well, thank you,' said John, 'but I think I will keep to the main road a little longer.'

He got out of the trap and turned to bid good-bye to Mr Enlightenment. Then a sudden thought came into his head, and he said:

'I am not sure that I have really understood all your arguments, sir. Is it absolutely certain that there is no Landlord?'

'Absolutely. I give you my word of honour.'

With these words they shook hands. Mr Enlightenment turned the pony's head up the by-road, gave it a touch with the whip, and in a few moments was out of sight.

2

THE HILL

*John abandons his religion with profound
relief – And forthwith has his first explicitly
moral experience*

Then I saw John bounding forward on his road so lightly that before he knew it he had come to the top of a little hill. It was not because the hill had tired him that he stopped there, but because he was too happy to move. 'There is no Landlord,' he cried. Such a weight had been lifted from his mind that he felt he could fly. All round him the frost was gleaming like silver; the sky was like blue glass; a robin sat in the hedge beside him; a cock was crowing in the distance. 'There is no Landlord.' He laughed when he thought of the old card of rules hung over his bed in the bedroom, so low and dark, in his father's house. 'There is no Landlord. There is no black hole.' He turned and looked back on the road he had come by: and when he did so he gasped with joy. For there in the East, under the morning light, he saw the mountains heaped up to the sky like clouds, green and violet and dark red; shadows were passing over the big rounded slopes, and water shone in the mountain pools, and up at the highest of all the sun was smiling steadily on the ultimate crags. These crags were indeed so shaped that you could easily take them for a castle: and now it came into John's head that he had never looked at the mountains before, because as long as he thought that the Landlord lived there, he had been afraid of them. But now that there was no Landlord he perceived that they were beautiful. For a moment he almost doubted whether the Island could be more beautiful, and whether he would not be wiser to go East, instead of West. But it did not seem to him to matter, for he said, 'If the world has the mountains at one end and the Island at the other, then every road leads to beauty, and the world is a glory among glories.'

At that moment he saw a man walking up the hill to meet him. Now I knew in my dream that this man's name was Mr Vertue, and he was about of an age with John, or a little older.

'What is the name of this place?' said John.

'It is called Jehovah-Jirah,' said Mr Vertue.

Then they both turned and continued their journey to the West. After they had gone a little way Mr Vertue stole a glance at John's face and then he smiled a little.

'Why do you smile?' said John.

'I was thinking that you looked very glad.'

'So would you be if you had lived in the fear of a Landlord all your life and had just discovered that you were a free man.'

'Oh, it's that, is it?'

'You don't believe in the Landlord, do you?'

'I know nothing about him – except by hearsay like the rest of us.'

'You wouldn't like to be under his thumb.'

'Wouldn't like? I wouldn't *be* under anyone's thumb.'

'You might have to, if he had a black hole.'

'I'd let him put me in the black hole sooner than take orders if the orders were not to my mind.'

'Why, I think you are right. I can hardly believe it yet – that I need not obey the rules. There's that robin again. To think that I could have a shot at it if I liked and no one would interfere with me!'

'Do you want to?'

'I'm not sure that I do,' said John, fingering his sling. But when he looked round on the sunshine and remembered his great happiness and looked twice at the bird, he said, 'No, I don't. There is nothing I want less. Still – I could if I liked.'

'You mean you could if you chose.'

'Where's the difference?'

'All the difference in the world.'

3

A LITTLE SOUTHWARD

*The Moral Imperative does not fully
understand itself – John decides that
Aesthetic Experience is the thing to pursue*

I thought that John would have questioned him further, but now they came in sight of a woman who was walking slower than they so that presently they came up with her and wished her good-day. When she turned, they saw that she was young and comely, though a little dark of complexion. She was friendly and frank, but not wanton like the brown girls, and the whole world became pleasanter to the young men because they were travelling the same way with her. But first they told her their names, and she told them hers, which was Media Halfways.

'And where are you travelling to, Mr Vertue?' she asked.

'To travel hopefully is better than to arrive,' said Vertue.

'Do you mean you are just out for a walk, just for exercise?'

'Certainly not,' said Vertue, who was becoming a little confused. 'I am on a pilgrimage. I must admit, now that you press me, I have not a very clear idea of the end. But that is not the important question. These speculations don't make one a better walker. The great thing is to do one's thirty miles a day.'

'Why?'

'Because that is the rule.'

'Ho-ho!' said John. 'So you *do* believe in the Landlord after all.'

'Not at all. I didn't say it was the Landlord's rule.'

'Whose is it then?'

'It is my own rule. I made it myself.'

'But why?'

'Well, that again is a speculative question. I have made the best rules I can. If I find any better ones I shall adopt them. In the meantime, the great thing is to have rules of some sort and to keep them.'

'And where are you going?' said Media, turning to John.

Then John began to tell his companions about the Island, and how he had first seen it, and was determined to give up everything for the hope of finding it.

'Then you had better come and see my father,' said she. 'He lives in the city of Thrill, and at the bottom of this hill there is a turn to the left which will bring us there in half an hour.'

'Has your Father been to the Island? Does he know the way?'

'He often talks about something very like it.'

'You had better come with us, Vertue,' said John, 'since you do not know where you are going and there can be no place better to go than the Island.'

'Certainly not,' said Vertue. 'We must keep to the road. We must keep on.'

'I don't see why,' said John.

'I dare say you don't,' said Vertue.

All this time they were going down the hill, and now they came to a little grassy lane on the left which went off through a wood. Then I thought that John had a little hesitation: but partly because the sun was now hot and the hard metal of the road was becoming sore to his feet, and partly because he felt a little angry with Vertue, and most of all because Media was going that way, he decided to turn down the lane. They said good-bye to Vertue, and he went on his way stumping up the next hill without ever looking back.

4

SOFT GOING

When they were in the lane they walked more gently. The grass was soft under their feet, and the afternoon sun beating down on the sheltered place made it warm. And presently they heard a sound of sweet and melancholy chimes.

'Those are the bells of the city,' said Media.

As they went on they walked closer together, and soon they were walking arm in arm. Then they kissed each other: and after that they went on their way kissing and talking in slow voices, of sad and beautiful things. And the shadow of the wood and the sweetness of the girl and the sleepy sound of the bells reminded John a little bit of the Island, and a little bit of the brown girls.

'This is what I have been looking for all my life,' said John. 'The brown girls were too gross and the Island was too fine. This is the real thing.'

'This is Love,' said Media with a deep sigh. 'This is the way to the *real* Island.'

Then I dreamed that they came in sight of the city, very old, and full of spires and turrets, all covered with ivy, where it lay in a little grassy valley, built on both sides of a lazy, winding river. And they passed the gate in the ruinous old city wall and came and knocked at a certain door and were let in. Then Media brought him in to a darkish room with a vaulted roof and windows of stained glass, and exquisite food was brought to them. With the food came old Mr Halfways. He was a gliding gentleman with soft, silver hair and a soft, silver voice, dressed in flowing robes: and he was so solemn, with his long beard, that John was reminded of the Steward with his mask on. 'But it is much better than the Steward,' thought John, 'because there is nothing to be afraid of. Also, he doesn't need a mask: his face is really like that.'

5

LEAH FOR RACHEL

*'Romantic' poetry professes to give what
hitherto John has only desired – For a
moment it seems to have kept its promise –
The rapture does not last but dwindles into
technical appreciation and sentiment*

As they ate John told him about the Island.

'You will find your Island here,' said Mr Halfways, looking into John's eyes.

'But how can it be here in the middle of the city?'

'It needs no place. It is everywhere and nowhere. It refuses entry to none who asks. It is an Island of the Soul,' said the old gentleman. 'Surely even in Puritania they told you that the Landlord's castle was within you?'

'But I don't want the castle,' said John. 'And I don't believe in the Landlord.'

'What is truth?' said the old man. 'They were mistaken when they told you of the Landlord: and yet they were not mistaken. What the imagination seizes as beauty must be truth, whether it existed before or not. The Landlord they dreamed to find, we find in our hearts: the Island you seek for, you already inhabit. The children of that country are never far from their fatherland.'

When the meal was ended the old gentleman took a harp, and at the first sweep of his hand across the strings John began to think of the music that he had heard by the window in the wall. Then came the voice: and it was no longer merely silver sweet and melancholy like Mr Halfways' speaking voice, but strong and noble and full of strange overtones, the noise of the sea, and of all birds, and sometimes of wind and thunder. And John began to see a picture of the Island with his eyes open: but it was more than a picture, for he sniffed the spicy smell and the sharp brine of the sea mixed with it. He seemed to be in the water, only a few yards from the sand of the Island. He could see more than he had ever seen before. But just as he had put down his feet and touched a sandy bottom and was beginning to wade ashore, the song ceased. The whole vision went away. John found himself back in the dusky room, seated on a low divan, with Media by his side.

'Now I shall sing you something else,' said Mr Halfways.

'Oh, no,' cried John, who was sobbing. 'Sing the same again. Please sing it again.'

'You had better not hear it twice in the same evening. I have plenty of other songs.'

'I would die to hear the first one again,' said John.

'Well, well,' said Mr Halfways, 'perhaps you know best. Indeed, what does it matter? It is as short to the Island one way as another.' Then he smiled indulgently and shook his head, and John could not help thinking that his talking voice and talking manner were almost silly after the singing. But as soon as the great deep wall of the music began again it swept everything else from his mind. It seemed to him that this time he got more pleasure from the first few notes, and even noticed delicious passages which had escaped him at the first hearing; and he said to himself, 'This is going to be even better than the other. I shall keep my head this time and sip all the pleasure at my ease.' I saw that he settled himself more comfortably to listen and Media slipped her hand into his. It pleased him to think that they were going to the Island together. Now came the vision of the Island again: but this time it was changed, for John scarcely noticed the Island because of a lady with a crown on her head who stood waiting for him on the shore. She was fair, divinely fair. 'At last,' said John, 'a girl with no trace of brown.' And he began again to wade ashore holding out his arms to embrace that queen: and his love for her appeared to him so great and so pure, and they had been parted for so long, that his pity for himself and her almost overwhelmed him. And as he was about to embrace her the song stopped.

'Sing it again, sing it again,' cried John, 'I liked it better the second time.'

'Well, if you insist,' said Mr Halfways with a shrug. 'It is nice to have a really appreciative audience.' So he sang it the third time. This time John noticed yet more about the music. He began to see how several of the effects were produced and that some parts were better than others. He wondered if it were not a trifle too long. The vision of the Island was a little shadowy this time, and he did not take much notice of it. He put his arm round Media and they lay cheek to cheek. He began to wonder if Mr Halfways would never end: and when at last the final passage closed, with a sobbing break in the singer's voice, the old gentleman looked up and saw how the young people lay in one another's arms. Then he rose and said:

'You have found your Island – you have found it in one another's hearts.'

Then he tiptoed from the room, wiping his eyes.

6

ICHABOD

*Rapture would finally turn into Lust, but
that in the nick of time the 'modern' literary
movement offers to 'debunk' it*

'Media, I love you,' said John.

'We have come to the *real* Island,' said Media.

'But oh, alas!' said he, 'so long our bodies why do we forbear?'

'Else a great prince in prison lies,' sighed she.

'No one else can understand the mystery of our love,' said he.

At that moment a brisk, hobnailed step was heard and a tall young man strode into the room carrying a light in his hand. He had coal-black hair and a straight mouth like the slit in a pillar-box, and he was dressed in various kinds of metal wire. As soon as he saw them he burst into a great guffaw. The lovers instantly sprang up and apart.

'Well, Brownie,' said he, 'at your tricks again?'

'Don't call me that name,' said Media, stamping her foot, 'I have told you before not to call me that.'

The young man made an obscene gesture at her, and then turned to John, 'I see that old fool of a father of mine has been at you?'

'You have no right to speak that way of Father,' said Media. Then, turning to John, her cheeks flaming, her breast heaving, she said, 'All is over. Our dream – is shattered. Our mystery – is profaned. I would have taught you all the secrets of love, and now you are lost to me for ever. We must part. I shall go and kill myself,' and with that she rushed from the room.

7

NON EST HIC

'Don't bother about her,' said the young man. 'She has threatened that a hundred times. She is only a brown girl, though she doesn't know it.'

'A brown girl!' cried John, 'And your father ...'

'My father has been in the pay of the Brownies all his life. He doesn't know it, the old chuckle-head. Calls them the Muses, or the Spirit, or some rot. In actual fact, he is by profession a pimp.'

'And the Island?' said John.

'We'll talk about it in the morning. Ain't the kind of Island you're thinking of. Tell you what. I don't live with my father and my precious sister. I live in Eschropolis and I am going back tomorrow. I'll take you down to the laboratory and show you some *real* poetry. Not fantasies. The real thing.'

'Thank you very much,' said John.

Then young Mr Halfways found his room for him and the whole of that household went to bed.

8

GREAT PROMISES

The poetry of the Machine Age is so
very pure

Gus Halfways was the name of Mr Halfways' son. As soon as he rose in the morning he called John down to breakfast with him so that they might start on their journey. There was no one to hinder them, for old Halfways was still asleep and Media always had breakfast in bed. When they had eaten, Gus brought him into a shed beside his father's house and showed him a machine on wheels.

'What is this?' said John.

'My old bus,' said young Halfways. Then he stood back with his head on one side and gazed at it for a bit: but presently he began to speak in a changed and reverent voice.

'She is a poem. She is the daughter of the spirit of the age. What was the speed of Atlanta to her speed? The beauty of Apollo to her beauty?'

Now beauty to John meant nothing save glimpses of his Island, and the machine did not remind him of his Island at all: so he held his tongue.

'Don't you see?' said Gus. 'Our fathers made images of what they called gods and goddesses; but they were really only brown girls and brown boys whitewashed – as anyone found out by looking at them too long. All self-deception and phallic sentiment. But here you have the real art. Nothing erotic about *her*, eh?'

'Certainly not,' said John, looking at the cog-wheels and coils of wire, 'it is certainly not at all like a brown girl.' It was, in fact, more like a nest of hedgehogs and serpents.

'I should say not,' said Gus. 'Sheer power, eh? Speed, ruthlessness, austerity, significant form, eh? Also' (and here he dropped his voice) 'very expensive indeed.'

Then he made John sit in the machine and he himself sat beside him. Then he began pulling the levers about and for a long time nothing happened: but at last there came a flash and a roar and the machine bounded into the air and then dashed forward. Before John had got his breath they had flashed across a broad thoroughfare which he recognised as the main road, and were racing through the country to the north of it – a flat country of square stony fields divided by barbed wire fences. A moment later they were standing still in a city where all the houses were built of steel.

BOOK 3

THROUGH DARKEST ZEITGEISTHEIM

And every shrewd turn was exalted among men ... and simple goodness, wherein nobility doth ever most participate, was mocked away and clean vanished.
THUCYDIDES

Now live the lesser, as lords of the world, The busy troublers. Banished is our glory, The earth's excellence grows old and sere.
ANON

The more ignorant men are, the more convinced are they that their little parish and their little chapel is an apex to which civilisation and philosophy has painfully struggled up.
SHAW

I

ESCHROPOLIS

The poetry of the Silly Twenties – The 'Courage' and mutual loyalty of Artists

Then I dreamed that he led John into a big room rather like a bathroom: it was full of steel and glass and the walls were nearly all window, and there was a crowd of people there, drinking what looked like medicine and talking at the tops of their voices. They were all either young, or dressed up to look as if they were young. The girls had short hair and flat breasts and flat buttocks so that they looked like boys: but the boys had pale, egg-shaped faces and slender waists and big hips so that they looked like girls – except for a few of them who had long hair and beards.

'What are they so angry about?' whispered John.

'They are not angry,' said Gus; 'they are talking about Art.'

Then he brought John into the middle of the room and said:

'Say! Here's a guy who has been taken in by my father and wants some real hundred per cent music to clean him out. We had better begin with something neo-romantic to make the transition.'

Then all the Clevers consulted together and presently they all agreed that Victoriana had better sing first. When Victoriana rose John at first thought that she was a school-girl: but after he had looked at her again he perceived that she was in fact about fifty. Before she began to sing she put on a dress which was a sort of exaggerated copy of Mr Halfways' robes, and a mask which was like the Steward's mask except that the nose had been painted bright red and one of the eyes had been closed in a permanent wink.

'Priceless!' exclaimed one half of the Clevers, 'too Puritanian.'

But the other half, which included all the bearded men, held their noses in the air and looked very stiff. Then Victoriana took a little toy harp and began. The noises of the toy harp were so strange that John could not think of them as music at all. Then, when she sang, he had a picture in his mind which was a little like the Island, but he saw at once that it was not the Island. And presently he saw people who looked rather like his father, and the Steward and old Mr Halfways, dressed up as clowns and doing a stiff sort of dance. Then there was a columbine, and some sort of love-story. But suddenly the whole Island turned into an aspidistra in a pot and the song was over.

'Priceless,' said the Clevers.

'I hope you like it,' said Gus to John.

'Well,' began John doubtfully, for he hardly knew what to say: but he got no further, for at that moment he had a very great surprise. Victoriana had thrown her mask away and walked up to him and slapped him in the face twice, as hard as she could.

'That's right,' said the Clevers, 'Victoriana has *courage*. We may not all agree with you, Vikky dear, but we admire your courage.'

'You may persecute me as much as you like,' said Victoriana to John. 'No doubt to see me thus with my back to the wall, wakes the hunting lust in you. You will always follow the cry of the majority. But I will fight to the end. So there,' and she began to cry.

'I am extremely sorry,' said John. 'But –'

'And I *know* it was a good song,' sobbed Victoriana, 'because all great singers are persecuted in their lifetime – and I'm per-persecuted – and therefore I *must* be a great singer.'

'She has you there,' said the Clevers, as Victoriana left the laboratory.

'Well, I must admit,' said one of the Clevers, 'now that she has gone, that I think that stuff of hers rather *vieux jeu*.'

'Can't stand it myself,' said another.

'I think it was *her* face that needed slapping,' said a third.

'She's been spoiled and flattered all her life,' said a fourth. 'That's what's the matter with her.'

'Quite,' said the rest in chorus.

2

A SOUTH WIND

*The swamp-literature of the Dirty Twenties
– It was a low-brow blunder to mention the
most obvious thing about it*

'Perhaps,' said Gus, 'someone else would give us a song.'

'I will,' cried thirty voices all together: but one cried much louder than the others and its owner had stepped into the middle of the room before anyone could do anything about it. He was one of the bearded men and wore nothing but a red shirt and a cod-piece made of the skins of crocodiles: and suddenly he began to beat on an African tom-tom and to croon with his voice, swaying his lean, half-clad body to and fro and staring at them all, out of eyes which were like burning coals. This time John saw no picture of an Island at all. He seemed to be in a dark green place full of tangled roots and hairy vegetable tubes: and all at once he saw in it shapes moving and writhing that were not vegetable but human. And the dark green grew darker, and a fierce heat came out of it: and suddenly all the shapes that were moving in the darkness came together to make a single obscene image which dominated the whole room. And the song was over.

'Priceless,' said the Clevers. 'Too stark! Too virile.'

John blinked and looked round and when he saw all the Clevers as cool as cucumbers, smoking their cigarettes and drinking the drinks that looked like medicines, all as if nothing remarkable had happened, he was troubled in his mind; for he thought that the song must have meant something different to them, and 'If so,' he argued, 'what very pure-minded people they must be.' Feeling himself among his betters, he became ashamed.

'You like it, *hein*?' said the bearded singer.

'I – I don't think I understood it,' said John.

'I make you like it, *hein*,' said the singer, snatching up his tom-tom again. 'It was what you *really* wanted all the time.'

'No, no,' cried John. 'I know you are wrong there. I grant you, that – that sort of thing – is what I always get if I think too long about the Island. But it can't be what I *want*.'

'No? Why not?'

'If it is what I wanted, why am I so disappointed when I get it? If what a man really wanted was food, how could he be disappointed when the food arrived? As well, I don't understand –'

'What you not understand? I explain to you.'

'Well, it's like this. I thought that you objected to Mr Halfways' singing because it led to brown girls in the end.'

'So we do.'

'Well, why is it better to lead to black girls in the beginning?'

A low whistle ran round the whole laboratory. John knew he had made a horrible blunder.

'Look here,' said the bearded singer in a new voice, 'what do you mean? You are not suggesting that there is anything of that kind about my singing, are you?'

'I – I suppose – perhaps it was my fault,' stammered John.

'In other words,' said the singer, 'you are not yet able to distinguish between art and pornography!' and advancing towards John very deliberately, he spat in his face and turned to walk out of the room.

'That's right, Phally,' cried the Clevers, 'serve him right.'

'Filthy-minded little beast,' said one.

'Yah! Puritanian!' said a girl.

'I expect he's impotent,' whispered another.

'You mustn't be too hard on him,' said Gus. 'He is full of inhibitions and everything he says is only a rationalisation of them. Perhaps he would get on better with something more formal. Why don't you sing, Glugly?'

3

FREEDOM OF THOUGHT

*The gibberish-literature of the Lunatic
Twenties – John abandons 'the Movement',
though a little damaged by it*

Glugly instantly rose. She was very tall and as lean as a post: and her mouth was not quite straight in her face. When she was in the middle of the room, and silence had been obtained, she began to make gestures. First of all she set her arms a-kimbo and cleverly turned her hands the wrong way so that it looked as if her wrists were sprained. Then she waddled to and fro with her toes pointing in. After that she twisted herself to make it look as if her hip bone was out of joint. Finally she made some grunts, and said:

'Globol abol ookle ogle globol gloogle gloo,' and ended by pursing up her lips and making a vulgar noise such as children make in their nurseries. Then she went back to her place and sat down.

'Thank you very much,' said John politely.

But Glugly made no reply, for Glugly could not talk, owing to an accident in infancy.

'I hoped you liked it,' said young Halfways.

'I didn't understand her.'

'Ah,' said a woman in spectacles who seemed to be Glugly's nurse or keeper, 'that is because you are looking for beauty. You are still thinking of your Island. You have got to realise that satire is the moving force in modern music.'

'It is the expression of a savage disillusionment,' said someone else.

'Reality has broken down,' said a fat boy who had drunk a great deal of the medicine and was lying flat on his back, smiling happily.

'Our art *must* be brutal,' said Glugly's nurse.

'We lost our ideals when there was a war in this country,' said a very young Clever, 'they were ground out of us in the mud and the flood and the blood. That is why we have to be so stark and brutal.'

'But, look here,' cried John, 'that war was years ago. It was your fathers who were in it: and they are all settled down and living ordinary lives.'

'Puritanian! Bourgeois!' cried the Clevers. Everyone seemed to have risen.

'Hold your tongue,' whispered Gus in John's ear. But already someone had struck John on the head, and as he bowed under the blow someone else hit him from behind.

'It was the mud and the blood,' hissed the girls all round him.

'Well,' said John, ducking to avoid a retort that had been flung at him, 'If you are really old enough to remember that war, why do you pretend to be so young?'

'We are young,' they howled; 'we are the new movement; we are the revolt.'

'We have got over humanitarianism,' bellowed one of the bearded men, kicking John on the kneecap.

'And prudery,' said a thin little old maid trying to wrench his clothes off from the neck. And at the same moment six girls leaped at his face with their nails, and he was kicked in the back and the belly, and tripped up so that he fell on his face, and hit again as he rose, and all the glass in the world seemed breaking round his head as he fled for his life from the laboratory. And all the dogs of Eschropolis joined in the chase as he ran along the street, and all the people followed pelting him with ordure, and crying:

'Puritanian! Bourgeois! Prurient!'

4

THE MAN BEHIND THE GUN

*What did the Revolutionary Intellectuals
live on?*

When John could run no further he sat down. The noise of the pursuers had died away and, looking back, he could see no sign of Eschropolis. He was covered with filth and blood, and his breathing hurt him. There seemed to be something wrong with one of his wrists. As he was too tired to walk he sat still and thought for a while. And first he thought that he would like to go back to Mr Halfways. 'It is true,' he said, 'that if you listened to him too long it would lead you to Media – and she *had* a trace of brown in her. But then you had a glimpse of the Island first. Now the Clevers took you straight to brown girls – or worse – without even a glimpse of the Island. I wonder would it be possible to keep always at the Island stage with Mr Halfways? Must it always end like that?' Then it came into his head that after all he did not want Mr Halfways' songs, but the Island itself: and that this was the only thing he wanted in the world. And when he remembered this he rose very painfully to continue his journey, looking round for the West. He was still in the flat country, but there seemed to be mountains ahead, and above them the sun was setting. A road ran towards them: so he began to limp along it. Soon the sunset disappeared and the sky was clouded over and a cold rain began.

When he had limped about a mile he passed a man who was mending the fence of his field and smoking a big cigar. John stopped and asked him if he knew the way to the sea.

'Nope,' said the man without looking up.

'Do you know of any place in this country where I could get a night's lodging?'

'Nope,' said the man.

'Could you give me a piece of bread?' said John.

'Certainly not,' said Mr Mammon, 'it would be contrary to all economic laws. It would pauperise you.' Then, when John lingered, he added, 'Move on. I don't want any loiterers about here.'

John limped on for about ten minutes. Suddenly he heard Mr Mammon calling out to him. He stopped and turned round.

'What do you want?' shouted John.

'Come back,' said Mr Mammon.

John was so tired and hungry that he humbled himself to walk back (and the way seemed long) in the hope that Mammon had relented. When he came again to the place where they had talked before, the man finished his work without speaking and then said:

'Where did you get your clothes torn?'

'I had a quarrel with the Clevers in Eschropolis.'

'Clevers?'

'Don't you know them?'

'Never heard of them.'

'You know Eschropolis?'

'Know it? I *own* Eschropolis.'

'How do you mean?'

'What do you suppose they live on?'

'I never thought of that.'

'Every man of them earns his living by writing for me or having shares in my land. I suppose the "Clevers" is some nonsense they do in their spare time – when they're not beating up tramps,' and he glanced at John. Then he resumed his work.

'You needn't wait,' he said presently.

5

UNDER ARREST

*John is hindered from pursuing his quest by
the Intellectual climate of the Age*

Then I turned round and immediately began to dream again and I saw John plodding westward in the dark and the rain, in great distress, because he was too tired to go on and too cold to stop. And after a time there came a north wind that drove the rain away and skinned the puddles with ice and set the bare boughs clashing in the trees. And the moon came out. Now John looked up with his teeth chattering and saw that he was entering into a long valley of rocks with high cliffs on the right and the left. And the far end of the valley was barred with a high cliff all across except for one narrow pass in the middle. The moonlight lay white on this cliff and right amidst it was a huge shadow like a man's head. John glanced over his shoulder and saw that the shadow was thrown by a mountain behind him, which he had passed in the darkness.

It was far too cold for a man to stay in the wind, and I dreamed of John going stumblingly forward up the valley till now he had come to the rock-wall and was about to enter the pass. But just as he rounded a great boulder and came full in sight of the pass he saw some armed men sitting in it by a brazier; and immediately they sprang up and barred his way.

'You can't pass here,' said their leader.

'Where can I pass?' said John.

'Where are you going to?'

'I am going to find the sea in order to set sail for an Island that I have seen in the West.'

'Then you cannot pass.'

'By whose orders?'

'Do you not know that all this country belongs to the Spirit of the Age?'

'I am sorry,' said John, 'I didn't know. I have no wish to trespass, I will go round some other way. I will not go through his country at all.'

'You fool,' said the captain, 'you are in his country *now*. This pass is the way out of it, not the way into it. He welcomes strangers. His quarrel is with runaways.' Then he called to one of his men and said, 'Here, Enlightenment, take this fugitive to our Master.'

A young man stepped out and clapped fetters upon John's hands: then putting the length of chain over his own shoulder and giving it a jerk he began to walk down the valley dragging John after him.

6

POISONING THE WELLS

*John is hindered especially by Freudianism –
All is only Wish-Fulfilment – A doctrine
which leads to the giant's prison*

Then I saw them going down the valley, the way John had come up, with the moon full in their faces: and up against the moon was the mountain which had cast the shadow, and now it looked more like a man than before.

'Mr Enlightenment,' said John at last. 'Is it really you?'

'Why should it not be?' said the guard.

'You looked so different when I met you before.'

'We have never met before.'

'What? Did you not meet me at the inn on the borders of Puritania and drive me five miles in your pony trap?'

'Oh, *that*?' said the other. 'That must have been my father, old Mr Enlightenment. He is a vain and ignorant old man, almost a Puritanian, and we never mention him in the family. I am Sigismund Enlightenment and I have long since quarrelled with my father.'

They went on in silence for a bit. Then Sigismund spoke again.

'It may save trouble if I tell you at once the best reason for not trying to escape: namely, that there is nowhere to escape to.'

'How do you know there is no such place as my Island?'

'Do you wish very much that there was?'

'I do.'

'Have you never before imagined anything to be true because you greatly wished for it?'

John thought for a little, and then he said, 'Yes.'

'And your Island is *like* an imagination – isn't it?'

'I suppose so.'

'It is just the sort of thing you *would* imagine merely through wanting it – the whole thing is very suspicious. But answer me another question. Have you ever – ever once yet – had a vision of the Island that did not end in brown girls?'

'I don't know that I have. But they weren't what I wanted.'

'No. What you wanted was to have them, and with them, the satisfaction of feeling that you were good. Hence the Island.'

'You mean –'

'The Island was the pretence that you put up to conceal your own lusts from yourself.'

'All the same – I was disappointed when it ended like that.'

'Yes. You were disappointed at finding that you could not have it both ways. But you lost no time in having it the way you could: you did not reject the brown girls.'

They went on in silence for a time and always the mountain with its odd shape grew bigger in front of them; and now they were in its shadow. Then John spoke again, half in his sleep, for he was very tired.

'After all, it isn't only my Island. I might go back – back East and try the mountains.'

'The mountains do not exist.'

'How do you know?'

'Have you ever been there? Have you ever seen them except at night or in a blaze of sunrise?'

'No.'

'And your ancestors must have enjoyed thinking that when their leases were out they would go up to the mountains and live in the Landlord's castle. It is a more cheerful prospect than going nowhere.'

'I suppose so.'

'It is clearly one more of the things people *wish* to believe.'

'But do we never do anything else? Are all the things I see at this moment there, only because I wish to see them.'

'Most of them,' said Sigismund. 'For example – you would like that thing in front of us to be a mountain; that is why you think it is a mountain.'

'Why?' cried John. 'What is it?'

And then in my nightmare I thought John became like a terrified child and put his hands over his eyes not to see the giant; but young Mr Enlightenment tore his hands away and forced his face round and made him see the Spirit of the Age where it sat like one of the stone giants, the size of a mountain, with its eyes shut. Then Mr Enlightenment opened a little door among the rocks and flung John into a pit made in the side of the hill, just opposite the giant, so that the giant could look into it through its gratings.

'He will open his eyes presently,' said Mr Enlightenment. Then he locked the door and left John in prison.

7

FACING THE FACTS

*John sees all humanity as bundles of
complexes*

John lay in his fetters all night in the cold and stench of the dungeon. And when morning came there was a little light at the grating, and looking round, John saw that he had many fellow prisoners, of all sexes and ages. But instead of speaking to him, they all huddled away from the light and drew as far back into the pit, away from the grating, as they could. But John thought that if he could breathe a little fresh air he would be better, and he crawled up to the grating. But as soon as he looked out and saw the giant, it crushed the heart out of him: and even as he looked, the giant began to open his eyes and John, without knowing why he did it, shrank from the grating. Now I dreamed that the giant's eyes had this property, that whatever they looked on became transparent. Consequently, when John looked round into the dungeon, he retreated from his fellow prisoners in terror, for the place seemed to be thronged with demons. A woman was seated near him, but he did not know it was a woman, because, through the face, he saw the skull and through that the brain and the passages of the nose, and the larynx, and the saliva moving in the glands and the blood in the veins: and lower down the lungs panting like sponges and the liver, and the intestines like a coil of snakes. And when he averted his eyes from her they fell on an old man, and this was worse for the old man had a cancer. And when John sat down and drooped his head, not to see the horrors, he saw only the working of his own innards. Then I dreamed of all these creatures living in that hole under the giant's eye for many days and nights. And John looked round on it all and suddenly he fell on his face and thrust his hands into his eyes and cried out, 'It is the black hole. There may be no Landlord, but it is true about the black hole. I am mad. I am dead. I am in hell for ever.'

8

PARROT DISEASE

At last John's commonsense revolts

Every day a jailor brought the prisoners their food, and as he laid down the dishes he would say a word to them. If their meal was flesh he would remind them that they were eating corpses, or give them some account of the slaughtering: or, if it was the innards of some beast, he would read them a lecture in anatomy and show the likeness of the mess to the same parts in themselves – which was the more easily done because the giant's eyes were always staring into the dungeon at dinner time. Or if the meal were eggs he would recall to them that they were eating the menstruum of a verminous fowl, and crack a few jokes with the female prisoners. So he went on day by day. Then I dreamed that one day there was nothing but milk for them, and the jailor said as he put down the pipkin:

'Our relations with the cow are not delicate – as you can easily see if you imagine eating any of her other secretions.'

Now John had been in the pit a shorter time than any of the others: and at these words something seemed to snap in his head and he gave a great sigh and suddenly spoke out in a loud, clear voice:

'Thank heaven! Now at last I know that you are talking nonsense.'

'What do you mean?' said the jailor, wheeling round upon him.

'You are trying to pretend that unlike things are like. You are trying to make us think that milk is the same sort of thing as sweat or dung.'

'And pray, what difference is there except by custom?'

'Are you a liar or only a fool, that you see no difference between that which Nature casts out as refuse and that which she stores up as food?'

'So Nature is a person, then, with purposes and consciousness,' said the jailor with a sneer. 'In fact, a Landlady. No doubt it comforts you to imagine you can believe that sort of thing'; and he turned to leave the prison with his nose in the air.

'I know nothing about that,' shouted John after him. 'I am talking of what happens. Milk does feed calves and dung does not.'

'Look here,' cried the jailor, coming back, 'we have had enough of this. It is high treason and I shall bring you before the Master.' Then he jerked John up by his chain and began to drag him towards the door; but John as he was being dragged, cried out to the others, 'Can't you see it's all a cheat?' Then the jailor struck him in the teeth so hard that his mouth was filled with blood and he became unable to speak: and while he was silent the jailor addressed the prisoners and said:

'You see he is trying to argue. Now tell me, someone, what is argument?'

There was a confused murmur.

'Come, come,' said the jailor. 'You must know your catechisms by now. You, there' (and he pointed to a prisoner little older than a boy whose name was Master Parrot), 'what is argument?'

'Argument,' said Master Parrot, 'is the attempted rationalisation of the arguer's desires.'

'Very good,' replied the jailor, 'but you should turn out your toes and put your hands behind your back. That is better. Now: what is the proper answer to an argument proving the existence of the Landlord?'

'The proper answer is, "You say that because you are a Steward."'

'Good boy. But hold your head up. That's right. And what is the answer to an argument proving that Mr Phally's songs are just as brown as Mr Halfways'?'

'There are two only generally necessary to damnation,' said Master Parrot. 'The first is, "You say that because you are a Puritanian," and the second is, "You say that because you are a sensualist."'

'Good. Now just one more. What is the answer to an argument turning on the belief that two and two make four?'

'The answer is, "You say that because you are a mathematician."'

'You are a very good boy,' said the jailor. 'And when I come back I shall bring you something nice. And now for *you*,' he added, giving John a kick and opening the grating.

9

THE GIANT SLAYER

*The spell begins to break – Once rational
argument is allowed a hearing the giant
is lost*

When they came out into the air John blinked a little, but not much, for they were still only in a half-light under the shadow of the giant, who was very angry, with smoke coming from his mouth, so that he looked more like a volcano than an ordinary mountain. And now John gave himself up for lost, but just as the jailor had dragged him up to the giant's feet, and had cleared his throat, and begun 'The case against this prisoner –' there was a commotion and a sound of a horse's hoofs. The jailor looked round, and even the giant took his terrible eyes off John and looked round: and last of all, John himself looked round too. They saw some of the guard coming towards them leading a great black stallion, and on it was seated a figure wound in a cloak of blue which was hooded over the head and came down concealing the face.

'Another prisoner, Lord,' said the leader of the guards.

Then very slowly the giant raised his great, heavy finger and pointed to the mouth of the dungeon.

'Not yet,' said the hooded figure. Then suddenly it stretched out its hands with the fetters on them and made a quick movement of the wrists. There was a tinkling sound as the fragments of the broken chain fell on the rock at the horse's feet: and the guardsmen let go the bridle and fell back, watching. Then the rider threw back the cloak and a flash of steel smote light into John's eyes and on the giant's face. John saw that it was a woman in the flower of her age: she was so tall that she seemed to him a Titaness, a sun-bright virgin clad in complete steel, with a sword naked in her hand. The giant bent forward in his chair and looked at her.

'Who are you?' he said.

'My name is Reason,' said the virgin.

'Make out her passport quickly,' said the giant in a low voice. 'And let her go through our dominion and be off with all the speed she wishes.'

'Not yet,' said Reason. 'I will ask you three riddles before I go, for a wager.'

'What is the pledge?' said the giant.

'Your head,' said Reason.

There was silence for a time among the mountains.

'Well,' said the giant at last, 'what must be, must be. Ask on.'

'This is my first riddle,' said Reason. 'What is the colour of things in dark places, of fish in the depth of the sea, or of the entrails in the body of man?'

'I cannot say,' said the giant.

'Well,' said Reason. 'Now hear my second riddle. There was a certain man who was going to his own house and his enemy went with him. And his house was beyond a river too swift to swim and too deep to wade. And he could go no faster than his enemy. While he was on his journey his wife sent to him and said, You know that there is only one bridge across the river: tell me, shall I destroy it that the enemy may not cross, or shall I leave it standing that you may cross? What should this man do?'

'It is too hard for me,' said the giant.

'Well,' said Reason. 'Try now to answer my third riddle. By what rule do you tell a copy from an original?'

The giant muttered and mumbled and could not answer, and Reason set spurs in her stallion and it leaped up on to the giant's mossy knees and galloped up his foreleg, till she plunged her sword into his heart. Then there was a noise and a crumbling like a landslide and the huge carcass settled down: and the Spirit of the Age became what he had seemed to be at first, a sprawling hummock of rock.

BOOK 4

BACK TO THE ROAD

Doth any man doubt, that if there were taken out of men's minds vain opinions, flattering hopes, false valuations, imaginations as one would, and the like: but it would leave the minds of a number of men poor shrunken things: full of melancholy and indisposition, and unpleasing to themselves?

BACON

I

LET GRILL BE GRILL

*Those who have been Freudianised too long
are incurable*

The guards had fled. Reason dismounted from her horse and wiped her sword clean on the moss of the foot hills which had been the giant's knees. Then she turned to the door of the pit and struck it so that it broke and she could look into the darkness of the pit and smell the filth.

'You can all come out,' she said.

But there was no movement from within: only, John could hear the prisoners wailing together and saying:

'It is one more wish-fulfilment dream: it is one more wish-fulfilment dream. Don't be taken in again.'

But presently Master Parrot came to the mouth of the pit and said, 'There is no good trying to fool us. Once bit twice shy.' Then he put out his tongue and retired.

'This psittacosis is a very obstinate disorder,' said Reason. And she turned to mount the black horse.

'May I come with you, lady?' said John.

'You may come until you are tired,' said Reason.

2

ARCHETYPE AND ECTYPE

*A question-begging argument exposed – The
sciences bring to the 'facts' the philosophy
they claim to derive from them*

In my dream I saw them set off together, John walking by the lady's stirrup: and I saw them go up the rocky valley where John had gone on the night of his capture. They found the pass unguarded and it gave back an echo to the horse's hoofs and then in a moment they were out of the mountain country and going down a grassy slope into the land beyond. There were few trees and bare, and it was cold: but presently John looked aside and saw a crocus in the grass. For the first time for many days the old sweetness pierced through John's heart: and the next moment he was trying to call back the sound of the birds wheeling over the Island and the green of the waves breaking on its sand – for they had all flashed about him so quickly that they were gone before he knew. His eyes were wet.

He turned to Reason and spoke.

'You can tell me, lady. Is there such a place as the Island in the West, or is it only a feeling of my own mind?'

'I cannot tell you,' said she, 'because you do not know.'

'But you know.'

'But I can tell you only what *you* know. I can bring things out of the dark part of your mind into the light part of it. But now you ask me what is not even in the dark part of your mind.'

'Even if it were only a feeling in my own mind, would it be a bad feeling?'

'I have nothing to tell you of good and bad.'

'I mean this,' said John. 'And this you can tell me. Is it true that it must always end in brown girls, or rather, that it really *begins* from brown girls? They say it is all a pretence, all a disguise for lust.'

'And what do you think of that saying?'

'It is very like that,' said John. 'Both are sweet. Both are full of longing. The one runs into the other. They *are* very alike.'

'Indeed they are,' said the lady. 'But do you not remember my third riddle?'

'About the copy and the original? I could not understand it.'

'Well, now you shall. The people in the country we have just left have seen that your love for the Island is very like your love for the brown girls. Therefore they say that one is a copy of the other. They would also say that you have followed me because I am like your mother, and that your trust in me is a copy of your love for your mother. And then they would say again that your love for your mother is a copy of your love for the brown girls; and so they would come full circle.'

'And what should I answer them?'

'You would say, perhaps one is a copy of the other. But which is the copy of which?'

'I never thought of that.'

'You are not yet of an age to have thought much,' said Reason. 'But you must see that if two things are alike, then it is a further question whether the first is copied from the second, or the second from the first, or both from a third.'

'What would the third be?'

'Some have thought that all these loves were copies of our love for the Landlord.'

'But surely they have considered that and rejected it. Their sciences have disproved it.'

'They could not have, for their sciences are not concerned at all with the general relations of this country to anything that may lie East of it or West of it. They indeed will tell you that their researches have proved that if two things are similar, the fair one is always the copy of the foul one. But their only reason to say so is that they have already decided that the fairest things of all – that is the Landlord, and, if you like, the mountains and the Island – are a mere copy of *this* country. They pretend that their researches lead to that doctrine: but in fact they assume that doctrine first and interpret their researches by it.'

'But they have reasons for assuming it.'

'They have none, for they have ceased to listen to the only people who can tell them anything about it.'

'Who are they?'

'They are younger sisters of mine, and their names are Philosophy and Theology.'

'Sisters! Who is your father?'

'You will know sooner than you wish.'

And now the evening was falling and they were near a little farm, so they turned in there and asked a night's lodging of the farmer, which was readily given them.

3

ESSE IS PERCIPI

*The Reason's duty not (even for life's sake)
to decide without evidence – Why all
accounts of the Unconscious are misleading –
Though they also have their use*

Next morning they continued their journey together. In my dream I saw them go through a country of little hills where the road was always winding to conform to the lie of the valleys: and John walked at the lady's stirrup. The fetter of his hands had broken at the moment when she killed the giant, but the handcuffs were still on his wrists. One half of the broken chain hung down from each hand. There was a greater mildness in the air this day and the buds were fully formed in the hedges.

'I have been thinking, lady,' said John, 'of what you said yesterday and I think I understand that though the Island is very like the place where I first met the brown girl, yet she might be the shadow and the Island the reality. But there is one thing that troubles me.'

'What is that?' said Reason.

'I cannot forget what I have seen in the giant's prison. If we are really like that inside, whatever we imagine must be abominable however innocent it looks. It may be true in general that the foul thing is not always the original and the fair thing not always the copy. But when we have to do with human imaginations, with things that come out of *us*, surely then the giant is right? There at least it is much more likely that whatever seems good is only a veil for the bad – only a part of our skin that has so far escaped the giant's eyes and not yet become transparent.'

'There are two things to be said about that,' replied the lady, 'and the first is this. Who told you that the Island was an imagination of yours?'

'Well, you would not assure me that it was anything real.'

'Nor that it was not.'

'But I must think it is one or the other.'

'By my father's soul, you must *not* – until you have some evidence. Can you not remain in doubt?'

'I don't know that I have ever tried.'

'You must learn to, if you are to come far with me. It is not hard to do it. In Eschropolis, indeed, it is impossible, for the people who live there have to give an opinion once a week or once a day, or else Mr Mammon would soon cut off their food. But out here in the country you can walk all day and all the next day with an unanswered question in your head: you need never speak until you have made up your mind.'

'But if a man wanted to know so badly that he would die unless the question was decided – and no more evidence turned up.'

'Then he would die, that would be all.'

They went on in silence for a while.

'You said there were two things to say,' said John. 'What was the second?'

'The second was this. Did you think that the things you saw in the dungeon were *real*: that we really are like that?'

'Of course I did. It is only our skin that hides them.'

'Then I must ask you the same question that I asked the giant. What is the colour of things in the dark?'

'I suppose, no colour at all.'

'And what of their shape? Have you any notion of it save as what could be seen or touched, or what you could collect from many seeings and touchings?'

'I don't know that I have.'

'Then do you not see how the giant has deceived you?'

'Not quite clearly.'

'He showed you by a trick what our innards *would* look like if they were visible. That is, he showed you something that is not, but something that would be if the world were made all other than it is. But in the real world our innards are invisible. They are not coloured shapes at all, they are feelings. The warmth in your limbs at this moment, the sweetness of your breath as you draw it in, the comfort in your belly because we breakfasted well, and your hunger for the next meal – these are the reality: all the sponges and tubes that you saw in the dungeon are the lie.'

'But if I cut a man open I should see them in him.'

'A man cut open is, so far, not a man: and if you did not sew him up speedily you would be seeing not organs, but death. I am not denying that death is ugly: but the giant made you believe that life is ugly.'

'I cannot forget the man with the cancer.'

'What you saw was unreality. The ugly lump was the giant's trick: the reality was pain, which has no colour or shape.'

'Is that much better?'

'That depends on the man.'

'I think I begin to see.'

'Is it surprising that things should look strange if you see them as they are not? If you take an organ out of a man's body – or a longing out of the dark part of a man's mind – and give to the one the shape and colour, and to the other the self-consciousness, which they never have in reality, would you expect them to be other than monstrous?'

'Is there, then, no truth at all in what I saw under the giant's eyes?'

'Such pictures are useful to physicians.'

'Then I really am clean,' said John. 'I am not – like those.'

Reason smiled. 'There, too,' she said, 'there is truth mixed up with the giant's conjuring tricks. It will do you no harm to remember from time to time the ugly sights inside. You come of a race that cannot afford to be proud.'

As she spoke John looked up, in doubt of her meaning: and for the first time since he came into her company he felt afraid. But the impression lasted only for a moment. 'Look,' said John, 'here is a little inn. Is it not time that we rested and ate something?'

4

ESCAPE

*If Religion is a Wish-fulfilment dream,
whose wishes does it fulfil? – Certainly not
John's! – He decides to stop reasoning at
this point*

In the warmth of the afternoon they went on again, and it came into John's mind to ask the lady the meaning of her second riddle.

'It has two meanings,' said she, 'and in the first the bridge signifies Reasoning. The Spirit of the Age wishes to allow argument and not to allow argument.'

'How is that?'

'You heard what they said. If anyone argues with them they say that he is rationalising his own desires, and therefore need not be answered. But if anyone listens to them they will then argue themselves to show that their own doctrines are true.'

'I see. And what is the cure for this?'

'You must ask them whether any reasoning is valid or not. If they say no, then their own doctrines, being reached by reasoning, fall to the ground. If they say yes, then they will have to examine your arguments and refute them on their merits: for if some reasoning is valid, for all they know, your bit of reasoning may be one of the valid bits.'

'I see,' said John. 'But what was the second interpretation?'

'In the second,' said Reason, 'the bridge signifies the giant's own favourite doctrine of the wish-fulfilment dream. For this also he wishes to use and not to use.'

'I don't see how he wishes *not* to use it.'

'Does he not keep on telling people that the Landlord is a wish-fulfilment dream?'

'Yes; surely that is true – the only true thing he did say.'

'Now think. Is it really true that the giant and Sigismund, and the people in Eschropolis, and Mr Halfways, are going about filled with a longing that there should be a Landlord, and cards of rules, and a mountain land beyond the brook, with a possibility of a black hole?'

Then John stood still on the road to think. And first he gave a shake of his shoulders, and then he put his hands to his sides, and then he began to laugh till he was almost shaken to pieces. And when he had nearly finished, the vastness and impudence and simplicity of the fraud which had been practised came over him all again, and he laughed harder. And just when he had nearly recovered and was beginning to get his breath again, suddenly he had a picture in his mind of Victoriana and Glugly and Gus Halfways and how they would look if a rumour reached them that there *was* a Landlord and he was coming to Eschropolis. This was too much for him, and he laughed so hard that the broken chains of the Spirit of the Age fell off his wrists altogether. But all the while Reason sat and watched him.

'You had better hear the rest of the argument,' she said at last. 'It may not be such a laughing matter as you suppose.'

'Oh, yes – the argument,' said John, wiping his eyes.

'You see now the direction in which the giant does *not* want the wish-fulfilment theory used?'

'I'm not sure that I do,' said John.

'Don't you see what follows if you adopt his own rules?'

'No,' said John, very loudly: for a terrible apprehension was stealing over him.

'But you must see,' said Reason, 'that for him and all his subjects *disbelief* in the Landlord is a wish-fulfilment dream.'

'I shall not adopt his rules.'

'You would be foolish not to have profited *at all* by your stay in his country,' said Reason. 'There is some force in the wish-fulfilment doctrine.'

'Some, perhaps, but very little.'

'I only wanted to make it clear that whatever force it had was in favour of the Landlord's existence, not against it – specially in your case.'

'Why specially in mine?' said John sulkily.

'Because the Landlord is the thing you have been most afraid of all your life. I do not say that any theory should be accepted because it is disagreeable, but if any should, then belief in the Landlord should be accepted first.'

As Reason said these words they had reached the top of a little hill, and John begged for a halt, being out of breath. He looked back and saw beyond the green, rolling country the dark line of mountains which was the frontier of the giant's land: but behind them, and far bigger, rose the old mountains of the East, picked out in the rays of the declining sun against a dark sky. They seemed no smaller than when John had looked at them long ago from Puritania.

'I do not know where you are leading me,' he said at last, 'and among all these winding roads I have lost my sense of direction. As well, I find the pace of your horse fatiguing. If you will excuse me, I think I will henceforth pursue my journey alone.'

'As you wish,' said Reason. 'But I would strongly advise you to take this turn to the left.'

'Where does it go to?' asked John suspiciously.

'It takes you back to the main road,' said Reason.

'That will do well enough,' said John. 'And now, lady, give me your blessing before I go.'

'I have no blessing to give,' said the Virgin. 'I do not deal in blessings and cursings.'

Then John bade her good-bye and took the road she had pointed out to him. As soon as she was out of sight, I dreamed that he put down his head and ran; for the silly fellow supposed that she might follow him. And he continued running until he found that he was going up a hill – a hill so steep that it left him no breath for running – and at the very top his road cut into another which ran left and right along the ridge. Then John looked one way along it to the East and the other way along it to the West, and saw that it was indeed the main road. He stayed for a minute to mop his brow. Then he turned to the right, with his face towards the setting sun, and resumed his journey.

BOOK 5

THE GRAND CANYON

Not by road and foot nor by sail and ocean
Shalt thou find any course that reaches
The world beyond the North.
PINDAR

The ephemerals have no help to give. Behold them;
They are deedless and cripple, like to
A dream. The kind of mortals
Is bound with a chain and their eyes are in darkness.
AESCHYLUS

Alas, what can they teach and not mislead,
Ignorant of themselves, of God much more,
And how the world began, and how man fell.
MILTON

I

THE GRAND CANYON

*John decides to live virtuously but at once
meets an obstacle – Conscience tells him he
can and must pass it by his own efforts –
Traditional Christianity says he cannot*

The main road soon began to ascend and after a short climb John found himself on a bleak tableland which continued to rise before him, but at a gentler angle. After he had walked a mile or so he saw the figure of a man ahead, outlined against the setting sun. At first the figure stood still: then it took a few paces to the left and to the right as if in indecision. Then it turned about to face him, and to his surprise hailed him as an old acquaintance. Because of the light in his face John could not at first see who it was, and they had joined hands before he knew that it was Vertue.

'What can have delayed you?' cried John, 'I thought by your pace when I left you that you would have been a week's journey ahead of me by now.'

'If you think that,' said Vertue, 'your way must have been easier than mine. Have you not crossed mountains?'

'I came through a pass,' said John.

'The main road took them without a bend,' said Vertue. 'And I often made scarcely ten miles a day. But that does not signify: I have learned something of climbing and sweated off a good deal of soft flesh. What has really delayed me is this – I have been here for several days.'

With that he motioned John to proceed and they went forward together to the brow of the slope. Then I saw John start back a pace or so with a cry, for he had found that he stood on the edge of a precipice. Then presently he re-approached it with caution and looked.

He saw that the road ran up without warning to the edge of a great gorge or chasm and ended in the air, as if it had been broken off. The chasm might be seven miles wide and as for its length, it stretched southward on his left and northward on his right as far as he could see. The sun shining in his face cast all the further side into shadow, so that he could not see much of it clearly. It seemed to him, however, a rich country from the verdure and the size of the trees.

'I have been exploring the cliffs,' said Vertue. 'And I think we could get half-way down. Come a little nearer. You see that ledge?'

'I have a very poor head for heights,' said John.

'That one,' said Vertue, pointing to a narrow strip of greenery a thousand feet below them.

'I could never reach it.'

'Oh, you could reach *that* easily enough. The difficulty is to know what happens beyond it. I am inclined to think that it overhangs: and though we could get down to it, I am not sure that we could get back if the rest of the descent was impracticable.'

'Then it would be madness to trust ourselves so far.'

'I don't know about that. It would be in accordance with the rule.'

'What rule?'

'The rule is,' said Vertue, 'that if we have one chance out of a hundred of surviving, we must attempt it: but if we have none, absolutely none, then it would be self-destruction, and we need not.'

'It is no rule of mine,' said John.

'But it is. We all have the same set of rules, really, you know.'

'If it is a rule of mine, it is one that I cannot obey.'

'I don't think I understand you,' said Vertue. 'But of course you may be such a bad climber that *you* wouldn't have even one chance ... that would make a difference, I allow.'

Then a third voice spoke.

'You have neither of you any chance at all unless I carry you down.'

Both the young men turned at the sound. An old woman was seated in a kind of rocky chair at the very edge of the precipice.

'Oh, it's you, Mother Kirk, is it?' said Vertue, and added in an undertone to John, 'I have seen her about the cliffs more than once. Some of the country people say she is second-sighted, and some that she is crazy.'

'I shouldn't trust her,' said John in the same tone. 'She looks to me much more like a witch.' Then he turned to the old woman and said aloud: 'And how could you carry us down, mother? We would be more fit to carry you.'

'I could do it, though,' said Mother Kirk, 'by the power that the Landlord has given me.'

'So you believe in the Landlord, too?' said John.

'How can I not, dear,' said she, 'when I am his own daughter-in-law?'

'He does not give you very fine clothes,' said John, glancing at the old woman's country cloak.

'They'll last my time,' said the old woman placidly.

'We ought to try her,' whispered Vertue to John. 'As long as there is any chance we are not allowed to neglect it.' But John frowned at him to be silent and addressed the old woman again.

'Do you not think this Landlord of yours is a very strange one?' he said.

'How so?' said she.

'Why does he make a road like this running up to the very edge of a precipice – unless it is to encourage travellers to break their necks in the dark?'

'Oh, bless you, he never left it like that,' said the old woman. 'It was a good road all round the world when it was new, and all this gorge is far later than the road.'

'You mean,' said Vertue, 'that there has been some sort of catastrophe.'

'Well,' said Mother Kirk, 'I see there will be no getting you down tonight, so I may as well tell you the story. Come and sit down by me. You are neither of you so wise that you need be ashamed of listening to an old wives' tale.'

2

MOTHER KIRK'S STORY

*The Sin of Adam – Because of it all his
posterity find a chasm across their road*

When they were seated, the old woman told the following story:
'You must know that once upon a time there were no tenants in this country at all, for the Landlord used to farm it himself. There were only the animals and the Landlord used to look after them, he and his sons and daughters. Every morning they used to come down from the mountains and milk the cows and lead out the sheep to pasture. And they needed less watching, for all the animals were tamer then: and there were no fences needed, for if a wolf got in among the flocks he would do them no harm. And one day the Landlord was going home from his day's work when he looked round on the country, and the beasts, and saw how the crops were springing, and it came into his head that the whole thing was too good to keep to himself. So he decided to let the country to tenants, and his first tenant was a young married man. But first the Landlord made a farm in the very centre of the land where the soil was the best and the air most wholesome, and that was the very spot where you are sitting now. They were to have the whole land, but that was too much for them to keep under cultivation. The Landlord's idea was that they could work the farm and leave the rest as a park for the time being: but later they could divide the park up into holdings for their children. For you must know that he drew up a very different lease from the kind you have nowadays. It was a lease in perpetuity on his side, for he promised never to turn them out; but on their side, they could leave when they chose, as long as one of their sons was there, to take the farm on, and then they could go up to live with him in the mountains. He thought that would be a good thing because it would broaden the minds of his own mountain children to mix with strangers. And they thought so too. But before he put the tenants in possession there was one thing he had to do. Up to this time the country had been full of a certain fruit which the Landlord had planted for the refreshment of himself and his children, if they were thirsty during the day as they worked down here. It was a very good fruit and up in the mountains they say it is even

more plentiful: but it is very strong and only those who are mountain-bred ought to eat it, for only they can digest it properly. Hitherto, while there were only beasts in the land, it had done no harm for these mountain-apples to be growing in every thicket; for you know that an animal will eat nothing but what is good for it. But now that there were to be men in the land, the Landlord was afraid that they might do themselves an injury; yet it was not to be thought of that he should dig up every sapling of that tree and make the country into a desert. So he decided that it was best to be frank with the young people, and when he found a great big mountain-apple tree growing in the very centre of the farm he said, "So much the better. If they are to learn sense, they may as well learn it from the beginning: and if they will not, there's no help for it. For if they did not find mountain-apples on the farm, they would soon find them somewhere else." So he left the apple tree standing, and put the man and his wife into their farm: but before he left them he explained the whole affair to them – as much of it as could be explained – and warned them on no account to eat any of the apples. Then he went home. And for a time the young man and his wife behaved very well, tending the animals and managing their farm, and abstaining from the mountain-apples; and for all I know they might never have done otherwise if the wife had not somehow made a new acquaintance. This new acquaintance was a landowner himself. He had been born in the mountains and was one of our Landlord's own children, but he had quarrelled with his father and set up on his own, and now had built up a very considerable estate in another country. His estate marches, however, with this country: and as he was a great land-grabber he always wanted to take this bit in – and he has very nearly succeeded.'

'I've never met any tenants of his,' said John.

'Not tenants in chief, my dear,' said the old woman. 'And so you didn't know them. But you may have met the Clevers, who are the tenants of Mr Mammon: and he is a tenant of the Spirit of the Age: who holds directly of the Enemy.'

'I am sure the Clevers would be very surprised,' said John, 'to hear that they had a Landlord at all. They would think this enemy, as you call him, no less a superstition than *your* Landlord.'

'But that is how business is managed,' said Mother Kirk. 'The little people do not know the big people to whom they belong. The big people do not intend that they should. No important transference of property could be carried out if all the small people at the bottom knew what was really happening. But this is not part of my story. As I was saying, the enemy got to know the farmer's wife: and, however he did it, or whatever he said to her, it wasn't long before he persuaded her that the one thing she needed was a nice mountain-apple. And she took one and ate it. And then – you know how it is with husbands – she made the farmer come round to her mind. And at the moment he put out his hand and plucked the fruit there was an earthquake, and the country cracked open all the way across from North to South; and ever since, instead of the farm, there has been this gorge, which the country people call the Grand Canyon. But in my language its name is *Peccatum Adae*.'

3

THE SELF-SUFFICIENCY

OF VERTUE

*Fear is too suspicious, and the natural
conscience too proud, to accept help –
Rejecting Christianity, John turns to
cultured Worldliness*

'And I suppose,' said John sourly, 'the Landlord was so annoyed that it was he who invented the rules and the black hole?'

'The story is not quite so simple as that,' said the old woman, 'so many things happened after the eating of the apple. For one thing, the taste created such a craving in the man and the woman that they thought they could never eat enough of it; and they were not content with all the wild apple trees, but planted more and more, and grafted mountain-apple on to every other kind of tree so that every fruit should have a dash of that taste in it. They succeeded so well that the whole vegetable system of the country is now infected: and there is hardly a fruit or a root in the land – certainly none this side of the canyon – that has not a little mountain-apple in it. You have never tasted anything that was quite free from it.'

'And what has that got to do with the card of rules?' said John.

'Everything,' said Mother Kirk. 'In a country where all the food is more or less poisoned – but some of it very much less than more – you need very complicated rules indeed to keep healthy.'

'Meanwhile,' said Vertue, 'we are not getting on with our journey.'

'I will carry you down in the morning, if you like,' said Mother Kirk. 'Only mind you, it is a dangerous place, and you must do exactly as I tell you.'

'If the place is so dangerous –' began John, when Vertue, who had been struck by the woman's last words, suddenly broke in:

'I am afraid it is no use, mother,' he said; 'I cannot put myself under anyone's orders. I must be the captain of my soul and the master of my fate. But thank you for your offer.'

'You are right,' said John hastily, and added in a whisper, 'The old creature is clearly insane. Our real business is to explore this chasm North and South until we find some place where the descent *is* practicable.'

Vertue had risen.

'We are thinking, mother,' he said, 'that we should like to make sure for ourselves that there is no place where we cannot get down without being carried. You see my own legs have served me so far – and I should not like to start being carried now.'

'It will do you no harm to try,' answered Mother Kirk. 'And I should not wonder if you find a way down. Getting up the other side is another question, to be sure; but perhaps we shall meet again when it comes to that.'

By this time it was quite dark. The two young men bade good night to the woman and drew back along the main road to discuss their plans. Two by-roads branched off from it about a quarter of a mile from the precipice: and as that which went to the north seemed rather the better, and also pointed a little backward and away from the cliffs (which John was anxious not to skirt in the darkness), they turned northward. It was a fine starlit night and grew colder as they proceeded.

4

MR SENSIBLE

*The pretentiousness and cold frivolity of
cultured Worldliness – Far from attacking
the spiritual life, the cultured World
patronises it – 'The philosophy of all sensible
men' – Its hatred of all systematic reasoning
– Its ignorant and dilettante scepticism*

When they had walked rather more than a mile John drew Vertue's attention to a light a little back from the road: and I saw them follow it till they came to a gateway and after that to a door, and there they knocked.

'Whose house is this?' said Vertue when the servant opened to them.

'This is Mr Sensible's house,' said the servant. 'And if you are benighted travellers he will receive you gladly.'

Then he brought them into a room where a lamp was burning clearly, but not very brightly, and an old gentleman was seated by a blazing wood fire with his dog at his feet and his book on his knees and a jig-saw puzzle at one side of him spread out on a wooden frame, and on the other a chessboard with the pieces set for a problem. He rose to greet them very cordially but not hastily.

'You are very welcome, gentlemen,' said Mr Sensible. 'Pray come and warm yourselves. Drudge' (and here he called to the servant) 'make some supper ready for three: the usual supper, Drudge. I shall not be able to offer you luxury, gentlemen. The wine of my own country, cowslip wine, shall be your drink. It will be rough to your palates, but to mine the draught that I owe to my own garden and my own kitchen will always have a flavour beyond Hippocrene. The radishes, also of my own growing, I think I may venture to praise. But I see by your looks that I have already betrayed my foible. I confess that my garden is my pride. But what then? We are all children, and I reckon him the wisest among us that can make most sport out of the toys suitable to that condition, without seeking to go beyond it. *Regum æquabit opes animis.* Contentment, my friends, contentment is the best riches. Do not let the dog tease you, sir. He has mange. Down, Rover! Alas, Rover! thou little knowest that sentence is passed upon thee.'

'You are surely not going to destroy him, sir?' said John.

'He begins to ail,' said Mr Sensible. 'And it would be foolish to keep him longer. What would you? *Omnes eodem cogimur*. He has lain in the sun and hunted fleas enough, and now, poor fellow, he must go *quo dives Tullus et Ancus*. We must take life on the terms it is given us.'

'You will miss your old companion.'

'Why, as to that you know, the great art of life is to moderate our passions. Objects of affection are like other belongings. We must love them enough to enrich our lives while we have them – not enough to impoverish our lives when they are gone. You see this puzzle here. While I am engaged on it it seems to me of sovereign importance to fit the pieces together: when it is done I think of it no more: and if I should fail to do it, why I should not break my heart. Confound that Drudge. Hi! whoreson, are we to wait all night for our supper?'

'Coming, sir,' said Drudge from the kitchen.

'I think the fellow goes to sleep over his pots and pans,' said Mr Sensible, 'but let us occupy the time by continuing our conversation. Good conversation I reckon among the finer sweets of life. But I would not include diatribe or lecturing or persistent discussion under that head. Your doctrinaire is the bane of all talk. As I sit here listening to your opinions – *nullius addictus* – and following the ball wherever it rolls, I defy system. I love to explore your minds *en déshabille*. Nothing comes amiss – *j'aime le jeu, l'amour, les livres, la musique, la ville et la champagne – enfin tout*! Chance is, after all, our best guide – need I call a better witness than the fortunate cast of the dice which has brought you beneath my roof tonight?'

'It wasn't exactly chance,' said Vertue, who had been restlessly waiting to speak. 'We are on a journey and we are looking for a way to cross the Grand Canyon.'

'*Haud equidem invideo*,' said the old gentleman. 'You do not insist on my accompanying you?'

'We hadn't thought of it,' said John.

'Why then I am very willing that you should go!' cried Mr Sensible with a burst of melodious laughter. 'And yet to what end? I often amuse myself with speculating on that curious restlessness in the mind which drives us, specially in youth, to climb up a mountain merely in order that we may then climb down, or to cross the seas in order that we may pay an inn-keeper for setting before us worse cheer than we might eat in our own house. *Caelum non animum mutamus*. Not that I would repress the impulse, you understand, any more than I would starve any other part of my nature. Here again, the secret of happiness lies in knowing where to stop. A moderate allowance of travelling – enough to quiet, without satiating, a liberal curiosity – is very well. One brings back a few rarities to store in one's inner cabinet against a dull day. But the Grand Canyon – surely a modest tour along the cliffs on *this* side of it would give you much the same sort of scenery, and save your necks.'

'It wasn't scenery we were looking for,' said John. 'I am trying to find the Island in the West.'

'You refer, no doubt, to some aesthetic experience. There again – I would not urge a young man to shut his eyes to that sort of thing. Who has not felt immortal longings at the lengthening of the shadow or the turning of the leaf? Who has not stretched out his hands for the ulterior shore? *Et ego in Arcadia!* We have all been fools once – aye, and are glad to have been fools too. But our imaginations, like our appetites, need discipline: not, heaven help us, in the interest of any transcendental ethic, but in the interests of our own solid good. That wild impulse must be tasted, not obeyed. The bees have stings, but we rob them of their honey. To hold all that urgent sweetness to our lips in the cup of one perfect moment, missing no faintest ingredient in the flavour of its μονόχρονος ἡδονή, yet ourselves, in a sense, unmoved – this is the true art. This tames in the service of the reasonable life even those pleasures whose loss might seem to be the heaviest, yet necessary, price we paid for rationality. Is it an audacity to hint that for the corrected palate the taste of the draught even owes its last sweetness to the knowledge that we have wrested it from an unwilling source? To cut off pleasures from the consequences and conditions which they have by nature, detaching, as it were, the precious phrase from its irrelevant context, is what distinguishes the man from the brute and the citizen from the savage. I cannot join with those moralists who inveigh against the Roman emetics in their banquets: still less with those who would forbid the even more beneficient contraceptive devices of our later times. That man who can eat as taste, not nature, prompts him and yet fear no aching belly, or who can indulge in Venus and fear no impertinent bastard, is a civilized man. In him I recognize Urbanity – the note of the centre.'

'Do you know of any way across the canyon?' said Vertue abruptly.

'I do not,' said their host, 'for I have never made inquiries. The proper study of mankind is man, and I have always left useless speculations alone. Suppose that there were a way across, to what purpose should I use it? Why should I scramble down this side and up the other to find after my labours the same soil still beneath me and the same heaven above? It would be laughable to suppose that the country beyond the gorge can be any different from the country on this side of it. *Eadem sunt omnia semper.* Nature has already done all she can for our comfort and amusement, and the man who does not find content at home will seek it vainly abroad. Confound that fellow! Drudge!! Will you bring us our supper or do you prefer to have every bone in your body broken?'

'Coming, sir,' said Drudge from the kitchen.

'There might be different *people* on the other side of the canyon,' suggested John in the momentary pause that followed.

'That is even less likely,' said Mr Sensible. 'Human nature is always the same. The dress and the manners may vary, but I detect the unchanging heart beneath the shifting disguises. If there are men beyond the canyon, rest assured that we know them already. They are born and they die: and in the interval between they are the same lovable rascals that we know at home.'

'Still,' said John, 'you can't really be certain that there is no such place as my Island. Reason left it an open question.'

'Reason!' exclaimed Mr Sensible. 'Do you mean the mad woman who goes riding about the country dressed up in armour? I trust that when I spoke of the reasonable life you did not think that I meant anything under *her* auspices? There is a strange confusion in our language here, for the reasonableness which I commend has no more dangerous enemy than Reason. Perhaps I should drop the use of the name altogether, and say that my deity is not reason but *le bon sens*.'

'What is the difference?' said Vertue.

'Sense is easy, Reason is hard. Sense knows where to stop with gracious inconsistency, while Reason slavishly follows an abstract logic whither she knows not. The one seeks comfort and finds it, the other seeks truth and is still seeking. *Le bon sens* is the father of a flourishing family: Reason is barren and a virgin. If I had my way I should clap this Reason of yours in the bridewell to pursue her meditations in the straw. The baggage has a pretty face, I allow: but she leads us from our true aim – joy, pleasure, ease, content, whate'er the name! She is a fanatic who has never learned from my master to pursue the golden mean, and, being a mortal, to think mortal thoughts. *Auream quis quis –*'

'It is very odd that you should say that,' interrupted Vertue, 'for I also was brought up on Aristotle. But I think my text must have differed from yours. In mine, the doctrine of the Mean does not bear the sense you have given it at all. He specially says that there is no excess of goodness. You cannot go too far in the right direction. The line that we should follow may start from a middle point in the base of a triangle: but the further off the apex is, the better. In that dimension –'

'*Do manus!*' broke out Mr Sensible. 'Spare us the rest, young man. We are not at a lecture, and I readily admit that your scholarship is more recent than mine. Philosophy should be our mistress, not our master: and the pursuit of a pedantic accuracy amidst the freedom of our social pleasures is as unwelcome as –'

'And the bit about thinking mortal thoughts,' continued Vertue, whose social experience, as I dreamed, was not extensive, 'the bit about mortal thoughts was quoted by Aristotle to say that he disagreed with it. He held that the end of mortal life was to put on immortality as much as might be. And he also said that the most useless of studies was the noblest.'

'I see you are letter-perfect, young man,' said Mr Sensible, with a rather chilly smile, 'and I am sure these pieces of information, if repeated to your teachers, would win the applause they deserve. Here, if you will forgive me, they are a little out of place. A gentleman's knowledge of the ancient authors is not that of a pedant: and I think you have misunderstood the place which philosophy ought to hold in the reasonable life. We do not memorise *systems*. What system can stand? What system does not leave us with the old refrain – *que sais-je?* It is in her power to remind us of the strangeness of things – in the brown charm of her secluded meditations – above all, in her decorative function – that philosophy becomes instrumental to the good life. We go to the Porch and the Academy to be spectators, not partisans. Drudge!!'

'Dinner is served, sir,' said Drudge, appearing at the door.

Then I dreamed that they went into the dining room and so to table.

5

TABLE TALK

*The cultured World's unacknowledged
dependences – 'The religion of all
sensible men'*

The cowslip wine came with the oysters. It was a little rough, as the old gentleman had prophesied, and the glasses were so very small that Vertue drained his at once. John was afraid that there might be no more to come and therefore dallied over his, partly because he feared that he might put his host out of countenance and partly because he disliked the taste. But his precautions were needless, for with the soup came sherry.

'*Dapibus mensas onerabat inemptis!*' said Mr Sensible. 'I hope that this wild garden vintage is not unpleasing to an unspoiled palate.'

'You don't mean to say that you have vines?' exclaimed John.

'I was referring to the cowslip wine,' said Mr Sensible. 'I hope to have some good vines soon, but at present I still rely a little on my neighbours. Is this our own sherry, Drudge?'

'No, sir,' said Drudge. 'This is that lot that Mr Broad sent.'

'Halibut!' said John. 'You surely don't –'

'No,' said Mr Sensible. 'Sea fish, I confess, I must get from my friends on the coast.'

As the meal went on, John's good manners forbade him to make further inquiries, and when a salad came with one or two very small radishes in it he was positively relieved that his host should be able to claim them as his own produce ('His humble sauce a radish or an egg,' said Mr Sensible). But in my dream I was privileged to know the sources of the whole meal. The cowslip wine and the radishes were home-grown; the joint had been a present from Mr Mammon: the entrées and savouries came from Eschropolis: the champagne and ices from old Mr Halfways. Some of the food was part of the stores which Mr Sensible had taken over when he came to live there, from his predecessors who had occupied this house before him: for on that tableland, and especially to the North of the main road, the air is so light and cold that things keep for a long time. The bread, the salt, and the apples had been left by Epicurus who was the builder of the house and its first inhabitant. Some very fine hock had belonged to Horace. The claret and also (as I remember) most of the silver, were Montaigne's. But the port, which was one in a thousand and the best thing on that table, had once belonged to Rabelais, who in his turn had it as a present from old Mother Kirk when they were friends. Then I dreamed that after dinner old Mr Sensible stood up and made a little speech in Latin thanking the Landlord for all they had received.

'What?' said John. 'Do *you* believe in the Landlord?'

'No part of our nature is to be suppressed,' said Mr Sensible. 'Least of all a part that has enshrined itself in beautiful traditions. The Landlord has his function like everything else as one element in the good life.'

Then presently Mr Sensible, who was turning very red, fixed his eyes intently on John and repeated:

'As one element. As one element.'

'I see,' said John, and there was a long silence.

'As well,' began Mr Sensible, with great energy some ten minutes later, 'it is part of good manners. Αθανάτους μὲν πρῶτα θεούς νόμω ὡς διάκειται— Τίμα. My dear Mr Vertue, my dear young friend, your glass is quite empty. I mean absolutely empty. *Cras ingens iterabimus.*'

There was another and longer pause. John began to wonder whether Mr Sensible were not asleep, when suddenly Mr Sensible said with great conviction:

'*Pellite cras ingens tum-tum* νόμω ὡς διάκειται.'

Then he smiled at them and finally went to sleep. And presently Drudge came in looking old and thin and dirty in the pale morning light – for I thought that the dawn was just then beginning to show through the chinks of the shutters – to carry his master to bed. Then I saw him come back and lead the guests to their beds. And then the third time I saw him come back into the dining-room and pour out the remains of the claret into a glass and drink it off. Then he stood for a moment or so blinking his red eyes and rubbing his bony, stubbly chin. At last he yawned and set about tidying the room for breakfast.

6

DRUDGE

The 'sensible' men are parasitic –
Their culture is precarious

I dreamed that John awoke feeling cold. The chamber in which he lay was luxuriously furnished and all the house was silent, so that John thought it would be useless to rise, and he piled all his clothes on him and tried to sleep again. But he only grew colder. Then he said to himself, 'Even if there is no chance of breakfast, I may save myself from freezing by walking about.' So he rose and huddled on all his clothes and went down into the house, but the fires were not yet lit. Finding the back door open he went out. It was full morning of a grey, sunless day. There were dark clouds, fairly low, and as John came out one snowflake fell at his feet, but no more. He found that he was in Mr Sensible's garden, but it was more of a yard than a garden. A high wall ran all about it and all within the wall was dry, brown earth, with a few stony paths. Dibbling the earth with his foot, John found that the soil was only half an inch deep: under it was solid rock. A little way from the house he found Drudge down on his hands and knees scraping together what seemed to be a little pile of dust, but it was in fact the soil of the garden. The little pile had been got together at the cost of leaving the rock uncovered for a big circle – like a bald patch – all round Drudge.

'Good morning, Drudge,' said John. 'What are you making?'
'Radish beds, sir.'
'Your master is a great gardener.'
'Talks about it, sir.'
'Does he not work in the garden himself?'
'No, sir.'
'It is a poor soil here. Does he manage to feed himself on his own produce in a good year?'
'Feeds me on it, sir.'
'What does the garden grow – besides radishes?'
'Nothing, sir.'
John passed on to the end of the garden and looked over the wall, which was lower here. He drew back with a little start for he found that he was

looking down an abyss: the garden was perched on the edge of the Grand Canyon. Below John's feet, at the bottom of the gorge, lay the forest, and on the opposite side he saw a mixture of wood and cliff. The cliffs were all shaggy with trailing and hanging greenery and streams, rendered immovable to sight by their distance, came down from the land beyond. Even on that cold morning the farther side looked richer and warmer than his own.

'We must get out of this,' said John. At that moment Drudge called to him.

'I shouldn't lean on that wall, sir,' he said. 'There's frequent landslides.'
'Landslides?'
'Yes, sir. I've rebuilt that wall a dozen times. The house used to be right out there – half-way across the gorge.'
'The canyon is getting wider, then?'
'At this point, sir. In Mr Epicurus' time –'
'You have been employed here under other masters, then?'
'Yes, sir. I've seen a good many of them. Whoever has lived here has always needed me. Choregia they used to call me in the old days, but now they just call me Drudge.'
'Tell me about your old masters,' said John.
'Mr Epicurus was the first. Mental case he was, poor gentleman: he had a chronic fear of the black hole. Something dreadful. I never had a better employer, though. Nice, kind, quiet-spoken sort of a man. I was very sorry when he went down the cliff –'
'Goodness me!' exclaimed John. 'Do you mean that some of your masters have lost their lives in these landslides?'
'Most of them, sir.'
At that moment a leonine roar came from one of the upper windows of the house.
'Drudge! Son of a bitch! Hot water.'
'Coming, sir,' said Drudge, rising very deliberately from his knees and giving a finishing pat to his heap of dust. 'I shall be leaving here soon,' he continued to John. 'I am thinking of going further North.'
'Further North?'
'Yes, sir. There are openings with Mr Savage up in the mountains. I was wondering if you and Mr Vertue were going that way –'
'Drudge!' bellowed Mr Sensible's voice from the house.
'Coming, sir,' said Drudge, beginning to untie two pieces of string with which he had confined his trousers beneath his knees. 'So you see, Mr John, I should be greatly obliged if you would allow me to travel with you.'
'Drudge! Am I to call you again?' shouted Mr Sensible.
'Coming, sir. If you was to agree I would give Mr Sensible notice this morning.'

'We are certainly going North for a bit,' said John. 'And I should have no objection, provided Mr Vertue agrees.'

'Very kind of you, I am sure, sir,' said Drudge. Then he turned and walked slowly into the house.

7

THE GAUCHERIE OF VERTUE

*Take away the cultured World's power
of commanding labour – And the whole
thing collapses*

Mr Sensible was not in good humour when they met at breakfast. 'That ungrateful blockhead of a servant of mine is leaving me in the lurch,' he said, 'and for the next few days we must shift for ourselves. I fear I am a wretched cook. Perhaps, Vertue, you would indulge me so far as to take the cooking on yourself until I get a new man? I dare say you could enable the three of us to live a very tolerable sort of picnic life for three days?'

The two young men informed him that they were continuing their journey after breakfast.

'This,' said Mr Sensible, 'is getting really serious. Do you mean to say that you are going to desert me? I am to be reduced to absolute solitude – deprived of the common decencies of life – compelled to spend my day in menial offices? Very well, sir, I am unacquainted with modern manners: no doubt this is the way in which young men now return hospitality.'

'I beg your pardon, sir,' said Vertue. 'I had not seen it in that light. I will certainly act as our servant for a day or so if you wish it. I had not understood that it would be such a burden to you to cook for yourself. I don't remember that you said anything about servants when you were outlining the good life last night.'

'Why, sir,' said Mr Sensible. 'When I outline the principles of the steam engine I do not explicitly state that I expect fire to burn or the laws of gravity to operate. There are certain things that one always takes for granted. When I speak of the art of life I presuppose the ordinary conditions of life which that art utilises.'

'Such as wealth,' said Vertue.

'A competence, a competence,' said Mr Sensible.

'And health, too?' said Vertue.

'Moderate health,' said Mr Sensible.

'Your art, then,' said Vertue, 'seems to teach men that the best way of being happy is to enjoy unbroken good fortune in every respect. They would not all find the advice helpful. And now, if Drudge will show me his scullery, I will wash up the breakfast things.'

'You may save yourself the trouble, sir,' said Mr Sensible drily. 'I cannot pretend to your intensity, and I do not choose to be lectured at the breakfast table. When you have mixed more with the world you will learn not to turn the social board into a school room. In the meantime, forgive me if I feel that I should find your continued society a little fatiguing. Conversation should be like the bee which darts to the next flower before the last has ceased swaying from its airy visit: you make it more like a wood beetle eating its way through a table.'

'As you wish,' said Vertue, 'but how will you do?'

'I shall shut up the house,' said Mr Sensible, 'and practise αὐτάρκεια in a hotel until I have fitted this place up with such mechanical devices as will henceforth render me wholly independent. I see that I have let myself get behind the times. I should have listened more to certain good friends of mine in the city of Claptrap who have kept abreast of modern invention. They assure me that machinery will soon put the good life beyond the reach of chance: and if mechanism alone will not do it I know a eugenist who promises to breed us a race of peons who will be psychologically incapable of playing me a trick like this of Drudge's.'

So it fell out that all four left the house together. Mr Sensible was astonished to find that Drudge (who parted from his employer very civilly) was accompanying the young men. He only shrugged his shoulders, however, and said, '*Vive la bagatelle*! You have stayed in my house which is called Thelema, and its motto is *Do what you will*. So many men, so many minds. I hope I can tolerate anything except intolerance.' Then he went his way and they saw him no more.

BOOK 6

NORTHWARD ALONG THE CANYON

*For being unlike the magnanimous man,
they yet ape him; and that in such particulars
as they can.*
ARISTOTLE

*Much of the soul they talk, but all awry,
And in themselves seek virtue.*
MILTON

*I do not admire the excess of some one virtue
unless I am shewn at the same time the
excess of the opposite virtue. A man does not
prove his greatness by standing at an
extremity, but by touching both extremities
at once and filling all that lies between them.*
PASCAL

*Contempt is a well-recognized defensive
reaction.*
I. A. RICHARDS

I

FIRST STEPS TO THE NORTH

*Accompanied by poverty and virtue – John
travels into sterner regions of the mind*

'It is of no use keeping to the road,' said Vertue. 'We must explore the cliff-edge as we go along and make trial descents from point to point.'

'Begging your pardon, sir,' said Drudge, 'I know these parts very well and there is no way down, at least within thirty miles. You'll miss nothing by keeping to the road for today at any rate.'

'How do you know?' asked Vertue. 'Have you ever tried?'

'Oh, bless you, yes,' said Drudge. 'I've often tried to get across the canyon when I was a youngster.'

'Clearly we had better follow the road,' said John.

'I do not feel quite satisfied,' said Vertue. 'But we can always take the cliffs on the way back. I have an idea that if there is a way down it will be at the extreme north where this gorge opens on the sea: or failing everything, we might manipulate the mouth of the gorge by boat. In the meantime I dare say we might do worse than press on by road.'

'I quite agree,' said John.

Then I saw the three set forward on a more desolate march than I had yet beheld. On every side of them the tableland seemed perfectly flat, but their muscles and lungs soon told them that there was a slight but continuous rise. There was little vegetation – here a shrub, and there some grass: but the most of it was brown earth and moss and rock, and the road beneath them was stone. The grey sky was never broken and I do not remember that they saw a single bird: and it was so bleak that if they stopped at any time to rest, the sweat grew cold on them instantly.

Vertue never abated his pace and Drudge kept even with him though always a respectful yard behind: but I saw that John grew footsore and began to lag. For some hours he was always inventing pretexts to stop and finally he said, 'Friends, it is no use, I can go no further.'

'But you must,' said Vertue.

'The young gentleman is soft, sir, very soft,' said Drudge. 'He is not used to this sort of thing. We'll have to help him along.'

So they took him, one by each arm, and helped him along for a few hours. They found nothing to eat or drink in the waste. Towards evening they heard a desolate voice crying 'Maiwi-maiwi', and looked up, and there was a seagull hanging in the currents of the wind as though it sauntered an invisible stair towards the low rain-clouds.

'Good!' cried Vertue. 'We are nearing the coast.'

'It's a good step yet, sir,' said Drudge. 'These gulls come forty miles inland and more in bad weather.'

Then they plodded on for many more miles. And the sky began to turn from sunless grey to starless black. And they looked and saw a little shanty by the roadside and there they knocked on the door.

2

THREE PALE MEN

Counter-romanticism makes strange bedfellows – Modern thought begets Freudianism on baser, Negativism on finer, souls – These men are interested in everything not for what it is but for what it is not

When they were let in they found three young men, all very thin and pale, seated by a stove under the low roof of the hut. There was some sacking on a bench along one wall and little comfort else.

'You will fare badly here,' said one of the three men. 'But I am a Steward and it is my duty according to my office to share my supper with you. You may come in.' His name was Mr Neo-Angular.

'I am sorry that my convictions do not allow me to repeat my friend's offer,' said one of the others. 'But I have had to abandon the humanitarian and egalitarian fallacies.' His name was Mr Neo-Classical.

'I hope,' said the third, 'that your wanderings in lonely places do not mean that you have any of the romantic virus still in your blood.' His name was Mr Humanist.

John was too tired and Drudge too respectful to reply: but Vertue said to Mr Neo-Angular, 'You are very kind. You are saving our lives.'

'I am not kind at all,' said Mr Neo-Angular with some warmth. 'I am doing my duty. My ethics are based on dogma, not on feeling.'

'I understand you very well,' said Vertue. 'May I shake hands with you?'

'Can it be,' said the other, 'that you are one of us? You are a Catholic? A scholastic?'

'I know nothing about that,' said Vertue, 'but I know that the rule is to be obeyed because it is a rule and not because it appeals to my feelings at the moment.'

'I see you are not one of us,' said Angular, 'and you are undoubtedly damned. *Virtutes paganorum splendida vitia.* Now let us eat.'

Then I dreamed that the three pale men produced three tins of bully beef and six biscuits, and Angular shared his with the guests. There was very little for each and I thought that the best share fell to John and Drudge, for Vertue and the young Steward entered into a kind of rivalry over who should leave most for the others.

'Our fare is simple,' said Mr Neo-Classical. 'And perhaps unwelcome to palates that have been reared on the kickshaws of lower countries. But you see the perfection of form. This beef is a perfect cube: this biscuit a true square.'

'You will admit,' said Mr Humanist, 'that, at least, our meal is quite free from any lingering flavour of the old romantic sauces.'

'Quite free,' said John, staring at the empty tin.

'It's better than radishes, sir,' said Drudge.

'Do you *live* here, gentlemen?' said Vertue when the empty tins had been removed.

'We do,' said Mr Humanist. 'We are founding a new community. At present we suffer the hardships of pioneers and have to import our food: but when we have brought the country under cultivation we shall have plenty – as much as is needed for the practice of temperance.'

'You interest me exceedingly,' said Vertue. 'What are the principles of this community?'

'Catholicism, Humanism, Classicism,' said all three.

'Catholicism! Then you are all Stewards?'

'Certainly not,' said Classical and Humanist.

'At least you all believe in the Landlord?'

'I have no interest in the question,' said Classical.

'And I,' said Humanist, 'know perfectly well that the Landlord is a fable.'

'And I,' said Angular, 'know perfectly well that he is a fact.'

'This is very surprising,' said Vertue. 'I do not see how you have come together, or what your common principles can possibly be.'

'We are united by a common antagonism to a common enemy,' said Humanist. 'You must understand that we are three brothers, the sons of old Mr Enlightenment of the town of Claptrap.'

'I know him,' said John.

'Our father was married, twice,' continued Humanist. 'Once to a lady named Epichaerecacia, and afterwards to Euphuia. By his first wife he had a son called Sigismund who is thus our step-brother.'

'I know him too,' said John.

'We are the children of his second marriage,' said Humanist.

'Then,' cried Vertue, 'we are related – if you care to acknowledge the kinship. You have probably heard that Euphuia had a child before she married your father. I was that child – though I confess that I never discovered who my father was and enemies have hinted that I am a bastard.'

'You have said quite sufficient,' replied Angular. 'You can hardly expect that the subject should be agreeable to us. I might add that my office, if there were nothing else, sets me apart even from my legitimate relations.'

'And what about the common antagonism?' said John.

'We were all brought up,' said Humanist, 'by our step-brother in the university at Eschropolis, and we learned there to see that whoever stays with Mr Halfways must either come on to Eschropolis or else remain at Thrill as the perpetual minion of his brown daughter.'

'You had not been with Mr Halfways yourselves, then?' asked John.

'Certainly not. We learned to hate him from watching the effect which his music had on other people. Hatred of him is the first thing that unites us. Next, we discovered how residence in Eschropolis inevitably leads to the giant's dungeon.'

'I know all about that too,' said John.

'Our common hatred therefore links us together against the giant, against Eschropolis, and against Mr Halfways.'

'But specially against the latter,' said Classical.

'I should rather say,' remarked Angular, 'against half measures and compromises of all sorts – against any pretence that there is any kind of goodness or decency, any even tolerable temporary resting place, on this side of the Grand Canyon.'

'And that,' said Classical, 'is why Angular is for me, in one sense, the enemy, but, in another, *the* friend. I cannot agree with his notions about the other side of the canyon: but just because he relegates his delusions to the *other* side, he is free to agree with me about this side and to be an implacable exposer (like myself) of all attempts to foist upon us any transcendental, romantical, optimistic trash.'

'My own feeling,' said Humanist, 'is rather that Angular is with me in guarding against any confusion of the *levels* of experience. He *canalises* all the mystical nonsense – the *sehnsucht* and *Wanderlust* and Nympholepsy – and transfers them to the far side: that prevents their drifting about on this side and hindering our real function. It leaves us free to establish a really tolerable and even comfortable civilisation here on the plateau; a culture based alike on those truths which Mr Sensible acknowledges and on those which the giant reveals, but throwing over both alike a graceful veil of illusion. And that way we shall remain human: we shall not become beasts with the giant nor abortive angels with Mr Halfways.'

'The young gentleman is asleep, sir,' said Drudge: and indeed John had sunk down some time ago.

'You must excuse him,' said Vertue. 'He found the road long today.'

Then I saw that all six men lay down together in the sacking. The night was far colder than the night they passed in Mr Sensible's house: but as there was here no pretence of comfort and they lay huddled together in the narrow hut, John slept warmer here than at Thelema.

3

NEO-ANGULAR

The men talk as if they had 'seen through'
things they have not even seen

When they rose in the morning John was so footsore and his limbs ached so that he knew not how to continue his journey. Drudge assured them that the coast could not now be very far. He thought that Vertue could reach it and return in a day and that John might await him in the hut. As for John himself, he was loth to burden hosts who lived in such apparent poverty: but Mr Angular constrained him to stay, when he had explained that the secular virtue of hospitality was worthless and care for the afflicted a sin if it proceeded from humanitarian sentiment, but that he was obliged to act as he did by the rules of his order. So, in my dream, I saw Drudge and Vertue set out northwards alone, while John remained with the three pale men.

In the forenoon he had a conversation with Angular.

'You believe then,' said John, 'that there is a way across the canyon?'

'I know there is. If you will let me take you to Mother Kirk she will carry you over in a moment.'

'And yet, I am not sure that I am not sailing under false colours. When I set out from home, crossing the canyon was never in my thoughts – still less was Mother Kirk.'

'It does not matter in the least what was in your thoughts.'

'It does, to me. You see, my only motive for crossing, is the hope that something I am looking for may be on the other side.'

'That is a dangerous, subjective motive. What is this something?'

'I saw an Island –'

'Then you must forget it as soon as you can. Islands are the Halfways' concern. I assure you, you must eradicate every trace of that nonsense from your mind before I can help you.'

'But how can you help me after removing the only thing that I want to be helped to? What is the use of telling a hungry man that you will grant him his desires, provided there is no question of eating?'

'If you do not *want* to cross the canyon, there is no more to be said. But, then, you must realise where you are. Go on with your Island, if you like, but do not pretend that it is anything but a part of the land of destruction this side of the canyon. If you are a sinner, for heaven's sake have the grace to be a cynic too.'

'But how can you say that the Island is all bad, when it is longing for the Island, and nothing else, that has brought me this far?'

'It makes no difference. All on this side of the canyon is much of a muchness. If you confine yourself to this side, then the Spirit of the Age is right.'

'But this is not what Mother Kirk said. She particularly insisted that some of the food was much less poisonous than the rest.'

'So you have met Mother Kirk? No wonder that you are confused. You had no business to talk to her except through a qualified Steward. Depend upon it, you have misunderstood every word she said.'

'Then there was Reason, too. She refused to say that the Island was an illusion. But perhaps, like Mr Sensible, you have quarrelled with Reason.'

'Reason is divine. But how should you understand her? You are a beginner. For you, the only safe commerce with Reason is to learn from your superiors the dogmata in which her deliverances have been codified for general use.'

'Look here,' said John. 'Have you ever seen my Island?'

'God forbid.'

'And you have never heard Mr Halfways either.'

'Never. And I never will. Do you take me for an escapist?'

'Then there is at least one object in the world of which I know more than you. I have *tasted* what you call romantic trash; you have only talked about it. You need not tell me that there is a danger in it and an element of evil. Do you suppose that I have not felt that danger and that evil a thousand times more than you? But I know also that the evil in it is not what I went to it to find, and that I should have sought nothing and found nothing without it. I know this by experience as I know a dozen things about it of which you betray your ignorance as often as you speak. Forgive me if I am rude: but how is it possible that you can advise me in this matter? Would you recommend a eunuch as confessor to a man whose difficulties lay in the realm of chastity? Would a man born blind be my best guide against the lust of the eye? But I am getting angry. And you have shared your biscuit with me. I ask your pardon.'

'It is part of my office to bear insults with patience,' said Mr Angular.

4

HUMANIST

*They boast of rejecting what was never in
fact within their reach*

In the afternoon Mr Humanist took John out to show him the garden, by whose produce, in time, the new culture was to become self-supporting. As there was no human, or indeed animal, habitation within sight, no wall or fence had been deemed necessary but the area of the garden had been marked out by a line of stones and sea-shells alternately arranged: and this was necessary as the garden would else have been indistinguishable from the waste. A few paths, also marked by stones and shells, were arranged in a geometrical pattern.

'You see,' said Mr Humanist, 'we have quite abandoned the ideas of the old romantic landscape gardeners. You notice a certain severity. A landscape gardener would have had a nodding grove over there on the right, and a mound on the left, and winding paths, and a pond, and flower-beds. He would have filled the obscurer parts with the means of sensuality – the formless potato and the romantically irregular cabbage. You see, there is nothing of the sort here.'

'Nothing at all,' said John.

'At present, of course, it is not very fruitful. But we are pioneers.'

'Do you ever try *digging* it?' suggested John.

'Why, no,' said Mr Humanist, 'you see, it is pure rock an inch below the surface, so we do not disturb the soil. That would remove the graceful veil of illusion which is so necessary to the *human* point of view.'

5

FOOD FROM THE NORTH

*This region has no strength to resist
philosophies more inhuman than its own*

Late that evening the door of the hut opened and Vertue staggered in and dropped to a sitting position by the stove. He was very exhausted and it was long before he had his breath to talk. When he had, his first words were:

'You must leave this place, gentlemen. It is in danger.'

'Where is Drudge?' said John.

'He stayed there.'

'And what is this danger?' asked Mr Humanist.

'I'm going to tell you. By the by, there's no way over the gorge northward.'

'We have been on a fool's errand, then,' said John, 'ever since we left the main road.'

'Except that now we know,' replied Vertue. 'But I must eat before I can tell my story. Tonight I am able to return our friends' hospitality,' and with that he produced from various parts of his clothing the remains of a handsome cold pie, two bottles of strong beer and a little flask of rum. For some time there was silence in the hut, and when the meal was finished and a little water had been boiled so that each had a glass of hot grog, Vertue began his story.

6

FURTHEST NORTH

*The revolutionary sub-men, whether of
the Left or the Right – Who are all alike
vassals of cruelty – Heroic Nihilism laughs
at the less thoroughgoing forms of Tough-
Mindedness*

'It is all like this as far as the mountains – about fifteen miles – and there is nothing to tell of our journey except rock and moss and a few gulls. The mountains are frightful as you approach them, but the road runs up to a pass and we had not much difficulty. Beyond the pass you get into a little rocky valley and it was here that we first found any signs of habitation. The valley is a regular warren of caves inhabited by dwarfs. There are several species of them, I gather, though I only distinguished two – a black kind with black shirts and a red kind who call themselves Marxomanni. They are all very fierce and apparently quarrel a good deal but they all acknowledge some kind of vassalage to this man Savage. At least they made no difficulty in letting me through when they heard that I wanted to see him – beyond insisting on giving me a guard. It was there I lost Drudge. He said he had come to join the red dwarfs and would I mind going on alone. He was just the same up to the end – civil as ever – but he was down one of their burrows and apparently quite at home before I could get in a word. Then my dwarfs took me on. I didn't care for the arrangements much. They were not men, you know, not dwarf men, but real dwarfs – trolls. They could talk, and they walk on two legs, but the structure must be quite different from ours. I felt all the time that if they killed me it wouldn't be murder, any more than if a crocodile or a gorilla killed me. It *is* a different species – however it came there. Different faces.

'Well, they kept taking me up and up. It was all rocky zig-zags, round and round. Fortunately, I do not get giddy. My chief danger was the wind whenever we got on a ridge – for of course my guides, being only some three feet high, did not offer it the same target. I had one or two narrow escapes. Savage's nest is a terrifying place. It is a long hall like a barn and when I first caught sight of it – half-way up the sky from where they were leading me – I thought to myself that wherever else we were going it could not be *there*; it looked so inaccessible. But on we went.

'One thing you must get into your heads is that there are caves all the way up, all inhabited. The whole mountain must be honeycombed. I saw thousands of the dwarfs. Like an ant-hill – and not a man in the place except me.

'From Savage's nest you look straight down to the sea. I should think it is the biggest sheer drop on any coast. It was from there that I saw the mouth of the gorge. The mouth is only a lowering of the cliff: from the lowest part of the opening it is still thousands of feet to the sea. There is no conceivable landing. It is no use to anyone but seagulls.

'But you want to hear about Savage. He sat on a high chair at the end of his barn – a very big man, almost a giant. When I say that I don't mean his height: I had the same feeling about him that I had about the dwarfs. That doubt about the *species*. He was dressed in skins and had an iron helmet on his head with horns stuck in it.

'He had a woman there, too, a great big woman with yellow hair and high cheek-bones. Grimhild her name is. And the funny thing is that she is the sister of an old friend of yours, John. She is Mr Halfways' elder daughter. Apparently Savage came down to Thrill and carried her off: and what is stranger still, both the girl and the old gentleman were rather pleased about it than otherwise.

'As soon as the dwarfs brought me in, Savage rapped on the table and bellowed out, "Lay the board for us men," and she set about laying it. He didn't say anything to me for a long time. He just sat and looked and sang. He had only one song and he was singing it off and on all the time I was there. I remember bits of it.

'Wind age, wolf age,
Ere the world crumbles:
Shard age, spear age,
Shields are broken...

'Then there was another bit began:

'East sits the Old 'Un
In Iron-forest;
Feeds amidst it
Fenris' children...

'I sat down after a bit, for I did not want him to think I was afraid of him. When the food was on the table he asked me to have some, so I had it. He offered me a sweet drink, very strong, in a horn, so I drank it. Then he shouted and drank himself and said that mead in a horn was all he could offer me at present: "But soon," he said, "I shall drink the blood of men from skulls." There was a lot of this sort of stuff. We ate roast pork, with our fingers. He kept on singing his song and shouting. It was only after dinner that he began to talk connectedly. I wish I could remember it all. This is the important part of my story.

'It is hard to understand it without being a biologist. These dwarfs *are* a different species and an older species than ours. But, then, the specific variation is always liable to reappear in human children. They revert to the dwarf. Consequently, they are multiplying very fast; they are being increased both by ordinary breeding among themselves and also from without by those hark-backs or changelings. He spoke of lots of sub-species besides the Marxomanni – Mussolimini, Swastici, Gangomanni ... I can't remember them all. For a long time I couldn't see where he himself came in.

'At last he told me. He is breeding and training them for a descent on this country. When I tried to find out why, for a long time he would only stare at me and sing his song. Finally – as near as I could get it – his theory seemed to be that fighting was an end in itself.

'Mind you, he was not drunk. He said that he could understand old-fashioned people who believed in the Landlord and kept the rules and hoped to go up and live in the Landlord's castle when they had to leave this country. "They have something to live for," he said. "And if their belief was true, their behaviour would be perfectly sensible. But as their belief is not true, there remains only one way of life fit for a man." This other way of life was something called Heroism, or Master-Morality, or Violence. "All the other people in between," he said, "are ploughing the sand." He went on railing at the people in Claptrap for ages, and also at Mr Sensible. "These are the dregs of man," he said. "They are always thinking of happiness. They are scraping together and storing up and trying to *build*. Can they not see that the law of the world is against them? Where will any of them be a hundred years hence?" I said they might be building for posterity. "And who will posterity build for?" he asked. "Can't you see that it is all bound to come to nothing in the end? And the end may come tomorrow: and however late it comes, to those who look back all their 'happiness' will seem but a moment that has slipped away and left nothing behind. You can't gather happiness. Do you go to bed with any more in hand on the day you have had a thousand pleasures?" I asked if his "Heroism" left anything behind it either: but he said it did. "The excellent deed," he said, "is eternal. The hero alone has this privilege, that death for him is not defeat, and the lamenting over him and the memory is part of the good he aimed for; and the moment of battle fears nothing from the future because it has already cast security away."

'He talked a lot like that. I asked him what he thought of the Eschropolitans and he roared with laughter and said: "When the Cruels meet the Clevers there will not be even the ghost of a tug of war." Then I asked him if he knew you three and he laughed louder still. He said that Angular might turn out an enemy worth fighting when he grew up. "But I don't know," he said. "Likely enough he is only an Eschropolitan turned inside-out – poacher turned gamekeeper. As for the other pair, they are the last even of the last men." I asked him what he meant. "The men of Claptrap," he said, "may have some excuse for their folly, for they at least still believe that your country is a place where Happiness is possible. But your two friends are madmen without qualification. They claim to have reached rock-bottom, they talk of being disillusioned. They think that they have reached the furthest North – as if I were not here to the North of them. They live on a rock that will never feed man, between a chasm that they cannot cross and the home of a giant to whom they dare not return: and still they maunder of a culture and a security. If all men who try to build are but polishing the brasses on a sinking ship, then your pale friends are the supreme fools who polish with the rest though they know and admit that the ship is sinking. Their Humanism and what not is but the old dream with a new name. The rot in the world is too deep and the leak in the world is too wide. They may patch and tinker as they please, they will not save it. Better give in. Better cut the wood with the grain. If I am to live in a world of destruction let me be its agent and not its patient."

'In the end he said: "I will make this concession to your friends. They do live further North than anyone but me. They are more like men than any of their race. They shall have this honour when I lead the dwarfs to war, that Humanist's skull shall be the first from which I drink the blood of a man: and Grimhild here shall have Classical's."

'That was about all he said. He made me go out on the cliffs with him. It was all I could do to keep my footing. He said, "This wind blows straight from the pole; it will make a man of you." I think he was trying to frighten me. In the end I got away. He loaded me with food for myself and you. "Feed them up," he said. "There is not enough blood in them at present to quench the thirst of a dwarfish sword." Then I came away. And I am very tired.'

7

FOOL'S PARADISE

The sub-men have no answer to it

'I should like to meet this Savage,' said Angular. 'He seems to be a very clear-headed man.'

'I don't know about that,' said Humanist. 'He and his dwarfs seem to me to be just the thing I am fighting against – the logical conclusion of Eschropolis against which I raise the banner of Humanism. All the wild atavistic emotions which old Halfways sets free under false pretences – I am not at all surprised that he likes a valkyrie for a daughter – and which young Halfways unmasks, but cherishes when he has unmasked them; where can they end but in a complete abandonment of the *human*? I am glad to hear of him. He shows how necessary I am.'

'I agree,' said John in great excitement, 'but how are you going to fight? Where are your troops? Where is your base of supplies? You can't feed an army on a garden of stones and sea-shells.'

'It is intelligence that counts,' said Humanist.

'It moves nothing,' said John. 'You see that Savage is scalding hot and you are cold. You must get heat to rival his heat. Do you think you can rout a million armed dwarfs by being "not romantic"?'

'If Mr Vertue will not be offended,' said Classical, 'I would suggest that he dreamed the whole thing. Mr Vertue is romantic: he is paying for his wish-fulfilment dreams as he will always pay – with a fear-fulfilment dream. It is well-known that nobody lives further North than we.' But Vertue was too tired to defend his story and soon all the occupants of the hut were asleep.

BOOK 7

SOUTHWARD ALONG THE CANYON

Now is the seventh winter since Troy fell, and we
Still search beneath unfriendly stars, through every sea
And desert isle, for Italy's retreating strand.
But here is kinsman's country and Acestes' land;
What hinders here to build a city and remain?
Oh fatherland, oh household spirits preserved in vain
From the enemy, shall no new Troy arise? Shall no
New Simois there, re-named for Hector's memory, flow?
Rather, come! – burn with me the boats that work us harm!

VIRGIL

Through this and through no other fault we fell,
Nor, being fallen, bear other pain than this,
– Always without hope in desire to dwell.

DANTE

Some also have wished that the next way to their Father's house were here that they might be troubled no more with either Hills or Mountains to go over; but the way is the way, there's an end.

BUNYAN

I

VERTUE IS SICK

*In the presence of these thoughts traditional
morality falters – Without Desire it finds no
motive: with Desire, no morality*

I saw the two travellers get up from their sacking and bid good-bye to their hosts, and set out southwards. The weather had not changed, nor did I ever see any other weather over that part of the country than clouds and wind without rain. Vertue himself was out of sorts and made haste without the spirit of haste. Then at last he opened his mind to his companion and said, 'John, I do not know what is coming over me. Long ago you asked me – or was it Media asked me – where I was going and why: and I remember that I brushed the question aside. At that time it seemed to me so much more important to keep my rules and do my thirty miles a day. But I am beginning to find that it will not do. In the old days it was always a question of doing what I chose instead of what I wanted: but now I am beginning to be uncertain what it is I choose.'

'How has this come about?' said John.

'Do you know that I nearly decided to stay with Savage?'

'With Savage?'

'It sounds like raving, but think it over. Supposing there is no Landlord, no mountains in the East, no Island in the West, nothing but this country. A few weeks ago I would have said that all those things made no difference. But now – I don't know. It is quite clear that all the ordinary ways of living in the country lead to something which I certainly do *not* choose. I know that, even if I don't know what I *do* choose. I know that I don't want to be a Halfways, or a Clever, or a Sensible. Then there is the life I have been leading myself – marching on I don't know where. I can't see that there is any other good in it except the mere fact of imposing my will on my inclinations. And that seems to be good *training*, but training for what? Suppose after all it was training for battle? Is it so absurd to think that that might be the thing we were born for? A fight in a narrow place, life or death; – that must be the final act of will – the conquest of the deepest inclination of all.'

'I think my heart will break,' said John after they had gone many paces in silence. 'I came out to find my Island. I am not high-minded like you,

Vertue: it was never anything but sweet desire that led me. I have not smelled the air from that Island since – since – it is so long that I cannot remember. I saw more of it at home. And now my only friend talks of selling himself to the dwarfs.'

'I am sorry for you,' said Vertue, 'and I am sorry for myself. I am sorry for every blade of grass and for this barren rock we are treading and the very sky above us. But I have no help to give you.'

'Perhaps,' said John, 'there are things East and West of this country after all.'

'Do you still understand me so little as that!' cried Vertue, turning on him. 'Things East and West! Don't you see that that is the other fatal possibility? Don't you see that I am caught either way?'

'Why?' said John: and then, 'Let us sit down. I am tired and we have nowhere to hurry to – not now.'

Vertue sat down as one not noticing that he did it.

'Don't you see?' he said. 'Suppose there is anything East and West. How can that give me a motive for going on? Because there is something pleasant ahead? That is a bribe. Because there is something dreadful behind? That is a threat. I meant to be a free man. I meant to choose things because I chose to choose them – not because I was paid for it. Do you think I am a child to be scared with rods and baited with sugar plums? It was for this reason that I never even enquired whether the stories about the Landlord were true; I saw that his castle and his black hole were there to corrupt my will and kill my freedom. If it was true it was a truth an honest man must not know.'

Evening darkened on the tableland and they sat for a long time, immovable.

'I believe that I am mad,' said Vertue presently. 'The world cannot be as it seems to me. If there is something to go to, it is a bribe, and I cannot go to it: if I can go, then there is nothing to go to.'

'Vertue,' said John, 'give in. For once yield to desire. Have done with your choosing. *Want* something.'

'I cannot,' said Vertue. 'I must choose because I choose because I choose: and it goes on for ever, and in the whole world I cannot find a reason for rising from this stone.'

'Is it not reason enough that the cold will presently kill us here?'

It had grown quite dark, and Vertue made no reply.

'Vertue!' said John, and then suddenly again in a louder voice, frightened, 'Vertue!!' But there was no answer. He groped for his friend in the dark and touched the cold dust of the tableland. He rose on his hands and knees and groped all about, calling. But he was confused and could not even find again the place whence he had risen himself. He could not tell how often he might have groped over the same ground or whether he was getting further and further from their resting-place. He could not be still; it was too cold. So all that night he rummaged to and fro in the dark, calling out Vertue's name: and often it came into his head that Vertue had been all along one of the phantoms of a dream and that he had followed a shade.

2

JOHN LEADING

*Conscience can guide John no longer. 'Sick,
wearied out with contrarieties, he yields up
moral questions in despair'*

I dreamed that morning broke over the plateau, and I saw John rise up, white and dirty, in the new twilight. He looked all round him and saw nothing but the heath. Then he walked this way and that, still looking, and so for a long time. And at last he sat down and wept: that also for a long time. And when he had wept enough he rose like a man determined and resumed his journey southward.

He had hardly gone twenty paces when he stopped with a cry, for there lay Vertue at his feet. I understood in my dream that during his groping in the darkness he had unwittingly gone further and further from the place where they had first sat down.

In a moment John was on his knees and feeling for Vertue's heart. It beat still. He laid his face to Vertue's lips. They breathed still. He caught him by the shoulder and shook him.

'Wake up,' he cried, 'the morning is here.'

Then Vertue opened his eyes and smiled at John, a little foolishly.

'Are you well?' said John. 'Are you fit to travel?'

But Vertue only smiled. He was dumb. Then John held out his hands and pulled Vertue to his feet: and Vertue stood up uncertainly, but as soon as he made a stride he stumbled and fell, for he was blind. It was long before John understood. Then at last I saw him take Vertue by the hand and, leading him, resume their journey to the South. And there fell upon John that last loneliness which comes when the comforter himself needs comforting, and the guide is to be guided.

3

THE MAIN ROAD AGAIN

They found Mr Sensible's house empty, as John had expected, with the shutters up and the chimneys smokeless. John decided to push on to the main road and then, if the worst came to the worst, they could go to Mother Kirk: but he hoped it would not come to that.

All their journey South had been a descent, from the northern mountains to Mr Sensible's: but after his house it began to rise again a little to the main road, which ran along a low ridge, so that, when they had gained the road, the country South of it was suddenly all opened before them. At the same moment there came a gleam of sunshine, the first for many days. The road was unfenced to the heath on its northern side, but on its southern side there was a hedge with a gate in it: and the first thing John saw through the gate was a long low mound of earth. He had not been a farmer's son for nothing. Having led Vertue to the bank of the road and seated him, he lost no time in climbing the gate and digging with both hands into the earthen mound. It contained, as he had expected, turnips; and in a minute he was seated by Vertue, cutting a fine root into chunks, feeding the blind man and teaching him how to feed himself. The sun grew warmer every moment. The spring seemed further on in this place, and the hedge behind them was already more green than brown. Among many notes of birds John thought he could distinguish a lark. They had breakfasted well, and as the warmth increased pleasantly over their aching limbs, they fell asleep.

4

GOING SOUTH

*John looks longingly towards less comfortless
modes of thought*

When John awoke his first look was towards Vertue, but Vertue was still sleeping. John stretched himself and rose: he was warm and well, but a little thirsty. It was a four-cross-road where they had been sitting, for the northern road, at which John looked with a shudder, was but the continuation of a road from the South. He stood and looked down the latter. To his eyes, long now accustomed to the dusty flats of the northern plateau, the country southward was as a rich counterpane. The sun had passed noon by an hour or so, and the slanting light freckled with rounded shadows a green land, that fell ever away before him, opening as it sank into valleys, and beyond them into deeper valleys again, so that places on the same level where now he stood, yonder were mountain tops. Nearer at hand were fields and hedgerows, ruddy ploughland, winding woods, and frequent farm-houses white among their trees. He went back and raised Vertue and was about to show it all to him when he remembered his blindness. Then, sighing, he took him by the hand and went down the new road.

Before they had gone far he heard a bubbling sound by the roadside, and found a little spring pouring itself into a stream that ran henceforth with the road, now at the left, now at the right, and often crossed their way. He filled his hat with water and gave Vertue to drink. Then he drank himself and they went on, always downhill. The road nestled deeper each half-mile between banks of grass. There were primroses, first one or two, then clustered, then innumerable. From many turns of the road John caught sight of the deeper valleys to which they were descending, blue with distance and rounded with the weight of trees: but often a little wood cut off all remoter prospect.

The first house they came to was a red house, old and ivied, and well back from the road, and John thought it had the look of a Steward's house: as they came nearer, there was the Steward himself, without his mask, pottering about at some light gardening labour on the sunny side of the hedge. John leaned over the gate and asked for hospitality, explaining at the same time his friend's condition.

'Come in, come in,' said the Steward. 'It will be a great pleasure.'

Now I dreamed that this Steward was the same Mr Broad who had sent a case of sherry to Mr Sensible. He was about sixty years of age.

5

TEA ON THE LAWN

*John meets Broad Church, modernising,
'religion' – It is friends with the World
and goes on no pilgrimage – It is fond of
wild-flowers*

'It is almost warm enough to have tea on the lawn,' said Mr Broad. 'Martha, I think we will have tea on the lawn.'

Chairs were set and all three sat down. On the smooth lawn, surrounded by laurels and laburnum, it was even warmer than in the road, and suddenly a sweet bird-note shot out from the thickets.

'Listen!' said Mr Broad, 'it is a thrush. I really believe it is a thrush.'

Maidservants in snowy aprons opened the long windows of the library and came over the grass carrying tables and trays, the silver teapot and the stand of cakes. There was honey for tea. Mr Broad asked John some questions about his travels.

'Dear me,' he said, when he heard of Mr Savage, 'dear me! I ought to go and see him. And such a clever man, too, by your account ... it is very sad.'

John went on to describe the three pale men.

'Ah, to be sure,' said Mr Broad. 'I knew their father very well. A very able man. I owed a good deal to him at one time. Indeed, as a young man, he formed my mind. I suppose I ought to go and see his boys. Young Angular I *have* met. He is a dear, good fellow – a little narrow; I would venture to say, even a little old-fashioned, though of course I wouldn't for the world – the two brothers are doing splendidly I have no doubt. I really ought to go and see them. But I am getting on, and I confess it never suits me up there.'

'It is a very different climate from this,' said John.

'I always think it is possible for a place to be *too* bracing. They call it the land of the Tough-minded – tough-skinned would be a better name. If one has a tendency to lumbago – But, dear me, if you have come from there you must have met my old friend Sensible?'

'You know him too?'

'Know him? He is my oldest friend. He is a kind of connection of mine, and then, you know, we are quite near neighbours. He is only a mile north of the road and I am about a mile south of it. I should think I did know him. I have passed many, many happy hours in his house. The dear old man. Poor Sensible, he is ageing fast. I don't think he has ever quite forgiven me for having kept most of my hair!'

'I should have thought his views differed from yours a good deal.'

'Ah, to be sure, to be sure! He is not very orthodox, perhaps, but as I grow older, I am inclined to set less and less store by mere orthodoxy. So often the orthodox view means the lifeless view, the barren formula. I am coming to look more and more at the language of the heart. Logic and definition divide us: it is those things which draw us together that I now value most – our common affections, our common struggle towards the light. Sensible's heart is in the right place.'

'I wonder,' said John, 'if he treats that servant of his very well.'

'His language is a little bit rough, I suppose. One must be charitable. You young people are so hard. Dear me, I remember when I was a boy myself ... And then a man of Sensible's age suffers a good deal. We are none of us perfect. Will you not have a little more tea?'

'Thank you,' said John, 'but if you can give me some directions I think I would like to continue my journey. I am trying to find an Island in the West –'

'That is a beautiful idea,' said Mr Broad. 'And if you will trust an older traveller, the seeking is the finding. How many happy days you have before you!'

'And I want to know,' continued John, 'whether it is really necessary to cross the canyon.'

'To be sure you do. I wouldn't for the world hold you back. At the same time, my dear boy, I think there is a very real danger at your age of trying to make these things too definite. That has been the great error of my profession in past ages. We have tried to enclose everything in formulae, to turn poetry into logic, and metaphor into dogma; and now that we are beginning to realise our mistake we find ourselves shackled by the formulae of dead men. I don't say that they were not adequate once: but they have ceased to be adequate for us with our wider knowledge. When I became a man, I put away childish things. These great truths need re-interpretation in every age.'

'I am not sure that I quite understand,' said John. 'Do you mean that I must cross the canyon or that I must not?'

'I see you want to pin me down,' said Mr Broad, with a smile, 'and I love to see it. I was like that myself once. But one loses faith in abstract logic as one grows older. Do you never feel that the truth is so great and so simple that no mere words can contain it? The heaven and the heaven of heavens ... how much less this house that I have builded.'

'Well, anyway,' said John, deciding to try a new question. 'Supposing a man *did* have to cross the canyon. Is it true that he would have to rely on Mother Kirk?'

'Ah, Mother Kirk! I love and honour her from the bottom of my heart, but I trust that loving her does not mean being blind to her faults. We are none of us infallible. If I sometimes feel that I must differ from her at present, it is because I honour all the more the *idea* that she stands for, the thing she may yet become. For the moment, there is no denying that she has let herself get a little out of date. Surely, for many of our generation, there is a truer, a more acceptable, message in all this beautiful world around us? I don't know whether you are anything of a botanist. If you would care –'

'I want my Island,' said John. 'Can you tell me how to reach it? I am afraid I am not specially interested in botany.'

'It would open a new world to you,' said Mr Broad. 'A new window on the Infinite. But perhaps this is not in your line. We must all find our own key to the mystery after all. I wouldn't for the world ...'

'I think I must be going,' said John. 'And I have enjoyed myself very much. If I follow this road, shall I find anywhere that will give me a night's lodging in a few miles?'

'Oh, easily,' said Mr Broad. 'I should be very glad to have you here if you would care to stay. But if not, there is Mr Wisdom within an easy walk. You will find him a delightful man. I used to go and see him quite often when I was younger, but it is a little too far for me now. A dear, good fellow – a *little* persistent, perhaps ... I sometimes wonder if he is really quite free from a trace of narrow-mindedness ... You should hear what Sensible says about him! But there: we are none of us perfect, and he is a very good sort of man on the whole. You will like him very much.'

The old Steward bade goodbye to John with almost fatherly kindness, and John, still leading Vertue, pursued his journey.

6

THE HOUSE OF WISDOM

John takes up the study of Metaphysics

The stream that they had followed to the Steward's house was now no longer a brook by the roadside, but a river that sometimes approached, sometimes receded from the road, sliding in swift amber reaches and descending silver rapids. The trees grew more thickly hereabouts and were of larger kinds – and as the valley deepened, tiers of forest rose one above the other on each side. They walked in shadow. But far above their heads the sun was still shining on the mountain tops, beyond the forest slopes and beyond the last steep fields, where there were domed summits of pale grass and winding water-glens, and cliffs the colour of doves, and cliffs the colour of wine. The moths were already flying when they reached an open place. The valley widened and a loop of the river made room for a wide and level lawn between its banks and the wooded mountains. Amidst the lawn stood a low, pillared house approachable by a bridge, and the door stood open. John led the sick man up to it and saw that the lamps were already lit within; and then he saw Wisdom sitting among his children, like an old man.

'You may stay here as long as you wish,' he said in answer to John's question. 'And it may be that we shall heal your friend if his sickness is not incurable. Sit and eat, and when you have eaten you shall tell us your story.'

Then I saw that chairs were brought for the travellers and some of the young men of the house carried water to them to wash. And when they had washed, a woman set a table before them and laid on it a loaf, and cheese, and a dish of fruit, with some curds, and butter-milk in a pitcher: 'For we can get no wine here,' said the old man with a sigh.

When the meal was over there was silence in the house, and John saw that they waited for his story. So he collected himself and cast back in his mind, a long time, in silence; and when at last he spoke he told the whole thing in order, from the first sight he had had of the Island down to his arrival among them.

Then Vertue was led away from John, and he himself was brought into a cell where there was a bed, and a table, and a pitcher of water. He lay on the bed, and it was hard, but not lumpy, and he was immediately in a deep sleep.

7

ACROSS THE CANYON
BY MOONLIGHT

John's imagination re-awakes

In the middle of the night he opened his eyes and saw the full moon, very large and low, shining at his window: and beside his bed stood a woman darkly clothed, who held up her hand for silence when he would have spoken.

'My name is Contemplation,' she said, 'and I am one of the daughters of Wisdom. You must rise and follow me.'

Then John rose and followed her out of the house on to the grassy lawn in the moonlight. She led him across it to its westward edge where the mountain began to rise under its cloak of forest. But as they came right up to the eaves of the forest he saw that there was a crack or crevasse in the earth between them and it, to which he could find no bottom, and though it was not very wide, it was too wide to jump.

'It is too wide a jump by day,' said the Lady, 'but in the moonlight you can jump it.'

John felt no doubt of her and gathered himself together and leaped. His leap carried him further than he had intended – though he felt no surprise – and he found himself flying over the tree tops and the steep fields, and he never alighted till he reached the mountain top; and the Lady was there by his side.

'Come,' she said, 'we have still far to go.'

Then they went on together over hills and dales, very fast, in the moonlight, till they came to the edge of a cliff, and he looked down and saw the sea below him: and out in the sea lay the Island. And because it was moonlight and night John could not see it so well as he had sometimes seen it, but either for that reason, or for some other, it seemed to him the more real.

'When you have learned to fly further, we can leap from here right into the Island,' said the Lady. 'But for this night, it is enough.'

As John turned to answer her, the Island and the sea and the Lady herself vanished, and he was awake, in daylight, in his cell in the house of Wisdom, and a bell was ringing.

8

THIS SIDE BY SUNLIGHT

*Idealist Philosophy rejects the literal truth of
religion – But also rejects Materialism – The
chasm is still not crossed – But this
Philosophy, while denying the Hope yet
spares the Desire, to cross it*

On the next day Mr Wisdom caused John and Vertue both to sit by him in a porch of his house looking westward. The wind was in the south and the sky was a little clouded and over the western mountains there was a delicate mist, so that they had the air of being in another world, though they were not more than a mile away. And Mr Wisdom instructed them.

'As to this Island in the West, and those eastern mountains, and as touching the Landlord also and the Enemy, there are two errors, my sons, which you must equally conquer, and pass right between them, before you can become wise. The first error is that of the southern people, and it consists in holding that these eastern and western places are real places – real as this valley is real, and places as this valley is a place. If any such thought lingers in your minds, I would have you root it out utterly, and give no quarter to that thought, whether it threatens you with fears, or tempts you with hopes. For this is Superstition, and all who believe it will come in the end to the swamps and the jungles of the far South, where they will live in the city of Magicians, transported with delight in things that help not, and haunted with terror of that which cannot hurt. And it is part of the same error to think that the Landlord is a real man: real as I am real, man as I am man. That is the first error. And the second is the opposite of it, and is chiefly current to the North of the road: it is the error of those who say that the eastern and western things are merely illusions in our own minds. This also it is my will that you should utterly reject: and you must be on your guard lest you ever embrace this error in your fear of the other, or run to and fro between the two as your hearts will prompt you to do, like some who will be Materialists (for that is the name of the second error) when the story of the black hole frightens them for their lawless living, or even when they are afraid of spectres, and then another day will believe in the Landlord and the castle because things in this country go hard with them, or because the lease of some dear friend is running out and they would gladly hope to meet him again. But the wise man, ruling his passions with reason and disciplined imagination, withdraws himself to the middle point between these two errors, having found that the truth lies there, and remains fixed immovably. But what that truth is you shall learn tomorrow; and for the present this sick man will be cared for, and you who are whole may do as you will.'

Then I saw Mr Wisdom rise and leave them, and Vertue was taken to another place. John spent the most part of that day walking in the neighbourhood of the house. He crossed the level grass of the valley and came to its western edge where the mountain began to rise under its cloak of forest. But as he came under the forest eaves, he saw that between him and the first trees there was a crack or crevasse in the earth to which he could find no bottom. It was very narrow, but not quite narrow enough to jump. There seemed also to be some vapour rising from it which made the further side indistinct: but the vapour was not so thick nor the chasm so wide but that he could see here a spray of foliage and there a stone with deep moss, and in one place falling water that caught the sunlight. His desire to pass and to go on to the Island was sharp, but not to the degree of pain. Mr Wisdom's words that the eastern and western things were neither wholly real nor wholly illusion, had spread over his mind a feeling of intent, yet quiet, comfort. Some fear was removed: the suspicion, never before wholly laid at rest, that his wanderings might lead him soon or late into the power of the Landlord, had passed away, and with it the gnawing anxiety lest the Island had never existed. The world seemed full of expectation, even as the misty veil between him and the forest seemed both to cover and discover sublimities that were without terror and beauties without sensuality; and every now and then a strengthening of the south wind would make a moment's clearness and show him, withdrawn in unexpected depth, remote reaches of the mountain valleys, desolate fields of flowers, the hint of snow beyond. He lay down in the grass. Presently one of the young men of the house passed that way and stopped to talk with him. They spoke of this and that, lazily, and at long intervals. Sometimes they discussed the regions further South where John had not been; sometimes, his own travels. The young man told him that if he had followed the road a few miles beyond the valley he would have come to a fork. The left hand turn would lead you, by a long way round, to the parts about Claptrap: the right went on to the southern forests, to the city of the Magicians and the country of Nycteris, 'and beyond that it is all swamp and sugar cane,' said he, 'and crocodiles and venomous spiders until the land sinks away altogether into the final salt swamp which becomes at last the southern ocean. There are no settlements there except a few lake-dwellers, Theosophists and what not, and it is very malarial.'

While they were speaking of the parts that John already knew, he asked his informant whether they in the House of Wisdom knew anything of the Grand Canyon or of the way down into it.

'Do you not know,' said the other, 'that we are in the bottom of the canyon here?' Then he made John sit up and showed him the lie of the land. The sides of the valley drew together northward, and at the same time grew more precipitous, so that at last they came together into a great V. 'And that V is the canyon, and you are looking into it endways from the southern end. The eastern face of the canyon is gentle and you were walking down into it all day yesterday, though you did not notice it.'

'So I am in the bottom of it already,' said John. 'And now there is nothing to prevent me from crossing it.'

The young man shook his head.

'There is no crossing it,' he said. 'When I told you we were now at the bottom, I meant the lowest point that can be reached by man. The real bottom is, of course, the bottom of this crevasse which we are sitting by: and that, of course – well, it would be a misunderstanding to talk of getting down it. There is no question of crossing or of getting to what you see over there.'

'Could it not be bridged?' said John.

'In a sense there is nothing to bridge – there is nowhere for this bridge to *arrive at*. You must not take literally the show of forest and mountain which we seem to see as we look across.'

'You don't mean that it is an illusion?'

'No. You will understand better when you have been longer with my father. It is not an illusion, it is an appearance. It is a true appearance, too, in a sense. You *must* see it as a mountain-side or the like – a continuation of the world we *do* know – and it does not mean that there is anything wrong with your eyes or any better way of seeing it to which you can attain. But don't think you can get there. Don't think there is any meaning in the idea of you (a man) going "there", as if it were really a place.'

'What? And the Island too! You would have me give up my heart's desire?'

'I would not. I would not have you cease to fix all your desires on the far side, for to wish to cross is simply to be a man, and to lose that wish is to be a beast. It is not desire that my father's doctrine kills: it is only hope.'

'And what is this valley called?'

'We call it now simply Wisdom's Valley: but the oldest maps mark it as the Valley of Humiliation.'

'The grass is quite wet,' said John, after a pause. 'The dew is beginning.'

'It is time that we went to supper,' said the young man.

9

WISDOM – EXOTERIC

Whence come logical categories? Whence come moral values? – Philosophy says that the existence of God would not answer the question – Philosophy will not explain away John's glimpse of the Transcendent – The Desired is real just because it is never an experience

Next day, as before, Wisdom had John and Vertue into the porch and continued to instruct them:

'You have heard what you are not to think of the eastern and western things, and now let us discover, as far as the imperfection of our faculty allows, what may rightly be thought. And first, consider this country in which we live. You see that it is full of roads, and no man remembers the making of these roads: neither have we any way to describe and order the land in our minds except by reference to them. You have seen how we determine the position of every other place by its relation to the main road: and though you may say that we have maps, you are to consider that the maps would be useless without the roads, for we find where we are on the map by the skeleton of roads which is common to it and to the country. We see that we have just passed such a turn to the right or the left, or that we are approaching such a bend in the road, and thus we know that we are near to some other place on the map which is not yet visible on the countryside. The people, indeed, say that the Landlord made these roads: and the Claptrapians say that we first made them on the map and have projected them, by some strange process, from it to the country. But I would have you hold fast to the truth, that we find them and do not make them: but also that no *man* could make them. For to make them he would need a bird's-eye view of the whole country, which he could have only from the sky. But no man could live in the sky. Again, this country is full of rules. The Claptrapians say that the Stewards made the rules. The servants of the giant say that we made them ourselves in order to restrain by them the lusts of our neighbours and to give a pompous colouring to our own. The people say that the Landlord made them.

'Let us consider these doctrines one by one. The Stewards made them? How then came they to be Stewards, and why did the rest of us consent to their rules? As soon as we ask this question, we are obliged to ask another. How comes it that those who have rejected the Stewards immediately set about making new rules of their own, and that these new rules are substantially the same as the old? A man says, "I have finished with rules: henceforth I will do what I want": but he finds that his deepest want, the only want that is constant through the flux of his appetites and despondencies, his moments of calm and of passion, is to keep the rules. Because these rules are a disguise for his desires, say the giant's following. But, I ask, what desires? Not any and every desire: the rules are frequently denials of these desires. The desire for self-approbation, shall we say? But why should we approve ourselves for keeping the rules unless we already thought that the rules were good? A man may find pleasure in supposing himself swifter or stronger than he really is, but only if he already loves speed or strength. The giant's doctrine thus destroys itself. If we wish to give a seemly colouring to our lusts we have already the idea of the seemly, and the seemly turns out to be nothing else than that which is according to the rules. The want to obey the rules is thus presupposed in every doctrine which describes our obedience to them, or to the rules themselves, as a self-flattery. Let us turn then to the old tale of the Landlord. Some mighty man beyond this country has made the rules. Suppose he has: then why do we obey them?'

Mr Wisdom turned to Vertue and said, 'This part is of great concern to you and to your cure,' then he continued:

'There can be only two reasons. Either because we respect the power of the Landlord, and are moved by fear of the penalties and hopes of the rewards with which he sanctions the rules: or else, because we freely agree with the Landlord, because we also think good the things that he thinks good. But neither explanation will serve. If we obey through hope and fear, in that very act we disobey: for the rule which we reverence most, whether we find it in our own hearts or on the Steward's card, is that rule which says that a man must act disinterestedly. To obey the Landlord thus, would be to disobey. But what if we obey freely, because we agree with him? Alas, this is even worse. To say that we agree, and obey because we agree, is only to say again that we find the same rule written in our hearts and obey *that*. If the Landlord enjoins *that*, he enjoins only what we already purposed to do, and his voice is idle: if he enjoins anything else, his voice again is idle, for we shall disobey him. In either case the mystery of the rules remains unsolved, and the Landlord is a meaningless addition to the problem. If he spoke, the rules were there before he spoke. If we and he agree about them, where is the common original which he and we both copy: what is the thing about which his doctrine and ours are both true?

'Of the rules, then as of the roads, we must say that indeed we find them and do not make them, but that it helps us not at all to assume a Landlord for their maker. And there is a third thing also' (here he looked to John) 'which specially concerns you. What of the Island in the West? The People in our age have all but forgotten it. The giant would say that it is, again, a delusion in your own mind trumped up to conceal lust. Of the Stewards, some do not know that there is such a thing: some agree with the giant, denouncing your Island as wickedness: some say that it is a blurred and confused sight from far off of the Landlord's castle. They have no common doctrine: but let us consider the question for ourselves.

'And first I would have you set aside all suspicion that the giant is right: and this will be the easier for you because you have already talked with Reason. They say it is there to conceal lust. But it does not conceal lust. If it is a screen, it is a very bad screen. The giant would make the dark part of our mind so strong and subtle that we never escape from its deceptions: and yet when this omnipotent conjuror has done all that he can, he produces an illusion which a solitary boy, in the fancies of his adolescence, can expose and see through in two years. This is but wild talk. There is no man and no nation at all capable of seeing the Island, who have not learned by experience, and that soon, how easily the vision ends in lust: and there is none also, not corrupted, who has not felt the disappointment of that ending, who has not known that it is the breaking of the vision, not its consummation. The words between you and Reason were true. What does not satisfy when we find it, was not the thing we were desiring. If water will not set a man at ease, then be sure it was not thirst, or not thirst only, that tormented him: he wanted drunkenness to cure his dullness, or talk to cure his solitude, or the like. How, indeed, do we know our desires save by their satisfaction? When do we know them until we say, "Ah, *this* was what I wanted"? And if there were any desire which it was natural for man to feel but impossible for man to satisfy, would not the nature of this desire remain to him always ambiguous? If old tales were true, if a man without putting off humanity could indeed pass the frontiers of our country, if he could be, and yet be a man, in that fabled East and fabled West, then indeed at the moment of fruition, the raising of the cup, the assumption of the crown, the kiss of the spouse – then first, to his backward glance, the long roads of desire that he had trodden would become plain in all their winding, and when he found, he would know what it was that he had sought. I am old and full of tears, and I see that you also begin to feel the sorrow that is born with us. Abandon hope: do not abandon desire. Feel no wonder that these glimpses of your Island so easily confuse themselves with viler things, and are so easily blasphemed. Above all, never try to keep them, never try to revisit the same place or time wherein the vision was accorded to you. You will pay the penalty of all who would bind down to one place or time within our country that which our country cannot contain. Have you not heard from the Stewards of the sin of idolatry, and how, in their old chronicles, the manna turned to worms if any tried to hoard it? Be not greedy, be not passionate; you will but crush dead on your own breast with hot, rough hands the thing you loved. But if ever you incline to doubt that the thing you long for is something real, remember what your own experience has taught you. Think that it is a *feeling*, and at once the feeling has no value. Stand sentinel at your own mind, watching for that feeling, and you will find – what shall I say? – a flutter in the heart, an image in the head, a sob in the throat; and was *that* your desire? You know that it was not, and that no feeling whatever will appease you; that *feeling*, refine it as you will, is but one more spurious claimant – spurious as the gross lusts of which the giant speaks. Let us conclude then that what you desire is no state of yourself at all, but something, for that very reason, Other and Outer. And knowing this you will find tolerable the truth that you cannot attain it. That the thing should *be* is so great a good that when you remember "it is" you will forget to be sorry that you can never have it. Nay, anything that you could have would be so much less than this that its fruition would be immeasurably below the mere hunger for this. Wanting is better than having. The glory of any world wherein you can live is in the end appearance: but then, as one of my sons has said, that leaves the world more glorious yet.'

10

WISDOM – ESOTERIC

*John finds that the real strength in the lives
of the Philosophers comes from sources
better, or worse, than any their philosophies
acknowledge – Marx really a Dwarf;
Spinoza a Jew; Kant a Puritan*

That day John spent as he had spent the other, wandering and often sleeping in the fields. In this valley the year came on with seven-leagued boots. Today the riverside was thick with fritillaries, the kingfisher flew, the dragon-flies darted, and when he sat it was in the shade. A pleasing melancholy rested upon him, and a great indolence. He talked that day with many of the people of the house, and when he went that night to his cell his mind was full of their resigned voices, and of their faces, so quiet and yet so alert, as though they waited in hourly expectation of something that would never happen. When next he opened his eyes moonlight filled his cell; and as he lay waking heard a low whistle from without his window. He put out his head. A dark figure stood in the shadow of the house. 'Come out and play,' said he. At the same time there came a sound of suppressed laughter from an angle of deeper shadow beyond the speaker.

'This window is too high for me to jump from,' said John.

'You forget that it is by moonlight,' said the other, and held up his hands. 'Jump!' he said.

John cast some clothes about him and bounded from the window. To his surprise, he reached the ground with no hurt or shock, and a moment later he found himself progressing over the lawn in a series of great leaps amidst a laughing crowd of the sons and daughters of the house: so that the valley in the moonlight, if any had watched, would have looked like nothing so much as a great salver which had been made into the arena for a troupe of performing fleas. Their dance or race led them to the dark border of a neighbouring wood and as John tumbled down breathless at the foot of a hawthorn, he heard with surprise all around him the sounds of silver and glass, of hampers opening, and bottles uncorking.

'My father's ideas of feeding are a little strict,' explained his host, 'and we younger ones have found it necessary to supplement the household meals a bit.'

'Here is champagne, from Mr Halfways,' said one.

'Cold chicken and tongue from Mr Mammon. What should we do without our friends?'

'Hashish from the south. Nycteris sent it up herself.'

'This claret,' said a girl beside him rather shyly, 'is from Mother Kirk.'

'I don't think we ought to drink that,' said another voice, 'that is really going a bit too far.'

'No further than your caviare from the Theosophists,' said the first girl, 'and anyway, I need it. It is only this that keeps me alive.'

'Try some of my brandy,' said another voice. 'All made by Savage's dwarfs.'

'I don't know how you can drink that stuff, Karl.[1] Plain, honest food from Claptrap is what you need.'

'So *you* say, Herbert,'[2] retorted a new speaker. 'But some of us find it rather heavy. For me, a morsel of lamb from the Shepherd's Country and a little mint sauce – that is really all you need to add to our Father's table.'

'We all know what you like, Benedict,'[3] said several.

'I have finished,' announced Karl, 'and now for a night with the dwarfs. Anyone come with me?'

'Not there,' cried another. 'I'm going South tonight to the magicians.'

'You had much better not, Rudolph,'[4] said someone. 'A few quiet hours in Puritania with me would be much better for you – much better.'

'Chuck it, Immanuel,'[5] said another. 'You might as well go to Mother Kirk straight away.'

'Bernard[6] does,' said the girl, who had contributed the claret.

By this time the party was rapidly decreasing, for most of the young people, after trying in vain to win converts to their several schemes of pleasure, had bounded off alone, plunging from treetop to treetop, and soon even the thin silvery sound of their laughter had died away. Those who were left swarmed round John soliciting his attention now for this, now for that, amusement. Some sat down beyond the shadow of the wood to work out puzzles in the light of the moon: others settled to serious leap-frog; the more frivolous ran to and fro chasing the moths, wrestling with and tickling one another, giggling and making giggle, till the wood rang with their shrill squeals of glee. It seemed to go on for a long time and if there was any more in that dream John did not remember it when he woke.

---

[1]Marx [2]Spencer [3]Spinoza [4]Steiner [5]Kant [6]Bosanquet

11

MUM'S THE WORD

At breakfast on the following morning John stole many furtive glances at the sons and daughters of Wisdom, but he could see no sign that they were conscious of having met him in such different guise during the night. Indeed, neither then, nor at any other time during his stay in the valley, did he find evidence that they were aware of their nocturnal holidays: and a few tentative questions assured him that, unless they were liars, they all believed themselves to be living exclusively on the spare diet of the house. Immanuel indeed admitted, as a speculative truth, that there were such things as dreams, and that he conceivably dreamed himself: but then he had a complex proof (which John never quite grasped) that no one could possibly remember a dream: and though his appearance and constitution were those of a prize-fighter he attributed this all to the excellent quality of the local fruit. Herbert was a lumpish sort of man who never could muster any appetite for his meals: but John discovered that Herbert put this down to his liver and had no notion that he had been stuffing himself with Claptrapian steak and gravy all night as hard as he could. Another of the family, Bernard by name, was in radiant health. John had seen him drinking Mother Kirk's wine with great relish and refreshment by moonlight: but the waking Bernard maintained that Mother Kirk's wine was merely a bad, early attempt at the admirable barley-water which his father sometimes brought out on birthdays and great occasions; and 'to this barley-water,' he said, 'I owe my health. It has made me what I am.' Still less could John discover, by all the traps that he laid for them, whether the younger members of the household had any recollection of their nightly leap-frog and other gambols. He was forced at last to conclude that either the whole thing had been a private dream of his own or else the secret was very well kept. A little irritation which some displayed when he questioned them, seemed to favour the second hypothesis.

12

MORE WISDOM

*John is taught that the finite self cannot
enter the Noumenal World – The doctrine of
the Absolute or Mind-as-such covers more of
the facts than any doctrine John has yet
encountered*

When they were seated in the porch, Wisdom continued his discourse. 'You have learned that there are these three things, the Island, the Roads, and the Rules: that they are certainly in some way real and that we have not made them; and further that it does not help us to invent a Landlord. Nor is it possible that there should really be a castle at one end of the world and an island at the other: for the world is round and we are everywhere at the end of the world, since the end of a sphere is its surface. The world is *all* end: but we can never pass beyond that end. And yet these things which our imagination impossibly places as a world beyond the world's end are, we have seen, in some sense real.

'You have told me how Reason refuted the lies of the giant by asking what was the colour of things in dark places. You learned from her that there is no colour without seeing, no hardness without touching: no *body*, to say all, save in the minds of those who perceive it. It follows, then, that all this choir of heaven and furniture of earth are imaginations: not your imaginations nor mine, for here we have met in the same world, which could not be if the world was shut up within my mind or yours. Without doubt, then, all this show of sky and earth floats within some mighty imagination. If you ask Whose, again the Landlord will not help you. He is a man: make him as great as you will, he still is other than we and his imagining inaccessible to us, as yours would be to me. Rather we must say that the world is not in this mind, or in that, but in Mind itself, in that impersonal principle of consciousness which flows eternally through us, its perishable forms.

'You see how this explains all the questions that have lain on our knees since we began. We find the roads, the reasonable skeleton in the countryside, the guiding-lines that enable us both to make maps and to use them when we have made them, because our country is the offspring of the rational. Consider also the Island. All that you know of it comes at last to this: that your first sight of it was yearning or wanting and that you have never ceased to want that first sight back, as though you wanted a wanting, as though the wanting were the having, and the having a wanting. What is the meaning of this hungry fruition and this emptiness which is the best filling? Surely, it becomes plain when you have learned that no man says "I" in an unambiguous sense. I am an old man who must soon go over the brook and be seen no more: I am eternal Mind in which time and place themselves are contained. I am the Imaginer: I am one of his imaginations. The Island is nothing else than that perfection and immortality which I possess as Spirit eternal, and vainly crave as mortal soul. Its voices sound at my very ear and are further than the stars; it is under my hand and will never be mine: I have it and lo! the very having is the losing: because at every moment I, as Spirit, am indeed abandoning my rich estate to become that perishing and imperfect creature in whose repeated deaths and births stands my eternity. And I as man in every moment still enjoy the perfection I have lost, since still, so far as I am at all, I am Spirit, and only by being Spirit maintain my short vitality as soul. See how life subsists by death and each becomes the other: for Spirit lives by dying perpetually into such things as we, and we also attain our truest life by dying to our mortal nature and relapsing, as far as may be, into the impersonality of our source: for this is the final meaning of all moral precepts, and the goodness of temperance and justice and of love itself is that they plunge the red heat of our separate and individual passions back in the ice brook of the Spirit, there to take eternal temper, though not endless duration.

'What I tell you is the *evangelium eternum*. This has been known always: ancients and moderns bear witness to it. The stories of the Landlord in our own time are but a picture-writing which show to the people as much of the truth as they can understand. Stewards must have told you – though it seems that you neither heeded nor understood them – the legend of the Landlord's Son. They say that after the eating of the mountain-apple and the earthquake, when things in our country had gone all awry, the Landlord's Son himself became one of his Father's tenants and lived among us, for no other purpose than that he should be killed. The Stewards themselves do not know clearly the meaning of their story: hence, if you ask them how the slaying of the Son should help us, they are driven to monstrous answers. But to us the meaning is clear and the story is beautiful. It is a picture of the life of Spirit itself. What the Son is in the legend, every man is in reality: for the whole world is nothing else than the Eternal thus giving itself to death that it may live – that we may live. Death is life's mode, and the increase of life is through repeated death.

'And what of the rules? You have seen that it is idle to make them the arbitrary commands of a Landlord: yet those who do so were not altogether astray, for it is equally an error to think that they are each man's personal choice. Remember what we have said of the Island. Because I am and am not Spirit, therefore I have and have not my desire. The same double nature of the word "I", explains the rules. I am the lawgiver: but I am also the subject. I, the Spirit, impose upon the soul which I become, the laws she must henceforth obey: and every conflict between the rules and our inclinations is but a conflict of the wishes of my mortal and apparent self against those of my real and eternal. "I ought but I do not wish" – how meaningless the words are, how close to saying, "I want and I do not want." But once we have learned to say "I, and yet not I, want," the mystery is plain.

'And now your sick friend is almost whole, and it is nearly noon.'

BOOK 8

AT BAY

He that hath understanding in himself is best;
He that lays up his brother's wisdom in his breast
Is good. But he that neither knoweth, nor will be taught
By the instruction of the wise – this man is naught.
HESIOD

Persons without education certainly do not
want either acuteness or strength of mind in
what concerns themselves, or in things
immediately within their observation; but
they have no power of abstraction – they see
their objects always near, never in the
horizon.
HAZLITT

I

TWO KINDS OF MONIST

But supposing one tries to live by Pantheistic philosophy – does it lead to a complacent Hegelian optimism? Or to Oriental pessimism and self-torture? – Adjustment between the two views seems impossible

That afternoon as John was walking in the water meadow he saw a man coming towards him who walked blunderingly like one whose legs were not his own. And as the man came nearer he saw that it was Vertue, with his face very pale.

'What,' cried John, 'are you cured? Can you see? Can you speak?'

'Yes,' said Vertue in a weak voice. 'I suppose I can see.' And he leaned heavily on a stile and breathed hard.

'You have walked too far,' said John. 'Are you ill?'

'I am still weak. It is nothing. I shall get my breath in a moment.'

'Sit down by me,' said John. 'And when you have rested we will go gently back to the house.'

'I am not going back to the house.'

'Not going back? You are not fit to travel – and where are you going?'

'I am not fit for anything, apparently,' said Vertue. 'But I must go on.'

'Go on where? You are not still hoping to cross the canyon? Do you not believe what Wisdom has told us?'

'I do. That is why I am going on.'

'Sit down at least for a moment,' said John, 'and explain yourself.'

'It is plain enough!'

'It isn't plain at all.'

Vertue spoke impatiently.

'Did you not hear what Wisdom said about the rules?' he asked.

'Of course I did,' said John.

'Well, then, he has given me back the rules. *That* puzzle is solved. The rules have to be obeyed, as I always thought. I know that now better than I have ever known it before.'

'Well?'

'And didn't you see what all the rest came to? The rules are from this Spirit or whatever he calls it, which is somehow also me. And any disinclination to obey the rules is the other part of me – the moral part. Does it not follow from that, and from everything else he said, that the real disobedience to the rules begins with being in this country at all? This country is simply *not* the Island, *not* the rules: that is its definition. My mortal self – that is, for all practical purposes, myself – can be defined, only as the part of me that is against the rules. Just as the Spirit answers to the Landlord, so this whole world answers to the black hole.'

'I take it all exactly the other way,' said John. 'Rather this world corresponds to the Landlord's castle. Everything is this Spirit's imagination, and therefore everything, properly understood, is good and happy. That the glory of this world in the end is appearance, leaves the world more glorious yet. I quite agree that the rules – the authority of the rules – becomes stronger than ever: but their content must be – well, easier. Perhaps I should say richer – more concrete.'

'Their content must become harsher. If the real good is simply "what is not here" and *here* means simply "the place where the good is not", what can the real rule be except to live here as little as possible, to commit ourselves as little as we can to the system of this world? I used to talk of innocent pleasures, fool that I was – as if anything could be innocent for us whose mere existence is a fall – as if all that a man eats or drinks or begets were not propagated curse.'

'Really, Vertue, this is a very strange view. The effect of Mr Wisdom's lessons on me has been just the opposite. I have been thinking how much of the Puritanian virus there must still be in me, to have held me back so long from the blameless generosity of Nature's breasts. Is not the meanest thing, in its degree, a mirror of the One; the lightest or the wildest pleasure as necessary to the perfection of the whole as the most heroic sacrifice? I am assured that in the Absolute, every flame even of carnal passion burns on –'

'Can even eating, even the coarsest food and the barest pittance, be justified? The flesh is but a living corruption –'

'There was a great deal to be said for Media after all –'

'I see that Savage was wiser than he knew –'

'It is true she had a dark complexion. And yet – is not brown as necessary to the spectrum as any other colour?'

'Is not every colour equally a corruption of the white radiance?'

'What we call evil – our greatest wickednesses – seen in the true setting is an element in the good. I am the doubter and the doubt.'

'What we call our righteousness is filthy rags. You are a fool, John, and I am going. I am going up into the rocks till I find where the wind is coldest and the ground hardest and the life of man furthest away. My notice to quit has not yet come, and I must be stained a while longer with the dye of our country. I shall still be part of that dark cloud which offends the white light:

but I shall make that part of the cloud which is called Me as thin, as nearly not a cloud, as I can. Body and mind shall pay for the crime of their existence. If there is any fasting, or watching, any mutilation or self-torture more harsh to nature than another, I shall find it out.'

'Are you mad?' said John.

'I have just become sane,' said Vertue. 'Why are you staring at me thus? I know I am pale and my pulse beats like a hammer. So much the saner! Disease is better than health and sees clearer, for it is one degree nearer to the Spirit, one degree less involved in the riot of our animal existence. But it will need stronger pains than this to kill the obscene thirst for life which I drank in with my mother's milk.'

'Why should we leave this pleasant valley?' John began, but Vertue cut him short.

'Who spoke of We? Do you think that I asked or expected *you* to accompany me? *You* to sleep on thorns and eat sloes?'

'You don't mean that we are to part?' said John.

'Pah!' said Vertue. 'You could not do the things I intend to do: and if you could, I would have none of you. Friendship – affection – what are these but the subtlest chains that tie us to our present country? He would be a fool indeed who mortified the body and left the mind free to be happy and thus still to affirm – to wallow in – her finite will. It is not this pleasure or that, but *all* that are to be cut off. No knife will cut deep enough to end the cancer. But I'll cut as deep as I can.'

He rose, still swaying, and continued his way over the meadow northward. He held his hand to his side as though he was in pain. Once or twice he nearly fell.

'What are you following me for?' he shouted to John. 'Go back.'

John stopped for a moment, checked by the hatred in his friend's face. Then, tentatively, he went on again. He thought that Vertue's illness had harmed his brain and had some indistinct hope that he might find means to humour him and bring him back. Before they had gone many paces, however, Vertue turned again and lifted a stone in his hand. 'Be off,' he said, 'or I'll throw it. We have nothing to do with one another, you and I. My own body and my own soul are enemies, and do you think I will spare *you*?'

John halted, undetermined, and then ducked, for the other had hurled the stone. I saw them go on like this for some way, John following at a distance, and stopping, and then continuing again, while Vertue every now and then stoned him and reviled him. But at last the distance between them was too great either for voice or stone to carry.

2

JOHN LED

John would turn back. Christ forces him on

As they went on thus John saw that the valley narrowed and the sides of it grew steeper. At the same time, the crevasse on his left hand which separated him from the western forest, became wider and wider; so that, what with that, and with the narrowing of the valley as a whole, the level piece where they were travelling was constantly diminished. Soon it was no longer the floor of the valley but only a ledge on its eastern side: and the crevasse revealed itself as being not a slot in the floor but the very floor. John saw that he was, in fact, walking on a shelf half-way down one side of the Grand Canyon. The cliff towered above him.

Presently a kind of spur or root of rock came out from the cliff and barred their way – crossing the ledge with a ruin of granite. And as Vertue began to scramble about the bases of this ascent, trying this grip and that to go up, John gained on him and came again within earshot. Before he came to the foot of the crags, however, Vertue had begun to climb. John heard his gasping as he struggled from hold to hold. Once he slipped back and left a little trail of blood where the rock skinned his ankle: but he went on again, and soon John saw him stand up, shaking and wiping the sweat out of his eyes, apparently at the top. He looked down and made gestures threateningly, and shouted, but he was too far for John to hear his words. Next moment John leaped aside to save his limbs, for Vertue had sent a great boulder rolling down: and as its thunder ceased echoing in the gorge and John looked up again, Vertue had gone over the spur out of sight and he saw no more of him.

John sat down in the desolate place. The grass here was finer and shorter, such grass as sheep love, which grows in the quiet intervals between the rocks. The windings of the gorge had already shut off the sight of Wisdom's Valley: yet I saw that John had no thought save of going back. There was indeed a confusion of shame and sorrow and bewilderment in his mind, but he put it all aside and held fast to his fear of the rocks and of meeting Vertue, now mad, in some narrow place whence he could not retreat. He thought,

'I will sit here and rest, till I get my wind, and then I will go back. I must live out the rest of my life as best I can.' Then suddenly he heard himself hailed from above. A Man was descending where Vertue had gone up.

'Hi!' shouted the Man. 'Your friend has gone on. Surely you will follow him?'

'He is mad, sir,' said John.

'No madder than you, and no saner,' said the Man. 'You will both recover if only you will keep together.'

'I cannot get up the rocks,' said John.

'I will give you a hand,' said the Man. And he came down till he was within reach of John, and held out his hand. And John grew pale as paper and nausea came upon him.

'It's now or never,' said the Man.

Then John set his teeth and took the hand that was offered him. He trembled at the very first grip he was made to take but he could not go back for they were speedily so high that he dared not attempt the return alone: and what with pushing and pulling the Man got him right up to the top and there he fell down on his belly in the grass to pant and to groan at the pains in his chest. When he sat up the Man was gone.

3

JOHN FORGETS HIMSELF

*As soon as he attempts seriously to live by
Philosophy, it turns into Religion*

John looked back and turned away with a shudder. All thought of descending again must be put aside at once and for ever. 'That fellow has left me in a nice fix,' he said bitterly. Next, he looked ahead. The cliffs still rose high above him and dropped far below him: but there was a ledge on a level with him, a narrow ledge, ten feet broad at its best and two at its worst, winding away along the cliff till it became but a green thread. His heart failed him. Then he tried to recall the lessons of Mr Wisdom, whether they would give him any strength. 'It is only myself,' he said. 'It is I myself, eternal Spirit, who drive this Me, the slave, along that ledge. I ought not to care whether he falls and breaks his neck or not. It is not he that is real, it is I – I – I. Can I remember that?' But then he felt so different from the eternal Spirit that he could call it 'I' no longer. 'It is all very well for *him*,' said John, 'but why does he give me no help? I want help. Help.' Then he gazed up at the cliffs and the narrow sky, blue and remote, between them, and he thought of that universal mind and of the shining tranquillity hidden somewhere behind the colours and the shapes, the pregnant silence under all the sounds, and he thought, 'If one drop of all that ocean would flow into me now – if I, the mortal, could but realise that I *am* that, all would be well. I know there is something there. I know the sensuous curtain is not a cheat.' In the bitterness of his soul he looked up again, saying: 'Help. Help. I want help.'

But as soon as the words were out of his mouth, a new fear, far deeper than his fear of the cliffs, sprang at him from the hiding-place, close to the surface, where it had lain against this moment. As a man in a dream talks without fear to his dead friend, and only afterwards bethinks himself, 'It was a ghost! I have talked with a ghost!' and wakes screaming: even so John sprang up as he saw what he had done.

'I have been *praying*,' he said. 'It is the Landlord under a new name. It is the rules and the black hole and the slavery dressed out in a new fashion to catch me. And I am caught. Who would have thought the old spider's web was so subtle?'

But this was insupportable to him and he said that he had only fallen into a metaphor. Even Mr Wisdom had confessed that Mother Kirk and the Stewards gave an account of the truth in picture-writing. And one must use metaphors. The feelings and the imagination needed that support. 'The great thing,' said John, 'is to keep the intellect free from them: to remember that they *are* metaphors.'

4

JOHN FINDS HIS VOICE

From Pantheism to Theism.
The transcendental I *becomes* Thou

He was much comforted by this idea of metaphor, and as he was now also rested, he began his journey along the cliff path with some degree of timid resolution. But it was very dreadful to him in the narrower places: and his courage seemed to him to decrease rather than to grow as he proceeded. Indeed he soon found that he could go forward at all only by remembering Mr Wisdom's Absolute incessantly. It was necessary by repeated efforts of the will to turn thither, consciously to draw from that endless reservoir the little share of vitality that he needed for the next narrow place. He knew now that he was praying, but he thought that he had drawn the fangs of that knowledge. In a sense, he said, Spirit is not. I am it, but I am not the whole of it. When I turn back to that part of it which is not I – that far greater part which my soul does not exhaust – surely that part is to me an Other. It must become, for my imagination, not really 'I' but 'Thou'. A metaphor – perhaps more than a metaphor. Of course there is no need at all to confuse it with the *mythical* Landlord ... However I think of it, I think of it inadequately.

Then a new thing happened to John, and he began to sing: and this is as much of his song as I remember from my dream:

He whom I bow to only knows to whom I bow
When I attempt the ineffable name, murmuring Thou;
And dream of Pheidian fancies and embrace in heart
Meanings, I know, that cannot be the thing thou art.
All prayers always, taken at their word, blaspheme,
Invoking with frail imageries a folk-lore dream;
And all men are idolaters, crying unheard
To senseless idols, if thou take them at their word,
And all men in their praying, self-deceived, address
One that is not (so saith that old rebuke) unless
Thou, of mere grace, appropriate, and to thee divert

Men's arrows, all at hazard aimed, beyond desert.
Take not, oh Lord, our literal sense, but in thy great,
Unbroken speech our halting metaphor translate.

When he came to think over the words that had gone out of him he began once more to be afraid of them. Day was declining and in the narrow chasm it was already almost dark.

5

FOOD AT A COST

*John must accept God's grace or die –
Having accepted His grace, he must
acknowledge His existence*

For a while he went on cautiously, but he was haunted by a picture in his mind of a place where the path would break off short when it was too dark for him to see, and he would step on air. This fear made him halt more and more frequently to examine his ground: and when he went on it was each time more slowly: till at last he came to a standstill. There seemed to be nothing for it but to rest where he was. The night was warm, but he was both hungry and thirsty. And he sat down. It was quite dark now.

Then I dreamed that once more a Man came to him in the darkness and said, 'You must pass the night where you are, but I have brought you a loaf and if you crawl along the ledge ten paces more you will find that a little fall of water comes down the cliff.'

'Sir,' said John. 'I do not know your name and I cannot see your face, but I thank you. Will you not sit down and eat, yourself?'

'I am full and not hungry,' said the Man. 'And I will pass on. But one word before I go. You cannot have it both ways.'

'What do you mean, sir?'

'Your life has been saved all this day by crying out to something which you call by many names, and you have said to yourself that you used metaphors.'

'Was I wrong, sir?'

'Perhaps not. But you must play fair. If its help is not a metaphor, neither are its commands. If it can answer when you call, then it can speak without your asking. If you can go to it, it can come to you.'

'I think I see, sir. You mean that I am not my own man: in some sense I have a Landlord after all?'

'Even so. But what is it that dismays you? You heard from Wisdom how the rules were yours and not yours. Did you not mean to keep them? And if so, can it scare you to know that there is one who will make you able to keep them?'

'Well,' said John. 'I suppose you have found me out. Perhaps I did not fully mean to keep them – not all – or not all the time. And yet, in a way, I think I did. It is like a thorn in your finger, sir. You know when you set about taking it out yourself – you mean to get it out – you know it will hurt – and it does hurt – but somehow it is not very serious business – well, I suppose, because you feel that you always *could* stop if it was very bad. Not that you intend to stop. But it is a very different thing to hold your hand out to a surgeon to be hurt as much as *he* thinks fit. And at *his* speed.'

The Man laughed. 'I see you understand me very well,' He said. 'But the great thing is to get the thorn out.' And then He went away.

6

CAUGHT

The terror of the Lord –
Where now is Sweet Desire?

John had no difficulty in finding the stream and when he had drunk he sat by it and ate. The bread had a rather flat taste which was somehow familiar and not very agreeable, but he was in no position to be dainty. Extreme weariness prevented him from thinking much of the conversation that had just passed. At the bottom of John's heart the stranger's words lay like a cold weight that he must some day take up and carry: but his mind was full of the pictures of cliff and chasm, of wondering about Vertue, and of smaller fears for the morrow and the moment, and, above all, the blessedness of food and of sitting still; and all these jumbled themselves together in an even dimmer confusion till at last he could no longer remember which he had been thinking of the moment before: and then he knew that he was sleeping: and last he was in deep sleep and knew nothing.

In the morning it was not so. With his first waking thought the full-grown horror leaped upon him. The blue sky above the cliffs was watching him: the cliffs themselves were imprisoning him: the rocks behind were cutting off his retreat: the path ahead was ordering him on. In one night the Landlord – call Him by what name you would – had come back to the world, and filled the world, quite full without a cranny. His eyes stared and His hand pointed and His voice commanded in everything that could be heard or seen, even from this place where John sat, to the end of the world: and if you passed the end of the world He would be there too. All things were indeed one – more truly one than Mr Wisdom dreamed – and all things said one word: CAUGHT – Caught into slavery again, to walk warily and on sufferance all his days, never to be alone; never the master of his own soul, to have no privacy, no corner whereof you could say to the whole universe: This is my own, here I can do as I please. Under that universal and inspecting gaze, John cowered like some small animal caught up in a giant's hands and held beneath a magnifying-glass.

When he had drunk and splashed his face in the stream he continued his way, and presently he made this song:

You rest upon me all my days
The inevitable Eye,
Dreadful and undeflected as the blaze
Of some Arabian sky;

Where, dead still, in their smothering tent
Pale travellers crouch, and, bright
About them, noon's long-drawn Astonishment
Hammers the rocks with light.

Oh, for but one cool breath in seven,
One air from northern climes,
The changing and the castle-clouded heaven
Of my old Pagan times!

But you have seized all in your rage
Of Oneness. Round about,
Beating my wings, all ways, within your cage,
I flutter, but not out.

And as he walked on, all day, in the strength of the bread he had eaten, not daring often to look down into the gulf and keeping his head mostly turned a little inward to the cliff, he had time to turn his trouble over in his mind and discover new sides to it. Above all it grew upon him that the return of the Landlord had blotted out the Island: for if there still were such a place he was no longer free to spend his soul in seeking it, but must follow whatever designs the Landlord had for him. And at the very best it now seemed that the last of things was at least more like a person than a place, so that the deepest thirst within him was not adapted to the deepest nature of the world. But sometimes he comforted himself by saying that this new and real Landlord must yet be very different from him whom the Stewards proclaimed and indeed from all images that men could make of him. There might still hang about him some of that promising darkness which had covered the Absolute.

7

THE HERMIT

*John begins to learn something of the history
of human thought – History has seen people
like the Counter-Romantics in many ages*

Presently he heard a bell struck, and he looked and saw a little chapel in a cave of the cliff beside him; and there sat a hermit whose name was History, so old and thin that his hands were transparent and John thought that a little wind would have blown him away.

'Turn in, my son,' said the hermit, 'and eat bread and then you shall go on your journey.' John was glad to hear the voice of a man among the rocks and he turned in and sat. The hermit gave him bread and water but he himself ate no bread and drank a little wine.

'Where are you going, son?' he said.

'It seems to me, Father, that I am going where I do not wish; for I set out to find an Island and I have found a Landlord instead.'

And the hermit sat looking at him, nodding almost imperceptibly with the tremors of age.

'The Clevers were right and the pale men were right,' said John, thinking aloud, 'since the world holds no allaying for the thirst I was born with, and seemingly the Island was an illusion after all. But I forget, Father, that you will not know these people.'

'I know all parts of this country,' said the hermit, 'and the genius of places. Where do these people live?'

'To the North of the road. The Clevers are in the country of Mammon, where a stone giant is the lord of the soil, and the pale men are on the Tableland of the Tough-Minded.'

'I have been in these countries a thousand times, for in my young days I was a pedlar and there is no land I have not been in. But tell me, do they still keep their old customs?'

'What customs were those?'

'Why, they all sprang from the ownership of the land there, for more than half of the country North of the road is now held by the Enemy's tenants. Eastward it was the giant, and under him Mammon and some others. But westward, on the Tableland, it was two daughters of the Enemy – let me see – yes, Ignorantia and Superbia. They always did impose strange customs on the smaller tenants. I remember many tenants there – Stoics and Manichees, Spartiates, and all sorts. One time they had a notion to eat better bread than is made of wheat. Another time their very nurses took up a strange ritual of always emptying the baby out along with the bath. Then once the Enemy sent a fox without a tail among them and it persuaded them that all animals should be without tails and they docked all their dogs and horses and cows. I remember they were very puzzled how to apply any corresponding treatment to themselves, until at last a wise man suggested that they could cut off their noses. But the strangest custom of all was one that they practised all the time through all their other changes of customs. It was this – that they never set anything to rights but destroyed it instead. When a dish was dirty they did not wash it, they broke it; and when their clothes were dirty they burned them.'

'It must have been a very expensive custom.'

'It was ruinous, and it meant, of course, that they were constantly importing new clothes and new crockery. But indeed they had to import everything, for that is the difficulty of the Tableland. It never has been able to support life and it never will. Its inhabitants have always lived on their neighbours.'

'They must always have been very rich men.'

'They always *were* very rich men. I don't think I remember a single case of a poor or a common person going there. When humble people go wrong they generally go South. The Tough-Minded nearly always go to the Tableland as colonists from Mammon's country. I would guess that your pale men are reformed Clevers.'

'In a kind of way I believe they are. But can you tell me, Father, why these Tough-Minded people behave so oddly?'

'Well, for one thing, they *know* very little. They never travel and consequently never learn anything. They really do not know that there are any places outside Mammon's country and their own Tableland – except that they have heard exaggerated rumours about the Southern swamps, and suppose that everything is swamp a few miles South of themselves. Thus, their disgust with bread came about through sheer ignorance. At home in Mammon's country they knew only the standard bread that Mammon makes, and a few sweet, sticky cakes which Mammon imported from the South – the only kind of Southern product that Mammon would be likely to let in. As they did not like either of these, they invented a biscuit of their own. It never occurred to them to walk a mile off the Tableland into the nearest cottage and try what an honest loaf tasted like. The same with the babies. They disliked babies because babies meant to them the various deformities spawned in the brothels of Mammon: again, a moderate walk would have shown them healthy children at play in the lanes. As for their poor noses – on the Tableland there is nothing to smell, good, bad, or indifferent, and in Mammon's land whatever does not reek of scent reeks of ordure. So they saw no good in noses, though five miles away from them the hay was being cut.'

'And what about the Island, Father?' said John. 'Were they equally wrong about that?'

'That is a longer story, my son. But I see it is beginning to rain, so perhaps you may as well hear it.'

John went to the mouth of the cave and looked out. The sky had grown dark while they talked and a warm rain, blotting out the cliffs like a steam, was descending as far as his eye could reach.

8

HISTORY'S WORDS

*There was a really Divine element in John's
Romanticism – For Morality is by no means
God's only witness in the sub-Christian world
– Even Pagan mythology contained a Divine
call – But the Jews, instead of a mythology,
had the Law – Conscience and Sweet Desire
must come together to make a Whole Man*

When John had returned and seated himself, the hermit resumed:
'You may be sure that they make the same mistake about the Island that they make about everything else. But what is the current lie at present?'

'They say it is all a device of Mr Halfways – who is in the pay of the Brown Girls.'

'Poor Halfways! They treat him very unfairly – as if he were anything more than the local representative of a thing as widespread and as necessary (though, withal, as dangerous) as the sky! Not a bad representative, either, if you take his songs in your stride and use them as they are meant to be used: of course people who go to him in cold blood to get as much *pleasure* as they can, and therefore hear the same song over and over again, have only themselves to thank if they wake in the arms of Media.'

'That is very true, Father. But they wouldn't believe that I had seen and longed for the Island before I met Mr Halfways – before I ever heard a song at all. They insist on treating it as his invention.'

'That is always the way with stay-at-homes. If they like something in their own village they take it for a thing universal and eternal, though perhaps it was never heard of five miles away; if they dislike something, they say it is a local, backward, provincial convention, though, in fact, it may be the law of nations.'

'Then it is really true that all men, all nations, have had this vision of an Island?'

'It does not always come in the form of an Island: and to some men, if they inherit particular diseases, it may not come at all.'

'But what *is* it, Father? And has it anything to do with the Landlord? I do not know how to fit things together.'

'It comes from the Landlord. We know this by its results. It has brought you to where you now are: and nothing leads back to him which did not at first proceed from him.'

'But the Stewards would say that it was the Rules which come from him.'

'Not all Stewards are equally travelled men. But those who are, know perfectly well that the Landlord has circulated other things besides the Rules. What use are Rules to people who cannot read?'

'But nearly everyone can.'

'No one is born able to read: so that the starting point for all of us must be a picture and not the Rules. And there are more than you suppose who are illiterate all their lives or who, at the best, never learn to read well.'

'And for these people the pictures are the right thing?'

'I would not quite say that. The pictures alone are dangerous, and the Rules alone are dangerous. That is why the best thing of all is to find Mother Kirk at the very beginning, and to live from infancy with a third thing which is neither the Rules nor the pictures and which was brought into the country by the Landlord's Son. That, I say, is the best: never to have known the quarrel between the Rules and the pictures. But it very rarely happens. The Enemy's agents are everywhere at work, spreading illiteracy in one district and blinding men to the pictures in another. Even where Mother Kirk is nominally the ruler men can grow old without knowing how to read the Rules. Her empire is always crumbling. But it never quite crumbles: for as often as men become Pagans again, the Landlord again sends them pictures and stirs up sweet desire and so leads them back to Mother Kirk even as he led the actual Pagans long ago. There is, indeed, no other way.'

'Pagans?' said John. 'I do not know that people.'

'I forgot that you had travelled so little. It may well be that you were never in the country of Pagus in the flesh, though in another sense, you have lived there all your life. The curious thing about Pagus was that the people there had not heard of the Landlord.'

'Surely, a great many other people don't know either?'

'Oh, a great many *deny* his existence. But you have to be told about a thing before you can deny it. The peculiarity of the Pagans was that they had not been told: or if they had, it is so long ago that the tradition had died out. You see, the Enemy had practically supplanted the Landlord, and he kept a sharp watch against any news from that quarter reaching the tenants.'

'Did he succeed?'

'No. It is commonly thought that he did, but that is a mistake. It is commonly thought that he fuddled the tenants by circulating a mass of false stories about the Landlord. But I have been through Pagus in my rounds too often to think it was quite so simple. What really happened was this: the Landlord succeeded in getting a lot of messages through.'

'What sort of messages?'

'Mostly pictures. You see, the Pagans couldn't read, because the Enemy shut up the schools as soon as he took over Pagus. But they had pictures. The moment you mentioned your Island I knew what you were at. I have seen that Island dozens of times in those pictures.'

'And what happened then?'

'Almost certainly the same thing has happened to you. These pictures woke desire. You understand me?'

'Very well.'

'And then the Pagans made mistakes. They would keep on trying to get the same picture again: and if it didn't come, they would make copies of it for themselves. Or even if it did come they would try to get out of it not desire but satisfaction. But you must know all this.'

'Yes, yes, indeed. But what came of it?

'They went on making up more and more stories for themselves about the pictures, and then pretending the stories were true. They turned to brown girls and tried to believe that that was what they wanted. They went far South, some of them and became magicians, and tried to believe it was that. There was no absurdity and no indecency they did not commit. But however far they went, the Landlord was too much for them. Just when their own stories seemed to have completely overgrown the original messages and hidden them beyond recovery, suddenly the Landlord would send them a new message and all their stories would look stale. Or just when they seemed to be growing really contented with lust or mystery mongering, a new message would arrive and the old desire, the real one, would sting them again, and they would say "Once more it has escaped us".'

'I know. And then the whole cycle would begin over again.'

'Yes. But all the while there was one people that could read. You have heard of the Shepherd People?'

'I had been hoping you would not come to that, Father. I have heard the Stewards talk of them and I think it is that more than anything else that sickened me of the whole story. It is so clear that the Shepherd People are just one of these Pagan peoples – and a peculiarly unattractive one. If the whole thing is hobbled by one leg to that special People...'

'This is merely a blunder,' said History. 'You, and those whom you trust, have not *travelled*. You have never been in Pagus, nor among the Shepherds. If you had lived on the roads as I have, you would never say that they were the same. The Shepherds could read: that is the thing to remember about them. And because they could read, they had from the Landlord, not pictures but Rules.'

'But who wants Rules instead of Islands?'

'That is like asking who wants cooking instead of dinner. Do you not see that the Pagans, because they were under the Enemy, were beginning at the wrong end? They were like lazy schoolboys attempting eloquence before they learn grammar. They had pictures for their eyes instead of roads for their feet, and that is why most of them could do nothing but desire and then, through starved desire, become corrupt in their imaginations, and so awake and despair, and so desire again. Now the Shepherds, because they were under the Landlord, were made to begin at the right end. Their feet were set on a road: and as the Landlord's Son once said, if the feet have been put right the hands and the head will come right sooner or later. It won't work the other way.'

'You know so much, Father,' said John, 'that I do not know how to answer you. But this is all unlike the accounts I have heard of those countries. Surely some of the Pagans did get somewhere.'

'They did. They got to Mother Kirk. That is the definition of a Pagan – a man so travelling that if all goes well he arrives at Mother Kirk's chair and is carried over this gorge. I saw it happen myself. But we define a thing by its perfection. The trouble about Pagus is that the perfect, and in that sense typical, Pagan, is so uncommon there. It must be so, must it not? These pictures – this ignorance of writing – this endless desire which so easily confuses itself with other desires and, at best, remains pure only by knowing what it does *not* want – you see that it is a starting point from which *one* road leads home and a thousand roads lead into the wilderness.'

'But were the Shepherds not just as bad in their own way? Is it not true that they were illiberal, narrow, bigoted?'

'They *were* narrow. The thing they had charge of was narrow: it was the Road. They found it. They sign-posted it. They kept it clear and repaired it. But you must not think I am setting them up against the Pagans. The truth is that a Shepherd is only half a man, and a Pagan is only half a man, so that neither people was well without the other, nor could either be healed until the Landlord's Son came into the country. And even so, my son, you will not be well until you have overtaken your fellow-traveller who slept in my cell last night.'

'Do you mean Vertue?' said John.

'That was his name. I knew him though he did not tell me, for I know his family; and his father, whom he does not know, was called Nomos and lived among the Shepherds. You will never do anything until you have sworn blood brotherhood with him: nor can he do anything without you.'

'I would gladly overtake him,' said John, 'but he is so angry with me that I am afraid to come near him. And even if we made it up, I don't see how we could help falling out again. Somehow we have never been able to be quite comfortable together for very long.'

'Of yourselves you never will. It is only a third that can reconcile you.'
'Who is that?'
'The same who reconciled the Shepherds and the Pagans. But you must go to Mother Kirk to find him.'
'It is raining harder than ever,' said John from the mouth of the cave.
'It will not stop tonight,' said Father History. 'You must stay with me till the morning.'

9

MATTER OF FACT

*It is dangerous to welcome Sweet Desire, but
fatal to reject it – Whether it comes as
Courtly Love in the Middle Ages – Or
nature-worship in the Nineteenth Century –
Every form has its proper corruption: but
'de-bunking' is not the cure*

'I see,' said John presently, 'that this question is harder than the Clevers and the pale men suppose. But they were right in distrusting the Island. From all that you have told me, it is a very dangerous thing.'

'There is no avoiding danger in our country,' said History. 'Do you know what happens to people who set about learning to skate with a determination to get no falls? They fall as often as the rest of us, and they cannot skate in the end.'

'But it is more than dangerous. You said it was beginning at the wrong end, while the Shepherd people began at the right end.'

'That is true. But if you are a Pagan by birth or by nature, you have no choice. It is better to begin at the wrong end than not to begin at all. And the most part of men are always Pagans. Their first step will always be the desire born of the pictures: and though that desire hides a thousand false trails it also hides the only true one for them, and those who preach down the desire under whatever pretext – Stoic, Ascetic, Rigorist, Realist, Classicist – are on the Enemy's side whether they know it or not.'

'Then there is always need for the Island?'

'It does not always take the form of an Island, as I have said. The Landlord sends pictures of many different kinds. What is universal is not the particular picture, but the arrival of some message, not perfectly intelligible, which wakes this desire and sets men longing for something East or West of the world: something possessed, if at all, only in the act of desiring it, and lost so quickly that the craving itself becomes craved; something that tends inevitably to be confused with common or even with vile satisfactions lying close to hand, yet which is able, if any man faithfully live through the dialectic of its successive births and deaths, to lead him at last where true joys are to be found. As for the shapes in which it comes, I have seen many in my travels. In Pagus it was sometimes, as I said, an Island. But it was often, too, a picture of people, stronger and fairer than we are. Sometimes it was a picture telling a story. The strangest shape it ever took was in Medium Aevum – that was a master stroke of the Landlord's diplomacy; for of course, since the Enemy has been in the country, the Landlord has had to become a politician. Medium Aevum was first inhabited by colonists from Pagus. They came there at the very worst period in the history of Pagus, when the enemy seemed to have succeeded completely in diverting all the desires that the Landlord could arouse into nothing but lust. These poor colonists were in such a state that they could not let their fancies wander for a minute without seeing images of black, craving eyes, and breasts, and gnawing kisses. It seemed hopeless to do anything with them. Then came the Landlord's crowning audacity. The very next picture he sent them was a picture of a Lady! Nobody had ever had the idea of a Lady before: and yet a Lady is a woman: so this was a new thing, which took the Enemy off his guard, and yet at the same time it was an old thing – in fact, the very thing which he was reckoning on as his strongest point. He got the shock of his life. The people went mad over the new picture, and made songs that are sung still, and looked away from the picture at the real women around them and saw them quite differently – so that ordinary love for women became, for a time, itself a form of the real desire, and not merely one of the spurious satisfactions offered to it. Of course the Landlord was playing a dangerous game (nearly all his games *are* dangerous) and the Enemy managed to mix up and corrupt the new message – as usual – but not so much as he wished, or as people afterwards said: and before he had recovered himself, one at least[1] of the tenants had carried this new form of the desire right up to its natural conclusion and found what he had really been wanting. He wrote it all down in what he called a *Comedy*.'

'And what about Mr Halfways?' said John. 'Where did his kind of song begin?'

'That was the last big arrival of new messages that we had,' said History. 'And it happened just before I retired from the world. It was in the land of Mr Enlightenment, but he was very different then. I do not know any man who has deteriorated so with advancing years. In those days Claptrap had not been built. The Enemy had agents in the country but did not come there often himself: it must have been just about that time that Mammon was taking it over, and building new towns and turning the people out of the fields into the factories. One of the results was a great deal of anaemia – though there were other causes for that too – and weak hearts. This time the Landlord did a curious thing: he sent them pictures of the country they were actually living in – as if he had sent them a number of mirrors. You

[1] Dante

see, he always does the last thing the Enemy is expecting. And just as the pictures of the Lady in Medium Aevum had made the real women look different, so when men looked at these pictures of the country and then turned to the real landscape, it was all changed. And a new idea was born in their minds, and they saw something – the old something, the Island West of the world, the Lady, the heart's desire – as it were hiding, yet not quite hidden, like something even more about to be, in every wood and stream and under every field. And because they saw this, the land seemed to be coming to life, and all the old stories of the Pagans came back to their minds and meant more than the Pagans themselves ever knew: and because women also were in the landscape, the old idea of the Lady came back too. For this is part of the Landlord's skill, that when one message has died he brings it to life again in the heart of the next. But out of this third revelation, which they called Romantic, so many songs were made that I cannot remember all of them: and many deeds were done, too, and many, through the usual false starts and disillusions and re-beginnings of desire, found their way home. Your Mr Halfways is one of the later and weaker followers of that school.'

'I don't think that the history of the Romantic pictures is quite as clear as the other histories. What exactly was the Landlord doing? And what did the Enemy do?'

'I thought you would have seen. This third stroke of policy was in a way one of the greatest. All the previous pictures had been of something that was *not there* in the world around you. This gave the Enemy the chance of making people believe that you *had* it in the picture, and *lacked* it elsewhere – in other words that the picture itself was the thing you wanted. And that, as you know, means idolatry, and then, when the idol disappoints you (as it must) there is an easy passage to all the spurious satisfactions. But this weapon was knocked out of the Enemy's hand when once the thing in the picture was the very same thing that you saw all round you. Even the stupidest tenant could see that you *had* the landscape, in the only sense in which it could be had, already: and still you *wanted*: therefore the landscape was not what you wanted. Idolatry became impossible. Of course the Enemy, when he had recovered himself, found a new method of defence. Just because the new message could not be idolised, it could be easily belittled. The desire awakened thus between the picture and the countryside could be confused with the ordinary *pleasure* that any healthy man feels in moving about out-of-doors: and when it had been so confused, the Enemy could pretend that the Romantics had made a great pother about nothing. And you can imagine that all the people who had not had pictures sent to them, and therefore not felt the desire, and therefore were itching with envy, would welcome this explanation.'

'I see,' said John. 'But still – on your own showing, all these messages get blurred and corrupted in the end, and then, surely, the thing to do is to look out for the new one. These pale men might be quite right to occupy themselves in cleaning away the rubbish of the old revelation. That might be the way to get ready for the next.'

'That is another notion they have which a little travel would soon blow to pieces. They think that the Landlord works like the factories in Claptrap, inventing every day a new machine which supersedes the old. As machines are among the very few things that they do know something about, they cannot help thinking that everything is like them. But this leads them into two mistakes. First of all, they have no conception how slowly the Landlord acts – the enormous intervals between these big changes in his type of picture. And secondly, they think that the new thing refutes and cancels the old, whereas, in reality it brings it to a fuller life. I have never known a case where the man who was engaged in ridiculing or rejecting the old message became the receiver of the new. For one thing it all takes so long. Why, bless my soul, I remember Homer in Pagus ridiculing some of the story pictures: but they had thousands of years to run still and thousands of souls were to get nourishment out of them. I remember Clopinel[2] in Medium Aevum, jeering at the pictures of the Lady before they had reached half his countrymen. But his jeer was no spell to evoke a new message, nor was he helping any cause but the Enemy's.'

---

[2] Jean de Meung

10

ARCHETYPE AND ECTYPE

*We know that the object of Sweet Desire is
not subjective – Nay, even the Desire ceases
to be our Desire – No matter; for it is God's
love, not ours, that moves us and all things*

There was a long silence in the cave except for the sound of the rain. Then John began once more:

'And yet ...' he said, 'and yet, Father, I am terribly afraid. I am afraid that the things the Landlord really intends for me may be utterly unlike the things he has taught me to desire.'

'They will be very unlike the things you imagine. But you already know that the objects which your desire imagines are always inadequate to that desire. Until you have it you will not know what you wanted.'

'I remember that Wisdom said that too. And I understand that. Perhaps what troubles me is a fear that my desires, after all you have said, do not really come from the Landlord – that there is some older and rival Beauty in the world which the Landlord will not allow me to get. How can we *prove* that the Island comes from him? Angular would say it did not.'

'You have proved it for yourself: you have *lived* the proof. Has not every object which fancy and sense suggested for the desire, proved a failure, confessed itself, after trial, not to be what you wanted? Have you not found by elimination that this desire is the perilous siege in which only One can sit?'

'But then,' said John, 'the very quality of it is so – so unlike what we think of the Landlord. I will confess to you what I had hoped to keep secret. It has been with me almost a bodily desire. There have been times ... I have felt the sweetness flow over from the soul into the body ... pass through me from head to foot. It's quite true, what the Clevers say. It *is* a thrill – a physical sensation.'

'That is an old story. You must fear thrills, but you must not fear them too much. It is only a foretaste of that which the real Desirable will be when you have found it. I remember well what an old friend of mine in Medium Aevum once said to me – "Out of the soul's bliss," he said, "there shall be a flowing over into the flesh."'

'Did he say that? I did not suppose that anyone except the Clevers knew it.

Do not laugh at me Father – or laugh if you will – I am indeed very ignorant and I have listened to people more ignorant still.'

Twilight, hastened by the rain, had fallen on the canyon, and in the cave it was quite dark. John heard the old man moving to and fro and presently there came the flame of a little lamp lighting up his pale bird-like face. He set food for supper before his guest and bade him eat and then sleep.

'Gladly, Father,' said John, 'for I am very tired. I do not know why I have plagued you with questions about the Island. It is all a story of what happened to me long ago. It was long ago that I saw it clearly. The visions, ever since the first one, have grown rarer, the desires fainter. I have been talking as if I still craved it, but I do not think I can find any craving in my heart now at all.'

The old man sat still, nodding a little as before.

Suddenly John spoke again.

'Why should it *wear out* if it is from the Landlord? It doesn't last, you know. Isn't it that which gives away the whole case?'

'Have you not heard men say, or have you forgotten, that it is like human love?' asked the hermit.

'What has that to do with it?'

'You would not ask if you had been married, or even if you had studied generation among the beasts. Do you not know how it is with love? First comes delight: then pain: then fruit. And then there is joy of the fruit, but that is different again from the first delight. And mortal lovers must not try to remain at the first step: for lasting passion is the dream of a harlot and from it we wake in despair. You must not try to keep the raptures: they have done their work. Manna kept, is worms. But you are full of sleep and we had better talk no more.'

Then I dreamed that John lay down on a hard bed in the cave; and as he lay between waking and sleeping, the hermit, as he thought, lit two candles at the back of the cave on an altar and went to and fro doing and saying his holy things. And on the very borders of sleep John heard him begin to sing, and this was the song:

My heart is empty. All the fountains that should run
　With longing, are in me
Dried up. In all my countryside there is not one
　That drips to find the sea.
I have no care for anything thy love can grant
　Except the moment's vain
And hardly noticed filling of the moment's want
　And to be free from pain.
Oh, thou that art unwearying, that dost neither sleep

> *Nor slumber, who didst take*
> *All care for Lazarus in the careless tomb, oh keep*
> > *Watch for me till I wake.*
> *If thou think for me what I cannot think, if thou*
> > *Desire for me what I*
> *Cannot desire, my soul's interior Form, though now*
> > *Deep-buried, will not die,*
> *– No more than the insensible dropp'd seed which grows*
> > *Through winter ripe for birth*
> *Because, while it forgets, the heaven remembering throws*
> > *Sweet influence still on earth,*
> *– Because the heaven, moved moth-like by thy beauty, goes*
> > *Still turning round the earth.*

BOOK 9

ACROSS THE CANYON

*Sholde nevere whete wexe bote whete
fyrste deyde;
And other sedes also, in the same wyse,
Thae ben leide on louh erthe, ylore as
hit were,
And thorwh the grete grace of God, of
greyn ded in erthe
Atte last launceth up wher-by we liven alle.*
LANGLAND

*You will not sleep, if you lie there a thousand
years, until you have opened your hand and
yielded that which is not yours to give or to
withhold. You may think you are dead, but
it will be only a dream; you may think you
have come awake, but it will still be only a
dream. Open your hand, and you will sleep
indeed – then wake indeed.*
GEORGE MACDONALD

You may as well come quiet.
POLICE MAXIM

I

ACROSS THE CANYON BY THE INNER LIGHT

John realises that he is in imminent danger of becoming a Christian – He struggles to withdraw

When John opened his eyes the day was still far off but there was light in the cave as though from a hundred candles. The hermit lay fast asleep by one wall of the cell as John lay by the other, and between them stood a woman, something like Reason and something like Mother Kirk, very bright.

'I am Contemplation,' she said. 'Rise and come with me.'

'You are not like the Contemplation that I know,' said John.

'It is one of my shadows whom you have met,' said the Lady. 'And there is little good in them and less harm. But rise and come.'

Then John rose and the Lady took him by the hand and led him out on to the ledge before the cave. And the night was still black with thunderous rain, but the Lady and he were in a sphere of light, so that the raindrops as they passed out of the darkness into it became bright like diamonds in the centre of the sphere and iridescent at the circumference. Held by the Lady's hand he crossed the chasm and passed up the glens of the mountains on the other side. When they had travelled a long way (and still the darkness lay everywhere save where they trod) they came to the sea. And they crossed the sea also, gliding a little above the water, and the water also was dark until it reached their light, but within that it was blue as though it lay in Mediterranean sunshine. But presently the surrounding darkness vanished away and the drop of light in which they had journeyed entered an ocean of light and was swallowed up. The sky was visible above them and it seemed to be early morning, for it was cool and dew soaked their feet. And John looked and saw fields going up before him and the light ran down as a river in the midst of the fields, singing with a voice like a river but more articulate and very loud, too bright to look at. There were many people with them. And as John looked round upon the people he saw that they were approaching some high walls and great gates. And, at the shape of the tower clustered above him, a memory, very deeply buried, stirred in his mind, first sweet, then uneasy, then spreading through the pool of his mind in widening circles of dismay, till at last with certainty, inevitable, unbearable, there flashed before him the picture of those turreted crags seen long ago from Puritania at the summit of the Eastern mountains, and he saw where he was – beyond the brook – where Uncle George had vanished – at the Landlord's castle – the good kind Landlord with the black hole. He began to draw his hand out of the Lady's hand. He could not get it free. She was leading him on to the castle gates and all the crowd of people were moving on in the same direction, with a sinister happiness on their faces. He struggled with Contemplation and screamed: and with that and the struggling he awoke.

2

THIS SIDE BY LIGHTNING

Reason will not let him withdraw

It was now pitchy black in the cave. Only the quiet breathing of the hermit recalled to John where he was: and with the first return of the knowledge he was already creeping out of the cave to dare the black night and the narrow ledge, to crawl the skin off his hands and his knees, to do and suffer anything so long as he was going back and not on – on in this direction where the next turning might lead him into the heart of his adversary's power. The rain fell in torrents and thunder echoed among the rocks: but the cool moisture on his back was better than the hot moisture on his forehead. He did not dare to stand up and walk, for the new terrors had not driven out the old, but rather joined with them in a phantasmagoric harmony, so that all in one moment his inner eye saw the black hole full of the spiders and scorpions – the narrow, narrow ledge sloping horribly the wrong way – the drop into the darkness and his own body bounced from crag to crag – the terrible face of Uncle George when the mask would not stay on it. And as the flashes came faster and the thunder followed faster on each flash, a new fear joined the dance: and in each flash the timeless unforgettable sight of the cliffs, lit up from end to end, gave a new edge to the old fear of climbing: and that again brought back the fear of Uncle George's face (so will mine look when I lie broken at the bottom of the gorge), until at last, when the complexity of fears seemed to admit no increase, a sharp, commanding voice out of the darkness suddenly startled him with such a shock that he seemed not to have been frightened till then.

'Back!' said the voice.

John crouched motionless from the balance of fears. He was not even sure that he *could* turn on this bit of the ledge.

'Back,' said the voice, 'or else show that you're the better man.'

The lightning tore open the darkness and flung it to again. But John had seen his enemy. It was Reason, this time on foot, but still mailed, and her sword drawn in her hand.

'Do you want to fight?' she said in the darkness.

John had a wild thought of catching one of the mailed ankles from where he crouched: but when he had a picture of Reason falling into the gulf he could not get it clear of another picture in which he fell with her.

'I can't turn here,' he said: but the steel was at his throat and turn he did. He shuffled along at a surprising speed, still on his hands and knees, till he had passed the cave again. It was no longer a question of plans or of ultimate escape. The hunted animal's impulse to prolong the chase kept him ragingly on the move. The flashes were growing rare and a star or two showed ahead. Then all of a sudden a wind shook the last raindrops fiercely in his face and there was moonlight all about him. But he drew back with a groan.

3

THIS SIDE BY THE DARKNESS

*John sees the face of Death and learns that
dying is the only escape from it*

Within an inch of him he had seen a face. Now a cloud crossed the moon and the face was no longer visible, but he knew that it was still looking at him – an aged, appalling face, crumbling and chaotic, larger than human. Presently its voice began:

'Do you still think it is the black hole you fear? Do you not know even now the deeper fear whereof the black hole is but the veil? Do you not know why they would all persuade you that there is nothing beyond the brook and that when a man's lease is out his story is done? Because, if this were true, they could in their reckoning make me equal to nought, therefore not dreadful: could say that where I am they are not, that while they are, I am not. They have prophesied soft things to you. I am no negation, and the deepest of your heart acknowledges it. Else why have you buried the memory of your uncle's face so carefully that it has needed all these things to bring it up? Do not think that you can escape me; do not think you can call me Nothing. To you I am not Nothing; I am the being blindfolded, the losing all power of self-defence, the surrender, not because any terms are offered, but because resistance is gone: the step into the dark: the defeat of all precautions: utter helplessness turned out to utter risk: the final loss of liberty. The Landlord's Son who feared nothing, feared me.'

'What am I to do?' said John.

'Which you choose,' said the voice. 'Jump, or be thrown. Shut your eyes or have them bandaged by force. Give in or struggle.'

'I would sooner do the first, if I could.'

'Then I am your servant and no more your master. The cure of death is dying. He who lays down his liberty in that act receives it back. Go down to Mother Kirk.'

John looked about him when next the moon shone. The bottom of the chasm was level far below him, and there he saw what seemed a concourse of dark figures. Amidst them they had left an open space, where there was a glimmer as of water: and near the water there was someone standing.

It seemed to him that he was waited for, and he began to explore the face of the cliff below him. To his surprise it was no longer sheer and smooth. He tried a few footholds and got five feet below the ledge. Then he sat down again, sick. But the kind of fear which he now suffered was cold and leaden: there was no panic in it: and soon he continued his descent.

4

SECURUS TE PROJICE

*John returns to the Church of Christ –
Though all the states of mind through which
he has ever passed rise up to dissuade him*

On the floor of *Peccatum Adae* stood Mother Kirk crowned and sceptred in the midst of the bright moonlit circle left by the silent people. All their faces were turned towards her, and she was looking eastward to where John slowly descended the cliff. Not far from her sat Vertue, mother-naked. They were both on the margin of a large pool which lay in a semicircle against the western cliff. On the far side of the water that cliff rose sheer to the edge of the canyon. There was deep silence for about half an hour.

At last the small, drooping figure of a man detached itself from the shadow of the crags and advanced towards them through the open moonlight. It was John.

'I have come to give myself up,' he said.

'It is well,' said Mother Kirk. 'You have come a long way round to reach this place, whither I would have carried you in a few moments. But it is very well.'

'What must I do?' said John.

'You must take off your rags,' said she, 'as your friend has done already, and then you must dive into this water.'

'Alas,' said he, 'I have never learned to dive.'

'There is nothing to learn,' said she. 'The art of diving is not to do anything new but simply to cease doing something. You have only to let yourself go.'

'It is only necessary,' said Vertue, with a smile, 'to abandon all efforts at self-preservation.'

'I think,' said John, 'that if it is all one, I would rather jump.'

'It is not all one,' said Mother Kirk. 'If you jump, you will be trying to save yourself and you may be hurt. As well, you would not go deep enough. You must dive so that you can go right down to the bottom of the pool: for you are not to come up again on this side. There is a tunnel in the cliff, far beneath the surface of the water, and it is through that that you must pass so that you may come up on the far side.'

'I see,' thought John to himself, 'that they have brought me here to kill me,' but he began, nevertheless, to take off his clothes. They were little loss to him, for they hung in shreds, plastered with blood and with the grime of every shire from Puritania to the canyon: but they were so stuck to him that they came away with pain and a little skin came with them. When he was naked Mother Kirk bade him come to the edge of the pool, where Vertue was already standing. It was a long way down to the water, and the reflected moon seemed to look up at him from the depth of a mine. He had had some thought of throwing himself in, with a run, the very instant he reached the edge, before he had time to be afraid. And the making of that resolution had seemed to be itself the bitterness of death, so that he half believed the worst must be over and that he would find himself in the water before he knew. But lo! he was still standing on the edge, still on this side. Then a stranger thing came to pass. From the great concourse of spectators, shadowy people came stealing out to his side, touching his arm and whispering to him: and every one of them appeared to be the wraith of some old acquaintance.

First came the wraith of old Enlightenment and said, 'There's still time. Get away and come back to me and all this will vanish like a nightmare.'

Then came the wraith of Media Halfways and said, 'Can you really risk losing me for ever? I know you do not desire me at this moment. But for ever? Think. Don't burn your boats.'

And the wraith of old Halfways said, 'After all – has this anything to do with the Island as you used to imagine it? Come back and hear my songs instead. You *know* them.'

The wraith of young Halfways said, 'Aren't you ashamed? Be a man. Move with the times and don't throw your life away for an old wives' tale.'

The wraith of Sigismund said, 'You know what this is, I suppose. Religious melancholia. Stop while there is time. If you dive, you dive into insanity.'

The wraith of Sensible said, 'Safety first. A touch of rational piety adds something to life: but this salvationist business ... well! Who knows where it will end? Never accept unlimited liabilities.'

The wraith of Humanist said, 'Mere atavism. You are diving to escape your real duties. All this emotionalism, after the first plunge, is so much *easier* than virtue in the classical sense.'

The wraith of Broad said, 'My dear boy, you are losing your head. These sudden conversions and violent struggles don't achieve anything. We have had to discard so much that our ancestors thought necessary. It is all far easier, far more gracious and beautiful than they supposed.'

But at that moment the voice of Vertue broke in:

'Come on, John,' he said, 'the longer we look at it the less we shall like it.' And with that he took a header into the pool and they saw him no more.

And how John managed it or what he felt I did not know, but he also rubbed his hands, shut his eyes, despaired, and let himself go. It was not a good dive, but, at least, he reached the water head first.

5

ACROSS THE CANYON

*John comes where Philosophy said no man
could come – The goal is, and is not, what he
had always Desired*

My dream grew darker so that I have a sense, but little clear memory of the things that John experienced both in the pool and in great catacombs, paved sometimes with water, sometimes with stone, and upon winding stairways in the live rocks, whereby he and Vertue ascended through the inwards of the mountain to the land beyond *Peccatum Adae*. He learned many mysteries in the earth and passed through many elements, dying many deaths. One thing has come through into my waking memory. Of all the people he had met in his journey only Wisdom appeared to him in the caverns, and troubled him by saying that no man could really come where he had come and that all his adventures were but figurative, for no professed experience of these places could be anything other than mythology. But then another voice spoke to him from behind him, saying:

'Child, if you will, it *is* mythology. It is but truth, not fact: an image, not the very real. But then it is My mythology. The words of Wisdom are also myth and metaphor: but since they do not know themselves for what they are, in them the hidden myth is master, where it should be servant: and it is but of man's inventing. But this is My inventing, this is the veil under which I have chosen to appear even from the first until now. For this end I made your senses and for this end your imagination, that you might see My face and live. What would you have? Have you not heard among the Pagans the story of Semele? Or was there any age in any land when men did not know that corn and wine were the blood and body of a dying and yet living God?'

And not long after that the light and colour, as with the sound of a trumpet, rushed back upon my dreaming eyes, and my ears were full of the sound of birds and the rustle of leaves, for John and Vertue had come up out of the earth into the green forests of the land beyond the canyon. Then I saw that they were received into a great company of other pilgrims who had all descended like them into the water and the earth and again come up, and now took their march westward along the banks of a clear river. All kinds of men were among them. And during the whole of this part of their journey Reason rode with the company, talking to them at will and not visiting them any longer by sudden starts, nor vanishing suddenly. It was a wonder to John to find so many companions: nor could he conceive how he had failed to run across them in the earlier parts of his journey.

I watched this journey in my dream a long time. At the outset their goal was heard of only by rumours as of something very far off: then, by continuous marching, winding their way among the peaked and valleyed lands, I saw where they came down to the white beaches of a bay of the sea, the western end of the world; a place very ancient, folded many miles deep in the silence of forests; a place, in some sort, lying rather at the world's beginning, as though men were born travelling away from it. It was early in the morning when they came there and heard the sound of the waves; and looking across the sea – at that hour still almost colourless – all these thousands became still. And what the others saw I do not know: but John saw the Island. And the morning wind, blowing off-shore from it, brought the sweet smell of its orchards to them, but rarefied and made faint with the thinness and purity of early air, and mixed with a little sharpness of the sea. But for John, because so many thousands looked at it with him, the pain and the longing were changed and all unlike what they had been of old: for humility was mixed with their wildness, and the sweetness came not with pride and with the lonely dreams of poets nor with the glamour of a secret, but with the homespun truth of folk-tales, and with the sadness of graves and freshness as of earth in the morning. There was fear in it also, and hope: and it began to seem well to him that the Island should be different from his desires, and so different that, if he had known it, he would not have sought it.

6

NELLA SUA VOLUNTADE

And the Christian life still to begin

How it fared with the other pilgrims I did not see, but presently a comely person took John and Vertue apart and said that he had been appointed to be their Guide. I dreamed that he was one born in the Mountain and they called him Slikisteinsauga because his sight was so sharp that the sight of any other who travelled with him would be sharpened by his company.

'Thank you,' said John. 'Pray, do we take ship from here?'

But Slikisteinsauga shook his head: and he asked them to look at the Island again and specially to consider the shape of the crags, or the castle (for they could not well see which at that distance) to which it rose at its highest point.

'I see,' said John presently.

'What do you see?' said the Guide.

'They are the very same shape as that summit of the Eastern Mountain which we called the Landlord's castle as we saw it from Puritania.'

'They are not only the same shape. They are the same.'

'How can that be?' said John with a sinking heart, 'for those mountains were in the extreme East, and we have been travelling West ever since we left home.'

'But the world is round,' said the Guide, 'and you have come nearly round it. The Island is the Mountains: or, if you will, the Island is the other side of the Mountains, and not, in truth, an Island at all.'

'And how do we go on from here?'

The Guide looked at him as a merciful man looks on an animal which he must hurt.

'The way to go on,' he said at last, 'is to go back. There are no ships. The only way is to go East again and cross the brook.'

'What must be must be,' said John. 'I deserve no better. You mean that I have been wasting my labour all my life, and I have gone half-round the world to reach what Uncle George reached in a mile or so.'

'Who knows what your uncle has reached, except the Landlord? Who knows what you would have reached if you had crossed the brook without ever leaving home? You may be sure the Landlord has brought you the shortest way: though I confess it would look an odd journey on a map.'

'How does it strike you, friend?' said John to Vertue.

'It cannot be helped,' said Vertue. 'But indeed, after the water and the earth, I thought we had already crossed the brook in a sense.'

'You will be always thinking that,' said the Guide. 'We call it Death in the Mountain language. It is too tough a morsel to eat at one bite. You will meet that brook more often than you think: and each time you will suppose that you have done with it for good. But some day you really will.'

They were all silent for a while.

'Come,' said the Guide at last, 'if you are ready let us start East again. But I should warn you of one thing – the country will look very different on the return journey.'

BOOK 10

THE REGRESS

And if, when he returned into the cave, he were constrained once more to contend with those that had always there been prisoners, in judgment of the said shadows, would they not mock him, and say of him that by going up out of the cave he had come down again with his eyes marred for his pains, and that it was lost labour for any so much as to try that ascent?
PLATO

First I must lead the human soul through all the range
Of heaven, that she may learn
How fortunate hath the turning of the wheel of change
How fate will never turn.
BERNARDUS SILVESTRIS

Let us suppose a person destitute of that knowledge which we have from our senses ... Let it be supposed that in his drought he puts golden dust into his eyes; when his eyes smart, he puts wine into his ears; that in his hunger, he puts gravel into his mouth; that in pain, he loads himself with the iron chains; that feeling cold, he puts his feet in the water; that being frighted at the fire, he runs away from it; that being weary, he makes a seat of his bread ... Let us suppose that some good being came to him, and showed him the nature and use of all the things that were about him.
LAW

I

THE SAME YET DIFFERENT

*John now first sees the real shape of the
world we live in – How we walk on a knife-
edge between Heaven and Hell*

Then I dreamed that the Guide armed John and Vertue at all points and led them back through the country they had just been travelling, and across the canyon again into this country. And they came up out of the canyon at the very place where the main road meets it by Mother Kirk's chair. I looked forward in the same direction where they were looking, expecting to see on my left the bare tableland rising to the North with Sensible's house a little way off, and on my right the house of Mr Broad and the pleasant valleys southward. But there was nothing of the kind: only the long straight road, very narrow, and on the left crags rising within a few paces of the road into ice and mist and, beyond that, black cloud: on the right, swamps and jungle sinking almost at once into black cloud. But, as it happens in dreams, I never doubted that this was the same country which I had seen before, although there was no similarity. John and Vertue came to a stand with their surprise.

'Courage,' said Slikisteinsauga, 'you are seeing the land as it really is. It is long but very narrow. Beyond these crags and cloud on the North it sinks immediately into the Arctic Sea, beyond which again lies the Enemy's country. But the Enemy's country is joined up with ours on the North by a land bridge called the Isthmus Sadisticus and right amid that Isthmus sits the cold dragon, the cold, costive, crustacean dragon who wishes to enfold all that he can get within the curl of his body and then to draw his body tighter round it so as to have it all inside himself. And you, John, when we pass the Isthmus must go up and contend with him that you may be hardened. But on the South, as soon as it passes into these swamps and this other cloud, the land sinks into the Southern Sea: and across that sea also there comes a land bridge, the Isthmus Mazochisticus, where the hot dragon crawls, the expansive, invertebrate dragon whose fiery breath makes all that she touches melt and corrupt. And to her you, Vertue, must go down that you may steal her heat and be made malleable.'

'Upon my soul,' said John, 'I think Mother Kirk treats us very ill. Since we have followed her and eaten her food the way seems twice as narrow and twice as dangerous as it did before.'

'You all know,' said the Guide, 'that security is mortals' greatest enemy.'

'It will do very well,' said Vertue, 'let us begin.'

Then they set out on their journey and Vertue sang this song:

'Thou only art alternative to God, oh, dark
And burning island among spirits, tenth hierarch,
Wormwood, immortal Satan, Ahriman, alone
Second to Him to whom no second else were known,
Being essential fire, sprung of His fire, but bound
Within the lightless furnace of thy Self, bricked round
To rage in the reverberated heat from seven
Containing walls: hence power thou hast to rival heaven.
Therefore, except the temperance of the eternal love
Only thy absolute lust is worth the thinking of.
All else is weak disguisings of the wishful heart,
All that seemed earth is Hell, or Heaven. God is: thou art:
The rest, illusion. How should man live save as glass
To let the white light without flame, the Father, pass
Unstained: or else – opaque, molten to thy desire,
Venus infernal starving in the strength of fire!'

'Lord, open not too often my weak eyes to this.'

2

THE SYNTHETIC MAN

'The World of all Sensible Men' becomes invisible

As they went on, Vertue glanced to the side of the road to see if there were any trace of Mr Sensible's house, but there was none.

'It is just as it was when you passed it before,' said the Guide, 'but your eyes are altered. You see nothing now but realities: and Mr Sensible was so near to nonentity – so shadowy even as an appearance – that he is now invisible to you. That mote will trouble your eyes no longer.'

'I am very surprised,' said Vertue, 'I should have thought that even if he was bad he was a singularly solid and four-square kind of evil.'

'All that solidity,' said the Guide, 'belonged not to him but to his predecessors in that house. There was an appearance of temperance about him, but it came from Epicurus. There was an appearance of poetry, but it came from Horace. A trace of old Pagan dignities lingered in his house – it was Montaigne's. His heart seemed warm for a moment, but the warmth was borrowed from Rabelais. He was a man of shreds and patches, and when you have taken from him what was not his own, the remainder equals nought.'

'But surely,' said Vertue, 'these things were not the less his own because he learned them from others.'

'He did not learn them. He learned only catchwords from them. He could talk like Epicurus of spare diet, but he was a glutton. He had from Montaigne the language of friendship, but no friend. He did not even know what these predecessors had really said. He never read one ode of Horace seriously in his life. And for his Rabelais, he can quote *Do what you will*. But he has no notion that Rabelais gave that liberty to his Thelemites on the condition that they should be bound by Honour, and for this reason alone free from laws positive. Still less does he know that Rabelais himself was following a great Steward of the olden days who said *Habe caritatem et fac quod vis*: and least of all that this Steward in his turn was only reducing to an epigram the words of his Master, when He said, "On these two commandments hang all the law and the prophets."'

3

LIMBO

God's mercy on philosophical Despair

Then I dreamed that John looked aside on the right hand of the road and saw a little island of willow trees amid the swamps, where ancient men sat robed in black, and the sound of their sighing reached his ears.

'That place,' said the Guide, 'is the same which you called the Valley of Wisdom when you passed it before: but now that you are going East you may call it Limbo, or the twilit porches of the black hole.'

'Who lives there?' asked John, 'and what do they suffer?'

'Very few live there, and they are all men like old Mr Wisdom – men who have kept alive and pure the deep desire of the soul but through some fatal flaw, of pride or sloth or, it may be, timidity, have refused till the end the only means to its fulfilment; taking huge pains, often, to prove to themselves that the fulfilment is impossible. They are very few because old Wisdom has few sons who are true to him, and the most part of those who come to him either go on and cross the canyon, or else, remaining his sons in name, secretly slip back to feed on worse fare than his. To stay long where he lives requires both a strange strength and a strange weakness. As for their sufferings, it is their doom to live for ever in desire without hope.'

'Is it not rather harsh of the Landlord to make them suffer at all?'

'I can answer that only by hearsay,' returned the Guide, 'for pain is a secret which he has shared with your race and not with mine; and you would find it as hard to explain suffering to me as I should find it to reveal to you the secrets of the Mountain people. But those who know best say this, that any liberal man would choose the pain of this desire, even for ever, rather than the peace of feeling it no longer: and that though the best thing is to have, the next best is to want, and the worst of all is not to want.'

'I see that,' said John. 'Even the wanting, though it is pain too, is more precious than anything else we experience.'

'It is as I foresaw, and you understand it already better than I can. But there is this also. The Landlord does not condemn them to lack of hope: they have done that themselves. The Landlord's interference is all on the other side. Left to itself, the desire without the hope would soon fall back to spurious satisfactions, and these souls would follow it of their own free will into far darker regions at the very bottom of the black hole. What the Landlord has done is to fix it forever: and by his art, though unfulfilled, it is uncorrupted. Men say that his love and his wrath are one thing. Of some places in the black hole you cannot see this, though you can believe it: but of that Island yonder under the willows, you can see it with your own eyes.'

'I see it very well,' said John.

Then the Guide sang:

'God in His mercy made
The fixèd pains of Hell.
That misery might be stayed,
God in His mercy made
Eternal bounds and bade
Its waves no further swell.
God in his mercy made
The fixèd pains of Hell.'

4

THE BLACK HOLE

*The Divine Justice – Hell as a tourniquet –
Human choice*

'Then there is, after all,' said John, 'a black hole such as my old Steward described to me.'

'I do not know what your Steward described. But there is a black hole.'

'And still the Landlord is "so kind and good"!'

'I see you have been among the Enemy's people. In these latter days there is no charge against the Landlord which the Enemy brings so often as cruelty. That is just like the Enemy: for he is, at bottom, very dull. He has never hit on the one slander against the Landlord which would be really plausible. Anyone can refute the charge of cruelty. If he really wants to damage the Landlord's character, he has a much stronger line than that to take. He ought to say that the Landlord is an inveterate gambler. That would not be true, but it would be plausible, for there is no denying that the Landlord does take risks.'

'But what about the charge of cruelty?'

'I was just coming to that. The Landlord has taken the risk of working the country with free tenants instead of slaves in chain gangs: and as they are free there is no way of making it impossible for them to go into forbidden places and eat forbidden fruits. Up to a certain point he can doctor them even when they have done so, and break them of the habit. But beyond that point – you can see for yourself. A man can go on eating mountain-apple so long that *nothing* will cure his craving for it: and the very worms it breeds inside him will make him more certain to eat more. You must not try to fix the point after which a return is impossible, but you can see that there will be such a point somewhere.'

'But surely the Landlord can do anything?'

'He cannot do what is contradictory: or, in other words, a meaningless sentence will not gain meaning simply because someone chooses to prefix to it the words "the Landlord can". And it is meaningless to talk of forcing a man to do freely what a man has freely made impossible for himself.'

'I see. But at least these poor creatures are unhappy enough: there is no need to add a black hole.'

'The Landlord does not make the blackness. The blackness is there already wherever the taste of mountain-apple has created the vermiculate will. What do you mean by a hole? Something that ends. A black hole is blackness enclosed, limited. And in that sense the Landlord *has* made the black hole. He has put into the world a Worst Thing. But evil of itself would never reach a worst: for evil is fissiparous and could never in a thousand eternities find any way to arrest its own reproduction. If it could, it would be no longer evil: for Form and Limit belong to the good. The walls of the black hole are the tourniquet on the wound through which the lost soul else would bleed to a death she never reached. It is the Landlord's last service to those who will let him do nothing better for them.'

Then the Guide sang:

'Nearly they stood who fall;
Themselves as they look back
See always in the track
The one false step, where all
Even yet, by lightest swerve
Of foot not yet enslaved,
By smallest tremor of the smallest nerve,
Might have been saved.

'Nearly they fell who stand,
And with cold after fear
Look back to mark how near
They grazed the Sirens' land,
Wondering that subtle fate,
By threads so spidery fine,
The choice of ways so small, the event so great,
Should thus entwine.

'Therefore oh, man, have fear
Lest oldest fears be true,
Lest thou too far pursue
The road that seems so clear,
And step, secure, a hair's
Breadth past the hair-breadth bourne,
Which, being once crossed forever unawares,
Denies return.'

5

SUPERBIA

*Tough-mindedness revealed as a form of
Pride – As virtue increases so does the
temptation to Pride – The vision of God is
the fountain of Humility*

Then they went further and saw in the rocks beside them on the left what seemed at first sight a skeleton, but as they drew nearer they saw that there was indeed skin stretched over its bones and eyes flaming in the sockets of its skull. And it was scrabbling and puddering to and fro on what appeared to be a mirror; but it was only the rock itself scraped clean of every speck of dust and fibre of lichen and polished by the continued activity of this famished creature.

'This is one of the Enemy's daughters,' said the Guide, 'and her name is Superbia. But when you last saw her, perhaps she wore the likeness of three pale men.'

As they passed her she began to croak out her song.

'*I have scraped clean the plateau from the filthy earth,
Earth the unchaste, the fruitful, the great grand maternal,
Sprawling creature, lolling at random and supine,
The broad-faced, sluttish helot, the slave wife
Grubby and warm, who opens unashamed
Her thousand wombs unguarded to the lickerous sun.
Now I have scoured my rock clean from the filthy earth,
On it no root can strike and no blade come to birth,
And though I starve of hunger it is plainly seen
That I have eaten nothing common or unclean.*

'*I have by fasting purged away the filthy flesh,
Flesh the hot, moist, salt scum, the obscenity
And parasitic tetter, from my noble bones.
I have torn from my breasts – I was an udder'd beast –
My child, for he was fleshly. Flesh is caught
By a contagion carried from impure
Generation to generation through the body's sewer.*

*And now though I am barren, yet no man can doubt
I am clean and my iniquities are blotted out.*

*'I have made my soul (once filthy) a hard, pure, bright
Mirror of steel: no damp breath breathes upon it
Warming and dimming: it would freeze the finger
If any touched it. I have a mineral soul.
Minerals eat no food and void no excrement.
So I, borrowing nothing and repaying
Nothing, neither growing nor decaying,
Myself am to myself, a mortal God, a self-contained
Unwindowed monad, unindebted and unstained.'*

John and the Guide were hurrying past, but Vertue hesitated.

'Her means may be wrong,' he said, 'but there is something to be said for her idea of the End.'

'What idea?' said the Guide.

'Why – self-sufficiency, integrity. Not to commit herself, you know. All said and done, there *is* something foul about all these natural processes.'

'You had better be careful of your thoughts here,' said the Guide. 'Do not confuse Repentance with Disgust: for the one comes from the Landlord and the other from the Enemy.'

'And yet disgust has saved many a man from worse evils.'

'By the power of the Landlord it may be so – now and then. But don't try to play that game for yourself. Fighting one vice with another is about the most dangerous strategy there is. You know what happens to kingdoms that use alien mercenaries.'

'I suppose you are right,' said Vertue, 'and yet this feeling goes very deep. Is it wholly wrong to be ashamed of being in the body?'

'The Landlord's Son was not. You know the verses – "When thou tookest upon thee to deliver man".'

'That was a special case.'

'It was a special case because it was the archetypal case. Has no one told you that that Lady spoke and acted for all that bears, in the presence of all that begets: for this country as against the things East and West: for matter as against form and patiency against agency? Is not the very word Mother akin to Matter? Be sure that the whole of this land, with all its warmth and wetness and fecundity, with all the dark and the heavy and the multitudinous for which you are too dainty, spoke through her lips when she said that He had regarded the lowliness of His hand-maiden. And if that Lady was a maid though a mother, you need not doubt that the nature which is, to human sense, impure, is also pure.'

'Well,' said Vertue, turning away from Superbia, 'I will think this over.'

'One thing you may as well know,' remarked the Guide, 'whatever virtues you may attribute to the Landlord, decency is not one of them. That is why so few of your national jokes have any point in my country.'

And as they continued their journey, Vertue sang:

'Because of endless pride
Reborn with endless error,
Each hour I look aside
Upon my secret mirror
Trying all postures there
To make my image fair.

'Thou givest grapes, and I,
Though starving, turn to see
How dark the cool globes lie
In the white hand of me,
And linger gazing thither
Till the live clusters wither.

'So should I quickly die
Narcissus-like of want,
But, in the glass, my eye
Catches such forms as haunt
Beyond nightmare, and make
Pride humble for pride's sake.

'Then and then only turning
The stiff neck round, I grow
A molten man all burning
And look behind and know
Who made the glass, whose light makes dark, whose fair
Makes foul, my shadowy form reflected there
That Self-Love, brought to bed of Love may die and bear
Her sweet son in despair.'

6

IGNORANTIA

*The change from classical to scientific
education strengthens our Ignorance –
Though the Machine Age, for good or ill,
will do less than is expected of it*

Still I lay dreaming and saw these three continue their journey through that long and narrow land with the rocks upon their left and the swamp on their right. They had much talk on the way of which I have remembered only snatches since I woke. I remember that they passed Ignorantia some miles beyond her sister Superbia and that led the pilgrims to question their Guide as to whether the Ignorance of the Tough-minded and the Clevers would some day be cured. He said there was less chance of that now than there had ever been: for till recently the Northern people had been made to learn the languages of Pagus 'and that meant', said the Guide, 'that at least they started no further from the light than the old Pagans themselves and had therefore the chance to come at last to Mother Kirk. But now they are cutting themselves off even from that roundabout route.'

'Why have they changed?' asked one of the others.

'Why did the shadow whom you call Sensible leave his old house and go to practise αὐτάρκεια in a hotel? Because his Drudge revolted. The same thing is happening all over the plateau and in Mammon's country: their slaves are escaping further north and becoming dwarfs, and therefore the masters are turning all their attention to machinery, by which they hope to be able to lead their old life without slaves. And this seems to them so important that they are suppressing every kind of knowledge except mechanical knowledge. I am speaking of the sub-tenants. No doubt the great landowners in the background have their own reasons for encouraging this movement.'

'There must be a good side somewhere to this revolution,' said Vertue. 'It is too solid – it looks too lasting – to be a mere evil. I cannot believe that the Landlord would otherwise allow the whole face of nature and the whole structure of life to be so permanently and radically changed.'

The Guide laughed. 'You are falling into their own error,' he said. 'The change is not radical, nor will it be permanent. That idea depends on a curious disease which they have all caught – an inability to dis-believe advertisements. To be sure, if the machines did what they promised, the change would be very deep indeed. Their next war, for example, would change the state of their country from disease to death. They are afraid of this themselves – though most of them are old enough to know by experience that a gun is no more likely than a toothpaste or a cosmetic to do the things its makers say it will do. It is the same with all their machines. Their labour-saving devices multiply drudgery; their aphrodisiacs make them impotent: their amusements bore them: their rapid production of food leaves half of them starving, and their devices for saving time have banished leisure from their country. There will be no radical change. And as for permanence – consider how quickly all machines are broken and obliterated. The black solitudes will some day be green again and of all cities that I have seen these iron cities will break most suddenly.'

And the Guide sang:

'Iron will eat the world's old beauty up.
Girder and grid and gantry will arise,
   Iron forest of engines will arise,
   Criss-cross of iron crotchet. For your eyes
   No green or growth. Over all, the skies
   Scribbled from end to end with boasts and lies.
(When Adam ate the irrevocable apple, Thou
Saw'st beyond death the resurrection of the dead.)

   'Clamour shall clean put out the voice of wisdom,
The printing-presses with their clapping wings,
Fouling your nourishment. Harpy wings,
Filling your minds all day with foolish things,
Will tame the eagle Thought: till she sings
Parrot-like in her cage to please dark kings.
(When Israel descended into Egypt, Thou
Didst purpose both the bondage and the coming out.)

   'The new age, the new art, the new ethic and thought,
And fools crying, Because it has begun
It will continue as it has begun!
The wheel runs fast, therefore the wheel will run
Faster for ever. The old age is done,
We have new lights and see without the sun.
(Though they lay flat the mountains and dry up the sea,
Wilt Thou yet change, as though God were a god?)'

7

LUXURIA

*Lechery means not simply forbidden
pleasure, but loss of the man's unity – Its
supreme mode of temptation is to make all
else insipid*

After this, John looked up and saw that they were approaching a concourse of living creatures beside the road. Their way was so long and desolate (and he was footsore too) that he welcomed any diversion, and he cast his eyes curiously upon this new thing. When he was nearer he saw that the concourse was of men, but they lay about in such attitudes and were so disfigured that he had not recognised them for men: moreover, the place was to the south of the road, and therefore the ground was very soft and some of them were half under water and some hidden in the reeds. All seemed to be suffering from some disease of a crumbling and disintegrating kind. It was doubtful whether all the life that pulsated in their bodies was their own: and soon John was certain, for he saw what seemed to be a growth on a man's arm slowly detach itself under his eyes and become a fat reddish creature, separable from the parent body, though it was in no hurry to separate itself. And once he had seen that, his eyes were opened and he saw the same thing happening all round him, and the whole assembly was but a fountain of writhing and reptilian life quickening as he watched and sprouting out of the human forms. But in each form the anguished eyes were alive, sending to him unutterable messages from the central life which survived, self-conscious, though the self were but a fountain of vermin. One old cripple, whose face was all gone but the mouth and eyes, was sitting up to receive drink from a cup which a woman held to his lips. When he had as much as she thought good, she snatched the cup from his hands and went on to her next patient. She was dark but beautiful.

'Don't lag,' said the Guide, 'this is a very dangerous place. You had better come away. This is Luxuria.'

But John's eyes were caught by a young man to whom the witch had just come in her rounds. The disease, by seeming, had hardly begun with him: there was an unpleasant suspicion about his fingers – something a little too supple for joints – a little independent of his other movements – but, on the whole, he was still a well-looking person. And as the witch came to him the hands shot out to the cup, and the man drew them back again: and the hands went crawling out for the cup a second time, and again the man wrenched them back, and turned his face away, and cried out:

'Quick! The black, sulphurous, never quenched,
Old festering fire begins to play
Once more within. Look! By brute force I have wrenched
Unmercifully my hands the other way.

'Quick, Lord! On the rack thus, stretched tight,
Nerves clamouring as at nature's wrong.
Scorched to the quick, whipp'd raw – Lord, in this plight
You see, you see no man can suffer long.

'Quick, Lord! Before new scorpions bring
New venom – ere fiends blow the fire
A second time – quick, show me that sweet thing
Which, 'spite of all, more deeply I desire.'

And all the while the witch stood saying nothing, but only holding out the cup and smiling kindly on him with her dark eyes and her dark, red mouth. Then, when she saw that he would not drink, she passed on to the next: but at the first step she took, the young man gave a sob and his hands flew out and grabbed the cup and he buried his head in it: and when she took it from him, his lips clung to it as a drowning man to a piece of wood. But at last he sank down in the swamp with a groan. And the worms where there should have been fingers were unmistakable.

'Come on,' said Vertue.

They resumed their journey, John lagging a bit. I dreamed that the witch came to him walking softly in the marshy ground by the roadside and holding out the cup to him also: when he went faster she kept pace with him.

'I will not deceive you,' she said. 'You see there is no pretence. I am not trying to make you believe that this cup will take you to your Island. I am not saying it will quench your thirst for long. But taste it, none the less, for you are very thirsty.'

But John walked forward in silence.

'It is true,' said the witch, 'that you never can tell when you have reached the point beyond which there is no return. But that cuts both ways. If you can never be certain that one more taste is safe, neither can you be certain that one more taste is fatal. But you can be certain that you are terribly thirsty.'

But John continued as before.

'At least,' said the witch, 'have one more taste of it, before you abandon it for ever. This is a bad moment to choose for resistance, when you are tired and miserable and have already listened to me too long. Taste this once, and I will leave you. I do not promise never to come back: but perhaps when I come again, you will be strong and happy and well able to resist me – not as you are now.'

And John continued as before.

'Come,' said the witch. 'You are only wasting time. You know you will give in, in the end. Look ahead at the hard road and the grey sky. What other pleasure is there in sight?'

So she accompanied him for a long way, till the weariness of her importunity tempted him far more than any positive desire. But he forced his mind to other things and kept himself occupied for a mile or so by making the following verses:

When Lilith means to draw me
Within her secret bower,
She does not overawe me
With beauty's pomp and power,
Nor, with angelic grace
Of courtesy, and the pace
Of gliding ships, comes veiled at evening hour.

Eager, unmasked, she lingers
Heart-sick and hunger sore;
With hot, dry, jewelled fingers
Stretched out, beside her door,
Offering with gnawing haste
Her cup, whereof who taste,
(She promises no better) thirst far more.

What moves me, then, to drink it?
– Her spells, which all around
So change the land, we think it
A great waste where a sound
Of wind like tales twice told
Blusters, and cloud is rolled
Always above yet no rain falls to ground.

Across drab iteration
Of bare hills, line on line,
The long road's sinuation

> *Leads on. The witch's wine,*
> *Though promising nothing, seems*
> *In that land of no streams,*
> *To promise best – the unrelished anodyne.*

And by the time he had reached the word '*anodyne*' the witch was gone. But he had never in his life felt more weary, and for a while the purpose of his pilgrimage woke no desire in him.

8

THE NORTHERN DRAGON

*The Northern and Southern diseases of the
Soul – The Northern tension, hardness,
possessiveness, coldness, anaemia – John
overcomes it – and wins from it some of the
needful hardness he lacked*

'Now,' said the Guide, 'our time is come.'
They looked at him inquiringly.

'We are come,' said he, 'to that point of the road which lies midway between the two land bridges that I spoke of. The cold dragon is here on our left, and the hot dragon on our right. Now is the time to show what you are made of. Wolf is waiting in the wood southward: in the rocks northward, raven wheeling, in hope of carrion. Behoves you both be on guard quickly. God defend you.'

'Well,' said Vertue. And he drew his sword and slung his shield round from his back. Then he held out his hand first to the Guide, and then to John. 'So long,' he said.

'Go where it is least green,' said the Guide, 'for there the ground is firmest. And good luck.'

Vertue left the road and began to pick his way cautiously southward, feeling out the fen-paths. The Guide turned to John.

'Have you any practice with a sword?' he said.

'None, sir,' answered John.

'None is better than a smattering. You must trust to mother-wit. Aim at his belly – an upward jab. I shouldn't try cutting, if I were you: you don't know enough.'

'I will do the best I can,' said John. And then, after a pause: 'There is only one dragon, I suppose. I don't need to guard my back.'

'Of course there is only one, for he has eaten all the others. Otherwise he would not be a dragon. You know the maxim – *serpens nisi serpentem comederit* –'

Then I saw John also settle his gear and step off the road to the left. The ascent began at once, and before he was ten yards from the road he was six feet above it: but the formation of the rocks was such that it was like mounting a huge stair, and was tiring rather than difficult. When he first stopped to wipe the sweat out of his eyes the mist was already so dense that he could hardly see the road beneath him. Ahead the grey darkness shaded quickly into black. Then suddenly John heard a dry, rattling sound in front of him, and a little above. He got a better grip on his sword, and took one pace towards it, listening intently. Then came the sound again: and after that he heard a croaking voice, as of a gigantic frog. The dragon was singing to himself:

'Once the worm-laid egg broke in the wood.
I came forth shining into the trembling world,
The sun was on my scales, dew upon the grasses,
The cool, sweet grasses and the budding leaves.
I wooed my speckled mate. We played at druery
And sucked warm milk dropping from the goats' teats.

'Now I keep watch on the gold in my rock cave
In a country of stones: old, deplorable dragon,
Watching my hoard. In winter night the gold
Freezes through toughest scales my cold belly.
The jagged crowns and twisted cruel rings
Knobbly and icy are old dragon's bed.

'Often I wish I hadn't eaten my wife,
Though worm grows not to dragon till he eat worm.
She could have helped me, watch and watch about,
Guarding the hoard. Gold would have been the safer.
I could uncoil my weariness at times and take
A little sleep, sometimes when she was watching.

'Last night under the moonset a fox barked,
Woke me. Then I knew I had been sleeping.
Often an owl flying over the country of stones
Startles me, and I think I must have slept.
Only a moment. That very moment a man
Might have come out of the cities, stealing, to get my gold.

'They make plots in the towns to steal my gold.
They whisper of me in a low voice, laying plans,
Merciless men. Have they not ale upon the benches,
Warm wife in bed, singing, and sleep the whole night?
But I leave not the cave but once in winter
To drink of the rock pool: in summer twice.

'They feel no pity for the old, lugubrious dragon.
Oh, Lord, that made the dragon, grant me Thy peace!
But ask not that I should give up the gold,
Nor more, nor die; others would get the gold.
Kill, rather, Lord, the men and the other dragons
That I may sleep, go when I will to drink.'

As John listened to this song he forgot to be afraid. Disgust first, and then pity, chased fear from his mind: and after them came a strange desire to speak with the dragon and to suggest some sort of terms and division of the spoil: not that he desired the gold, but it seemed to him a not all ignoble desire to surround and contain so much within oneself. But while these things passed through his imagination, his body took care of him, keeping his grip steady on the sword hilt, his eyes strained into the darkness, and his feet ready to spring: so that he was not taken by surprise when he saw that in the rolling of the mist above him something else was rolling, and rolling round him to enclose him. But still he did not move. The dragon was paying its body out like a rope from a cave just above him. At first it swayed, the great head bobbing vertically, as a caterpillar sways searching for a new grip with half its length while the other half rests still on the leaf. Then the head dived and went behind him. He kept turning round to watch it, and it led the volume of the dragon's body round in a circle and finally went back into the cave, leaving a loop of dragon all round the man. Still John waited till the loop began to tighten, about on a level with his chest. Then he ducked and came up again with a jab of his sword into the under-side of the brute. It went in to the hilt, but there was no blood. At once the head came twisting back out of the cave. Eyes full of cruelty – cold cruelty without a spark of rage in it – stared into his face. The mouth was wide open – it was not red within, but grey like lead – and the breath of the creature was freezing cold. As soon as it touched John's face, everything was changed. A corselet of ice seemed to be closed about him, seemed to shut in his heart, so that it could never again flutter with panic or with greed. His strength was multiplied. His arms seemed to him iron. He found he was laughing and making thrust after thrust into the brute's throat. He found that the struggle was already over – perhaps hours ago. He was standing unwearied in a lonely place among rocks with a dead reptile at his feet. He remembered that he had killed it. And the time before he had killed it seemed very long ago.

9

THE SOUTHERN DRAGON

*Meanwhile John's Moral Self must meet the
Southern evil – And take into him its heat,
which will make Virtue itself henceforth
a passion*

John came leaping down the rocks into the road, whistling a tune. The Guide came to greet him, but before they had spoken a word, they both turned round in wonder at a great cry from the South. The sun had come out so that the whole marsh glittered like dirty copper: and at first they thought that it was the sun upon his arms that made Vertue flash like flame as he came leaping, running, and dancing towards them. But as he drew nearer they saw that he was veritably on fire. Smoke came from him, and where his feet slipped into the bog holes there were little puffs of steam. Hurtless flames ran up and down his sword and licked over his hand. His breast heaved and he reeled like a drunk man. They made towards him, but he cried out:

'I have come back with victory got –
But stand away – touch me not
Even with your clothes. I burn red-hot.

'The worm was bitter. When she saw
My shield glitter beside the shaw
She spat flame from her golden jaw.

'When on my sword her vomit spilt
The blade took fire. On the hilt
Beryl cracked, and bubbled gilt.

'When sword and sword arm were all flame
With the very heat that came
Out of the brute, I flogged her tame.

'In her own spew the worm died.
I rolled her round and tore her wide
And plucked the heart from her boiling side.

'When my teeth were in the heart
I felt a pulse within me start
As though my breast would break apart.

'It shook the hills and made them reel
And spun the woods round like a wheel.
The grass singed where I set my heel.

'Behemoth is my serving man!
Before the conquered hosts of Pan
Riding tamed Leviathan,
Loud I sing for well I can
*R*ESVRGAM *and* I*O* P*AEAN;*
*I*O, I*O,* I*O,* P*AEAN!!*

'Now I know the stake I played for,
Now I know what a worm's made for!'

10

THE BROOK

Death is at hand. Morality still seeks no
reward and desires no resurrection –
But Faith, being humbler, asks more –
The Angel sings

My dream was full of light and noise. I thought they went on their way singing and laughing like schoolboys. Vertue lost all his dignity, and John was never tired: and for ten miles or so they picked up an old fiddler who was going that way, who played them such jigs and they danced more than they walked. And Vertue invented doggerels to his tunes to mock the old Pagan virtues in which he had been bred.

But in the midst of all this gaiety, suddenly John stood still and his eyes filled with tears. They had come to a little cottage, beside a river, which was empty and ruinous. Then they all asked John what ailed him.

'We have come back to Puritania,' he said, 'and that was my father's house. I see that my father and mother are gone already beyond the brook. I had much I would have said to them. But it is no matter.'

'No matter indeed,' said the Guide, 'since you will cross the brook yourself before nightfall.'

'For the last time?' said Vertue.

'For the last time,' said the Guide, 'all being well.'

And now the day was declining and the Eastern Mountains loomed big and black ahead of them. Their shadows lengthened as they went down towards the brook.

'I am cured of playing the Stoic,' said Vertue, 'and I confess that I go down in fear and sadness. I also – there were many people I would have spoken to. There were many years I would call back. Whatever there is beyond the brook, it cannot be the same. Something is being ended. It is a real brook.

'I am not one that easily flits past in thought
The ominous stream, imagining death made for nought.
This person, mixed of body and breath, to which concurred
Once only one articulation of thy word,
Will be resolved eternally: nor can time bring

(Else time were vain) once back again the self-same thing.
Therefore among the riddles that no man has read
I put thy paradox, Who liveth and was dead.
As Thou hast made substantially, thou wilt unmake
In earnest and for everlasting. Let none take
Comfort in frail supposal that some hour and place
To those who mourn recovers the wished voice and face.
Whom Thy great Exit *banishes, no after age*
Of epilogue leads back upon the lighted stage.
Where is Prince Hamlet when the curtain's down? Where fled
Dreams at the dawn, or colours when the light is sped?
We are thy colours, fugitive, never restored,
Never repeated again. Thou only art the Lord,
Thou only art holy. In the shadowy vast
Of thine Osirian wings Thou dost enfold the past.
There sit in throne antediluvian, cruel kings,
There the first nightingale that sang to Eve yet sings,
There are the irrecoverable guiltless years,
There, yet unfallen, Lucifer among his peers.
For thou art also a deity of the dead, a god
Of graves, with necromancies in thy potent rod;
Thou art Lord of the unbreathable transmortal air
Where mortal thinking fails: night's nuptial darkness, where
All lost embraces intermingle and are bless'd.
And all die, but all are, while Thou continuest.'

The twilight was now far advanced and they were in sight of the brook. And John said, 'I thought all those things when I was in the house of Wisdom. But now I think better things. Be sure it is not for nothing that the Landlord has knit our hearts so closely to time and place – to one friend rather than another and one shire more than all the land.

'Passing today by a cottage, I shed tears
When I remembered how once I had dwelled there
With my mortal friends who are dead. Years
Little had healed the wound that was laid bare.

'Out, little spear that stabs. I, fool, believed
I had outgrown the local, unique sting,
I had transmuted away (I was deceived)
Into love universal the lov'd thing.

'But Thou, Lord, surely knewest Thine own plan
When the angelic indifferences with no bar
Universally loved but Thou gav'st man
The tether and pang of the particular;

'Which, like a chemic drop, infinitesimal,
Plashed into pure water, changing the whole,
Embodies and embitters and turns all
Spirit's sweet water to astringent soul.

'That we, though small, may quiver with fire's same
Substantial form as Thou – not reflect merely,
As lunar angel, back to thee, cold flame.
Gods we are, Thou has said: and we pay dearly.'

And now they were already at the brook, and it was so dark that I did not see them go over. Only, as my dream ended, and the voice of the birds at my window began to reach my ear (for it was a summer morning), I heard the voice of the Guide, mixed with theirs and not unlike them, singing this song:

'I know not, I,
    What the men together say,
How lovers, lovers die
    And youth passes away.

'Cannot understand
    Love that mortal bears
For native, native land
    – All lands are theirs.

'Why at grave they grieve
  For one voice and face,
And not, and not receive
  Another in its place.

'I, above the cone
  Of the circling night
Flying, never have known
  More or lesser light.

'Sorrow it is they call
  This cup: whence my lip,
Woe's me, never in all
  My endless days must sip.'

PRAYER: LETTERS TO MALCOLM

I

I am all in favour of your idea that we should go back to your old plan of having a more or less set subject – an *agendum* – for our letters. When we were last separated the correspondence languished for lack of it. How much better we did in our undergraduate days with our interminable letters on the *Republic*, and classical metres, and what was then the 'new' psychology! Nothing makes an absent friend so present as a disagreement.

Prayer, which you suggest, is a subject that is a good deal in my mind. I mean, private prayer. If you were thinking of corporate prayer, I won't play. There is no subject in the world (always excepting sport) on which I have less to say than liturgiology. And the almost nothing which I have to say may as well be disposed of in this letter.

I think our business as laymen is to take what we are given and make the best of it. And I think we should find this a great deal easier if what we were given was always and everywhere the same.

To judge from their practice, very few Anglican clergymen take this view. It looks as if they believed people can be lured to go to church by incessant brightenings, lightenings, lengthenings, abridgements, simplifications and complications of the service. And it is probably true that a new, keen vicar will usually be able to form within his parish a minority who are in favour of his innovations. The majority, I believe, never are. Those who remain – many give up churchgoing altogether – merely endure.

Is this simply because the majority are hide-bound? I think not. They have a good reason for their conservatism. Novelty, simply as such, can have only an entertainment value. And they don't go to church to be entertained. They go to *use* the service, or, if you prefer, to *enact* it. Every service is a structure of acts and words through which we receive a sacrament, or repent, or supplicate, or adore. And it enables us to do these things best – if you like, it 'works' best – when, through long familiarity, we don't have to think about it. As long as you notice, and have to count, the steps, you are not yet dancing but only learning to dance. A good shoe is a shoe you don't notice. Good reading becomes possible when you need not consciously think about eyes, or light, or print, or spelling. The perfect church service would be one we were almost unaware of; our attention would have been on God.

But every novelty prevents this. It fixes our attention on the service itself; and thinking about worship is a different thing from worshipping. The important question about the Grail was 'for what does it serve?' ''Tis mad idolatry that makes the service greater than the god.'

A still worse thing may happen. Novelty may fix our attention not even on the service but on the celebrant. You know what I mean. Try as one may to exclude it, the question, 'What on earth is he up to now?' will intrude. It lays one's devotion waste. There is really some excuse for the man who said, 'I wish they'd remember that the charge to Peter was Feed my sheep; not Try experiments on my rats, or even, Teach my performing dogs new tricks.'

Thus my whole liturgiological position really boils down to an entreaty for permanence and uniformity. I can make do with almost any kind of service whatever, if only it will stay put. But if each form is snatched away just when I am beginning to feel at home in it, then I can never make any progress in the art of worship. You give me no chance to acquire the trained habit – *habito dell' arte*.

It may well be that some variations which seem to me merely matters of taste really involve grave doctrinal differences. But surely not all? For if grave doctrinal differences are really as numerous as variations in practice, then we shall have to conclude that no such thing as the Church of England exists. And anyway, the Liturgical Fidget is not a purely Anglican phenomenon; I have heard Roman Catholics complain of it too.

And that brings me back to my starting point. The business of us laymen is simply to endure and make the best of it. Any tendency to a passionate preference for one type of service must be regarded simply as a temptation. Partisan 'Churchmanships' are my *bête noire*. And if we avoid them, may we not possibly perform a very useful function? The shepherds go off, 'every one to his own way' and vanish over diverse points of the horizon. If the sheep huddle patiently together and go on bleating, might they finally recall the shepherds? (Haven't English victories sometimes been won by the rank and file in spite of the generals?)

As to the words of the service – liturgy in the narrower sense – the question is rather different. If you have a vernacular liturgy you must have a changing liturgy; otherwise it will finally be vernacular only in name. The ideal of 'timeless English' is sheer nonsense. No living language can be timeless. You might as well ask for a motionless river.

I think it would have been best, if it were possible, that necessary change should have occurred gradually and (to most people) imperceptibly; here a little and there a little; one obsolete word replaced in a century – like the gradual change of spelling in successive editions of Shakespeare. As things are we must reconcile ourselves, if we can also reconcile government, to a new Book.

If we were – I thank my stars I'm not – in a position to give its authors advice, would you have any advice to give them? Mine could hardly go beyond unhelpful cautions: 'Take care. It is so easy to break eggs without making omelettes.'

Already our liturgy is one of the very few remaining elements of unity in our hideously divided Church. The good to be done by revision needs to be very great and very certain before we throw that away. Can you imagine any new Book which will not be a source of new schism?

Most of those who press for revision seem to wish that it should serve two purposes: that of modernising the language in the interests of intelligibility, and that of doctrinal improvement. Ought the two operations – each painful and each dangerous – to be carried out at the same time? Will the patient survive?

What are the agreed doctrines which are to be embodied in the new Book and how long will agreement on them continue? I ask with trepidation because I read a man the other day who seemed to wish that everything in the old Book which was inconsistent with orthodox Freudianism should be deleted.

For whom are we to cater in revising the language? A country parson I know asked his sexton what he understood by *indifferently* in the phrase 'truly and indifferently administer justice'. The man replied, 'It means making no difference between one chap and another.' 'And what would it mean if it said *impartially*?' asked the parson. 'Don't know. Never heard of it,' said the sexton. Here, you see, we have a change intended to make things easier. But it does so neither for the educated, who understand *indifferently* already, nor for the wholly uneducated, who don't understand *impartially*. It helps only some middle area of the congregation which may not even be a majority. Let us hope the revisers will prepare for their work by a prolonged empirical study of popular speech as it actually is, not as we (*a priori*) assume it to be. How many scholars know (what I discovered by accident) that when uneducated people say *impersonal* they sometimes mean *incorporeal*?

What of expressions which are archaic but not unintelligible? ('Be ye lift up.') I find that people react to archaism most diversely. It antagonises some: makes what is said unreal. To others, not necessarily more learned, it is highly numinous and a real aid to devotion. We can't please both.

I know there must be change. But is this the right moment? Two signs of the right moment occur to me. One would be a unity among us which enabled the Church – not some momentarily triumphant party – to speak through the new work with a united voice. The other would be the manifest presence, somewhere in the Church, of the specifically literary talent needed for composing a good prayer. Prose needs to be not only very good but very good in a very special way, if it is to stand up to reiterated reading aloud. Cranmer may have his defects as a theologian; as a stylist, he can play all the moderns, and many of his predecessors, off the field. I don't see either sign at the moment.

Yet we all want to be tinkering. Even I would gladly see 'Let your light so shine before men' removed from the offertory. It sounds, in that context, so like an exhortation to do our alms that they may be seen by men.

I'd meant to follow up what you say about Rose Macaulay's letters, but that must wait till next week.

2

I can't understand why you say that my view of church services is 'man-centred' and too concentrated with 'mere edification'. How does this follow from anything I said? Actually my ideas about the sacrament would probably be called 'magical' by a good many modern theologians. Surely, the more fully one believes that a strictly supernatural event takes place, the less one can attach any great importance to the dress, gestures, and position of the priest? I agree with you that he is there not only to edify the people but to glorify God. But how can a man glorify God by placing obstacles in the way of the people? Especially if the slightest element of 'clerical one-upmanship' – I owe the phrase to a cleric – underlines some of his eccentricities? How right is that passage in the *Imitation* where the celebrant is told, 'Consult not your own devotion but the edification of your flock.' I've forgotten how the Latin runs.

Now about the Rose Macaulay *Letters*. Like you, I was staggered by this continual search for more and more prayers. If she were merely collecting them as *objets d'art* I could understand it; she was a born collector. But I get the impression that she collected them in order to use them; that her whole prayer-life depended on what we may call 'ready-made' prayers – prayers written by other people.

But though, like you, staggered, I was not, like you, repelled. One reason is that I had – and you hadn't – the luck to meet her. Make no mistake. She was the right sort; one of the most fully civilised people I ever knew. The other reason, as I have so often told you, is that you are a bigot. Broaden your mind, Malcolm, broaden your mind! It takes all sorts to make a world; or a church. This may be even truer of a church. If grace perfects nature it must expand all our natures into the full richness of the diversity which God intended when He made them, and heaven will display far more variety than hell. 'One fold' doesn't mean 'one pool'. Cultivated roses and daffodils are no more alike than wild roses and daffodils. What pleased me most about a Greek Orthodox mass I once attended was that there seemed to be no prescribed behaviour for the congregation. Some stood, some knelt, some sat, some walked; one crawled about the floor like a caterpillar. And the beauty of it was that nobody took the slightest notice of what anyone else was doing. I wish we Anglicans would follow their example. One meets people who are perturbed because someone in the next pew does, or does not, cross himself. They oughtn't even to have seen, let alone censured. 'Who art thou that judgest Another's servant?'

I don't doubt, then, that Rose Macaulay's method was the right one for her. It wouldn't be for me, any more than for you.

All the same, I am not quite such a purist in this matter as I used to be. For many years after my conversion I never used any ready-made forms except the Lord's Prayer. In fact I tried to pray without words at all – not to verbalise the mental acts. Even in praying for others I believe I tended to avoid their names and substituted mental images of them. I still think the prayer without words is the best – if one can really achieve it. But I now see that in trying to make it my daily bread I was counting on a greater mental and spiritual strength than I really have. To pray successfully without words one needs to be 'at the top of one's form'. Otherwise the mental acts become merely imaginative or emotional acts – and a fabricated emotion is a miserable affair. When the golden moments come, when God enables one really to pray without words, who but a fool would reject the gift? But He does not give it – anyway not to me – day in, day out. My mistake was what Pascal, if I remember rightly, calls 'Error of Stoicism': thinking we can do always what we can do sometimes.

And this, you see, makes the choice between ready-made prayers and one's own words rather less important for me than it apparently is for you. For me words are in any case secondary. They are only an anchor. Or, shall I say, they are the movements of a conductor's baton: not the music. They serve to canalise the worship or penitence or petition which might without them – such are our minds – spread into wide and shallow puddles. It does not matter very much who first put them together. If they are our own words they will soon, by unavoidable repetition, harden into a formula. If they are someone else's, we shall continually pour into them our own meaning.

At present – for one's practice changes and, I think, ought to change – I find it best to make 'my own words' the staple but introduce a modicum of the ready-made.

Writing to you, I need not stress the importance of the home-made staple. As Solomon said at the dedication of the temple, each man who prays knows 'the plague of his own heart'. Also, the comforts of his own heart. No other creature is identical with me; no other situation identical with mine. Indeed, I myself and my situation are in continual change. A ready-made form can't serve for my intercourse with God any more than it could serve for my intercourse with you.

This is obvious. Perhaps I shan't find it so easy to persuade you that the ready-made modicum has also its use: for me, I mean – I'm not suggesting rules for anyone else in the whole world.

First, it keeps me in touch with 'sound doctrine'. Left to oneself, one could easily slide away from 'the faith once given' into a phantom called 'my religion'.

Secondly, it reminds me 'what things I ought to ask' (perhaps especially when I am praying for other people). The crisis of the present moment, like the nearest telegraph-post, will always loom largest. Isn't there a danger that our great, permanent, objective necessities – often more important – may get crowded out? By the way, that's another thing to be avoided in a revised Prayer Book. 'Contemporary problems' may claim an undue share. And the more 'up to date' the Book is, the sooner it will be dated.

Finally, they provide an element of the ceremonial. On your view, that is just what we don't want. On mine, it is part of what we want. I see what you mean when you say that using ready-made prayers would be like 'making love to your own wife out of Petrarch or Donne'. (Incidentally might you not *quote* them – to such a literary wife as Betty?) The parallel won't do.

I fully agree that the relationship between God and a man is more private and intimate than any possible relation between two fellow creatures. Yes, but at the same time there is, in another way, a greater distance between the participants. We are approaching – well I won't say 'the Wholly Other', for I suspect that is meaningless, but the Unimaginably and Insupportably Other. We ought to be – sometimes I hope one is – simultaneously aware of closest proximity and infinite distance. You make things far too snug and confiding. Your erotic analogy needs to be supplemented by 'I fell at His feet as one dead.'

I think the 'low' church *milieu* that I grew up in did tend to be too cosily at ease in Sion. My grandfather, I'm told, used to say that he 'looked forward to having some very interesting conversations with St Paul when he got to heaven.' Two clerical gentlemen talking at ease in a club! It never seemed to cross his mind that an encounter with St Paul might be rather an overwhelming experience even for an Evangelical clergyman of good family. But when Dante saw the great apostles in heaven they affected him like *mountains*. There's lots to be said against devotions to saints; but at least they keep on reminding us that we are very small people compared with them. How much smaller before their Master?

A few formal, ready-made, prayers serve me as a corrective of – well, let's call it 'cheek'. They keep one side of the paradox alive. Of course it is only one side. It would be better not to be reverent at all than to have a reverence which denied the proximity.

3

Oh for Mercy's sake. Not you too! Why, just because I raise an objection to your parallel between prayer and a man making love to his own wife, must you trot out all the rigmarole about the 'holiness' of sex and start lecturing me as if I were a Manichaean? I know that in most circles nowadays one need only mention sex to set everyone in the room emitting this gas. But, I did hope, not you. Didn't I make it plain that I objected to your image solely on the ground of its nonchalance, or presumption?

I'm not saying anything against (or for) 'sex'. Sex in itself cannot be moral or immoral any more than gravitation or nutrition. The sexual behaviour of human beings can. And like their economic, or political, or agricultural, or parental, or filial behaviour, it is sometimes good and sometimes bad. And the sexual act, when lawful – which means chiefly when consistent with good faith and charity – can, like all other merely natural acts ('whether we eat or drink, etc.', as the apostle says), be done to the glory of God, and will then be holy. And like other natural acts it is sometimes so done, and sometimes not. This may be what the poor Bishop of Woolwich was trying to say. Anyway, what more is there to be said? And can we now get this red herring out of the way? I'd be glad if we could; for the moderns have achieved the feat, which I should have thought impossible, of making the whole subject a bore. Poor Aphrodite! They have sandpapered most of the Homeric laughter off her face.

Apparently I have been myself guilty of introducing another red herring by mentioning devotions to saints. I didn't in the least want to go off into a discussion on that subject. There is clearly a theological defence for it; if you can ask for the prayers of the living, why should you not ask for the prayers of the dead? There is clearly also a great danger. In some popular practice we see it leading off into an infinitely silly picture of heaven as an earthly court where applicants will be wise to pull the right wires, discover the best 'channels', and attach themselves to the most influential pressure groups. But I have nothing to do with all this. I am not thinking of adopting the practice myself; and who am I to judge the practices of others? I only hope there'll be no scheme for canonisations in the Church of England. Can you imagine a better hot-bed for yet more divisions between us?

The consoling thing is that while Christendom is divided about the rationality, and even the lawfulness, of praying *to* the saints, we are all agreed about praying *with* them. 'With angels and archangels and all the company of heaven.' Will you believe it? It is only quite recently I made that quotation a part of my private prayers – I festoon it round 'hallowed be Thy name'. This, by the way, illustrates what I was saying last week about the uses of ready-made forms. They remind one. And I have found this quotation a great enrichment. One always accepted this *with* theoretically. But it is quite different when one brings it into consciousness at an appropriate moment and wills the association of one's own little twitter with the voice of the great saints and (we hope) of our own dear dead. They may drown some of the uglier qualities and set off any tiny value it has.

You may say that the distinction between the communion of the saints as I find it in that act and full-fledged prayers to saints is not, after all, very great. All the better if so. I sometimes have a bright dream of reunion engulfing us unawares, like a great wave from behind our backs, perhaps at the very moment when our official representatives are still pronouncing it impossible. Discussions usually separate us; actions sometimes unite us.

When I spoke of prayer without words I don't think I meant anything so exalted as what mystics call the 'prayer of silence'. And when I spoke of being 'at the top of one's form' I didn't mean it purely in a spiritual sense. The condition of the body comes in; for I suppose a man may be in a state of grace and yet very sleepy.

And, talking of sleepiness, I entirely agree with you that no one in his senses, if he has any power of ordering his own day, would reserve his chief prayers for bedtime – obviously the worst possible hour for any action which needs concentration. The trouble is that thousands of unfortunate people can hardly find any other. Even for us, who are the lucky ones, it is not always easy. My own plan, when hard pressed, is to seize any time, and place, however unsuitable, in preference to the last waking moment. On a day of travelling – with, perhaps, some ghastly meeting at the end of it – I'd rather pray sitting in a crowded train than put it off till midnight when one reaches a hotel bedroom with aching head and dry throat and one's mind partly in a stupor and partly in a whirl. On other, and slightly less crowded, days a bench in a park, or a back street where one can pace up and down, will do.

A man to whom I was explaining this said, 'But why don't you turn into a church?' Partly because, for nine months of the year, it will be freezingly cold but also because I have bad luck with churches. No sooner do I enter one and compose my mind than one or other of two things happens. Either someone starts practising the organ. Or else, with resolute tread, there appears from nowhere a pious woman in elastic-side boots, carrying mop, bucket, and dust-pan, and begins beating hassocks and rolling up carpets and doing things to flower vases. Of course (blessings on her) 'work is prayer', and her enacted *oratio* is probably worth ten times my spoken one. But it doesn't help mine to become worth more.

When one prays in strange places and at strange times one can't kneel, to be sure. I won't say this doesn't matter. The body ought to pray as well as the soul. Body and soul are both the better for it. Bless the body. Mine has led me into many scrapes, but I've led it into far more. If the imagination were obedient the appetites would give us very little trouble. And from how much it has saved me! And but for our body one whole realm of God's glory – all that we receive through the senses – would go unpraised. For the beasts can't appreciate it and the angels are, I suppose, pure intelligences. They *understand* colours and tastes better than our greatest scientists; but have they retinas or palates? I fancy the 'beauties of nature' are a secret God has shared with us alone. That may be one of the reasons why we were made – and why the resurrection of the body is an important doctrine.

But I'm being led into a digression; perhaps because I am still smarting under the charge of being a Manichee! The relevant point is that kneeling does matter, but other things matter even more. A concentrated mind and a sitting body make for better prayer than a kneeling body and a mind half asleep. Sometimes these are the only alternatives. (Since the osteoporosis I can hardly kneel at all in most places, myself.)

A clergyman once said to me that a railway compartment, if one has it to oneself, is an extremely good place to pray in 'because there is just the right amount of distraction'. When I asked him to explain, he said that perfect silence and solitude left one more open to the distractions which come from within, and that a moderate amount of external distraction was easier to cope with. I don't find this so myself, but I can imagine it.

The Jones boy's name is Cyril – though why you find it so important to pray for people by their Christian names I can't imagine. I always assume God knows their surnames as well. I am afraid many people appear in my prayers only as 'that old man at Crewe' or 'the waitress' or even 'that man'. One may have lost, or may never have known, their names and yet remember how badly they need to be prayed for.

No letter next week. I shall be in the thick of exams.

4

Of the two difficulties you mention I think that only one is often a practical problem for believers. The other is in my experience usually raised by people who are attacking Christianity.

The ideal opening for their attacks – if they know the Bible – is the phrase in Philippians about 'making your requests known to God'. I mean, the words making known bring out most clearly the apparent absurdity with which they charge us. We say that we believe God to be omniscient; yet a great deal of prayer seems to consist of giving Him information. And indeed we have been reminded by Our Lord too not to pray as if we forgot the omniscience – 'for your heavenly Father knows you need all these things.'

This is final against one very silly sort of prayer. I have heard a man offer a prayer for a sick person which really amounted to a diagnosis followed by advice as to how God should treat the patient. And I have heard prayers nominally for peace, but really so concerned for various devices which the petitioner believed to be means to peace, that they were open to the same criticism.

But even when that kind of thing is ruled out, the unbeliever's objection remains. To confess our sins before God is certainly to tell Him what He knows much better than we. And also, any petition is a kind of telling. If it does not strictly exclude the belief that God knows our need, it at least seems to solicit His attention. Some traditional formulae make that implication very clear: 'Hear us, good Lord' – 'O let thine ears consider well the voice of my complaint.' As if, though God does not need to be informed, He does need, and even rather frequently, to be reminded. But we cannot really believe that degrees of attention, and therefore of inattention, and therefore of something like forgetfulness, exist in the Absolute Mind. I presume that only God's attention keeps me (or anything else) in existence at all.

What, then, are we really doing? Our whole conception of, so to call it, the prayer-situation depends on the answer.

We are always completely, and therefore equally, known to God. That is our destiny whether we like it or not. But though this knowledge never varies, the quality of our being known can. A school of thought holds that 'freedom is willed necessity'. Never mind if they are right or not. I want this idea only as an analogy. Ordinarily, to be known by God is to be, for this purpose, in the category of things. We are, like earthworms, cabbages, and nebulae, objects of Divine knowledge. But when we (a) become aware of the fact – the present fact, not the generalisation – and (b) assent with all our will to be so known, then we treat ourselves, in relation to God, not as things but as persons. We have unveiled. Not that any veil could have baffled His sight. The change is in us. The passive changes to the active. Instead of merely being known, we show, we tell, we offer ourselves to view.

To put ourselves thus on a personal footing with God could, in itself and without warrant, be nothing but presumption and illusion. But we are taught that it is not; that it is God who gives us that footing. For it is by the Holy Spirit that we cry 'Father'. By unveiling, by confessing our sins and 'making known' our requests, we assume the high rank of persons before Him. And He, descending, becomes a Person to us.

But I should not have said 'becomes'. In Him there is no becoming. He reveals Himself as Person: or reveals that in Him which is Person. For – dare one say it? In a book it would need pages of qualification and insurance – God is in some measure to a man as that man is to God. The door in God that opens is the door he knocks at. (At least, I think so, usually.) The Person in Him – He is more than a person – meets those who can welcome or at least face it. He speaks as 'I' when we truly call Him 'Thou'. (How good Buber is!)

This talk of 'meeting' is, no doubt, anthropomorphic; as if God and I could be face to face, like two fellow-creatures, when in reality He is above me and within me and below me and all about me. That is why it must be balanced by all manner of metaphysical and theological abstractions. But never, here or anywhere else, let us think that while anthropomorphic images are a concession to our weakness, the abstractions are the literal truth. Both are equally concessions; each singly misleading, and the two together mutually corrective. Unless you sit to it very lightly, continually murmuring 'Not thus, not thus, neither is this Thou', the abstraction is fatal. It will make the life of lives inanimate and the love of loves impersonal. The *naïf* image is mischievous chiefly in so far as it holds unbelievers back from conversion. It does believers, even at its crudest, no harm. What soul ever perished for believing that God the Father really has a beard?

Your other question is one which, I think, really gets in pious people's way. It was, you remember, 'How important must a need or desire be before we can properly make it the subject of petition?' *Properly*, I take it, here means either 'Without irreverence' or 'Without silliness', or both.

When I'd thought about it for a bit, it seemed to me that there are really two questions involved.

1. How important must an object be before we can, without sin and folly, allow our desire for it to become a matter of serious concern to us? This, you see, is a question about what old writers call our 'frame'; that is, our 'frame of mind'.

2. Granted the existence of such a serious concern in our minds, can it always be properly laid before God in prayer?

We all know the answer to the first of these in theory. We must aim at what St Augustine (is it?) called 'ordinate loves'. Our deepest concern should be for first things, and our next deepest for second things, and so on down to zero – to total absence of concern for things that are not really good, nor means to good, at all.

Meantime, however, we want to know not how we should pray if we were perfect but how we should pray being as we now are. And if my idea of prayer as 'unveiling' is accepted, we have already answered this. It is no use to ask God with factitious earnestness for A when our whole mind is in reality filled with the desire for B. We must lay before Him what is in us, not what ought to be in us.

Even an intimate human friend is ill used if we talk to him about one thing while our mind is really on another, and even a human friend will soon become aware when we are doing so. You yourself came to see me a few years ago when the great blow had fallen upon me. I tried to talk to you as if nothing were wrong. You saw through it in five minutes. Then I confessed. And you said things which made me ashamed of my attempt at concealment.

It may well be that the desire can be laid before God only as a sin to be repented; but one of the best ways of learning this is to lay it before God. Your problem, however, was not about sinful desires in that sense; rather about desires, intrinsically innocent and sinning, if at all, only by being stronger than the triviality of their object warrants. I have no doubt at all that if they are the subject of our thoughts they must be the subject of our prayers – whether in penitence or in petition or in a little of both: penitence for the excess, yet petition for the thing we desire.

If one forcibly excludes them, don't they wreck all the rest of our prayers? If we lay all the cards on the table, God will help us to moderate the excesses. But the pressure of things we are trying to keep out of our mind is a hopeless distraction. As someone said, 'No noise is so emphatic as one you are trying not to listen to.'

The ordinate frame of mind is one of the blessings we must pray for, not a fancy-dress we must put on when we pray.

And perhaps, as those who do not turn to God in petty trials will have no *habit* or such resort to help them when the great trials come, so those who have not learned to ask Him for childish things will have less readiness to ask Him for great ones. We must not be too high-minded. I fancy we may sometimes be deterred from small prayers by a sense of our own dignity rather than of God's.

5

I don't very much like the job of telling you 'more about my festoonings' – the private overtones I give to certain petitions. I make two conditions: (a) That you will in return tell me some of yours. (b) That you will understand I am not in the least *recommending* mine either to you or to anyone else. There could be many better; and my present festoons will very probably change.

I call them 'festoons', by the way, because they don't (I trust) obliterate the plain, public sense of the petition but are merely hung on it.

What I do about 'hallowed be Thy name' I told a fortnight ago.

Thy kingdom come. That is, may your reign be realised here, as it is realised there. But I tend to take *there* on three levels. First, as in the sinless world beyond the horrors of animal and human life; in the behaviour of stars and trees and water, in sunrise and wind. May there be *here* (in my heart) the beginning of a like beauty. Secondly, as in the best human lives I have known: in all the people who really bear the burdens and ring true, the people we call bricks, and in the quiet, busy, ordered life of really good families and really good religious houses. May that too be 'here'. Finally, of course, in the usual sense: as in heaven, as among the blessed dead.

And *here* can of course be taken not only for 'in my heart', but for 'in this college' – in England – in the world in general. But prayer is not the time for pressing our own favourite social or political panacea. Even Queen Victoria didn't like 'being talked to as if she were a public meeting'.

Thy will be done. My festoons on this have been added gradually. At first I took it exclusively as an act of submission, attempting to do with it what Our Lord did in Gethsemane. I thought of God's will purely as something that would come upon me, something of which I should be the patient. And I also thought of it as a will which would be embodied in pains and disappointments. Not, to be sure, that I suppose God's will for me to consist entirely of disagreeables. But I thought it was only the disagreeables that called for this preliminary submission – the agreeables could look after themselves for the present. When they turned up, one could give thanks.

This interpretation is, I expect, the commonest. And so it must be. And such are the miseries of human life that it must often fill our whole mind. But at other times other meanings can be added. So I added one more.

The peg for it is, I admit, much more obvious in the English version than in the Greek or Latin. No matter: this is where the liberty of festooning comes in. 'Thy will be *done*.' But a great deal of it is to be done by God's creatures; including me. The petition, then, is not merely that I may patiently suffer God's will but also that I may vigorously do it. I must be an agent as well as a patient. I am asking that I may be enabled to do it. In the long run I am asking to be given 'the same mind which was also in Christ'.

Taken this way, I find the words have a more regular daily application. For there isn't always – or we don't always have reason to suspect that there is – some great affliction looming in the near future, but there are always duties to be done; usually, for me, neglected duties to be caught up with. 'Thy will be *done* – by me – now' brings one back to brass tacks.

But more than that, I am at this very moment contemplating a new festoon. Tell me if you think it a vain subtlety. I am beginning to feel that we need a preliminary act of submission not only towards possible future afflictions but also towards possible future blessings. I know it sounds fantastic; but think it over. It seems to me that we often, almost sulkily, reject the good that God offers us because, at that moment, we expected some other good. Do you know what I mean? On every level of our life – in our religious experience, in our gastronomic, erotic, aesthetic and social experience – we are always harking back to some occasion which seemed to us to reach perfection, setting that up as a norm, and depreciating all other occasions by comparison. But these other occasions, I now suspect, are often full of their own new blessings if only we would lay ourselves open to it. God shows us a new facet of the glory, and we refuse to look at it because we're still looking for the old one. And of course we don't get that. You can't, at the twentieth reading, get again the experience of reading *Lycidas* for the first time. But what you do get can be in its own way as good.

This applies especially to the devotional life. Many religious people lament that the first fervours of their conversion have died away. They think – sometimes rightly, but not, I believe always – that their sins account for this. They may even try by pitiful efforts of will to revive what now seem to have been the golden days. But were those fervours – the operative word is *those* – ever intended to last?

It would be rash to say that there is any prayer which God *never* grants. But the strongest candidate is the prayer we might express in the single word *encore*. And how should the Infinite repeat Himself? All space and time are too little for Him to utter Himself in them *once*.

And the joke, or tragedy, of it all is that these golden moments in the past, which are so tormenting if we erect them into a norm, are entirely nourishing, wholesome, and enchanting if we are content to accept them for what they are, for memories. Properly bedded down in a past which we do not miserably try to conjure back, they will send up exquisite growths. Leave the bulbs alone, and the new flowers will come up. Grub them up and hope, by fondling and sniffing, to get last year's blooms, and you will get nothing. 'Unless a seed die...'

I expect we all do much the same with the prayer for our *daily bread*. It means, doesn't it, all we need for the day – 'things requisite and necessary as well for the body as for the soul'. I should hate to make this clause 'purely religious' by thinking of 'spiritual' needs alone. One of its uses, to me, is to remind us daily that what Burnaby calls the *naif* view of prayer is firmly built into Our Lord's teaching.

Forgive us ... as we forgive. Unfortunately there's no need to do any festooning here. To forgive for the moment is not difficult. But to go on forgiving, to forgive the same offence again every time it recurs to the memory – there's the real tussle. My resource is to look for some action of my own which is open to the same charge as the one I'm resenting. If I still smart to remember how A let me down, I must still remember how I let B down. If I find it difficult to forgive those who bullied me at school, let me, at that very moment, remember, and pray for, those I bullied. (Not that we called it *bullying* of course. That is where prayer without words can be so useful. In it there are no names; therefore no aliases.)

I was never worried myself by the words *lead us not into temptation*, but a great many of my correspondents are. The words suggest to them what someone has called 'a fiend-like conception of God', as one who first forbids us certain fruits and then lures us to taste them. But the Greek word (πειρασμός) means 'trial' – 'trying circumstances' – of every sort; a far larger word than English 'temptation'. So that the petition essentially is, 'Make straight our paths. Spare us, where possible, from all crises, whether of temptation or affliction.' By the way, you yourself, though you've doubtless forgotten it, gave me an excellent gloss on it: years ago in the pub at Coton. You said it added a sort of reservation to all our preceding prayers. As if we said, 'In my ignorance I have asked for A, B and C. But don't give me them if you foresee that they would in reality be to me either snares or sorrows.' And you quoted Juvenal, *numinibus vota exaudita malignis*, 'enormous prayers which heaven in vengeance grants'. For we make plenty of such prayers. If God had granted all the silly prayers I've made in my life, where should I be now?

I don't often use *the kingdom, the power and the glory*. When I do, I have an idea of the *kingdom* as sovereignty *de jure*; God, as good, would have a claim on my obedience even if He had no power. The *power* is the sovereignty *de facto* – He is omnipotent. And the *glory* is – well, the glory; the 'beauty so old and new', the 'light from behind the sun'.

6

I can't remember exactly what I said about not making the petition for our daily bread too 'religious', and I'm not quite sure what you mean – nor how ironically – by asking if I've become 'one of Vidler's young men'!

About Vidler. I never heard the programme which created all that scandal, and naturally one wouldn't condemn a dog on newspaper extracts. But I have now read his essay in *Soundings* and I believe I go a good deal further with him than you would. Much of what he quotes from F. D. Maurice and Bonhoeffer seems to me very good; and so, I think, are his own arguments for the Establishment.

At any rate I can well understand how a man who is trying to love God and his neighbour should come to dislike the very word *religion*; a word, by the way, which hardly ever appears in the New Testament. Newman makes my blood run cold when he says in one of the *Parochial and Plain Sermons* that Heaven is like a church because in both, 'one single sovereign subject religion – is brought before us'. He forgets that there is no temple in the new Jerusalem.

He has substituted *religion* for God – as if navigation were substituted for arrival, or battle for victory, or wooing for marriage, or in general the means for the end. But even in this present life, there is danger in the very concept of *religion*. It carries the suggestion that this is one more department of life, an extra department added to the economic, the social, the intellectual, the recreational, and all the rest. But that whose claims are infinite can have no standing as a department. Either it is an illusion or else our whole life falls under it. We have no non-religious activities; only religious and irreligious.

Religion, nevertheless, appears to exist as a department, and, in some ages, to thrive as such. It thrives partly because there exists in many people a 'love of religious observances', which I think Simone Weil is quite right in regarding as a merely natural taste. There exists also – Vidler is rather good on this – the delight in religious (as in any other) organisation. Then all sorts of aesthetic, sentimental, historical, political interests are drawn in. Finally sales of work, the parish magazine, and bell-ringing, and Santa Claus.

None of them bad things. But none of them is necessarily of more spiritual value than the activities we call secular. And they are infinitely dangerous when this is not understood. This department of life, labelled 'sacred', can become an end in itself; an idol that hides both God and my neighbours. ('When the means are autonomous they are deadly.') It may even come about that a man's most genuinely Christian actions fall entirely outside that part of his life which he calls *religious*.

I read in a religious paper, 'Nothing is more important than to teach children to use the sign of the cross.' Nothing? Not compassion, nor veracity, nor justice? *Voila l'ennemi.*

One must, however, walk warily, for the truth that *religion* as a department has really no right to exist can be misunderstood.

Some will conclude that this illegitimate department ought to be abolished. Others will think, coming nearer to the truth, that it ought to cease to be departmental by being extended to the whole of life, but will misinterpret this. They will think it means that more and more of our secular transactions should be 'opened with prayer', that a wearisomely explicit pietism should infest our talk, that there should be no more cakes and ale. A third sort, well aware that God still rules a very small part of their lives, and that 'a departmental religion' is no good, may despair. It would have to be carefully explained to them that to be 'still only a part' is not the same as being a permanent department. In all of us God 'still' holds only a part. D-Day is only a week ago. The bite so far taken out of Normandy shows small on the map of Europe. The resistance is strong, the casualties heavy, and the event uncertain. There is, we have to admit, a line of demarcation between God's part in us and the enemy's region. But it is, we hope, a fighting line; not a frontier fixed by agreement.

But I suspect the real misunderstanding of Vidler's talk lay elsewhere. We have been speaking of *religion* as a pattern of behaviour – which, if contentedly departmental, cannot really be Christian behaviour. But people also, and more often, use *religion* to mean a system of beliefs. When they heard that Vidler wanted a church with 'less religion', they thought he meant that the little – the very little – which liberal theology has still left of the 'faith once given' was to be emptied out. Hence someone asked, 'Is he a Theist?'

Well, he certainly is. He wants – I think he wants very earnestly – to retain some Christian doctrines. But he is prepared to scrap a good deal. 'Traditional doctrines' are to be tested. Many things will have to be 'outgrown' or 'survive chiefly as venerable archaisms or as fairy-stories'. He feels quite happy about this undefined programme of jettison because he trusts in the continued guidance of the Holy Spirit. A noble faith; provided, of course, there is any such being as the Holy Spirit. But I suppose His existence is itself one of the 'traditional doctrines' which, on Vidler's premises, we might any day find we had outgrown. So with the doctrine – Vidler calls it 'the fact' – that man is 'a twofold creature – not only a political creature, but also a spiritual being'. Vidler and you and I (and Plato) think it a fact. Tens of thousands, perhaps millions, think it a fantasy. The neutral description of it is 'a traditional doctrine'. Do you think he means that these two doctrines – and why just these two? – are the hard core of his belief, exempt from the threat of rejection which overhangs all other doctrines? Or would he say that, as the title of the book implies, he is only 'taking soundings' – and if the line is not long enough to reach bottom, soundings can yield only negative information to the navigator?

I was interested in the things you said about *forgive us our trespasses*. Often, to be sure, there is something definite for which to ask forgiveness. This is plain sailing. But, like you, I often find one or other of two less manageable states: either a vague feeling of guilt or a sly, and equally vague, self-approval. What are we to do with these?

Many modern psychologists tell us always to distrust this vague feeling of guilt, as something purely pathological. And if they had stopped at that, I might believe them. But when they go on, as some do, to apply the same treatment to all guilt-feelings whatever, to suggest that one's feeling about a particular unkind act or a particular insincerity is also and equally untrustworthy – I can't help thinking they are talking nonsense. One sees this the moment one looks at other people. I have talked to some who felt guilt when they jolly well ought to have felt it; they have behaved like brutes and know it. I've also met others who felt guilty and weren't guilty by any standard I can apply. And thirdly, I've met people who were guilty and didn't seem to feel guilt. And isn't this what we should expect? People can be *malades imaginaires* who are well and think they are ill; and others, especially consumptives, are ill and think they are well; and thirdly – far the largest class – people are ill and know they are ill. It would be very odd if there were any region in which all mistakes were in one direction.

Some Christians would tell us to go on rummaging and scratching till we find something specific. We may be sure, they say, that there are real sins enough to justify the guilt-feeling or to overthrow the feeling that all is well. I think they are right in saying that if we hunt long enough we shall find, or think we have found, something. But that is just what wakens suspicion. A theory which could never by any experience be falsified can for that reason hardly be verified. And just as, when we are yielding to temptation, we make ourselves believe that what we have always thought a sin will on this occasion, for some strange reason, not be a sin, shan't we persuade ourselves that something we have always (rightly) thought to be innocent was really wrong? We may create scruples. And scruples are always a bad thing – if only because they usually distract us from real duties.

I don't at all know whether I'm right or not, but I have, on the whole, come to the conclusion that one can't directly *do* anything about either feeling. One is not to believe either – indeed, how can one believe a fog? I come back to St John: 'if our heart condemn us, God is greater than our heart.' And equally, if our heart flatter us, God is greater than our heart. I sometimes pray not for self-knowledge in general but for just so much self-knowledge at the moment as I can bear and use at the moment; the little daily dose.

Have we any reason to suppose that total self-knowledge, if it were given us, would be for our good? Children and fools, we are told, should never look at half-done work; and we are not yet, I trust, even half-done. You and I wouldn't, at all stages, think it wise to tell a pupil exactly what we thought of his quality. It is much more important that he should know what to do next.

If one said this in public one would have all the Freudians on one's back. And, mind you, we are greatly indebted to them. They did expose the cowardly evasions of really useful selfknowledge which we had all been practising from the beginning of the world. But there is also a merely morbid and fidgety curiosity about one's self – the slop-over from modern psychology – which surely does no good? The unfinished picture would so like to jump off the easel and have a look at itself! And analysis doesn't cure that. We all know people who have undergone it and seem to have made themselves a lifelong subject of research ever since.

If I am right, the conclusion is that when our conscience won't come down to brass-tacks but will only vaguely accuse or vaguely approve, we must say to it, like Herbert, 'Peace, prattler' – and get on.

7

If you meant in your last letter that we can scrap the whole idea of petitionary prayer – prayer which, as you put it, calls upon God to 'engineer' particular events in the objective world – and confine ourselves to acts of penitence and adoration, I disagree with you. It may be true that Christianity would be, intellectually, a far easier religion if it told us to do this. And I can understand the people who think it would also be a more high-minded religion. But remember the psalm: 'Lord, I am not high minded.' Or better still, remember the New Testament. The most unblushingly petitionary prayers are there recommended to us both by precept and example. Our Lord in Gethsemane made a petitionary prayer (and did not get what He asked for).

You'll remind me that He asked with a reservation – 'nevertheless, not my will but thine'. This makes an enormous difference. But the difference which it precisely does not make is that of removing the prayer's petitionary character. When poor Bill, on a famous occasion, asked us to advance him £100, he said, 'If you are sure you can spare it,' and, 'I shall quite understand if you'd rather not.' This made his request very different from the nagging or even threatening request which a different sort of man might have made. But it was still a request.

The servant is not greater, and must not be more high-minded, than the master. Whatever the theoretical difficulties are, we must continue to make requests of God. And on this point we can get no help from those who keep on reminding us that this is the lowest and least essential kind of prayer. They may be right; but so what? Diamonds are more precious than cairngorms, but the cairngorms still exist and must be taken into account like anything else.

But don't let us be too easily brow-beaten. Some of the popular objections to petitionary prayer, if they are valid against it, are equally valid against other things which we all do whether we are Christians or not, and have done ever since the world began, and shall certainly continue to do. I don't think the burden of answering these rests especially on us.

There is, for example, the Determinism which, whether under that name or another, seems to be implicit in a scientific view of the world. Determinism does not deny the existence of human behaviour. It rejects as an illusion our spontaneous conviction that our behaviour has its ultimate origin in ourselves. What I call 'my act' is the conduit-pipe through which the torrent of the universal process passes, and was bound to pass, at a particular time and place. The distinction between what we call the 'voluntary' and the 'involuntary' movements of our own bodies is not obliterated, but turns out (on this view) to be not exactly the sort of difference we supposed. What I call the 'involuntary' movements necessarily – and, if we know enough, predictably – result from mechanical causes outside my body or from pathological or organic processes within it. The 'voluntary' ones result from conscious psychological factors which themselves result from unconscious psychological factors dependent on my economic situation, my infantile and prenatal experience, my heredity... and so on back to the beginnings of organic life and beyond. I am a conductor, not a source. I never make an original contribution to the world-process. I move with that process not even as a floating log moves with the river but as a particular pint of the water itself moves.

But even those who believe this will, like anyone else, ask you to hand them the salt. Every form of behaviour, including speech, can go on just the same, and will. If a strict Determinist believed in God (and I think he might) petitionary prayer would be no more irrational in him than in anyone else.

Another argument, put up (but not accepted) by Burnaby in *Soundings*, is this. If man's freedom is to be of any value, if he is to have any power of planning and of adapting means to ends, he must live in a predictable world. But if God alters the course of events in answer to prayer, then the world will be unpredictable. Therefore, if man is to be effectively free, God must be in this respect un-free.

But is it not plain that this predictable world, whether it is necessary to our freedom or no, is not the world we live in? This is a world of bets and insurance policies, of hopes and anxieties, where 'nothing is certain but the unexpected' and prudence lies in 'the masterly administration of the unforeseen'. Nearly all the things people pray about are unpredictable: the result of a battle or an operation, the losing or getting of a job, the reciprocation of a love. We don't pray about eclipses.

But, you will reply, we once did. Every advance of science makes predictable something that was formerly unpredictable. It is only our ignorance that makes petitionary prayer possible. Would it not be rational to assume that all those events we now pray about are in principle just as predictable – though we don't yet know enough to predict them – as things like eclipses? But that is no answer to the point I'm making. I am not now trying to refute

Determinism. I am only arguing that a world where the future is unknown cannot be inconsistent with planned and purposive action since we are actually planning and purposing in such a world now and have been doing so for thousands of years.

Also, between ourselves, I think this objection involves a false idea of what the sciences do. You are here a better judge than I, but I give it for what it may be worth. It is true in one sense that the mark of a genuine science is its power to predict. But does this mean that a perfected science, or a perfected synthesis of all the sciences, would be able to write reliable histories of the future? And would the scientists even want to do so? Doesn't science predict a future event only in so far as, and only because, that event is the instance of some universal law? Everything that makes the event unique – in other words, everything that makes it a concrete historical event – is deliberately ruled out; not only as something which science can't, or can't yet, include, but also as something in which science, as such, has no interest. No one sunrise has ever been exactly like another. Take away from the sunrises that in which they differ and what is left will be identical. Such abstracted identicals are what science predicts. But life as we live it is not reducible to such identities. Every real physical event, much more every human experience, has behind it, in the long run, the whole previous history of the real universe which is not itself an 'instance' of anything – and is therefore always festooned with those particularities which science for her own purposes quite rightly discounts. Doesn't the whole art of contriving a good experiment consist in devising means whereby the irrelevancies – that is, the historical particularities – can be reduced to the minimum?

Later in his essay Burnaby seems to suggest that human wills are the only radically unpredictable factor in history. I'm not happy about this. Partly because I don't see how the gigantic negative which it involves could be proved; partly because I agree with Bradley that unpredictability is not the essence, nor even a symptom, of freedom. (Did you see they've reprinted *Ethical Studies*? The baiting of Arnold, wholly just and in Arnold's own manner, is exquisite.) But suppose it were true. Even then, it would make such a huge rent in the predictability of events that the whole idea of predictability as somehow necessary to human life would be in ruins. Think of the countless human acts, acts of copulation, spread over millennia, that led to the birth of Plato, Attila, or Napoleon. Yet it is on these unpredictables that human history largely depends. Twenty-five years ago you asked Betty to marry you. And now, as a result, we have young George (I hope he's got over his gastric flu?). A thousand years hence he might have a good many descendants, and only modesty could conceal from you the possibility that one of these might have as huge a historical effect as Aristotle – or Hitler!

8

What froth and bubble my last letter must have seemed to you! I had hardly posted it when I got Betty's card with the disquieting news about George – turning my jocular reference to his descendants into a stab (at least I suppose it did) and making our whole discussion on prayer seem to you, as it now does to me, utterly unreal. The distance between the abstract, 'Does God hear petitionary prayers?' and the concrete, 'Will He – can He – grant our prayers for George?' is apparently infinite.

Not of course that I can pretend for a moment to be able to feel it as you do. If I did, you would say to yourself (like the man in *Macbeth*), 'He has no children.' A few years ago when I was in my own trouble you said as much to me. You wrote, 'I know I'm outside. My voice can hardly reach you.' And that was one reason why your letter was more like the real grasp of a real hand than any other I got.

The temptation is to attempt reassurances: to remind you how often a GP's preliminary diagnosis is wrong, that the symptoms are admittedly ambiguous, that threatened men sometimes live to a ripe old age. And it would all in fact be true. But what, in that way, could I say which you are not saying to yourself every hour? And you would know my motive. You'd know how little real scientific candour – or knowledge – lay behind my words. And if, which God forbid, your suspense ended as terribly as mine did, these reassurances would sound like mockeries. So at least I found. The memory of the false hopes was an additional torment. Even now certain remembered moments of fallacious comfort twist my heart more than the remembered moment of despair.

All may yet be well. This is true. Meanwhile you have the waiting – waiting till the X-rays are developed and till the specialist has completed his observations. And while you wait, you still have to go on living – if only one could go underground, hibernate, sleep it out. And then (for me – I believe you are stronger) the horrible by-products of anxiety; the incessant, circular movement of the thoughts, even the Pagan temptation to keep watch for irrational omens. And one prays; but mainly such prayers as are themselves a form of anguish.

Some people feel guilty about their anxieties and regard them as a defect of faith. I don't agree at all. They are afflictions, not sins. Like all afflictions, they are, if we can so take them, our share in the Passion of Christ. For the beginning of the Passion – the first move, so to speak – is in Gethsemane. In Gethsemane a very strange and significant thing seems to have happened.

It is clear from many of His sayings that Our Lord had long foreseen His death. He knew what conduct such as His, in a world such as we have made of this, must inevitably lead to. But it is clear that this knowledge must somehow have been withdrawn from Him before He prayed in Gethsemane. He could not, with whatever reservation about the Father's will, have prayed that the cup might pass and simultaneously known that it would not. That is both a logical and a psychological impossibility. You see what this involves? Lest any trial incident to humanity should be lacking, the torments of hope – of suspense, anxiety – were at the last moment loosed upon Him – the supposed possibility that, after all, He might, He just conceivably might, be spared the supreme horror. There was precedent. Isaac had been spared: he too at the last moment, he also against all apparent probability. It was not quite impossible ... and doubtless He had seen other men crucified ... a sight very unlike most of our religious pictures and images.

But for this last (and erroneous) hope against hope, and the consequent tumult of the soul, the sweat of blood, perhaps He would not have been very Man. To live in a fully predictable world is not to be a man.

At the end, I know, we are told that an angel appeared 'comforting' him. But neither *comforting* in Sixteenth Century English nor ἐννισχύων in Greek means 'consoling'. 'Strengthening' is more the word. May not the strengthening have consisted in the renewed certainty – cold comfort this – that the thing must be endured and therefore could be?

We all try to accept with some sort of submission our afflictions when they actually arrive. But the prayer in Gethsemane shows that the preceding anxiety is equally God's will and equally part of our human destiny. The perfect Man experienced it. And the servant is not greater than the master. We are Christians, not Stoics.

Does not every movement in the Passion write large some common element in the sufferings of our race? First, the prayer of anguish; not granted. Then He turns to His friends. They are asleep – as ours, or we, are so often, or busy, or away, or pre-occupied. Then He faces the Church; the very Church that He brought into existence. It condemns Him. This is also characteristic. In every Church, in every institution, there is something which sooner or later works against the very purpose for which it came into existence. But there seems to be another chance. There is the State; in this case, the Roman state. Its pretensions are far lower than those of the Jewish church, but for that very reason it may be free from local fanaticisms. It claims to be just, on a rough, worldly level. Yes, but only so far as is consistent with political expediency and *raison d'état*. One becomes a counter in a complicated game. But even now all is not lost. There is still an appeal to the People – the poor and simple whom He had blessed, whom He had healed and fed and taught, to whom He himself belongs. But they have become over-night (it is nothing unusual) a murderous rabble shouting for His blood. There is, then, nothing left but God. And to God, God's last words are, 'Why hast thou forsaken me?'

You see how characteristic, how representative it all is. The human situation writ large. These are among the things it means to be a man. Every rope breaks when you seize it. Every door is slammed shut as you reach it. To be like the fox at the end of the run; the earths all staked.

As for the last dereliction of all, how can we either understand or endure it? Is it that God Himself cannot be Man unless God seems to vanish at His greatest need? And if so, why? I sometimes wonder if we have even begun to understand what is involved in the very concept of creation. If God will create, He will make something to be, and yet to be not Himself. To be created is, in some sense, to be ejected or separated. Can it be that the more perfect the creature is, the further this separation must at some point be pushed? It is saints, not common people, who experience the 'dark night'. It is men and angels, not beasts, who rebel. Inanimate matter sleeps in the bosom of the Father. The 'hiddenness' of God perhaps presses most painfully on those who are in another way nearest to Him, and therefore God Himself, made man, will of all men be by God most forsaken? One of the Seventeenth Century divines says: 'By pretending to be visible God could only deceive the world.' Perhaps He does pretend just a little to simple souls who need a full measure of 'sensible consolation'. Not deceiving them, but tempering the wind to the shorn lamb. Of course I'm not saying like Niebühr that evil is inherent in finitude. That would identify the creation with the fall and make God the author of evil. But perhaps there is an anguish, an alienation, a crucifixion involved in the creative act. Yet He who alone can judge judges the far-off consummation to be worth it.

I am, you see, a Job's comforter. Far from lightening the dark valley where you now find yourself, I blacken it. And you know why. Your darkness has brought back my own. But on second thoughts I don't regret what I have written. I think it is only in a shared darkness that you and I can really meet at present; shared with one another and, what matters most, with our Master. We are not on an untrodden path. Rather, on the main road.

Certainly we were talking too lightly and easily about these things a fortnight ago. We were playing with counters. One used to be told as a child:

'Think what you're saying.' Apparently we need also to be told: 'Think what you're thinking.' The stakes have to be raised before we take the game quite seriously. I know this is the opposite of what is often said about the necessity of keeping all emotion out of our intellectual processes – 'You can't think straight unless you are cool.' But then neither can you think deep if you are. I suppose one must try every problem in both states. You remember that the ancient Persians debated everything twice: once when they were drunk and once when they were sober.

I know one of you will let me have news as soon as there is any.

9

Thank God. What a mare's nest! Or, more grimly, what a rehearsal! It is only twenty-four hours since I got Betty's wire, and already the crisis seems curiously far away. Like at sea. Once you have doubled the point and got into smooth water, the point doesn't take long to hide below the horizon.

And now, your letter. I'm not at all surprised at your feeling flattened rather than joyful. That isn't ingratitude. It's only exhaustion. Weren't there moments even during those terrible days when you glided into a sort of apathy – for the same reason? The body (bless it) will not continue indefinitely supplying us with the physical media of emotion.

Surely there's no difficulty about the prayer in Gethsemane on the ground that if the disciples were asleep they couldn't have heard it and therefore couldn't have recorded it? The words they did record would hardly have taken three seconds to utter. He was only 'a stone's throw' away. The silence of night was around them. And we may be sure He prayed aloud. People did everything aloud in those days. You remember how astonished St Augustine was – some centuries later in a far more sophisticated society – to discover that when St Ambrose was reading (to himself) you couldn't hear the words even if you went and stood just beside him? The disciples heard the opening words of the prayer before they went to sleep. They record those opening words as if they were the whole.

There is a rather amusing instance of the same thing in Acts 24. The Jews had got down a professional orator called Tertullos to conduct the prosecution of St Paul. The speech as recorded by St Luke takes eighty-four words in the Greek, if I've counted correctly. Eighty-four words are impossibly short for a Greek advocate on a full-dress occasion. Presumably, then, they are a *précis*? But of those eighty-odd words forty are taken up with preliminary compliments to the bench – stuff, which, in a *précis* on that tiny scale, ought not to have come in at all. It is easy to guess what has happened. St Luke, though an excellent narrator, was no good as a reporter. He starts off by trying to memorise, or to get down, the whole speech *verbatim*. And he succeeds in reproducing a certain amount of the exordium. (The style [is] unmistakable. Only a practising *rhetor* ever talks that way.) But he is soon defeated. The whole of the rest of the speech has to be represented by a ludicrously inadequate abstract. But he doesn't tell us what has happened, and thus seems to attribute to Tertullos a performance which would have spelled professional ruin.

As you say, the problems about prayer which really press upon a man when he is praying for dear life are not the general and philosophical ones; they are those that arise within Christianity itself. At least, this is so for you and me. We have long since agreed that if our prayers are granted at all they are granted from the foundation of the world. God and His acts are not in time. Intercourse between God and man occurs at particular moments for the man, but not for God. If there is – as the very concept of prayer presupposes – an adaptation between the free actions of men in prayer and the course of events, this adaptation is from the beginning inherent in the great single creative act. Our prayers are heard – don't say 'have been heard' or you are putting God into time – not only before we make them but before we are made ourselves.

The real problems are different. Is it our faith that prayers, or some prayers, are real causes? But they are not magical causes: they don't, like spells, act directly on nature. They act, then, on nature through God? This would seem to imply that they act on God. But God, we believe, is impassible. All theology would reject the idea of a transaction in which a creature was the agent and God the patient.

It is quite useless to try to answer this empirically by producing stories – though you and I could tell strange ones – of striking answers to prayer. We shall be told, reasonably enough, that *post hoc* is not *propter hoc*. The thing we prayed for was going to happen anyway. Our action was irrelevant. Even a fellow-creature's action which fulfils our request may not be caused by it; he does what we ask, but perhaps he would equally have done so without our asking. Some cynics will tell us that no woman ever married a man because he proposed to her: she always elicits the proposal because she has determined to marry him.

In these human instances we believe, when we do believe, that our request was the cause, or a cause, of the other party's action, because we have from deep acquaintance a certain impression of that party's character. Certainly not by applying the scientific procedures – control experiments, etc. – for establishing causes. Similarly we believe, when we do believe, that the relation between our prayer and the event is not a mere coincidence only because we have a certain idea of God's character. Only faith vouches for the connection. No empirical proof could establish it. Even a miracle, if one occurred, 'might have been going to happen anyway'.

Again, in the most intimate human instances we really feel that the category of cause and effect will not contain what actually happens. In a real 'proposal' – as distinct from one in an old-fashioned novel – is there any agent-patient relation? Which drop on the window pane moves to join the other?

Now I am going to suggest that strictly causal thinking is even more inadequate when applied to the relation between God and man. I don't mean only when we are thinking of prayer, but whenever we are thinking about what happens at the Frontier, at the mysterious point of junction and separation where absolute being utters derivative being.

One attempt to define causally what happens there has led to the whole puzzle about Grace and free will. You will notice that Scripture just sails over the problem. 'Work out your own salvation in fear and trembling' – pure Pelagianism. But why? 'For it is God who worketh in you' – pure Augustinianism. It is presumably only our presuppositions that make this appear nonsensical. We profanely assume that divine and human action exclude one another like the actions of two fellow-creatures so that 'God did this' and 'I did this' cannot both be true of the same act except in the sense that each contributed a share.

In the end we must admit a two-way traffic at the junction. At first sight no passive verb in the world would seem to be so utterly passive as 'to be created'. Does it not mean 'to *have been* nonentity'? Yet, for us rational creatures, to be created also means 'to be made agents'. We have nothing that we have not received; but part of what we have received is the power of being something more than receptacles. We exercise it, no doubt, briefly by our sins. But they, for my present argument, will do as well as anything else. For God forgives sins. He would not do so if we committed none – 'whereto serves Mercy but to confront the visage of offence?' In that sense the Divine action is consequent upon, conditioned by, elicited by, our behaviour. Does this mean that we can 'act upon' God? I suppose you could put it that way if you wanted. If you do, then we must interpret His 'impassibility' in a way which admits this; for we know that God forgives much better than we know what 'impassible' means. I would rather say that from before all worlds His providential and creative act (for they are all one) takes into account all the situations produced by the acts of His creatures. And if He takes our sins into account, why not our petitions?

10

I see your point. But you must admit that Scripture doesn't take the slightest pains to guard the doctrine of Divine Impassibility. We are constantly represented as exciting the Divine wrath or pity – even as 'grieving' God. I know this language is analogical. But when we say that, we must not smuggle in the idea that we can throw the analogy away and, as it were, get in behind it to a purely literal truth. All we can really substitute for the analogical expression is some theological abstraction. And the abstraction's value is almost entirely negative. It warns us against drawing absurd consequences from the analogical expression by prosaic extrapolations. By itself, the abstraction 'impassible' can get us nowhere. It might even suggest something far more misleading than the most *naif* Old Testament picture of a stormily emotional Jehovah. Either something inert, or something which was 'Pure Act' in such a sense that it could take no account of events within the universe it had created.

I suggest two rules for exegetics. (1) Never take the images literally. (2) When the *purport* of the images – what they say to our fear and hope and will and affections – seems to conflict with the theological abstractions, trust the purport of the images every time. For our abstract thinking is itself a tissue of analogies: a continual modelling of spiritual reality in legal or chemical or mechanical terms. Are these likely to be more adequate than the sensuous, organic, and personal images of Scripture – light and darkness, river and well, seed and harvest, master and servant, hen and chickens, father and child? The footprints of the Divine are more visible in that rich soil than across rocks or slag-heaps. Hence what they now call 'de-mythologising' Christianity can easily be 're-mythologising' it – and substituting a poorer mythology for a richer.

I agree that my deliberately vague expression about our prayers being 'taken into account' is a retreat from Pascal's magnificent dictum ('God has instituted prayer so as to confer upon His creatures the dignity of being causes'). But Pascal really does suggest a far too explicit agent-and-patient relation, with God as the patient. And I have another ground for preferring my own more modest formula. To think of our prayers as just 'causes' would suggest that the whole importance of petitionary prayer lay in the achievement of the thing asked for. But really, for our spiritual life as a whole, the 'being taken into account', or 'considered', matters more than the being granted. Religious people don't talk about the 'results' of prayer; they talk of its being 'answered' or 'heard'. Someone said 'A suitor wants his suit to be heard as well as granted.' In suits to God, if they are really religious acts at all and not merely attempts at magic, this is even more so. We can bear to be refused but not to be ignored. In other words, our faith can survive many refusals if they really are refusals and not mere disregards. The apparent stone will be bread to us if we believe that a Father's hand put it into ours, in mercy or in justice or even in rebuke. It is hard and bitter; yet it can be chewed and swallowed. But if, having prayed for our heart's desire and got it, we then became convinced that this was a mere accident – that providential designs which had only some quite different end just couldn't help throwing out this satisfaction for us as a by-product – then the apparent bread would become a stone. A pretty stone, perhaps, or even a precious stone. But not edible to the soul.

What we must fight against is Pope's maxim:

the first Almighty Cause
Acts not by partial, but by general laws.

The odd thing is that Pope thought, and all who agree with him think, that this philosophical theology is an advance beyond the religion of the child and the savage (and the New Testament). It seems to them less *naïf* and anthropomorphic. The real difference, however, is that the anthropomorphism is more subtly hidden and of a far more disastrous type.

For the implication is that there exists on the Divine level a distinction with which we are very familiar on our own: that between the plan (or the main plan) and its unintended but unavoidable by-products. Whatever we do, even if it achieves its object, will also scatter round it a spray of consequences which were not its object at all. This is so even in private life. I throw out crumbs for the birds and provide, incidentally, a breakfast for the rats. Much more so in what may be called managerial life. The governing body of the college alters the time of dinner in hall; our object being to let the servants get home earlier. But by doing so we alter the daily pattern of life for every undergraduate. To some the new arrangement will be a convenience, to others the reverse. But we had no special favour for the first lot and no spite against the second. Our arrangement drags these unforeseen and undesired consequences after it. We can't help this.

On Pope's view God has to work in the same way. He has His grand design for the sum of things. Nothing we can say will deflect it. It leaves Him little freedom (or none?) for granting, or even for deliberately refusing, our prayers. The grand design churns out innumerable blessings and curses for individuals. God can't help that. They're all by-products.

I suggest that the distinction between plan and by-product must vanish entirely on the level of omniscience, omnipotence, and perfect goodness. I believe this because even on the human level it diminishes the higher you go. The better a human plan is made, the fewer unconsidered by-products it will have and the more birds it will kill with one stone, the more diverse needs and interests it will meet; the nearer it will come – it can never come very near – to being a plan for each individual. Bad laws make hard cases. But let us go beyond the managerial altogether. Surely a man of genius composing a poem or symphony must be less unlike God than a ruler? But the man of genius has no mere by-products in his work. Every note or word will be more than a means, more than a consequence. Nothing will be present *solely* for the sake of other things. If each note or word were conscious it would say: 'The maker had me myself in view and chose for me, with the whole force of his genius, exactly the context I required.' And it would be right – provided it remembered that every other note or word could say no less.

How should the true Creator work by 'general laws'? 'To generalise is to be an idiot,' said Blake. Perhaps he went too far. But to generalise is to be a finite mind. Generalities are the lenses with which our intellects have to manage. How should God sully the infinite lucidity of this vision with such makeshifts? One might as well think He had to consult books of reference, or that, if He ever considered me individually, He would begin by saying, 'Gabriel, bring me Mr Lewis's file.'

The God of the New Testament who takes into account the death of every sparrow is not more, but far less, anthropomorphic than Pope's.

I will not believe in the Managerial God and his general laws. If there is Providence at all, everything is providential and every providence is a special providence. It is an old and pious saying that Christ died not only for Man but for each man, just as much as if each had been the only man there was. Can I not believe the same of this creative act – which, as spread out in time, we call destiny or history? It is for the sake of each human soul. Each is an end. Perhaps for each beast. Perhaps even each particle of matter – the night sky suggests that the inanimate also has for God some value we cannot imagine. His ways are not (not there, anyway) like ours.

If you ask why I believe all this, I can only reply that we are taught, both by precept and example, to pray, and that prayer would be meaningless in the sort of universe Pope pictured. One of the purposes for which God instituted prayer may have been to bear witness that the course of events is not governed like a state but created like a work of art to which every being makes its contribution and (in prayer) a conscious contribution, and in which every being is both an end and a means. And since I have momentarily considered prayer itself as a means let me hasten to add that it is also an end. The world was made partly that there might be prayer; partly that our prayers for George might be answered. But let's have finished with 'partly'. The great work of art was made for the sake of all it does and is, down to the curve of every wave and the flight of every insect.

11

I see you won't let me off. And the longer I look at it the less I shall like it. I must face – or else explicitly decline – the difficulties that really torment us when we cry for mercy in earnest. I have found no book that helps me with them all. I have so little confidence in my own power to tackle them that, if it were possible, I would let sleeping dogs lie. But the dogs are not sleeping. They are awake and snapping. We both bear the marks of their teeth. That being so, we had better share our bewilderments. By hiding them from each other we should not hide them from ourselves.

The New Testament contains embarrassing promises that what we pray for with faith we shall receive. Mark 11:24 is the most staggering. Whatever we ask for, believing that we'll get it, we'll get. No question, it seems, of confining it to spiritual gifts; *whatever* we ask for. No question of a merely general faith in God, but a belief that you will get the particular thing you ask. No question of getting either it or else something that is really far better for you; you'll get precisely it. And to heap paradox on paradox, the Greek doesn't even say, 'believing that you *will* get it'. It uses the aorist, ἐλάβετε, which one is tempted to translate 'believing that you *got* it'. But this final difficulty I shall ignore. I don't expect Aramaic had anything which we – brought up on Latin grammar – would recognise as tenses at all.

How is this astonishing promise to be reconciled – (a) With the observed facts? (b) With the prayer in Gethsemane, and (as a result of that prayer) the universally accepted view that we should ask everything with a reservation ('if it be Thy will')?

As regards (a), no evasion is possible. Every war, every famine or plague, almost every death-bed, is the monument to a petition that was not granted. At this very moment thousands of people in this one island are facing a *fait accompli*, the very thing against which they have prayed night and day, pouring out their whole soul in prayer, and, as they thought, with faith. They have sought and not found. They have knocked and it has not been opened. 'That which they greatly feared has come upon them.'

But (b), though much less often mentioned, is surely an equal difficulty. How is it possible at one and the same moment to have a perfect faith – an untroubled or unhesitating faith as St James says (1:6) – that you will get what you ask and yet also prepare yourself submissively in advance for a possible refusal? If you envisage a refusal as possible, how can you have simultaneously a perfect confidence that what you ask will not be refused? If you have that confidence, how can you take refusal into account at all?

It is easy to see why so much more is written about worship and contemplation than about 'crudely' or 'naïvely' petitionary prayer. They may be – I think they are – nobler forms of prayer. But they are also a good deal easier to write about.

As regards the first difficulty, I'm not asking why our petitions are so often refused. Anyone can see in general that this must be so. In our ignorance we ask what is not good for us or for others, or not even intrinsically possible. Or again, to grant one man's prayer involves refusing another's. There is much here which it is hard for our will to accept but nothing that is hard for our intellect to understand. The real problem is different; not why refusal is so frequent, but why the opposite result is so lavishly promised.

Shall we then proceed on Vidler's principles and scrap the embarrassing promises as 'venerable archaisms' which have to be 'outgrown'? Surely, even if there were no other objection, that method is too easy. If we are free to delete all inconvenient data we shall certainly have no theological difficulties; but for the same reason no solutions and no progress. The very writers of the 'Tekkies', not to mention the scientists, know better. The troublesome fact, the apparent absurdity which can't be fitted into any synthesis we have yet made, is precisely the one we must not ignore. Ten to one, it's in that covert the fox is lurking. There is always hope if we keep an unsolved problem fairly in view; there's none if we pretend it's not there.

Before going any further, I want to make two purely practical points: 1. These lavish promises are the worst possible place at which to begin Christian instruction in dealing with a child or a Pagan. You remember what happened when the Widow started Huck Finn off with the idea he could get what he wanted by praying for it. He tried the experiment and then, not unnaturally, never gave Christianity a second thought; we had better not talk about the view of prayer embodied in Mark 11:24 as 'naïf' or 'elementary'. If that passage contains a truth, it is a truth for very advanced pupils indeed. I don't think it is 'addressed to our condition' (yours and mine) at all. It is a coping-stone, not a foundation. For most of us the prayer in Gethsemane is the only model. Removing mountains can wait.

2. We must not encourage in ourselves or others any tendency to work up a subjective state which, if we succeeded, we should describe as 'faith', with the idea that this will somehow ensure the granting of our prayer. We have

probably all done this as children. But the state of mind which desperate desire working on a strong imagination can manufacture is not faith in the Christian sense. It is a feat of psychological gymnastics.

It seems to me we must conclude that such promises about prayer with faith refer to a degree or kind of faith which most believers never experience. A far inferior degree is, I hope, acceptable to God. Even the kind that says, 'Help thou my unbelief', may make way for a miracle. Again, the absence of such faith as ensures the granting of the prayer is not even necessarily a sin; for Our Lord had no such assurance when He prayed in Gethsemane.

How or why does such faith occur sometimes, but not always, even in the perfect petitioner? We, or I, can only guess. My own idea is that it occurs only when the one who prays does so as God's fellow-worker, demanding what is needed for the joint work. It is the prophet's, the apostle's, the missionary's, the healer's prayer that is made with this confidence and finds the confidence justified by the event. The difference, we are told, between a servant and a friend is that a servant is not in his master's secrets. For him, 'orders is orders'. He has only his own surmises as to the plans he helps to execute. But the fellow-worker, the companion or (dare we say?) the colleague of God is so united with Him at certain moments that something of the divine fore-knowledge enters his mind. Hence his faith is the 'evidence' – that is, the evidentness, the obviousness – of things not seen.

As the friend is above the servant, the servant is above the suitor, the man praying on his own behalf. It is no sin to be a suitor. Our Lord descends into the humiliation of being a suitor, or praying on His own behalf, in Gethsemane. But when He does so the certitude about His Father's will is apparently withdrawn.

After that it would be no true faith – it would be idle presumption – for us, who are habitually suitors and do not often rise to the level of servants, to imagine that we shall have any assurance which is not an illusion – or correct only by accident – about the events of our prayers. Our struggle is, isn't it? – to achieve and retain faith on a lower level. To believe that, whether He can grant them or not, God will listen to our prayers, will take them into account. Even to go on believing that there is a Listener at all. For as the situation grows more and more desperate, the grisly fears intrude. Are we only talking to ourselves in an empty universe? The silence is often so emphatic. And we have prayed so much already.

What do you think about these things? I have offered only guesses.

12

My experience is the same as yours. I have never met a book on prayer which was much use to people in our position. There are many little books *of* prayers, which may be helpful to those who share Rose Macaulay's approach, but you and I wouldn't know what to do with them. It's not words we lack! And there are books *on* prayer, but they nearly all have a strongly conventual background. Even the *Imitation* is sometimes, to an almost comic degree, 'not addressed to my condition'. The author assumes that you will want to be chatting in the kitchen when you ought to be in your cell. Our temptation is to be in our studies when we ought to be chatting in the kitchen. (Perhaps if our studies were as cold as those cells it would be different.)

You and I are people of the foothills. In the happy days when I was still a walker, I loved the hills, and even mountain walks, but I was no climber. I hadn't the head. So now, I do not attempt the precipices of mysticism. On the other hand, there is, apparently, a level of prayer-life lower even than ours. I don't mean that people who occupy it are spiritually lower than we. They may far excel us. But their praying is of an astonishingly underdeveloped type.

I have only just learned about it – from our Vicar. He assures me that, so far as he has been able to discover, the overwhelming majority of his parishioners mean by 'saying their prayers' repeating whatever little formula they were taught in childhood by their mothers. I wonder how this can come about. It can't be that they are never penitent or thankful – they're dear people, many of them – or have no needs. Is it that there is a sort of watertight bulk-head between their 'religion' and their 'real life', in which case the part of their life which they call 'religious' is really the irreligious part?

But however badly needed a good book on prayer is, I shall never try to write it. Two people on the foothills comparing notes in private are all very well. But in a book one would inevitably seem to be attempting, not discussion, but instruction. And for me to offer the world instruction about prayer would be impudence.

About the higher level – the crags up which the mystics vanish out of my sight – the glaciers and the *aiguilles* – I have only two things to say. One is that I don't think we are all 'called' to that ascent. 'If it were so, He would have told us.'

The second is this. The following position is gaining ground and is extremely plausible. Mystics (it is said) starting from the most diverse religious premises all find the same things. These things have singularly little to do with the professed doctrines of any particular religion – Christianity, Hinduism, Buddhism, Neo-Platonism, etc. Therefore, mysticism is, by empirical evidence, the only real contact Man has ever had with the unseen. The agreement of the explorers proves that they are all in touch with something objective. It is therefore the one true religion. And what we call the 'religions' are either mere delusions or, at best, so many porches through which an entrance into transcendent reality can be effected –

And when he hath the kernel eatn,
Who doth not throw away the shell?

I am doubtful about the premises. Did Plotinus and Lady Julian and St John of the Cross really find 'the same things'? But even admitting some similarity, one thing common to all mysticisms is the temporary shattering of our ordinary spatial and temporal consciousness and of our discursive intellect. The value of this negative experience must depend on the nature of that positive, whatever it is, for which it makes room. But should we not expect that the negative would always *feel* the same? If wine-glasses were conscious, I suppose that *being emptied* would be the same experience for each, even if some were to remain empty and some to be filled with wine and some broken. All who leave the land and put to the sea will 'find the same things' – the land sinking below the horizon, the gulls dropping behind, the salty breeze. Tourists, merchants, sailors, pirates, missionaries – it's all one. But this identical experience vouches for nothing about the utility or unlawfulness or final event of their voyages –

It may be that the gulfs will wash them down,
It may be they will touch the Happy Isles.

I do not at all regard mystical experience as an illusion. I think it shows that there is a way to go, before death, out of what may be called 'this world' – out of the stage set. Out of this; but into what? That's like asking an Englishman, 'Where does the sea lead to?' He will reply, 'To everywhere on earth, including Davy Jones's locker, except England.' The lawfulness, safety, and utility of the mystical voyage depends not at all on its being mystical – that is, on its being a departure – but on the motives, skill, and constancy of the voyager, and on the grace of God. The true religion gives value to its own mysticism; mysticism does not invalidate the religion in which it happens to occur.

I shouldn't be at all disturbed if it could be shown that a diabolical mysticism, or drugs, produced experiences indistinguishable (by introspection) from those of the great Christian mystics. Departures are all alike; it is the landfall that crowns the voyage. The saint, by being a saint, proves that his mysticism (if he was a mystic; not all saints are) led him aright; the fact that he has practised mysticism could never prove his sanctity.

You may wonder that my intense desire to peep behind the scenes has not led me to attempt the mystic way. But would it not be the worst of all possible motives? The saint may win 'a mortal glimpse of death's immortal rose', but it is a by-product. He took ship simply in humble and selfless love.

There can be a desire (like mine) with no carnal element in it at all which is nevertheless, in St Paul's sense, 'flesh' and not 'spirit'. That is, there can be a merely impulsive, headstrong, greedy desire even for spiritual things. It is, like our other appetites, 'cross-fodder'. Yet, being crucified, it can be raised from the dead, and made part of our bliss.

Turning now to quite a different point in your letter. I too had noticed that our prayers for others flow more easily than those we offer on our own behalf. And it would be nice to accept your view that this just shows we are made to live by charity. I'm afraid, however, I detect two much less attractive reasons for the ease of my own intercessory prayers. One is that I am often, I believe, praying for others when I should be doing things for them. It's so much easier to pray for a bore than to go and see him. And the other is like unto it. Suppose I pray that you may be given grace to withstand your besetting sin (a short-list of candidates for this post will be forwarded on demand). Well, all the work has to be done by God and you. If I pray against my own besetting sin there will be work for me. One sometimes fights shy of admitting an act to be a sin for this very reason.

The increasing list of people to be prayed for is, nevertheless, one of the burdens of old age. I have a scruple about crossing anyone off the list. When I say a scruple, I mean precisely a scruple. I don't really think that if one prays for a man at all it is a duty to pray for him all my life. But when it comes to dropping him *now*, this particular day, it somehow goes against the grain. And as the list lengthens, it is hard to make it more than a mere string of names. But here – in some measure – a curious law comes into play. Don't you find that, if you keep your mind fixed upon God, you will automatically think of the person you are praying for; but that there is no tendency for it to work the other way round?

13

I've just found in an old notebook a poem, with no author's name attached, which is rather relevant to something we were talking about a few weeks ago – I mean, the haunting fear that there is no one listening, and that what we call prayer is soliloquy: someone talking to himself. This writer takes the bull by the horns and says in effect: 'Very well, suppose it is,' and gets a surprising result. Here is the poem:

They tell me, Lord that when I seem
    To be in speech with you,
Since but one voice is heard, it's all a dream,
    One talker aping two.

Sometimes it is, yet not as they
    Conceive it. Rather, I
Seek in myself the things I hoped to say,
    But lo!, my wells are dry.

Then, seeing me empty, you forsake
    The listener's role and through
My dumb lips breathe and into utterance wake
    The thoughts I never knew.

And thus you neither need reply
    Nor can; thus, while we seem
Two talkers, thou art One forever, and I
    No dreamer, but thy dream.

Dream makes it too like Pantheism and was perhaps dragged in for the rhyme. But is he not right in thinking that prayer in its most perfect state is a soliloquy? If the Holy Spirit speaks in the man, then in prayer God speaks to God. But the human petitioner does not therefore become a 'dream'. As you said the other day, God and man cannot exclude one another, as man excludes man, at the point of junction, so to call it, between Creator and creature; the point where the mystery of creation – timeless for God, and incessant in time for us – is actually taking place. 'God did (or said) it' and 'I did (or said) it' can both be true.

You remember the two maxims Owen [Barfield] lays down in *Saving the Appearances*? On the one hand, the man who does not regard God as other than himself cannot be said to have a religion at all. On the other hand, if I think God other than myself in the same way in which my fellow-men, and objects in general, are other than myself, I am beginning to make Him an idol. I am daring to treat His existence as somehow *parallel* to my own. But He is the ground of our being. He is always both within us and over against us. Our reality is so much from His reality as He, moment by moment, projects into us. The deeper the level within ourselves from which our prayer, or any other act, wells up, the more it is His, but not at all the less ours. Rather, most ours when most His. Arnold speaks of us as 'enisled' from one another in 'the sea of life'. But we can't be similarly 'enisled' from God. To be discontinuous from God as I am discontinuous from you would be annihilation.

A question at once arises. Is it still God speaking when a liar or a blasphemer speaks? In one sense, almost Yes. Apart from God he could not speak at all; there are no words not derived from the Word; no acts not derived from Him who is *Actus purus*. And indeed the only way in which I can make real to myself what theology teaches about the heinousness of sin is to remember that every sin is the distortion of an energy breathed into us – an energy which, if not thus distorted, would have blossomed into one of those holy acts whereof 'God did it' and 'I did it' are both true descriptions. We poison the wine as He decants it into us; murder a melody He would play with us as the instrument. We caricature the self-portrait He would paint. Hence all sin, whatever else it is, is sacrilege.

We must, no doubt, distinguish the ontological continuity between Creator and creature which is, so to speak, 'given' by the relation between them, from the union of wills which, under Grace, is reached by a life of sanctity. The ontological continuity is, I take it, unchangeable, and exists between God and a reprobate (or a devil) no less than between God and a saint. 'Whither shall I go then from thy presence? If I go down to hell, thou art there also.'

Where there is prayer at all we may suppose that there is some effort, however feeble, towards the second condition, the union of wills. What God labours to do or say through the man comes back to God with a distortion which at any rate is not total.

Do you object to the apparent 'roundaboutness' – it could easily be made comic – of the whole picture? Why should God speak to Himself through man? I ask, in reply, why should He do anything through His creatures? Why should He achieve, the long way round, through the labours of angels, men (always imperfectly obedient and efficient), and the activity of irrational and inanimate beings, ends which, presumably, the mere *fiat* of omnipotence would achieve with instantaneous perfection?

Creation seems to be delegation through and through. He will do nothing simply of Himself which can be done by creatures. I suppose this is because He is a giver. And He has nothing to give but Himself. And to give Himself is to do His deeds – in a sense, and on varying levels to be Himself – through the things He has made.

In Pantheism God is all. But the whole point of creation surely is that He was not content to be all. He intends to be 'all *in all*'.

One must be careful not to put this in a way which would blur the distinction between the creation of a man and the Incarnation of God. Could one, as a mere model, put it thus? In creation God makes – invents – a person and 'utters' – injects – him into the realm of Nature. In the Incarnation, God the Son takes the body and human soul of Jesus, and, through that, the whole environment of Nature, all the creaturely predicament, into His own being. So that 'He came down from Heaven' can almost be transposed into 'Heaven drew earth up into it', and locality, limitation, sleep, sweat, footsore weariness, frustration, pain, doubt and death, are, from before all worlds, known by God from within. The pure light walks the earth; the darkness, received into the heart of Deity, is there swallowed up. Where, except in uncreated light, can the darkness be drowned?

14

I won't admit without a struggle that when I speak of God 'uttering' or 'inventing' the creatures I am 'watering down the concept of creation'. I am trying to give it, by remote analogies, some sort of content. I know that to create is defined as 'to make out of nothing', *ex nihilo*. But I take that to mean '*not* out of any pre-existing material'. It can't mean that God makes what God has not thought of, or that He gives His creatures any powers or beauties that He Himself does not possess. Why, we think that even human work comes nearest to creation when the maker has 'got it all out of his own head'.

Nor am I suggesting a theory of 'emanations'. The differentia of an 'emanation' – literally an overflowing, a trickling out – would be that it suggests something involuntary. But my words – 'uttering' and 'inventing' – are meant to suggest an act.

This act, as it is for God, must always remain totally inconceivable to man. For we – even our poets and musicians and inventors – never, in the ultimate sense, *make*. We only build. We always have materials to build from. All we can know about the act of creation must be derived from what we can gather about the relation of the creatures to their Creator.

Now the very Pagans knew that any beggar at your door might be a god in disguise: and the parable of the sheep and the goats is Our Lord's comment. What you do, or don't do, to the beggar, you do, or don't do, to Him. Taken at the Pantheist extreme, this could mean that men are only appearances of God – dramatic representations, as it were. Taken at the Legalist extreme, it could mean that God, by a sort of Legal fiction, will 'deem' your kindness to the beggar a kindness done to Himself. Or again, as Our Lord's own words suggest, that since the least of men are His 'brethren', the whole action is, so to speak, 'within the family'. And in what sense brethren? Biologically, because Jesus is Man? Ontologically, because the light lightens them all? Or simply 'loved like brethren'. (It cannot refer only to the regenerate.) I would ask first whether any one of these formulations is 'right' in a sense which makes the others simply wrong? It seems to me improbable. If I ever see more clearly I will speak more surely.

Meanwhile, I stick to Owen's view. All creatures, from the angel to the atom, are other than God; with an otherness to which there is no parallel: incommensurable. The very word 'to be' cannot be applied to Him and to them in exactly the same sense. But also, no creature is other than He in the same way in which it is other than all the rest. He is in it as they can never be in one another. In each of them as the ground and root and continual supply of its reality. And also in good rational creatures as light; in bad ones as fire, as at first the smouldering unease, and later the flaming anguish, of an unwelcome and vainly resisted presence.

Therefore of each creature we can say, 'This also is Thou: neither is this Thou.'

Simple faith leaps to this with astonishing ease. I once talked to a Continental pastor who had seen Hitler, and had, by all human standards, good cause to hate him. 'What did he look like?' I asked. 'Like all men,' he replied, 'that is, like Christ.'

One is always fighting on at least two fronts. When one is among Pantheists one must emphasise the distinctness, and relative independence, of the creatures. Among Deists – or perhaps in Woolwich, if the laity there really think God is to be sought in the sky – one must emphasise the divine presence in my neighbour, my dog, my cabbage-patch.

It is much wiser, I believe, to think of that presence in particular objects than just of 'omnipresence'. The latter gives very *naïf* people (Woolwich again, perhaps?) the idea of something spatially extended, like a gas. It also blurs the distinctions, the truth that God is present in each thing but not necessarily in the same mode; not in a man as in the consecrated bread and wine, nor in a bad man as in a good one, nor in a beast as in a man, nor in a tree as in a beast, nor in inanimate matter as in a tree. I take it there is a paradox here. The higher the creature, the more and also the less God is in it; the more present by grace, and the less present (by a sort of abdication) as mere power. By grace He gives the higher creatures power to will His will ('and wield their little tridents'): the lower ones simply execute it automatically.

It is well to have specifically holy places, and things, and days, for, without these focal points or reminders, the belief that all is holy and 'big with God' will soon dwindle into a mere sentiment. But if these holy places, things, and days cease to remind us, if they obliterate our awareness that all ground is holy and every bush (could we but perceive it) a Burning Bush, then the hallows begin to do harm. Hence both the necessity, and the perennial danger, of 'religion'.

Boehme advises us once an hour 'to fling ourselves beyond every creature'. But in order to find God it is perhaps not always necessary to leave the creatures behind. We may ignore, but we can nowhere evade, the presence of God. The world is crowded with Him. He walks everywhere *incognito*. And the *incognito* is not always hard to penetrate. The real labour is to remember, to attend. In fact, to come awake. Still more, to remain awake.

Oddly enough, what corroborates me in this faith is the fact, otherwise so infinitely deplorable, that the awareness of this presence has so often been unwelcome. I call upon Him in prayer. Often He might reply – I think He does reply – 'But you have been evading me for hours.' For He comes not only to raise up but to cast down; to deny, to rebuke, to interrupt. The prayer 'prevent us in all our doings' is often answered as if the word *prevent* had its modern meaning. The presence which we voluntarily evade is often, and we know it, His presence in wrath.

And out of this evil comes a good. If I never fled from His presence, then I should suspect those moments when I seemed to delight in it of being wish-fulfilment dreams. That, by the way, explains the feebleness of all those watered versions of Christianity which leave out all the darker elements and try to establish a religion of pure consolation. No real belief in the watered versions can last. Bemused and besotted as we are, we still dimly know at heart that nothing which is at all times and in every way agreeable to us can have objective reality. It is of the very nature of the real that it should have sharp corners and rough edges, that it should be resistant, should be itself. Dream-furniture is the only kind on which you never stub your toes or bang your knee. You and I have both known happy marriage. But how different our wives were from the imaginary mistresses of our adolescent dreams! So much less exquisitely adapted to all our wishes; and for that very reason (among others) so incomparably better.

Servile fear is, to be sure, the lowest form of religion. But a god such that there could never be occasion for even servile fear, a *safe* god, a tame god, soon proclaims himself to any sound mind as a fantasy. I have met no people who fully disbelieved in Hell and also had a living and life-giving belief in Heaven.

There is, I know, a belief in both, which is of no religious significance. It makes these spiritual things, or some travesty of them, objects of purely carnal, prudential, self-centred fear and hope. The deeper levels, those things which only immortal spirit can desire or dread, are not concerned at all. Such belief is fortunately very brittle. The old divines exhausted their eloquence especially in arousing such fear: but, as they themselves rather naïvely complain, the effect did not last for more than a few hours after the sermon.

The soul that has once been waked, or stung, or uplifted by the desire of God, will inevitably (I think) awake to the fear of losing Him.

15

I hadn't realised that Betty was the silent third in this dialogue. I ought to have guessed it. Not that her worst enemy ever accused her of being The Silent Woman – remember the night at Mullingar – but that her silences during a prolonged argument between you and me are usually of a very emphatic, audible, and even dialectical character. One knows she is getting her broom ready and will soon sweep up all our breakages. On the present point she is right. I *am* making very heavy weather of what most believers find a very simple matter. What is more natural, and easier, if you believe in God, than to address Him? How could one not?

Yes. But it depends who one is. For those in my position – adult converts from the *intelligentsia* – that simplicity and spontaneity can't always be the starting point. One can't just jump back into one's childhood. If one tries to, the result will only be an archaising revival, like Victorian Gothic – a parody of being born again. We have to work back to the simplicity a long way round.

In actual practice, in my prayers, I often have to use that long way at the very beginning of the prayer.

St François de Sales begins every meditation with the command: *Mettez-vous en la présence de Dieu.* I wonder how many different mental operations have been carried out in intended obedience to that?

What happens to me if I try to take it – as Betty would tell me – 'simply', is the juxtaposition of two 'representations' or ideas or phantoms. One is the bright blur in the mind which stands for God. The other is the ideal I call 'me'. But I can't leave it at that, because I know – and it's useless to pretend I don't know – that they are both phantasmal. The real I has created them both – or, rather, built them up in the vaguest way from all sorts of psychological odds and ends.

Very often, paradoxically, the first step is to banish the 'bright blur' – or, in statelier language, to break the idol. Let's get back to what has at least some degree of resistant reality. Here are the four walls of the room. And here am I. But both terms are merely the façade of impenetrable mysteries.

The walls, they say, are matter. That is, as the physicists will try to tell me, something totally unimaginable, only mathematically describable, existing in a curved space, charged with appalling energies. If I could penetrate far enough into that mystery I should perhaps finally reach what is sheerly real.

And what am I? The façade is what I call consciousness. I am at least conscious of the colour of those walls. I am not, in the same way, or to the same degree, conscious of what I call my thoughts: for if I try to examine what happens when I am thinking, it would, I well know, turn out to be the thinnest possible film on the surface of a vast deep. The psychologists have taught us that. Their real error lies in underestimating the depth and the variety of its contents. Dazzling lightness as well as dark clouds come up. And if all the enchanting visions are, as they rashly claim, mere disguises for sex, where lives the hidden artist who, from such monotonous and claustrophobic material, can make works of such various and liberating art? And depths of time too. All my past; my ancestral past; perhaps my pre-human past.

Here again, if I could dive deeply enough, I might again reach at the bottom that which simply is.

And only now am I ready, in my own fashion, to 'place myself in the presence of God'. Either mystery, if I could follow it far enough, would lead me to the same point – the point where something, in each case unimaginable, leaps forth from God's naked hand. The Indian, looking at the material world, says 'I am that'. I say, 'That and I grow from one root.' *Verbum supernum prodiens*, the Word coming forth from the Father, has made both, and brought them together in this subject-object embrace.

And what, you ask, is the advantage of all this? Well, for me – I am not talking about anyone else – it plants the prayer right in the present reality. For, whatever else is or is not real, this momentary confrontation of subject and object is certainly occurring: always occurring except when I am asleep. Here is the actual meeting of God's activity and man's – not some imaginary meeting that might occur if I were an angel or if God incarnate entered the room. There is here no question of a God 'up there' or 'out there'; rather, the present operation of God 'in here', as the ground of my own being, and God 'in there', as the ground of the matter that surrounds me, and God embracing and uniting both in the daily miracle of finite consciousness.

The two façades – the 'I' as I perceive myself and the room as I perceive it – were obstacles as long as I mistook them for ultimate realities. But the moment I recognised them as façades, as mere surfaces, they became conductors. Do you see? A lie is a delusion only so long as we believe it; but a recognised lie is a reality – a real lie – and as such may be highly instructive. A dream ceases to be a delusion as soon as we wake. But it does not become a nonentity. It is a real dream: and it also may be instructive. A stage set is not a real wood or drawing room: it is a real stage set, and may be a good one. (In fact we should never ask of anything 'Is it real?', for everything is real. The proper question is 'A real *what*?' – e.g. a real snake or a real *delirium tremens*?) The objects around me, and my idea of 'me', will deceive if taken at their face value. But they are momentous if taken as the end-products of divine activities. Thus and not otherwise, the creation of matter and the creation of mind meet one another and the circuit is closed.

Or put it this way. I have called my material surroundings a stage set. A stage set is not a dream nor a nonentity. But if you attack a stage house with a chisel you will not get chips of brick or stone; you'll only get a hole in a piece of canvas and, beyond that, windy darkness. Similarly, if you start investigating the nature of matter, you will not find anything like what imagination has always supposed matter to be. You will get mathematics. From that unimaginable physical reality my senses select a few stimuli. These they translate or symbolise into sensations, which have no likeness at all to the reality of matter. Of these sensations my associative power, very much directed by my practical needs and influenced by social training, makes up little bundles into what I call 'things' (labelled by nouns). Out of these I build myself a neat little box stage, suitably provided with properties such as hills, fields, houses, and the rest. In this I can act.

And you may well say 'act'. For what I call 'myself' (for all practical, everyday purposes) is also a dramatic construction; memories, glimpses in the shaving-glass, and snatches of the very fallible activity called 'introspection', are the principal ingredients. Normally I call this construction 'me', and the stage set 'the real world'.

Now the moment of prayer is for me – or involves for me as its condition – the awareness, the reawakened awareness, that this 'real world' and 'real self' are very far from being rock-bottom realities. I cannot, in the flesh, leave the stage, either to go behind the scenes or to take my seat in the pit; but I can remember that these regions exist. And I also remember that my apparent self – this clown or hero or super – under his grease-paint is a real person with an off-stage life. The dramatic person could not tread the stage unless he concealed a real person: unless the real and unknown I existed, I would not even make mistakes about the imagined me. And in prayer this real I struggles to speak, for once, from his real being, and to address, for once, not the other actors, but – what shall I call Him? The Author, for He invented us all? The Producer, for He controls all? Or the Audience, for He watches, and will judge, the performance?

The attempt is not to escape from space and time and from my creaturely situation as a subject facing objects. It is more modest: to reawake the awareness of that situation. If that can be done, there is no need to go anywhere else. This situation itself, is, at every moment, a possible theophany. Here is the holy ground; the Bush is burning now.

Of course this attempt may be attended with almost every degree of success or failure. The prayer preceding all prayers is, 'May it be the real I who speaks. May it be the real Thou that I speak to.' Infinitely various are the levels from which we pray. Emotional intensity is in itself no proof of spiritual depth. If we pray in terror we shall pray earnestly; it only proves that terror is an earnest emotion. Only God Himself can let the bucket down to the depths in us. And, on the other side, He must constantly work as the iconoclast. Every idea of Him we form, He must in mercy shatter. The most blessed result of prayer would be to rise thinking, 'But I never knew before. I never dreamed...' I suppose it was at such a moment that Thomas Aquinas said of all his own theology: 'It reminds me of straw.'

16

I didn't mean that a 'bright blur' is my only idea of God. I meant that something of that sort tends to be there when I start praying, and would remain if I made no effort to do better. And 'bright blur' is not a very good description. In fact you can't have a good description of anything so vague. If the description became good it would become false.

Betty's recipe – 'use images as the rest of us do' – doesn't help me much. And which does she mean? Images in the outer world, things made of wood or plaster? Or mental images?

As regards the first kind, I am not, as she suggests, suffering from a phobia about 'idolatry'. I don't think people of our type are in danger of that. We shall always be aware that the image is only a bit of matter. But its use, for me, is very limited. I think the mere fact of keeping one's eyes focused on something – almost any object will do – is some help towards concentration. The visual concentration symbolises, and promotes, the mental. That's one of the ways the body teaches the soul. The lines of a well designed church, free from stunts, drawing one's eyes to the altar, have something of the same effect.

But I think that is all an image does for me. If I tried to get more out of it, I think it would get in the way. For one thing, it will have some artistic merits or (more probably) demerits. Both are a distraction. Again, since there can be no plausible images of the Father or the Spirit, it will usually be an image of Our Lord. The continual and exclusive addressing our prayers to Him surely tends to what has been called 'Jesus-worship'? A religion which has its value; but not, in isolation, the religion Jesus taught.

Mental images may have the same defect, but they give rise to another problem as well.

St Ignatius Loyola (I think it was) advised his pupils to begin their meditations with what he called a *compositio loci*. The Nativity or the Marriage at Cana, or whatever the theme might be, was to be visualised in the fullest possible detail. One of his English followers would even have us look up 'what good Authors write of those places' so as to get the topography, 'the height of the hills and the situation of the townes', correct. Now for two different reasons this is not 'addressed to my condition'.

One is that I live in an archaeological age. We can no longer, as St Ignatius could, believingly introduce the clothes, furniture, and utensils of our age into ancient Palestine. I'd know I wasn't getting them right. I'd know that the very sky and sunlight of those latitudes were different from any my northern imagination could supply. I could no doubt pretend to myself a *naïveté* I don't really possess; but that would cast an unreality over the whole exercise.

The second reason is more important. St Ignatius was a great master, and I am sure he knew what his pupils needed. I conclude that they were people whose visual imagination was weak and needed to be stimulated. But the trouble with people like ourselves is the exact reverse. We can say this to one another because, in our mouths, it is not a boast but a confession. We are agreed that the power – indeed, the compulsion – to visualise is not 'Imagination' in the higher sense, not the Imagination which makes a man either a great author or a sensitive reader. Ridden on a *very* tight rein, this visualising power can sometimes serve true Imagination; very often it merely gets in the way.

If I started with a *compositio loci* I should never reach the meditation. The picture would go on elaborating itself indefinitely and becoming every moment of less spiritual relevance.

There is indeed one mental image which does not lure me away into trivial elaborations. I mean the Crucifixion itself; not seen in terms of all the pictures and crucifixes, but as we must suppose it to have been in its raw, historical reality. But even this is of less spiritual value than one might expect. Compunction, compassion, gratitude – all the fruitful emotions – are strangled. Sheer physical horror leaves no room for them. Nightmare. Even so, the image ought to be periodically faced. But no one could live with it. It did not become a frequent motif of Christian art until the generations which had seen real crucifixions were all dead. As for many hymns and sermons on the subject – endlessly harping on blood, as if that were all that mattered – they must be the work either of people so far above me that they can't reach me, or else of people with no imagination at all. (Some might be cut off from me by both these gulfs.)

Yet mental images play an important part in my prayers. I doubt if any act of will or thought or emotion occurs in me without them. But they seem to help me most when they are most fugitive and fragmentary – rising and bursting like bubbles in champagne or wheeling like rooks in a windy sky: contradicting one another (in logic) as the crowded metaphors of a swift poet may do. Fix on any one, and it goes dead. You must do as Blake would do with a joy; kiss it as it flies. And then, in their total effect, they do mediate to me something very important. It is always something qualitative – more like an adjective than a noun. That, for me, gives it the impact of reality. For I think we respect nouns (and what we think they stand for) too much. All my deepest, and certainly all my earliest, experiences seem to be of sheer quality. The terrible and the lovely are older and solider than terrible and lovely things. If a musical phrase could be translated into words at all it would become an adjective. A great lyric is very like a long, utterly adequate, adjective. Plato was not so silly as the Moderns think when he elevated abstract nouns – that is, adjectives disguised as nouns – into the supreme realities – the Forms.

I know very well that in logic God is a 'substance'. Yet my thirst for quality is authorised even here: 'We give thanks to thee for thy great glory.' He *is* this glory. What He is (the quality) is no abstraction from Him. A personal God, to be sure; but so much more than personal. To speak more soberly, our whole distinction between 'things' and 'qualities', 'substances' and 'attitudes', has no application to Him. Perhaps it has much less than we suppose even to the created universe. Perhaps it is only part of the stage set.

The wave of images, thrown off like a spray from the prayer, all momentary, all correcting, refining, 'inter-animating' one another, and giving a kind of spiritual body to the unimaginable, occurs more, I find, in acts of worship than in petitionary prayers. Of which, perhaps, we have written enough. But I don't regret it. They are the right starting point. They raise all the problems. If anyone attempted to practise, or to discuss, the higher forms without going through this turnstile, I should distrust him. 'The higher does not stand without the lower.' An omission or disdain of petitionary prayer can sometimes, I think, spring not from superior sanctity but from a lack of faith and a consequent preference for levels where the question: 'Am I only doing things to myself?' does not jut out in such apparent crudity.

17

It's comical that you, of all people, should ask my views about prayer as worship or adoration. On this subject you yourself taught me nearly all I know. On a walk in the Forest of Dean. Can you have forgotten?

You first taught me the great principle, 'Begin where you are.' I had thought one had to start by summoning up what we believe about the goodness and greatness of God, by thinking about creation and redemption and 'all the blessings of this life'. You turned to the brook and once more splashed your burning face and hands in the little waterfall and said: 'Why not begin with this?'

And it worked. Apparently you have never guessed how much. That cushiony moss, that coldness and sound and dancing light were no doubt very minor blessings compared with 'the means of grace and the hope of glory'. But then they were manifest. So far as they were concerned, sight had replaced faith. They were not the hope of glory, they were an exposition of the glory itself.

Yet you were not – or so it seemed to me – telling me that 'Nature', or 'the beauties of Nature', manifest the glory. No such abstraction as 'Nature' comes into it. I was learning the far more secret doctrine that *pleasures* are shafts of the glory as it strikes our sensibility. As it impinges on our will or our understanding, we give it different names – goodness or truth or the like. But its flash upon our senses and mood is pleasure.

But aren't there bad, unlawful pleasures? Certainly there are. But in calling them 'bad pleasures' I take it we are using a kind of shorthand. We mean 'pleasures snatched by unlawful acts'. It is the stealing of the apple that is bad, not the sweetness. The sweetness is still a beam from the glory. That does not palliate the stealing. It makes it worse. There is sacrilege in the theft. We have abused a holy thing.

I have tried, since that moment, to make every pleasure into a channel of adoration. I don't mean simply by giving thanks for it. One must of course give thanks, but I mean something different. How shall I put it?

We can't – or I can't – hear the song of a bird simply as a sound. Its meaning or message ('That's a bird') comes with it inevitably – just as one can't see a familiar word in print as a merely visual pattern. The reading is as involuntary as the seeing. When the wind roars I don't just hear the roar; I 'hear the wind'. In the same way it is possible to 'read' as well as to 'have' a pleasure. Or not even 'as well as'. The distinction ought to become, and sometimes is, impossible; to receive it and to recognise its divine source are a single experience. This heavenly fruit is instantly redolent of the orchard where it grew. This sweet air whispers of the country from whence it blows. It is a message. We know we are being touched by a finger of that right hand at which there are pleasures for evermore. There need be no question of thanks or praise as a separate event, something done afterwards. To experience the tiny theophany is itself to adore.

Gratitude exclaims, very properly: 'How good of God to give me this.' Adoration says: 'What must be the quality of that Being whose far-off and momentary coruscations are like this!' One's mind runs back up the sunbeam to the sun.

If I could always be what I aim at being, no pleasure would be too ordinary or too usual for such reception; from the first taste of the air when I look out of the window – one's whole cheek becomes a sort of palate – down to one's soft slippers at bedtime.

I don't always achieve it. One obstacle is inattention. Another is the wrong kind of attention. One could, if one practised, hear simply a roar and not the roaring-of-the-wind. In the same way, only far too easily, one can concentrate on the pleasure as an event in one's own nervous system – subjectify it – and ignore the smell of Deity that hangs about it. A third obstacle is greed. Instead of saying: 'This also is Thou', one may say the fatal word *Encore*. There is also conceit: the dangerous reflection that not everyone can find God in a plain slice of bread and butter, or that others would condemn as simply 'grey' the sky in which I am delightedly observing such delicacies of pearl and dove and silver.

You notice that I am drawing no distinction between sensuous and aesthetic pleasures. But why should I? The line is almost impossible to draw and what use would it be if one succeeded in drawing it?

If this is Hedonism, it is also a somewhat arduous discipline. But it is worth some labour: for in so far as it succeeds, almost every day furnishes us with, so to speak, 'bearings' on the Bright Blur. It becomes brighter but less blurry.

William Law remarks that people are merely 'amusing themselves by asking for the patience which a famine or a persecution would call for if, in the meantime, the weather and every other inconvenience sets them grumbling. One must learn to walk before one can run. So here. We – or at least I – shall not be able to adore God on the highest occasions if we have learned no habit of doing so on the lowest. At best, our faith and reason will tell us that He is adorable, but we shall not have *found* Him so, not have 'tasted and seen'. Any patch of sunlight in a wood will show you something about the sun which you could never get from reading books on astronomy. These pure and spontaneous pleasures are 'patches of Godlight' in the woods of our experience.

Of course one wants the books too. One wants a great many things besides this 'adoration in infinitesimals' which I am preaching. And if I were preaching it in public, instead of feeding it back to the very man who taught it me (though he may by now find the lesson nearly unrecognisable?), I should have to pack it in ice, enclose it in barbed-wire reservations, and stick up warning notices in every direction.

Don't imagine I am forgetting that the simplest act of mere obedience is worship of a far more important sort than what I've been describing (to obey is better than sacrifice). Or that God, besides being the Great Creator, is the Tragic Redeemer. Perhaps the Tragic Creator too. For I am not sure that the great canyon of anguish which lies across our lives is *solely* due to some prehistoric catastrophe. Something tragic may, as I think I've said before, be inherent in the very act of creation. So that one sometimes wonders why God thinks the game worth the candle. But then we share, in some degree, the cost of the candle and have not yet seen the 'game'.

There! I've done it again. I know that my tendency to use images like play and dance for the highest things is a stumbling-block to you. You don't, I admit, accuse me of profanity, as you used to – like the night we nearly came to blows at Edinburgh. You now, much more reasonably, call it 'heartless'. You feel it a brutal mockery of every martyr and every slave that a world-process which is so desperately serious to the actors should, at whatever celestial apex, be seen in terms of frivolities. And you add that it comes with a ludicrously ill grace from me who never enjoyed any game and can dance no better than a centipede with wooden legs. But I still think you don't see the real point.

I do *not* think that the life of Heaven bears any analogy to play or dance in respect of frivolity. I do think that while we are in this 'valley of tears', cursed with labour, hemmed round with necessities, tripped up with frustrations, doomed to perpetual plannings, puzzlings, and anxieties, certain qualities that must belong to the celestial condition have no chance to get through, can project no image of themselves, except in activities which, for us here and now, are frivolous. For surely we must suppose the life of the blessed to be an end in itself, indeed The End: to be utterly spontaneous; to be the complete reconciliation of boundless freedom with order – with the most delicately adjusted, supple, intricate, and beautiful order? How can you find any image of this in the 'serious' activities either of our natural or of our (present) spiritual life? – either in our precarious and heart-broken affections or in the Way which is always, in some degree, a *via crucis*: No, Malcolm. It is only in our 'hours-off', only in our moments of permitted festivity, that we find an analogy. Dance and game *are* frivolous, unimportant down here; for 'down here' is not their natural place. Here, they are a moment's rest from the life we were placed here to live. But in this world everything is upside down. That which, if it could be prolonged here, would be a truancy, is likest that which in a better country is the End of ends. Joy is the serious business of Heaven.

18

I plead guilty. When I was writing about pleasures last week I had quite forgotten about the *mala mentis gaudia* – the pleasures of the mind which are intrinsically evil. The pleasure, say, of having a grievance. What a disappointment it is – for one self-revealing moment – to discover that the other party was not really to blame? And how a resentment, while it lasts, draws one back and back to nurse and fondle and encourage it! It behaves just like a lust. But I don't think this leaves my theory (and experience) of ordinary pleasures in ruins. Aren't these intrinsically vicious pleasures, as Plato said, 'mixed'. To use his own image, given the itch, one wants to scratch it. And if you abstain, the temptation is very severe, and if you scratch there is a sort of pleasure in the momentary and deceptive relief. But one didn't want to itch. The scratch is not a pleasure simply, but only by comparison with the context. In the same way, resentment is pleasant only as a relief from, or alternative to, humiliation. I still think that those experiences which are pleasures in their own right can all be regarded as I suggest.

The mere mention of the horrible pleasures – the dainties of Hell – very naturally led you away from the subject of adoration to that of repentance. I'm going to follow you into your digression, for you said something I disagreed with.

I admit of course that penitential prayers – 'acts' of penitence, as I believe they are called – can be on very different levels. At the lowest, what you call 'Pagan penitence', there is simply the attempt to placate a supposedly angry power – 'I'm sorry. I won't do it again. Let me off this time.' At the highest level, you say, the attempt is rather to restore an infinitely valued and vulnerable personal relation which has been shattered by an action of one's own, and if forgiveness, in the 'crude' sense of remission of penalty, comes in, this is valued chiefly as a symptom or seal or even by-product of the reconciliation. I expect you are right about that. I say 'expect' because I can't claim to know much by experience about the highest level either of penitence or of anything else. The ceiling, if there is one, is a long way off.

All the same, there is a difference between us. I can't agree to call your lowest level 'Pagan penitence'. Doesn't your description cover a great deal of Old Testament penitence? Look at the psalms. Doesn't it cover a good deal of Christian penitence – a good deal that is embodied in Christian liturgies? 'Neither take thou vengeance for our sins . . . be not angry with us forever . . . *neque secundum iniquitates nostras retribuas nobis.*'

Here, as nearly always, what we regard as 'crude' and 'low', and what presumably is in fact lowest, spreads far further up the Christian life than we like to admit. And do we find anywhere in Scripture or in the Fathers that explicit and resounding rejection of it which would be so welcome?

I fully grant you that 'wrath' can be attributed to God only by an analogy. The situation of the penitent before God isn't, but is somehow like, that of one appearing before a justly angered sovereign, lover, father, master, or teacher. But what more can we know about it than just this likeness? Trying to get in behind the analogy, you go further and fare worse. You suggest that what is traditionally regarded as our experience of God's anger would be more helpfully regarded as what inevitably happens to us if we behave inappropriately towards a reality of immense power. As you say, 'The live wire doesn't feel angry with us, but if we blunder against it we get a shock.'

My dear Malcolm, what do you suppose you have gained by substituting the image of a live wire for that of angered majesty? You have shut us all up in despair; for the angry can forgive, and electricity can't.

And you give as your reason that 'even by analogy the sort of pardon which arises because a fit of temper is spent cannot worthily be attributed to God nor gratefully accepted by man.' But the belittling words 'fit of temper' are your own choice. Think of the fullest reconciliation between mortals. Is cool disapproval coolly assuaged? Is the culprit let down lightly in a view of 'extenuating circumstances'? Was peace restored by a moral lecture? Was the offence said not to 'matter'? Was it hushed up or passed over? Blake knew better:

I was angry with my friend;
I told my wrath. My wrath did end.
I was angry with my foe;
I hid my wrath. My wrath did grow.

You too know better. Anger – no peevish fit of temper, but just, generous, scalding indignation – passes (not necessarily at once) into embracing, exultant, re-welcoming love. That is how friends and lovers are truly reconciled. Hot wrath, hot love. Such anger is the fluid that love bleeds when you cut it. The *angers*, not the measured remonstrances, of lovers are love's renewal. Wrath and pardon are both, as applied to God, analogies; but they belong together to the same circle of analogy – the circle of life, and love, and deeply personal relationships. All the liberalising and 'civilising' analogies only lead us astray. Turn God's wrath into mere enlightened disapproval, and you also turn His love into mere humanitarianism. The 'consuming fire' and the 'perfect beauty' both vanish. We have, instead, a judicious headmistress or a conscientious magistrate. It comes of being high-minded.

I know that 'the wrath of man worketh not the righteousness of God'. That is not because wrath is wrath but because man is (fallen) man.

But perhaps I've already said too much. All that any imagery can do is to facilitate, or at least not to impede, man's act of penitence and reception of pardon. We cannot see the matter 'from God's side'.

The crude picture of penitence as something like apology or even placation has, for me, the value of making penitence an act. The more high-minded views involve some danger of regarding it simply as a state of feeling. Do you agree that this would be unwholesome?

The question is before my mind at present because I've been reading Alexander Whyte. Morris lent him to me. He was a Presbyterian divine of the last century, whom I'd never heard of. Very well worth reading, and strangely broad-minded – Dante, Pascal, and even Newman, are among his heroes. But I mention him at the moment for a different reason. He brought me violently face to face with a characteristic of Puritanism which I had almost forgotten. For him, one essential symptom of the regenerate life is a permanent, and permanently horrified, perception of one's natural and (it seems) unalterable corruption. The true Christian's nostril is to be continually attentive to the inner cess-pool. I knew that the experience was a regular feature of the old conversion stories. As in *Grace Abounding*: 'But my inward and original corruption ... that I had the guilt of to amazement ... I was more loathsome in mine own eyes than was a toad ... sin and corruption, I said, would as naturally bubble out of my heart, as water would bubble out of a fountain.' Another author, quoted in Haller's *Rise of Puritanism* says that when he looked into his heart, it was 'as if I had in the heat of summer lookt down into the Filth of a Dungeon, where I discerned Millions of crawling living things in the midst of that Sink and liquid Corruption.'

I won't listen to those who describe that vision as merely pathological. I have seen the 'slimy things that crawled with legs' in my own dungeon. I thought the glimpse taught me sense. But Whyte seems to think it should be not a glimpse but a daily, lifelong scrutiny. Can he be right? It sounds so very unlike the New Testament fruits of the spirit – love, joy, peace. And very unlike the Pauline programme; 'forgetting those things which are behind and reaching forth unto those things that are before.' And very unlike St François de Sales' green, dewy chapter on *la douceur* towards one's self. Anyway, what's the use of laying down a programme of permanent emotions? They can be permanent only by being factitious.

What do you think? I know that a spiritual emetic, at the right moment, may be needed. But not a regular diet of emetics! If one survived, one would develop a 'tolerance' of them. This poring over the 'sink' might breed its own perverse pride:

over-just and self-displeased
For self-offence more than for God offended.

Anyway, in solitude, and also in confession, I have found (to my regret) that the degrees of shame and disgust which I actually feel at my own sins do not at all correspond to what my reason tells me about their comparative gravity. Just as the degree to which, in daily life, I feel the emotion of fear has very little to do with my rational judgment of the danger. I'd sooner have really nasty seas when I'm in an open boat than look down in perfect (actual) safety from the edge of a cliff. Similarly, I have confessed ghastly uncharities with less reluctance than small unmentionables – or those sins which happen to be ungentlemanly as well as un-Christian. Our emotional reactions to our own behaviour are of limited ethical significance.

19

Tell Betty that if you hadn't whisked me off on to the subject of repentance, I was just going to say the very thing she blames me for not saying. I was going to say that in adoration, more than in any other kind of prayer, the public or communal act is of the utmost importance. One would lose incomparably more by being prevented from going to church on Easter than on Good Friday. And, even in private, adoration should be communal – 'with angels and archangels and all the company', all the transparent publicity of Heaven. On the other hand, I find that the prayers to which I can most fully attend in church are always those I have most often used in my bedroom.

I deny, with some warmth, the charge of being 'choosy about services'. My whole point was that any form will do me if only I'm given time to get used to it. The idea of allowing myself to be put off by mere inadequacy – an ugly church, a gawky server, a badly turned out celebrant – is horrible. On the contrary, it constantly surprises me how little these things matter, as if

never anything can be amiss
When simpleness and duty tender it.

One of the golden Communions of my life was in a Nissen hut. Sometimes the cockney accent of a choir has a singularly touching quality. A tin mug for a chalice, if there were good reason for it, would not distress me in the least. (I wonder what sort of crockery was used at the Last Supper?)

You ask me why I've never written anything about the Holy Communion. For the very simple reason that I am not good enough at Theology. I have nothing to offer. Hiding any light I think I've got under a bushel is not my besetting sin! I am much more prone to prattle unseasonably. But there is a point at which even I would gladly keep silent. The trouble is that people draw conclusions even from silence. Someone said in print the other day that I seemed to 'admit rather than welcome' the sacraments.

I wouldn't like you and Betty to think the same. But as soon as I try to tell you anything more, I see another reason for silence. It is almost impossible to state the negative effect which certain doctrines have on me – my failure to be nourished by them – without seeming to mount an attack against them. But the very last thing I want to do is to unsettle in the mind of any Christian, whatever his denomination, the concepts – for him traditional – by which he finds it profitable to represent to himself what is happening when he receives the bread and wine. I could wish that no definitions had ever been felt to be necessary; and, still more, that none had been allowed to make divisions between churches.

Some people seem able to discuss different theories of this act as if they understood them all and needed only evidence as to which was best. This light has been withheld from me. I do not know and can't imagine what the disciples understood Our Lord to mean when, His body still unbroken and His blood unshed, He handed them the bread and wine, saying *they* were His body and blood. I can find within the forms of my human understanding no connection between eating a man – and it is as Man that the Lord has flesh – and entering into any spiritual oneness or community or κοινωνία with him. And I find 'substance' (in Aristotle's sense), when stripped of its own accidents and endowed with the accidents of some other substance, an object I cannot think. My effort to do so produces mere nursery-thinking – a picture of something like very rarefied Plasticine. On the other hand, I get on no better with those who tell me that the elements are mere bread and mere wine, used symbolically to remind me of the death of Christ. They are, on the natural level, such a very odd symbol of *that*. But it would be profane to suppose that they are as arbitrary as they seem to me. I well believe there is in reality an appropriateness, even a necessity, in their selection. But it remains, for me, hidden. Again, if they are, if the whole act is, simply memorial, it would seem to follow that its value must be purely psychological, and dependent on the recipient's sensibility at the moment of reception. And I cannot see why *this* particular reminder – a hundred other things may, psychologically, remind me of Christ's death, equally, or perhaps more – should be so uniquely important as all Christendom (and my own heart) unhesitatingly declare.

However, then, it may be for others, for me the something which holds together and 'informs' all the objects, words, and actions of this rite, is unknown and unimaginable. I am not saying to any one in the world: 'Your explanation is wrong.' I am saying: 'Your explanation leaves the mystery for me still a mystery.'

Yet I find no difficulty in believing that the veil between the worlds, nowhere else (for me) so opaque to the intellect, is nowhere else so thin and permeable to divine operation. Here a hand from the hidden country touches not only my soul but my body. Here the prig, the don, the modern, in me have no privilege over the savage or the child. Here is big medicine and strong magic. *Favete linguis*.

When I say 'Magic' I am not thinking of the paltry and pathetic techniques by which fools attempt and quacks pretend to control Nature. I mean rather what is suggested by fairy-tale sentences like: 'This is a magic flower, and if you carry it the seven gates will open to you of their own accord', or: 'This is a magic cave and those who enter it will renew their youth.' I should define magic in this sense as 'objective efficacy which cannot be further analysed'.

Magic, in this sense, will always win a response from a normal imagination because it is in principle so 'true to nature'. Mix these two powders and there will be an explosion. Eat a grain of this and you will die. Admittedly, the 'magical' element in such truths can be got rid of by explanation; that is, by seeing them to be instances or consequences of larger truths. Which larger truths remain 'magical' till they also are, in the same way, explained. In that fashion, the sciences are always pushing further back the realm of mere 'brute fact'. But no scientist, I suppose, believes that the process could ever reach completion. At the very least, there must always remain the utterly 'brute' fact, the completely opaque *datum*, that a universe – or rather *this* universe with its determinate character – exists; as 'magical' as the magic flower in the fairy tale.

Now the value, for me, of the magical element in Christianity is this. It is a permanent witness that the heavenly realm, certainly no less than the natural universe and perhaps very much more, is a realm of objective facts – hard, determinate facts, not to be constructed *a priori*, and not to be dissolved into maxims, ideals, values, and the like. One cannot conceive a more completely 'given', or, if you like, a more 'magical', fact than the existence of God as *causa sui*.

Enlightened people want to get rid of this magical element in favour of what they would call the 'spiritual' element. But the spiritual, conceived as something thus antithetical to 'magical', seems to become merely the psychological or ethical. And neither that by itself, nor the magical by itself, is a religion. I am not going to lay down rules as to the share – quantitatively considered – which the magical should have in anyone's religious life. Individual differences may be permissible. What I insist on is that it can never be reduced to zero. If it is, what remains is only morality, or culture, or philosophy.

What makes some theological works like sawdust to me is the way the authors can go on discussing how far certain positions are adjustable to contemporary thought, or beneficial in relation to social problems, or 'have a future' before them, but never squarely ask what grounds we have for supposing them to be true accounts of any objective reality. As if we were trying to make rather than to learn. Have we no Other to reckon with?

I hope I do not offend God by making my communions in the frame of mind I have been describing. The command, after all, was Take, eat: not Take, understand. Particularly, I hope I need not be tormented by the question 'What is this?' – this wafer, this sip of wine. That has a dreadful effect on me. It invites me to take 'this' out of its holy context and regard it as an object among objects, indeed as part of nature. It is like taking a red coal out of the fire to examine it: it becomes a dead coal. To me, I mean. All this is autobiography, not theology.

20

I really must digress to tell you a bit of good news. Last week, while at prayer, I suddenly discovered – or felt as if I did – that I had forgiven someone I had been trying to forgive for over thirty years. Trying, and praying that I might. When the thing actually happened – sudden as the longed-for cessation of one's neighbour's radio – my feeling was 'But it's so easy. Why didn't you do it ages ago?' So many things are done easily the moment you can do them at all. But till then, sheerly impossible, like learning to swim. There are months during which no efforts will keep you up; then comes the day and hour and minute after which, and ever after, it becomes almost impossible to sink. It also seemed to me that forgiving (that man's cruelty) and being forgiven (my resentment) were the very same thing. 'Forgive and you shall be forgiven' sounds like a bargain. But perhaps it is something much more. By heavenly standards, that is, for pure intelligence, it is perhaps a tautology – forgiving and being forgiven are two names for the same thing. The important thing is that a discord has been resolved, and it is certainly the great Resolver who has done it. Finally, and perhaps best of all, I believed anew what is taught us in the parable of the Unjust Judge. No evil habit is so ingrained nor so long prayed against (as it seemed) in vain, that it cannot, even in dry old age, be whisked away.

I wonder, do the long dead know it when we at last, after countless failures, succeed in forgiving them? It would be a pity if they don't. A pardon given but not received would be frustrated. Which brings me to your question.

Of course I pray for the dead. The action is so spontaneous, so all but inevitable, that only the most compulsive theological case against it would deter me. And I hardly know how the rest of my prayers would survive if those for the dead were forbidden. At our age the majority of those we love best are dead. What sort of intercourse with God could I have if what I love best were unmentionable to Him?

On the traditional Protestant view, all the dead are damned or saved. If they are damned, prayer for them is useless. If they are saved, it is equally useless. God has already done all for them. What more should we ask?

But don't we believe that God has already done and is already doing all that He can for the living? What more should we ask? Yet we are told to ask.

'Yes,' it will be answered, 'but the living are still on the road. Further trials, developments, possibilities of error, await them. But the saved have been made perfect. They have finished the course. To pray for them presupposes that progress and difficulty are still possible. In fact, you are bringing in something like Purgatory.'

Well, I suppose I am. Though even in Heaven some perpetual increase of beatitude, reached by a continually more ecstatic selfsurrender, without the possibility of failure but not perhaps without its own ardours and exertions – for delight also has its severities and steep ascents, as lovers know – might be supposed. But I won't press, or guess, that side for the moment. I believe in Purgatory.

Mind you, the Reformers had good reasons for throwing doubt on 'the Romish doctrine concerning Purgatory' as that Romish doctrine had then become. I don't mean merely the commercial scandal. If you turn from Dante's *Purgatorio* to the Sixteenth Century you will be appalled by the degradation. In Thomas More's *Supplication of Souls* Purgatory is simply temporary Hell. In it the souls are tormented by devils, whose presence is 'more horrible and grievous to us than is the pain itself'. Worse still, Fisher, in his Sermon on Psalm VI, says the tortures are so intense that the spirit who suffers them cannot, for pain, 'remember God as he ought to do'. In fact, the very etymology of the word *purgatory* has dropped out of sight. Its pains do not bring us nearer to God, but make us forget Him. It is a place not of purification but purely of retributive punishment.

The right view returns magnificently in Newman's *Dream*. There, if I remember rightly, the saved soul, at the very foot of the throne, begs to be taken away and cleansed. It cannot bear for a moment longer 'With its darkness to affront that light.' Religion has reclaimed Purgatory.

Our souls *demand* Purgatory, don't they? Would it not break the heart if God said to us, 'It is true, my son, that your breath smells and your rags drip with mud and slime, but we are charitable here and no one will upbraid you with these things, nor draw away from you. Enter into the joy'? Should we not reply, 'With submission, sir, and if there is no objection, I'd *rather* be cleaned first.' 'It may hurt, you know.' – 'Even so, sir.'

I assume that the process of purification will normally involve suffering. Partly from tradition; partly because most real good that has been done me in this life has involved it. But I don't think suffering is the purpose of the purgation. I can well believe that people neither much worse nor much better than I will suffer less than I or more. 'No nonsense about merit.'

The treatment given will be the one required, whether it hurts little or much.

My favourite image on this matter comes from the dentist's chair. I hope that when the tooth of life is drawn and I am 'coming round', a voice will say, 'Rinse your mouth out with this.' *This* will be Purgatory. The rinsing may take longer than I can now imagine. The taste of *this* may be more fiery and astringent than my present sensibility could endure. But More and Fisher shall not persuade me that it will be disgusting and unhallowed.

Your own peculiar difficulty – that the dead are not in time – is another matter.

How do you know they are not? I certainly believe that to be God is to enjoy an infinite present, where nothing has yet passed away and nothing is still to come. Does it follow that we can say the same of saints and angels? Or at any rate exactly the same? The dead might experience a time which was not quite so linear as ours – it might, so to speak, have thickness as well as length. Already in this life we get some thickness whenever we learn to attend to more than one thing at once. One can suppose this increased to any extent, so that though, for them as for us, the present is always becoming the past, yet each present contains unimaginably more than ours.

I *feel* – can you work it out for me and tell me if it is more than a feeling – that to make the life of the blessed dead strictly timeless is inconsistent with the resurrection of the body.

Again, as you and I have agreed, whether we pray on behalf of the living or the dead, the causes which will prevent or exclude the events we pray for are in fact already at work. Indeed they are part of a series which, I suppose, goes back as far as the creation of the universe. The causes which made George's illness a trivial one were already operating while we prayed about it; if it had been what we feared, the causes of that would have been operative. That is why, as I hold, our prayers are granted, or not, in eternity. The task of dovetailing the spiritual and physical histories of the world into each other is accomplished in the total act of creation itself. Our prayers, and other free acts, are known to us only as we come to the moment of doing them. But they are eternally in the score of the great symphony. Not 'predetermined'; the syllable *pre* lets in the notion of eternity as simply an older time. For though we cannot experience our life as an endless present, we are eternal in God's eyes; that is, in our deepest reality. When I say we are 'in time' I don't mean that we are, impossibly, outside the endless present in which He beholds us as He beholds all else. I mean, our creaturely limitation is that our fundamentally timeless reality can be experienced by us only in the mode of succession.

In fact we began by putting the question wrongly. The question is not whether the dead are part of timeless reality. They are; so is a flash of lightning. The question is whether they share the divine perception of timelessness.

Tell George I should be delighted. *Rendez-vous* in my rooms at 7.15. We do *not* dress for dinner on ordinary nights.

21

Betty is quite right – 'all this about prayer and never a word on the practical problem: its irksomeness.' And she sees fit to add, 'Anyone might think it was a correspondence between two saints!'

That was a barbed shaft and went home. And yet I don't really think we are being hypocritical. Doesn't the mere fact of putting something into words of itself involve an exaggeration? Prose words, I mean. Only poetry can speak low enough to catch the faint murmur of the mind, the 'litel winde, unethe hit might be lesse'. The other day I tried to describe to you a very minimal experience – the tiny wisps of adoration with which (sometimes) I salute my pleasures. But I now see that putting it down in black and white made it sound far bigger than it really is. The truth is, I haven't any language weak enough to depict the weakness of my spiritual life. If I weakened it enough it would cease to be language at all. Like when you try to turn the gas-ring a little lower still, and it merely goes out.

Then again, by talking at this length about prayer at all, we seem to give it a much bigger place in our lives than, I'm afraid, it has. For while we talk about it, all the rest of our experience, which in reality crowds our prayer into the margin or sometimes off the page altogether, is not mentioned. Hence, in the talk, an error of proportion which amounts to, though it was not intended for, a lie.

Well, let's now at any rate come clean. Prayer *is* irksome. An excuse to omit it is never unwelcome. When it is over, this casts a feeling of relief and holiday over the rest of the day. We are reluctant to begin. We are delighted to finish. While we are at prayer, but not while we are reading a novel or solving a crossword puzzle, any trifle is enough to distract us.

And we know that we are not alone in this. The fact that prayers are constantly set as penances tells its own tale.

The odd thing is that this reluctance to pray is not confined to periods of dryness. When yesterday's prayers were full of comfort and exaltation, today's will still be felt as, in some degree, a burden.

Now the disquieting thing is not simply that we skimp and begrudge the duty of prayer. The really disquieting thing is it should have to be numbered among duties at all. For we believe that we were created to 'glorify God and enjoy Him forever'. And if the few, the very few, minutes we now spend on intercourse with God are a burden to us rather than a delight, what then? If I were a Calvinist this symptom would fill me with despair. What can be done *for* – or what should be done *with* – a rose-tree that *dislikes* producing roses? Surely it ought to want to?

Much of our backwardness in prayer is no doubt due to our sins, as every teacher will tell us; to our avoidable immersion in the things of this world, to our neglect of mental discipline. And also to the very worst kind of 'fear of God'. We shrink from too naked a contact, because we are afraid of the divine demands upon us which it might make too audible. As some old writer says, many a Christian prays faintly 'lest God might really hear him, which he, poor man, never intended.' But sins – at any rate, our actual and individual sins – are not perhaps the only cause.

By the very constitution of our minds as they now are – whatever they may have been when God first made man – it is difficult for us to concentrate on anything which is neither sensible (like potatoes) nor abstract (like numbers). What is concrete but immaterial can be kept in view only by painful effort. Some would say, 'Because it does not exist.' But the rest of our experience cannot accept that solution. For we ourselves, and all that we most care about, seem to come in the class 'concrete (that is, individual) and insensible'. If reality consists of nothing but physical objects and abstract concepts, then reality has, in the last resort, nothing to say to us. We are in the wrong universe. Man is a *passion inutile*; and so, good night. And yet, the supposedly real universe has been quarried out of man's sensuous experiences.

The painful effort which prayer involves is no proof that we are doing something we were not created to do.

If we were perfected, prayer would not be a duty, it would be delight. Some day, please God, it will be. The same is true of many other behaviours which now appear as duties. If I loved my neighbour as myself, most of the actions which are now my moral duty would flow out of me as spontaneously as song from a lark or fragrance from a flower. Why is this not so yet? Well, we know, don't we? Aristotle has taught us that delight is the 'bloom' on an unimpeded activity. 'But the very activities for which we were created are, while we live on earth, variously impeded: by evil in ourselves or in others. Not to practise them is to abandon our humanity. To practise them spontaneously and delightfully is not yet possible. This situation creates the category of duty, the whole specifically *moral* realm.

It exists to be transcended. Here is the paradox of Christianity. As practical imperatives for here and now the two great commandments have to be translated 'Behave *as if* you loved God and man.' For no man can love because he is told to. Yet obedience on this practical level is not really obedience at all. And if a man really loved God and man, once again this would hardly be obedience; for if he did, he would be unable to help it. Thus the command really says to us, 'Ye must be born again.' Till then, we have duty, morality, the Law. A schoolmaster, as St Paul says, to bring us to Christ. We must expect no more of it than of a schoolmaster; we must allow it no less. I must say my prayers today whether I feel devout or not; but that is only as I must learn my grammar if I am ever to read the poets.

But the school-days, please God, are numbered. There is no morality in Heaven. The angels never knew (from within) the meaning of the word *ought*, and the blessed dead have long since gladly forgotten it. This is why Dante's Heaven is so right, and Milton's, with its military discipline, so silly. This also explains – to pick up an earlier point – why we have to picture that world in terms which seem almost frivolous. In this world our most momentous actions are impeded. We can picture unimpeded, and therefore delighted, action only by the analogy of our present play and leisure. Thus we get the notion that what is as free as they would have to matter as little.

I said, mind you, that 'most' of the behaviour which is now duty would be spontaneous and delightful if we were, so to speak, good rose-trees. Most, not all. There is, or might be, martyrdom. We are not called upon to like it. Our Master didn't. But the principle holds, that duty is always conditioned by evil. Martyrdom, by the evil in the persecutor; other duties, by lack of love in myself or by the general diffused evil of the world. In the perfect and eternal world the Law will vanish. But the results of having lived faithfully under it will not.

I am therefore not really deeply worried by the fact that prayer is at present a duty, and even an irksome one. This is humiliating. It is frustrating. It is terribly time-wasting – the worse one is praying, the longer one's prayers take. But we are still only at school. Or, like Donne, 'I tune my instrument here at the door.' And even now – how can I weaken the words enough, how speak at all without exaggeration? – we have what seem rich moments. Most frequently, perhaps, in our momentary, only just voluntary, ejaculations; refreshments 'unimplored, unsought, Happy for man so coming'.

But I don't rest much on that; nor would I if it were ten times as much as it is. I have a notion that what seem our worst prayers may really be, in God's eyes, our best. Those, I mean, which are least supported by devotional feeling and contend with the greatest disinclination. For these, perhaps, being nearly all will, come from a deeper level than feeling. In feeling there is so much that is really not ours – so much that comes from weather and health or from the last book read. One thing seems certain. It is no good angling for the rich moments. God sometimes seems to speak to us most intimately when He catches us, as it were, off our guard. Our preparations to receive Him sometimes have the opposite effect. Doesn't Charles Williams say somewhere that 'the altar must often be built in one place in order that the fire from heaven may descend *somewhere else*'?

22

By not belonging to a press-cutting agency I miss most of the bouquets and brickbats which are aimed at me. So I never saw the article you write about. But I have seen others of that kind, and they'll break no bones of mine. Don't, however, misjudge these 'liberal Christians'. They genuinely believe that writers of my sort are doing a great deal of harm.

They themselves find it impossible to accept most of the articles of the 'faith once given to the saints'. They are nevertheless extremely anxious that some vestigial religion which they (not we) can describe as 'Christianity' should continue to exist and make numerous converts. They think these converts will come in only if this religion is sufficiently 'de-mythologised'. The ship must be lightened if she is to keep afloat.

It follows that, to them, the most mischievous people in the world are those who, like myself, proclaim that Christianity essentially involves the supernatural. They are quite sure that belief in the supernatural never will, nor should, be revived, and that if we convince the world that it must choose between accepting the supernatural and abandoning all pretence of Christianity, the world will undoubtedly choose the second alternative. It will thus be we, not the liberals, who have really sold the pass. We shall have re-attached to the name *Christian* a deadly scandal from which, but for us, they might have succeeded in decontaminating it.

If, then, some tone of resentment creeps into their comments on our work, can you blame them? But it would be unpardonable if we allowed ourselves any resentment against them. We do in some measure queer their pitch. But they make no similar contribution to the forces of secularism. It has already a hundred champions who carry far more weight than they. Liberal Christianity can only supply an ineffectual echo to the massive chorus of agreed and admitted unbelief. Don't be deceived by the fact that this echo so often 'hits the headlines'. That is because attacks on Christian doctrine which would pass unnoticed if they were launched (as they are daily launched) by anyone else, become News when the attacker is a clergyman;

just as a very commonplace protest against make-up would be News if it came from a film star.

By the way, did you ever meet, or hear of, anyone who was converted from scepticism to a 'liberal' or 'demythologised' Christianity? I think that when unbelievers come in at all, they come in a good deal further.

Not, of course, that either group is to be judged by its success, as if the question were one of tactics. The liberals are honest men and preach their version of Christianity, as we preach ours, because they believe it to be true. A man who first tried to guess 'what the public wants,' and then preached that as Christianity *because* the public wants it, would be a pretty mixture of fool and knave.

I am enlarging on this because even you, in your last letter, seemed to hint that there was too much of the supernatural in my position; especially in the sense that 'the next world' loomed so large. But how can it loom less than large if it is believed in at all?

You know my history. You know why my withers are quite unwrung by the fear that I was bribed – that I was lured into Christianity by the hope of everlasting life. I believed in God before I believed in Heaven. And even now, even if – let's make an impossible supposition – His voice, unmistakably His, said to me, They have misled you. I can do nothing of that sort for you. My long struggle with the blind forces is nearly over. I die, children. The story is ending' – would that be a moment for changing sides? Would not you and I take the Viking way: 'The Giants and Trolls win. Let us die on the right side, with Father Odin.'

But if it is not so, if that other world is once admitted, how can it, except by sensual or bustling preoccupations, be kept in the background of our minds? How can the 'rest of Christianity' – what is this 'rest'? – be disentangled from it? How can we untwine this idea, if once admitted, from our present experience, in which, even before we believed, so many things at least *looked* like 'bright shoots of everlastingness'?

And yet ... after all, I know. It is a venture. We don't *know* it will be. There is our freedom, our chance for a little generosity, a little sportsmanship.

Isn't it possible that many 'liberals' have a highly illiberal motive for banishing the idea of Heaven? They want the gilt-edged security of a religion so contrived that no possible fact could ever refute it. In such a religion they have the comfortable feeling that, whatever the real universe may be like, they will not have 'been had' or 'backed the wrong horse'. It is close to the spirit of the man who hid his talent in a napkin – 'I know you are a hard man and I'm taking no risks.' But surely the sort of religion they want would consist of nothing but tautologies?

About the resurrection of the body. I agree with you that the old picture of the soul reassuming the corpse – perhaps blown to bits or long since usefully dissipated through nature – is absurd. Nor is it what St Paul's words imply. And I admit that if you ask what I substitute for this, I have only speculations to offer.

The principle behind these speculations is this. We are not, in this doctrine, concerned with matter as such at all: with waves and atoms and all that. What the soul cries out for is the resurrection of the senses. Even in this life matter would be nothing to us if it were not the source of sensations.

Now we already have some feeble and intermittent power of raising dead sensations from their graves. I mean, of course, memory.

You see the way my thought is moving. But don't run away with the idea that when I speak of the resurrection of the body I mean merely that the blessed dead will have excellent memories of their sensuous experiences on earth. I mean it the other way round: that memory as we now know it is a dim foretaste, a mirage even, of a power which the soul, or rather Christ in the soul (he 'went to prepare a place for us') will exercise hereafter. It need no longer be intermittent. Above all, it need no longer be private to the soul in which it occurs. I can now communicate to you the vanished fields of my boyhood – they are building-estates today – only imperfectly by words. Perhaps the day is coming when I can take you for a walk through them.

At present we tend to think of the soul as somehow 'inside' the body. But the glorified body of the resurrection as I conceive it – the sensuous life raised from its death – will be inside the soul. As God is not in space but space is in God.

I have slipped in 'glorified' almost unawares. But this glorification is not only promised, it is already foreshadowed. The dullest of us knows how memory can transfigure; how often some momentary glimpse of beauty in boyhood is

... a whisper
Which memory will warehouse as a shout.

Don't talk to me of the 'illusions' of memory. Why should what we see at the moment be more 'real' than what we see from ten years' distance? It is indeed an illusion to believe that the blue hills on the horizon would still look blue if you went to them. But the fact that they are blue five miles away, and the fact that they are green when you are on them, are equally good facts. Traherne's 'orient and immortal wheat' or Wordsworth's landscape 'apparelled in celestial light' may not have been so radiant in the past when it was present as in the remembered past. That is the beginning of the glorification. One day they will be more radiant still. Thus in the sense-bodies of the redeemed the whole New Earth will arise. The same yet not the same as this. It was sown in corruption, it is raised in incorruption.

I dare not omit, though it may be mocked and misunderstood, the extreme example. The strangest discovery of a widower's life is the possibility, sometimes, of recalling with detailed and uninhibited imagination, with tenderness and gratitude, a passage of carnal love, yet with no re-awakening of concupiscence. And when this occurs (it must not be sought) awe comes upon us. It is like seeing Nature itself rising from its grave. What was sown in momentariness is raised in still permanence. What was sown as a becoming rises as being. Sown in subjectivity, it rises in objectivity. The transitory secret of two is now a chord in the ultimate music.

'But this,' you protest, 'is no resurrection of the *body*. You have given the dead a sort of dream world and dream bodies. They are not real.' Surely neither less nor more real than those you have always known: you know better than I that the 'real world' of our present experience (coloured, resonant, soft or hard, cool or warm, all corseted by perspective) has no place in the world described by physics or even physiology. Matter enters our experience only by becoming sensation (when we perceive it) or conception (when we understand it). That is, by becoming soul. That element in the soul which it becomes will, in my view, be raised and glorified; the hills and valleys of Heaven will be to those you now experience not as a copy is to an original, nor as a substitute to the genuine article, but as the flower to the root, or the diamond to the coal. It will be eternally true that they originate with matter; let us therefore bless matter. But in entering our soul as alone it can enter – that is, by being perceived and known – matter has turned into soul (like the Undines who acquired a soul by marriage with a mortal).

I don't say the resurrection of this body will happen at once. It may well be that this part of us sleeps in death and the intellectual soul is sent to Lenten lands where she fasts in naked spirituality – a ghostlike and imperfectly human condition. I don't imply that an angel is a ghost. But naked spirituality is in accordance with his nature: not, I think, with ours. (A two-legged horse is maimed but not a two-legged man.) Yet from that fact my hope is that we shall return and re-assume the wealth we laid down.

Then the new earth and sky, the same yet not the same as these, will rise in us as we have risen in Christ. And once again, after who knows what aeons of the silence and the dark, the birds will sing out and the waters flow, and lights and shadows move across the hills and the faces of our friends laugh upon us with amazed recognition.

Guesses, of course, only guesses. If they are not true, something better will be. For we know that we shall be made like Him, for we shall see Him as He is.

Thank Betty for her note. I'll come by the later train, the 3.40. And tell her not to bother about a bed on the ground floor. I can manage stairs again now, provided I take them 'in bottom'. Till Saturday.

REFLECTIONS ON THE PSALMS

To
Austin and Katharine Farrer

Contents

1	Introductory	309
2	'Judgement' in the Psalms	313
3	The Cursings	319
4	Death in the Psalms	327
5	'The fair beauty of the Lord'	333
6	'Sweeter than Honey'	338
7	Connivance	344
8	Nature	350
9	A Word about Praising	358
10	Second Meanings	363
11	Scripture	369
12	Second Meanings in the Psalms	375
	Appendix I – Selected Psalms	385
	Appendix II – Psalms discussed or mentioned	392

I

INTRODUCTORY

This is not a work of scholarship. I am no Hebraist, no higher critic, no ancient historian, no archaeologist. I write for the unlearned about things in which I am unlearned myself. If an excuse is needed (and perhaps it is) for writing such a book, my excuse would be something like this. It often happens that two schoolboys can solve difficulties in their work for one another better than the master can. When you took the problem to a master, as we all remember, he was very likely to explain what you understood already, to add a great deal of information which you didn't want, and say nothing at all about the thing that was puzzling you. I have watched this from both sides of the net; for when, as a teacher myself, I have tried to answer questions brought me by pupils, I have sometimes, after a minute, seen that expression settle down on their faces which assured me that they were suffering exactly the same frustration which I had suffered from my own teachers. The fellow-pupil can help more than the master because he knows less. The difficulty we want him to explain is one he has recently met. The expert met it so long ago that he has forgotten. He sees the whole subject, by now, in such a different light that he cannot conceive what is really troubling the pupil; he sees a dozen other difficulties which ought to be troubling him but aren't.

In this book, then, I write as one amateur to another, talking about difficulties I have met, or lights I have gained, when reading the Psalms, with the hope that this might at any rate interest, and sometimes even help, other inexpert readers. I am 'comparing notes', not presuming to instruct. It may appear to some that I have used the Psalms merely as pegs on which to hang a series of miscellaneous essays. I do not know that it would have done any harm if I had written the book that way, and I shall have no grievance against anyone who reads it that way. But that is not how it was in fact written. The thoughts it contains are those to which I found myself driven in reading the Psalms; sometimes by my enjoyment of them, sometimes by meeting with what at first I could not enjoy.

The Psalms were written by many poets and at many different dates. Some, I believe, are allowed to go back to the reign of David; I think certain scholars allow that Psalm 18 (of which a slightly different version occurs in 2 Samuel 22) might be by David himself. But many are later than the 'captivity', which we should call the deportation to Babylon. In a scholarly work, chronology would be the first thing to settle: in a book of this sort nothing more need, or can, be said about it.

What must be said, however, is that the Psalms are poems, and poems intended to be sung: not doctrinal treatises, nor even sermons. Those who talk of reading the Bible 'as literature' sometimes mean, I think, reading it without attending to the main thing it is about; like reading Burke with no interest in politics, or reading the *Aeneid* with no interest in Rome. That seems to me to be nonsense. But there is a saner sense in which the Bible, since it is after all literature, cannot properly be read except as literature; and the different parts of it as the different sorts of literature they are. Most emphatically the Psalms must be read as poems; as lyrics, with all the licences and all the formalities, the hyperboles, the emotional rather than logical connections, which are proper to lyric poetry. They must be read as poems if they are to be understood; no less than French must be read as French or English as English. Otherwise we shall miss what is in them and think we see what is not.

Their chief formal characteristic, the most obvious element of pattern, is fortunately one that survives in translation. Most readers will know that I mean what the scholars call 'parallelism'; that is, the practice of saying the same thing twice in different words. A perfect example is 'He that dwelleth in heaven shall laugh them to scorn: the Lord shall have them in derision' (2:4), or again, 'He shall make thy righteousness as clear as the light; and thy just dealing as the noon-day' (37:6). If this is not recognised as pattern, the reader will either find mares' nests (as some of the older preachers did) in his effort to get a different meaning out of each half of the verse or else feel that it is rather silly.

In reality it is a very pure example of what all pattern, and therefore all art, involves. The principle of art has been defined by someone as 'the same in the other'. Thus in a country dance you take three steps and then three steps again. That is the same. But the first three are to the right and the second three to the left. That is the other. In a building there may be a wing on one side and a wing on the other, but both of the same shape. In music the composer may say ABC, and then abc, and then $\alpha\beta\gamma$. Rhyme consists in putting together two syllables that have the same sound except for their initial consonants, which are other. 'Parallelism' is the characteristically Hebrew form of the same in the other, but it occurs in many English poets too: for example, in Marlowe's

*Cut is the branch that might have grown full straight
And burned is Apollo's laurel bough,*

or in the childishly simple form used by the *Cherry Tree Carol,*

Joseph was an old man and an old man was he.

Of course the Parallelism is often partially concealed on purpose (as the balances between masses in a picture may be something far subtler than complete symmetry). And of course other and more complex patterns may be worked in across it, as in Psalm 119, or in 107 with its refrain. I mention only what is most obvious, the Parallelism itself. It is (according to one's point of view) either a wonderful piece of luck or a wise provision of God's, that poetry which was to be turned into all languages should have as its chief formal characteristic one that does not disappear (as mere metre does) in translation.

If we have any taste for poetry we shall enjoy this feature of the Psalms. Even those Christians who cannot enjoy it will respect it; for Our Lord, soaked in the poetic tradition of His country, delighted to use it. 'For with what judgement ye judge, ye shall be judged; and with what measure ye mete, it shall be measured to you again' (Matthew 7:2). The second half of the verse makes no logical addition; it echoes, with variation, the first, 'Ask, and it shall be given you; seek, and ye shall find; knock and it shall be opened unto you' (7:7). The advice is given in the first phrase, then twice repeated with different images. We may, if we like, see in this an exclusively practical and didactic purpose; by giving to truths which are infinitely worth remembering this rhythmic and incantatory expression, He made them almost impossible to forget. I like to suspect more. It seems to me appropriate, almost inevitable, that when that great Imagination which in the beginning, for Its own delight and for the delight of men and angels and (in their proper mode) of beasts, had invented and formed the whole world of Nature, submitted to express Itself in human speech, that speech should sometimes be poetry. For poetry too is a little incarnation, giving body to what had been before invisible and inaudible.

I think, too, it will do us no harm to remember that, in becoming Man, He bowed His neck beneath the sweet yoke of a heredity and early environment. Humanly speaking, He would have learned this style, if from no one else (but it was all about Him) from His Mother. 'That we should be saved from our enemies and from the hands of all that hate us; to perform the mercy promised to our fathers, and to remember his holy covenant.' Here is the same parallelism. (And incidentally, is this the only aspect in which we can say of His human nature 'He was His Mother's own son'? There is a fierceness, even a touch of Deborah, mixed with the sweetness in the Magnificat to which most painted Madonnas do little justice; matching the frequent severity of His own sayings. I am sure the private life of the holy family was, in many senses, 'mild' and 'gentle', but perhaps hardly in the way some hymn writers have in mind. One may suspect, on proper occasions, a certain astringency; and all in what people at Jerusalem regarded as a rough north-country dialect.)

I have not attempted of course to 'cover the subject' even on my own amateurish level. I have stressed, and omitted, as my own interests led me. I say nothing about the long historical Psalms, partly because they have meant less to me, and partly because they seem to call for little comment. I say the least I can about the history of the Psalms as parts of various 'services'; a wide subject, and not for me. And I begin with those characteristics of the Psalter which are at first most repellent. Other men of my age will know why. Our generation was brought up to eat everything on the plate; and it was the sound principle of nursery gastronomy to polish off the nasty things first and leave the titbits to the end.

I have worked in the main from the translation which Anglicans find in their Prayer Book; that of Coverdale. Even of the old translators he is by no means the most accurate; and of course a sound modern scholar has more Hebrew in his little finger than poor Coverdale had in his whole body. But in beauty, in poetry, he, and St Jerome, the great Latin translator, are beyond all whom I know. I have usually checked, and sometimes corrected, his version from that of Dr Moffatt.

Finally, as will soon be apparent to any reader, this is not what is called an 'apologetic' work. I am nowhere trying to convince unbelievers that Christianity is true. I address those who already believe it, or those who are ready, while reading, to 'suspend their disbelief'. A man can't be always defending the truth; there must be a time to feed on it.

I have written, too, as a member of the Church of England, but I have avoided controversial questions as much as possible. At one point I had to explain how I differed on a certain matter both from Roman Catholics and from Fundamentalists: I hope I shall not for this forfeit the goodwill or the prayers of either. Nor do I much fear it. In my experience the bitterest opposition comes neither from them nor from any other thorough-going believers, and not often from atheists, but from semi-believers of all complexions. There are some enlightened and progressive old gentlemen of this sort whom no courtesy can propitiate and no modesty disarm. But then I dare say I am a much more annoying person than I know. (Shall we, perhaps, in Purgatory, see our own faces and hear our own voices as they really were?)

2

'JUDGEMENT' IN THE PSALMS

If there is any thought at which a Christian trembles it is the thought of God's 'judgement'. The 'Day' of Judgement is 'that day of wrath, that dreadful day'. We pray for God to deliver us 'in the hour of death and at the day of judgement'. Christian art and literature for centuries have depicted its terrors. This note in Christianity certainly goes back to the teaching of Our Lord Himself; especially to the terrible parable of the Sheep and the Goats. This can leave no conscience untouched, for in it the 'Goats' are condemned entirely for their sins of omission; as if to make us fairly sure that the heaviest charge against each of us turns not upon the things he has done but on those he never did – perhaps never dreamed of doing.

It was therefore with great surprise that I first noticed how the Psalmists talk about the judgements of God. They talk like this: 'O let the nations rejoice and be glad, for thou shalt judge the folk righteously' (67:4), 'Let the field be joyful ... all the trees of the wood shall rejoice before the Lord, for he cometh, for he cometh to judge the earth' (96:12, 13). Judgement is apparently an occasion of universal rejoicing. People ask for it: 'Judge me, O Lord my God, according to thy righteousness' (35:24).

The reason for this soon becomes very plain. The ancient Jews, like ourselves, think of God's judgement in terms of an earthly court of justice. The difference is that the Christian pictures the case to be tried as a criminal case with himself in the dock; the Jew pictures it as a civil case with himself as the plaintiff. The one hopes for acquittal, or rather for pardon; the other hopes for a resounding triumph with heavy damages. Hence he prays 'judge my quarrel', or 'avenge my cause' (35:23). And though, as I said a minute ago, Our Lord in the parable of the Sheep and the Goats painted the characteristically Christian picture, in another place He is very characteristically Jewish. Notice what He means by 'an unjust judge'. By those words most of us would mean someone like Judge Jeffreys or the creatures who sat on the benches of German tribunals during the Nazi *régime*: someone who bullies witnesses and jurymen in order to convict, and then savagely to punish, innocent men. Once again, we are thinking of a criminal trial. We hope we shall never appear in the dock before such a judge. But the Unjust Judge in the parable is quite a different character. There is no danger of appearing in his court against your will: the difficulty is the opposite – to get into it. It is clearly a civil action. The poor woman (Luke 18:1–5) has had her little strip of land – room for a pigsty or a hen-run – taken away from her by a richer and more powerful neighbour (nowadays it would be Town-Planners or some other 'Body'). And she knows she has a perfectly watertight case. If once she could get it into court and have it tried by the laws of the land, she would be bound to get that strip back. But no one will listen to her, she can't get it tried. No wonder she is anxious for 'judgement'.

Behind this lies an age-old and almost world-wide experience which we have been spared. In most places and times it has been very difficult for the 'small man' to get his case heard. The judge (and, doubtless, one or two of his underlings) has to be bribed. If you can't afford to 'oil his palm' your case will never reach court. Our judges do not receive bribes. (We probably take this blessing too much for granted; it will not remain with us automatically.) We need not therefore be surprised if the Psalms, and the Prophets, are full of the longing for judgement, and regard the announcement that 'judgement' is coming as good news. Hundreds and thousands of people who have been stripped of all they possess and who have the right entirely on their side will at last be heard. Of course they are not afraid of judgement. They know their case is unanswerable – if only it could be heard. When God comes to judge, at last it will.

Dozens of passages make the point clear. In Psalm 9 we are told that God will 'minister true judgement' (v. 8), and that is because He 'forgetteth not the complaint of the poor' (v. 12). He 'defendeth the cause' (that is, the 'case') 'of the widows' (68:5). The good king in Psalm 72:2 will 'judge' the people rightly; that is, he will 'defend the poor'. When God 'arises to judgement' he will 'help all the meek upon earth' (76:9), all the timid, helpless people whose wrongs have never been righted yet. When God accuses earthly judges of 'wrong judgement', He follows it up by telling them to see that the poor 'have right' (82:2, 3).

The 'just' judge, then, is primarily he who rights a wrong in a civil case. He would, no doubt, also try a criminal case justly, but that is hardly ever what the Psalmists are thinking of. Christians cry to God for mercy instead of justice; *they* cried to God for justice instead of injustice. The Divine Judge is the defender, the rescuer. Scholars tell me that in the Book of Judges the word we so translate might almost be rendered 'champions'; for though these 'judges' do sometimes perform what we should call judicial functions many of them are much more concerned with rescuing the oppressed Israelites from Philistines and others by force of arms. They are more like

Jack the Giant Killer than like a modern judge in a wig. The knights in romances of chivalry who go about rescuing distressed damsels and widows from giants and other tyrants are acting almost as 'judges' in the old Hebrew sense: so is the modern solicitor (and I have known such) who does unpaid work for poor clients to save them from wrong.

I think there are very good reasons for regarding the Christian picture of God's judgement as far more profound and far safer for our souls than the Jewish. But this does not mean that the Jewish conception must simply be thrown away. I, at least, believe I can still get a good deal of nourishment out of it.

It supplements the Christian picture in one important way. For what alarms us in the Christian picture is the infinite purity of the standard against which our actions will be judged. But then we know that none of us will ever come up to that standard. We are all in the same boat. We must all pin our hopes on the mercy of God and the work of Christ, not on our own goodness. Now the Jewish picture of a civil action sharply reminds us that perhaps we are faulty not only by the Divine standard (that is a matter of course) but also by a very human standard which all reasonable people admit and which we ourselves usually wish to enforce upon others. Almost certainly there are unsatisfied claims, human claims, against each one of us. For who can really believe that in all his dealings with employers and employees, with husband or wife, with parents and children, in quarrels and in collaborations, he has always attained (let alone charity or generosity) mere honesty and fairness? Of course we forget most of the injuries we have done. But the injured parties do not forget even if they forgive. And God does not forget. And even what we can remember is formidable enough. Few of us have always, in full measure, given our pupils or patients or clients (or whatever our particular 'consumers' may be called) what we were being paid for. We have not always done quite our fair share of some tiresome work if we found a colleague or partner who could be beguiled into carrying the heavy end.

Our quarrels provide a very good example of the way in which the Christian and Jewish conceptions differ, while yet both should be kept in mind. As Christians we must of course repent of all the anger, malice, and self-will which allowed the discussion to become, on our side, a quarrel at all. But there is also the question on a far lower level: 'granted the quarrel (we'll go into that later) did you fight fair?' Or did we not quite unknowingly falsify the whole issue? Did we pretend to be angry about one thing when we knew, or could have known, that our anger had a different and much less presentable cause? Did we pretend to be 'hurt' in our sensitive and tender feelings (fine natures like ours are so vulnerable) when envy, ungratified vanity, or thwarted self-will was our real trouble? Such tactics often succeed. The other parties give in. They give in not because they don't know what is really wrong with us but because they have long known it only too well, and that sleeping dog can be roused, that skeleton brought out of its cupboard, only at the cost of imperilling their whole relationship with us. It needs surgery which they know we will never face. And so we win; by cheating. But the unfairness is very deeply felt. Indeed what is commonly called 'sensitiveness' is the most powerful engine of domestic tyranny, sometimes a lifelong tyranny. How we should deal with it in others I am not sure; but we should be merciless to its first appearances in ourselves.

The constant protests in the Psalms against those who oppress 'the poor' might seem at first to have less application to our own society than to most. But perhaps this is superficial; perhaps what changes is not the oppression but only the identity of 'the poor'. It often happens that someone in my acquaintance gets a demand from the Income Tax people which he queries. As a result it sometimes comes back to him reduced by anything up to 50 per cent. One man whom I knew, a solicitor, went round to the office and asked what they had meant by the original demand. The creature behind the counter tittered and said, 'Well, there's never any harm in trying it on.' Now when the cheat is thus attempted against men of the world who know how to look after themselves, no great harm is done. Some time has been wasted, and we all in some measure share the disgrace of belonging to a community where such practices are tolerated, but that is all. When, however, that kind of publican sends a similarly dishonest demand to a poor widow, already half starving on a highly taxable 'unearned' income (actually earned by years of self-denial on her husband's part) which inflation has reduced to almost nothing, a very different result probably follows. She cannot afford legal help; she understands nothing; she is terrified, and pays – cutting down on the meals and the fuel which were already wholly insufficient. The publican who has successfully 'tried it on' with her is precisely 'the ungodly' who 'for his own lust doth persecute the poor' (10:2). To be sure, he does this, not like the ancient publican, for his own immediate rake-off; only to advance himself in the service or to please his masters. This makes a difference. How important that difference is in the eyes of Him who avenges the fatherless and the widow I do not know. The publican may consider the question in the hour of death and will learn the answer at the day of 'judgement'. (But – who knows? – I may be doing the publicans an injustice. Perhaps they regard their work as a sport and observe game laws; and as other sportsmen will not shoot a sitting bird, so they may reserve their illegal demands for those who can defend themselves and hit back, and would never dream of 'trying it on' with the helpless. If so, I can only apologise for my error. If what I have said is unjustified as a rebuke of what they are, it may still be useful as a warning of what they may yet become. Falsehood is habit-forming.)

It will be noticed, however, that I make the Jewish conception of a civil judgement available for my Christian profit by picturing myself as the defendant, not the plaintiff. The writers of the Psalms do not do this. They look forward to 'judgement' because they think they have been wronged and hope to see their wrongs righted. There are, indeed, some passages in which the Psalmists approach to Christian humility and wisely lose their self-confidence. Thus in Psalm 50 (one of the finest) God is the accuser (vv. 6–21); and in 143:2, we have the words which most Christians often repeat – 'Enter not into judgement with Thy servant, for in Thy sight shall no man living be justified.' But these are exceptional. Nearly always the Psalmist is the indignant plaintiff.

He is quite sure, apparently, that his own hands are clean. He never did to others the horrid things that others are doing to him. 'If I have done any such thing' – If I ever behaved like so-and-so, then let so-and-so 'tread my life down upon the earth' (7:3–5). But of course I haven't. It is not as if my enemies are paying me out for any ill turn I ever did them. On the contrary, they have 'rewarded me evil for good'. Even after that, I went on exercising the utmost charity towards them. When they were ill I prayed and fasted on their behalf (35:12–14).

All this of course has its spiritual danger. It leads into that typically Jewish prison of self-righteousness which Our Lord so often terribly rebuked. We shall have to consider that presently. For the moment, however, I think it is important to make a distinction: between the conviction that one is in the right and the conviction that one is 'righteous', is a good man. Since none of us is righteous, the second conviction is always a delusion. But any of us may be, probably all of us at one time or another are, in the right about some particular issue. What is more, the worse man may be in the right against the better man. Their general characters have nothing to do with it. The question whether the disputed pencil belongs to Tommy or Charles is quite distinct from the question which is the nicer little boy, and the parents who allowed the one to influence their decision about the other would be very unfair. (It would be still worse if they said Tommy ought to let Charles have the pencil whether it belonged to him or not, because this would show he had a nice disposition. That may be true, but it is an untimely truth. An exhortation to charity should not come as a rider to a refusal of justice. It is likely to give Tommy a lifelong conviction that charity is a sanctimonious dodge for condoning theft and white-washing favouritism.) We need therefore by no means assume that the Psalmists are deceived or lying when they assert that, as against their particular enemies at some particular moment, they are completely in the right. Their voices while they say so may grate harshly on our ear and suggest to us that they are unamiable people. But that is another matter. And to be wronged does not commonly make people amiable.

But of course the fatal confusion between being in the right and being righteous soon falls upon them. In Psalm 7, from which I have already quoted, we see the transition. In verses 3 to 5 the poet is merely in the right; by verse 8 he is saying 'give sentence with me, O Lord, according to my righteousness and according to the innocency that is in me'. There is also in many of the Psalms a still more fatal confusion – that between the desire for justice and the desire for revenge. These important topics will have to be treated separately. The self-righteous Psalms can be dealt with only at a much later stage; the vindictive Psalms, the cursings, we may turn to at once. It is these that have made the Psalter largely a closed book to many modern church-goers. Vicars, not unnaturally, are afraid to set before their congregations poems so full of that passion to which Our Lord's teaching allows no quarter. Yet there must be some Christian use to be made of them; if, at least, we still believe (as I do) that all Holy Scripture is in some sense – though not all parts of it in the same sense – the word of God. (The sense in which I understand this will be explained later.)

3

THE CURSINGS

In some of the Psalms the spirit of hatred which strikes us in the face is like the heat from a furnace mouth. In others the same spirit ceases to be frightful only by becoming (to a modern mind) almost comic in its naïvety.

Examples of the first can be found all over the Psalter, but perhaps the worst is in Psalm 109. The poet prays that an ungodly man may rule over his enemy and that 'Satan' may stand at his right hand (v. 5). This probably does not mean what a Christian reader naturally supposes. The 'Satan' is an accuser, perhaps an informer. When the enemy is tried, let him be convicted and sentenced, 'and let his prayer be turned into sin' (v. 6). This again means, I think, not his prayers to God, but his supplications to a human judge, which are to make things all the hotter for him (double the sentence because he begged for it to be halved). May his days be few, may his job be given to someone else (v. 7). When he is dead may his orphans be beggars (v. 9). May he look in vain for anyone in the world to pity him (v. 11). Let God always remember against him the sins of his parents (v. 13). Even more devilish in one verse is the otherwise beautiful Psalm 137 where a blessing is pronounced on anyone who will snatch up a Babylonian baby and beat its brains out against the pavement (v. 9). And we get the refinement of malice in 69:23, 'Let their table be made a snare to take themselves withal; and let the things that should have been for their wealth be unto them an occasion of falling.'

The examples which (in me at any rate) can hardly fail to produce a smile may occur most disquietingly in Psalms we love: 143, after proceeding for 11 verses in a strain that brings tears to the eyes, adds in the 12th, almost like an afterthought, 'and of thy goodness slay mine enemies'. Even more naïvely, almost childishly, Psalm 139, in the middle of its hymn of praise throws in (v. 19), 'Wilt thou not slay the wicked, O God?' – as if it were surprising that such a simple remedy for human ills had not occurred to the Almighty. Worst of all in 'The Lord is my shepherd' (Psalm 23), after the green pasture, the waters of comfort, the sure confidence in the valley of the shadow, we suddenly run across (v. 5) 'Thou shalt prepare a table for me *against them that trouble me*' – or, as Dr Moffatt translates it, 'Thou art my host, spreading a feast for me *while my enemies have to look on*.' The poet's enjoyment of his present prosperity would not be complete unless those horrid enemies (who used to look down their noses at him) were watching it all and hating it. This may not be so diabolical as the passages I have quoted above; but the pettiness and vulgarity of it, especially in such surroundings, are hard to endure.

One way of dealing with these terrible or (dare we say?) contemptible Psalms is simply to leave them alone. But unfortunately the bad parts will not 'come away clean'; they may, as we have noticed, be intertwined with the most exquisite things. And if we still believe that all Holy Scripture is 'written for our learning' or that the age-old use of the Psalms in Christian worship was not entirely contrary to the will of God, and if we remember that Our Lord's mind and language were clearly steeped in the Psalter, we shall prefer, if possible, to make some use of them. What use can be made?

Part of the answer to this question cannot be given until we come to consider the subject of allegory. For the moment I can only describe, on the chance that it may help others, the use which I have, undesignedly and gradually, come to make of them myself.

At the outset I felt sure, and I feel sure still, that we must not either try to explain them away or to yield for one moment to the idea that, because it comes in the Bible, all this vindictive hatred must somehow be good and pious. We must face both facts squarely. The hatred is there – festering, gloating, undisguised – and also we should be wicked if we in any way condoned or approved it, or (worse still) used it to justify similar passions in ourselves. Only after these two admissions have been made can we safely proceed.

The first thing that helped me – this is a common experience – came from an angle that did not seem to be religious at all. I found that these maledictions were in one way extremely interesting. For here one saw a feeling we all know only too well. Resentment, expressing itself with perfect freedom, without disguise, without self-consciousness, without shame – as few but children would express it today. I did not of course think that this was because the ancient Hebrews had no conventions or restraints. Ancient and oriental cultures are in many ways more conventional, more ceremonious, and more courteous than our own. But their restraints came in different places. Hatred did not need to be disguised for the sake of social decorum or for fear anyone would accuse you of a neurosis. We therefore see it in its 'wild' or natural condition.

One might have expected that this would immediately, and usefully, have turned my attention to the same thing in my own heart. And that, no doubt, is one very good use we can make of the maledictory Psalms. To be sure, the hates which we fight against in ourselves do not dream of quite such appalling revenges. We live – at least, in some countries we still live – in a milder age. These poets lived in a world of savage punishments, of massacre and violence, of blood sacrifice in all countries and human sacrifice in many. And of course, too, we are far more subtle than they in disguising our ill will from others and from ourselves. 'Well,' we say, 'he'll live to be sorry for it,' as if we were merely, even regretfully, predicting; not noticing, certainly not admitting, that what we predict gives us a certain satisfaction. Still more in the Psalmists' tendency to chew over and over the cud of some injury, to dwell in a kind of self-torture on every circumstance that aggravates it, most of us can recognise something we have met in ourselves. We are, after all, blood-brothers to these ferocious, self-pitying, barbaric men.

That, as I say, is a good use to make of the cursings. In fact, however, something else occurred to me first. It seemed to me that, seeing in them hatred undisguised, I saw also the natural result of injuring a human being. The word *natural* is here important. This result can be obliterated by grace, suppressed by prudence or social convention, and (which is dangerous) wholly disguised by self-deception. But just as the natural result of throwing a lighted match into a pile of shavings is to produce a fire – though damp or the intervention of some more sensible person may prevent it – so the natural result of cheating a man, or 'keeping him down' or neglecting him, is to arouse resentment; that is, to impose upon him the temptation of becoming what the Psalmists were when they wrote the vindictive passages. He may succeed in resisting the temptation; or he may not. If he fails, if he dies spiritually because of his hatred for me, how do I, who provoked that hatred, stand? For in addition to the original injury I have done him a far worse one. I have introduced into his inner life, at best a new temptation, at worst a new besetting sin. If that sin utterly corrupts him, I have in a sense debauched or seduced him. I was the tempter.

There is no use talking as if forgiveness were easy. We all know the old joke, 'You've given up smoking once; I've given it up a dozen times.' In the same way I could say of a certain man, 'Have I forgiven him for what he did that day? I've forgiven him more times than I can count.' For we find that the work of forgiveness has to be done over and over again. We forgive, we mortify our resentment; a week later some chain of thought carries us back to the original offence and we discover the old resentment blazing away as if nothing had been done about it at all. We need to forgive our brother seventy times seven not only for 490 offences but for one offence. Thus the man I am thinking of has introduced a new, and difficult temptation into a soul which had the devil's plenty of them already. And what he has done to me, doubtless I have done to others; I, who am exceptionally blessed in having been allowed a way of life in which, having little power, I have had little opportunity of oppressing and embittering others. Let all of us who have never been school prefects, NCOs, schoolmasters, matrons of hospitals, prison warders, or even magistrates, give hearty thanks for it.

It is monstrously simple-minded to read the cursings in the Psalms with no feeling except one of horror at the uncharity of the poets. They are indeed devilish. But we must also think of those who made them so. Their hatreds are the reaction to something. Such hatreds are the kind of thing that cruelty and injustice, by a sort of natural law, produce. This, among other things, is what wrong-doing means. Take from a man his freedom or his goods and you may have taken his innocence, almost his humanity, as well. Not all the victims go and hang themselves like Mr Pilgrim; they may live and hate.

Then another thought occurred which led me in an unexpected, and at first unwelcome, direction. The reaction of the Psalmists to injury, though profoundly natural, is profoundly wrong. One may try to excuse it on the ground that they were not Christians and knew no better. But there are two reasons why this defence, though it will go some way, will not go very far.

The first is that within Judaism itself the corrective to this natural reaction already existed. 'Thou shalt not hate thy brother in thine heart ... thou shalt not avenge or bear any grudge against the children of thy people, but thou shalt love thy neighbour as thyself,' says Leviticus (19:17, 18). In Exodus we read, 'If thou seest the ass of him that hateth thee lying under his burden ... thou shalt surely help with him,' and 'if thou meet thine enemy's ox or his ass going astray, thou shalt surely bring it back to him' (23:4, 5). 'Rejoice not when thine enemy falleth, and let not thine heart be glad when he stumbleth' (Proverbs 24:17). And I shall never forget my surprise when I first discovered that St Paul's 'If thine enemy hunger, give him bread', etc., is a direct quotation from the same book (Proverbs 25:21). But this is one of the rewards of reading the Old Testament regularly. You keep on discovering more and more what a tissue of quotations from it the New Testament is; how constantly Our Lord repeated, reinforced, continued, refined, and sublimated, the Judaic ethics, how very seldom He introduced a novelty. This indeed was perfectly well known – was almost axiomatic – to millions of unlearned Christians as long as Bible-reading was habitual. Nowadays it seems to be so forgotten that people think they have somehow discredited Our Lord if they can show that some pre-Christian document (or what they take to be pre-Christian) such as the Dead Sea Scrolls has 'anticipated' Him. As if we supposed Him to be a cheapjack, like Nietzsche, inventing a new ethic! Every good teacher, within Judaism as without, has anticipated Him. The whole religious history of the pre-Christian world, on its better side, anticipates Him. It could not be otherwise. The Light which has lightened every man from the beginning may shine more clearly but cannot change. The Origin cannot suddenly start being, in the popular sense of the word, 'original'.

The second reason is more disquieting. If we are to excuse the poets of the Psalms on the ground that they were not Christians, we ought to be able to point to the same sort of thing, and worse, in Pagan authors. Perhaps if I knew more Pagan literature I should be able to do this. But in what I do know (a little Greek, a little Latin, and of Old Norse very little indeed) I am not at all sure that I can. I can find in them lasciviousness, much brutal insensibility, cold cruelties taken for granted, but not this fury or luxury of hatred. I mean, of course, where writers are speaking in their own person; speeches put into the mouths of angry characters in a play are a different matter. One's first impression is that the Jews were much more vindictive and vitriolic than the Pagans.

If we are not Christians we shall dismiss this with the old gibe 'How odd of God to choose the Jews'. That is impossible for us who believe that God chose that race for the vehicle of His own Incarnation, and who are indebted to Israel beyond all possible repayment.

Where we find a difficulty we may always expect that a discovery awaits us. Where there is cover we hope for game. This particular difficulty is well worth exploring.

It seems that there is a general rule in the moral universe which may be formulated, 'The higher, the more in danger'. The 'average sensual man' who is sometimes unfaithful to his wife, sometimes tipsy, always a little selfish, now and then (within the law) a trifle sharp in his deals, is certainly, by ordinary standards, a 'lower' type than the man whose soul is filled with some great Cause, to which he will subordinate his appetites, his fortune, and even his safety. But it is out of the second man that something really fiendish can be made; an Inquisitor, a Member of the Committee of Public Safety. It is great men, potential saints, not little men, who become merciless fanatics. Those who are readiest to die for a cause may easily become those who are readiest to kill for it. One sees the same principle at work in a field (comparatively) so unimportant as literary criticism; the most brutal work, the most rankling hatred of all other critics and of nearly all authors, may come from the most honest and disinterested critic, the man who cares most passionately and selflessly about literature. The higher the stakes, the greater the temptation to lose your temper over the game. We must not over-value the relative harmlessness of the little, sensual, frivolous people. They are not above, but below, some temptations.

If I am never tempted, and cannot even imagine myself being tempted, to gamble, this does not mean that I am better than those who are. The timidity and pessimism which exempt me from that temptation themselves tempt me to draw back from those risks and adventures which every man ought to take. In the same way we cannot be certain that the comparative absence of vindictiveness in the Pagans, though certainly a good thing in itself, is a good symptom. This was borne in upon me during a night journey taken early in the Second World War in a compartment full of young soldiers. Their conversation made it clear that they totally disbelieved all that they had read in the papers about the wholesale cruelties of the Nazi *régime*. They took it for granted, without argument, that this was all lies, all propaganda put out by our own government to 'pep up' our troops. And the shattering thing was, that, believing this, they expressed not the slightest anger. That our rulers should falsely attribute the worst of crimes to some of their fellow-men in order to induce other men to shed their blood seemed to them a matter of course. They weren't even particularly interested. They saw nothing wrong in it. Now it seemed to me that the most violent of the Psalmists – or, for that matter any child wailing out 'But it's not fair' – was in a more hopeful condition than these young men. If they had perceived, and felt as a man should feel, the diabolical wickedness which they believed our rulers to be committing, and then forgiven them, they would have been saints. But not to perceive it at all – not even to be tempted to resentment – to accept it as the most ordinary thing in the world – argues a terrifying insensibility. Clearly these young men had (on that subject anyway) no conception of good and evil whatsoever.

Thus the absence of anger, especially that sort of anger which we call *indignation*, can, in my opinion, be a most alarming symptom. And the presence of indignation may be a good one. Even when that indignation passes into bitter personal vindictiveness, it may still be a good symptom, though bad in itself. It is a sin; but it at least shows that those who commit it have not sunk below the level at which the temptation to that sin exists – just as the sins (often quite appalling) of the great patriot or great reformer point to something in him above mere self. If the Jews cursed more bitterly than the Pagans this was, I think, at least in part because they took right and wrong more seriously. For if we look at their railings we find they are usually angry not simply because these things have been done to them but because these things are manifestly wrong, are hateful to God as well as to the victim. The thought of the 'righteous Lord' – who surely must hate such doings as much as they do, who surely therefore must (but how terribly He delays!) 'judge' or avenge, is always there, if only in the background. Sometimes it comes into the foreground; as in Psalm 58:9, 10, 'The righteous shall rejoice when he seeth the vengeance ... so that a man shall say ... Doubtless there is a God that judgeth the earth.' This is something different from mere anger without indignation – the almost animal rage at finding that a man's enemy has done to him exactly what he would have done to his enemy if he had been strong enough or quick enough.

Different, certainly higher, a better symptom; yet also leading to a more terrible sin. For it encourages a man to think that his own worst passions are holy. It encourages him to add, explicitly or implicitly, 'Thus saith the Lord' to the expression of his own emotions or even his own opinions; as Carlyle and Kipling and some politicians, and even, in their own way, some modern critics, so horribly do. (It is this, by the way, rather than mere idle 'profane swearing' that we ought to mean by 'taking God's name in vain'. The man who says 'Damn that chair!' does not really wish that it should first be endowed with an immortal soul and then sent to eternal perdition.) For here also it is true, 'the higher, the more in danger'. The Jews sinned in this matter worse than the Pagans not because they were further from God but because they were nearer to Him. For the Supernatural, entering a human soul, opens to it new possibilities of both good and evil. From that point the road branches: one way to sanctity, love, humility, the other to spiritual pride, self-righteousness, persecuting zeal. And no way back to the mere humdrum virtues and vices of the unawakened soul. If the Divine call does not make us better, it will make us very much worse. Of all bad men religious bad men are the worst. Of all created beings the wickedest is one who originally stood in the immediate presence of God. There seems no way out of this. It gives a new application to Our Lord's words about 'counting the cost'.

For we can still see, in the worst of their maledictions, how these old poets were, in a sense, near to God. Though hideously distorted by the human instrument, something of the Divine voice can be heard in these passages. Not, we trust, that God looks upon their enemies as they do: He 'desireth not the death of a sinner'. But doubtless He has for the sin of those enemies just the implacable hostility which the poets express. Implacable? Yes, not to the sinner but to sin. It will not be tolerated nor condoned, no treaty will be made with it. That tooth must come out, that right hand must be amputated, if the man is to be saved. In that way the relentlessness of the Psalmists is far nearer to one side of the truth than many modern attitudes which can be mistaken, by those who hold them, for Christian charity. It is, for example, obviously nearer than the total moral indifference of the young soldiers. It is nearer than the pseudo-scientific tolerance which reduces all wickedness to neurosis (though of course some apparent wickedness is). It even contains a streak of sanity absent from the old woman presiding at a juvenile court who – I heard it myself – told some young hooligans, convicted of a well-planned robbery for gain (they had already sold the swag and some had previous convictions against them) that they must, they really must, give up such 'stupid pranks'. Against all this the ferocious parts of the Psalms serve as a reminder that there is in the world such a thing as wickedness and that it (if not its perpetrators) is hateful to God. In that way, however dangerous the human distortion may be, His word sounds through these passages too.

But can we, besides learning from these terrible Psalms, also use them in our devotional life? I believe we can; but that topic must be reserved for a later chapter.

4

DEATH IN THE PSALMS

According to my policy of taking first what is most unattractive, I should now proceed to the self-righteousness in many of the Psalms. But we cannot deal with that properly until some other matters have been noticed. I turn first to a very different subject.

Our ancestors seem to have read the Psalms and the rest of the Old Testament under the impression that the authors wrote with a pretty full understanding of Christian Theology; the main difference being that the Incarnation, which for us is something recorded, was for them something predicted. In particular, they seldom doubted that the old authors were, like ourselves, concerned with a life beyond death, that they feared damnation and hoped for eternal joy.

In our own Prayer Book version, and probably in many others, some passages make this impression almost irresistibly. Thus in Psalm 17:14, we read of wicked men 'which have their portion in this life'. The Christian reader inevitably reads into this (and Coverdale, the translator, obviously did so too) Our Lord's contrast between the Rich Man who had his good things here and Lazarus who had them hereafter; the same contrast which is implied in Luke 6:24 – 'Woe unto you that are rich, for ye have received your consolation.' But modern translators can find nothing like this in the actual Hebrew. In reality this passage is merely one of the cursings we were considering in the previous chapter. In Psalm 17:13 the poet prays God to 'cast down' (in Dr Moffatt, 'crush') the ungodly; in verse 14, a refinement occurs to him. Yes, crush them, but first let them 'have their portion in this life'. Kill them, but first give them a bad time while alive.

Again, in Psalm 49, we have, 'No man may deliver his brother ... for it cost more to redeem their souls; so that he must let that alone forever' (vv. 7, 8). Who would not think that this referred to the redeeming work of Christ? No man can 'save' the soul of another. The price of salvation is one that only the Son of God could pay; as the hymn says, there was no other 'good enough to pay the price'. The very phrasing of our version strengthens the effect – the verb 'redeem' which (outside the pawnbroking business) is now used only in a theological sense, and the past tense of 'cost'. Not it 'costs', but it did cost, more, once and for all on Calvary. But apparently the Hebrew poet meant something quite different and much more ordinary. He means merely that death is inevitable. As Dr Moffatt translates it: 'None can buy himself off. Not one can purchase for a price from God (soul's ransom is too dear) life that shall never end.'

At this point I can imagine a lifelong lover of the Psalms exclaiming: 'Oh bother the great scholars and modern translators! I'm not going to let them spoil the whole Bible for me. At least let me ask two questions. (i) Is it not stretching the arm of coincidence rather far to ask me to believe that, not once but twice, in the same book, mere accident (wrong translations, bad manuscripts, or what not) should have so successfully imitated the language of Christianity? (ii) Do you mean that the old meanings which we have always attached to these verses simply have to be scrapped?' Both questions will come up for consideration in a later chapter. For the moment I will only say that, to the second, my personal answer is a confident No. I return to what I believe to be the facts.

It seems quite clear that in most parts of the Old Testament there is little or no belief in a future life; certainly no belief that is of any religious importance. The word translated 'soul' in our version of the Psalms means simply 'life'; the word translated 'hell' means simply 'the land of the dead', the state of all the dead, good and bad alike, *Sheol*.

It is difficult to know how an ancient Jew thought of *Sheol*. He did not like thinking about it. His religion did not encourage him to think about it. No good could come of thinking about it. Evil might. It was a condition from which very wicked people like the Witch of Endor were believed to be able to conjure up a ghost. But the ghost told you nothing about Sheol; it was called up solely to tell you things about our own world. Or again, if you allowed yourself an unhealthy interest in Sheol you might be lured into one of the neighbouring forms of Paganism and 'eat the offerings of the dead' (Psalm 106:28).

Behind all this one can discern a conception not specifically Jewish but common to many ancient religions. The Greek Hades is the most familiar example to modern people. Hades is neither Heaven nor Hell; it is almost nothing. I am speaking of the popular beliefs; of course philosophers like Plato have a vivid and positive doctrine of immortality. And of course poets may write fantasies about the world of the dead. These have often no more to do with the real Pagan religion than the fantasies we may write about other planets have to do with real astronomy. In real Pagan belief, Hades was hardly worth talking about; a world of shadows, of decay. Homer (probably far closer to actual beliefs than the later and more sophisticated poets) represents the ghosts as witless. They gibber meaninglessly until some living man gives them sacrificial blood to drink. How the Greeks felt about it in his time is startlingly shown at the beginning of the *Iliad* where he says of men killed in battle that 'their souls' went to Hades but 'the men themselves' were devoured by dogs and carrion birds. It is the body, even the dead body which is the man himself; the ghost is only a sort of reflection or echo. (The grim impulse sometimes has crossed my mind to wonder whether all this was, is, in fact true; that the merely natural fate of humanity, the fate of unredeemed humanity, is just this – to disintegrate in soul as in body, to be a witless psychic sediment. If so, Homer's idea that only a drink of sacrificial blood can restore a ghost to rationality would be one of the most striking among many Pagan anticipations of the truth.)

Such a conception, vague and marginal even in Paganism, becomes more so in Judaism. Sheol is even dimmer, further in the background, than Hades. It is a thousand miles away from the centre of Jewish religion; especially in the Psalms. They speak of Sheol (or 'hell' or 'the pit') very much as a man speaks of 'death' or 'the grave' who has no belief in any sort of future state whatever – a man to whom the dead are simply dead, nothing, and there's no more to be said.

In many passages this is quite clear, even in our translation, to every attentive reader. The clearest of all is the cry in Psalm 89:46: 'O remember how short my time is: why hast thou made all men for nought?' We all come to nothing in the end. Therefore 'every man living is altogether vanity' (39:6). Wise and foolish have the same fate (49:10). Once dead, a man worships God no more: 'Shall the dust give thanks unto thee?' (30:10); 'for in death, no man remembereth thee' (6:5). Death is 'the land' where, not only worldly things, but all things, 'are forgotten' (88:12). When a man dies, 'all his thoughts perish' (146:3). Every man will 'follow the generation of his fathers, and shall never see light' (49:19): he goes into a darkness which will never end.

Elsewhere, I admit, it sounds as if the poet were praying for the 'salvation of his soul' in the Christian sense. Almost certainly he is not. In Psalm 30:3, 'Thou hast brought my soul out of hell' means 'you have saved me from death'. 'The snares of death compassed me round about, and the pains of hell gat hold upon me' (116:3) means 'Death was setting snares for me, I felt the anguish of a dying man' – as we should say, 'I was at death's door.'

As we all know from our New Testaments, Judaism had greatly changed in this respect by Our Lord's time. The Sadducees held to the old view. The Pharisees, and apparently many more, believed in the life of the world to come. When, and by what stages, and (under God) from what sources, this new belief crept in, is not part of our present subject. I am more concerned to try to understand the absence of such a belief, in the midst of intense religious feeling, over the earlier period. To some it may seem astonishing that God, having revealed so much of Himself to that people, should not have taught them this.

It does not now astonish me. For one thing there were nations close to the Jews whose religion was overwhelmingly concerned with the after life. In reading about ancient Egypt one gets the impression of a culture in which the main business of life was the attempt to secure the well-being of the dead. It looks as if God did not want the chosen people to follow that example. We may ask why. Is it possible for men to be too much concerned with their eternal destiny? In one sense, paradoxical though it sounds, I should reply, Yes.

For the truth seems to me to be that happiness or misery beyond death, simply in themselves, are not even religious subjects at all. A man who believes in them will of course be prudent to seek the one and avoid the other. But that seems to have no more to do with religion than looking after one's health or saving money for one's old age. The only difference here is that the stakes are so very much higher. And this means that, granted a real and steady conviction, the hopes and anxieties aroused are overwhelming. But they are not on that account the more religious. They are hopes for oneself, anxieties for oneself. God is not in the centre. He is still important only for the sake of something else. Indeed such a belief can exist without a belief in God at all. Buddhists are much concerned with what will happen to them after death, but are not, in any true sense, Theists.

It is surely, therefore, very possible that when God began to reveal Himself to men, to show them that He and nothing else is their true goal and the satisfaction of their needs, and that He has a claim upon them simply by being what He is, quite apart from anything He can bestow or deny, it may have been absolutely necessary that this revelation should not begin with any hint of future Beatitude or Perdition. These are not the right points to begin at. An effective belief in them, coming too soon, may even render almost impossible the development of (so to call it) the appetite for God; personal hopes and fears, too obviously exciting, have got in first. Later, when, after centuries of spiritual training, men have learned to desire and adore God, to pant after Him 'as pants the hart', it is another matter. For then those who love God will desire not only to enjoy Him but 'to enjoy Him forever', and will fear to lose Him. And it is by that door that a truly religious hope of Heaven and fear of Hell can enter; as corollaries to a faith already centred upon God, not as things of any independent or intrinsic weight. It is even arguable that the moment 'Heaven' ceases to mean union with God and 'Hell' to mean separation from Him, the belief in either is a mischievous superstition; for then we have, on the one hand, a merely 'compensatory' belief (a 'sequel' to life's sad story, in which everything will 'come all right') and, on the other, a nightmare which drives men into asylums or makes them persecutors.

Fortunately, by God's good providence, a strong and steady belief of that self-seeking and sub-religious kind is extremely difficult to maintain, and is perhaps possible only to those who are slightly neurotic. Most of us find that our belief in the future life is strong only when God is in the centre of our thoughts; that if we try to use the hope of 'Heaven' as a compensation (even for the most innocent and natural misery, that of bereavement) it crumbles away. It can, on those terms, be maintained only by arduous efforts of controlled imagination; and we know in our hearts that the imagination is our own. As for Hell, I have often been struck, in reading the 'hell-fire sermons' of our older divines, at the desperate efforts they make to render these horrors vivid to their hearers, at their astonishment that men, with such horrors hanging over them, can live as carelessly as they do. But perhaps it is not really astonishing. Perhaps the divines are appealing, on the level of self-centred prudence and self-centred terror, to a belief which, on that level, cannot really exist as a permanent influence on conduct – though doubtless it may be worked up for a few excited minutes or even hours.

All this is only one man's opinion. And it may be unduly influenced by my own experience. For I (I have said it in another book, but the repetition is unavoidable) was allowed for a whole year to believe in God and try – in some stumbling fashion – to obey Him before any belief in the future life was given me. And that year always seems to me to have been of very great value. It is therefore perhaps natural that I should suspect a similar value in the centuries during which the Jews were in the same position. Other views no doubt can be taken.

Of course among ancient Jews, as among us, there were many levels. They were not all of them, not perhaps any of them at all times, disinterested, any more than we. What then filled the place which was later taken by the hope of Heaven (too often, I am afraid, desired chiefly as an escape from Hell) was of course the hope of peace and plenty on earth. This was in itself no less (but really no more) sub-religious than prudential cares about the next world. It was not quite so personal and self-centred as our own wishes for earthly prosperity. The individual, as such, seems to have been less aware of himself, much less separated from others, in those ancient times. He did not so sharply distinguish his own prosperity from that of the nation and especially of his own descendants. Blessings on one's remote posterity were blessings on oneself. Indeed it is not always easy to know whether the speaker in a Psalm is the individual poet or Israel itself. I suspect that sometimes the poet had never raised the question.

But we should be quite mistaken if we supposed that these worldly hopes were the only thing in Judaism. They are not the characteristic thing about it, the thing that sets it apart from ancient religion in general. And notice here the strange roads by which God leads His people. Century after century, by blows which seem to us merciless, by defeat, deportation, and massacre, it was hammered into the Jews that earthly prosperity is not in fact the certain, or even the probable, reward of seeing God. Every hope was disappointed. The lesson taught in the Book of Job was grimly illustrated in practice. Such experience would surely have destroyed a religion which had no other centre than the hope of peace and plenty with 'every man under his own vine and his own fig tree'. We know that many did 'fall off'. But the astonishing thing is that the religion is not destroyed. In its best representatives it grows purer, stronger, and more profound. It is being, by this terrible discipline, directed more and more to its real centre. That will be the subject of the next chapter.

5

'THE FAIR BEAUTY OF THE LORD'

'Now let us stint all this and speak of mirth.' So far – I couldn't help it – this book has been what the old woman in Scott described as 'a cauld clatter o' morality'. At last we can turn to better things. If we think 'mirth' an unsuitable word for them, that may show how badly we need something which the Psalms can give us perhaps better than any other book in the world.

David, we know, danced before the Ark. He danced with such abandon that one of his wives (presumably a more modern, though not a better type than he) thought he was making a fool of himself. David didn't care whether he was making a fool of himself or not. He was rejoicing in the Lord. This helps to remind us at the outset that Judaism, though it is the worship of the one true and eternal God, is an ancient religion. That means that its externals, and many of its attitudes, were much more like those of Paganism than they were like all that stuffiness – all that regimen of tiptoe tread and lowered voice – which the word 'religion' suggests to so many people now. In one way, of course, this puts a barrier between it and us. We should not have enjoyed the ancient rituals. Every temple in the world, the elegant Parthenon at Athens and the holy Temple at Jerusalem, was a sacred slaughterhouse. (Even the Jews seem to shrink from a return to this. They have not rebuilt the Temple nor revived the sacrifices.) But even that has two sides. If temples smelled of blood, they also smelled of roast meat; they struck a festive and homely note, as well as a sacred.

When I read the Bible as a boy I got the idea that the Temple of Jerusalem was related to the local synagogues very much as a great cathedral is related to the parish churches in a Christian country. In reality there is no such parallel. What happened in the synagogues was quite unlike what happened in the Temple. The synagogues were meeting-houses where the Law was read and where an address might be given – often by some distinguished visitor (as in Luke 4:20 or Acts 13:15). The Temple was the place of sacrifice, the place where the essential worship of Jahweh was enacted. Every parish church is the descendant of both. By its sermons and lessons it shows its ancestry in the synagogue. But because the Eucharist is celebrated and all other sacraments administered in it, it is like the Temple; it is a place where the adoration of the Deity can be fully enacted. Judaism without the Temple was mutilated, deprived of its central operation; any church, barn, sickroom, or field, can be the Christian's temple.

The most valuable thing the Psalms do for me is to express that same delight in God which made David dance. I am not saying that this is so pure or so profound a thing as the love of God reached by the greatest Christian saints and mystics. But I am not comparing it with that, I am comparing it with the merely dutiful 'churchgoing' and laborious 'saying our prayers' to which most of us are, thank God not always, but often, reduced. Against that it stands out as something astonishingly robust, virile, and spontaneous; something we may regard with an innocent envy and may hope to be infected by as we read.

For the reason I have given, this delight is very much centred on the Temple. The simpler poets do not in fact distinguish between the love of God in what we might (rather dangerously) call 'a spiritual sense' and their enjoyment of the festivals in the Temple. We must not misunderstand this. The Jews were not, like the Greeks, an analytical and logical people; indeed, except the Greeks, no ancient peoples were. The sort of distinction which we can easily make between those who are really worshipping God in church and those who enjoy 'a beautiful service' for musical, antiquarian, or merely sentimental reasons, would have been impossible to them. We get nearest to their state of mind if we think of a pious modern farm-labourer at church on Christmas Day or at the harvest thanksgiving. I mean, of course, one who really believes, who is a regular communicant; not one who goes only on these occasions and is thus (not in the worst but in the best sense of that word) a Pagan, practising Pagan piety, making his bow to the Unknown – and at other times Forgotten – on the great annual festivals. The man I picture is a real Christian. But you would do him wrong by asking him to separate out, at such moments, some exclusively religious element in his mind from all the rest – from his hearty social pleasure in a corporate act, his enjoyment of the hymns (and the crowd), his memory of other such services since childhood, his well-earned anticipation of rest after harvest or Christmas dinner after church. They are all one in his mind. This would have been even truer of any ancient man, and especially of an ancient Jew. He was a peasant, very close to the soil. He had never heard of music, or festivity, or agriculture as things separate from religion, nor of religion as something separate from them. Life was one. This assuredly laid him open to spiritual dangers which more sophisticated people can avoid; it also gave him privileges which they lack.

Thus when the Psalmists speak of 'seeing' the Lord, or long to 'see' Him, most of them mean something that happened to them in the Temple. The fatal way of putting this would be to say 'they only mean they have seen the festival'. It would be better to say, 'If we had been there we should have seen only the festival'. Thus in Psalm 68, 'It is well seen, O God, how thou goest[1] ... in the sanctuary ... the singers go before, the minstrels follow after; in the midst are the damsels playing with the timbrels' (vv. 24–25), it is almost as if the poet said, 'Look, here He comes'. If I had been there I should have seen the musicians and the girls with the tambourines; in addition, as another thing, I might or might not have (as we say) 'felt' the presence of God. The ancient worshipper would have been aware of no such dualism. Similarly, if a modern man wished to 'dwell in the house of the Lord all the days of his life, to behold the fair beauty of the Lord' (27:4), he would mean, I suppose, that he hoped to receive, not of course without the mediation of the sacraments and the help of other 'services', but as something distinguishable from them and not to be presumed upon as their inevitable result, frequent moments of spiritual vision and the 'sensible' love of God. But I suspect that the poet of that Psalm drew no distinction between 'beholding the fair beauty of the Lord' and the acts of worship themselves.

When the mind becomes more capable of abstraction and analysis this old unity breaks up. And no sooner is it possible to distinguish the rite from the vision of God than there is a danger of the rite becoming a substitute for, and a rival to, God Himself. Once it can be thought of separately, it will; and it may then take on a rebellious, cancerous life of its own. There is a stage in a child's life at which it cannot separate the religious from the merely festal character of Christmas or Easter. I have been told of a very small and very devout boy who was heard murmuring to himself on Easter morning a poem of his own composition which began 'Chocolate eggs and Jesus risen'. This seems to me, for his age, both admirable poetry and admirable piety. But of course the time will soon come when such a child can no longer effortlessly and spontaneously enjoy that unity. He will become able to distinguish the spiritual from the ritual and festal aspect of Easter; chocolate eggs will no longer be sacramental. And once he has distinguished he must put one or the other first. If he puts the spiritual first he can still taste something of Easter in the chocolate eggs; if he puts the eggs first they will soon be no more than any other sweetmeat. They have taken on an independent, and therefore a soon withering, life. Either at some period in Judaism, or else in the experience of some Jews, a roughly parallel situation occurred. The unity falls apart; the sacrificial rites become distinguishable from the

---

[1] This was perhaps sung while the Ark itself was carried round.

meeting with God. This does not unfortunately mean that they will cease or become less important. They may, in various evil modes, become even more important than before. They may be valued as a sort of commercial transaction with a greedy God who somehow really wants or needs large quantities of carcasses and whose favours cannot be secured on any other terms. Worse still, they may be regarded as the only thing He wants, so that their punctual performance will satisfy Him without obedience to His demands for mercy, 'judgement', and truth. To the priests themselves the whole system will seem important simply because it is both their art and their livelihood; all their pedantry, all their pride, all their economic position, is bound up with it. They will elaborate their art more and more. And of course the corrective to these views of sacrifice can be found within Judaism itself. The prophets continually fulminate against it. Even the Psalter, though largely a Temple collection, can do so; as in Psalm 50 where God tells His people that all this Temple worship, considered in itself, is not the real point at all, and particularly ridicules the genuinely Pagan notion that He really needs to be fed with roast meat. 'If I were hungry, do you think I would apply to *you*?' (v. 12). I have sometimes fancied He might similarly ask a certain type of modern clergyman, 'If I wanted music – if I were conducting research into the more recondite details of the history of the Western Rite – do you really think *you* are the source I would rely on?'

This possible degradation of sacrifice and the rebukes of it are, however, so well known that there is no need to stress them here. I want to stress what I think that we (or at least I) need more; the joy and delight in God which meet us in the Psalms, however loosely or closely, in this or that instance, they may be connected with the Temple. This is the living centre of Judaism. These poets knew far less reason than we for loving God. They did not know that He offered them eternal joy; still less that He would die to win it for them. Yet they express a longing for Him, for His mere presence, which comes only to the best Christians or to Christians in their best moments. They long to live all their days in the Temple so that they may constantly see 'the fair beauty of the Lord' (27:4). Their longing to go up to Jerusalem and 'appear before the presence of God' is like a physical thirst (42). From Jerusalem His presence flashes out 'in perfect beauty' (50:2). Lacking that encounter with Him, their souls are parched like a waterless countryside (63:2). They crave to be 'satisfied with the pleasures' of His house (65:4). Only there can they be at ease, like a bird in the nest (84:3). One day of those 'pleasures' is better than a lifetime spent elsewhere (v. 10).

I have rather – though the expression may seem harsh to some – called this the 'appetite for God' than 'the love of God'. The 'love of God' too easily suggests the word 'spiritual' in all those negative or restrictive senses which it has unhappily acquired. These old poets do not seem to think that they are meritorious or pious for having such feelings; nor, on the other hand, that they are privileged in being given the grace to have them. They are at once less priggish about it than the worst of us and less humble – one might almost say, less surprised – than the best of us. It has all the cheerful spontaneity of a natural, even a physical, desire. It is gay and jocund. They are glad and rejoice (9:2). Their fingers itch for the harp (43:4), for the lute and the harp – wake up, lute and harp! – (57:9); let's have a song, bring the tambourine, bring the 'merry harp with the lute', we're going to sing merrily and make a cheerful noise (81:1, 2). Noise, you may well say. Mere music is not enough. Let everyone, even the benighted Gentiles,[2] clap their hands (47:1). Let us have clashing cymbals, not only well tuned, but *loud*, and dances too (150:5). Let even the remote islands (all islands were remote, for the Jews were no sailors) share the exultation (97:1).

I am not saying that this gusto – if you like, this rowdiness – can or should be revived. Some of it cannot be revived because it is not dead but with us still. It would be idle to pretend that we Anglicans are a striking example. The Romans, the Orthodox, and the Salvation Army all, I think, have retained more of it than we. We have a terrible concern about good taste. Yet even we can still exult. The second reason goes far deeper. All Christians know something the Jews did not know about what it 'cost to redeem their souls'. Our life as Christians begins by being baptised into a death; our most joyous festivals begin with, and centre upon, the broken body and the shed blood. There is thus a tragic depth in our worship which Judaism lacked. Our joy has to be the sort of joy which can coexist with that; there is for us a spiritual counterpoint where they had simple melody. But this does not in the least cancel the delighted debt which I, for one, feel that I owe to the most jocund Psalms. There, despite the presence of elements we should now find it hard to regard as religious at all, and the absence of elements which some might think essential to religion, I find an experience fully God-centred, asking of God no gift more urgently than His presence, the gift of Himself, joyous to the highest degree, and unmistakably real. What I see (so to speak) in the faces of these old poets tells me more about the God whom they and we adore.

But this characteristically Hebraic delight or gusto finds also another channel. We must follow it in the next chapter.

---

[2] Not 'all ye people' as in our version, but 'all ye nations' (*Goyim*).

6

'SWEETER THAN HONEY'

In Racine's tragedy of *Athalie* the chorus of Jewish girls sing an ode about the original giving of the Law on Mount Sinai, which has the remarkable refrain *ô charmante loi* (Act 1, scene iv). Of course it will not do – it will border on the comic – to translate this 'oh charming Law'. *Charming* in English has come to be a tepid and even patronising word; we use it of a pretty cottage, of a book that is something less than great or a woman who is something less than beautiful. How we should translate *charmante* I don't know; 'enchanting'? 'delightful'? 'beautiful'? None of them quite fits. What is, however, certain is that Racine (a mighty poet and steeped in the Bible) is here coming nearer than any modern writer I know to a feeling very characteristic of certain Psalms. And it is a feeling which I at first found utterly bewildering.

'More to be desired are they than gold, yea than much fine gold: sweeter also than honey and the honey-comb' (19:10). One can well understand this being said of God's mercies, God's visitations, His attributes. But what the poet is actually talking about is God's law, His commands; His 'rulings' as Dr Moffatt well translates in verse 9 (for 'judgements' here plainly means decisions about conduct). What are being compared to gold and honey are those 'statutes' (in the Latin version 'decrees') which, we are told, 'rejoice the heart' (v. 8). For the whole poem is about the Law, not about 'judgement' in the sense to which Chapter 1 was devoted.

This was to me at first very mysterious. 'Thou shalt not steal, thou shalt not commit adultery' – I can understand that a man can, and must, respect these 'statutes', and try to obey them, and assent to them in his heart. But it is very hard to find how they could be, so to speak, delicious, how they exhilarate. If this is difficult at any time, it is doubly so when obedience to either is opposed to some strong, and perhaps *in itself* innocent, desire. A man held back by his unfortunate previous marriage to some lunatic or criminal who never dies from some woman whom he faithfully loves, or a hungry man left alone, without money, in a shop filled with the smell and sight of new bread, roasting coffee, or fresh strawberries – can these find the prohibition of adultery or of theft at all like honey? They may obey, they may still respect the 'statute'. But surely it could be more aptly compared to the dentist's forceps or the front line than to anything enjoyable and sweet.

A fine Christian and a great scholar to whom I once put this question said he thought that the poets were referring to the satisfaction men felt in knowing they had obeyed the Law; in other words, to the 'pleasures of a good conscience'. They would, on his view, be meaning something very like what Wordsworth meant when he said we know nothing more beautiful than the 'smile' on Duty's face – her smile when her orders have been carried out. It is rash for me to differ from such a man, and his view certainly makes excellent sense. The difficulty is that the Psalmists never seem to me to say anything very like this.

In Psalm 1:2 we are told that the good man's 'delight is in the law of the Lord, and in his law will he exercise himself day and night'. To 'exercise himself' in it apparently does not mean to obey it (though no doubt the good man will do that too) but to study it, as Dr Moffatt says to 'pore over it'. Of course 'the Law' does not here mean simply the ten commandments, it means the whole complex legislation (religious, moral, civil, criminal and even constitutional) contained in Leviticus, Numbers and Deuteronomy. The man who 'pores upon it' is obeying Joshua's command (Joshua 1:8), 'the book of the Law shall not depart out of thy mouth; but thou shalt meditate therein day and night.' This means, among other things, that the Law was a study or, as we should say, a 'subject'; a thing on which there would be commentaries, lectures, and examinations. There were. Thus part (religiously, the least important part) of what an ancient Jew meant when he said he 'delighted in the Law' was very like what one of us would mean if he said that somebody 'loved' history, or physics, or archaeology. This might imply a wholly innocent – though, of course, merely natural – delight in one's favourite subject; or, on the other hand, the pleasures of conceit, pride in one's own learning and consequent contempt for the outsiders who don't share it, or even a venal admiration for the studies which secure one's own stipend and social position.

The danger of this second development is obviously increased tenfold when the study in question is from the outset stamped as sacred. For then the danger of spiritual pride is added to that of mere ordinary pedantry and conceit. One is sometimes (not often) glad not to be a great theologian; one might so easily mistake it for being a good Christian. The temptations to which a great philologist or a great chemist is exposed are trivial in comparison. When the subject is sacred, proud and clever men may come to think that the outsiders who don't know it are not merely inferior to them in skill but lower in God's eyes; as the priests said (John 7:49), 'All that rabble who are not experts in the Torah are accursed.' And as this pride increases, the 'subject' or study which confers such privilege will grow more and more complicated, the list of things forbidden will increase, till to get through a single day without supposed sin becomes like an elaborate step-dance, and this horrible network breeds self-righteousness in some and haunting anxiety in others. Meanwhile the 'weightier matters of the Law', righteousness itself, shrinks into insignificance under this vast overgrowth, so that the legalists strain at a gnat and swallow a camel.

Thus the Law, like the sacrifice, can take on a cancerous life of its own and work against the thing for whose sake it existed. As Charles Williams wrote, 'When the means are autonomous they are deadly.' This morbid condition of the Law contributed to – I do not suggest it is the sole or main cause of – St Paul's joyous sense of Christ as the Deliverer from Law. It is against this same morbid condition that Our Lord uttered some of His sternest words; it is the sin, and simultaneously the punishment, of the Scribes and Pharisees. But that is not the side of the matter I want to stress here, nor does it by this time need stressing. I would rather let the Psalms show me again the good thing of which this bad thing is the corruption.

As everyone knows, the Psalm specially devoted to the Law is 119, the longest in the whole collection. And everyone has probably noticed that from the literary or technical point of view, it is the most formal and elaborate of them all. The technique consists in taking a series of words which are all, for purposes of this poem, more or less synonyms (*word, statutes, commandments, testimonies*, etc.), and ringing the changes on them through each of its eight-verse sections – which themselves correspond to the letters of the alphabet. (This may have given an ancient ear something of the same sort of pleasure we get from the Italian metre called the *Sestina*, where instead of rhymes we have the same end words repeated in varying orders in each stanza.) In other words, this poem is not, and does not pretend to be, a sudden outpouring of the heart like, say, Psalm 18. It is a pattern, a thing done like embroidery, stitch by stitch, through long, quiet hours, for love of the subject and for the delight in leisurely, disciplined craftsmanship.

Now this, in itself, seems to me very important because it lets us into the mind and mood of the poet. We can guess at once that he felt about the Law somewhat as he felt about his poetry; both involved exact and loving conformity to an intricate pattern. This at once suggests an attitude from which the Pharisaic conception could later grow but which in itself, though not necessarily religious, is quite innocent. It will look like priggery or pedantry (or else like a neurotic fussiness) to those who cannot sympathise with it, but it need not be any of these things. It may be the delight in Order, the pleasure in getting a thing 'just so' – as in dancing a minuet. Of course the poet is well aware that something incomparably more serious than a minuet is here in question. He is also aware that he is very unlikely, himself, to achieve this perfection of discipline: 'O that my ways *were* made so straight that I *might* keep thy statutes!' (v. 5). At present they aren't, and he can't. But his effort to do so does not spring from servile fear. The Order of the Divine mind, embodied in the Divine Law, is beautiful. What should a man do but try to reproduce it, so far as possible, in his daily life? His 'delight' is in those statutes (v. 16); to study them is like finding treasure (v. 14); they affect him like music, are his 'songs' (v. 54); they taste like honey (v. 103); they are better than silver and gold (v. 72). As one's eyes are more and more opened, one sees more and more in them, and it excites wonder (v. 18). This is not priggery nor even scrupulosity; it is the language of a man ravished by a moral beauty. If we cannot at all share his experience, we shall be the losers. Yet I cannot help fancying that a Chinese Christian – one whose own traditional culture had been the 'schoolmaster to bring him to Christ' – would appreciate this Psalm more than most of us; for it is an old idea in that culture that life should above all things be ordered and that its order should reproduce a Divine order.

But there is something else to our purpose in this grave poem. On three occasions the poet asserts that the Law is 'true' or 'the truth' (vv. 86, 138, 142). We find the same in Psalm 111:7, 'all his commandments are true'. (The word, I understand, could also be translated 'faithful', or 'sound'; what is, in the Hebrew sense, 'true' is what 'holds water', what doesn't 'give way' or collapse.) A modern logician would say that the Law is a command and that to call a command 'true' makes no sense; 'The door is shut' may be true or false but 'Shut the door' can't. But I think we all see pretty well what the Psalmists mean. They mean that in the Law you find the 'real' or 'correct' or stable, well-grounded, directions for living. The Law answers the question 'Wherewithal shall a young man cleanse his way?' (119:9). It is like a lamp, a guide (v. 105). There are many rival directions for living, as the Pagan cultures all round us show. When the poets call the directions or 'rulings' of Jahweh 'true' they are expressing the assurance that these, and not those others, are the 'real' or 'valid' or unassailable ones; that they are based on the very nature of things and the very nature of God.

By this assurance they put themselves, implicitly, on the right side of a controversy which arose far later among Christians. There were in the eighteenth century terrible theologians who held that 'God did not command certain things because they are right, but certain things are right because God commanded them.' To make the position perfectly clear, one of them even said that though God has, as it happens, commanded us to love Him and one another, He might equally well have commanded us to hate Him and one another, and hatred would then have been right. It was apparently a mere toss-up which He decided on. Such a view in effect makes God a mere arbitrary tyrant. It would be better and less irreligious to believe in no God and to have no ethics than to have such an ethics and such a theology as this. The Jews of course never discuss this in abstract and philosophical terms. But at once, and completely, they assume the right view, knowing better than they know. They know that the Lord (not merely obedience to the Lord) is 'righteous' and commands 'righteousness' because He loves it (11:8). He enjoins what is good because it is good, because He is good. Hence His laws have *emeth*, 'truth', intrinsic validity, rock-bottom reality, being rooted in His own nature, and are therefore as solid as that Nature which He has created. But the Psalmists themselves can say it best; 'thy righteousness standeth like the strong mountains, thy judgements are like the great deep' (36:6).[1] Their delight in the Law is a delight in having touched firmness; like the pedestrian's delight in feeling the hard road beneath his feet after a false short cut has long entangled him in muddy fields.

For there were other roads, which lacked 'truth'. The Jews had as their immediate neighbours, close to them in race as well as in position, Pagans of the worst kind, Pagans whose religion was marked by none of that beauty or (sometimes) wisdom which we can find among the Greeks. That background made the 'beauty' or 'sweetness' of the Law more visible; not least because these neighbouring Paganisms were a constant temptation to the Jew and may in some of their externals have been not unlike his own religion. The temptation was to turn to those terrible rites in times of terror – when, for example, the Assyrians were pressing on. We who not so long ago waited daily for invasion by enemies, like the Assyrians, skilled and constant in systematic cruelty, know how they may have felt. They were tempted, since the Lord seemed deaf, to try those appalling deities who demanded so much more and might therefore perhaps give more in return. But when a Jew in some happier hour, or a better Jew even in that hour, looked at those worships – when he thought of sacred prostitution, sacred sodomy, and the babies thrown into the fire for Moloch – his own 'Law' as he turned back to it must have shone with an extraordinary radiance. Sweeter than honey; or if that metaphor does not suit us who have not such a sweet tooth as all ancient peoples (partly because we have plenty of sugar), let us say like mountain water, like fresh air after a dungeon, like sanity after a nightmare. But, once again, the best image is in a Psalm, the 19th.[2]

I take this to be the greatest poem in the Psalter and one of the greatest lyrics in the world. Most readers will remember its structure; six verses about Nature, five about Law, and four of personal prayer. The actual words supply no logical connection between the first and second movements. In this way its technique resembles that of the most modern poetry. A modern

---

[1] See Appendix I, p. 720.
[2] See Appendix I, p. 719.

poet would pass with similar abruptness from one theme to another and leave you to find out the connecting link for yourself. But then he would possibly be doing this quite deliberately; he might have, though he chose to conceal, a perfectly clear and conscious link in his own mind which he could express to you in logical prose if he wanted to. I doubt if the ancient poet was like that. I think he felt, effortlessly and without reflecting on it, so close a connection, indeed (for his imagination) such an identity, between his first theme and his second that he passed from the one to the other without realising that he had made any transition. First he thinks of the sky; how, day after day, the pageantry we see there shows us the splendour of its Creator. Then he thinks of the sun, the bridal joyousness of its rising, the unimaginable speed of its daily voyage from east to west. Finally, of its heat; not of course the mild heats of our climate but the cloudless, blinding, tyrannous rays hammering the hills, searching every cranny. The key phrase on which the whole poem depends is 'there is nothing hid from the heat thereof'. It pierces everywhere with its strong, clean ardour. Then at once, in verse 7 he is talking of something else, which hardly seems to him something else because it is so like the all-piercing, all-detecting sunshine. The Law is 'undefiled', the Law gives light, it is clean and everlasting, it is 'sweet'. No one can improve on this and nothing can more fully admit us to the old Jewish feeling about the Law; luminous, severe, disinfectant, exultant. One hardly needs to add that this poet is wholly free from self-righteousness and the last section is concerned with his 'secret faults'. As he has felt the sun, perhaps in the desert, searching him out in every nook of shade where he attempted to hide from it, so he feels the Law searching out all the hiding-places of his soul.

In so far as this idea of the Law's beauty, sweetness, or preciousness, arose from the contrast of the surrounding Paganisms, we may soon find occasion to recover it. Christians increasingly live on a spiritual island; new and rival ways of life surround it in all directions and their tides come further up the beach every time. None of these new ways is yet so filthy or cruel as some Semitic Paganism. But many of them ignore all individual rights and are already cruel enough. Some give morality a wholly new meaning which we cannot accept, some deny its possibility. Perhaps we shall all learn, sharply enough, to value the clean air and 'sweet reasonableness' of the Christian ethics which in a more Christian age we might have taken for granted. But of course, if we do, we shall then be exposed to the danger of priggery. We might come to 'thank God that we are not as other men'. This introduces the greatest difficulty which the Psalms have raised in my mind.

7

CONNIVANCE

Every attentive reader of the Psalms will have noticed that they speak to us severely not merely about doing evil ourselves but about something else. In Psalm 26:4, the good man is not only free from 'vanity' (falsehood) but has not even 'dwelled with', been on intimate terms with, those who are 'vain'. He has 'hated' them (v. 5). So in 31:7, he has 'hated' idolaters. In 50:18, God blames a man not for being a thief but for 'consenting to' a thief (in Dr Moffatt, 'you are a friend to any thief you see'). In 141:4–6, where our translation appears to be rather wrong, the general sense nevertheless comes through and expresses the same attitude. Almost comically the Psalmist of 139 asks, 'Don't I hate those who hate thee, Lord? ... Why, I hate them as if they were *my* enemies!' (vv. 21, 22).

Now obviously all this – taking upon oneself to hate those whom one thinks God's enemies, avoiding the society of those one thinks wicked, judging our neighbours, thinking oneself 'too good' for some of them (not in the snobbish way, which is a trivial sin in comparison, but in the deepest meaning of the words 'too good') – is an extremely dangerous, almost a fatal, game. It leads straight to 'Pharisaism' in the sense which Our Lord's own teaching has given to that word. It leads not only to the wickedness but to the absurdity of those who in later times came to be called the 'unco guid'. This I assume from the outset, and I think that even in the Psalms this evil is already at work. But we must not be Pharisaical even to the Pharisees. It is foolish to read such passages without realising that a quite genuine problem is involved. And I am not at all confident about the solution.

We hear it said again and again that the editor of some newspaper is a rascal, that some politician is a liar, that some official person is a tyrannical Jack-in-office and even dishonest, that someone has treated his wife abominably, that some celebrity (film-star, author, or what not) leads a most vile and mischievous life. And the general rule in modern society is that no one refuses to meet any of these people and to behave towards them in the friendliest and most cordial manner. People will even go out of their way to meet them. They will not even stop buying the rascally newspaper, thus paying the owner for the lies, the detestable intrusions upon private life and private tragedy, the blasphemies and the pornography, which they profess to condemn.

I have said there is a problem here, but there are really two. One is social and almost political. It may be asked whether that state of society in which rascality undergoes no social penalty is a healthy one; whether we should not be a happier country if certain important people were pariahs as the hangman once was – blackballed at every club, dropped by every acquaintance, and liable to the print of riding-crop or fingers across the face if they were ever bold enough to speak to a respectable woman. It leads into the larger question whether the great evil of our civil life is not the fact that there seems now no medium between hopeless submission and full-dress revolution. Rioting has died out, moderate rioting. It can be argued that if the windows of various ministries and newspapers were more often broken, if certain people were more often put under pumps and (mildly – mud, not stones) pelted in the streets, we should get on a great deal better. It is not wholly desirable that any man should be allowed at once the pleasures of a tyrant or a wolf's-head and also those of an honest freeman among his equals. To this question I do not know the answer. The dangers of a change in the direction I have outlined are very great; so are the evils of our present tameness.

I am concerned here only with the problem that appears in our individual and private lives. How ought we to behave in the presence of very bad people? I will limit this by changing 'very bad people' to 'very bad people who are powerful, prosperous and impenitent'. If they are outcasts, poor and miserable, whose wickedness obviously has not 'paid', then every Christian knows the answer. Christ speaking to the Samaritan woman at the well, Christ with the woman taken in adultery, Christ dining with publicans, is our example. I mean, of course, that His humility, His love, His total indifference to the social discredit and misrepresentation He might incur are examples for us; not, Heaven knows, that any of us who was not specially qualified to do so by priesthood, age, old acquaintance, or the earnest request of the sinners themselves, could without insolence and presumption assume the least trace of His authority to rebuke and pardon. (One has to be very careful lest the desire to patronise and the itch to be a busybody should disguise itself as a vocation to help the 'fallen', or tend to obscure our knowledge that we are fallen – perhaps in God's eyes far more so – ourselves.) But we may be sure there were others who equally consorted with 'publicans and sinners' and whose motives were very unlike those of Our Lord.

The publicans were the lowest members of what may be called the Vichy or Collaborationist movement in Palestine; men who fleeced their fellow-countrymen to get money for the occupying power in return for a fat percentage of the swag. As such they were like the hangman, outside all decent social intercourse. But some of them did pretty well financially, and no doubt most of them enjoyed, up to a point, the protection and contemptuous favours of the Roman government. One may guess that some consorted with them for very bad reasons – to get 'pickings', to be on good terms with such dangerous neighbours. Besides Our Lord there would have been among their guests toadies and those who wanted to be 'on the bandwagon'; people in fact like a young man I once knew.

He had been a strict socialist at Oxford. Everything ought to be run by the State; private enterprise and independent professions were for him the great evil. He then went away and became a schoolmaster. After about ten years of that he came to see me. He said his political views had been wholly reversed. You never heard a fuller recantation. He now saw that State interference was fatal. What had converted him was his experience as a schoolmaster of the Ministry of Education – a set of ignorant meddlers armed with insufferable powers to pester, hamper and interrupt the work of real, practical teachers who knew the subjects they taught, who knew boys, parents, and all the real conditions of their work. It makes no difference to the point of the story whether you agree with his view of the Ministry; the important thing is that he held that view. For the real point of the story, and of his visit, when it came, nearly took my breath away. Thinking thus, he had come to see whether I had any influence which might help him to get a job in the Ministry of Education.

Here is the perfect band-wagoner. Immediately on the decision 'This is a revolting tyranny', follows the question 'How can I as quickly as possible cease to be one of the victims and become one of the tyrants?' If I had been able to introduce the young man to someone in the Ministry, I think we may be sure that his manners to that hated 'meddler' would have been genial and friendly in the extreme. Thus someone who had heard his previous invective against the meddling and then witnessed his actual behaviour to the meddler, might possibly (for charity 'believeth all things') have concluded that this young man was full of the purest Christianity and loved one he thought a sinner while hating what he thought his sin.

Of course this is an instance of band-wagoning so crude and unabashed as to be farcical. Not many of us perhaps commit the like. But there are subtler, more social or intellectual forms of band-wagoning which might deceive us. Many people have a very strong desire to meet celebrated or 'important' people, including those of whom they disapprove, from curiosity or vanity. It gives them something to talk or even (anyone may produce a book of reminiscences) to write about. It is felt to confer distinction if the great, though odious, man recognises you in the street. And where such motives are in play it is better still to know him quite well, to be intimate with him.

It would be delightful if he shouted out 'Hallo Bill' while you were walking down the Strand with an impressionable country cousin. I don't know that the desire is itself a very serious defect. But I am inclined to think a Christian would be wise to avoid, where he decently can, any meeting with people who are bullies, lascivious, cruel, dishonest, spiteful and so forth.

Not because we are 'too good' for them. In a sense because we are not good enough. We are not good enough to cope with all the temptations, nor clever enough to cope with all the problems, which an evening spent in such society produces. The temptation is to condone, to connive at; by our words, looks and laughter, to 'consent'. The temptation was never greater than now when we are all (and very rightly) so afraid of priggery or 'smugness'. And of course, even if we do not seek them out, we shall constantly be in such company whether we wish it or not. This is the real and unavoidable difficulty.

We shall hear vile stories told as funny; not merely licentious stories but (to me far more serious and less noticed) stories which the teller could not be telling unless he was betraying someone's confidence. We shall hear infamous detraction of the absent, often disguised as pity or humour. Things we hold sacred will be mocked. Cruelty will be slyly advocated by the assumption that its only opposite is 'sentimentality'. The very presuppositions of any possible good life – all disinterested motives, all heroism, all genuine forgiveness – will be, not explicitly denied (for then the matter could be discussed), but assumed to be phantasmal, idiotic, believed in only by children.

What is one to do? For on the one hand, quite certainly, there is a degree of unprotesting participation in such talk which is very bad. We are strengthening the hands of the enemy. We are encouraging him to believe that 'those Christians', once you get them off their guard and round a dinner table, really think and feel exactly as he does. By implication we are denying our Master; behaving as if we 'knew not the Man'. On the other hand is one to show that, like Queen Victoria, one is 'not amused'? Is one to be contentious, interrupting the flow of conversation at every moment with 'I don't agree, I don't agree'? Or rise and go away? But by these courses we may also confirm some of their worst suspicions of 'those Christians'. We are just the sort of ill-mannered prigs they always said.

Silence is a good refuge. People will not notice it nearly so easily as we tend to suppose. And (better still) few of us enjoy it as we might be in danger of enjoying more forcible methods. Disagreement can, I think, sometimes be expressed without the appearance of priggery, if it is done argumentatively not dictatorially; support will often come from some most unlikely member of the party, or from more than one, till we discover that those who were silently dissentient were actually a majority. A discussion of real interest may follow. Of course the right side may be defeated in it. That matters very much less than I used to think. The very man who has argued you down will sometimes be found, years later, to have been influenced by what you said.

There comes, however, a degree of evil against which a protest will have to be made, however little chance it has of success. There are cheery agreements in cynicism or brutality which one must contract out of unambiguously. If it can't be done without seeming priggish, then priggish we must seem.

For what really matters is not seeming but being a prig. If we sufficiently dislike making the protest, if we are strongly tempted not to, we are unlikely to be priggish in reality. Those who positively enjoy, as they call it, 'testifying' are in a different and more dangerous position. As for the mere seeming – well, though it is very bad to be a prig, there are social atmospheres so foul that in them it is almost an alarming symptom if a man has never been called one. Just in the same way, though pedantry is a folly and snobbery a vice, yet there are circles in which only a man indifferent to all accuracy will escape being called a pedant, and others where manners are so coarse, flashy and shameless that a man (whatever his social position) of any natural good taste will be called a snob.

What makes this contact with wicked people so difficult is that to handle the situation successfully requires not merely good intentions, even with humility and courage thrown in; it may call for social and even intellectual talents which God has not given us. It is therefore not self-righteousness but mere prudence to avoid it when we can. The Psalmists were not quite wrong when they described the good man as avoiding 'the seat of the scornful' and fearing to consort with the ungodly lest he should 'eat of' (shall we say, laugh at, admire, approve, justify?) 'such things as please them'. As usual in their attitude, with all its dangers, there is a core of very good sense. 'Lead us not into temptation' often means, among other things, 'Deny me those gratifying invitations, those highly interesting contacts, that participation in the brilliant movements of our age, which I so often, at such risk, desire.'

Closely connected with these warnings against what I have called 'connivance' are the protests of the Psalter[1] against other sins of the tongue. I think that when I began to read it these surprised me a little; I had half expected that in a simpler and more violent age when more evil was done with the knife, the big stick, and the firebrand, less would be done by talk. But in reality the Psalmists mention hardly any kind of evil more often than this one, which the most civilised societies share. 'Their throat is an open sepulchre, they flatter' (5:10), 'under his tongue is ungodliness and vanity', or 'perjury' as Dr Moffatt translates it (10:7), 'deceitful lips' (12:3), 'lying

---

[1] Some of these probably involve archaic, and even magical, ideas of a power intrinsic in words themselves, so that all blessings and cursings would be efficacious.

lips' (31:20), 'words full of deceit' (36:3), the 'whispering' of evil men (41:7), cruel lies that 'cut like a razor' (52:3), talk that sounds 'smooth as oil' and will wound like a sword (55:22), pitiless jeering (102:8). It is all over the Psalter. One almost hears the incessant whispering, tattling, lying, scolding, flattery, and circulation of rumours. No historical readjustments are here required, we are in the world we know. We even detect in that muttering and wheedling chorus voices which are familiar. One of them may be too familiar for recognition.

8

NATURE

Two factors determine the Psalmists' approach to Nature. The first they share with the vast majority of ancient writers; the second was in their time, if not absolutely unique, extremely rare.

(i) They belong to a nation chiefly of peasants. For us the very name Jew is associated with finance, shop-keeping, money-lending and the like. This however, dates from the Middle Ages when the Jews were not allowed to own land and were driven into occupations remote from the soil. Whatever characteristics the modern Jew has acquired from millennia of such occupations, they cannot have been those of his ancient ancestors. Those were peasants or farmers. When even a king covets a piece of his neighbour's property, the piece is a vineyard; he is more like a wicked squire than a wicked king. Everyone was close to the land; everyone vividly aware of our dependence on soils and weather. So, till a late age, was every Greek and Roman. Thus part of what we should now, perhaps, call 'appreciation of Nature' could not then exist – all that part which is really delight in 'the country' as a contrast to the town. Where towns are few and very small and where nearly everyone is on the land, one is not aware of any special thing called 'the country'. Hence a certain sort of 'nature poetry' never existed in the ancient world till really vast cities like Alexandria arose; and, after the fall of ancient civilisation, it never existed again until the eighteenth century. At other periods what we call 'the country' is simply the world, what water is to a fish. Nevertheless appreciation of Nature can exist; a delight which is both utilitarian and poetic. Homer can enjoy a landscape, but what he means by a beautiful landscape is one that is useful – good deep soil, plenty of fresh water, pasture that will make the cows really fat, and some nice timber. Being one of a seafaring race he adds, as a Jew would not, a good harbour. The Psalmists, who are writing lyrics not romances, naturally give us little landscape. What they do give us, far more sensuously and delightedly than anything I have seen in Greek, is the very feel of weather – weather seen with a real countryman's eyes, enjoyed almost as a vegetable might be supposed to enjoy it. 'Thou art good to the earth ... thou waterest her furrows ... thou makest it soft with drops of rain ... the little hills shall rejoice on every side ... the valleys shall stand so thick with corn that they shall laugh and sing; (65:9–14). In 104:16 (better in Dr Moffatt than in the Prayer Book), 'the great trees drink their fill'.

(ii) The Jews, as we all know, believed in one God, maker of heaven and earth. Nature and God were distinct; the One had made the other; the One ruled and the other obeyed. This, I say, we all know. But for various reasons its real significance can easily escape a modern reader if his studies happen not to have led him in certain directions.

In the first place it is for us a platitude. We take it for granted. Indeed I suspect that many people assume that some clear doctrine of creation underlies all religions: that in Paganism the gods, or one of the gods, usually created the world; even that religions normally begin by answering the question, 'Who made the world?' In reality, creation, in any unambiguous sense, seems to be a surprisingly rare doctrine; and when stories about it occur in Paganism they are often religiously unimportant, not in the least central to the religions in which we find them. They are on the fringe where religion tails off into what was perhaps felt, even at the time, to be more like fairy-tale. In one Egyptian story a god called Atum came up out of the water and, being apparently a hermaphrodite, begot and bore the two next gods; after that, things could get on. In another, the whole senate of the gods came up out of Nun, the Deep. According to a Babylonian myth, before heaven and earth were made a being called Apsu begot, and a being called Tiamat bore, Lahmu and Lahamu, who in their turn produced Anshar and Kishar. We are expressly told that this pair were greater than their parents, so that it is more like a myth of evolution than of creation. In the Norse myth we begin with ice and fire, and indeed with a north and south, amidst all which, somehow, a giant comes to life, who bears (from his arm-pit) a son and daughter. Greek mythology starts with heaven and earth already in existence.

I do not mention these myths to indulge in a cheap laugh at their crudity. All our language about such things, that of the theologian as well as that of the child, is crude. The real point is that the myths, even in their own terms, do not reach the idea of Creation in our sense at all. Things 'come up out of' something or 'are formed in' something. If the stories could, for the moment, be supposed true, they would still be stories about very early events in a process of development, a world-history, which was already going on. When the curtain rises in these myths there are always some 'properties' already on the stage and some sort of drama is proceeding. You may say they answer the question 'How did the play begin?' But that is an ambiguous question. Asked by the man who arrived ten minutes late it would be properly answered, say, with the words, 'Oh, first three witches came in, and then there was a scene between an old king and a wounded soldier.' That is the sort of question the myths are in fact answering. But the very different question: 'How does a play originate? Does it write itself? Do the actors make it up as they go along? Or is there someone – not on the stage, not like the people on the stage – someone we don't see – who invented it all and caused it to be?' – this is rarely asked or answered.

Admittedly we find in Plato a clear Theology of Creation in the Judaic and Christian sense; the whole universe – the very conditions of time and space under which it exists – are produced by the will of a perfect, timeless, unconditioned God who is above and outside all that He makes. But this is an amazing leap (though not made without the help of Him who is the Father of lights) by an overwhelming theological genius; it is not ordinary Pagan religion.

Now we all understand of course the importance of this peculiarity in Judaic thought from a strictly and obviously religious point of view. But its total consequences, the ways in which it changes a man's whole mind and imagination, might escape us.

To say that God created Nature, while it brings God and Nature into relation, also separates them. What makes and what is made must be two, not one. Thus the doctrine of Creation in one sense empties Nature of divinity. How very hard this was to do and, still more, to keep on doing, we do not now easily realise. A passage from Job (not without its own wild poetry in it) may help us. 'If I beheld the sun when it shined, or the moon walking in brightness; and my heart hath been secretly enticed, or my mouth kissed my hand; this also would be an iniquity' (31:26–28). There is here no question of turning, in a time of desperate need, to devilish gods. The speaker is obviously referring to an utterly spontaneous impulse, a thing you might find yourself acting upon almost unawares. To pay some reverence to the sun or moon is apparently so natural; so apparently innocent. Perhaps in certain times and places it was really innocent. I would gladly believe that the gesture of homage offered to the moon was sometimes accepted by her Maker; in those times of ignorance which God 'winked at' (Acts 17:30). The author of Job, however, was not in that ignorance. If he had kissed his hand to the moon it would have been iniquity. The impulse was a temptation; one which no European has felt for the last thousand years.

But in another sense the same doctrine which empties Nature of her divinity also makes her an index, a symbol, a manifestation, of the Divine. I must recall two passages quoted in an earlier chapter. One is that from Psalm 19 where the searching and cleansing sun becomes an image of the searching and cleansing Law. The other is from Psalm 36: 'Thy mercy, O Lord, reacheth unto the heavens, and thy faithfulness unto the clouds. Thy righteousness standeth like the strong mountains, thy judgements are like the great deep'

(vv. 5, 6). It is surely just because the natural objects are no longer taken to be themselves Divine that they can now be magnificent symbols of Divinity. There is little point in comparing a Sun-god with the sun or Neptune with the great deep; there is much in comparing the Law with the sun or saying that God's judgements are an abyss and a mystery like the sea.

But of course the doctrine of Creation leaves Nature full of manifestations which show the presence of God, and created energies which serve Him. The light is His garment, the thing we partially see Him through (Psalm 104:2), the thunder can be His voice (29:3–5). He dwells in the dark thundercloud (18:11), the eruption of a volcano comes in answer to His touch (104:32). The world is full of his emissaries and executors. He makes winds His messengers and flames His servants (104:4), rides upon cherubim (18:10), commands the army of angels.

All this is clearly in one way very close to Paganism. Thor and Zeus also spoke in the thunder; Hermes or Iris was the messenger of the gods. But the difference, though subtle, is momentous, between hearing in the thunder the voice of God or the voice of a god. As we have seen, even in the creation-myths, gods have beginnings. Most of them have fathers and mothers; often we know their birth-places. There is no question of self-existence or the timeless. Being is imposed upon them, as upon us, by preceding causes. They are, like us, creatures or products; though they are luckier than we in being stronger, more beautiful, and exempt from death. They are, like us, actors in the cosmic drama, not its authors. Plato fully understood this. His God creates the gods and preserves them from death by His own power; they have no inherent immortality. In other words, the difference between believing in God and in many gods is not one of arithmetic. As someone has said 'gods' is not really the plural of God; God has no plural. Thus, when you hear in the thunder the voice of a god, you are stopping short, for the voice of a god is not really a voice from beyond the world, from the uncreated. By taking the god's voice away – or envisaging the god as an angel, a servant of that Other – you go further. The thunder becomes not less divine but more. By emptying Nature of divinity – or, let us say, of divinities – you may fill her with Deity, for she is now the bearer of messages. There is a sense in which Nature-worship silences her – as if a child or a savage were so impressed with the postman's uniform that he omitted to take in the letters.

Another result of believing in Creation is to see Nature not as a mere datum but as an achievement. Some of the Psalmists are delighted with its mere solidity and permanence. God has given to His works His own character of *emeth*; they are watertight, faithful, reliable, not at all vague or phantasmal. 'All His works are *faithful* – He spake and it was done, He commanded and it stood fast' (33:4, 9). By His might (Dr Moffatt's version) 'the mountains are made firm and strongly fixed' (65:6). God has laid the foundations of the earth with perfect thoroughness (104:5). He has made everything firm and permanent and imposed boundaries which limit each thing's operation (148:6). Notice how in Psalm 136 the poet passes from God's creation of Nature to the delivering of Israel out of Egypt: both are equally great deeds, great victories.

But the most surprising result of all is still to be mentioned. I said that the Jews, like nearly all the ancients, were agricultural and approached Nature with a gardener's and a farmer's interest, concerned with rain, with grass 'for the service of man', wine to cheer man up and olive-oil to make his face shine – to make it look, as Homer says somewhere, like a peeled onion (104:14, 15). But we find them led on beyond this. Their gusto, or even gratitude, embraces things that are no use to man. In the great Psalm especially devoted to Nature, from which I have just quoted (104),[1] we have not only the useful cattle, the cheering vine, and the nourishing corn. We have springs where the wild asses quench their thirst (v. 11), fir trees for the storks (v. 17), hill country for the wild goats and 'conies' (perhaps marmots, v. 18), finally even the lions (v. 21); and even with a glance far out to sea, where no Jew willingly went, the great whales playing, enjoying themselves (v. 26).

Of course this appreciation of, almost this sympathy with, creatures useless or hurtful or wholly irrelevant to man, is not our modern 'kindness to animals'. That is a virtue most easily practised by those who have never, tired and hungry, had to work with animals for a bare living, and who inhabit a country where all dangerous wild beasts have been exterminated.[2] The Jewish feeling, however, is vivid, fresh, and impartial. In Norse stories a pestilent creature such as a dragon tends to be conceived as the enemy not only of men but of gods. In classical stories, more disquietingly, it tends to be sent by a god for the destruction of men whom he has a grudge against. The Psalmist's clear objective view – noting the lions and whales side by side with men and men's cattle – is unusual. And I think it is certainly reached through the idea of God as Creator and sustainer of all. In 104:21, the point about the lions is that they, like us, 'do seek their meat from God'. All these creatures, like us, 'wait upon' God at feeding-time (v. 27). It is the same in 147:9; though the raven was an unclean bird to Jews, God 'feedeth the young ravens that call upon him'. The thought which gives these creatures a place in the Psalmist's gusto for Nature is surely obvious. They are our fellow-dependents; we all – lions, storks, ravens, whales – live, as our fathers said, 'at God's charges', and mention of all equally redounds to His praise.

---

[1] See Appendix 1, pp. 723–4.
[2] Heaven forbid, however, that I should be thought to slight it. I only mean that for those of us who meet beasts solely as pets it is not a costly virtue. We may properly be kicked if we lack it, but must not pat ourselves on the back for having it. When a hard-worked shepherd or carter remains kind to animals his back may well be patted; not ours.

One curious bit of evidence strengthens my belief that there is such a connection between this sort of nature poetry and the doctrine of creation; and it is also so interesting in itself that I think it worth a digression. I have said that Paganism in general fails to get out of nature something that the Jews got. There is one apparent instance to the contrary; one ancient Gentile poem which provides a fairly close parallel to Psalm 104. But then, when we come to examine it, we find that this poem is not Pagan in the sense of Polytheistic at all. It is addressed to a Monotheistic God and salutes Him as the Creator of the whole earth. It is therefore no exception to my generalisation. Where ancient Gentile literature (in some measure) anticipates the nature poetry of the Jews, it has also (in some measure) anticipated their theology. And that, in my view, is what we might have expected.

The poem in question is an Egyptian *Hymn to the Sun* dating from the 14th century BC. Its author is that Pharaoh whose real name was Amenhetep IV, but who called himself Akhenaten. Many of my readers will know his story already. He was a spiritual revolutionary. He broke away from the Polytheism of his fathers and nearly tore Egypt into shreds in his efforts to establish by force the worship of a single God. In the eyes of the established priesthood, whose property he transferred to the service of this new religion, he must have seemed a monster; a sort of Henry VIII plundering the abbeys. His Monotheism appears to have been of an extremely pure and conceptual kind. He did not, as a man of that age might have been expected to do, even identify God with the Sun. The visible disc was only His manifestation. It is an astonishing leap, more astonishing in some ways than Plato's, and, like Plato's, in sharp contrast to ordinary Paganism. And as far as we can see, it was a total failure. Akhenaten's religion died with him. Nothing, apparently, came of it.

Unless of course, as is just possible, Judaism itself partly came of it. It is conceivable that ideas derived from Akhenaten's system formed part of that Egyptian 'Wisdom' in which Moses was bred. There is nothing to disquiet us in such a possibility. Whatever was true in Akhenaten's creed came to him, in some mode or other, as all truth comes to all men, from God. There is no reason why traditions descending from Akhenaten should not have been among the instruments which God used in making Himself known to Moses. But we have no evidence that this is what actually happened. Nor do we know how fit Akhenatenism would really have been to serve as an instrument for this purpose. Its inside, its spirituality, the quality of life from which it sprang and which it encouraged, escape us. The man himself still has the power, after 34 centuries, to evoke the most violent, and contradictory, reactions. To one modern scholar he is the 'first individual' whom history records; to another, he is a crank, a faddist, half insane, possibly cretinous. We may well hope that he was accepted and blessed by God; but that his religion, at any rate on the historical level, was not so blessed and so accepted, is pretty clear. Perhaps the seed was good seed but fell on stony ground. Or perhaps it was not after all exactly the right sort of seed. To us moderns, no doubt, such a simple, enlightened, reasonable Monotheism looks very much more like the good seed than those earliest documents of Judaism in which Jahweh seems little more than a tribal deity. We might be wrong. Perhaps if Man is finally to know the bodiless, timeless, transcendent Ground of the whole universe not as a mere philosophical abstraction but as the Lord who, despite this transcendence, is 'not far from any one of us', as an utterly concrete Being (far more concrete than we) whom Man can fear, love, address, and 'taste', he must begin far more humbly and far nearer home, with the local altar, the traditional feast, and the treasured memories of God's judgements, promises, and mercies. It is possible that a certain sort of enlightenment can come too soon and too easily. At that early stage it may not be fruitful to typify God by anything so remote, so neutral, so international and (as it were) interdenominational, so featureless, as the solar disc. Since in the end we are to come to baptism and the Eucharist, to the stable at Bethlehem, the hill of Calvary, and the emptied rock-tomb, perhaps it is better to begin with circumcision, the Passover, the Ark, and the Temple. For 'the highest does not stand without the lowest'. Does not stand, does not stay; rises, rather, and expands, and finally loses itself in endless space. For the entrance is low: we must stoop till we are no taller than children in order to get in.

It would therefore be rash to assume that Akhenaten's Monotheism was, in those ways which are religiously most important, an exact anticipation of the Judaic; so that if only the priests and people of Egypt had accepted it, God could have dispensed with Israel altogether and revealed Himself to us henceforward through a long line of Egyptian prophets. What concerns us at the moment, however, is simply to note that Akhenaten's religion, being certainly in some respects like that of the Jews, sets him free to write nature-poetry in some degree like theirs. The degree could be exaggerated. The *Hymn to the Sun* remains different from the Psalms. It is magnificently like Psalm 139 (vv. 13–16) when it praises God for making the embryo grow in the mother's body, so that He is 'our nurse even in the womb': or for teaching the chick to break the eggshell and come forth 'chirping as loud as he can'. In the verse, 'Thou didst create the earth, according to thy desire,' Akhenaten even anticipates the New Testament – 'thou hast created all things, and for thy pleasure they are, and were created' (Revelation 4:11). But he does not quite see the lions as our fellow-pensioners. He brings them in, to be sure, but notice how: 'when thou settest, the world is in darkness like the dead. Out come the lions: all serpents sting.' Thus coupled with death and poisonous snakes, they are clearly envisaged in their capacity of enemies. It almost sounds as if the night itself were an enemy, out of God's reach. There is just a trace of dualism. But if there is difference, the likeness also is real. And it is the likeness which is relevant to the theme of this chapter. In Akhenaten as in the Psalms, a certain kind of poetry seems to go with a certain kind of theology. But the full and abiding development of both is Jewish.

(Meanwhile, what gentle heart can leave the topic without a prayer that this lonely ancient king, crank and doctrinaire though perhaps he was, has long seen and now enjoys the truth which so far transcends his own glimpse of it?)

9

A WORD ABOUT PRAISING

It is possible (and it is to be hoped) that this chapter will be unnecessary for most people. Those who were never thick-headed enough to get into the difficulty it deals with may even find it funny. I have not the least objection to their laughing; a little comic relief in a discussion does no harm, however serious the topic may be. (In my own experience the funniest things have occurred in the gravest and most sincere conversations.)

When I first began to draw near to belief in God and even for some time after it had been given to me, I found a stumbling block in the demand so clamorously made by all religious people that we should 'praise' God; still more in the suggestion that God Himself demanded it. We all despise the man who demands continued assurance of his own virtue, intelligence or delightfulness; we despise still more the crowd of people round every dictator, every millionaire, every celebrity, who gratify that demand. Thus a picture, at once ludicrous and horrible, both of God and of His worshippers, threatened to appear in my mind. The Psalms were especially troublesome in this way – 'Praise the Lord', 'O praise the Lord with me', 'Praise Him'. (And why, incidentally, did praising God so often consist in telling other people to praise Him? Even in telling whales, snowstorms, etc., to go on doing what they would certainly do whether we told them or not?) Worse still was the statement put into God's own mouth, 'whoso offereth me thanks and praise, he honoureth me' (50:23). It was hideously like saying, 'What I most want is to be told that I am good and great.' Worst of all was the suggestion of the very silliest Pagan bargaining, that of the savage who makes offerings to his idol when the fishing is good and beats it when he has caught nothing. More than once the Psalmists seemed to be saying, 'You like praise. Do this for me, and you shall have some.' Thus in Psalm 54 the poet begins 'save me' (v. 1), and in verse 6 adds an inducement, 'An offering of a free heart will I give thee, and praise thy Name.' Again and again the speaker asks to be saved from death on the ground that if God lets His suppliants die He will get no more praise from them, for the ghosts in Sheol cannot praise (30:10; 88:10; 119:175). And mere quantity of praise seemed to count; 'seven times a day do I praise thee' (119:164). It was extremely distressing. It made one think what one least wanted to think. Gratitude to God, reverence to Him, obedience to Him, I thought I could understand; not this perpetual eulogy. Nor were matters mended by a modern author who talked of God's 'right' to be praised.

I still think 'right' is a bad way of expressing it, but I believe I now see what the author meant. It is perhaps easiest to begin with inanimate objects which can have no rights. What do we mean when we say that a picture is 'admirable'? We certainly don't mean that it is admired (that's as may be) for bad work is admired by thousands and good work may be ignored. Nor that it 'deserves' admiration in the sense in which a candidate 'deserves' a high mark from the examiners – i.e. that a human being will have suffered injustice if it is not awarded. The sense in which the picture 'deserves' or 'demands' admiration is rather this; that admiration is the correct, adequate or appropriate, response to it, that, if paid, admiration will not be 'thrown away', and that if we do not admire we shall be stupid, insensible, and great losers, we shall have missed something. In that way many objects both in Nature and in Art may be said to deserve, or merit, or demand, admiration. It was from this end, which will seem to some irreverent, that I found it best to approach the idea that God 'demands' praise. He is that Object to admire which (or, if you like, to appreciate which) is simply to be awake, to have entered the real world; not to appreciate which is to have lost the greatest experience, and in the end to have lost all. The incomplete and crippled lives of those who are tone-deaf, have never been in love, never known true friendship, never cared for a good book, never enjoyed the feel of the morning air on their cheeks, never (I am one of these) enjoyed football, are faint images of it.

But of course this is not all. God does not only 'demand' praise as the supremely beautiful and all-satisfying Object. He does apparently command it as lawgiver. The Jews were told to sacrifice. We are under an obligation to go to church. But this was a difficulty only because I did not then understand any of what I have tried to say above in Chapter 5. I did not see that it is in the process of being worshipped that God communicates His presence to men. It is not indeed the only way. But for many people at many times the 'fair beauty of the Lord' is revealed chiefly or only while they worship Him together. Even in Judaism the essence of the sacrifice was not really that men gave bulls and goats to God, but that by their so doing God gave Himself to men; in the central act of our own worship of course this is far clearer – there is manifestly, even physically, God who gives and we who receive. The miserable idea that God should in any sense need, or crave for, our worship like a vain woman wanting compliments, or a vain author presenting his new books to people who have never met or heard of him, is implicitly answered by the words, 'If I be hungry I will not tell *thee*' (50:12). Even if such an absurd Deity could be conceived, He would hardly come to *us*, the lowest of rational creatures, to gratify His appetite. I don't want my dog to bark approval of my books. Now that I come to think of it, there are some humans whose enthusiastically favourable criticism would not much gratify me.

But the most obvious fact about praise – whether of God or anything – strangely escaped me. I thought of it in terms of compliment, approval, or the giving of honour. I had never noticed that all enjoyment spontaneously overflows into praise unless (sometimes even if) shyness or the fear of boring others is deliberately brought in to check it. The world rings with praise – lovers praising their mistresses, readers their favourite poet, walkers praising the countryside, players praising their favourite game – praise of weather, wines, dishes, actors, motors, horses, colleges, countries, historical personages, children, flowers, mountains, rare stamps, rare beetles, even sometimes politicians or scholars. I had not noticed how the humblest, and at the same time most balanced and capacious, minds, praised most, while the cranks, misfits and malcontents praised least. The good critics found something to praise in many imperfect works; the bad ones continually narrowed the list of books we might be allowed to read. The healthy and unaffected man, even if luxuriously brought up and widely experienced in good cookery, could praise a very modest meal: the dyspeptic and the snob found fault with all. Except where intolerably adverse circumstances interfere, praise almost seems to be inner health made audible. Nor does it cease to be so when, through lack of skill, the forms of its expression are very uncouth or even ridiculous. Heaven knows, many poems of praise addressed to an earthly beloved are as bad as our bad hymns, and an anthology of love poems for public and perpetual use would probably be as sore a trial to literary taste as *Hymns Ancient and Modern.* I had not noticed either that just as men spontaneously praise whatever they value, so they spontaneously urge us to join them in praising it: 'Isn't she lovely? Wasn't it glorious? Don't you think that magnificent?' The Psalmists in telling everyone to praise God are doing what all men do when they speak of what they care about. My whole, more general, difficulty about the praise of God depended on my absurdly denying to us, as regards the supremely Valuable, what we delight to do, what indeed we can't help doing, about everything else we value.

I think we delight to praise what we enjoy because the praise not merely expresses but completes the enjoyment; it is its appointed consummation. It is not out of compliment that lovers keep on telling one another how beautiful they are; the delight is incomplete till it is expressed. It is frustrating to have discovered a new author and not to be able to tell anyone how good he is; to come suddenly, at the turn of the road, upon some mountain valley of unexpected grandeur and then to have to keep silent because the people with you care for it no more than for a tin can in the ditch; to hear a good joke and find no one to share it with (the perfect hearer died a year ago). This is so even when our expressions are inadequate, as of course they usually are. But how if one could really and fully praise even such things to perfection – utterly 'get out' in poetry or music or paint the upsurge of appreciation which almost bursts you? Then indeed the object would be fully appreciated and our delight would have attained perfect development. The worthier the object, the more intense this delight would be. If it were possible for a created soul fully (I mean, up to the full measure conceivable in a finite being) to 'appreciate', that is to love and delight in, the worthiest object of all, and simultaneously at every moment to give this delight perfect expression, then that soul would be in supreme beatitude. It is along these lines that I find it easiest to understand the Christian doctrine that 'Heaven' is a state in which angels now, and men hereafter, are perpetually employed in praising God. This does not mean, as it can so dismally suggest, that it is like 'being in church'. For our 'services' both in their conduct and in our power to participate, are merely attempts at worship; never fully successful, often 99.9 per cent failures, sometimes total failures. We are not riders but pupils in the riding school; for most of us the falls and bruises, the aching muscles and the severity of the exercise, far outweigh those few moments in which we were, to our own astonishment, actually galloping without terror and without disaster. To see what the doctrine really means, we must suppose ourselves to be in perfect love with God – drunk with, drowned in, dissolved by, that delight which, far from remaining pent up within ourselves as incommunicable, hence hardly tolerable, bliss, flows out from us incessantly again in effortless and perfect expression, our joy no more separable from the praise in which it liberates and utters itself than the brightness a mirror receives is separable from the brightness it sheds. The Scotch catechism says that man's chief end is 'to glorify God and enjoy Him forever'. But we shall then know that these are the same thing. Fully to enjoy is to glorify. In commanding us to glorify Him, God is inviting us to enjoy Him.

Meanwhile of course we are merely, as Donne says, tuning our instruments. The tuning up of the orchestra can be itself delightful, but only to those who can in some measure, however little, anticipate the symphony. The Jewish sacrifices, and even our own most sacred rites, as they actually occur in human experience, are, like the tuning, promise, not performance. Hence, like the tuning, they may have in them much duty and little delight; or none. But the duty exists for the delight. When we carry out our 'religious duties' we are like people digging channels in a waterless land, in order that when at last the water comes, it may find them ready. I mean, for the most part. There are happy moments, even now, when a trickle creeps along the dry beds; and happy souls to whom this happens often.

As for the element of bargaining in the Psalms (Do this and I will praise you), that silly dash of Paganism certainly existed. The flame does not ascend pure from the altar. But the impurities are not its essence. And we are not all in a position to despise even the crudest Psalmists on this score. Of course we would not blunder in our words like them. But there is, for ill as well as for good, a wordless prayer. I have often, on my knees, been shocked to find what sort of thoughts I have, for a moment, been addressing to God; what infantile placations I was really offering, what claims I have really made, even what absurd adjustments or compromises I was, half-consciously, proposing. There is a Pagan, savage heart in me somewhere. For unfortunately the folly and idiot-cunning of Paganism seem to have far more power of surviving than its innocent or even beautiful elements. It is easy, once you have power, to silence the pipes, still the dances, disfigure the statues, and forget the stories; but not easy to kill the savage, the greedy, frightened creature now cringing, now blustering, in one's soul – the creature to whom God may well say, 'thou thoughtest I am even such a one as thyself' (50:21).

But all this, as I have said, will be illuminating to only a few of my readers. To the others, such a comedy of errors, so circuitous a journey to reach the obvious, will furnish occasion for charitable laughter.

10

SECOND MEANINGS

I must now turn to something far more difficult. Hitherto we have been trying to read the Psalms as we suppose – or I suppose – their poets meant them to be read. But this of course is not the way in which they have chiefly been used by Christians. They have been believed to contain a second or hidden meaning, an 'allegorical' sense, concerned with the central truths of Christianity, with the Incarnation, the Passion, the Resurrection, the Ascension, and with the Redemption of man. All the Old Testament has been treated in the same way. The full significance of what the writers are saying is, on this view, apparent only in the light of events which happened after they were dead.

Such a doctrine, not without reason, arouses deep distrust in a modern mind. Because, as we know, almost anything can be read into any book if you are determined enough. This will be especially impressed on anyone who has written fantastic fiction. He will find reviewers, both favourable and hostile, reading into his stories all manner of allegorical meanings which he never intended. (Some of the allegories thus imposed on my own books have been so ingenious and interesting that I often wish I had thought of them myself.) Apparently it is impossible for the wit of man to devise a narrative in which the wit of some other man cannot, and with some plausibility, find a hidden sense.

The field for self-deception, once we accept such methods of interpretation, is therefore obviously very wide. Yet in spite of this I think it impossible – for a reason I will give later – to abandon the method wholly when we are dealing, as Christians, with the Bible. We have, therefore, a steep hill before us. I will not attempt the cliffs. I must take a roundabout route which will look first as if it could never lead us to the top at all.

I begin far away from Scripture and even from Christianity, with instances of something said or written which takes on a new significance in the light of later events.

One of the Roman historians tells us about a fire in a provincial town which was thought to have originated in the public baths. What gave some colour to the suspicion of deliberate incendiarism was the fact that, earlier that day, a gentleman had complained that the water in the hot bath was only lukewarm and had received from an attendant the reply, *it will soon be hot enough*. Now of course if there really had been a plot, and the slave was in it, and fool enough to risk discovery by this veiled threat, then the story would not concern us. But let us suppose the fire was an accident (i.e. was intended by nobody). In that case the slave would have said something truer, or more importantly true, than he himself supposed. Clearly, there need to be nothing here but chance coincidence. The slave's reply is fully explained by the customer's complaint; it is just what any bath attendant would say. The deeper significance which his words turned out to have during the next few hours was, as we should say, accidental.

Now let us take a somewhat tougher instance. (The non-classical reader needs to know that to a Roman the 'age' or 'reign' of Saturn meant the lost age of innocence and peace. That is, it roughly corresponded to the Garden of Eden before the Fall; though it was never, except among the Stoics, of anything like comparable importance.) Virgil, writing not very long before the birth of Christ, begins a poem thus: 'The great procession of the ages begins anew. Now the Virgin returns, the reign of Saturn returns, and the new child is sent down from high heaven.' It goes on to describe the paradisal age which this nativity will usher in. And of course throughout the Middle Ages it was taken that some dim prophetic knowledge of the birth of Christ had reached Virgil, probably through the Sibylline Books. He ranked as a Pagan prophet. Modern scholars would, I suppose, laugh at the idea. They might differ as to what noble or imperial couple were being thus extravagantly complimented by a court poet on the birth of a son; but the resemblance to the birth of Christ would be regarded, once more, as an accident. To say the least of it, however, this is a much more striking accident than the slave's words to the man in the baths. If this is luck, it is extraordinary luck. If one were a fanatical opponent of Christianity one would be tempted to say, in an unguarded moment, that it was diabolically lucky.

I now turn to two examples which I think to be on a different level. In them, as in those we have been considering, someone says what is truer and more important than he knows; but it does not seem to me that he could have done so by chance. I hasten to add that the alternative to chance which I have in mind is not 'prophecy' in the sense of clear prevision, miraculously bestowed. Nor of course have I the slightest intention of using the examples I shall cite as evidences for the truth of Christianity. Evidences are not here our subject. We are merely considering how we should regard those second meanings which things said or written sometimes take on in the light of fuller knowledge than their author possessed. And I am suggesting that different instances demand that we should regard them in different ways.

Sometimes we may regard this overtone as the result of simple coincidence, however striking. But there are other cases in which the later truth (which the speaker did not know) is intimately related to the truth he did know; so that, in hitting on something like it, he was in touch with that very same reality in which the fuller truth is rooted. Reading his words in the light of that fuller truth and hearing it in them as an overtone or second meaning, we are not foisting on them something alien to his mind, an arbitrary addition. We are prolonging his meaning in a direction congenial to it. The basic reality behind his words and behind the full truth is one and the same.

The status I claim for such things, then, is neither that of coincidence on the one hand nor that of supernatural prevision on the other. I will try to illustrate it by three imaginable cases. (i) A holy person, explicitly claiming to prophesy by the Spirit, tells us that there is in the universe such and such a creature. Later we learn (which God forbid) to travel in space and distribute upon new worlds the vomit of our own corruption; and, sure enough, on the remote planet of some remote star, we find that very creature. This would be prophecy in the strictest sense. This would be evidence for the prophet's miraculous gift and strong presumptive evidence for the truth of anything else he had said. (ii) A wholly unscientific writer of fantasies invents a creature for purely artistic reasons. Later on, we find a creature recognisably like it. This would be just the writer's luck. A man who knows nothing about racing may once in his life back a winner. (iii) A great biologist, illustrating the relation between animal organisms and their environment, invents for this purpose a hypothetical animal adapted to a hypothetical environment. Later, we find a creature very like it (of course in an environment very like the one he had supposed). This resemblance is not in the least accidental. Insight and knowledge, not luck, led to his invention. The real nature of life explains both why there is such a creature in the universe and also why there was such a creature in his lectures. If, while we re-read the lectures, we think of the reality, we are not bringing arbitrary fancies of our own to bear on the text. This second meaning is congenial to it. The examples I have in mind correspond to this third case; though, as we shall see, something more sensitive and personal than scientific knowledge is involved – what the writer or speaker was, not only what he knew.

Plato in his *Republic* is arguing that righteousness is often praised for the rewards it brings – honour, popularity, and the like – but that to see it in its true nature we must separate it from all these, strip it naked. He asks us therefore to imagine a perfectly righteous man treated by all around him as a monster of wickedness. We must picture him, still perfect, while he is bound, scourged, and finally impaled (the Persian equivalent of crucifixion). At this passage a Christian reader starts and rubs his eyes. What is happening? Yet another of these lucky coincidences? But presently he sees that there is something here which cannot be called luck at all.

Virgil, in the poem I have quoted, may have been, and the slave in the baths almost certainly was, 'talking about something else', some matter other than that of which their words were most importantly true. Plato is talking, and knows he is talking, about the fate of goodness in a wicked and misunderstanding world. But that is not something simply other than the Passion of Christ. It is the very same thing of which that Passion is the supreme illustration. If Plato was in some measure moved to write of it by the recent death – we may almost say the martyrdom – of his master Socrates then that again is not something simply other than the Passion of Christ. The imperfect, yet very venerable, goodness of Socrates led to the easy death of the hemlock, and the perfect goodness of Christ led to the death of the cross, not by chance but for the same reason; because goodness is what it is, and because the fallen world is what it is. If Plato, starting from one example and from his insight into the nature of goodness and the nature of the world, was led on to see the possibility of a perfect example, and thus to depict something extremely like the Passion of Christ, this happened not because he was lucky but because he was wise. If a man who knew only England and had observed that, the higher a mountain was, the longer it retained the snow in early spring, were led on to suppose a mountain so high that it retained the snow all the year round, the similarity between his imagined mountain and the real Alps would not be merely a lucky accident. He might not know that there were any such mountains in reality; just as Plato probably did not know that the ideally perfect instance of crucified goodness which he had depicted would ever become actual and historical. But if that man ever saw the Alps he would not say, 'What a curious coincidence.' He would be more likely to say, 'There! What did I tell you?'

And what are we to say of those gods in various Pagan mythologies who are killed and rise again and who thereby renew or transform the life of their worshippers or of nature? The odd thing is that here those anthropologists who are most hostile to our faith would agree with many Christians in saying, 'The resemblance is not accidental.' Of course the two parties would say this for different reasons. The anthropologists would mean: 'All these superstitions have a common source in the mind and experience, especially the agricultural experience, of early man. Your myth of Christ is like the myth of Balder because it has the same origin. The likeness is a family likeness.' The Christians would fall into two schools of thought. The early Fathers (or some of them), who believed that Paganism was nothing but the direct work of the Devil, would say: 'The Devil has from the beginning tried to mislead humanity with lies. As all accomplished liars do, he makes his lies as like the truth as he can; provided they lead man astray on the main issue, the more closely they imitate truth the more effective they will be. That is why we call him God's Ape; he is always imitating God. The resemblance of Adonis to Christ is therefore not at all accidental; it is the resemblance we expect to find between a counterfeit and the real thing, between a parody and the original, between imitation pearls and pearls.' Other Christians who think, as I do, that in mythology divine and diabolical and human elements (the desire for a good story), all play a part, would say: 'It is not accidental. In the sequence of night and day, in the annual death and rebirth of the crops, in the myths which these processes gave rise to, in the strong, if half-articulate, feeling (embodied in many Pagan "Mysteries") that man himself must undergo some sort of death if he would truly live, there is already a likeness permitted by God to that truth on which all depends. The resemblance between these myths and the Christian truth is no more accidental than the resemblance between the sun and the sun's reflection in a pond, or that between a historical fact and the somewhat garbled version of it which lives in popular report, or between the trees and hills of the real world and the trees and hills in our dreams.' Thus all three views alike would regard the 'Pagan Christs' and the true Christ as things really related and would find the resemblance significant.

In other words, when we examine things said which take on, in the light of later knowledge, a meaning they could not have had for those who said them, they turn out to be of different sorts. To be sure, of whatever sort they may be, we can often profitably read them with that second meaning in mind. If I think (as I cannot help thinking) about the birth of Christ while I read that poem of Virgil's, or even if I make it a regular part of my Christmas reading, this may be quite a sensible and edifying thing to do. But the resemblance which makes such a reading possible may after all be a mere coincidence (though I am not sure that it is). I may be reading into Virgil what is wholly irrelevant to all he was, and did, and intended; irrelevant as the sinister meaning which the bathman's word in the Roman story acquired from later events may have been to anything that slave was or meant. But when I meditate on the Passion while reading Plato's picture of the Righteous One, or on the Resurrection while reading about Adonis or Balder, the case is altered. There is a real connection between what Plato and the myth-makers most deeply were and meant and what I believe to be the truth. I know that connection and they do not. But it is really there. It is not an arbitrary fancy of my own thrust upon the old words. One can, without any absurdity, imagine Plato or the myth-makers if they learned the truth, saying, 'I see ... so that was what I was really talking about. Of course. That is what my words really meant, and I never knew it.' The bath attendant if innocent, on hearing the second meaning given to his words, would no doubt have said, 'So help me, I never meant no such thing. Never come into my head. I hadn't a clue.' What Virgil would have said, if he had learned the truth, I have no idea. (Or may we more charitably speak, not of what Plato and Virgil and the myth-makers 'would have said' but of what they said? For we can pray with good hope that they now know and have long since welcomed the truth. 'Many shall come from the east and the west and sit down in the kingdom.')

Thus, long before we come to the Psalms or the Bible, there are good reasons for not throwing away all second meanings as rubbish. Keble said of the Pagan poets, 'Thoughts beyond their thoughts to those high bards were given.' But let us now turn to Scripture itself.

11

SCRIPTURE

If even pagan utterances can carry a second meaning, not quite accidentally but because, in the sense I have suggested, they have a sort of right to it, we shall expect the Scriptures to do this more momentously and more often. We have two grounds for doing so if we are Christians.

(i) For us these writings are 'holy', or 'inspired', or, as St Paul says, 'the Oracles of God'. But this has been understood in more than one way, and I must try to explain how I understand it, at least so far as the Old Testament is concerned. I have been suspected of being what is called a Fundamentalist. That is because I never regard any narrative as unhistorical simply on the ground that it includes the miraculous. Some people find the miraculous so hard to believe that they cannot imagine any reason for my acceptance of it other than a prior belief that every sentence of the Old Testament has historical or scientific truth. But this I do not hold, any more than St Jerome did when he said that Moses described Creation 'after the manner of a popular poet' (as we should say, mythically) or than Calvin did when he doubted whether the story of Job were history or fiction. The real reason why I can accept as historical a story in which a miracle occurs is that I have never found any philosophical grounds for the universal negative proposition that miracles do not happen. I have to decide on quite other grounds (if I decide at all) whether a given narrative is historical or not. The Book of Job appears to me unhistorical because it begins about a man quite unconnected with all history or even legend, with no genealogy, living in a country of which the Bible elsewhere has hardly anything to say; because, in fact, the author quite obviously writes as a story-teller not as a chronicler.

I have therefore no difficulty in accepting, say, the view of those scholars who tell us that the account of Creation in Genesis is derived from earlier Semitic stories which were Pagan and mythical. We must of course be quite clear what 'derived from' means. Stories do not reproduce their species like mice. They are told by men. Each re-teller either repeats exactly what his predecessor had told him or else changes it. He may change it unknowingly or deliberately. If he changes it deliberately, his invention, his sense of form, his ethics, his ideas of what is fit, or edifying, or merely interesting, all come in. If unknowingly, then his unconscious (which is so largely responsible for our forgettings) has been at work. Thus at every step in what is called – a little misleadingly – the 'evolution' of a story, a man, all he is and all his attitudes, are involved. And no good work is done anywhere without aid from the Father of Lights. When a series of such re-tellings turns a creation story which at first had almost no religious or metaphysical significance into a story which achieves the idea of true Creation and of a transcendent Creator (as Genesis does), then nothing will make me believe that some of the re-tellers, or some one of them, has not been guided by God.

Thus something originally merely natural – the kind of myth that is found amongst most nations – will have been raised by God above itself, qualified by Him and compelled by Him to serve purposes which of itself it would not have served. Generalising thus, I take it that the whole Old Testament consists of the same sort of material as any other literature – chronicle (some of it obviously pretty accurate), poems, moral and political diatribes, romances, and what not; but all taken into the service of God's word. Not all, I suppose, in the same way. There are prophets who write with the clearest awareness that Divine compulsion is upon them. There are chroniclers whose intention may have been merely to record. There are poets like those in the Song of Songs who probably never dreamed of any but a secular and natural purpose in what they composed. There is (and it is no less important) the work first of the Jewish and then of the Christian Church in preserving and canonising just these books. There is the work of redactors and editors in modifying them. On all of these I suppose a Divine pressure; of which not by any means all need have been conscious.

The human qualities of the raw materials show through. Naïvety, error, contradiction, even (as in the cursing Psalms) wickedness are not removed. The total result is not 'the Word of God' in the sense that every passage, in itself, gives impeccable science or history. It carries the Word of God; and we (under grace, with attention to tradition and to interpreters wiser than ourselves, and with the use of such intelligence and learning as we may have) receive that Word from it not by using it as an encyclopaedia or an encyclical but by steeping ourselves in its tone or temper and so learning its overall message.

To a human mind this working up (in a sense imperfectly), this sublimation (incomplete) of human material, seems, no doubt, an untidy and leaky vehicle. We might have expected, we may think we should have preferred, an unrefracted light giving us ultimate truth in systematic form – something we could have tabulated and memorised and relied on like the multiplication table. One can respect, and at moments envy, both the Fundamentalist's view of the Bible and the Roman Catholic's view of the Church. But there is one argument which we should beware of using for either position: God must have done what is best; this is best, therefore God has done this. For we are mortals and do not know what is best for us, and it is dangerous to prescribe what God must have done – especially when we cannot, for the life of us, see that He has after all done it.

We may observe that the teaching of Our Lord Himself, in which there is no imperfection, is not given us in that cut-and-dried, fool-proof, systematic fashion we might have expected or desired. He wrote no book. We have only reported sayings, most of them uttered in answer to questions, shaped in some degree by their context. And when we have collected them all we cannot reduce them to a system. He preaches but He does not lecture. He uses paradox, proverb, exaggeration, parable, irony; even (I mean no irreverence) the 'wisecrack'. He utters maxims which, like popular proverbs, if rigorously taken, may seem to contradict one another. His teaching therefore cannot be grasped by the intellect alone, cannot be 'got up' as if it were a 'subject'. If we try to do that with it, we shall find Him the most elusive of teachers. He hardly ever gave a straight answer to a straight question. He will not be, in the way we want, 'pinned down'. The attempt is (again, I mean no irreverence) like trying to bottle a sunbeam.

Descending lower, we find a somewhat similar difficulty with St Paul. I cannot be the only reader who has wondered why God, having given him so many gifts, withheld from him (what would to us seem so necessary for the first Christian theologian) that of lucidity and orderly exposition.

Thus on three levels, in appropriate degrees, we meet the same refusal of what we might have thought best for us – in the Word Himself, in the Apostle of the Gentiles, in Scripture as a whole. Since this is what God has done, this, we must conclude, was best. It may be that what we should have liked would have been fatal to us if granted. It may be indispensable that Our Lord's teaching, by that elusiveness (to our systematising intellect), should demand a response from the whole man, should make it so clear that there is no question of learning a subject but of steeping ourselves in a Personality, acquiring a new outlook and temper, breathing a new atmosphere, suffering Him, in His own way, to rebuild in us the defaced image of Himself. So in St Paul. Perhaps the sort of works I should wish him to have written would have been useless. The crabbedness, the appearance of inconsequence and even of sophistry, the turbulent mixture of petty detail, personal complaint, practical advice, and lyrical rapture, finally let through what matters more than ideas – a whole Christian life in operation – better say, Christ Himself operating in a man's life. And in the same way, the value of the Old Testament may be dependent on what seems its imperfection. It may repel one use in order that we may be forced to use it in another way – to find the Word in it, not without repeated and leisurely reading nor without discriminations made by our conscience and our critical faculties, to relive, while we read, the whole Jewish experience of God's gradual and graded self-revelation, to feel the very contentions between the Word and the human material through which it works. For here again, it is our total response that has to be elicited.

Certainly it seems to me that from having had to reach what is really the Voice of God in the cursing Psalms through all the horrible distortions of the human medium, I have gained something I might not have gained from a flawless, ethical exposition. The shadows have indicated (at least to my heart) something more about the light. Nor would I (now) willingly spare from my Bible something in itself so anti-religious as the nihilism of Ecclesiastes. We get there a clear, cold picture of man's life without God. That statement is itself part of God's word. We need to have heard it. Even to have assimilated Ecclesiastes and no other book in the Bible would be to have advanced further towards truth than some men do.

Admittedly these conjectures as to why God does what He does are probably of no more value than my dog's ideas of what I am up to when I sit and read. But though we can only guess the reasons, we can at least observe the consistency, of His ways. We read in Genesis (2:7) that God formed man of the dust and breathed life into him. For all the first writer knew of it, this passage might merely illustrate the survival, even in a truly creational story, of the Pagan inability to conceive true Creation, the savage, pictorial tendency to imagine God making things 'out of' something as the potter or the carpenter does. Nevertheless, whether by lucky accident or (as I think) by God's guidance, it embodies a profound principle. For on any view man is in one sense clearly made 'out of' something else. He is an animal; but an animal called to be, or raised to be, or (if you like) doomed to be, something more than an animal. On the ordinary biological view (what difficulties I have about evolution are not religious) one of the primates is changed so that he becomes man; but he remains still a primate and an animal. He is taken up into a new life without relinquishing the old. In the same way, all organic life takes up and uses processes merely chemical. But we can trace the principle higher as well as lower. For we are taught that the Incarnation itself proceeded 'not by the conversion of the godhead into flesh, but by taking of (the) manhood into God'; in it human life becomes the vehicle of Divine life. If the Scriptures proceed not by conversion of God's word into a literature but by taking up of a literature to be a vehicle of God's word, this is not anomalous.

Of course, on almost all levels, that method seems to us precarious or, as I have said, leaky. None of these up-gradings is, as we should have wished, self-evident. Because the lower nature, in being taken up and loaded with a new burden and advanced to a new privilege remains, and is not annihilated, it will always be possible to ignore the up-grading and see nothing but the lower. Thus men can read the life of Our Lord (because it is a human life) as nothing but a human life. Many, perhaps most, modern philosophies read human life merely as an animal life of unusual complexity. The Cartesians read animal life as mechanism. Just in the same way Scripture can be read as merely human literature. No new discovery, no new method, will ever give a final victory to either interpretation. For what is required, on all these levels alike, is not merely knowledge but a certain insight; getting the focus right. Those who can see in each of these instances only the lower will always be plausible. One who contended that a poem was nothing but black marks on white paper would be unanswerable if he addressed an audience who couldn't read. Look at it through microscopes, analyse the printer's ink and the paper, study it (in that way) as long as you like; you will never find something over and above all the products of analysis whereof you can say 'This is the poem'. Those who can read, however, will continue to say the poem exists.

If the Old Testament is a literature thus 'taken up', made the vehicle of what is more than human, we can hardly set any limit to the weight or multiplicity of meanings which may have been laid upon it. If any writer may say more than he knows and mean more than he meant, then these writers will be especially likely to do so. And not by accident.

(ii) The second reason for accepting the Old Testament in this way can be put more simply and is of course far more compulsive. We are committed to it in principle by Our Lord Himself. On that famous journey to Emmaus He found fault with the two disciples for not believing what the prophets had said. They ought to have known from their Bibles that the Anointed One, when He came, would enter his glory through suffering. He then explained, from 'Moses' (i.e. the Pentateuch) down, all the places in the Old Testament 'concerning Himself' (Luke 24:25–27). He clearly identified Himself with a figure often mentioned in the Scriptures; appropriated to Himself many passages where a modern scholar might see no such reference. In the predictions of His Own Passion which He had previously made to the disciples, He was obviously doing the same thing. He accepted – indeed He claimed to be – the second meaning of Scripture.

We do not know – or anyway I do not know – what all these passages were. We can be pretty sure about one of them. The Ethiopian eunuch who met Philip (Acts 8:27–38) was reading Isaiah 53. He did not know whether in that passage the prophet was talking about himself or about someone else. Philip, in answering the question, 'preached unto him Jesus'. The answer, in fact, was 'Isaiah is speaking of Jesus'. We need have no doubt that Philip's authority for this interpretation was Our Lord. (Our ancestors would have thought that Isaiah consciously foresaw the sufferings of Christ as people see the future in the sort of dreams recorded by Mr Dunne. Modern scholars would say, that on the conscious level, he was referring to Israel itself, the whole nation personified. I do not see that it matters which view we take.) We can, again, be pretty sure, from the words on the cross (Mark 15:34), that Our Lord identified Himself with the sufferer in Psalm 22. Or when He asked (Mark 12:35–36) how Christ could be both David's son and David's lord, He clearly identified Christ, and therefore Himself, with the 'my Lord' of Psalm 110 – was in fact hinting at the mystery of the Incarnation by pointing out a difficulty which only it could solve. In Matthew 4:6 the words of Psalm 91:11, 12, 'He shall give his angels charge over thee ... that thou hurt not thy foot against a stone,' are applied to Him, and we may be sure the application was His own since only He could be the source of the temptation story. In Mark 12:10 He implicitly appropriates to Himself the words of Psalm 118:22 about the stone which the builders rejected. 'Thou shalt not leave my soul in hell, neither shalt thou suffer thy Holy One to see corruption' (16:11) is treated as a prophecy of His Resurrection in Acts 2:27, and was doubtless so taken by Himself, since we find it so taken in the earliest Christian tradition – that is, by people likely to be closer both to the spirit and to the letter of His words than any scholarship (I do not say, 'any sanctity') will bring a modern. Yet it is, perhaps, idle to speak here of spirit and letter. There is almost no 'letter' in the words of Jesus. Taken by a literalist, He will always prove the most elusive of teachers. Systems cannot keep up with that darting illumination. No net less wide than a man's whole heart, nor less fine of mesh than love, will hold the sacred Fish.

12

SECOND MEANINGS IN THE PSALMS

In a certain sense Our Lord's interpretation of the Psalms was common ground between Himself and His opponents. The question we mentioned a moment ago, how David can call Christ 'my Lord' (Mark 12:35–37), would lose its point unless it were addressed to those who took it for granted that the 'my Lord' referred to in Psalm 110 was the Messiah, the regal and anointed deliverer who would subject the world to Israel. This method was accepted by all. The 'scriptures' all had a 'spiritual' or second sense. Even a Gentile 'God-fearer'[1] like the Ethiopian eunuch (Acts 8:27–38) knew that the sacred books of Israel could not be understood without a guide, trained in the Judaic tradition, who could open the hidden meanings. Probably all instructed Jews in the first century saw references to the Messiah in most of those passages where Our Lord saw them; what was controversial was His identification of the Messianic King with another Old Testament figure and of both with Himself.

Two figures meet us in the Psalms, that of the sufferer and that of the conquering and liberating king. In 13, 28, 55 or 102, we have the Sufferer; in 2 or 72, the King. The Sufferer was, I think, by this time generally identified with (and may sometimes have originally been intended as) the whole nation, Israel itself – they would have said 'himself'. The King was the successor of David, the coming Messiah. Our Lord identified Himself with both these characters.

In principle, then, the allegorical way of reading the Psalms can claim the highest possible authority. But of course this does not mean that all the countless applications of it are fruitful, legitimate, or even rational. What we see when we think we are looking into the depths of Scripture may sometimes be only the reflection of our own silly faces. Many allegorical interpretations which were once popular seem to me, as perhaps to most moderns, to be

---

[1] The 'god-fearers' (*sebomenoi* or *metuentes*) were a recognised class of Gentiles who worshipped Jahveh without submitting to circumcision and the other ceremonial obligations of the Law. Cf. Psalm 118 (v. 2, Jewish laity, v. 3 Jewish priests; v. 4 God-fearers) and Acts 10:2.

strained, arbitrary and ridiculous. I think we may be sure that some of them really are; we ought to be much less sure that we know which. What seems strained – a mere triumph of perverse ingenuity – to one age, seems plain and obvious to another, so that our ancestors would often wonder how we could possibly miss what we wonder how they could have been silly-clever enough to find. And between different ages there is no impartial judge on earth, for no one stands outside the historical process; and of course no one is so completely enslaved to it as those who take our own age to be, not one more period, but a final and permanent platform from which we can see all other ages objectively.

Interpretations which were already established in the New Testament naturally have a special claim on our attention. We find in our Prayer Book that Psalm 110[2] is one of those appointed for Christmas Day. We may at first be surprised by this. There is nothing in it about peace and goodwill, nothing remotely suggestive of the stable at Bethlehem. It seems to have been originally either a coronation ode for a new king, promising conquest and empire, or a poem addressed to some king on the eve of a war, promising victory. It is full of threats. The 'rod' of the king's power is to go forth from Jerusalem, foreign kings are to be wounded, battle fields to be covered with carnage, skulls cracked. The note is not 'Peace and goodwill' but 'Beware. He's coming.' Two things attach it to Christ with an authority far beyond that of the Prayer Book. The first of course (already mentioned) is that He Himself did so; He is the 'lord' whom 'David' calls 'my Lord'. The second is the reference to Melchizedek (v. 4). The identification of this very mysterious person as a symbol or prophecy of Christ is made in Hebrews 7. The exact form of the comment there made on Genesis 14 is no doubt alien to our minds, but I think the essentials can all be retained in our own idiom. We should certainly not argue from the failure of Genesis to give Melchizedek any genealogy or even parents that he has neither beginning nor end (if it comes to that, Job has no genealogy either); but we should be vividly aware that his unrelated, unaccounted for, appearance sets him strangely apart from the texture of the surrounding narrative. He comes from nowhere, blesses in the name of the 'most high God, possessor of heaven and earth', and utterly disappears. This gives him the effect of belonging, if not to *the* Other World, at any rate to *another* world; other than the story of Abraham in general. He assumes without question, as the writer of Hebrews saw, a superiority over Abraham which Abraham accepts. He is an august, a 'numinous' figure. What the teller, or last re-teller, of Genesis would have said if we asked him why he brought

---

[2] See Appendix 1, p. 725.

this episode in or where he had got it from, I do not know. I think, as I have explained, that a pressure from God lay upon these tellings and re-tellings. And one effect which the episode of Melchizedek was to have is quite clear. It puts in, with unforgettable impressiveness, the idea of a priesthood, not Pagan but a priesthood to the one God, far earlier than the Jewish priesthood which descends from Aaron, independent of the call to Abraham, somehow superior to Abraham's vocation. And this older, pre-Judaic, priesthood is united with royalty; Melchizedek is a priest-king. In some communities priest-kings were normal, but not in Israel. It is thus simply a fact that Melchizedek resembles (in his peculiar way he is the only Old Testament character who resembles) Christ Himself. For He, like Melchizedek, claims to be Priest, though not of the priestly tribe, and also King. Melchizedek really does point to Him; and so of course does the hero of Psalm 110 who is a king but also has the same sort of priesthood.

For a Jewish convert to Christianity this was extremely important and removed a difficulty. He might be brought to see how Christ was the successor of David; it would be impossible to say that He was, in a similar sense, the successor of Aaron. The idea of His priesthood therefore involved the recognition of a priesthood independent of and superior to Aaron's. Melchizedek was there to give this conception the sanction of the Scriptures. For us Gentile Christians it is rather the other way round. We are more likely to start from the priestly, sacrificial, and intercessory character of Christ and under-stress that of king and conqueror. Psalm 110, with three other Christmas Psalms, corrects this. In 45 we have again the almost threatening tone: 'Gird thee with thy sword upon thy thigh, O thou most mighty ... thy right hand shall teach thee terrible things ... thy arrows are very sharp' (vv. 4–6). In 89 we have the promises to David (who would certainly mean all, or any, of David's successors, just as 'Jacob' can mean all his descendants). Foes are to fall before him (v. 24). 'David' will call God 'Father', and God says 'I will make him my first-born' (vv. 27–28), that is 'I will make him an eldest son', make him my heir, give him the whole world. In 132 we have 'David' again; 'As for his enemies, I shall clothe them with shame, but upon himself shall his crown flourish' (v. 19). All this emphasises an aspect of the Nativity to which our later sentiment about Christmas (excellent in itself) does less than justice. For those who first read these Psalms as poems about the birth of Christ, that birth primarily meant something very militant; the hero, the 'judge' or champion or giant-killer, who was to fight and beat death, hell and the devils, had at last arrived, and the evidence suggests that Our Lord also thought of Himself in those terms. (Milton's poem on the *Nativity* well recaptures this side of Christmas.)

The assignment of Psalm 68[3] to Whitsunday has some obvious reasons, even at a first reading. Verse 8, 'The earth shook and the heavens dropped at the presence of God, even as Sinai also was moved,' was, no doubt, for the original writer a reference to the miracles mentioned in Exodus, and thus foreshadows that very different descent of God which came with the tongues of fire. Verse 11 is a beautiful instance of the way in which the old texts, almost inevitably, charge themselves with the new weight of meaning. The Prayer Book version gives it as, 'The Lord gave the word, great was the company of the preachers.' The 'word' would be the order for battle and its 'preachers' (in rather a grim sense) the triumphant Jewish warriors. But that translation appears to be wrong. The verse really means that there were many to spread 'word' (i.e. the news) of the victory. This will suit Pentecost quite as well. But I think the real New Testament authority for assigning this Psalm to Whitsunday appears in verse 18 (in the Prayer Book, 'Thou art gone up on high, thou hast led captivity captive, and received gifts for men'). According to the scholars the Hebrew text here means that God, with the armies of Israel as his agents, had taken huge masses of prisoners and received 'gifts' (booty or tribute) *from* men. St Paul, however (Ephesians 4:8), quotes a different reading: 'When He ascended up on high He led captivity captive and *gave* gifts *to* men.' This must be the passage which first associated the Psalm with the coming of the Holy Ghost, for St Paul is there speaking of the gifts of the Spirit (vv. 4–7) and stressing the fact that they come after the Ascension. After ascending, as a result of ascending, Christ gives these gifts to men, or receives these gifts (notice how the Prayer Book version will now do well enough) from His Father 'for men', for the use of men, in order to transmit them to men. And this relation between the Ascension and the coming of the Spirit is of course in full accordance with Our Lord's own words, 'It is expedient for you that I go away, for if I go not away the Comforter will not come unto you' (John 16:7); as if the one were somehow impossible without the other, as if the Ascension, the withdrawal from the space–time in which our present senses operate, of the incarnate God, were the necessary condition of God's presence in another mode. There is a mystery here that I will not even attempt to sound.

That Psalm has led us through some complications; those in which Christ appears as the sufferer are very much easier. And it is here too that the second meaning is most inevitable. If Christ 'tasted death for all men', became the archetypal sufferer, then the expressions of all who ever suffered in the world are, from the very nature of things, related to His. Here (to speak in ludicrously human terms) we feel that it needed no Divine guidance to give the old texts their second meaning but would rather have needed a special

[3] See Appendix 1, p. 722.

miracle to keep it out. In Psalm 22, the terrible poem which Christ quoted in His final torture, it is not 'they pierced my hands and my feet' (v. 17), striking though this anticipation must always be, that really matters most. It is the union of total privation with total adherence to God, to a God who makes no response, simply because of what God is: 'and thou continuest holy' (v. 3). All the sufferings of the righteous speak here; but in 40:15, all the sufferings of the guilty too – 'my sins have taken such hold upon me that I am not able to look up.' But this too is for us the voice of Christ, for we have been taught that He who was without sin became sin for our sakes, plumbed the depth of that worst suffering which comes to evil men who at last know their own evil. Notice how this, in the original or literal sense, is hardly consistent with verses 8 and 9, and what counterpoint of truth this apparent contradiction takes on once the speaker is understood to be Christ.

But to say more of these suffering Psalms would be to labour the obvious. What I, at any rate, took longer to see was the full richness of that Christmas Psalm we have already mentioned, Psalm 45,[4] which shows us so many aspects of the Nativity we could never get from the carols or even (easily) from the Gospels. This in its original intention was obviously a laureate ode on a royal wedding. (We are nowadays surprised to find that such an official bit of work, made 'to order' by a court poet for a special occasion, should be good poetry. But in ages when the arts had their full health no one would have understood our surprise. All the great poets, painters, and musicians of old could produce great work 'to order'. One who could not would have seemed as great a humbug as a captain who could navigate or a farmer who could farm only when the fit took him.) And simply as a marriage ode – what the Greeks call an *Epithalamium* – it is magnificent. But it is far more valuable for the light it throws on the Incarnation.

Few things once seemed to me more frigid and far-fetched than those interpretations, whether of this Psalm or of the Song of Songs, which identify the Bridegroom with Christ and the Bride with the Church. Indeed, as we read the frank erotic poetry of the latter and contrast it with the edifying headlines in our Bibles, it is easy to be moved to a smile, even a cynically knowing smile, as if the pious interpreters were feigning an absurd innocence. I should still find it very hard to believe that anything like the 'spiritual' sense was remotely intended by the original writers. But no one now (I fancy) who accepts that spiritual or second sense is denying, or saying anything against, the very plain sense which the writers did intend. The Psalm remains a rich, festive Epithalamium, the Song remains fine, sometimes exquisite, love poetry, and this is not in the least obliterated by the burden of

---

[4] See Appendix I, p. 721.

the new meaning. (Man is still one of the primates; a poem is still black marks on white paper.) And later I began to see that the new meaning is not arbitrary and springs from depths I had not suspected. First, the language of nearly all great mystics, not even in a common tradition, some of them Pagan, some Islamic, most Christian, confronts us with evidence that the image of marriage, of sexual union, is not only profoundly natural but almost inevitable as a means of expressing the desired union between God and man. The very word 'union' has already entailed some such idea. Secondly, the god as bridegroom, his 'holy marriage' with the goddess, is a recurrent theme and a recurrent ritual in many forms of Paganism – Paganism not at what we should call its purest or most enlightened, but perhaps at its most religious, at its most serious and convinced. And if, as I believe, Christ, in transcending and thus abrogating, also fulfils, both Paganism and Judaism, then we may expect that He fulfils this side of it too. This, as well as all else, is to be 'summed up' in Him. Thirdly, the idea appears, in a slightly different form, within Judaism. For the mystics God is the Bridegroom of the individual soul. For the Pagans, the god is the bridegroom of the mother-goddess, the earth, but his union with her also makes fertile the whole tribe and its livestock, so that in a sense he is their bridegroom too. The Judaic conception is in some ways closer to the Pagan than to that of the mystics, for in it the Bride of God is the whole nation, Israel. This is worked out in one of the most moving and graphic chapters of the whole Old Testament (Ezekiel 16). Finally, this is transferred in the Apocalypse from the old Israel to the new, and the Bride becomes the Church, 'the whole blessed company of faithful people'. It is this which has, like the unworthy bride in Ezekiel, been rescued, washed, clothed, and married by God – a marriage like King Cophetua's. Thus the allegory which at first seemed so arbitrary – the ingenuity of some prudish commentator who was determined to force flat edifications upon the most unpromising texts – turned out, when you seriously tugged at it, to have roots in the whole history of religion, to be loaded with poetry, to yield insights. To reject it because it does not immediately appeal to our own age is to be provincial, to have the self-complacent blindness of the stay-at-home.

Read in this sense, the Psalm restores Christmas to its proper complexity. The birth of Christ is the arrival of the great warrior and the great king. Also of the Lover, the Bridegroom, whose beauty surpasses that of man. But not only the Bridegroom as the lover, the desired; the Bridegroom also as he who makes fruitful, the father of children still to be begotten and born. (Certainly the image of a Child in a manger by no means suggests to us a king, giant-killer, bridegroom, and father. But it would not suggest the eternal Word either – if we didn't know. All alike are aspects of the same central paradox.) Then the poet turns to the Bride, with the exhortation, 'forget also thine own people and thy father's house' (v. 11). This sentence has a plain, and to us painful, sense while we read the Psalm as the poet probably intended it. One thinks of home-sickness, of a girl (probably a mere child) secretly crying in a strange *hareem*, of all the miseries which may underlie any dynastic marriage, especially an Oriental one. The poet (who of course knew all about this – he probably had a daughter of his own) consoles her: 'Never mind, you have lost your parents but you will presently have children instead, and children who will be great men.' But all this has also its poignant relevance when the Bride is the Church. A vocation is a terrible thing. To be called out of nature into the supernatural life is at first (or perhaps not quite at first – the wrench of the parting may be felt later) a costly honour. Even to be called from one natural level to another is loss as well as gain. Man has difficulties and sorrows which the other primates escape. But to be called up higher costs still more. 'Get thee out of thy country, and from thy kindred, and from thy father's house,' said God to Abraham (Genesis 12:1). It is a terrible command; turn your back on all you know. The consolation (if it will at that moment console) is very like that which the Psalmist offers to the bride: 'I will make of thee a great nation.' This 'turn your back' is of course terribly repeated, one may say aggravated, by Our Lord – 'he that hateth not father and mother and his own life'. He speaks, as so often, in the proverbial, paradoxical manner; hatred (in cold prose) is not enjoined; only the resolute, the apparently ruthless, rejection of natural claims when, and if, the terrible choice comes to that point. (Even so, this text is, I take it, profitable only to those who read it with horror. The man who finds it easy enough to hate his father, the woman whose life is a long struggle not to hate her mother, had probably best keep clear of it.) The consolation of the Bride, in this allegory, consists, not (where the mystics would put it) in the embraces of the Spouse, but in her fruitfulness. If she does not bear fruit, is not the mother of saints and sanctity, it may be supposed that the marriage was an illusion – for 'a god's embraces never are in vain'.

The choice of Psalm 8[5] for Ascension Day again depends on an interpretation found in the New Testament. In its literal sense this short, exquisite lyric is simplicity itself – an expression of wonder at man and man's place in Nature (there is a chorus in Sophocles not unlike it) and therefore at God who appointed it. God is wonderful both as champion or 'judge' and as Creator. When one looks up at the sky, and all the stars which are His work, it seems strange that He should be concerned at all with such things as man. Yet in fact, though He has made us inferior to the celestial beings, He has,

[5] See Appendix I, p. 719.

down here on earth, given us extraordinary honour – made us lords of all the other creatures. But to the writer of Hebrews (2:6–9) this suggested something which we, of ourselves, would never have thought of. The Psalmist said, 'Thou hast put all things in subjection under his (man's) feet' (v. 6). The Christian writer observes that, in the actual state of the universe, this is not strictly true. Man is often killed, and still more often defeated, by beasts, poisonous vegetables, weather, earthquakes, etc. It would seem to us merely perverse and captious thus to take a poetic expression as if it were intended for a scientific universal. We can get nearest to the point of view if we imagine the commentator arguing not (as I think he actually does), 'Since this is not true of the present, and since all the scriptures must be true, the statement must really refer to the future,' but rather, 'This is of course true in the poetic – and therefore, to a logician, the loose – sense which the poet intended; but how if it were far truer than he knew?' This will lead us, by a route that is easier for our habits of mind, to what he thinks the real meaning – or I should say the 'over-meaning', the new weight laid upon the poet's words. Christ has ascended into Heaven. And in due time all things, quite strictly all, will be subjected to Him. It is He who, having been made (for a while) 'lower than the angels', will become the conqueror and ruler of all things, including death and (death's patron) the devil.

To most of us this will seem a wire-drawn allegory. But it is the very same which St Paul obviously has in mind in 1 Corinthians 15:20–28. This, with the passage in Hebrews, makes it pretty certain that the interpretation was established in the earliest Christian tradition. It may even descend from Our Lord. There was, after all, no description of Himself which He delighted in more than the 'Son of Man'; and of course, just as 'daughter of Babylon' means Babylon, so 'Son of Man' means Man, the Man, the archetypal Man, in whose suffering, resurrection, and victories all men (unless they refuse) can share.

And it is this, I believe, that most modern Christians need to be reminded of. It seems to me that I seldom meet any strong or exultant sense of the continued, never-to-be-abandoned, Humanity of Christ in glory, in eternity. We stress the Humanity too exclusively at Christmas, and the Deity too exclusively after the Resurrection; almost as if Christ once became a man and then presently reverted to being simply a God. We think of the Resurrection and Ascension (rightly) as great acts of God; less often as the triumph of Man. The ancient interpretation of Psalm 8, however arrived at, is a cheering corrective. Nor, on further consideration, is the analogy of humanity's place in the universe (its greatness and littleness, its humble origins and – even on the natural level – amazing destiny) to the humiliation and victories of Christ, really strained and far-fetched. At least it does not seem so to me. As I have already indicated, there seems to me to be something more than analogy between the taking up of animality into man and the taking up of man into God.

But I walk in wonders beyond myself. It is time to conclude with a brief notice of some simpler things.

One is the apparent (and often no doubt real) self-righteousness of the Psalms: 'Thou shalt find no wickedness in me' (17:3), 'I have walked innocently' (26:1), 'Preserve thou my soul, for I am holy' (86:2). For many people it will not much mend matters if we say, as we probably can with truth, that sometimes the speaker was from the first intended to be Israel, not the individual; and even, within Israel, the faithful remnant. Yet it makes some difference; up to a certain point that remnant was holy and innocent compared with some of the surrounding Pagan cultures. It was often an 'innocent sufferer' in the sense that it had not deserved what was inflicted on it, nor deserved it at the hands of those who inflicted it. But of course there was to come a Sufferer who was in fact holy and innocent. Plato's imaginary case was to become actual. All these assertions were to become true in His mouth. And if true, it was necessary they should be made. The lesson that perfect, unretaliating, forgiving innocence can lead, as the world is, not to love but to the screaming curses of the mob and to death, is essential. Our Lord therefore becomes the speaker in these passages when a Christian reads them; by right – it would be an obscuring of the real issue if He did not. For He denied all sin of Himself. (That, indeed, is no small argument of His Deity. For He has not often made even on the enemies of Christianity the impression of arrogance; many of them do not seem as shocked as we should expect at His claim to be 'meek and lowly of heart'. Yet He said such things as, on any hypothesis but one, would be the arrogance of a paranoiac. It is as if, even where the hypothesis is rejected, some of the reality which implies its truth 'got across'.)

Of the cursing Psalms I suppose most of us make our own moral allegories – well aware that these are personal and on a quite different level from the high matters I have been trying to handle. We know the proper object of utter hostility – wickedness, especially our own. Thus in 36, 'My heart sheweth me the wickedness of the ungodly,' each can reflect that his own heart is the specimen of that wickedness best known to him. After that, the upward plunge at verse 5 into the mercy high as heaven and the righteousness solid as the mountains takes on even more force and beauty. From this point of view I can use even the horrible passage in 137 about dashing the Babylonian babies against the stones. I know things in the inner world which are like babies; the infantile beginnings of small indulgences, small resentments, which may one day become dipsomania or settled hatred, but which woo us and wheedle us with special pleadings and seem so tiny, so helpless that in resisting them we feel we are being cruel to animals. They begin whimpering to us, 'I don't ask much, but', or 'I had at least hoped', or 'you owe yourself *some* consideration'. Against all such pretty infants (the dears have such winning ways) the advice of the Psalm is the best. Knock the little bastards' brains out. And 'blessed' he who can, for it's easier said than done.

Sometimes with no prompting from tradition a second meaning will impose itself upon a reader irresistibly. When the poet of Psalm 84 said (v. 10), 'For one day in thy courts is better than a thousand,' he doubtless meant that one day there was better than a thousand elsewhere. I find it impossible to exclude while I read this the thought which, so far as I know, the Old Testament never quite reaches. It is there in the New, beautifully introduced not by laying a new weight on old words but more simply by adding to them. In Psalm 90 (v. 4) it had been said that a thousand years were to God like a single yesterday; in 2 Peter 3:8 – not the first place in the world where one would have looked for so metaphysical a theology – we read not only that a thousand years are as one day but also that 'one day is as a thousand years'. The Psalmist only meant, I think, that God was everlasting, that His life was infinite in time. But the epistle takes us out of the time-series altogether. As nothing outlasts God, so nothing slips away from Him into a past. The later conception (later in Christian thought – Plato had reached it) of the timeless as an eternal present has been achieved. Ever afterwards, for some of us, the 'one day' in God's courts which is better than a thousand, must carry a double meaning. The Eternal may meet us in what is, by our present measurements, a day, or (more likely) a minute or a second; but we have touched what is not in any way commensurable with lengths of time, whether long or short. Hence our hope finally to emerge, if not altogether from time (that might not suit our humanity) at any rate from the tyranny, the unlinear poverty, of time, to ride it not to be ridden by it, and so to cure that always aching wound ('the wound man was born for') which mere succession and mutability inflict on us, almost equally when we are happy and when we are unhappy. For we are so little reconciled to time that we are even astonished at it. 'How he's grown!' we exclaim, 'How time flies!' as though the universal form of our experience were again and again a novelty. It is as strange as if a fish were repeatedly surprised at the wetness of water. And that would be strange indeed; unless of course the fish were destined to become, one day, a land animal.

APPENDIX I

SELECTED PSALMS

PSALM 8 *Domine, Dominus noster*
O Lord our Governor, how excellent is thy Name in all the world: thou that hast set thy glory above the heavens!

2. Out of the mouth of very babes and sucklings hast thou ordained strength, because of thine enemies: that thou mightest still the enemy and the avenger.

3. For I will consider thy heavens, even the works of thy fingers: the moon and the stars, which thou hast ordained.

4. What is man, that thou art mindful of him: and the son of man, that thou visitest him?

5. Thou madest him lower than the angels: to crown him with glory and worship.

6. Thou makest him to have dominion of the works of thy hands: and thou hast put all things in subjection under his feet;

7. All sheep and oxen: yea, and the beasts of the field;

8. The fowls of the air, and the fishes of the sea: and whatsoever walketh through the paths of the seas.

9. O Lord our Governor: how excellent is thy Name in all the world!

PSALM 19 *Coeli enarrant*
The heavens declare the glory of God: and the firmament sheweth his handywork.

2. One day telleth another: and one night certifieth another.

3. There is neither speech nor language: but their voices are heard among them.

4. Their sound is gone out into all lands: and their words into the ends of the world.

5. In them hath he set a tabernacle for the sun: which cometh forth as a bridegroom out of his chamber, and rejoiceth as a giant to run his course.

6. It goeth forth from the uttermost part of the heaven, and runneth about unto the end of it again: and there is nothing hid from the heat thereof.

7. The law of the Lord is an undefiled law, converting the soul: the testimony of the Lord is sure, and giveth wisdom unto the simple.

8. The statutes of the Lord are right, and rejoice the heart: the commandment of the Lord is pure, and giveth light unto the eyes.

9. The fear of the Lord is clean, and endureth for ever: the judgements of the Lord are true, and righteous altogether.

10. More to be desired are they than gold, yea, than much fine gold: sweeter also than honey, and the honeycomb.

11. Moreover, by them is thy servant taught: and in keeping of them there is great reward.

12. Who can tell how oft he offendeth: O cleanse thou me from my secret faults.

13. Keep thy servant also from presumptuous sins, lest they get the dominion over me: so shall I be undefiled, and innocent from the great offence.

14. Let the words of my mouth, and the meditation of my heart: be alway acceptable in thy sight,

15. O Lord: my strength, and my redeemer.

PSALM 36 *Dixit injustus*

My heart sheweth me the wickedness of the ungodly: that there is no fear of God before his eyes.

2. For he flattereth himself in his own sight: until his abominable sin be found out.

3. The words of his mouth are unrighteous, and full of deceit: he hath left off to behave himself wisely, and to do good.

4. He imagineth mischief upon his bed, and hath set himself in no good way: neither doth he abhor any thing that is evil.

5. Thy mercy, O Lord, reacheth unto the heavens: and thy faithfulness unto the clouds.

6. Thy righteousness standeth like the strong mountains: thy judgements are like the great deep.

7. Thou, Lord, shalt save both man and beast; How excellent is thy mercy, O God: and the children of men shall put their trust under the shadow of thy wings.

8. They shall be satisfied with the plenteousness of thy house: and thou shalt give them drink of thy pleasures, as out of the river.

9. For with thee is the well of life: and in thy light shall we see light.

10. O continue forth thy loving-kindness unto them that know thee: and thy righteousness unto them that are true of heart.

11. O let not the foot of pride come against me: and let not the hand of the ungodly cast me down.

12. There are they fallen, all that work wickedness: they are cast down, and shall not be able to stand.

PSALM 45 *Eructavit cor meum*

My heart is inditing of a good matter: I speak of the things which I have made unto the King.

2. My tongue is the pen: of a ready writer.

3. Thou art fairer than the children of men: full of grace are thy lips, because God hath blessed thee for ever.

4. Gird thee with thy sword upon thy thigh, O thou most Mighty: according to thy worship and renown.

5. Good luck have thou with thine honour: ride on, because of the word of truth, of meekness, and righteousness; and thy right hand shall teach thee terrible things.

6. The arrows are very sharp, and the people shall be subdued unto thee: even in the midst among the King's enemies.

7. Thy seat, O God, endureth for ever: the sceptre of thy kingdom is a right sceptre.

8. Thou hast loved righteousness, and hated iniquity: wherefore God, even thy God, hath anointed thee with the oil of gladness above thy fellows.

9. All the garments smell of myrrh, aloes, and cassia: out of the ivory palaces, whereby they have made thee glad.

10. King's daughters were among thy honourable women: upon thy right hand did stand the queen in a vesture of gold, wrought about with divers colours.

11. Hearken, O daughter, and consider, incline thine ear: forget also thine own people, and thy father's house.

12. So shall the King have pleasure in thy beauty: for he is thy Lord God, and worship thou him.

13. And the daughter of Tyre shall be there with a gift: like as the rich also among the people shall make their supplication before thee.

14. The King's daughter is all glorious within: her clothing is of wrought gold.

15. She shall be brought unto the King in raiment of needlework: the virgins that be her fellows shall bear her company, and shall be brought unto thee.

16. With joy and gladness shall they be brought: and shall enter into the King's palace.

17. Instead of thy fathers thou shalt have children: whom thou mayest make princes in all lands.

18. I will remember thy Name from one generation to another: therefore shall the people give thanks unto thee, world without end.

PSALM 68 *Exurgat Deus*

Let God arise, and let his enemies be scattered: let them also that hate him flee before him.

2. Like as the smoke vanisheth, so shalt thou drive them away: and like as wax melteth at the fire, so let the ungodly perish at the presence of God.

3. But let the righteous be glad and rejoice before God: let them also be merry and joyful.

4. O sing unto God, and sing praises unto his Name: magnify him that rideth upon the heavens, as it were upon an horse; praise him in his Name JAH, and rejoice before him.

5. He is a Father of the fatherless, and defendeth the cause of the widows: even God in his Holy habitation.

6. He is the God that maketh men to be of one mind in an house, and bringeth the prisoners out of captivity: but letteth the runagates continue in scarceness.

7. O God, when thou wentest forth before the people: when thou wentest through the wilderness,

8. The earth shook, and the heavens dropped at the presence of God: even as Sinai also was moved at the presence of God, who is the God of Israel.

9. Thou, O God, sentest a gracious rain upon thine inheritance: and refreshedst it when it was weary.

10. Thy congregation shall dwell therein: for thou, O God, hast of thy goodness prepared for the poor.

11. The Lord gave the word: great was the company of the preachers.

12. Kings with their armies did flee, and were discomfited: and they of the household divided the spoil.

13. Though ye have lien among the pots, yet shall ye be as the wings of a dove: that is covered with silver wings, and her feathers like gold.

14. When the Almighty scattered kings for their sake: then were they as white as snow in Salmon.

15. As the hill of Basan, so is God's hill: even an high hill, as the hill of Basan.

16. Why hop ye so, ye high hills? this is God's hill, in which it pleaseth him to dwell: yea, the Lord will abide in it for ever.

17. The chariots of God are twenty thousand, even thousands of angels: and the Lord is among them, as in the holy place of Sinai.

18. Thou art gone up on high, thou hast led captivity captive, and received gifts for men: yea, even from thine enemies, that the Lord God might dwell among them.

19. Praised be the Lord daily: even the God who helpeth us, and poureth his benefits upon us.

20. He is our God, even the God of whom cometh salvation: God is the Lord, by whom we escape death.

21. God shall wound the head of his enemies: and the hairy scalp of such a one as goeth on still in wickedness.

22. The Lord hath said, I will bring my people again, as I did from Basan: mine own will I bring again, as I did sometime from the deep of the sea.

23. That thy foot may be dipped in the blood of thine enemies: and that the tongue of thy dogs may be red through the same.

24. It is well seen, O God, how thou goest: how thou, my God and King, goest in the sanctuary.

25. The singers go before, the minstrels follow after: in the midst are the damsels playing with the timbrels.

26. Give thanks, O Israel, unto God the Lord in the congregations: from the ground of the heart.

27. There is little Benjamin, their ruler, and the princes of Judah their counsel: the princes of Zabulon, and the princes of Nephthali.

28. Thy God hath sent forth strength for thee: stablish the thing, O God, that thou hast wrought in us.

29. For thy temple's sake at Jerusalem: so shall kings bring presents unto thee.

30. When the company of the spear-men, and multitude of the mighty are scattered abroad among the beasts of the people, so that they humbly bring pieces of silver: and when he hath scattered the people that delight in war;

31. Then shall the princes come out of Egypt: the Morians' land shall soon stretch out her hands unto God.

32. Sing unto God, O ye kingdoms of the earth: O sing praises unto the Lord;

33. Who sitteth in the heavens over all from the beginning: lo, he doth send out his voice, yea, and that a mighty voice.

34. Ascribe ye the power to God over Israel: his worship and strength is in the clouds.

35. O God, wonderful art thou in thy holy places: even the God of Israel; he will give strength and power unto his people; blessed be God.

PSALM 104 *Benedic, anima mea*

Praise the Lord, O my soul: O Lord my God, thou art become exceeding glorious; thou art clothed with majesty and honour.

2. Thou deckest thyself with light as it were with a garment: and spreadest out the heavens like a curtain.

3. Who layeth the beams of his chambers in the waters: and maketh the clouds his chariot, and walketh upon the wings of the wind.

4. He maketh his angels spirits: and his ministers a flaming fire.

5. He laid the foundations of the earth: that it never should move at any time.

6. Thou coveredst it with the deep like as with a garment: the waters stand in the hills.

7. At thy rebuke they flee: at the voice of thy thunder they are afraid.

8. They go up as high as the hills, and down to the valleys beneath: even unto the place which thou hast appointed for them.

9. Thou hast set them their bounds which they shall not pass: neither turn again to cover the earth.

10. He sendeth the springs into the rivers: which run among the hills.

11. All beasts of the field drink thereof: and the wild asses quench their thirst.

12. Beside them shall the fowls of the air have their habitation: and sing among the branches.

13. He watereth the hills from above: the earth is filled with the fruit of thy works.

14. He bringeth forth grass for the cattle: and green herb for the service of men.

15. That he may bring food out of the earth, and wine that maketh glad the heart of man: and oil to make him a cheerful countenance, and bread to strengthen man's heart.

16. The trees of the Lord also are full of sap: even the cedars of Libanus which he hath planted;

17. Wherein the birds make their nests: and the fir-trees are a dwelling for the stork.

18. The high hills are a refuge for the wild goats: and so are the stony rocks for the conies.

19. He appointed the moon for certain seasons: and the sun knoweth his going down.

20. Thou makest darkness that it may be night: wherein all the beasts of the forest do move.

21. The lions roaring after their prey: do seek their meat from God.

22. The sun ariseth, and they get them away together: and lay them down in their dens.

23. Man goeth forth to his work, and to his labour: until the evening.

24. O Lord, how manifold are thy works: in wisdom hast thou made them all; the earth is full of thy riches.

25. So is the great and wide sea also: wherein are things creeping innumerable, both small and great beasts.

26. There go the ships, and there is that Leviathan: whom thou hast made to take his pastime therein.

27. These wait all upon thee: that thou mayest give them their meat in due season.

28. When thou givest it them they gather it: and when thou openest thy hand they are filled with good.

29. When thou hidest thy face they are troubled: when thou takest away their breath they die, and are turned again to their dust.

30. When thou lettest thy breath go forth they shall be made: and thou shalt renew the face of the earth.

31. The glorious majesty of the Lord shall endure for ever: the Lord shall rejoice in his works.

32. The earth shall tremble at the look of him: if he do but touch the hills, they shall smoke.

33. I will sing unto the Lord as long as I live: I will praise my God while I have my being.

34. And so shall my words please him: my joy shall be in the Lord.

35. As for sinners, they shall be consumed out of the earth, and the ungodly shall come to an end: praise thou the Lord, O my soul, praise the Lord.

PSALM 110 *Dixit Dominus*

The Lord said unto my Lord: Sit thou on my right hand, until I make thine enemies thy footstool.

2. The Lord shall send the rod of thy power out of Sion: be thou ruler, even in the midst among thine enemies.

3. In the day of thy power shall the people offer thee free-will offerings with an holy worship: the dew of thy birth is of the womb of the morning.

4. The Lord sware, and will not repent: Thou art a Priest for ever after the order of Melchisedech.

5. The Lord upon thy right hand: shall wound even kings in the day of his wrath.

6. He shall judge among the heathen; he shall fill the places with the dead bodies: and smite in sunder the heads over divers countries.

7. He shall drink of the brook in the way: therefore shall he lift up his head.

APPENDIX II

PSALMS DISCUSSED OR MENTIONED

PSALM
1. Blessed is the man (*Beatus vir*) — 673
2. Why do the heathen (*Quare fremuerunt*) — 644, 709
5. Ponder my words (*Verba mea auribus*) — 682
6. O Lord, rebuke me not (*Domine ne in furore*) — 663
7. O Lord my God (*Domine Deus Meus*) — 651, 652
8. O Lord our governor (*Domine, Dominus noster*) — 715–17
9. I will give thanks (*Confitebor tibi*) — 648, 671
10. Why standest thou so far off (*Ut quid Domine?*) — 650, 682
11. In the Lord put I my trust (*In Domino confido*) — 676
12. Help me, Lord (*Salvum me fac*) — 682
13. How long wilt thou forget me (*Usque quo, Domine?*) — 709
16. Preserve me, O God (*Conserva me, Domine*) — 708
17. Hear the right, O Lord (*Exaudi Domine*) — 661, 717
18. I will love thee (*Diligam te, Domine*) — 644, 674, 687
19. The heavens declare (*Coeli enarrant*) — 672, 676–7, 686
22. My God, My God, look upon me (*Deus, Deus me*) — 708, 713
23. The Lord is my shepherd (*Dominus regit me*) — 653
26. Be thou my Judge (*Judica me, Domine*) — 678, 717
27. The Lord is my light (*Dominus illuminatio*) — 669, 670
28. Unto thee will I cry (*Ad te, Domine*) — 709
29. Bring unto the Lord (*Afferte Domino*) — 687
30. I will magnify thee (*Exaltabo te, Domine*) — 663, 693
31. In thee, O Lord (*In te, Domine, speravi*) — 678, 683
33. Rejoice in the Lord (*Exultate, justi*) — 687
35. Plead thou my cause (*Judica, Domine*) — 647, 651
36. My heart sheweth me (*Dixit injustus*) — 676, 683, 686, 717
37. Fret not thyself (*Noli aemulari*) — 644
39. I said, I will take heed (*Dixi, custodiam*) — 663
40. I waited patiently (*Expectans expectavi*) — 713

41.	Blessed is he that considereth (*Beatus qui intelligit*)	683
42.	Like as the hart (*Quemadmodum*)	670
43.	Give sentence with me, O God (*Judica me, Deus*)	671
45.	My heart is inditing (*Eructavit cor meum*)	711, 713–15
47.	O clap your hands (*Omnes gentes, plaudite*)	671
49.	O hear ye this (*Audite haec, omnes*)	661, 663
50.	The Lord, even the most mighty God (*Deus deorum*)	651, 670, 678, 692, 694, 696
52.	Why boastest thou thyself (*Quid gloriaris?*)	683
54.	Save me, O God (*Deus in nomine*)	692
55.	Hear my prayer, O God (*Exaudi Deus*)	683, 709
57.	Be merciful unto me (*Miserere mei, Deus*)	671
58.	Are your minds set (*Si vere utique*)	658
63.	O God, thou art my God (*Deus, Deus meus*)	670
65.	Thou, O God, art praised (*Te decet hymnus*)	670, 685, 687
67.	God be merciful unto us (*Deus misereatur*)	647
68.	Let God arise (*Exurgat Deus*)	648, 669, 712
69.	Save me, O God (*Salvum me fac*)	653
72.	Give the King thy judgements (*Deus judicium*)	648, 709
76.	In Jewry is God known (*Notus in Judaea*)	648
81.	Sing we merrily (*Exultate Deo*)	671
82.	God standeth in the congregation (*Deus stetit*)	648
84.	How amiable (*Quam dilecta!*)	670
86.	Bow down thine ear (*Inclina, Domine*)	717
88.	O Lord God of my salvation (*Domine Deus*)	663, 693
89.	My song shall be alway (*Misericordias Domini*)	663, 711
90.	Lord, thou hast been our refuge (*Domine, refugium*)	718
91.	Whoso dwelleth (*Qui habitat*)	708
96.	O sing unto the Lord (*Cantate Domino*)	647
97.	The Lord is King (*Dominus regnavit*)	671
102.	Hear my prayer, O Lord (*Domine exaudi*)	683, 709
104.	Praise the Lord, O my soul (*Benedic, anima mea*)	685, 687, 688, 689
106.	O give thanks (*Confitemini Domino*)	662
107.	O give thanks (*Confitemini Domino*)	645
109.	Hold not thy tongue (*Deus laudem*)	653
110.	The Lord said unto my Lord (*Dixit Dominus*)	708, 709, 710–11
111.	I will give thanks (*Confitebor tibi*)	675
116.	I am well pleased (*Dilexi, quoniam*)	663
118.	O give thanks (*Confitemini Domino*)	708
119.	Blessed are those (*Beati immaculati*)	645, 674–6, 693

132.	Lord, remember David (*Memento Domine*)	711
136.	O give thanks (*Confitemini*)	688
137.	By the waters of Babylon (*Super flumina*)	653, 717
139.	O Lord, thou hast searched me out (*Domine probasti*)	653, 678, 690
141.	Lord, I call upon thee (*Domine, clamavi*)	678
143.	Hear my prayer (*Domine, exaudi*)	651, 653
146.	Praise the Lord, O my soul (*Lauda, anima mea*)	663
147.	O praise the Lord (*Laudate Dominum*)	688
148.	O praise the Lord (*Laudate Dominum*)	688
150.	O praise God (*Laudate Dominum*)	671

THE ABOLITION OF MAN

or

Reflections on education with special reference to the teaching of English in the upper forms of schools

The Master said, He who sets to work on a different strand destroys the whole fabric
Confucius, Analects ii. 16

Contents

1	Men without Chests	399
2	The Way	409
3	The Abolition of Man	419
	Appendix	
	Illustrations of the *Tao*	430
	Notes	438

I

MEN WITHOUT CHESTS

So he sent the word to slay
And slew the little childer
CAROL

I doubt whether we are sufficiently attentive to the importance of elementary text books. That is why I have chosen as the starting-point for these lectures a little book on English intended for 'boys and girls in the upper forms of schools'. I do not think the authors of this book (there were two of them) intended any harm, and I owe them, or their publisher, good language for sending me a complimentary copy. At the same time I shall have nothing good to say of them. Here is a pretty predicament. I do not want to pillory two modest practising schoolmasters who were doing the best they knew: but I cannot be silent about what I think the actual tendency of their work. I therefore propose to conceal their names. I shall refer to these gentlemen as Gaius and Titius and to their book as *The Green Book*. But I promise you there is such a book and I have it on my shelves.

In their second chapter Gaius and Titius quote the well-known story of Coleridge at the waterfall. You remember that there were two tourists present: that one called it 'sublime' and the other 'pretty'; and that Coleridge mentally endorsed the first judgement and rejected the second with disgust. Gaius and Titius comment as follows: 'When the man said *This is sublime*, he appeared to be making a remark about the waterfall ... Actually ... he was not making a remark about the waterfall, but a remark about his own feelings. What he was saying was really *I have feelings associated in my mind with the word "Sublime"*, or shortly, *I have sublime feelings*.' Here are a good many deep questions settled in a pretty summary fashion. But the authors are not yet finished. They add: 'This confusion is continually present in language as we use it. We appear to be saying something very important about something: and actually we are only saying something about our own feelings.'[1]

Before considering the issues really raised by this momentous little paragraph (designed, you will remember, for 'the upper forms of schools') we must eliminate one mere confusion into which Gaius and Titius have fallen. Even on their own view – on any conceivable view – the man who says *This is sublime* cannot mean *I have sublime feelings*. Even if it were granted that such qualities as sublimity were simply and solely projected into things from our own emotions, yet the emotions which prompt the projection are the correlatives, and therefore almost the opposites, of the qualities projected. The feelings which make a man call an object sublime are not sublime feelings but feelings of veneration. If *This is sublime* is to be reduced at all to a statement about the speaker's feelings, the proper translation would be *I have humble feelings*. If the view held by Gaius and Titius were consistently applied it would lead to obvious absurdities. It would force them to maintain that *You are contemptible* means *I have contemptible feelings*: in fact that *Your feelings are contemptible* means *My feelings are contemptible*. But we need not delay over this which is the very *pons asinorum* of our subject. It would be unjust to Gaius and Titius themselves to emphasize what was doubtless a mere inadvertence.

The schoolboy who reads this passage in *The Green Book* will believe two propositions: firstly, that all sentences containing a predicate of value are statements about the emotional state of the speaker, and secondly, that all such statements are unimportant. It is true that Gaius and Titius have said neither of these things in so many words. They have treated only one particular predicate of value (*sublime*) as a word descriptive of the speaker's emotions. The pupils are left to do for themselves the work of extending the same treatment to all predicates of value: and no slightest obstacle to such extension is placed in their way. The authors may or may not desire the extension: they may never have given the question five minutes' serious thought in their lives. I am not concerned with what they desired but with the effect their book will certainly have on the schoolboy's mind. In the same way, they have not said that judgements of value are unimportant. Their words are that we '*appear* to be saying something very important' when in reality we are '*only* saying something about our own feelings'. No schoolboy will be able to resist the suggestion brought to bear upon him by that word *only*. I do not mean, of course, that he will make any conscious inference from what he reads to a general philosophical theory that all values are subjective and trivial. The very power of Gaius and Titius depends on the fact that they are dealing with a boy: a boy who thinks he is 'doing' his 'English prep' and has no notion that ethics, theology, and politics are all at stake. It is not a theory they put into his mind, but an assumption, which ten years hence, its origin forgotten and its presence unconscious, will condition him to take one side in a controversy which he has never recognized as a controversy at all. The authors themselves, I suspect, hardly know what they are doing to the boy, and he cannot know what is being done to him.

Before considering the philosophical credentials of the position which Gaius and Titius have adopted about value, I should like to show its practical results on the educational procedure. In their fourth chapter they quote a silly advertisement of a pleasure cruise and proceed to inoculate their pupils against the sort of writing it exhibits.[2] The advertisement tells us that those who buy tickets for this cruise will go 'across the Western Ocean where Drake of Devon sailed', 'adventuring after the treasures of the Indies', and bringing home themselves also a 'treasure' of 'golden hours' and 'glowing colours'. It is a bad bit of writing, of course: a venal and bathetic exploitation of those emotions of awe and pleasure which men feel in visiting places that have striking associations with history or legend. If Gaius and Titius were to stick to their last and teach their readers (as they promised to do) the art of English composition, it was their business to put this advertisement side by side with passages from great writers in which the very emotion is well expressed, and then show where the difference lies.

They might have used Johnson's famous passage from the *Western Islands*, which concludes: 'That man is little to be envied, whose patriotism would not gain force upon the plain of Marathon, or whose piety would not grow warmer among the ruins of Iona.'[3] They might have taken that place in *The Prelude* where Wordsworth describes how the antiquity of London first descended on his mind with 'Weight and power, Power growing under weight'.[4] A lesson which had laid such literature beside the advertisement and really discriminated the good from the bad would have been a lesson worth teaching. There would have been some blood and sap in it – the trees of knowledge and of life growing together. It would also have had the merit of being a lesson in literature: a subject of which Gaius and Titius, despite their professed purpose, are uncommonly shy.

What they actually do is to point out that the luxurious motor-vessel won't really sail where Drake did, that the tourists will not have any adventures, that the treasures they bring home will be of a purely metaphorical nature, and that a trip to Margate might provide 'all the pleasure and rest' they required.[5] All this is very true: talents inferior to those of Gaius and Titius would have sufficed to discover it. What they have not noticed, or not cared about, is that a very similar treatment could be applied to much good literature which treats the same emotion. What, after all, can the history of early British Christianity, in pure reason, add to the motives for piety as they exist in the eighteenth century? Why should Mr Wordsworth's inn be more comfortable or the air of London more healthy because London has existed for a long time? Or, if there is indeed any obstacle which will prevent a critic from 'debunking' Johnson and Wordsworth (and Lamb, and Virgil, and Thomas Browne, and Mr de la Mare) as *The Green Book* debunks the advertisement, Gaius and Titius have given their schoolboy readers no faintest help to its discovery.

From this passage the schoolboy will learn about literature precisely nothing. What he will learn quickly enough, and perhaps indelibly, is the belief that all emotions aroused by local association are in themselves contrary to reason and contemptible. He will have no notion that there are two ways of being immune to such an advertisement – that it falls equally flat on those who are above it and those who are below it, on the man of real sensibility and on the mere trousered ape who has never been able to conceive the Atlantic as anything more than so many million tons of cold salt water. There are two men to whom we offer in vain a false leading article on patriotism and honour: one is the coward, the other is the honourable and patriotic man. None of this is brought before the schoolboy's mind. On the contrary, he is encouraged to reject the lure of the 'Western Ocean' on the very dangerous ground that in so doing he will prove himself a knowing fellow who can't be bubbled out of his cash. Gaius and Titius, while teaching him nothing about letters, have cut out of his soul, long before he is old enough to choose, the possibility of having certain experiences which thinkers of more authority than they have held to be generous, fruitful, and humane.

But it is not only Gaius and Titius. In another little book, whose author I will call Orbilius, I find that the same operation, under the same general anaesthetic, is being carried out. Orbilius chooses for 'debunking' a silly bit of writing on horses, where these animals are praised as the 'willing servants' of the early colonists in Australia.[6] And he falls into the same trap as Gaius and Titius. Of Ruksh and Sleipnir and the weeping horses of Achilles and the war-horse in the Book of Job – nay even of Brer Rabbit and of Peter Rabbit – of man's prehistoric piety to 'our brother the ox' – of all that this semi-anthropomorphic treatment of beasts has meant in human history and of the literature where it finds noble or piquant expression – he has not a word to say.[7] Even of the problems of animal psychology as they exist for science he says nothing. He contents himself with explaining that horses are not, *secundum litteram*, interested in colonial expansion.[8] This piece of information is really all that his pupils get from him. Why the composition before them is bad, when others that lie open to the same charge are good, they do not hear. Much less do they learn of the two classes of men who are, respectively, above and below the danger of such writing – the man who really knows horses and really loves them, not with anthropomorphic illusions, but with ordinate love, and the irredeemable urban blockhead to whom a horse is merely an old-fashioned means of transport. Some pleasure in their own ponies and dogs they will have lost; some incentive to cruelty or neglect they will have received; some pleasure in their own knowingness will have entered their minds. That is their day's lesson in English, though of English they have learned nothing. Another little portion of the human heritage has been quietly taken from them before they were old enough to understand.

I have hitherto been assuming that such teachers as Gaius and Titius do not fully realize what they are doing and do not intend the far-reaching consequences it will actually have. There is, of course, another possibility. What I have called (presuming on their concurrence in a certain traditional system of values) the 'trousered ape' and the 'urban blockhead' may be precisely the kind of man they really wish to produce. The differences between us may go all the way down. They may really hold that the ordinary human feelings about the past or animals or large waterfalls are contrary to reason and contemptible and ought to be eradicated. They may be intending to make a clean sweep of traditional values and start with a new set. That position will be discussed later. If it is the position which Gaius and Titius are holding, I must, for the moment, content myself with pointing out that it is a philosophical and not a literary position. In filling their book with it they have been unjust to the parent or headmaster who buys it and who has got the work of amateur philosophers where he expected the work of professional grammarians. A man would be annoyed if his son returned from the dentist with his teeth untouched and his head crammed with the dentist's *obiter dicta* on bimetallism or the Baconian theory.

But I doubt whether Gaius and Titius have really planned, under cover of teaching English, to propagate their philosophy. I think they have slipped into it for the following reasons. In the first place, literary criticism is difficult, and what they actually do is very much easier. To explain why a bad treatment of some basic human emotion is bad literature is, if we exclude all question-begging attacks on the emotion itself, a very hard thing to do. Even Dr Richards, who first seriously tackled the problem of badness in literature, failed, I think, to do it. To 'debunk' the emotion, on the basis of a commonplace rationalism, is within almost anyone's capacity. In the second place, I think Gaius and Titius may have honestly misunderstood the pressing educational need of the moment. They see the world around them swayed by emotional propaganda – they have learned from tradition that youth is sentimental – and they conclude that the best thing they can do is to fortify the minds of young people against emotion. My own experience as a teacher tells an opposite tale. For every one pupil who needs to be guarded from a weak excess of sensibility there are three who need to be awakened from the slumber of cold vulgarity. The task of the modern educator is not to cut down jungles but to irrigate deserts. The right defence against false sentiments is to inculcate just sentiments. By starving the sensibility of our pupils we only make them easier prey to the propagandist when he comes. For famished nature will be avenged and a hard heart is no infallible protection against a soft head.

But there is a third, and a profounder, reason for the procedure which Gaius and Titius adopt. They may be perfectly ready to admit that a good education should build some sentiments while destroying others. They may endeavour to do so. But it is impossible that they should succeed. Do what they will, it is the 'debunking' side of their work, and this side alone, which will really tell. In order to grasp this necessity clearly I must digress for a moment to show that what may be called the educational predicament of Gaius and Titius is different from that of all their predecessors.

Until quite modern times all teachers and even all men believed the universe to be such that certain emotional reactions on our part could be either congruous or incongruous to it – believed, in fact, that objects did not merely receive, but could *merit*, our approval or disapproval, our reverence or our contempt. The reason why Coleridge agreed with the tourist who called the cataract sublime and disagreed with the one who called it pretty was of course that he believed inanimate nature to be such that certain responses could be more 'just' or 'ordinate' or 'appropriate' to it than others. And he believed (correctly) that the tourists thought the same. The man who called the cataract sublime was not intending simply to describe his own emotions about it: he was also claiming that the object was one which *merited* those emotions. But for this claim there would be nothing to agree or disagree about. To disagree with *This is pretty* if those words simply described the lady's feelings, would be absurd: if she had said *I feel sick* Coleridge would hardly have replied *No; I feel quite well*. When Shelley, having compared the human sensibility to an Aeolian lyre, goes on to add that it differs from a lyre in having a power of 'internal adjustment' whereby it can 'accommodate its chords to the motions of that which strikes them',[9] he is assuming the same belief. 'Can you be righteous', asks Traherne, 'unless you be just in rendering to things their due esteem? All things were made to be yours and you were made to prize them according to their value.'[10]

St Augustine defines virtue as *ordo amoris*, the ordinate condition of the affections in which every object is accorded that kind of degree of love which is appropriate to it.[11] Aristotle says that the aim of education is to make the pupil like and dislike what he ought.[12] When the age for reflective thought comes, the pupil who has been thus trained in 'ordinate affections' or 'just sentiments' will easily find the first principles in Ethics; but to the corrupt man they will never be visible at all and he can make no progress in that science.[13] Plato before him had said the same. The little human animal will not at first have the right responses. It must be trained to feel pleasure, liking, disgust, and hatred at those things which really are pleasant, likeable, disgusting and hateful.[14] In the *Republic*, the well-nurtured youth is one 'who would see most clearly whatever was amiss in ill-made works of man or ill-grown works of nature, and with a just distaste would blame and hate the ugly even from his earliest years and would give delighted praise to beauty, receiving it into his soul and being nourished by it, so that he becomes a man of gentle heart. All this before he is of an age to reason; so that when Reason at length comes to him, then, bred as he has been, he will hold out his hands in welcome and recognize her because of the affinity he bears to her.'[15] In early Hinduism that conduct in men which can be called good consists in conformity to, or almost participation in, the *Rta* – that great ritual or pattern of nature and supernature which is revealed alike in the cosmic order, the moral virtues, and the ceremonial of the temple. Righteousness, correctness, order, the *Rta*, is constantly identified with *satya* or truth, correspondence to reality. As Plato said that the Good was 'beyond existence' and Wordsworth that through virtue the stars were strong, so the Indian masters say that the gods themselves are born of the *Rta* and obey it.[16]

The Chinese also speak of a great thing (the greatest thing) called the *Tao*. It is the reality beyond all predicates, the abyss that was before the Creator Himself. It is Nature, it is the Way, the Road. It is the Way in which the universe goes on, the Way in which things everlastingly emerge, stilly and tranquilly, into space and time. It is also the Way which every man should tread in imitation of that cosmic and supercosmic progression, conforming all activities to that great exemplar.[17] 'In ritual', say the *Analects*, 'it is harmony with Nature that is prized.'[18] The ancient Jews likewise praise the Law as being 'true'.[19]

This conception in all its forms, Platonic, Aristotelian, Stoic, Christian, and Oriental alike, I shall henceforth refer to for brevity simply as 'the *Tao*'. Some of the accounts of it which I have quoted will seem, perhaps, to many of you merely quaint or even magical. But what is common to them all is something we cannot neglect. It is the doctrine of objective value, the belief that certain attitudes are really true, and others really false, to the kind of thing the universe is and the kind of things we are. Those who know the *Tao* can hold that to call children delightful or old men venerable is not simply to record a psychological fact about our own parental or filial emotions at the moment, but to recognize a quality which *demands* a certain response from us whether we make it or not. I myself do not enjoy the society of small children: because I speak from within the *Tao* I recognize this as a defect in myself – just as a man may have to recognize that he is tone deaf or colour blind. And because our approvals and disapprovals are thus recognitions of objective value or responses to an objective order, therefore emotional states can be in harmony with reason (when we feel liking for what ought to be approved) or out of harmony with reason (when we perceive that liking is due but cannot feel it). No emotion is, in itself, a judgement; in that sense all emotions and sentiments are alogical. But they can be reasonable or unreasonable as they conform to Reason or fail to conform. The heart never takes the place of the head: but it can, and should, obey it.

Over against this stands the world of *The Green Book*. In it the very possibility of a sentiment being reasonable – or even unreasonable – has been excluded from the outset. It can be reasonable or unreasonable only if it conforms or fails to conform to something else. To say that the cataract is sublime means saying that our emotion of humility is appropriate or ordinate to the reality, and thus to speak of something else besides the emotion; just as to say that a shoe fits is to speak not only of shoes but of feet. But this reference to something beyond the emotion is what Gaius and Titius exclude from every sentence containing a predicate of value. Such statements, for them, refer solely to the emotion. Now the emotion, thus considered by itself, cannot be either in agreement or disagreement with Reason. It is irrational not as a paralogism is irrational, but as a physical event is irrational: it does not rise even to the dignity of error. On this view, the world of facts, without one trace of value, and the world of feelings, without one trace of truth or falsehood, justice or injustice, confront one another, and no *rapprochement* is possible.

Hence the educational problem is wholly different according as you stand within or without the *Tao*. For those within, the task is to train in the pupil those responses which are in themselves appropriate, whether anyone is making them or not, and in making which the very nature of man consists. Those without, if they are logical, must regard all sentiments as equally nonrational, as mere mists between us and the real objects. As a result, they must either decide to remove all sentiments, as far as possible, from the pupil's mind; or else to encourage some sentiments for reasons that have nothing to do with their intrinsic 'justness' or 'ordinacy'. The latter course involves them in the questionable process of creating in others by 'suggestion' or incantation a mirage which their own reason has successfully dissipated.

Perhaps this will become clearer if we take a concrete instance. When a Roman father told his son that it was a sweet and seemly thing to die for his country, he believed what he said. He was communicating to the son an emotion which he himself shared and which he believed to be in accord with the value which his judgement discerned in noble death. He was giving the boy the best he had, giving of his spirit to humanize him as he had given of his body to beget him. But Gaius and Titius cannot believe that in calling such a death sweet and seemly they would be saying 'something important about something'. Their own method of debunking would cry out against them if they attempted to do so. For death is not something to eat and therefore cannot be *dulce* in the literal sense, and it is unlikely that the real sensations preceding it will be *dulce* even by analogy. And as for *decorum* –

that is only a word describing how some other people will feel about your death when they happen to think of it, which won't be often, and will certainly do you no good. There are only two courses open to Gaius and Titius. Either they must go the whole way and debunk this sentiment like any other, or must set themselves to work to produce, from outside, a sentiment which they believe to be of no value to the pupil and which may cost him his life, because it is useful to us (the survivors) that our young men should feel it. If they embark on this course the difference between the old and the new education will be an important one. Where the old initiated, the new merely 'conditions'. The old dealt with its pupils as grown birds deal with young birds when they teach them to fly; the new deals with them more as the poultry-keeper deals with young birds – making them thus or thus for purposes of which the birds know nothing. In a word, the old was a kind of propagation – men transmitting manhood to men; the new is merely propaganda.

It is to their credit that Gaius and Titius embrace the first alternative. Propaganda is their abomination: not because their own philosophy gives a ground for condemning it (or anything else) but because they are better than their principles. They probably have some vague notion (I will examine it in my next lecture) that valour and good faith and justice could be sufficiently commended to the pupil on what they would call 'rational' or 'biological' or 'modern' grounds, if it should ever become necessary. In the meantime, they leave the matter alone and get on with the business of debunking.

But this course, though less inhuman, is not less disastrous than the opposite alternative of cynical propaganda. Let us suppose for a moment that the harder virtues could really be theoretically justifed with no appeal to objective value. It still remains true that no justification of virtue will enable a man to be virtuous. Without the aid of trained emotions the intellect is powerless against the animal organism. I had sooner play cards against a man who was quite sceptical about ethics, but bred to believe that 'a gentleman does not cheat', than against an irreproachable moral philosopher who had been brought up among sharpers. In battle it is not syllogisms that will keep the reluctant nerves and muscles to their post in the third hour of the bombardment. The crudest sentimentalism (such as Gaius and Titius would wince at) about a flag or a country or a regiment will be of more use. We were told it all long ago by Plato. As the king governs by his executive, so Reason in man must rule the mere appetites by means of the 'spirited element'.[20] The head rules the belly through the chest – the seat, as Alanus tells us, of Magnanimity,[21] of emotions organized by trained habit into stable sentiments. The Chest – Magnanimity – Sentiment – these are the indispensable liaison officers between cerebral man and visceral man. It may even be said that it is by this middle element that man is man: for by his intellect he is mere spirit and by his appetite mere animal.

The operation of *The Green Book* and its kind is to produce what may be called Men without Chests. It is an outrage that they should be commonly spoken of as Intellectuals. This gives them the chance to say that he who attacks them attacks Intelligence. It is not so. They are not distinguished from other men by any unusual skill in finding truth nor any virginal ardour to pursue her. Indeed it would be strange if they were: a persevering devotion to truth, a nice sense of intellectual honour, cannot be long maintained without the aid of a sentiment which Gaius and Titius could debunk as easily as any other. It is not excess of thought but defect of fertile and generous emotion that marks them out. Their heads are no bigger than the ordinary: it is the atrophy of the chest beneath that makes them seem so.

And all the time – such is the tragi-comedy of our situation – we continue to clamour for those very qualities we are rendering impossible. You can hardly open a periodical without coming across the statement that what our civilization needs is more 'drive', or dynamism, or self-sacrifice, or 'creativity'. In a sort of ghastly simplicity we remove the organ and demand the function. We make men without chests and expect of them virtue and enterprise. We laugh at honour and are shocked to find traitors in our midst. We castrate and bid the geldings be fruitful.

2

THE WAY

It is upon the Trunk that a gentleman works.
ANALECTS OF CONFUCIUS, 1.2

The practical result of education in the spirit of *The Green Book* must be the destruction of the society which accepts it. But this is not necessarily a refutation of subjectivism about values as a theory. The true doctrine might be a doctrine which if we accept we die. No one who speaks from within the *Tao* could reject it on that account: ἐν δὲ φάει καὶ ολεσσου. But it has not yet come to that. There are theoretical difficulties in the philosophy of Gaius and Titius.

However subjective they may be about some traditional values, Gaius and Titius have shown by the very act of writing *The Green Book* that there must be some other values about which they are not subjective at all. They write in order to produce certain states of mind in the rising generation, if not because they think those states of mind intrinsically just or good, yet certainly because they think them to be the means to some state of society which they regard as desirable. It would not be difficult to collect from various passages in *The Green Book* what their ideal is. But we need not. The important point is not the precise nature of their end, but the fact that they have an end at all. They must have, or their book (being purely practical in intention) is written to no purpose. And this end must have real value in their eyes. To abstain from calling it good and to use, instead, such predicates as 'necessary' or 'progressive' or 'efficient' would be a subterfuge. They could be forced by argument to answer the questions 'necessary for what?', 'progressing towards what?', 'effecting what?'; in the last resort they would have to admit that some state of affairs was in their opinion good for its own sake. And this time they could not maintain that 'good' simply described their own emotion about it. For the whole purpose of their book is so to condition the young reader that he will share their approval, and this would be either a fool's or a villain's undertaking unless they held that their approval was in some way valid or correct.

In actual fact Gaius and Titius will be found to hold, with complete uncritical dogmatism, the whole system of values which happened to be in vogue among moderately educated young men of the professional classes during the period between the two wars.' Their scepticism about values is on the surface: it is for use on other people's values; about the values current in their own set they are not nearly sceptical enough. And this phenomenon is very usual. A great many of those who 'debunk' traditional or (as they would say) 'sentimental' values have in the background values of their own which they believe to be immune from the debunking process. They claim to be cutting away the parasitic growth of emotion, religious sanction, and inherited taboos, in order that 'real' or 'basic' values may emerge. I will now try to find out what happens if this is seriously attempted.

Let us continue to use the previous example – that of death for a good cause – not, of course, because virtue is the only value or martyrdom the only virtue, but because this is the *experimentum crucis* which shows different systems of thought in the clearest light. Let us suppose that an Innovator in values regards *dulce et decorum* and *greater love hath no man* as mere irrational sentiments which are to be stripped off in order that we may get down to the 'realistic' or 'basic' ground of this value. Where will he find such a ground?

First of all, he might say that the real value lay in the utility of such sacrifice to the community. 'Good', he might say, '*means* what is useful to the community.' But of course the death of the community is not useful to the community – only the death of some of its members. What is really meant is that the death of some men is useful to other men. That is very true. But on what ground are some men being asked to die for the benefit of others? Every appeal to pride, honour, shame, or love is excluded by hypothesis. To use these would be to return to sentiment and the Innovator's task is, having cut all that away, to explain to men, in terms of pure reasoning, why they will be well advised to die that others may live. He may say 'Unless some of us *risk* death all of us are *certain* to die.' But that will be true only in a limited number of cases; and even when it is true it provokes the very reasonable counter question 'Why should I be one of those who take the risk?'

At this point the Innovator may ask why, after all, selfishness should be more 'rational' or 'intelligent' than altruism. The question is welcome. If by Reason we mean the process actually employed by Gaius and Titius when engaged in debunking (that is, the connecting by inference of propositions, ultimately derived from sense data, with further propositions), then the answer must be that a refusal to sacrifice oneself is no more rational than a consent to do so. And no less rational. Neither choice is rational – or irrational – at all. From propositions about fact alone no *practical* conclusion can ever be drawn. *This will preserve society* cannot lead to *do this* except by the mediation of *society ought to be preserved*. *This will cost you your life* cannot lead directly to *do not do this*: it can lead to it only through a felt desire or an acknowledged duty of self-preservation. The Innovator is trying to get a conclusion in the imperative mood out of premisses in the indicative mood: and though he continues trying to all eternity he cannot succeed, for the thing is impossible. We must therefore either extend the word Reason to include what our ancestors called Practical Reason and confess that judgements such as *society ought to be preserved* (though they can support themselves by no reason of the sort that Gaius and Titius demand) are not mere sentiments but are rationality itself; or else we must give up at once, and for ever, the attempt to find a core of 'rational' value behind all the sentiments we have debunked. The Innovator will not take the first alternative, for practical principles known to all men by Reason are simply the *Tao* which he has set out to supersede. He is more likely to give up the quest for a 'rational' core and to hunt for some other ground even more 'basic' and 'realistic'.

This he will probably feel that he has found in Instinct. The preservation of society, and of the species itself, are ends that do not hang on the precarious thread of Reason: they are given by Instinct. That is why there is no need to argue against the man who does not acknowledge them. We have an instinctive urge to preserve our own species. That is why men ought to work for posterity. We have no instinctive urge to keep promises or to respect individual life: that is why scruples of justice and humanity – in fact the *Tao* – can be properly swept away when they conflict with our real end, the preservation of the species. That, again, is why the modern situation permits and demands a new sexual morality: the old taboos served some real purpose in helping to preserve the species, but contraceptives have modified this and we can now abandon many of the taboos. For of course sexual desire, being instinctive, is to be gratified whenever it does not conflict with the preservation of the species. It looks, in fact, as if an ethics based on instinct will give the Innovator all he wants and nothing that he does not want.

In reality we have not advanced one step. I will not insist on the point that Instinct is a name for we know not what (to say that migratory birds find their way by instinct is only to say that we do not know how migratory birds find their way), for I think it is here being used in a fairly definite sense, to mean an unreflective or spontaneous impulse widely felt by the members of a given species. In what way does Instinct, thus conceived, help us to find 'real' values? Is it maintained that we *must* obey Instinct, that we cannot do otherwise? But if so, why are *Green Books* and the like written? Why this stream of exhortation to drive us where we cannot help going? Why such praise for those who have submitted to the inevitable? Or is it maintained that if we do obey Instinct we shall be happy and satisfied? But the very question we are considering was that of facing death which (so far as the Innovator knows) cuts off every possible satisfaction: and if we have an instinctive desire for the good of posterity then this desire, by the very nature of the case, can never be satisfied, since its aim is achieved, if at all, when we are dead. It looks very much as if the Innovator would have to say not that we must obey Instinct, nor that it will satisfy us to do so, but that we *ought* to obey it.[2]

But why ought we to obey Instinct? Is there another instinct of a higher order directing us to do so, and a third of a still higher order directing us to obey *it*? – an infinite regress of instincts? This is presumably impossible, but nothing else will serve. From the statement about psychological fact 'I have an impulse to do so and so' we cannot by any ingenuity derive the practical principle 'I ought to obey this impulse'. Even if it were true that men had a spontaneous, unreflective impulse to sacrifice their own lives for the preservation of their fellows, it remains a quite separate question whether this is an impulse they should control or one they should indulge. For even the Innovator admits that many impulses (those which conflict with the preservation of the species) have to be controlled. And this admission surely introduces us to a yet more fundamental difficulty.

Telling us to obey Instinct is like telling us to obey 'people'. People say different things: so do instincts. Our instincts are at war. If it is held that the instinct for preserving the species should always be obeyed at the expense of other instincts, whence do we derive this rule of precedence? To listen to that instinct speaking in its own cause and deciding it in its own favour would be rather simple-minded. Each instinct, if you listen to it, will claim to be gratified at the expense of all the rest. By the very act of listening to one rather than to others we have already prejudged the case. If we did not bring to the examination of our instincts a knowledge of their comparative dignity we could never learn it from them. And that knowledge cannot itself be instinctive: the judge cannot be one of the parties judged; or, if he is, the decision is worthless and there is no ground for placing the preservation of the species above self-preservation or sexual appetite.

The idea that, without appealing to any court higher than the instincts themselves, we can yet find grounds for preferring one instinct above its fellows dies very hard. We grasp at useless words: we call it the 'basic', or 'fundamental', or 'primal', or 'deepest' instinct. It is of no avail. Either these words conceal a value judgement passed *upon* the instinct and therefore not derivable *from* it, or else they merely record its felt intensity, the frequency of its operation and its wide distribution. If the former, the whole attempt to base value upon instinct has been abandoned: if the latter, these observations about the quantitative aspects of a psychological event lead to no practical conclusion. It is the old dilemma. Either the premises already concealed an imperative or the conclusion remains merely in the indicative.³

Finally, it is worth inquiry whether there *is* any instinct to care for posterity or preserve the species. I do not discover it in myself: and yet I am a man rather prone to think of remote futurity – a man who can read Mr Olaf Stapledon with delight. Much less do I find it easy to believe that the majority of people who have sat opposite me in buses or stood with me in queues feel an unreflective impulse to do anything at all about the species, or posterity. Only people educated in a particular way have ever had the idea 'posterity' before their minds at all. It is difficult to assign to instinct our attitude towards an object which exists only for reflective men. What we have by nature is an impulse to preserve our own children and grandchildren; an impulse which grows progressively feebler as the imagination looks forward and finally dies out in the 'deserts of vast futurity'. No parents who were guided by this instinct would dream for a moment of setting up the claims of their hypothetical descendants against those of the baby actually crowing and kicking in the room. Those of us who accept the *Tao* may, perhaps, say that they ought to do so: but that is not open to those who treat instinct as the source of value. As we pass from mother love to rational planning for the future we are passing away from the realm of instinct into that of choice and reflection: and if instinct is the source of value, planning for the future ought to be less respectable and less obligatory than the baby language and cuddling of the fondest mother or the most fatuous nursery anecdotes of a doting father. If we are to base ourselves upon instinct, these things are the substance, and care for posterity the shadow – the huge, flickering shadow of the nursery happiness cast upon the screen of the unknown future. I do not say this projection is a bad thing: but then I do not believe that instinct is the ground of value judgements. What is absurd is to claim that your care for posterity finds its justification in instinct and then flout at every turn the only instinct on which it could be supposed to rest, tearing the child almost from the breast to crèche and kindergarten in the interests of progress and the coming race.

The truth finally becomes apparent that neither in any operation with factual propositions nor in any appeal to instinct can the Innovator find the basis for a system of values. None of the principles he requires are to be found there: but they are all to be found somewhere else. 'All within the four seas are his brothers' (xii. 5) says Confucius of the *Chün-tzu*, the *cuor gentil* or gentleman. *Humani nihil a me alienum puto* says the Stoic. 'Do as you would be done by,' says Jesus. 'Humanity is to be preserved,' says Locke.⁴ All the practical principles behind the Innovator's case for posterity, or society, or the species, are there from time immemorial in the *Tao*. But they are nowhere else. Unless you accept these without question as being to the world of action what axioms are to the world of theory, you can have no practical principles whatever. You cannot reach them as conclusions: they are premisses. You may, since they can give no 'reason' for themselves of a kind to silence Gaius and Titius, regard them as sentiments: but then you must give up contrasting 'real' or 'rational' value with sentimental value. All value will be sentimental; and you must confess (on pain of abandoning every value) that all sentiment is not 'merely' subjective. You may, on the other hand, regard them as rational – nay as rationality itself – as things so obviously reasonable that they neither demand nor admit proof. But then you must allow that Reason can be practical, that an *ought* must not be dismissed because it cannot produce some *is* as its credential. If nothing is self-evident, nothing can be proved. Similarly if nothing is obligatory for its own sake, nothing is obligatory at all.

To some it will appear that I have merely restored under another name what they always meant by basic or fundamental instinct. But much more than a choice of words is involved. The Innovator attacks traditional values (the *Tao*) in defence of what he at first supposes to be (in some special sense) 'rational' or 'biological' values. But as we have seen, all the values which he uses in attacking the *Tao*, and even claims to be substituting for it, are themselves derived from the *Tao*. If he had really started from scratch, from right outside the human tradition of value, no jugglery could have advanced him an inch towards the conception that a man should die for the community or work for posterity. If the *Tao* falls, all his own conceptions of value fall with it. Not one of them can claim any authority other than that of the *Tao*. Only by such shreds of the *Tao* as he has inherited is he enabled even to attack it. The question therefore arises what title he has to select bits of it for acceptance and to reject others. For if the bits he rejects have no authority, neither have those he retains: if what he retains is valid, what he rejects is equally valid too.

The Innovator, for example, rates high the claims of posterity. He cannot get any valid claim for posterity out of instinct or (in the modern sense) reason. He is really deriving our duty to posterity from the *Tao*; our duty to do good to all men is an axiom of Practical Reason, and our duty to do good to our descendants is a clear deduction from it. But then, in every form of the *Tao* which has come down to us, side by side with the duty to children and descendants lies the duty to parents and ancestors. By what right do we reject one and accept the other? Again, the Innovator may place economic value first. To get people fed and clothed is the great end, and in pursuit of its scruples about justice and good faith may be set aside. The *Tao* of course agrees with him about the importance of getting the people fed and clothed. Unless the Innovator were himself using the *Tao* he could never have learned of such a duty. But side by side with it in the *Tao* lie those duties of justice and good faith which he is ready to debunk. What is his warrant? He may be a Jingoist, a Racialist, an extreme nationalist, who maintains that the advance-ment of his own people is the object to which all else ought to yield. But no kind of factual observation and no appeal to instinct will give him a ground for this option. Once more, he is in fact deriving it from the *Tao*: a duty to our own kin, because they are our own kin, is a part of traditional morality. But side by side with it in the *Tao*, and limiting it, lie the inflexible demands of justice, and the rule that, in the long run, all men are our brothers. Whence comes the Innovator's authority to pick and choose?

Since I can see no answer to these questions, I draw the following conclusions. This thing which I have called for convenience the *Tao*, and which others may call Natural Law or Traditional Morality or the First Principles of Practical Reason or the First Platitudes, is not one among a series of possible systems of value. It is the sole source of all value judgements. If it is rejected, all value is rejected. If any value is retained, it is retained. The effort to refute it and raise a new system of value in its place is self-contradictory. There has never been, and never will be, a radically new judgement of value in the history of the world. What purport to be new systems or (as they now call them) 'ideologies', all consist of fragments from the *Tao* itself, arbitrarily wrenched from their context in the whole and then swollen to madness in their isolation, yet still owing to the *Tao* and to it alone such validity as they possess. If my duty to my parents is a superstition, then so is my duty to posterity. If justice is a superstition, then so is my duty to my country or my race. If the pursuit of scientific knowledge is a real value, then so is conjugal fidelity. The rebellion of new ideologies against the *Tao* is a rebellion of the branches against the tree: if the rebels could succeed they would find that they had destroyed themselves. The human mind has no more power of inventing a new value than of imagining a new primary colour, or, indeed, of creating a new sun and a new sky for it to move in.

Does this mean, then, that no progress in our perceptions of value can ever take place? That we are bound down for ever to an unchanging code given once for all? And is it, in any event, possible to talk of obeying what I call the *Tao*? If we lump together, as I have done, the traditional moralities of East and West, the Christian, the Pagan, and the Jew, shall we not find many contradictions and some absurdities? I admit all this. Some criticism, some removal of contradictions, even some real development, is required. But there are two very different kinds of criticism.

A theorist about language may approach his native tongue, as it were from outside, regarding its genius as a thing that has no claim on him and advocating wholesale alterations of its idiom and spelling in the interests of commercial convenience or scientific accuracy. That is one thing. A great poet, who has 'loved, and been well nurtured in, his mother tongue', may also make great alterations in it, but his changes of the language are made in the spirit of the language itself: he works from within. The language which suffers, has also inspired the changes. That is a different thing – as different as the works of Shakespeare are from Basic English. It is the difference between alteration from within and alteration from without: between the organic and the surgical.

In the same way, the *Tao* admits development from within. There is a difference between a real moral advance and a mere innovation. From the Confucian 'Do not do to others what you would not like them to do to you' to the Christian 'Do as you would be done by' is a real advance. The morality of Nietzsche is a mere innovation. The first is an advance because no one who did not admit the validity of the old maxim could see reason for accepting the new one, and anyone who accepted the old would at once recognize the new as an extension of the same principle. If he rejected it, he would have to reject it as a superfluity, something that went too far, not as something simply heterogeneous from his own ideas of value. But the Nietzschean ethic can be accepted only if we are ready to scrap traditional morals as a mere error and then to put ourselves in a position where we can find no ground for any value judgements at all. It is the difference between a man who says to us: 'You like your vegetables moderately fresh; why not grow your own and have them perfectly fresh?' and a man who says, 'Throw away that loaf and try eating bricks and centipedes instead.'

Those who understand the spirit of the *Tao* and who have been led by that spirit can modify it in directions which that spirit itself demands. Only they can know what those directions are. The outsider knows nothing about the matter. His attempts at alteration, as we have seen, contradict themselves. So far from being able to harmonize discrepancies in its letter by penetration to its spirit, he merely snatches at some one precept, on which the accidents of time and place happen to have riveted his attention, and then rides it to death – for no reason that he can give. From within the *Tao* itself comes the only authority to modify the *Tao*. This is what Confucius meant when he said 'With those who follow a different Way it is useless to take counsel'.[5] This is why Aristotle said that only those who have been well brought up can usefully study ethics: to the corrupted man, the man who stands outside the *Tao*, the very starting point of this science is invisible.[6] He may be hostile, but he cannot be critical: he does not know what is being discussed. This is why it was also said 'This people that knoweth not the Law is accursed'[7] and 'He that believeth not shall be damned'.[8] An open mind, in questions that are not ultimate, is useful. But an open mind about the ultimate foundations either of Theoretical or of

Practical Reason is idiocy. If a man's mind is open on these things, let his mouth at least be shut. He can say nothing to the purpose. Outside the *Tao* there is no ground for criticizing either the *Tao* or anything else.

In particular instances it may, no doubt, be a matter of some delicacy to decide where the legitimate internal criticism ends and the fatal external kind begins. But wherever any precept of traditional morality is simply challenged to produce its credentials, as though the burden of proof lay on it, we have taken the wrong position. The legitimate reformer endeavours to show that the precept in question conflicts with some precept which its defenders allow to be more fundamental, or that it does not really embody the judgement of value it professes to embody. The direct frontal attack 'Why?' – 'What good does it do?' – 'Who said so?' is never permissible; not because it is harsh or offensive but because no values at all can justify themselves on that level. If you persist in *that* kind of trial you will destroy all values, and so destroy the bases of your own criticism as well as the thing criticized. You must not hold a pistol to the head of the *Tao*. Nor must we postpone obedience to a precept until its credentials have been examined. Only those who are practising the *Tao* will understand it. It is the well-nurtured man, the *cuor gentil*, and he alone, who can recognize Reason when it comes.[9] It is Paul, the Pharisee, the man 'perfect as touching the Law' who learns where and how that Law was deficient.[10]

In order to avoid misunderstanding, I may add that though I myself am a Theist, and indeed a Christian, I am not here attempting any indirect argument for Theism. I am simply arguing that if we are to have values at all we must accept the ultimate platitudes of Practical Reason as having absolute validity: that any attempt, having become sceptical about these, to reintroduce value lower down on some supposedly more 'realistic' basis, is doomed. Whether this position implies a supernatural origin for the *Tao* is a question I am not here concerned with.

Yet how can the modern mind be expected to embrace the conclusion we have reached? This *Tao* which, it seems, we must treat as an absolute is simply a phenomenon like any other – the reflection upon the minds of our ancestors of the agricultural rhythm in which they lived or even of their physiology. We know already in principle how such things are produced: soon we shall know in detail: eventually we shall be able to produce them at will. Of course, while we did not know how minds were made, we accepted this mental furniture as a datum, even as a master. But many things in nature which were once our masters have become our servants. Why not this? Why must our conquest of nature stop short, in stupid reverence, before this final and toughest bit of 'nature' which has hitherto been called the conscience of man? You threaten us with some obscure disaster if we step outside it: but we have been threatened in that way by obscurantists at every step in our advance, and each time the threat has proved false. You say we shall have no values at all if we step outside the *Tao*. Very well: we shall probably find that we can get on quite comfortably without them. Let us regard all ideas of what we *ought* to do simply as an interesting psychological survival: let us step right out of all that and start doing what we like. Let us decide for ourselves what man is to be and make him into that: not on any ground of imagined value, but because we want him to be such. Having mastered our environment, let us now master ourselves and choose our own destiny.

This is a very possible position: and those who hold it cannot be accused of self-contradiction like the half-hearted sceptics who still hope to find 'real' values when they have debunked the traditional ones. This is the rejection of the concept of value altogether. I shall need another lecture to consider it.

3

THE ABOLITION OF MAN

*It came burning hot into my mind, whatever
he said and however he flattered, when he
got me home to his house, he would sell me
for a slave.*
BUNYAN

'Man's conquest of Nature' is an expression often used to describe the progress of applied science. 'Man has Nature whacked,' said someone to a friend of mine not long ago. In their context the words had a certain tragic beauty, for the speaker was dying of tuberculosis. 'No matter,' he said, 'I know I'm one of the casualties. Of course there are casualties on the winning as well as on the losing side. But that doesn't alter the fact that it is winning.' I have chosen this story as my point of departure in order to make it clear that I do not wish to disparage all that is really beneficial in the process described as 'Man's conquest', much less all the real devotion and self-sacrifice that has gone to make it possible. But having done so I must proceed to analyse this conception a little more closely. In what sense is Man the possessor of increasing power over Nature?

Let us consider three typical examples: the aeroplane, the wireless, and the contraceptive. In a civilized community, in peace-time, anyone who can pay for them may use these things. But it cannot strictly be said that when he does so he is exercising his own proper or individual power over Nature. If I pay you to carry me, I am not therefore myself a strong man. Any or all of the three things I have mentioned can be withheld from some men by other men – by those who sell, or those who allow the sale, or those who own the sources of production, or those who make the goods. What we call Man's power is, in reality, a power possessed by some men which they may, or may not, allow other men to profit by. Again, as regards the powers manifested in the aeroplane or the wireless, Man is as much the patient or subject as the possessor, since he is the target both for bombs and for propaganda. And as regards contraceptives, there is a paradoxical, negative sense in which all possible future generations are the patients or subjects of a power wielded by those already alive. By contraception simply, they are denied existence; by contraception used as a means of selective breeding, they are, without their concurring voice, made to be what one generation, for its own reasons, may choose to prefer. From this point of view, what we call Man's power over Nature turns out to be a power exercised by some men over other men with Nature as its instrument.

It is, of course, a commonplace to complain that men have hitherto used badly, and against their fellows, the powers that science has given them. But that is not the point I am trying to make. I am not speaking of particular corruptions and abuses which an increase of moral virtue would cure: I am considering what the thing called 'Man's power over Nature' must always and essentially be. No doubt, the picture could be modified by public ownership of raw materials and factories and public control of scientific research. But unless we have a world state this will still mean the power of one nation over others. And even within the world state or the nation it will mean (in principle) the power of majorities over minorities, and (in the concrete) of a government over the people. And all long-term exercises of power, especially in breeding, must mean the power of earlier generations over later ones.

The latter point is not always sufficiently emphasized, because those who write on social matters have not yet learned to imitate the physicists by always including Time among the dimensions. In order to understand fully what Man's power over Nature, and therefore the power of some men over other men, really means, we must picture the race extended in time from the date of its emergence to that of its extinction. Each generation exercises power over its successors: and each, in so far as it modifies the environment bequeathed to it and rebels against tradition, resists and limits the power of its predecessors. This modifies the picture which is sometimes painted of a progressive emancipation from tradition and a progressive control of natural processes resulting in a continual increase of human power. In reality, of course, if any one age really attains, by eugenics and scientific education, the power to make its descendants what it pleases, all men who live after it are the patients of that power. They are weaker, not stronger: for though we may have put wonderful machines in their hands we have pre-ordained how they are to use them. And if, as is almost certain, the age which had thus attained maximum power over posterity were also the age most emancipated from tradition, it would be engaged in reducing the power of its predecessors almost as drastically as that of its successors. And we must also remember that, quite apart from this, the later a generation comes – the nearer it lives to that date at which the species becomes extinct – the less power it will have in the forward direction, because its subjects will be so few. There is therefore no question of a power vested in the race as a whole steadily growing as long as the race survives. The last men, far from being the heirs of power, will be of all men most subject to the dead hand of the great planners and conditioners and will themselves exercise least power upon the future.

The real picture is that of one dominant age – let us suppose the hundredth century AD – which resists all previous ages most successfully and dominates all subsequent ages most irresistibly, and thus is the real master of the human species. But then within this master generation (itself an infinitesimal minority of the species) the power will be exercised by a minority smaller still. Man's conquest of Nature, if the dreams of some scientific planners are realized, means the rule of a few hundreds of men over billions upon billions of men. There neither is nor can be any simple increase of power on Man's side. Each new power won *by* man is a power *over* man as well. Each advance leaves him weaker as well as stronger. In every victory, besides being the general who triumphs, he is also the prisoner who follows the triumphal car.

I am not yet considering whether the total result of such ambivalent victories is a good thing or a bad. I am only making clear what Man's conquest of Nature really means and especially that final stage in the conquest, which, perhaps, is not far off. The final stage is come when Man by eugenics, by pre-natal conditioning, and by an education and propaganda based on a perfect applied psychology, has obtained full control over himself. *Human* nature will be the last part of Nature to surrender to Man. The battle will then be won. We shall have 'taken the thread of life out of the hand of Clotho' and be henceforth free to make our species whatever we wish it to be. The battle will indeed be won. But who, precisely, will have won it?

For the power of Man to make himself what he pleases means, as we have seen, the power of some men to make other men what *they* please. In all ages, no doubt, nurture and instruction have, in some sense, attempted to exercise this power. But the situation to which we must look forward will be novel in two respects. In the first place, the power will be enormously increased. Hitherto the plans of educationalists have achieved very little of what they attempted and indeed, when we read them – how Plato would have every infant 'a bastard nursed in a bureau', and Elyot would have the boy see no men before the age of seven and, after that, no women,[1] and how Locke wants children to have leaky shoes and no turn for poetry[2] – we may well thank the beneficent obstinacy of real mothers, real nurses, and (above all) real children for preserving the human race in such sanity as it still possesses. But the man-moulders of the new age will be armed with the powers of an omnicompetent state and an irresistible scientific technique: we shall get at last a race of conditioners who really can cut out all posterity in what shape they please.

The second difference is even more important. In the older systems both the kind of man the teachers wished to produce and their motives for producing him were prescribed by the *Tao* – a norm to which the teachers themselves were subject and from which they claimed no liberty to depart.

They did not cut men to some pattern they had chosen. They handed on what they had received: they initiated the young neophyte into the mystery of humanity which over-arched him and them alike. It was but old birds teaching young birds to fly. This will be changed. Values are now mere natural phenomena. Judgements of value are to be produced in the pupil as part of the conditioning. Whatever *Tao* there is will be the product, not the motive, of education. The conditioners have been emancipated from all that. It is one more part of Nature which they have conquered. The ultimate springs of human action are no longer, for them, something given. They have surrendered – like electricity: it is the function of the Conditioners to control, not to obey them. They know how to *produce* conscience and decide what kind of conscience they will produce. They themselves are outside, above. For we are assuming the last stage of Man's struggle with Nature. The final victory has been won. Human nature has been conquered – and, of course, has conquered, in whatever sense those words may now bear.

The Conditioners, then, are to choose what kind of artificial *Tao* they will, for their own good reasons, produce in the Human race. They are the motivators, the creators of motives. But how are they going to be motivated themselves?

For a time, perhaps, by survivals, within their own minds, of the old 'natural' *Tao*. Thus at first they may look upon themselves as servants and guardians of humanity and conceive that they have a 'duty' to do it 'good'. But it is only by confusion that they can remain in this state. They recognize the concept of duty as the result of certain processes which they can now control. Their victory has consisted precisely in emerging from the state in which they were acted upon by those processes to the state in which they use them as tools. One of the things they now have to decide is whether they will, or will not, so condition the rest of us that we can go on having the old idea of duty and the old reactions to it. How can duty help them to decide that? Duty itself is up for trial: it cannot also be the judge. And 'good' fares no better. They know quite well how to produce a dozen different conceptions of good in us. The question is which, if any, they should produce. No conception of good can help them to decide. It is absurd to fix on one of the things they are comparing and make it the standard of comparison.

To some it will appear that I am inventing a factitious difficulty for my Conditioners. Other, more simple-minded, critics may ask, 'Why should you suppose they will be such bad men?' But I am not supposing them to be bad men. They are, rather, not men (in the old sense) at all. They are, if you like, men who have sacrificed their own share in traditional humanity in order to devote themselves to the task of deciding what 'Humanity' shall henceforth mean. 'Good' and 'bad', applied to them, are words without content: for it is from them that the content of these words is henceforward to be derived. Nor is their difficulty factitious. We might suppose that it was possible to say 'After all, most of us want more or less the same things – food and drink and sexual intercourse, amusement, art, science, and the longest possible life for individuals and for the species. Let them simply say, This is what we happen to like, and go on to condition men in the way most likely to produce it. Where's the trouble?' But this will not answer. In the first place, it is false that we all really like the same things. But even if we did, what motive is to impel the Conditioners to scorn delights and live laborious days in order that we, and posterity, may have what we like? Their duty? But that is only the *Tao*, which they may decide to impose on us, but which cannot be valid for them. If they accept it, then they are no longer the makers of conscience but still its subjects, and their final conquest over Nature has not really happened. The preservation of the species? But why should the species be preserved? One of the questions before them is whether this feeling for posterity (they know well how it is produced) shall be continued or not. However far they go back, or down, they can find no ground to stand on. Every motive they try to act on becomes at once a *petitio*. It is not that they are bad men. They are not men at all. Stepping outside the *Tao*, they have stepped into the void. Nor are their subjects necessarily unhappy men. They are not men at all: they are artefacts. Man's final conquest has proved to be the abolition of Man.

Yet the Conditioners will act. When I said just now that all motives fail them, I should have said all motives except one. All motives that claim any validity other than that of their felt emotional weight at a given moment have failed them. Everything except the *sic volo, sic jubeo* has been explained away. But what never claimed objectivity cannot be destroyed by subjectivism. The impulse to scratch when I itch or to pull to pieces when I am inquisitive is immune from the solvent which is fatal to my justice, or honour, or care for posterity. When all that says 'it is good' has been debunked, what says 'I want' remains. It cannot be exploded or 'seen through' because it never had any pretentions. The Conditioners, therefore, must come to be motivated simply by their own pleasure. I am not here speaking of the corrupting influence of power nor expressing the fear that under it our Conditioners will degenerate. The very words *corrupt* and *degenerate* imply a doctrine of value and are therefore meaningless in this context. My point is that those who stand outside all judgements of value cannot have any ground for preferring one of their own impulses to another except the emotional strength of that impulse.

We may legitimately hope that among the impulses which arise in minds thus emptied of all 'rational' or 'spiritual' motives, some will be benevolent. I am very doubtful myself whether the benevolent impulses, stripped of that preference and encouragement which the *Tao* teaches us to give them and left to their merely natural strength and frequency as psychological events, will have much influence. I am very doubtful whether history shows us one example of a man who, having stepped outside traditional morality and attained power, has used that power benevolently. I am inclined to think that the Conditioners will hate the conditioned. Though regarding as an illusion the artificial conscience which they produce in us their subjects, they will yet perceive that it creates in us an illusion of meaning for our lives which compares favourably with the futility of their own: and they will envy us as eunuchs envy men. But I do not insist on this, for it is a mere conjecture. What is not conjecture is that our hope even of a 'conditioned' happiness rests on what is ordinarily called 'chance' – the chance that benevolent impulses may on the whole predominate in our Conditioners. For without the judgement 'Benevolence is good' – that is, without re-entering the *Tao* – they can have no ground for promoting or stabilizing these impulses rather than any others. By the logic of their position they must just take their impulses as they come, from chance. And Chance here means Nature. It is from heredity, digestion, the weather, and the association of ideas, that the motives of the Conditioners will spring. Their extreme rationalism, by 'seeing through' all 'rational' motives, leaves them creatures of wholly irrational behaviour. If you will not obey the *Tao*, or else commit suicide, obedience to impulse (and therefore, in the long run, to mere 'nature') is the only course left open.

At the moment, then, of Man's victory over Nature, we find the whole human race subjected to some individual men, and those individuals subjected to that in themselves which is purely 'natural' – to their irrational impulses. Nature, untrammelled by values, rules the Conditioners and, through them, all humanity. Man's conquest of Nature turns out, in the moment of its consummation, to be Nature's conquest of Man. Every victory we seemed to win has led us, step by step, to this conclusion. All Nature's apparent reverses have been but tactical withdrawals. We thought we were beating her back when she was luring us on. What looked to us like hands held up in surrender was really the opening of arms to enfold us for ever. If the fully planned and conditioned world (with its *Tao* a mere product of the planning) comes into existence, Nature will be troubled no more by the restive species that rose in revolt against her so many millions of years ago, will be vexed no longer by its chatter of truth and mercy and beauty and happiness. *Ferum victorem cepit*: and if the eugenics are efficient enough there will be no second revolt, but all snug beneath the Conditioners, and the Conditioners beneath her, till the moon falls or the sun grows cold.

My point may be clearer to some if it is put in a different form. Nature is a word of varying meanings, which can best be understood if we consider its various opposites. The Natural is the opposite of the Artificial, the Civil, the Human, the Spiritual, and the Supernatural. The Artificial does not now concern us. If we take the rest of the list of opposites, however, I think we can get a rough idea of what men have meant by Nature and what it is they oppose to her. Nature seems to be the spatial and temporal, as distinct from what is less fully so or not so at all. She seems to be the world of quantity, as against the world of quality; of objects as against consciousness; of the bound, as against the wholly or partially autonomous; of that which knows no values as against that which both has and perceives value; of efficient causes (or, in some modern systems, of no causality at all) as against final causes. Now I take it that when we understand a thing analytically and then dominate and use it for our own convenience, we reduce it to the level of 'Nature' in the sense that we suspend our judgements of value about it, ignore its final cause (if any), and treat it in terms of quantity. This repression of elements in what would otherwise be our total reaction to it is sometimes very noticeable and even painful: something has to be overcome before we can cut up a dead man or a live animal in a dissecting room. These objects *resist* the movement of the mind whereby we thrust them into the world of mere Nature. But in other instances too, a similar price is exacted for our analytical knowledge and manipulative power, even if we have ceased to count it. We do not look at trees either as Dryads or as beautiful objects while we cut them into beams: the first man who did so may have felt the price keenly, and the bleeding trees in Virgil and Spenser may be far-off echoes of that primeval sense of impiety. The stars lost their divinity as astronomy developed, and the Dying God has no place in chemical agriculture. To many, no doubt, this process is simply the gradual discovery that the real world is different from what we expected, and the old opposition to Galileo or to 'body-snatchers' is simply obscurantism. But that is not the whole story. It is not the greatest of modern scientists who feel most sure that the object, stripped of its qualitative properties and reduced to mere quantity, is wholly real. Little scientists, and little unscientific followers of science, may think so. The great minds know very well that the object, so treated, is an artificial abstraction, that something of its reality has been lost.

From this point of view the conquest of Nature appears in a new light. We reduce things to mere Nature *in order that* we may 'conquer' them. We are always conquering Nature, *because* 'Nature' is the name for what we have, to some extent, conquered. The price of conquest is to treat a thing as mere Nature. Every conquest over Nature increases her domain. The stars do not become Nature till we can weigh and measure them: the soul does not become Nature till we can psychoanalyse her. The wresting of powers *from* Nature is also the surrendering of things *to* Nature. As long as this process stops short of the final stage we may well hold that the gain outweighs the loss. But as soon as we take the final step of reducing our own species to the level of mere Nature, the whole process is stultified, for this time the being who stood to gain and the being who has been sacrificed are one and the same. This is one of the many instances where to carry a principle to what seems its logical conclusion produces absurdity. It is like the famous Irishman who found that a certain kind of stove reduced his fuel bill by half and thence concluded that two stoves of the same kind would enable him to warm his house with no fuel at all. It is the magician's bargain: give up our soul, get power in return. But once our souls, that is, ourselves, have been given up, the power thus conferred will not belong to us. We shall in fact be the slaves and puppets of that to which we have given our souls. It is in Man's power to treat himself as a mere 'natural object' and his own judgements of value as raw material for scientific manipulation to alter at will. The objection to his doing so does not lie in the fact that this point of view (like one's first day in a dissecting room) is painful and shocking till we grow used to it. The pain and the shock are at most a warning and a symptom. The real objection is that if man chooses to treat himself as raw material, raw material he will be: not raw material to be manipulated, as he fondly imagined, by himself, but by mere appetite, that is, mere Nature, in the person of his de-humanized Conditioners.

We have been trying, like Lear, to have it both ways: to lay down our human prerogative and yet at the same time to retain it. It is impossible. Either we are rational spirit obliged for ever to obey the absolute values of the *Tao*, or else we are mere nature to be kneaded and cut into new shapes for the pleasures of masters who must, by hypothesis, have no motive but their own 'natural' impulses. Only the *Tao* provides a common human law of action which can over-arch rulers and ruled alike. A dogmatic belief in objective value is necessary to the very idea of a rule which is not tyranny or an obedience which is not slavery.

I am not here thinking solely, perhaps not even chiefly, of those who are our public enemies at the moment. The process which, if not checked, will abolish Man goes on apace among Communists and Democrats no less than among Fascists. The methods may (at first) differ in brutality. But many a mild-eyed scientist in pince-nez, many a popular dramatist, many an amateur philosopher in our midst, means in the long run just the same as the Nazi rulers of Germany. Traditional values are to be 'debunked' and mankind to be cut out into some fresh shape at the will (which must, by hypothesis, be an arbitrary will) of some few lucky people in one lucky generation which has learned how to do it. The belief that we can invent 'ideologies' at pleasure, and the consequent treatment of mankind as mere ὑλη, specimens, preparations, begins to affect our very language. Once we killed bad men: now we liquidate unsocial elements. Virtue has become *integration* and diligence *dynamism*, and boys likely to be worthy of a commission are 'potential officer material'. Most wonderful of all, the virtues of thrift and temperance, and even of ordinary intelligence, are *sales-resistance*.

The true significance of what is going on has been concealed by the use of the abstraction Man. Not that the word Man is necessarily a pure abstraction. In the *Tao* itself, as long as we remain within it, we find the concrete reality in which to participate is to be truly human: the real common will and common reason of humanity, alive, and growing like a tree, and branching out, as the situation varies, into ever new beauties and dignities of application. While we speak from within the *Tao* we can speak of Man having power over himself in a sense truly analogous to an individual's self-control. But the moment we step outside and regard the *Tao* as a mere subjective product, this possibility has disappeared. What is now common to all men is a mere abstract universal, an H.C.F., and Man's conquest of himself means simply the rule of the Conditioners over the conditioned human material, the world of post-humanity which, some knowingly and some unknowingly, nearly all men in all nations are at present labouring to produce.

Nothing I can say will prevent some people from describing this lecture as an attack on science. I deny the charge, of course: and real Natural Philosophers (there are some now alive) will perceive that in defending value I defend *inter alia* the value of knowledge, which must die like every other when its roots in the *Tao* are cut. But I can go further than that. I even suggest that from Science herself the cure might come.

I have described as a 'magician's bargain' that process whereby man surrenders object after object, and finally himself, to Nature in return for power. And I meant what I said. The fact that the scientist has succeeded where the magician failed has put such a wide contrast between them in popular thought that the real story of the birth of Science is misunderstood. You will even find people who write about the sixteenth century as if Magic were a medieval survival and Science the new thing that came in to sweep it away. Those who have studied the period know better. There was very little magic in the Middle Ages: the sixteenth and seventeenth centuries are the high noon of magic. The serious magical endeavour and the serious scientific endeavour are twins: one was sickly and died, the other strong and throve. But they were twins. They were born of the same impulse. I allow that some (certainly not all) of the early scientists were actuated by a pure love of knowledge. But if we consider the temper of that age as a whole we can discern the impulse of which I speak.

There is something which unites magic and applied science while separating both from the 'wisdom' of earlier ages. For the wise men of old the cardinal problem had been how to conform the soul to reality, and the solution had been knowledge, self-discipline, and virtue. For magic and applied science alike the problem is how to subdue reality to the wishes of men: the solution is a technique; and both, in the practice of this technique, are ready to do things hitherto regarded as disgusting and impious – such as digging up and mutilating the dead.

If we compare the chief trumpeter of the new era (Bacon) with Marlowe's Faustus, the similarity is striking. You will read in some critics that Faustus has a thirst for knowledge. In reality, he hardly mentions it. It is not truth he wants from the devils, but gold and guns and girls. 'All things that move between the quiet poles shall be at his command' and 'a sound magician is a mighty god'.[3] In the same spirit Bacon condemns those who value knowledge as an end in itself: this, for him, is to use as a mistress for pleasure what ought to be a spouse for fruit.[4] The true object is to extend Man's power to the performance of all things possible. He rejects magic because it does not work;[5] but his goal is that of the magician. In Paracelsus the characters of magician and scientist are combined. No doubt those who really founded modern science were usually those whose love of truth exceeded their love of power; in every mixed movement the efficacy comes from the good elements not from the bad. But the presence of the bad elements is not irrelevant to the direction the efficacy takes. It might be going too far to say that the modern scientific movement was tainted from its birth: but I think it would be true to say that it was born in an unhealthy neighbourhood and at an inauspicious hour. Its triumphs may have been too rapid and purchased at too high a price: reconsideration, and something like repentance, may be required.

Is it, then, possible to imagine a new Natural Philosophy, continually conscious that the 'natural object' produced by analysis and abstraction is not reality but only a view, and always correcting the abstraction? I hardly know what I am asking for. I hear rumours that Goethe's approach to nature deserves fuller consideration – that even Dr Steiner may have seen something that orthodox researchers have missed. The regenerate science which I have in mind would not do even to minerals and vegetables what modern science threatens to do to man himself. When it explained it would not explain away. When it spoke of the parts it would remember the whole. While studying the *It* it would not lose what Martin Buber calls the *Thou*-situation. The analogy between the *Tao* of Man and the instincts of an animal species would mean for it new light cast on the unknown thing, Instinct, by the inly known reality of conscience and not a reduction of conscience to the category of Instinct. Its followers would not be free with the words *only* and *merely*. In a word, it would conquer Nature without being at the same time conquered by her and buy knowledge at a lower cost than that of life.

Perhaps I am asking impossibilities. Perhaps, in the nature of things, analytical understanding must always be a basilisk which kills what it sees and only sees by killing. But if the scientists themselves cannot arrest this process before it reaches the common Reason and kills that too, then someone else must arrest it. What I most fear is the reply that I am 'only one more' obscurantist, that this barrier, like all previous barriers set up against the advance of science, can be safely passed. Such a reply springs from the fatal serialism of the modern imagination – the image of infinite unilinear progression which so haunts our minds. Because we have to use numbers so much we tend to think of every process as if it must be like the numeral series, where every step, to all eternity, is the same kind of step as the one before. I implore you to remember the Irishman and his two stoves. There are progressions in which the last step is *sui generis* – incommensurable with the others – and in which to go the whole way is to undo all the labour of your previous journey. To reduce the *Tao* to a mere natural product is a step of that kind. Up to that point, the kind of explanation which explains things away may give us something, though at a heavy cost. But you cannot go on 'explaining away' for ever: you will find that you have explained explanation itself away. You cannot go on 'seeing through' things for ever. The whole point of seeing through something is to see something through it. It is good that the window should be transparent, because the street or garden beyond it is opaque. How if you saw through the garden too? It is no use trying to 'see through' first principles. If you see through everything, then everything is transparent. But a wholly transparent world is an invisible world. To 'see through' all things is the same as not to see.

APPENDIX

ILLUSTRATIONS OF THE TAO

The following illustrations of the Natural Law are collected from such sources as come readily to the hand of one who is not a professional historian. The list makes no pretence of completeness. It will be noticed that writers such as Locke and Hooker, who wrote within the Christian tradition, are quoted side by side with the New Testament. This would, of course, be absurd if I were trying to collect independent testimonies to the *Tao*. But (1) I am not trying to *prove* its validity by the argument from common consent. Its validity cannot be deduced. For those who do not perceive its rationality, even universal consent could not prove it. (2) The idea of collecting *independent* testimonies presupposes that 'civilizations' have arisen in the world independently of one another; or even that humanity has had several independent emergences on this planet. The biology and anthropology involved in such an assumption are extremely doubtful. It is by no means certain that there has ever (in the sense required) been more than one civilization in all history. It is at least arguable that every civilization we find has been derived from another civilization and, in the last resort, from a single centre – 'carried' like an infectious disease or like the Apostolical succession.

1. The Law of General Beneficence
(a) NEGATIVE

'I have not slain men.' (Ancient Egyptian. From the Confession of the Righteous Soul, 'Book of the Dead'. v. *Encyclopedia of Religion and Ethics* [= *ERE*], vol. v, p. 478)

'Do not murder.' (Ancient Jewish. Exodus 20:13)

'Terrify not men or God will terrify thee.' (Ancient Egyptian. Precepts of Ptahhetep. H. R. Hall, *Ancient History of the Near East*, p. 133n)

'In Nástrond (= Hell) I saw ... murderers.' (Old Norse. *Volospá* 38, 39)

'I have not brought misery upon my fellows. I have not made the beginning of every day laborious in the sight of him who worked for me.' (Ancient Egyptian. Confession of the Righteous Soul. *ERE* v. 478)

'I have not been grasping.' (Ancient Egyptian. Ibid.)

'Who meditates oppression, his dwelling is overturned.' (Babylonian. *Hymn to Samas. ERE* v. 445)

'He who is cruel and calumnious has the character of a cat.' (Hindu. Laws of Manu. Janet, *Histoire de la Science Politique*, vol. i, p. 6)

'Slander not.' (Babylonian. *Hymn to Samaš. ERE* v. 445)

'Thou shalt not bear false witness against thy neighbour.' (Ancient Jewish. Exodus 20:16)

'Utter not a word by which anyone could be wounded.' (Hindu. Janet, p. 7)

'Has he ... driven an honest man from his family? Broken up a well cemented clan?' (Babylonian. List of Sins from incantation tablets. *ERE* v. 446)

'I have not caused hunger. I have not caused weeping.' (Ancient Egyptian. *ERE* v. 478)

'Never do to others what you would not like them to do to you.' (Ancient Chinese. *Analects of Confucius*, trans. A. Waley, xv. 23; cf. xii. 2)

'Thou shalt not hate thy brother in thy heart.' (Ancient Jewish. Leviticus 19:17)

'He whose heart is in the smallest degree set upon goodness will dislike no one.' (Ancient Chinese. *Analects*, iv. 4)

(b) POSITIVE

'Nature urges that a man should wish human society to exist and should wish to enter it.' (Roman. Cicero, *De Officiis*, I. iv)

'By the fundamental Law of Nature Man [is] to be preserved as much as possible.' (Locke, *Treatises of Civil Govt.* ii. 3)

'When the people have multiplied, what next should be done for them? The Master said, Enrich them. Jan Ch'iu said, When one has enriched them, what next should be done for them? The Master said, Instruct them.' (Ancient Chinese. *Analects*, xiii. 9)

'Speak kindness ... show good will.' (Babylonian. *Hymn to Samaš. ERE* v. 445)

'Men were brought into existence for the sake of men that they might do one another good.' (Roman. Cicero. *De Off*. i. vii)

'Man is man's delight.' (Old Norse. *Hávamál* 47)

'He who is asked for alms should always give.' (Hindu. Janet, i. 7)

'What good man regards any misfortune as no concern of his?' (Roman. Juvenal xv. 140)

'I am a man: nothing human is alien to me.' (Roman. Terence, *Heaut. Tim.*)

'Love thy neighbour as thyself.' (Ancient Jewish. Leviticus 19:18)
'Love the stranger as thyself.' (Ancient Jewish. Ibid. 33, 34)
'Do to men what you wish men to do to you.' (Christian. Matthew 7:12)

2. The Law of Special Beneficence

'It is upon the trunk that a gentleman works. When that is firmly set up, the Way grows. And surely proper behaviour to parents and elder brothers is the trunk of goodness.' (Ancient Chinese. *Analects*, i. 2)

'Brothers shall fight and be each others' bane.' (Old Norse. Account of the Evil Age before the World's end, *Volospá* 45)

'Has he insulted his elder sister?' (Babylonian. List of Sins. *ERE* v. 446)

'You will see them take care of their kindred [and] the children of their friends ... never reproaching them in the least.' (Redskin. Le Jeune, quoted *ERE* v. 437)

'Love thy wife studiously. Gladden her heart all thy life long.' (Ancient Egyptian. *ERE* v. 481)

'Nothing can ever change the claims of kinship for a right thinking man.' (Anglo-Saxon. *Beowulf*, 2600)

'Did not Socrates love his own children, though he did so as a free man and as one not forgetting that the gods have the first claim on our friendship?' (Greek, Epictetus, iii. 24)

'Natural affection is a thing right and according to Nature.' (Greek. Ibid. 1. xi)

'I ought not to be unfeeling like a statue but should fulfil both my natural and artificial relations, as a worshipper, a son, a brother, a father, and a citizen.' (Greek. Ibid. III. ii)

'This first I rede thee: be blameless to thy kindred. Take no vengeance even though they do thee wrong.' (Old Norse. *Sigdrifumál*, 22)

'Is it only the sons of Atreus who love their wives? For every good man, who is right-minded, loves and cherishes his own.' (Greek. Homer, *Iliad*, ix. 340)

'The union and fellowship of men will be best preserved if each receives from us the more kindness in proportion as he is more closely connected with us.' (Roman. Cicero. *De Off.* 1. xvi)

'Part of us is claimed by our country, part by our parents, part by our friends.' (Roman. Ibid. 1. vii)

'If a ruler ... compassed the salvation of the whole state, surely you would call him Good? The Master said, It would no longer be a matter of "Good". He would without doubt be a Divine Sage.' (Ancient Chinese. *Analects*, vi. 28)

'Has it escaped you that, in the eyes of gods and good men, your native land deserves from you more honour, worship, and reverence than your mother and father and all your ancestors? That you should give a softer answer to its anger than to a father's anger? That if you cannot persuade it to alter its mind you must obey it in all quietness, whether it binds you or beats you or sends you to a war where you may get wounds or death?' (Greek. Plato, *Crito*, 51, a, b)

'If any provide not for his own, and specially for those of his own house, he hath denied the faith.' (Christian. 1 Timothy 5:8)

'Put them in mind to obey magistrates.' ... 'I exhort that prayers be made for kings and all that are in authority.' (Christian. Titus 3:1 and 1 Timothy 2:1, 2)

3. Duties to Parents, Elders, Ancestors

'Your father is an image of the Lord of Creation, your mother an image of the Earth. For him who fails to honour them, every work of piety is in vain. This is the first duty.' (Hindu. Janet, i. 9)

'Has he despised Father and Mother?' (Babylonian. List of Sins. *ERE* v. 446)

'I was a staff by my Father's side ... I went in and out at his command.' (Ancient Egyptian. Confession of the Righteous Soul. *ERE* v. 481)

'Honour thy Father and thy Mother.' (Ancient Jewish. Exodus 20:12)

'To care for parents.' (Greek. List of duties in Epictetus, III. vii)

'Children, old men, the poor, and the sick, should be considered as the lords of the atmosphere.' (Hindu. Janet, i. 8)

'Rise up before the hoary head and honour the old man.' (Ancient Jewish. Leviticus 19:32)

'I tended the old man, I gave him my staff.' (Ancient Egyptian. *ERE* v. 481)

'You will see them take care ... of old men.' (Redskin. Le Jeune, quoted *ERE* v. 437)

'I have not taken away the oblations of the blessed dead.' (Ancient Egyptian. Confession of the Righteous Soul. *ERE* v. 478)

'When proper respect towards the dead is shown at the end and continued after they are far away, the moral force (*tê*) of a people has reached its highest point.' (Ancient Chinese. *Analects*, i. 9)

4. Duties to Children and Posterity

'Children, the old, the poor, etc. should be considered as lords of the atmosphere.' (Hindu. Janet, i. 8)

'To marry and to beget children.' (Greek. List of duties. Epictetus, III. vii)

'Can you conceive an Epicurean commonwealth? ... What will happen? Whence is the population to be kept up? Who will educate them? Who will be Director of Adolescents? Who will be Director of Physical Training? What will be taught?' (Greek. Ibid.)

'Nature produces a special love of offspring' and 'To live according to Nature is the supreme good.' (Roman. Cicero, *De Off.* I. iv, and *De Legibus*, I. xxi)

'The second of these achievements is no less glorious than the first; for while the first did good on one occasion, the second will continue to benefit the state for ever.' (Roman. Cicero. *De Off.* I. xxii)

'Great reverence is owed to a child.' (Roman. Juvenal, xiv. 47)

'The Master said, Respect the young.' (Ancient Chinese. *Analects*, ix. 22)

'The killing of the women and more especially of the young boys and girls who are to go to make up the future strength of the people, is the saddest part ... and we feel it very sorely.' (Redskin. Account of the Battle of Wounded Knee. *ERE* v. 432)

5. The Law of Justice

(a) SEXUAL JUSTICE

'Has he approached his neighbour's wife?' (Babylonian. List of Sins. *ERE* v. 446)

'Thou shalt not commit adultery.' (Ancient Jewish. Exodus 20:14)

'I saw in Nástrond (= Hell) ... beguilers of others' wives.' (Old Norse. *Volospá* 38, 39)

(b) HONESTY

'Has he drawn false boundaries?' (Babylonian. List of Sins. *ERE* v. 446)

'To wrong, to rob, to cause to be robbed.' (Babylonian. Ibid.)

'I have not stolen.' (Ancient Egyptian. Confession of the Righteous Soul. *ERE* v. 478)

'Thou shalt not steal.' (Ancient Jewish. Exodus 20:15)

'Choose loss rather than shameful gains.' (Greek. Chilon Fr. 10. Diels)

'Justice is the settled and permanent intention of rendering to each man his rights.' (Roman. Justinian, *Institutions*, 1. i)

'If the native made a "find" of any kind (e.g. a honey tree) and marked it, it was thereafter safe for him, as far as his own tribesmen were concerned, no matter how long he left it.' (Australian Aborigines. *ERE* v. 441)

'The first point of justice is that none should do any mischief to another unless he has first been attacked by the other's wrongdoing. The second is that a man should treat common property as common property, and private property as his own. There is no such thing as private property by nature, but things have become private either through prior occupation (as when men of old came into empty territory) or by conquest, or law, or agreement, or stipulation, or casting lots.' (Roman. Cicero, *De Off.* 1. vii)

(c) JUSTICE IN COURT, &C.
'Whoso takes no bribe ... well pleasing is this to Samaš.' (Babylonian. *ERE* v. 445)
'I have not traduced the slave to him who is set over him.' (Ancient Egyptian. Confession of the Righteous Soul. *ERE* v. 478)
'Thou shalt not bear false witness against thy neighbour.' (Ancient Jewish. Exodus 20:16)
'Regard him whom thou knowest like him whom thou knowest not.' (Ancient Egyptian. *ERE* v. 482)
'Do no unrighteousness in judgement. You must not consider the fact that one party is poor nor the fact that the other is a great man.' (Ancient Jewish. Leviticus 19:15)

6. The Law of Good Faith and Veracity
'A sacrifice is obliterated by a lie and the merit of alms by an act of fraud.' (Hindu. Janet, i. 6)
'Whose mouth, full of lying, avails not before thee: thou burnest their utterance.' (Babylonian. *Hymn to Samaš. ERE* v. 445)
'With his mouth was he full of *Yea*, in his heart full of *Nay*?' (Babylonian. *ERE* v. 446)
'I have not spoken falsehood.' (Ancient Egyptian. Confession of the Righteous Soul. *ERE* v. 478)
'I sought no trickery, nor swore false oaths.' (Anglo-Saxon. *Beowulf*, 2738)
'The Master said, Be of unwavering good faith.' (Ancient Chinese. *Analects*, viii. 13)
'In Nástrond (= Hell) I saw the perjurers.' (Old Norse. *Volospá* 39)
'Hateful to me as are the gates of Hades is that man who says one thing, and hides another in his heart.' (Greek. Homer. *Iliad*, ix. 312)
'The foundation of justice is good faith.' (Roman. Cicero, *De Off.* 1. vii)
'[The gentleman] must learn to be faithful to his superiors and to keep promises.' (Ancient Chinese. *Analects*, i. 8)
'Anything is better than treachery.' (Old Norse. *Hávamál* 124)

7. The Law of Mercy
'The poor and the sick should be regarded as lords of the atmosphere.' (Hindu. Janet, i. 8)

'Whoso makes intercession for the weak, well pleasing is this to Samaš.' (Babylonian. *ERE* v. 445)

'Has he failed to set a prisoner free?' (Babylonian. List of Sins. *ERE* v. 446)

'I have given bread to the hungry, water to the thirsty, clothes to the naked, a ferry boat to the boatless.' (Ancient Egyptian. *ERE* v. 446)

'One should never strike a woman; not even with a flower.' (Hindu. Janet, i. 8)

'There, Thor, you got disgrace, when you beat women.' (Old Norse. *Hárbarthsljóth* 38)

'In the Dalebura tribe a woman, a cripple from birth, was carried about by the tribes-people in turn until her death at the age of sixty-six.' ... 'They never desert the sick.' (Australian Aborigines. *ERE* v. 443)

'You will see them take care of ... widows, orphans, and old men, never reproaching them.' (Redskin. *ERE* v. 439)

'Nature confesses that she has given to the human race the tenderest hearts, by giving us the power to weep. This is the best part of us.' (Roman. Juvenal, xv. 131)

'They said that he had been the mildest and gentlest of the kings of the world.' (Anglo-Saxon. Praise of the hero in *Beowulf*, 3180)

'When thou cuttest down thine harvest ... and hast forgot a sheaf ... thou shalt not go again to fetch it: it shall be for the stranger, for the fatherless, and for the widow.' (Ancient Jewish. Deuteronomy 24:19)

8. The Law of Magnanimity

(a)

'There are two kinds of injustice: the first is found in those who do an injury, the second in those who fail to protect another from injury when they can.' (Roman. Cicero, *De Off.* 1. vii)

'Men always knew that when force and injury was offered they might be defenders of themselves; they knew that howsoever men may seek their own commodity, yet if this were done with injury unto others it was not to be suffered, but by all men and by all good means to be withstood.' (English. Hooker, *Laws of Eccl. Polity*, 1. ix. 4)

'To take no notice of a violent attack is to strengthen the heart of the enemy. Vigour is valiant, but cowardice is vile.' (Ancient Egyptian. The Pharaoh Senusert III, cit. H. R. Hall, *Ancient History of the Near East*, p. 161)

'They came to the fields of joy, the fresh turf of the Fortunate Woods and the dwellings of the Blessed ... here was the company of those who had suffered wounds fighting for their fatherland.' (Roman. Virgil, *Aeneid*, vi. 638–9, 660)

'Courage has got to be harder, heart the stouter, spirit the sterner, as our strength weakens. Here lies our lord, cut to pieces, out best man in the dust. If anyone thinks of leaving this battle, he can howl forever.' (Anglo-Saxon. *Maldon*, 312)

'Praise and imitate that man to whom, while life is pleasing, death is not grievous.' (Stoic. Seneca, *Ep.* liv)

'The Master said, Love learning and if attacked be ready to die for the Good Way.' (Ancient Chinese. *Analects*, viii. 13)

(b)

'Death is to be chosen before slavery and base deeds.' (Roman. Cicero, *De Off.* 1, xxiii)

'Death is better for every man than life with shame.' (Anglo-Saxon. *Beowulf*, 2890)

'Nature and Reason command that nothing uncomely, nothing effeminate, nothing lascivious be done or thought.' (Roman. Cicero, *De Off.* 1. iv)

'We must not listen to those who advise us "being men to think human thoughts, and being mortal to think mortal thoughts," but must put on immortality as much as is possible and strain every nerve to live according to that best part of us, which, being small in bulk, yet much more in its power and honour surpasses all else.' (Ancient Greek. Aristotle, *Eth. Nic.* 1177 B)

'The soul then ought to conduct the body, and the spirit of our minds the soul. This is therefore the first Law, whereby the highest power of the mind requireth obedience at the hands of all the rest.' (Hooker, op. cit. 1. viii. 6)

'Let him not desire to die, let him not desire to live, let him wait for his time ... let him patiently bear hard words, entirely abstaining from bodily pleasures.' (Ancient Indian. Laws of Manu. *ERE* ii. 98)

'He who is unmoved, who has restrained his senses ... is said to be devoted. As a flame in a windless place that flickers not, so is the devoted.' (Ancient Indian. *Bhagavad gita. ERE* ii 90)

(c)

'Is not the love of Wisdom a practice of death?' (Ancient Greek. Plato, *Phadeo*, 81 A)

'I know that I hung on the gallows for nine nights, wounded with the spear as a sacrifice to Odin, myself offered to Myself.' (Old Norse. *Hávamál*, 1. 10 in *Corpus Poeticum Boreale*; stanza 139 in Hildebrand's *Lieder der Älteren Edda*. 1922)

'Verily, verily I say to you unless a grain of wheat falls into the earth and dies, it remains alone, but if it dies it bears much fruit. He who loves his life loses it.' (Christian. John 12:24, 25)

NOTES

1 Men without Chests
1 *The Green Book*, pp. 19, 20.
2 Ibid., p 53.
3 *Journey to the Western Islands* (Samuel Johnson).
4 *The Prelude*, viii, ll. 549–59.
5 *The Green Book*, pp. 53–5.
6 Orbilius' book, p 5.
7 Orbilius is so far superior to Gaius and Titius that he does (pp. 19–22) contrast a piece of good writing to animals with the piece condemned. Unfortunately, however, the only superiority he really demonstrates in the second extract is its superiority in factual truth. The specifically literary problem (the use and abuse of expressions which are false *secundum litteram*) is not tackled. Orbilius indeed tells us (p. 97) that we must 'learn to distinguish between legitimate and illegitimate figurative statement', but he gives us very little help in doing so. At the same time it is fair to record my opinion that his work is on quite a different level from *The Green Book*.
8 Ibid., p 9.
9 *Defence of Poetry*.
10 *Centuries of Meditations*, i, 12.
11 *De Civ. Dei*, xv. 22. Cf. ibid. ix. 5, xi. 28.
12 *Eth. Nic.* 1104 B.
13 Ibid. 1095 B.
14 *Laws*, 653.
15 *Republic*, 402 A.
16 A. B. Keith, s.v. 'Righteousness (Hindu)' *Enc. Religion and Ethics*, vol. x.
17 Ibid., vol. ii, p. 454 B; iv. 12 B; ix. 87 A.
18 *The Analects of Confucius*, trans. Arthur Waley, London, 1938, i. 12
19 Psalm 119:151. The word is *emeth*, 'truth'. Where the *Satya* of the Indian sources emphasizes truth as 'correspondence', *emeth* (connected with a verb that means 'to be firm') emphasizes rather the reliability or trustworthiness of truth. *Faithfulness* and *permanence* are suggested by Hebraists as alternative renderings.

Emeth is that which does not deceive, does not 'give', does not change, that which holds water. (See T. K. Cheyne in *Encyclopedia Biblica*, 1914, s.v. 'Truth'.)
20 *Republic*, 442 B, C.
21 Alanus ab Insulis. *De Planctu Naturae Prosa*, iii.

2 The Way

1 The real (perhaps unconscious) philosophy of Gaius and Titius becomes clear if we contrast the two following lists of disapprovals and approvals.
A. *Disapprovals*: A mother's appeal to a child to be 'brave' is 'nonsense' (*Green Book*, p. 62). The reference of the word 'gentleman' is 'extremely vague' (ibid.) 'To call a man a coward tells us really nothing about what he does' (p. 64). Feelings about a country or empire are feelings 'about nothing in particular' (p. 77).
B. *Approvals*: Those who prefer the arts of peace to the arts of war (it is not said in what circumstances) are such that 'we may want to call them wise men' (p. 65). The pupil is expected 'to believe in a demo-cratic community life' (p. 67). 'Contact with the ideas of other people is, as we know, healthy' (p. 86). The reason for bathrooms ('that people are healthier and pleasanter to meet when they are clean') is 'too obvious to need mentioning' (p. 142). It will be seen that comfort and security, as known to a suburban street in peace-time, are the ultimate values: those things which can alone produce or spiritualize comfort and security are mocked. Man lives by bread alone, and the ultimate source of bread is the baker's van: peace matters more than honour and can be preserved by jeering at colonels and reading newspapers.

2 The most determined effort which I know to construct a theory of value on the basis of 'satisfaction of impulses' is that of Dr I. A. Richards (*Principles of Literary Criticism*, 1924). The old objection to defining Value as Satisfaction is the universal value judgement that 'it is better to be Socrates dissatisfied than a pig satisfied'. To meet this Dr Richards endeavours to show that our impulses can be arranged in a hierarchy and some satisfactions preferred to others without an appeal to any criterion other than satisfaction. He does this by the doctrine that some impulses are more 'important' than others – an *important* impulse being one whose frustration involves the frustration of other impulses. A good systematization (i.e. the good life) consists in satisfying as many impulses as possible; which entails satisfying the 'important' at the expense of the 'unimportant'. The objections to this scheme seem to me to be two:

(1) Without a theory of immortality it leaves no room for the value of noble death. It may, of course, be said that a man who has saved his life by treachery will suffer for the rest of that life from frustration. But not, surely, frustration of *all* his impulses? Whereas the dead man will have *no* satisfaction. Or is it maintained that since he had no unsatisfied impulses he is better off than the disgraced and living man? This at once raises the second objection.

(2) Is the value of a systematization to be judged by the presence of satisfactions or the absence of dissatisfactions? The extreme case is that of the dead man in whom satisfactions and dissatisfactions (on the modern view) both equal zero, as against the successful traitor who can still eat, drink, sleep, scratch and copulate, even if he cannot have friendship or love or self-respect. But it arises at other levels. Suppose A has only 500 impulses and all are satisfied, and that B has 1200 impulses whereof 700 are satisfied and 500 not: which has the better systematization? There is no doubt which Dr Richards actually prefers – he even praises art on the ground that it makes us 'discontented' with ordinary crudities! (op. cit., p. 230). The only trace I find of a philosophical basis for this preference is the statement that 'the more complex an activity the more conscious it is' (p. 109). But if satisfaction is the only value, why should increase of consciousness be good? For consciousness is the condition of all dissatisfactions as well as of all satisfactions. Dr Richards's system gives no support to his (and our) actual preference for civil life over savage and human over animal – or even for life over death.

(3) The desperate expedients to which a man can be driven if he attempts to base value on fact are well illustrated by Dr C. H. Waddington's fate in *Science and Ethics*. Dr Waddington here explains that 'existence is its own justification' (p. 14), and writes: 'An existence which is essentially evolutionary is itself the justification for an evolution towards a more comprehensive existence' (p. 17). I do not think Dr Waddington is himself at ease in this view, for he does endeavour to recommend the course of evolution to us on three grounds other than its mere occurrence. (*a*) That the later stages include or 'comprehend' the earlier. (*b*) That T. H. Huxley's picture of Evolution will not revolt you if you regard it from an 'actuarial' point of view. (*c*) That, any way, after all, it isn't half so bad as people make out ('not so morally offensive that we cannot accept it', p. 18). These three palliatives are more creditable to Dr Waddington's heart than his head and seem to me to give up the main position. If Evolution is praised (or, at least, apologized for) on the ground of *any* properties it exhibits, then we are using an external standard and the attempt to make existence its own justification has been abandoned. If that attempt is maintained, why does Dr Waddington concentrate on Evolution: i.e. on a temporary phase of organic existence in one planet? This is 'geocentric'. If Good = 'whatever Nature happens to be doing', then surely we should notice what Nature is doing as a whole; and Nature as a whole, I understand, is working steadily and irreversibly towards the final extinction of all life in every part of the universe, so that Dr Waddington's ethics, stripped of their unaccountable bias towards such a parochial affair as tellurian biology, would leave murder and suicide our only duties. Even this, I confess, seems to me a lesser objection than the discrepancy between Dr Waddington's first principle and the value judgements men actually make. To value anything simply because it occurs is in fact to worship success, like Quislings or men of Vichy. Other philosophies more wicked have been devised: none more vulgar. I am far from suggesting that Dr Waddington practises in real life such grovelling prostration

before the *fait accompli*. Let us hope that *Rasselas*, chap. 22, gives the right picture of what his philosophy amounts to in action. ('The philosopher, supposing the rest vanquished, rose up and departed with the air of a man that had co-operated with the present system.')

4 See Appendix.

5 *Analects of Confucius*, xv. 39.

6 *Eth. Nic.* 1095 B, 1140 B, 1151 A.

7 John 7:49. The speaker said it in malice, but with more truth than he meant. Cf. John 13:51.

8 Mark 16:6.

9 *Republic*, 402 A

10 Philippians 3:6.

3 The Abolition of Man

1 *The Boke Named the Governour*, 1. iv: 'Al men except physitions only shulde be excluded and kepte out of the norisery.' 1 vi: 'After that a childe is come to seuen yeres of age ... the most sure counsaile is to withdrawe him from all company of women.'

2 *Some Thoughts concerning Education*, §7: 'I will also advise his *Feet to be wash'd* every Day in cold Water, and to have his Shoes so thin that they might leak and *let in Water*, whenever he comes near it.' § 174: 'If he have a poetick vein, 'tis to me the strangest thing in the World that the Father should desire or suffer it to be cherished or improved. Methinks the Parents should labour to have it stifled and suppressed as much as may be.' Yet Locke is one of our most sensible writers on education.

3 *Dr Faustus*, 77–90.

4 *Advancement of Learning*, Bk 1 (p. 60 in Ellis and Spedding, 1905; p. 35 in Everyman Edition).

5 *Filum Labyrinthi*, i.

TILL WE HAVE FACES

A Myth Retold

Love is too young to know what conscience is
SHAKESPEARE

To Joy Davidman

NOTE

The story of Cupid and Psyche first occurs in one of the few surviving Latin novels, the *Metamorphoses* (sometimes called *The Golden Ass*) of Lucius Apuleius Platonicus, who was born about 125 A.D. The relevant parts are as follows:

A king and queen had three daughters of whom the youngest was so beautiful that men worshipped her as a goddess and neglected the worship of Venus for her sake. One result was that Psyche (as the youngest was called) had no suitors; men reverenced her supposed deity too much to aspire to her hand. When her father consulted the oracle of Apollo about her marriage he received the answer: 'Hope for no human son-in-law. You must expose Psyche on a mountain to be the prey of a dragon.' This he obediently did.

But Venus, jealous of Psyche's beauty, had already devised a different punishment for her, she had ordered her son Cupid to afflict the girl with an irresistible passion for the basest of men. Cupid set off to do so but, on seeing Psyche, fell in love with her himself. As soon as she was left on the mountain he therefore had her carried off by the West-Wind (Zephyrus) to a secret place where he had prepared a stately palace. Here he visited her by night and enjoyed her love; but he forbade her to see his face. Presently she begged that she might receive a visit from her two sisters. The god reluctantly consented and wafted them to her palace. Here they were royally feasted and expressed great delight at all the splendours they saw. But inwardly they were devoured with envy, for their husbands were not gods and their houses not so fine as hers.

They therefore plotted to destroy her happiness. At their next visit they persuaded her that her mysterious husband must really be a monstrous serpent. 'You must take into your bedroom tonight,' they said, 'a lamp covered with a cloak and a sharp knife. When he sleeps uncover the lamp – see the horror that is lying in your bed – and stab it to death.' All this the gullible Psyche promised to do.

When she uncovered the lamp and saw the sleeping god she gazed on him with insatiable love, till a drop of hot oil from her lamp fell on his shoulder and woke him. Starting up, he spread his shining wings, rebuked her, and vanished from her sight.

The two sisters did not long enjoy their malice, for Cupid took such measures as led both to their death. Psyche meanwhile wandered away, wretched and desolate, and attempted to drown herself in the first river she came to; but the god Pan frustrated her attempt and warned her never to repeat it. After many miseries she fell into the hands of her bitterest enemy, Venus, who seized her for a slave, beat her, and set her what were meant to be impossible tasks. The first, that of sorting out seeds into separate heaps, she did by the help of some friendly ants. Next, she had to get a hank of golden wool from some man-killing sheep; a reed by a river bank whispered to her that this could be achieved by plucking the wool off the bushes. After that, she had to fetch a cupful of the water of the Styx, which could be reached only by climbing certain impracticable mountains, but an eagle met her, took the cup from her hand, and returned with it full of the water. Finally she was sent down to the lower world to bring back to Venus, in a box, the beauty of Persephone, the Queen of the Dead. A mysterious voice told her how she could reach Persephone and yet return to our world; on the way she would be asked for help by various people who seemed to deserve her pity, but she must refuse them all. And when Persephone gave her the box (full of beauty) she must on no account open the lid to look inside. Psyche obeyed all this and returned to the upper world with the box; but then at last curiosity overcame her and she looked into it. She immediately lost consciousness.

Cupid now came to her again, but this time he forgave her. He interceded with Jupiter, who agreed to permit his marriage and make Psyche a goddess. Venus was reconciled and they all lived happily ever after.

The central alteration in my own version consists in making Psyche's palace invisible to normal, mortal eyes – if 'making' is not the wrong word for something which forced itself upon me, almost at my first reading of the story, as the way the thing must have been. This change of course brings with it a more ambivalent motive and a different character for my heroine and finally modifies the whole quality of the tale. I felt quite free to go behind Apuleius, whom I suppose to have been its transmitter, not its inventor. Nothing was further from my aim than to recapture the peculiar quality of the *Metamorphoses* – that strange compound of picaresque novel, horror comic, mystagogue's tract, pornography, and stylistic experiment. Apuleius was of course a man of genius: but in relation to my work he is a 'source', not an 'influence' nor a 'model'.

His version has been followed pretty closely by William Morris (in *The Earthly Paradise*) and by Robert Bridges (*Eros and Psyche*). Neither poem, in my opinion, shows its author at his best. The whole *Metamorphoses* was last translated by Mr Robert Graves (Penguin Books, 1950).

C.S.L.

On another occasion, C.S. Lewis wrote of TILL WE HAVE FACES:

This re-interpretation of an old story has lived in the author's mind, thickening and hardening with the years, ever since he was an undergraduate. That way, he could be said to have worked at it most of his life. Recently, what seemed to be the right form presented itself and themes suddenly interlocked: the straight tale of barbarism, the mind of an ugly woman, dark idolatry and pale enlightenment at war with each other and with vision, and the havoc which a vocation, or even a faith, works on human life.

PART I

I

I am old now and have not much to fear from the anger of gods. I have neither husband nor child, nor hardly a friend, through whom they can hurt me. My body, this lean carrion that still has to be washed and fed and have clothes hung about it daily with so many changes, they may kill as soon as they please. The succession is provided for. My crown passes to my nephew.

Being, for all these reasons, free from fear, I will write in this book what no one who has happiness would dare to write. I will accuse the gods; especially the god who lives on the Grey Mountain. That is, I will tell all he has done to me from the very beginning, as if I were making my complaint of him before a judge. But there is no judge between gods and men, and the god of the mountain will not answer me. Terrors and plagues are not an answer. I write in Greek as my old master taught it to me. It may some day happen that a traveller from the Greeklands will again lodge in this palace and read the book. Then he will talk of it among the Greeks, where there is great freedom of speech even about the gods themselves. Perhaps their wise men will know whether my complaint is right or whether the god could have defended himself if he had made an answer

I was Orual the eldest daughter of Trom, King of Glome. The city of Glome stands on the left hand of the river Shennit to a traveller who is coming up from the south-east, not more than a day's journey above Ringal, which is the last town southward that belongs to the land of Glome. The city is built about as far back from the river as a woman can walk in the third of an hour; for the Shennit overflows her banks in the spring. In summer there was then dry mud on each side of it, and reeds, and plenty of waterfowl. About as far beyond the ford of the Shennit as our city is on this side of it you come to the holy house of Ungit. And beyond the house of Ungit (going all the time east and north) you come quickly to the foothills of the Grey Mountain. The god of the Grey Mountain, who hates me, is the son of Ungit. He does not, however, live in the house of Ungit, but Ungit sits there alone.

In the furthest recess of her house where she sits it is so dark that you cannot see her well, but in summer enough light may come down from the smokeholes in the roof to show her a little. She is a black stone without head or hands or face, and a very great goddess. My old master, whom we called the Fox, said she was the same whom the Greeks call Aphrodite; but I write all the names of people and places in our own language.

I will begin my writing with the day my mother died, and they cut off my hair, as the custom is. The Fox – but he was not with us then – said it is a custom we learned from the Greeks. Batta, the nurse, shore me and my sister Redival outside the palace, at the foot of the garden which runs steeply up the hill behind. Redival was my sister, three years younger than I, and we two were still the only children. While Batta was using the shears many other of the slave women were standing round, from time to time wailing for the Queen's death and beating their breasts; but in between they were eating nuts and joking. As the shears snipped and Redival's curls fell off, the slaves said, 'Oh, what a pity! All the gold gone!' They had not said anything like that while I was being shorn. But what I remember best is the coolness of my head and the hot sun on the back of my neck when we were building mud houses, Redival and I, all that summer afternoon.

Our nurse Batta was a big-boned, fair-haired, hard-handed woman whom my father had bought from traders who got her further north. When we plagued her she would say, 'Only wait till your father brings home a new queen to be your stepmother. It'll be changed times for you then. You'll have hard cheese instead of honey-cakes then and skim milk instead of red wine. Wait and see.'

As things fell out, we got something else before we got a stepmother. There was a bitter frost that day. Redival and I were booted (we mostly went barefoot or sandalled) and trying to slide in the yard which is at the back of the oldest part of the palace, where the walls are wooden. There was ice enough all the way from the byre-door to the big dunghill, what with frozen spills of milk and puddles and the stale of the beasts; but too rough for sliding. And out comes Batta, with the cold reddening her nose, calling out, 'Quick, quick! Ah, you filthies! Come and be cleaned and then to the King. You'll see who's waiting for you there. My word! This'll be a change for you.'

'Is it the Stepmother?' said Redival.

'Oh, worse than that, worse than that; you'll see,' said Batta, polishing Redival's face with the end of her apron. 'Lots of whippings for the pair of you; lots of ear-pullings; lots of hard work.' Then we were led off and over to the new parts of the palace, where it is built of painted brick, and there were guards in their armour, and skins and heads of animals hung up on the walls. In the Pillar Room our father was standing by the hearth, and opposite him there were three men in travelling dress whom we knew well enough – traders who came to Glome three times a year. They were just packing up their scales, so we knew they had been paid for something, and one was putting up a fetter, so we knew they must have sold our father a slave. There was a short, thick-set man standing before them, and we knew this must be the man they had sold, for you could still see the sore places on his legs where the irons had been. But he did not look like any other slave we had ever known. He was very bright-eyed, and whatever of his hair and beard was not grey was reddish.

'Now, Greekling,' said my father to this man, 'I trust to beget a prince one of these days and I have a mind to see him brought up in all the wisdom of your people. Meanwhile practise on *them*.' (He pointed at us children.) 'If a man can teach a girl, he can teach anything.' Then, just before he sent us away, he said, 'Especially the elder. See if you can make her wise; it's about all she'll ever be good for.' I didn't understand that, but I knew it was like things I had heard people say of me ever since I could remember.

I loved the Fox, as my father called him, better than anyone I had yet known. You would have thought that a man who had been free in the Greeklands, and then been taken in war and sold far away among the barbarians, would be downcast. And so he was sometimes; possibly more often than I, in my childishness, guessed. But I never heard him complain; and I never heard him boast (as all the other foreign slaves did) about the great man he had been in his own country. He had all sorts of sayings to cheer himself up with: 'No man can be an exile if he remembers that all the world is one city,' and, 'Everything is as good or bad as our opinion makes it.' But I think what really kept him cheerful was his inquisitiveness. I never knew such a man for questions. He wanted to know everything about our country and language and ancestors and gods, and even our plants and flowers.

That was how I came to tell him all about Ungit, about the girls who are kept in her house, and the presents that brides have to make to her, and how we sometimes, in a bad year, have to cut someone's throat and pour the blood over her. He shuddered when I said that and muttered something under his breath; but a moment later he said, 'Yes, she is undoubtedly Aphrodite, though more like the Babylonian than the Greek. But come, I'll tell you a tale of our Aphrodite.'

Then he deepened and lilted his voice and told how their Aphrodite once fell in love with the prince Anchises while he kept his father's sheep on the slopes of a mountain called Ida. And as she came down the grassy slopes towards his shepherd's hut, lions and lynxes and bears and all sorts of beasts came about her fawning like dogs, and all went from her again in pairs to the delights of love. But she dimmed her glory and made herself like a mortal woman and came to Anchises and beguiled him and they went up together into his bed. I think the Fox had meant to end here, but the song now had him in its grip, and he went on to tell what followed; how Anchises woke from sleep and saw Aphrodite standing in the door of the hut, not now like a mortal but with the glory. So he knew he had lain with a goddess, and he covered his eyes and shrieked, 'Kill me at once.'

'Not that this ever really happened,' the Fox said in haste. 'It's only lies of poets, lies of poets, child. Not in accordance with nature.' But he had said enough to let me see that if the goddess was more beautiful in Greece than in Glome she was equally terrible in each.

It was always like that with the Fox; he was ashamed of loving poetry ('All folly, child') and I had to work much at my reading and writing and what he called philosophy in order to get a poem out of him. But thus, little by little, he taught me many. *Virtue, sought by man with travail and toil* was the one he praised most, but I was never deceived by that. The real lilt came into his voice and the real brightness into his eyes when we were off into *Take me to the apple-laden land* or

> *The Moon's gone down, but*
> *Alone I lie.*

He always sang that one very tenderly and as if he pitied me for something. He liked me better than Redival, who hated study and mocked and plagued him and set the other slaves on to play tricks on him.

We worked most often (in summer) on the little grass plot behind the pear trees, and it was there one day that the King found us. We all stood up of course, two children and a slave with our eyes on the ground and our hands crossed on our breasts. The King smacked the Fox heartily on the back and said, 'Courage, Fox. There'll be a prince for you to work on yet, please the gods. And thank them too, Fox, for it can't often have fallen to the lot of a mere Greekling to rule the grandson of so great a king as my father-in-law that is to be. Not that you'll know or care more about it than an ass. You're all pedlars and hucksters down in the Greeklands, eh?'

'Are not all men of one blood, Master?' said the Fox.

'Of one blood?' said the King with a stare and a great bull-laugh. 'I'd be sorry to think so.'

Thus in the end it was the King himself and not Batta who first told us that the Stepmother was really at hand. My father had made a great match. He was to have the third daughter of the King of Caphad, who is the biggest king in all our part of the world. (I know now why Caphad wanted an alliance with so poor a kingdom as we are, and I have wondered how my father did not see that his father-in-law must already be a sinking man. The marriage itself was a proof of it.)

It cannot have been many weeks before the marriage took place, but in my memory the preparations seem to have lasted for almost a year. All the brick work round the great gate was painted scarlet, and there were new hangings for the Pillar Room, and a great new royal bed which cost the King far more than he was wise to give. It was made of an eastern wood which was said to have such virtue that four of every five children begotten in such a bed would be male. ('All folly, child,' said the Fox, 'these things come about by natural causes.') And as the day drew nearer there was nothing but driving in of beasts and slaughtering of beasts – the whole courtyard reeked with the skins of them – and baking and brewing. But we children had not much time to wander from room to room and stare and hinder, for the King suddenly took it into his head that Redival and I and twelve other girls, daughters of nobles, were to sing the bridal hymn. And nothing would do him but a Greek hymn, which was a thing no other neighbouring king could have provided. 'But, Master—' said the Fox, almost with tears in his eyes. 'Teach 'em, Fox, teach 'em,' roared my father. 'What's the use of my spending good food and drink on your Greek belly if I'm not to get a Greek song out of you on my wedding night? What's that? No one's asking you to teach them Greek. Of course they won't understand what they're singing, but they can make the noises. See to it, or your back'll be redder than ever your beard was.'

It was a crazy scheme, and the Fox said afterwards that the teaching of that hymn to us barbarians was what greyed the last red hair. 'I was a fox,' he said, 'now I am a badger.'

When we had made some progress in our task the King brought the Priest of Ungit in to hear us. I had a fear of that Priest which was quite different from my fear of my father. I think that what frightened me (in those early days) was the holiness of the smell that hung about him – a temple-smell of blood (mostly pigeons' blood, but he had sacrificed men too) and burnt fat and singed hair and wine and stale incense. It is the Ungit smell. Perhaps I was afraid of his clothes too; all the skins they were made of, and the dried bladders, and the great mask shaped like a bird's head which hung on his chest. It looked as if there were a bird growing out of his body.

He did not understand a word of the hymn, nor the music either, but he asked, 'Are the young women to be veiled or unveiled?'

'Need you ask?' said the King with one of his great laughs, jerking his thumb in my direction. 'Do you think I want my queen frightened out of her senses? Veils of course. And good thick veils too.' One of the other girls tittered, and I think that was the first time I clearly understood that I am ugly.

This made me more afraid of the Stepmother than ever. I thought she would be crueller to me than to Redival because of my ugliness. It wasn't only what Batta had said that frightened me; I had heard of stepmothers in plenty of stories. And when the night came and we were all in the pillared porch, nearly dazzled with the torches and trying hard to sing our hymn as the Fox had taught us to – and he kept on frowning and smiling and nodding at us while we sang, and once he held up his hands in horror – pictures of things that had been done to girls in the stories were dancing in my mind. Then came the shouts from outside, and more torches, and next moment they were lifting the bride out of the chariot. She was as thickly veiled as we, and all I could see was that she was very small; it was as if they were lifting a child. That didn't ease my fears; 'the little are the spiteful', our proverb says. Then (still singing) we got her into the bridal chamber and took off her veil.

I know now that the face I saw was beautiful, but I did not think of that then. All I saw was that she was frightened, more frightened than I; indeed terrified. It made me see my father as he must have looked to her, a moment since, when she had her first sight of him standing to greet her in the porch. His was not a brow, a mouth, a girth, a stance, or a voice to quiet a girl's fear.

We took off layer after layer of her finery, making her yet smaller, and left the shivering, white body with its staring eyes in the King's bed, and filed out. We had sung very badly.

2

I can say very little about my father's second wife, for she did not live till the end of her first year in Glome. She was with child as soon as anyone could reasonably look for it, and the King was in high spirits and hardly ever ran across the Fox without saying something about the prince who was to be born. He made great sacrifices to Ungit every month after that. How it was between him and the Queen I do not know; except that once, after messengers had come from Caphad, I heard the King say to her, 'It begins to look, girl, as if I had driven my sheep to a bad market. I learn now that your father has lost two towns – no, three, though he tries to mince the matter. I would thank him to have told me he was sinking before he persuaded me to embark in the same bottom.' (I was leaning my head on my windowsill to dry my hair after the bath, and they were walking in the garden.) However that might be, it is certain that she was very homesick, and I think our winter was too hard for her southern body. She was soon pale and thin. I learned that I had nothing to fear from her. She was at first more afraid of me; after that, very loving in her timid way, and more like a sister than a stepmother.

Of course no one in the house went to bed on the night of the birth, for that, they say, will make the child refuse to wake into the world. We all sat in the great hall between the Pillar Room and the Bedchamber, in a red glare of birth-torches. The flames swayed and guttered terribly, for all doors must be open; the shutting of a door might shut up the mother's womb. In the middle of the hall burned a great fire. Every hour the Priest of Ungit walked round it nine times and threw in the proper things. The King sat in his chair and never moved all night, not even his head. I was sitting next to the Fox.

'Grandfather,' I whispered to him, 'I am terribly afraid.'

'We must learn, child, not to fear anything that nature brings,' he whispered back.

I must have slept after that, for the next thing I knew was the sound of women wailing and beating the breast as I had heard them do it the day my mother died. Everything had changed while I slept. I was shivering with cold.

The fire had sunk low, the King's chair was empty, the door of the Bedchamber was at last shut, and the terrible sounds from within it had stopped. There must have been some sacrifice too, for there was a smell of slaughtering, and blood on the floor, and the Priest was cleaning his holy knife. I was all in a daze from my sleep, for I started up with the wildest idea; I would go and see the Queen. The Fox was after me long before I reached the door of the Bedchamber. 'Daughter, daughter,' he was saying. 'Not now. Are you mad? The King—'

At that moment the door was flung open and out came my father. His face shocked me full awake, for he was in his pale rage. I knew that in his red rage he would storm and threaten, and little might come of it, but when he was pale he was deadly. 'Wine,' he said, not very loud; and that too was a bad sign. The other slaves pushed forward a boy who was rather a favourite, as slaves do when they are afraid. The child, white as his master and in all his finery (my father dressed the younger slaves very fine) came running with the flagon and the royal cup, slipped in the blood, reeled, and dropped both. Quick as thought, my father whipped out his dagger and stabbed him in the side. The boy dropped dead in the blood and wine, and the fall of his body sent the flagon rolling over and over. It made a great noise in that silence; I hadn't thought till then that the floor of the hall was so uneven. (I have re-paved it since.)

My father stared for a moment at his own dagger; stupidly, it seemed. Then he goes very gently up to the Priest.

'What have you to say for Ungit now?' he asked, still in that low voice. 'You had better recover what she owes me. When are you going to pay me for my good cattle?' Then, after a pause, 'Tell me, prophet, what would happen if I hammered Ungit into powder and tied you between the hammers and the stone?'

But the Priest was not in the least afraid of the King.

'Ungit hears, King, even at this moment,' he said. 'And Ungit will remember. You have already said enough to call down doom upon all your descendants.'

'Descendants,' says the King. 'You talk of descendants,' still very quiet, but now he was shaking. The ice of his rage would break any moment. The body of the dead boy caught his eye. 'Who did that?' he asked. Then he saw the Fox and me. All the blood rushed into his face, and now at last the voice came roaring out of his chest loud enough to lift the roof.

'Girls, girls, girls,' he bellowed. 'And now one girl more. Is there no end to it? Is there a plague of girls in heaven that the gods send me this flood of them? You – you—' He caught me by the hair, shook me to and fro, and flung me from him so that I fell in a heap. There are times when even a child knows better than to cry. When the blackness passed and I could see again, he was shaking the Fox by his throat.

'Here's an old babbler who has eaten my bread long enough,' he said. 'It would have paid me better to buy a dog as things turn out. But I'll feed you in idleness no longer. Some of you take him to the mines tomorrow. There might be a week's work in his old bones even now.'

Again there was dead silence in the hall. Suddenly the King flung up his hands, stamped, and cried, 'Faces, faces, faces! What are you all gaping at? It'd make a man mad. Be off! Away! Out of my sight, the whole pack of you!'

We were out of the hall as quick as the doorways would let us.

The Fox and I went out of the little door by the herb-garden on the east. It was nearly daylight now and there was a small rain beginning.

'Grandfather,' said I, sobbing, 'you must fly at once. This moment, before they come to take you to the mines.'

He shook his head. 'I'm too old to run far,' he said. 'And you know what the King does to runaway slaves.'

'But the mines, the mines! Look, I'll come with you. If we're caught I'll say I made you come. We shall be almost out of Glome once we're over *that*.' I pointed to the ridge of the Grey Mountain, now dark with a white daybreak behind it, seen through the slanting rain.

'That is foolishness, daughter,' said he, petting me like a small child. 'They would think I was stealing you to sell. No; I must fly further. And help me you shall. Down by the river; you know the little plant with the purple spots on its stalks. It's the roots of it I need.'

'The poison?'

'Why, yes. (Child, child, don't cry so.) Have I not told you often that to depart from life of a man's own will when there's good reason is one of the things that are according to nature? We are to look on life as—'

'They say that those who go that way lie wallowing in filth – down there in the land of the dead.'

'Hush, hush. Are you also still a barbarian? At death we are resolved into our elements. Shall I accept birth and cavil at—'

'Oh, I know, I know. But, Grandfather—do you really in your heart believe nothing of what is said about the gods and Those Below? But you do, you do. You are trembling.'

'That's my disgrace. The body is shaking. I needn't let it shake the god within me. Have I not already carried this body too long if it makes such a fool of me at the end? But we are wasting time.'

'Listen!' said I. 'What's that?' For I was in a state to be scared by every sound.

'Horses,' said the Fox, peering through the quick-hedge with his eyes screwed up to see against the rain. 'They are coming to the great door. Messengers from Phars, by the look of them. And that will not sweeten the

King's mood either. Will you – ah, Zeus, it is already too late.' For there was a call from within doors, 'The Fox, the Fox, the Fox to the King.'

'As well go as be dragged,' said the Fox. 'Farewell, daughter,' and he kissed me, Greek fashion, on the eyes and the head. But I went in with him. I had an idea I would face the King; though whether I meant to beseech him or curse him or kill him I hardly knew. But as we came to the Pillar Room we saw many strangers within, and the King shouted through the open door, 'Here, Fox, I've work for you.' Then he saw me and said, 'And you, curd-face, be off to the women's quarters and don't come here to sour the morning drink for the men.'

I do not know that I have ever (to speak of things merely mortal) been in such dread as I was for the rest of that day; dread that feels as if there were an empty place between your belly and your chest. I didn't know whether I dared be comforted by the King's last words or not; for they sounded as if his anger had passed, but it might blaze out again. Moreover, I had known him do a cruel thing not in anger but in a kind of murderous joke, or because he remembered he had sworn to do it when he was angry. He had sent old house-slaves to the mines before. And I could not be alone with my terror, for now comes Batta to shear my head and Redival's again as they had been shorn when my mother died, and to make a great tale (clicking her tongue) of how the Queen was dead in childbed, which I had known ever since I heard the mourning, and how she had borne a daughter alive. I sat for the shearing and thought that, if the Fox must die in the mines, it was very fit I should offer my hair. Lank and dull and little it lay on the floor beside Redival's rings of gold.

In the evening the Fox came and told me that there was no more talk of the mines; for the present. A thing that had often irked me had now been our salvation. More and more, of late, the King had taken the Fox away from us girls to work for him in the Pillar Room; he had begun to find that the Fox could calculate and read and write letters (at first only in Greek but now in the speech of our parts too) and give advice better than any man in Glome. This very day the Fox had taught him to drive a better bargain with the King of Phars than he would ever have thought of for himself. The Fox was a true Greek; where my father could give only a Yes or a No to some neighbouring king or dangerous noble, he could pare the Yes to the very quick and sweeten the No till it went down like wine. He could make your weak enemy believe that you were his best friend and make your strong enemy believe you were twice as strong as you really were. He was far too useful to be sent to the mines.

They burnt the dead Queen on the third day, and my father named the child Istra. 'It is a good name,' said the Fox, 'a very good name. And you know enough now to tell me what it would be in Greek.'

'It would be Psyche, Grandfather,' said I.

New-born children were no rarity in the palace; the place sprawled with the slaves' babies and my father's bastards. Sometimes my father would say, 'Lecherous rascals! Anyone'd think this was Ungit's house, not mine,' and threaten to drown a dozen of them like blind puppies. But in his heart he thought the better of a man-slave if he could get half the maids in the place with child, especially if they bore boys. (The girls, unless they took his own fancy, were mostly sold when they were ripe; some were given to the house of Ungit.) Nevertheless, because I had (a little) loved the Queen, I went to see Psyche that very evening as soon as the Fox had set my mind at rest. And so, in one hour, I passed out of the worst anguish I had yet suffered into the beginning of all my joys.

The child was very big, not a wearish little thing as you might have expected from her mother's stature, and very fair of skin. You would have thought she made bright all the corner of the room in which she lay. She slept (tiny was the sound of her breathing). But there never was a child like Psyche for quietness in her cradle days. As I gazed at her the Fox came in on tiptoes and looked over my shoulder. 'Now by all the gods,' he whispered, 'old fool that I am, I could almost believe that there really is divine blood in your family. Helen herself, new-hatched, must have looked so.'

Batta had put her to nurse with a red-haired woman who was sullen and (like Batta herself) too fond of the wine-jar. I soon had the child out of their hands. I got for her nurse a free woman, a peasant's wife, as honest and wholesome as I could find, and after that both were in my own chamber day and night. Batta was only too pleased to have her work done for her, and the King knew and cared nothing about it. The Fox said to me, 'Don't wear yourself out, daughter, with too much toil, even if the child is as beautiful as a goddess.' But I laughed in his face. I think I laughed more in those days than in all my life before. Toil? I lost more sleep looking on Psyche for the joy of it than in any other way. And I laughed because she was always laughing. She laughed before the third month. She knew me for certain (though the Fox said not) before the second.

This was the beginning of my best times. The Fox's love for the child was wonderful; I guessed that long before, when he was free, he must have had a daughter of his own. He was like a true grandfather now. And it was now always we three – the Fox, and Psyche, and I – alone together. Redival had always hated our lessons and, but for the fear of the King, would never have come near the Fox. Now, it seemed, the King had put all his three daughters out of his mind, and Redival had her own way. She was growing tall, her breasts rounding, her long legs getting their shape. She promised to have beauty enough, but not like Psyche's.

Of Psyche's beauty – at every age the beauty proper to that age – there is only this to be said, that there were no two opinions about it, from man or woman, once she had been seen. It was beauty that did not astonish you till afterwards when you had gone out of sight of her and reflected on it. While she was with you, you were not astonished. It seemed the most natural thing in the world. As the Fox delighted to say, she was 'according to nature'; what every woman, or even every thing, ought to have been and meant to be, but had missed by some trip of chance. Indeed, when you looked at her you believed, for a moment, that they had not missed it. She made beauty all round her. When she trod on mud, the mud was beautiful; when she ran in the rain, the rain was silver. When she picked up a toad – she had the strangest and, I thought, unchanciest love for all manner of brutes – the toad became beautiful.

The years, doubtless, went round then as now, but in my memory it seems to have been all springs and summers. I think the almonds and the cherries blossomed earlier in those years and the blossoms lasted longer; how they hung on in such winds I don't know, for I see the boughs always rocking and dancing against blue-and-white skies, and their shadows flowing water-like over all the hills and valleys of Psyche's body. I wanted to be a wife so that I could have been her real mother. I wanted to be a boy so that she could be in love with me. I wanted her to be my full sister instead of my half sister. I wanted her to be a slave so that I could set her free and make her rich.

The Fox was so trusted by now that when my father did not need him he was allowed to take us anywhere, even miles from the palace. We were often out all day in summer on the hill-top to the south-west, looking down on all Glome and across to the Grey Mountain. We stared our eyes out on that jagged ridge till we knew every tooth and notch of it, for none of us had ever gone there or seen what was on the other side. Psyche, almost from the beginning (for she was a very quick, thinking child), was half in love with the Mountain. She made herself stories about it. 'When I'm big,' she said, 'I will be a great, great queen, married to the greatest king of all, and he will build me a castle of gold and amber up there on the very top.'

The Fox clapped his hands and sang, 'Prettier than Andromeda, prettier than Helen, prettier than Aphrodite herself.'

'Speak words of better omen, Grandfather,' I said, though I knew he would scold and mock me for saying it. For at his words, though on that summer day the rocks were too hot to touch, it was as if a soft, cold hand had been laid on my left side, and I shivered.

'Babai!' said the Fox. 'It is your words that are ill-omened. The divine nature is not like that. It has no envy.'

But whatever he said, I knew it is not good to talk that way about Ungit.

3

It was Redival who ended the good time. She had always been featherheaded and now grew wanton, and what must she do but stand kissing and whispering love-talk with a young officer of the guard (one Tarin) right under Batta's window an hour after midnight. Batta had slept off her wine in the earlier part of the night and was now wakeful. Being a busybody and tattler in grain, she went off straight and woke the King, who cursed her roundly but believed her. He was up, and had a few armed men with him, and was out into the garden and surprised the lovers before they knew that anything was amiss. The whole house was raised by the noise of it. The King had the barber to make a eunuch of Tarin there and then (as soon as he was healed, they sold him down at Ringal). The boy's screams had hardly sunk to a whimper before the King turned on the Fox and me, and made us to blame for the whole thing. Why had the Fox not looked to his pupil? Why had I not looked to my sister? The end of it was a strict command that we were never to let her out of our sight. 'Go where you will and do what you will,' said my father. 'But the salt bitch must be with you. I tell you, Fox, if she loses her maidenhead before I find her a husband, you'll yell louder for it than she. Look to your hide. And you, goblin daughter, do what you're good for, you'd best. Name of Ungit! if you with that face can't frighten the men away, it's a wonder.'

Redival was utterly cowed by the King's anger and obeyed him. She was always with us. And that soon cooled any love she had for Psyche or me. She yawned and she quarrelled and she mocked. Psyche, who was a child so merry, so truthful, so obedient that in her (the Fox said) Virtue herself had put on a human form, could do no right in Redival's eyes. One day Redival hit her. Then I hardly knew myself again till I found that I was astride of Redival, she on the ground with her face a lather of blood, and my hands about her throat. It was the Fox who pulled me off and, in the end, some kind of peace was made between us.

Thus all the comfort we three had had was destroyed when Redival joined us. And after that, little by little, one by one, came the first knocks of the hammer that finally destroyed us all.

The year after I fought Redival was the first of the bad harvests. That same year my father tried to marry himself (as the Fox told me) into two royal houses among the neighbouring kings, and they would have none of him. The world was changing, the great alliance with Caphad had proved a snare. The tide was against Glome.

That same year, too, a small thing happened which cost me many a shuddering. The Fox and I, up behind the pear trees, were deep in his philosophy. Psyche had wandered off, singing to herself, among the trees, to the edge of the royal gardens where they overlook the lane. Redival went after her. I had one eye on the pair of them, and one ear for the Fox. Then it seemed they were talking to someone in the lane, and shortly after that they came back.

Redival, sneering, bowed double before Psyche and went through the actions of pouring dust on her head. 'Why don't you honour the goddess?' she said to us.

'What do you mean, Redival?' asked I, wearily, for I knew she meant some new spite.

'Did you not know our stepsister had become a goddess?'

'What does she mean, Istra?' said I. (I never called her Psyche now that Redival had joined us.)

'Come on, stepsister goddess, speak up,' said Redival. 'I'm sure I've been told often enough how truthful you are, so you'll not deny that you have been worshipped.'

'It's not true,' said Psyche. 'All that happened was that a woman with child asked me to kiss her.'

'Ah, but why?' said Redival.

'Because – because she said her baby would be beautiful if I did.'

'*Because you are so beautiful yourself.* Don't forget that. She said that.'

'And what did you do, Istra?' asked I.

'I kissed her. She was a nice woman. I liked her.'

'And don't forget that she then laid down a branch of myrtle at your feet and bowed and put dust on her head,' said Redival.

'Has this happened before, Istra?' said I.

'Yes. Sometimes.'

'How often?'

'Don't know.'

'Twice before?'

'More than that.'

'Well, ten times?'

'No, more. I don't know. I can't remember. What are you looking at me like that for? Is it wrong?'

'Oh, it's dangerous, dangerous,' said I. 'The gods are jealous. They can't bear—'

'Daughter, it doesn't matter a straw,' said the Fox. 'The divine nature is without jealousy. Those gods – the sort of gods you are always thinking about – are all folly and lies of poets. We have discussed this a hundred times.'

'Heigh-ho,' yawns Redival, lying flat on her back in the grass and kicking her legs in the air till you could see all there was of her (which she did purely to put the Fox out of countenance, for the old man was very modest). 'Heigh-ho, a stepsister for goddess and a slave for counsellor. Who'd be a princess in Glome? I wonder what Ungit thinks of our new goddess.'

'It is not very easy to find out what Ungit thinks,' said the Fox.

Redival rolled round and laid her cheek on the grass. Then, looking up at him, she said softly, 'But it would be easy to find out what the Priest of Ungit thinks. Shall I try?'

All my old fear of the Priest, and more fears for the future than I could put a name to, stabbed into me.

'Sister,' said Redival to me, 'give me your necklace with the blue stones, the one our mother gave you.'

'Take it,' said I. 'I'll give it you when we go in.'

'And you, slave,' she said to the Fox. 'Mend your manners. And get my father to give me to some king in marriage; and it must be a young king, brave, yellow-bearded, and lusty. You can do what you like with my father when you're shut up with him in the Pillar Room. Everyone knows that you are the real King of Glome.'

The year after that we had rebellion. It came of my father's gelding Tarin. Tarin himself was of no great lineage (to be about a king's house at all) and the King had thought his father would have no power to avenge him. But the father made common cause with bigger men than himself, and about nine strong lords in our north-west rose against us. My father took the field himself (and when I saw him ride out in his armour, I came nearer to loving him than I had been yet) and beat the rebels; but with great slaughter on both parts and, I think, more slaughter of the beaten men than was needed. The thing left a stench and a disaffection behind it; when all was done, the King was weaker than he had been.

That year was the second bad harvest and the beginning of the fever. In the autumn the Fox took it and nearly died. I could not be with him, for as soon as the Fox fell sick the King said, 'Now, girl, you can read and write and chatter Greek. I'll have work for you. You must take the Fox's place.' So I was nearly always in the Pillar Room, for there was much business at the time. Though I was sick with fear for the Fox, the work with my father was far less dreadful to me than I expected. He came, for the time, to hate me less. In the end he would speak to me, not, certainly, with love, but friendly as one man might to another. I learned how desperate his affairs were. No neighbouring houses of divine blood (and ours cannot lawfully marry into any other) would take his daughters or give him theirs. The nobles were muttering about the succession. There were threats of war from every side, and no strength to meet any of them.

It was Psyche who nursed the Fox, however often forbidden. She would fight, yes, and bite, any who stood between her and his door; for she, too, had our father's hot blood, though her angers were all the sort that come from love. The Fox won through his illness, thinner and greyer than before. Now mark the subtlety of the god who is against us. The story of his recovery and Psyche's nursing got abroad; Batta alone was conduit-pipe enough, and there were a score of other talkers. It became a story of how the beautiful princess could cure the fever by her touch; soon, that her touch was the only thing that could cure it. Within two days half the city was at the palace gate – such scarecrows, risen from their beds, old dotards as eager to save their lives as if their lives in any event were worth a year's purchase, babies, sick men half dead and carried on beds. I stood looking at them from behind barred windows; all the pity and dread of it, the smell of sweat and fever and garlic and foul clothes.

'The Princess Istra,' they cried. 'Send out the Princess with her healing hands. We die! Healing, healing, healing!'

'And bread,' came other voices. 'The royal granaries! We are starving.'

This was at first, while they stood a little way off from the gate. But they got nearer. Soon they were hammering at it. Someone was saying, 'Bring fire.' But, behind them, the weaker voices wailed on, 'Heal us, heal us. The Princess with the healing hands!'

'She'll have to go out,' said my father. 'We can't hold them.' (Two-thirds of our guards were down with the fever.)

'Can she heal them?' said I to the Fox. 'Did she heal you?'

'It is possible,' said the Fox. 'It might be in accordance with nature that some hands can heal. Who knows?'

'Let me go out,' said Psyche. 'They are our people.'

'Our rump!' said my father. 'They shall smart for this day's work if ever I get the whip hand of them again. But quick. Dress the girl. She has beauty enough, that's one thing. And spirit.'

They put a queen's dress on her and a chaplet on her head and opened the door. You know how it is when you shed few tears or none, but there is a weight and pressure of weeping through your whole head. It is like that with me even now when I remember her going out, slim and straight as a sceptre, out of the darkness and cool of the hall into the hot, pestilential glare of that day. The people drew back, thrusting one another, the moment the doors opened. I think they expected a rush of spearmen. But a minute later the wailing and shouting died utterly away. Every man (and many a woman too) in that crowd was kneeling. Her beauty, which most of them had never seen, worked on them as a terror might work. Then a low murmur, almost a sob, began; swelled, broke into the gasping cry, 'A goddess, a goddess.' One woman's voice rang out clear. 'It is Ungit herself in mortal shape.'

Psyche went on, walking slowly and gravely, like a child going to say a lesson, right in among all the foulness. She touched and she touched. They fell at her feet and kissed her feet and the edge of her robe and her shadow and the ground where she had trodden. And still she touched and touched. There seemed to be no end of it; the crowd increased instead of diminishing. For hours she touched. The air was stifling even for us who stood in the shadow of the porch. The whole earth and air ached for the thunderstorm which (we knew now) would not come. I saw her growing paler and paler. Her walk had become a stagger.

'King,' said I, 'it will kill her.'

'Then more's the pity,' said the King. 'They'll kill us all if she stops.'

It was over in the end, somewhere about sunset. We carried her to her bed, and next day the fever was on her. But she won through it. In her wanderings she talked most of her gold and amber castle on the ridge of the Grey Mountain. At her worst, there was no look of death upon her face. It was as if he dared not come near her. And when her strength came back she was more beautiful than before. The childishness had gone. There was a new and severer radiance. 'Ah, no wonder,' sang the Fox, 'if the Trojans and the Achaeans suffer long woes for such a woman. Terribly does she resemble an undying spirit.'

Some of the sick in the town died and some recovered. Only the gods know if those who recovered were those whom Psyche had touched, and gods do not tell. But the people had, at first, no doubts. Every morning there were offerings left for her outside the palace; myrtle branches and garlands and soon honey-cakes and then pigeons, which are specially sacred to Ungit. 'Can this be well?' I said to the Fox.

'I should be greatly afraid,' said he, 'but for one thing. The Priest of Ungit lies sick with the fever himself. I do not think he can do us much mischief at present.'

About this time Redival became very pious and went often to the house of Ungit to make offerings. The Fox and I saw to it that she always had with her a trusty old slave who would let her get into no mischief. I thought she was praying for a husband (she wanted one badly since the King had, in a manner, chained her to the Fox and me) and also that she was as glad to be out of our sight for an hour as we were to be out of hers. Yet I warned her to speak to no one on the way.

'Oh, make your mind easy, Sister,' says Redival. 'It's not me they worship, you know. I'm not the goddess. The men are as likely to look at you as at me, now they've seen Istra.'

4

Up till now I had not known what the common people are like. That was why their adorings of Psyche, which in one way made me afraid, comforted me in another. For I was confused in my mind, sometimes thinking of what Ungit by her own divine power might do to any mortal who thus stole her honour, and sometimes of what the Priest and our enemies in the city (my father had many now) might do with their tongues, or stones, or spears. Against the latter the people's love for Psyche seemed to me a protection.

It did not last long. For one thing, the mob had now learned that a palace door can be opened by banging on it. Before Psyche was out of her fever they were back at our gates crying, 'Corn, corn! We are starving. Open the royal granaries.' That time the King gave them a dole. 'But don't come again,' he said. 'I've no more to give you. Name of Ungit! d'you think I can make corn if the fields don't bear it?'

'And why don't they?' said a voice from the back of the crowd.

'Where are your sons, King?' said another. 'Where's the prince?'

'The King of Phars has thirteen sons,' said another.

'Barren king makes barren land,' said a fourth. This time the King saw who had spoken and nodded to one of the bowmen who stood beside him. Before you'd wink the arrow went through the speaker's throat and the mob took to its heels. But it was foolishly done; my father ought to have killed either none of them or nearly all. He was right enough, though, in saying we could give them no more doles. This was the second of the bad harvests and there was little in the granary but our own seedcorn. Even in the palace we were already living for the most part on leeks and bean-bread and small beer. It took me endless contrivance to get anything good for Psyche when she was mending from the fever.

The next thing was this. Shortly after Psyche was well, I left the Pillar Room where I had been working for the King (and he still kept the Fox with him after he let me go) and set out to look for Redival, that care being always on my mind. The King would have thought nothing of keeping me away from her at his own business all the day and then blaming me for not having my eyes on her. But as it happened I met her at once, just coming in from one of her visits to the house of Ungit, and Batta with her. Batta and she were as thick as thieves these days.

'You needn't come looking for me, sister-jailer,' says Redival. 'I'm safe enough. It isn't here the danger lies. When did you last see the little goddess? Where's your darling stepsister?'

'In the gardens most likely,' said I. 'And as for *little*, she's half a head taller than yourself.'

'Oh mercy! Have I blasphemed? Will she smite me with thunder? Yes, she's tall enough. Tall enough to see her a long way off – half an hour ago – in a little lane near the market place. A king's daughter doesn't usually walk the back streets alone; but I suppose a goddess can.'

'Istra out in the town and alone?' said I.

'Indeed she was then,' chattered Batta. 'Scuttling along with her robe caught up. Like this ... like this.' (Batta was a bad mimic but always mimicking; I remembered that from my earliest years.) 'I'd have followed her, the young boldface, but she went in at a doorway, so she did.'

'Well, well,' said I. 'The child ought to have known better. But she'll do no harm and come to none.'

'Come to no harm!' said Batta. 'That's more than any of us know.'

'You are mad, Nurse,' said I. 'The people were worshipping her not six days ago.'

'I don't know anything about that,' said Batta (who knew perfectly well). 'But she'll get little worship today. I knew what would come of all that touching and blessing. Fine goings on indeed! The plague's worse than ever it was. There were a hundred died yesterday, the smith's wife's brother-in-law tells me. They say the touchings didn't heal the fever but gave it. I've spoken to a woman whose old father was touched by the Princess, and he was dead before they had carried him home. And he wasn't the only one. If anyone had listened to old Batta—'

But I at least listened no more. I went out to the porch and looked towards the city; a long half-hour. I watched the shadows of the pillars slowly changing their position and it was then I first saw how the things we have known ever since we were weaned can look new and strange, like enemies. And at last I saw Psyche coming, very tired but in great haste. She caught me by the wrist and swallowed, like one that has a sob in the throat, and began leading me away and never stopped till we were in my own chamber. Then she put me in my chair and fell down and laid her head on my knees. I thought she was crying, but when at last she raised her face there were no tears on it.

'Sister,' she said. 'What is wrong? I mean, about me.'

'About you, Psyche?' said I. 'Nothing. What do you mean?'

'Why do they call me the Accursed?'

'Who has dared? We'll have his tongue torn out. Where have you been?'

Then it all came out. She had gone (very foolishly, I thought) into the city without a word to any of us. She had heard that her old nurse, the freewoman whom I had hired to suckle her and who now lived in town, was sick with the fever. And Psyche had gone to touch her – 'For they all said my hands cured it, and who knows? It might be. I felt as if they did.'

I told her she had done very wrong, and it was then that I fully perceived how much older she had grown since her sickness. For she neither accepted the rebuke like a child nor defended herself like a child, but looked at me with a grave quietness, almost as if she were older than I. It gave me a pang at the heart.

'But who cursed you?' I asked.

'Nothing happened till I had left Nurse's house; except that no one in the streets had saluted me, and I thought that one or two women gathered their skirts together and drew away from me as I passed. Well, on the way back, first there was a boy – a lovely boy he was, not eight years old – who stared at me and spat on the ground. 'Oh rude!' said I, and laughed and held out my hand to him. He scowled at me as black as a little fiend and then lost his courage and ran howling into a doorway. After that the street was empty for a space, but presently I had to pass a knot of men. They gave me black looks as I was passing, and as soon as my back was towards them they were all saying, 'The Accursed, the Accursed! She made herself a goddess.' And one said, 'She is the curse itself.' Then they threw stones. No, I'm not hurt. But I had to run. What does it mean? What did I do to them?'

'Do?' said I. 'You healed them, and blessed them, and took their filthy diseases upon yourself. And these are their thanks. Oh, I could tear them in pieces! Get up, child. Let me go. Even now – we are king's daughters still. I'll go to the King. He may beat me and drag me by the hair as he pleases, but this he shall hear. Bread for them indeed. I'll – I'll—'

'Hush, sister, hush,' said Psyche. 'I can't bear it when he hurts you. And I'm so tired. And I want my supper. There, don't be angry. You look just like our father when you say those things. Let us have supper here, you and I. There is some bad thing coming towards us – I have felt it a long time – but I don't think it will come tonight. I'll clap my hands to call your maids.'

Though the words *You look just like our father*, and from her, had hurt me with a wound that sometimes aches still, I let go my anger and yielded. We supped together and turned our poor meal into a joke and a game and were in a fashion happy. One thing the gods have not taken from me; I can remember all that she said or did that night and how she looked from moment to moment.

But whatever my heart boded, our ruin (and even now I had no clear foresight what it would be) did not fall upon us the next day. A whole train of days went past in which nothing happened, except for the slow, steady worsening of everything in Glome. The Shennit was now no more than a trickle between one puddle and another amid dry mud-flats; it was the corpse of a river and stank. Her fish were dead, her birds dead or gone away. The cattle had all died or been killed or were not worth the killing. The bees were dead. Lions, which had not been heard of in the land for forty years, came over the ridge of the Grey Mountain and took most of the few sheep we had left. The plague never ceased. All through these days I was waiting and listening, watching (when I could) everyone who went out of the palace or came in. It was well for me that the King found plenty of work both for the Fox and me in the Pillar Room. Messengers and letters from the neighbouring kings were coming in every day, demanding impossible things and contrary things, dragging up old quarrels or claiming old promises. They knew how things were in Glome and clustered round us like flies and crows round a dying sheep. My father would pass in and out of his rages a dozen times in one morning. When he was in them he would slap the Fox about the face and pull me by the ears or the hair; and then, between the fits, the tears would stand in his eyes, and he would speak to us more like a child imploring help than a king asking counsel.

'Trapped!' he would say. 'No way out. They will kill me by inches. What have I done that all these miseries should fall upon me? I've been a god-fearing man all my life.'

The only betterment in these days was that the fever seemed to have left the palace. We had lost a good many slaves, but we had better luck with the soldiers. Only one died and all the rest were now back at duty.

Then we heard that the Priest of Ungit had recovered from his fever. His sickness had been very long, for he had taken the fever and won over it and then taken it again, so that it was a wonder he should be alive. But it was noticed for a strange and unlucky thing about this sickness that it killed the young more easily than the old. On the seventh day after this news the Priest came to the palace. The King, who saw his coming (as I did too) from the windows of the Pillar Room, said, 'What does the old carrion mean by coming here with half an army?' There were indeed a good many spears behind his litter, for the house of Ungit has its own guards and he had brought a big handful with him. They grounded their spears some distance from our gates, and only the litter was carried to the porch. 'They'd better come no nearer,' said the King. 'Is this treason or only pride?' Then he gave some order to the captain of his own guard. I don't think he expected it would come to a fight, but that was what I, being still young, looked for. I had never seen men fight and, being as big a fool in that way as most girls, I felt no dread; rather, a little tingling that I liked well enough.

The bearers set down the litter and the Priest was lifted out of it. He was very old now and blind, and he had two temple girls with him to lead him. I had seen their kind before, but only by torchlight in the house of Ungit. They looked strange under the sun, with their gilt paps and their huge flaxen wigs and their faces painted till they looked like wooden masks. Only these two and the Priest, with one hand on a shoulder of each, came into the palace. As soon as they were in, my father called out to our men to shut and bar the door. 'The old wolf would hardly walk into such a trap if he meant mischief,' he said. 'But we'll make sure.'

The temple girls led the Priest into the Pillar Room, and a chair was set for him and he was helped into it. He was out of breath and sat for a long time before he spoke, making a chewing motion with his gums as old men do. The girls stood stiffly at each side of his chair, their meaningless eyes looking always straight ahead out of the mask of their painting. The smell of old age, and the smell of the oils and essences they put on those girls, and the Ungit smell, filled the room. It became very holy.

5

My father greeted the Priest and wished him joy of his recovery and called for wine to be given him. But the Priest held up his hand and said, 'No, King. I am under a strong vow, and neither food nor drink must pass my lips till I have given my message.' He spoke well enough now, though weakly, and I noticed how much thinner he was since his sickness.

'As you please, servant of Ungit,' said the King. 'What's this of a message?'

'I am speaking to you, King, with the voice of Ungit and the voice of all the people and elders and nobles of Glome.'

'Did all these, then, send you with a message?'

'Yes. We were all gathered – or those who could speak for all were gathered – last night, and even till this day's daybreak, in the house of Ungit.'

'Were you, death and scabs?' said my father, frowning. 'It's a new fashion to hold an assembly without the King's bidding; and newer still to hold it without bidding the King to it.'

'There would have been no reason in bidding you to it, King, seeing that we came together not to hear what you would say to us but to determine what we would say to you.'

My father's look grew very black.

'And being gathered together,' said the Priest, 'we reckoned up all the woes that have come upon us. First, the famine, which still increases. Second, the pestilence. Third, the drought. Fourth, the certain expectation of war by next spring at the latest. Fifth, the lions. And lastly, King, your own barrenness of sons which is hateful to Ungit—'

'That's enough,' shouted the King. 'You old fool, do you think I need you or any of the other wiseacres to tell me where my own belly aches? Hateful to Ungit, is it? Why does Ungit not mend it then? She's had bulls and rams and goats from me in plenty; blood enough to sail a ship on if all was reckoned.'

The Priest jerked up his head as if, though blind, he was looking at the King. And now I saw better how his thinness had changed him. He looked like a vulture. I was more afraid of him than I had been. The King dropped his eyes.

'Bulls and rams and goats will not win Ungit's favour while the land is impure,' said the Priest. 'I have served Ungit these fifty – no, sixty-three years, and I have learned one thing for certain. Her anger never comes upon us without cause, and it never ceases without expiation. I have made offerings to her for your father and your father's father, and it has always been the same. We were overthrown long before your day by the King of Essur; and that was because there was a man in your grandfather's army who had lain with his sister and killed the child. He was the Accursed. We found him out and expiated his sin, and then the men of Glome chased the men of Essur like sheep. Your father himself could have told you how one woman, little more than a child, cursed Ungit's son, the god of the Mountain, in secret. For her sake the floods came. She was the Accursed. We found her out and expiated her sin, and Shennit returned into her banks. And now, by all the signs I have reckoned over to you, we know that Ungit's anger is far greater than ever within my memory. Thus we all said in her house last night. We all said, We must find the Accursed. Though every man knew that he himself might be the Accursed, no man spoke against it. I too – I had not a word to say against it, though I knew that the Accursed might be I; or you, King. For we all knew (and you may hold it for certain) that there will be no mending of all our ills till the land is purged. Ungit will be avenged. It's not a bull or a ram that will quiet her now.'

'You mean she wants Man?' said the King.

'Yes,' said the Priest. 'Or Woman.'

'If they think I can get them a captive in war at present, they must be mad. The next time I take a thief you can cut his throat over Ungit if you like.'

'That is not enough, King. And you know it. We must find the Accursed. And she (or he) must die by the rite of the Great Offering. What is a thief more than a bull or a ram? This is not to be a common sacrifice. We must make the Great Offering. The Brute has been seen again. And when it comes the Great Offering must be made. That is how the Accursed must be offered.'

'The Brute? It's the first I've heard of it.'

'It may be so. Kings seem to hear very little. They do not know even what goes on in their own palaces. But I hear. I lie awake in the nights, very long awake, and Ungit tells me things. I hear of terrible doings in this land; mortals aping the gods and stealing the worship due to the gods—'

I looked at the Fox and said, soundlessly, by the shaping of my lips, 'Redival.'

The King was walking up and down the room with his hands clasped behind his back and his fingers working.

'You're doting,' he said. 'The Brute's a tale of my grandmother's.'

'It may well be,' said the Priest, 'for it was in her time that the Brute was last seen. And we made the Great Offering and it went away.'

'Who has ever seen this Brute?' asked by father. 'What is it like, eh?'

'Those who have seen it closest can least say what it is like, King. And many have seen it of late. Your own chief shepherd on the Grey Mountain saw it the night the first lion came. He fell upon the lion with a burning torch. And in the light of the torch he saw the Brute – behind the lion – very black and big, a terrible shape.'

As the Priest said this the King's walk had brought him close to the table where I and the Fox sat with our tablets and other tools for writing. The Fox slid along the bench and whispered something in my father's ear.

'Well said, Fox,' muttered my father. 'Speak up. Say it to the Priest.'

'By the King's permission,' said the Fox, 'the shepherd's tale is very questionable. If the man had a torch, of necessity the lion would have a big black shadow behind it. The man was scared and new waked from sleep. He took a shadow for a monster.'

'That is the wisdom of the Greeks,' said the Priest. 'But Glome does not take counsel with slaves, not even if they are king's favourites. And if the Brute was a shadow, King, what then? Many say it *is* a shadow. But if that shadow begins coming down into the city, look to yourself. You are of divine blood and doubtless fear nothing. But the people will fear. Their fear will be so great that not even I will be able to hold them. They will burn your palace about your ears. They will bar you in before they burn it. You would be wiser to make the Great Offering.'

'How is it made?' said the King. 'It has never happened in my time.'

'It is not done in the house of Ungit,' said the Priest. 'The victim must be given to the Brute. For the Brute is, in a mystery, Ungit herself or Ungit's son, the god of the Mountain; or both. The victim is led up the mountain to the Holy Tree, and bound to the Tree and left. Then the Brute comes. That is why you angered Ungit just now, King, when you spoke of offering a thief. In the Great Offering the victim must be perfect. For in holy language a man so offered is said to be Ungit's husband, and a woman is said to be the bride of Ungit's son. And both are called the Brute's Supper. And when the Brute is Ungit it lies with the man, and when it is her son it lies with the woman. And either way there is a devouring … many different things are said … many sacred stories … many great mysteries. Some say the loving and the devouring are all the same thing. For in sacred language we say that a woman who lies with a man devours the man. That is why you are so wide of the mark, King, when you think a thief, or an old worn-out slave, or a coward taken in battle, would do for the Great Offering. The best in the land is not too good for this office.'

The King's forehead, I saw, was clammy now. The holiness and horror of divine things were continually thickening in that room. All at once, the Fox burst out, 'Master, Master, let me speak.'

'Speak on,' said the King.

'Do you not see, Master,' said the Fox, 'that the Priest is talking nonsense? A shadow is to be an animal which is also a goddess which is also a god, and loving is to be eating – a child of six would talk more sense. And a moment ago the victim of this abominable sacrifice was to be the Accursed, the wickedest person in the whole land, offered as a punishment. And now it is to be the best person in the whole land – the perfect victim – married to the god as a reward. Ask him which he means. It can't be both.'

If any hope had put up its head within me when the Fox began, it was killed. This sort of talk could do no good. I knew what had happened to the Fox; he had forgotten all his wiles, even, in a way, his love and fears for Psyche, simply because things such as the Priest had been saying put him beyond all patience. (I have noticed that all men, not only Greek men, if they have clear wits and ready tongues, will do the same.)

'We are hearing much Greek wisdom this morning, King,' said the Priest. 'And I have heard most of it before. I did not need a slave to teach it to me. It is very subtle. But it brings no rain and grows no corn; sacrifice does both. It does not even give them boldness to die. That Greek there is your slave because in some battle he threw down his arms and let them bind his hands and lead him away and sell him, rather than take a spear-thrust in his heart. Much less does it give them understanding of holy things. They demand to see such things clearly, as if the gods were no more than letters written in a book. I, King, have dealt with the gods for three generations of men, and I know that they dazzle our eyes and flow in and out of one another like eddies on a river, and nothing that is said clearly can be said truly about them. Holy places are dark places. It is life and strength, not knowledge and words, that we get in them. Holy wisdom is not clear and thin like water, but thick and dark like blood. Why should the Accursed not be both the best and the worst?'

The Priest looked more and more like a gaunt bird as he was speaking; not unlike the bird-mask that lay on his knees. And his voice, though not loud, was no longer shaking like an old man's. The Fox sat hunched together with his eyes fixed on the table. The taunt about being taken in war, I guessed, had been hot iron to some old ulcer in his soul. Certainly, I would that moment have hanged the Priest and made the Fox a king if power had been given me; but it was easy to see on which side the strength lay.

'Well, well,' says the King, quickening his stride, 'this may be all very true. I'm neither priest nor Greekling, I. They used to tell me I was the King. What's next?'

'Being determined, therefore,' said the Priest, 'to seek out the Accursed, we cast the holy lots. First we asked whether the Accursed were to be found among the commons. And the lots said No.'

'Go on, go on,' said the King.

'I cannot speak quickly,' said the Priest. 'I have not breath for it now. Then we asked if it was among the Elders. And the lots said No.'

There was a queer mottled colour on the King's face now; his fear and his anger were just on the balance, and neither he nor anyone else knew at all which would have the victory.

'Then we asked if it were among the nobles. And the lots said No.'

'And then you asked?' says the King, stepping up close to him and speaking low. And the Priest says:

'Then we asked, Is it in the King's house? And the lots said Yes.'

'Aye,' says the King, rather breathless. 'Aye. I thought as much. I smelled it from the beginning. Treason in a new cloak. Treason.' Then louder, 'Treason.' Next moment he was at the door, roaring, 'Treason! Treason! Guards! Bardia! Where are my guards? Where's Bardia? Send Bardia.'

There was a rush and a jingle of iron and guards came running. Bardia their captain, a very honest man, came in.

'Bardia,' said the King, 'there are too many people about my door today. Take what men you think you need and fall on those rebels who are standing with spears out yonder over against the gate. Don't scatter them but kill. Kill, do you see? Don't leave one of them alive.'

'Kill the temple guards, King?' said Bardia, looking from the King to the Priest and back at the King again.

'Temple rats! Temple pimps!' shouted the King. 'Are you deaf? Are you afraid? I – I—' And his rage choked him.

'This is foolishness, King,' said the Priest. 'All Glome is in arms. There is a party of armed men at every door of the palace by now. Your guards are outnumbered ten to one. And they won't fight. Would you fight against Ungit, Bardia?'

'Will you slink away from my side, Bardia?' said the King. 'After eating my bread? You were glad of my shield to cover you one day at Varin's wood.'

'You saved my head that day, King,' said Bardia. 'I'll never say otherwise. May Ungit send me to do as much for you (there may be chance enough next spring). I'm for the King of Glome and the gods of Glome while I live. But if the King and the gods fall out, you great ones must settle it between you. I'll not fight against powers and spirits.'

'You – you girl!' squealed the King, his voice shrill as a pipe. Then, 'Be off! I'll talk with you presently.' Bardia saluted and went out; you could see from his face that he cared no more for the insult than a great dog cares for a puppy making believe to fight him.

The moment the door was shut, the King, all quiet and white again, whipped out his dagger (the same he killed the page with the night Psyche was born), stepped up to the Priest's chair in three long cat's strides, shouldered the two girls away, and had the point of the dagger through the Priest's robes and his skin.

'You old fool,' he said. 'Where is your plot now? Eh? Can you feel my bodkin? Does it tickle you? As that? Or that? I can drive it into your heart as quickly or slowly as I please. The wasps may be outside but I've the queen wasp here. And now, what'll you do?'

I have never (to speak of things merely mortal) seen anything more wonderful than the Priest's stillness. Hardly any man can be quite still when a finger, much less a dagger, is thrust into the place between two ribs. The Priest was. Even his hands did not tighten on the arms of the chair. Never moving his head or changing his voice, he said:

'Drive it in, King, swift or slow, if it pleases you. It will make no difference. Be sure the Great Offering will be made whether I am dead or living. I am here in the strength of Ungit. While I have breath I am Ungit's voice. Perhaps longer. A priest does not wholly die. I may visit your palace more often, both by day and night, if you kill me. The others will not see me. I think you will.'

This was the worst yet. The Fox had taught me to think – at any rate to speak – of the Priest as of a mere schemer and a politic man who put into the mouth of Ungit whatever might most increase his own power and lands or most harm his enemies. I saw it was not so. He was sure of Ungit. Looking at him as he sat with the dagger pricking him and his blind eyes unwinking, fixed on the King, and his face like an eagle's face, I was sure too. Our real enemy was not a mortal. The room was full of spirits, and the horror of holiness.

With a beastly noise, all groan and snarl in one, my father turned away from the Priest and flung himself into his own chair and leaned back and passed his hands over his face and ruffled his hair like a man who is tired.

'Go on. Finish it,' he said.

'And then,' said the Priest, 'we asked whether it was the King who was the Accursed, and the lots said No.'

'What?' said the King. And this is the greatest shame I have to tell of in my whole life. His face cleared. He was only a hair's breadth from smiling. I had thought that he had seen the arrow pointed at Psyche all along, had been afraid for her, fighting for her. He had not thought of her at all, nor of any of us. Yet I am credibly told that he was a brave enough man in a fight.

'Go on,' he said. But his voice was changed; freshened, as if ten years of his age had slipped off him.

'The lot fell on your youngest daughter, King. She is the Accursed. The Princess Istra must be the Great Offering.'

'It's very hard,' said the King; gravely and glum enough, but I saw he was acting. He was hiding the greatness of his own relief. I went mad. In a moment I was at his feet, clinging to his knees as suppliants cling, babbling out I didn't know what, weeping, begging, calling him Father – a name I never used before. I believe he was glad of the diversion. He tried to kick me away, and when I still clung to his feet, rolling over and over, bruised in face and breast, he rose, gathered me up by my shoulders, and flung me from him with all his power.

'You!' he shouted. 'You! You to raise your voice among the counsels of men? You trull, you quean, you mandrake root! Have I not woes and miseries and horrors enough heaped upon me by the gods but you also must come scrabbling and clawing me? and it would have come to biting in a trice if I'd let you. There's vixen in your face this minute. For two straws I'd have you to the guardhouse to be flogged. Name of Ungit! are gods and priests and lions and shadowbrutes and traitors and cowards not enough unless I'm plagued with girls as well?'

I think he felt better the longer he railed. The breath had been knocked out of me so that I could neither sob nor rise nor speak. Somewhere above my head I heard them talking on, making all the plans for Psyche's death. She was to be kept prisoner in her chamber – or no, better in the room with five sides, which was more secure. The temple guards would reinforce our own; the whole house must be guarded, for the people were weathercocks – there might be a change of mood, even a rescue. They were talking soberly and prudently like men providing for a journey or a feast. Then I lost myself in darkness and a roaring noise.

6

'She's coming to her mind again,' said my father's voice. 'Take that side of her, Fox, and we'll get her to the chair.' The two of them were lifting me; my father's hands were gentler than I expected. I have found since that a soldier's hands often are. The three of us were alone.

'Here, lass, this'll do you good,' he said when they had put me in the chair, holding a cup of wine to my lips. 'Faugh, you're spilling it like a baby. Take it easy. So; that's better. If there's a bit of raw meat still to be had in this dog-hole of a palace, you must lay it on your bruises. And look, daughter, you shouldn't have crossed me like that. A man can't have women (and his own daughters, what's worse) meddling in business.'

There was a sort of shame about him; whether for beating me or for giving up Psyche without a struggle, who knows? He seemed to me now a very vile, pitiable king.

He set down the cup. 'The thing has to be done,' he said. 'Screaming and scrabbling won't help. Why, the Fox here was just telling me it's done even in your darling Greeklands – which I begin to think I was a fool ever to let you hear of.'

'Master,' said the Fox, 'I had not finished telling you. It is very true that a Greek king sacrificed his own daughter. But afterwards his wife murdered him, and his son murdered the wife, and Those Below drove the son mad.'

At this the King scratched his head and looked very blank. 'That's just like the gods,' he muttered. 'Drive you to do a thing and then punish you for doing it. The comfort is I've no wife or son, Fox.'

I had got my voice again now. 'King,' I said, 'you can't mean to do it. Istra is your daughter. You can't do it. You have not even tried to save her. There must be some way. Surely between now and the day—'

'Listen to her!' says the King. 'You fool, it's tomorrow they offer her.'

I was within an inch of fainting again. To hear this was as bad as to hear that she must be offered at all. As bad? It was worse. I felt that I had had no sorrow till now. I felt that if she could be spared only for a month – a month, why, a month was like eternity – we should all be happy.

'It's better so, dear,' whispered the Fox to me in Greek. 'Better for her and for us.'

'What are you mumbling about, Fox?' said the King. 'You both look at me as if I were some sort of two-headed giant they frighten children with, but what'd you have me do? What would you do yourself, Fox, with all your cleverness, if you were in my place?'

'I'd fight about the day first. I'd get a little time somehow. I'd say the Princess was at the wrong time of the month to be a bride. I'd say I'd been warned in a dream not to make the Great Offering till the new moon. I'd bribe men to swear that the Priest had cheated over the lots. There's half a dozen men across the river who hold land from him and don't love their landlord. I'd make a party. Anything to gain time. Give me ten days and I'd have a secret messenger to the King of Phars. I'd offer him all he wants without war – offer him anything if he'd come in and save the Princess – offer him Glome itself and my own crown.'

'What?' snarled the King. 'Be a little less free with other men's wealth, you'd best.'

'But, Master, I'd lose not only my throne but my life to save the Princess, if I were a king and a father. Let us fight. Arm the slaves and promise them their freedom if they play the man. We can make a stand, we of your household, even now. At the worst, we should all die innocent. Better than going Down Yonder with a daughter's blood on your hands.'

The King flung himself once more into his chair and began speaking with a desperate patience, like a teacher to a very stupid child (I had seen the Fox do it with Redival).

'I am a King. I have asked you for counsel. Those who counsel kings commonly tell them how to strengthen or save their kingship and their land. That is what counselling a king means. And your counsel is that I should throw my crown over the roof, sell my country to Phars, and get my throat cut. You'll tell me next that the best way to cure a man's headache is to cut off his head.'

'I see, Master,' said the Fox. 'I ask your pardon. I had forgotten that your own safety was the thing we must work for at all costs.' I, who knew the Fox so well, could see such a look in his face that he could not have done the King much more dishonour if he had spat on him. Indeed I had often seen him look at the King like that, and the King never knew. I was determined he should know something now.

'King,' said I, 'the blood of the gods is in us. Can such a house as ours bear the shame? How will it sound if men say when you are dead that you took shelter behind a girl to save your own life?'

'You hear her, Fox, you hear her,' said the King. 'And then she wonders that I black her eyes! I'll not say mar her face, for that's impossible. Look, mistress, I'd be sorry to beat you twice in a day, but don't try me too far.' He leaped up and began pacing the floor again.

'Death and scabs!' he said. 'You'd make a man mad. Anyone'd think it was *your* daughter they were giving to the Brute. Sheltering behind a girl, you say. No one seems to remember whose girl she is. She's mine; fruit of my own body. My loss. It's I who have a right to rage and blubber if anyone has. What did I beget her for if I can't do what I think best with my own? What is it to you? There's some cursed cunning that I haven't yet smelled out behind all your sobbing and scolding. You're not asking me to believe that any woman, let alone such a fright as you, has much love for a pretty half-sister. It's not in nature. But I'll sift you yet.'

I don't know whether he really believed this or not, but it is possible he did. He could believe anything in his moods, and everyone in the palace knew more than he about the life of us girls.

'Yes,' he said, more quietly now. 'It's I who should be pitied. It's I who am asked to give up part of myself. But I'll do my duty. I'll not ruin the land to save my own girl. The pair of you have talked me into making too much work about it. It has happened before. I'm sorry for the girl. But the Priest's right. Ungit must have her due. What's one girl – why, what would one man be – against the safety of us all? It's only sense that one should die for many. It happens in every battle.'

Wine and passion had brought my strength back. I rose from my chair and found that I could stand.

'Father,' said I. 'You are right. It is fit that one should die for the people. Give me to the Brute instead of Istra.'

The King, without a word, came up to me, took me (softly enough) by the wrist and led me the whole length of the room, to where his great mirror hung. You might wonder that he did not keep it in his bedchamber, but the truth is he was too proud of it for that and wanted every stranger to see it. It had been made in some distant land and no king in our parts had one to match it. Our common mirrors were false and dull; in this you could see your perfect image. As I had never been in the Pillar Room alone, I had never looked in it. He stood me before it and we saw our two selves, side by side.

'Ungit asked for the best in the land as her son's bride,' he said. 'And you'd give her *that*.' He held me there a full minute in silence; perhaps he thought I would weep or turn my eyes away. At last he said, 'Now be off. A man can't keep pace with your moods today. Get the beefsteak for your face. The Fox and I must be busy.'

As I came out of the Pillar Room I first noticed the pain in my side; I had twisted myself somehow in my fall. But I forgot it again when I saw how, in that little time, our house had changed. It seemed crowded. All the slaves, whether they had anything to do or not, were walking about and gathering in knots, wearing looks of importance; chattering under their breath, too, with a sort of mournful cheerfulness. (They always will when there's great news in a house, and now it troubles me not at all.) There were many of the temple guard lounging in the porch; some temple girls sitting in the hall. From the courtyard came the smell of incense, and sacrifice was going on. Ungit had taken the house; the reek of holiness was everywhere.

At the foot of the staircase who should meet me but Redival, running to me all in tears, and a great babble pouring out of her mouth – 'Oh Sister, Sister, how dreadful! Oh, poor Psyche! It's only Psyche, isn't it? They're not going to do it to all of us, are they? I never thought – I didn't mean any harm – it wasn't I – and oh, oh, oh....'

I put my face close up to hers and said very low but distinctly, 'Redival: if there is one single hour when I am queen of Glome, or even mistress of this house, I'll hang you by the thumbs at a slow fire till you die.'

'Oh, cruel, cruel,' sobbed Redival. 'How can you say such things, and when I'm so miserable already? Sister, don't be angry, comfort me—'

I pushed her away from me and passed on. I had known Redival's tears ever since I could remember. They were not wholly feigned; nor much dearer than ditchwater. I know now, as I felt sure then, that she had carried tattle about Psyche to the house of Ungit, and that with malice. It's likely enough she meant less mischief than she had done (she never knew how much she meant) and was now, in her fashion, sorry; but a new brooch, much more a new lover, would have had her drying her eyes and laughing in no time.

As I came to the top of the stairs (for we have upper rooms and even galleries in the palace; it is not like a Greek house) I was a little out of breath and the pain in my side came on me worse. I seemed to be somewhat lame in one foot too. I went on with all the haste I could to that five-sided room where they had shut Psyche up. The door was bolted on the outside (I have used that room for a courteous prison myself) and an armed man stood before it. It was Bardia.

'Bardia,' I panted, 'let me in. I must see the Princess Istra.'

He looked at me kindly but shook his head. 'It can't be done, Lady,' he said.

'But, Bardia, you can lock us both in. There's no way out but the door.'

'That's how all escapes begin, Lady. I am sorry for you and for the other Princess, but it can't be done. I'm under the sternest orders.'

'Bardia,' I said, with tears, my left hand to my side (for the pain was bad now), 'It's her last night alive.'

He looked away from me and said again, 'I'm sorry.'

I turned from him without another word. Though his was the kindest face (always excepting the Fox) I had seen that day, for the moment I hated him more than my father or the Priest or even Redival. What I did next shows how near I was to madness. I went as fast as I could to the Bedchamber. I knew the King had arms there. I took a plain, good sword, drew it, looked at it, and weighed it in my hand. It was not at all too heavy for me. I felt the edges and the point; they were what I then thought sharp, though a smart soldier would not have called them so. Quickly I was back at Psyche's door. Even in my woman's rage I had man enough about me to cry out, 'Ward yourself, Bardia,' before I fell on him.

It was of course the craziest attempt for a girl who had never had a weapon in her hand before. Even if I had known my work, the lame foot and the pain in my side (to breathe deep was agony) disabled me. Yet I made him use some of his skill; chiefly, of course, because he was not fighting to hurt me. In a moment he had twisted my sword out of my grip. I stood before him, with my hand pressed harder than ever to my side, all in a muck sweat and a tremble. His brow was dry and his breathing unchanged; it had been as easy as that for him. The knowledge that I was so helpless came over me like a new woe, or gathered the other woe up into itself. I burst into utterly childish weeping; like Redival.

'It's a thousand pities, Lady, that you weren't a man,' said Bardia. 'You've a man's reach and a quick eye. There are none of the recruits would do as well at a first attempt; I'd like to have the training of you. It's a thousand—'

'Ah, Bardia, Bardia,' I sobbed, 'if only you'd killed me. I'd be out of my misery now.'

'No, you wouldn't,' said he. 'You'd be dying, not dead. It's only in tales that a man dies the moment the steel's gone in and come out. Unless of course you swap off his head.'

I could talk no more at all now. The whole world seemed to me to be in my weeping.

'Curse it,' said Bardia, 'I can't bear this.' There were tears in his own eyes now; he was a very tender man. 'I wouldn't mind so much if the one weren't so brave and the other so beautiful. Here! Lady! Stop it. I'll risk my life, and Ungit's wrath too.'

I gazed at him, but was still not able to speak.

'I'd give my own life for the girl in there, if it would do any good. You may have wondered why I, the captain of the guard, am standing here like a common sentry. I wouldn't let anyone else do it. I thought if the poor girl called, or if I had to go in to her for any reason, I'd be homelier for her than a stranger. She sat on my knees when she was little. ... I wonder do the gods know what it feels like to be a man.'

'You'll let me in?' I said.

'On one condition, Lady. You must swear to come out when I knock. It's quiet up here now, but there'll be comings and goings later. There'll be two temple girls coming to her presently; I was warned of that. I'll give you as long as I can. But I must be sure of your coming out when I give the sign. Three knocks – like this.'

'I'll come out at once when you do that.'

'Swear it, Lady; here on my sword.'

I swore it. He looked to left and right, did back the bolt, and said, 'Quick. In you go. Heaven comfort you both.'

7

The window in that room is so small and high up that men need lights there at noon. That is why it can serve as a prison; it was built as the second story of a tower which my great-grandfather began and never finished.

Psyche sat upon the bed with a lamp burning beside her. Of course I was at once in her arms and saw this only in a flash; but the picture – Psyche, a bed, and a lamp – is everlasting.

Long before I could speak she said, 'Sister, what have they done to you? Your face, your eye! He has been beating you again.' Then I realised somewhat slowly that all this time she had been petting and comforting me as if it were I who was the child and the victim. And this, even in the midst of the great anguish, made its own little eddy of pain. It was so unlike the sort of love that used to be between us in our happy times.

She was so quick and tender that she knew at once what I was thinking, and at once she called me *Maia*, the old baby's name that the Fox had taught her. It was one of the first words she ever learned to say.

'Maia, Maia, tell me. What has he done to you?'

'Oh, Psyche,' said I, 'what does it matter? If only he had killed me! If only they would take me instead of you!'

But she would not be put off. She forced the whole tale out of me (how could one deny her?) wasting on it the little time we had.

'Sister, no more,' I said at last. 'What is it to me? What is he to either of us? I'll not shame your mother or mine to say he's not our father. If so, the name *father* is a curse. I'll believe now that he would hide behind a woman in a battle.'

And then (it was a kind of terror to me) she smiled. She had wept very little, and mostly, I think, for love and pity of me. Now she sat tall and queenly and still. There was no sign about her of coming death, except that her hands were very cold.

'Orual,' she said, 'you make me think I have learned the Fox's lessons better than you. Have you forgotten what we are to say to ourselves every morning? "Today I shall meet cruel men, cowards and liars, the envious and the drunken. They will be like that because they do not know what is good from what is bad. This is an evil which has fallen upon them not upon me. They are to be pitied, not—"' She was speaking with a loving mimicry of the Fox's voice; she could do this as well as Batta did it badly.

'Oh child, how can—' But I was choked again. All she was saying seemed to me so light, so far away from our sorrow. I felt we ought not to be talking that way, not now. What I thought it would be better to talk of, I did not know.

'Maia,' said Psyche. 'You must make me a promise. You'll not do anything outrageous? You'll not kill yourself? You mustn't, for the Fox's sake. We have been three loving friends.' (Why must she say bare *friends*?) 'Now it's only he and you; you must hold together and stand the closer. No, Maia, you must. Like soldiers in a hard battle.'

'Oh, your heart is of iron,' I said.

'As for the King, give him my duty – or whatever is proper. Bardia is a prudent and courteous man. He'll tell you what dying girls ought to say to fathers. One would not seem rude or ignorant at the last. But I can send the King no other message. The man is a stranger to me; I know the henwife's baby better than him. And for Redival—'

'Send her your curse. And if the dead can—'

'No, no. She also does what she doesn't know.'

'Not even for you, Psyche, will I pity Redival, whatever the Fox says.'

'Would you like to be Redival? What? No? Then she's pitiable. If I am allowed to give my jewels as I please, you must keep all the things that you and I have really loved. Let her have all that's big and costly and doesn't matter. You and the Fox take what you please.'

I could bear no more for a while, so I laid my head down in her lap and wept. If only she would so have laid her head in mine!

'Look up, Maia,' she said presently. 'You'll break my heart, and I to be a bride.' She could bear to say that. I could not bear to hear it.

'Orual,' she said, very softly, 'we are the blood of the gods. We must not shame our lineage. Maia, it was you who taught me not to cry when I fell.'

'I believe you are not afraid at all,' said I; almost, though I had not meant it to sound so, as if I were rebuking her for it.

'Only of one thing,' she said. 'There is a cold doubt, a horrid shadow, in some corner of my soul. Supposing – supposing – how if there were no god of the Mountain and even no holy Shadowbrute, and those who are tied to the tree only die, day by day, from thirst and hunger and wind and sun, or are eaten piecemeal by the crows and catamountains? And it is this – oh, Maia, Maia …'

And now she did weep and now she was a child again. What could I do but fondle and weep with her? But this is a great shame to write; there was now (for me) a kind of sweetness in our misery for the first time. This was what I had come to her in her prison to do.

She recovered before I did. She raised her head, queenlike again, and said, 'But I'll not believe it. The Priest has been with me. I never knew him before. He is not what the Fox thinks. Do you know, Sister, I have come to feel more and more that the Fox hasn't the whole truth. Oh, he has much of it. It'd be dark as a dungeon within me but for his teaching. And yet ... I can't say it properly. He calls the whole world a city. But what's a city built on? There's earth beneath. And outside the wall? Doesn't all the food come from there as well as all the dangers? ... things growing and rotting, strengthening and poisoning, things shining wet ... in one way (I don't know which way) more like, yes, even more like the House of—'

'Yes, of Ungit,' said I. 'Doesn't the whole land smell of her? Do you and I need to flatter gods any more? They're tearing us apart ... oh, how shall I bear it? ... and what worse can they do? Of course the Fox is wrong. He knows nothing about her. He thought too well of the world. He thought there were no gods, or else (the fool!) that they were better than men. It never entered his mind – he was too good – to believe that the gods are real, and viler than the vilest man.'

'Or else,' said Psyche, 'they are real gods but don't really do these things. Or even – mightn't it be – they do these things and the things are not what they seem to be? How if I am indeed to wed a god?'

She made me, in a way, angry. I would have died for her (this, at least, I know is true) and yet, the night before her death, I could feel anger. She spoke so steadily and thoughtfully; as if we had been disputing with the Fox, up behind the pear trees, with hours and days still before us. The parting between her and me seemed to cost her so little.

'Oh, Psyche,' I said, almost in a shriek, 'what can these things be except the cowardly murder they seem? To take you – you whom they have worshipped and who never hurt so much as a toad – to make you food for a monster ...'

You will say – I have said it many thousand times to myself – that, if I saw in her any readiness to dwell on the better part of the Priest's talk and to think she would be a god's bride more than a Brute's prey, I ought to have fallen in with her and encouraged it. Had I not come to her to give comfort, if I could? Surely not to take it away. But I could not rule myself. Perhaps it was a sort of pride in me, a little like her own; not to blind our eyes, not to hide terrible things; or a bitter impulse in anguish itself to say, and to keep on saying, the worst.

'I see,' said Psyche in a low voice. 'You think it devours the offering. I mostly think so myself. Anyway, it means death. Orual, you didn't think I was such a child as not to know that? How can I be the ransom for all Glome unless I die? And if I am to go to the god, of course it must be through death. That way, even what is strangest in the holy sayings might be true. To be eaten and to be married to the god might not be so different. We don't understand. There must be so much that neither the Priest nor the Fox knows.'

This time I bit my lip and said nothing. Unspeakable foulness seethed in my mind; did she think the Brute's lust better than its hunger? To be mated with a worm, or a giant eft, or a spectre?

'And as for death,' she said, 'why, Bardia there (I love Bardia) will look on it six times a day and whistle a tune as he goes to find it. We have made little use of the Fox's teaching if we're to be scared by death. And you know, Sister, he has sometimes let out that there were other Greek masters than those he follows himself; masters who have taught that death opens a door out of a little, dark room (that's all the life we have known before it) into a great, real place where the true sun shines and we shall meet—'

'Oh, cruel, cruel!' I wailed. 'Is it nothing to you that you leave me here alone? Psyche; did you ever love me at all?'

'Love you? Why, Maia, what have I ever had to love save you and our grandfather the Fox?' (But I did not want her to bring even the Fox in now.) 'But, Sister, you will follow me soon. You don't think any mortal life seems a long thing to me tonight? And how would it be better if I had lived? I suppose I should have been given to some king in the end; perhaps such another as our father. And there you can see again how little difference there is between dying and being married. To leave your home – to lose you, Maia, and the Fox – to lose one's maidenhead – to bear a child – they are all deaths. Indeed, indeed, Orual, I am not sure that this which I go to is not the best.'

'This!'

'Yes. What had I to look for if I lived? Is the world – this palace, this father – so much to lose? We have already had what would have been the best of our time. I must tell you something, Orual, which I never told to anyone, not even you.'

I know now that this must be so even between the lovingest hearts. But her saying it that night was like stabbing me.

'What is it?' said I, looking down at her lap where our four hands were joined.

'This,' she said, 'I have always – at least, ever since I can remember – had a kind of longing for death.'

'Ah, Psyche,' I said, 'have I made you so little happy as that?'

'No, no, no,' she said. 'You don't understand. Not that kind of longing. It was when I was happiest that I longed most. It was on happy days when we were up there on the hills, the three of us, with the wind and the sunshine ... where you couldn't see Glome or the palace. Do you remember? The colour and the smell, and looking across at the Grey Mountain in the distance? And because it was so beautiful, it set me longing, always longing. Somewhere else there must be more of it. Everything seemed to be saying, Psyche come! But I couldn't (not yet) come and I didn't know where I was to come to. It almost hurt me. I felt like a bird in a cage when the other birds of its kind are flying home.'

She kissed both my hands, flung them free, and stood up. She had her father's trick of walking to and fro when she talked of something that moved her. And from now till the end I felt (and this horribly) that I was losing her already, that the sacrifice tomorrow would only finish something that had already begun. She was (how long had she been, and I not to know?) out of my reach; in some place of her own.

Since I write this book against the gods, it is just that I should put into it whatever can be said against myself. So let me set this down; as she spoke I felt, amid all my love, a bitterness. Though the things she was saying gave her (that was plain enough) courage and comfort, I grudged her that courage and comfort. It was as if someone or something else had come in between us. If this grudging is the sin for which the gods hate me, it is one I have committed.

'Orual,' she said, her eyes shining. 'I am going, you see, to the Mountain. You remember how we used to look and long? And all the stories of my gold and amber house, up there against the sky, where we thought we should never really go? The greatest King of all was going to build it for me. If only you could believe it, Sister! No, listen. Do not let grief shut up your ears and harden your heart—'

'Is it *my* heart that is hardened?'

'Never to me; nor mine to you at all. But listen. Are these things so evil as they seemed? The gods will have mortal blood. But they say whose. If they had chosen any other in the land, that would have been only terror and cruel misery. But they chose me. And I am the one who has been made ready for it ever since I was a little child in your arms, Maia. The sweetest thing in all my life has been the longing – to reach the Mountain, to find the place where all the beauty came from—'

'And that was the sweetest? Oh, cruel, cruel. Your heart is not of iron; stone, rather,' I sobbed. I don't think she even heard me.

'— my country, the place where I ought to have been born. Do you think it all meant nothing, all the longing? The longing for home? For indeed it now feels not like going, but like going back. All my life the god of the Mountain has been wooing me. Oh, look up once at least before the end and wish me joy. I am going to my lover. Do you not see now—?'

'I only see that you have never loved me,' said I. 'It may well be you are going to the gods. You are becoming cruel like them.'

'Oh, Maia!' cried Psyche, tears at last coming into her eyes again. 'Maia, I—'

Bardia knocked on the door. No time for better words, no time to unsay anything. Bardia knocked again, and louder. My oath on his sword, itself like a sword, was upon us.

So, the last, spoiled embrace. Those are happy who have no such in their memory. For those who have – would they endure that I should write of it?

8

As soon as I was out in the gallery my pains, which I had not perceived while I was with Psyche, came strongly back upon me. My grief, even, was deadened for a while, though my wits became very sharp and clear. I was determined to go with Psyche to the Mountain and the Holy Tree, unless they bound me with chains. I even thought I might hide up there and set her free when the Priest and the King and all the rest had turned to come home. 'Or if there is a real Shadowbrute,' I thought, 'and I cannot save her from it, I'll kill her with my own hand before I'll leave her to its clutches.' To do all this I knew I must eat and drink and rest. (It was now nearly twilight and I was still fasting.) But first of all I must find out when their murder, their Offering, was to be. So I limped, holding my side, along the gallery and found an old slave, the King's butler, who was able to tell me all. The procession, he said, was to leave the palace an hour before sunrise. Then I went to my own chamber and told my women to bring me food. I sat down to wait till it came. A great dullness and heaviness crept over me; I thought and felt nothing, except that I was very cold. When the food came I could not eat, though I tried to force myself to it; it was like putting cloth in my mouth. But I drank; a little of the small beer which was all they had to give me, and then (for my stomach rose against the beer) a great deal of water. I must have been almost sleeping before I finished, for I remember that I knew I was in some great sorrow but I could not recall what it was.

They lifted me into the bed (I shrank and cried out a little at their touch) and I fell at once into a dead stupidity of sleep; so that it seemed only a heartbeat later that they were waking me – two hours before sunrise, as I had bidden them. I woke screaming, for all my sore places had stiffened while I slept and it was like hot pincers when I tried to move. One eye had closed up so that I might as well have been blind on that side. When they found how much they hurt me in raising me from the bed, they begged me to lie still. Some said it was useless for me to rise, for the King had said that neither of the Princesses should go to the Offering. One asked if she should bring Batta to me. I told that one, with bitter words, to hold her tongue, and if I had had the strength I would have hit her; which would have been ill done, for she was a good girl. (I have always been fortunate with my women since first I had them to myself and out of the reach of Batta's meddling.)

They dressed me somehow and tried to make me eat. One even had a little wine for me; stolen, I guess, from a flagon intended for the King. They were all weeping; I was not.

Dressing me (so sore I was) had taken a great time, so that I had hardly swallowed the wine before we heard the music beginning: temple music, Ungit's music, the drums and the horns and rattles and castanets, all holy, deadly; dark, detestable, maddening noises.

'Quick!' said I. 'It's time. They're going. Oh, I can't get up. Help me, girls. No, quicker! Drag me, if need be. Take no heed of my groaning and screaming.'

They got me with great torture as far as the head of the staircase. I could now see down into the great hall between the Pillar Room and the Bedchamber. It was ablaze with torches, and very crowded. There were many guards. There were some girls of noble blood veiled and chapleted like a bride's party. My father was there in very splendid robes. And there was a great bird-headed man. By the smell and the smoke there seemed to have been much killing already, at the altar in the courtyard. (Food for the gods must always be found somehow, even when the land starves.) The great gateway was opened. I could see cold, early twilight through it. Outside, priests and girls were singing. There must have been a great mob of the rabble too; in the pauses you could hear (who can mistake it?) their noise. No herd of other beasts, gathered together, has so ugly a voice as Man.

For a long time I could not see Psyche at all. The gods are cleverer than we and can always think of some vileness it never entered our heads to fear. When at last I saw her, that was the worst of all. She sat upright on an open litter between the King and the Priest. The reason I had not known her was that they had painted and gilded and be-wigged her like a temple girl. I could not even tell whether she saw me or not. Her eyes, peering out of the heavy, lifeless mask which they had made of her face, were utterly strange; you couldn't even see in what direction she was looking.

It is, in its way, admirable, this divine skill. It was not enough for the gods to kill her, they must make her father the murderer. It was not enough to take her from me, they must take her from me three times over, tear out my heart three times. First her sentence; then her strange, cold talk last night; and now this painted and gilded horror to poison my last sight of her. Ungit had taken the most beautiful thing that was ever born and made it into an ugly doll.

They told me afterwards that I tried to start going down the stairway, and fell. They carried me to my bed.

For many days after that I was sick, and most of them I do not remember. I was not in my right mind, and slept (they tell me) not at all. My ravings – what I can recall of them – were a ceaseless torture of tangled diversity, yet also of sameness. Everything changed into something else before you could understand it, yet the new thing always stabbed you in the very same place. One thread ran through all the delusions. Now mark yet again the cruelty of the gods. There is no escape from them into sleep or madness, for they can pursue you into them with dreams. Indeed you are then most at their mercy. The nearest thing we have to a defence against them (but there is no real defence) is to be very wide awake and sober and hard at work, to hear no music, never to look at earth or sky, and (above all) to love no one. And now, finding me heart-shattered for Psyche's sake, they made it the common burden of all my fantasies that Psyche was my greatest enemy. All my sense of intolerable wrong was directed against her. It was she who hated me; it was on her that I wanted to be revenged. Sometimes she and Redival and I were all children together, and then Psyche and Redival would drive me away and put me out of the game and stand with their arms linked laughing at me. Sometimes I was beautiful and had a lover who looked (absurdly) a little like poor, eunuch'd Tarin or a little like Bardia (I suppose because his was the last man's face, almost, that I had seen before I fell ill). But on the very threshold of the bridal chamber, or from the very bedside, Psyche, wigged and masked and no bigger than my forearm, would lead him away with one finger. And when they got to the door they would turn round and mock and point at me. But these were the clearest visions. More often it was all confused and dim – Psyche throwing me down high precipices, Psyche (now very like the King, but still Psyche) kicking me and dragging me by the hair, Psyche with a torch or a sword or a whip pursuing me over vast swamps and dark mountains; I running to save my life. But always wrong, hatred, mockery, and my determination to be avenged.

The beginning of my recovery was when the visions ceased and left behind them only a settled sense of some great injury that Psyche had done me, though I could not gather my wits to think what it was. They say I lay for hours saying, 'Cruel girl. Cruel Psyche. Her heart is of stone.' And soon I was in my right mind again and knew how I loved her and that she had never willingly done me any wrong; though it hurt me somewhat that she should have found time, at our last meeting of all, talking so little of me, to talk so much about the god of the Mountain, and the King, and the Fox, and Redival, and even Bardia.

Soon after that I was aware of a pleasant noise that had already been going on a long time.

'What is it?' I asked (and was astonished at the weak croak of my voice).

'What is what, child?' said the voice of the Fox; and I knew somehow that he had been sitting by my bed for many hours.

'The noise, Grandfather. Above our heads.'

'That is the rain, dear,' he said. 'Give thanks to Zeus for that and for your own recovery. And I – but you must sleep again. And drink this first.' I saw the tears on his face as he gave me the cup.

I had no broken bones, the bruises were gone, and my other pains with them. But I was very weak. Weakness, and work, are two comforts the gods have not taken from us. I'd not write it (it might move them to take these also away) except that they must know it already. I was too weak now to feel much grief or anger. These days, before my strength came back, were almost happy. The Fox was very loving and tender (and much weakened himself) and so were my women. I was loved; more than I had thought. And my sleeps were sweet now and there was much rain and, between-whiles, the kind south wind blowing in at the window; and sunshine. For a long time we never spoke of Psyche. We talked, when we talked at all, of common things.

They had much to tell me. The weather had changed the very day after my sickness began. The Shennit was full again. The breaking of the drought had come too late to save the crops (for the most part; one or two fields put up a little) but garden stuff was growing. Above all, the grass was reviving wonderfully; we should save far more of the cattle than we had hoped. And the fever was clean gone. My own sickness had been of another kind. And birds were coming back to Glome, so that every woman whose husband could shoot with a bow or set a snare might soon have something in the pot.

These things I heard of from the women as well as from the Fox. When we were alone he told me other news. My father was now, while it lasted, the darling of his people. It seemed (this was how we first came round to the matter nearest our hearts) he had been much pitied and praised at the Great Offering. Up there at the holy Tree he had wailed and wept and torn his robes and embraced Psyche countless times (he had never done it before) but said again and again that he would not withhold his heart's dearest when the good of the people called for her death. The whole crowd was in tears, as the Fox had been told; he himself, as a slave and an alien, had not been there.

'Did you know, Grandfather,' said I, 'that the King was such a mountebank?' (We were talking in Greek of course.)

'Not wholly that, child,' said the Fox. 'He believed it while he did it. His tears are no falser – or truer – than Redival's.'

Then he went on to tell me of the great news from Phars. A fool in the crowd had said the King of Phars had thirteen sons. The truth is he had begotten eight, whereof one died in childhood. The eldest was simple and could never rule, and the King (as some said their laws allowed him) had named Argan, the third, as his successor. And now, it seemed, his second son, Trunia, taking it ill to be put out of the succession – and, doubtless, fomenting some other discontents such as are never far to seek in any land –

had risen in rebellion, with a strong following, to recover what he called his right. The upshot was that all Phars was likely to be busy with civil war for a twelvemonth at least, and both parties were already as soft as butter towards Glome, so that we were safe from any threat in that quarter.

A few days later when the Fox was with me (often he could not be, for the King needed him) I said:

'Grandfather, do you still think that Ungit is only lies of poets and priests?'

'Why not, child?'

'If she were indeed a goddess what more could have followed my poor sister's death than has followed it? All the dangers and plagues that hung over us have been scattered. Why, the wind must have changed the very day after they had—' I found, now, I could not give it a name. The grief was coming back with my strength. So was the Fox's.

'Cursed chance, cursed chance,' he muttered, his face all screwed up, partly in anger and partly to keep back his tears (Greek men cry easily as women). 'It is these chances that nourish the beliefs of barbarians.'

'How often, Grandfather, you have told me there's no such thing as chance?'

'You're right. It was an old trick of the tongue. I meant that all these things had no more to do with that murder than with anything else. They and it are all part of the same web, which is called Nature, or the Whole. That south-west wind came over a thousand miles of sea and land. The weather of the whole world would have to have been different from the beginning if that wind was not to blow. It's all one web; you can't pick threads out nor put them in.'

'And so,' said I, raising myself on my elbow, 'she died to no purpose. If the King had waited a few days later we could have saved her, for all would have begun to go well of itself. And this you call comfort?'

'Not this. Their evil-doing was vain and ignorant, as all evil deeds are. This is our comfort, that the evil was theirs, not hers. They say there was not a tear in her eye, nor did so much as her hand shake, when they put her to the Tree. Not even when they turned away and left her did she cry out. She died full of all things that are really good; courage, and patience, and – and – Aiai! Aiai – oh Psyche, oh my little one—' Then his love got the better of his philosophy and he pulled his mantle over his head and at last, still weeping, left me.

Next day he said, 'You saw yesterday, Daughter, how little progress I have made. I began to philosophise too late. You are younger and can go further. To love, and to lose what we love, are equally things appointed for our nature. If we cannot bear the second well, that evil is ours. It did not befall Psyche. If we look at it with reason's eyes and not with our passions, what good that life offers did she not win? Chastity, temperance, prudence, meekness, clemency, valour – and, though fame is froth, yet, if we should reckon it at all, a name that stands with Iphigenia's and Antigone's.'

Of course he had long since told me those stories, so often that I had them by heart, mostly in the very words of the poets. Nevertheless, I asked him to tell me them again; chiefly for his sake, for I was now old enough to know that a man (above all, a Greek man) can find comfort in words coming out of his own mouth. But I was glad to hear them too. These were peaceful, familiar things and would keep at bay the great desolation which now, with my returning health, was beginning to mix itself in every thought.

Next day, being then for the first time risen, I said to him, 'Grandfather, I have missed being Iphigenia. I can be Antigone.'

'Antigone? How, child?'

'She gave her brother burial. I too – there may be something left. Even the Brute would not eat bones and all. I must go up to the Tree. I will bring it ... them ... back if I can and burn them rightly. Or, if there's too much, I'll bury it up there.'

'It would be pious,' said the Fox. 'It would accord with custom, if not with Nature. If you can. It's late in the year now for going up the Mountain.'

'That's why it must be done speedily. I think it will be about five-and-twenty days before the earliest snow.'

'If you can, child. You have been very sick.'

'It's all I can do,' said I.

9

I was soon able to go about the house and in the gardens again. I did it in some stealth, for the Fox told the King I was still sick. Otherwise he would have had me off to the Pillar Room to work for him. He often asked, 'Where's that girl got to? Does she mean to slug abed for the rest of her life? I'll not feed drones in my hive for ever.' The loss of Psyche had not at all softened him to Redival and me. Rather, the opposite. 'To hear him talk,' said the Fox, 'you'd think no father ever loved a child better than he Psyche.' The gods had taken his darling and left him the dross: the young whore (that was Redival) and the hobgoblin (which was I). But I could guess it all without the Fox's reports to help me.

For my own part, I was busily thinking out how I could make my journey to the Tree on the Mountain and gather whatever might remain of Psyche. I had talked lightly enough of doing this and was determined that I would do it, but the difficulties were very great. I had never been taught to ride any beast, so I must go on foot. I knew it would take a man who knew the way about six hours to go from the palace to the Tree. I, a woman, and one who had to find her way, must allow myself eight at the least. And two more for the work I went to do; and, say, six for the journey home. There were sixteen hours in all. It could not be done in one stitch. I must reckon to lie out a night on the Mountain, and must take food (water I should find) and warm clothing. It could not be done till I recovered my full strength.

And in truth (as I now see) I had the wish to put off my journey as long as I could. Not for any peril or labour it might cost; but because I could see nothing in the whole world for me to do once it was accomplished. As long as this act lay before me, there was, as it were, some barrier between me and the dead desert which the rest of my life must be. Once I had gathered Psyche's bones, then, it seemed, all that concerned her would be over and done with. Already, even with the great act still ahead, there was flowing in upon me, from the barren years beyond it, a dejection such as I had never conceived. It was not at all like the agonies I had endured before and have endured since. I did not weep nor wring my hands. I was like water put into a bottle and left in a cellar; utterly motionless, never to be drunk, poured out, spilled or shaken. The days were endless. The very shadows seemed nailed to the ground, as if the sun no longer moved.

One day when this deadness was at its worst I came into the house by the little door that leads into a narrow passage between the guards' quarters and the dairy. I sat down on the threshold, less weary of body (for the gods, not out of mercy, have made me strong) than unable to find a reason for going a step further in any direction or for doing anything at all. A fat fly was crawling up the doorpost. I remember thinking that its sluggish crawling, seemingly without aim, was like my life, or even the life of the whole world. 'Lady,' said a voice behind me. I looked up; it was Bardia.

'Lady,' he said, 'I'll make free with you. I've known sorrow too. I have been as you are now; I have sat and felt the hours drawn out to the length of years. What cured me was the wars. I don't think there's any other cure.'

'But I can't go to the wars, Bardia,' said I.

'You can, almost,' he said. 'When you fought me outside the other Princess's door (peace be on her, the Blessed!) I told you you had a good eye and a good reach. You thought I was saying it to cheer you. Well, so perhaps I was. But it was true too. There's no one in the quarters, and there are blunt swords. Come in and let me give you a lesson.'

'No,' said I dully. 'I don't want to. What would be the use?'

'Use? Try it and see. No one can be sad while they're using wrist and hand and eye and every muscle of their body. That's truth, Lady, whether you believe it or not. As well, it would be a hundred shames not to train anyone who has such a gift for the sport as you look like having.'

'No,' said I. 'Leave me alone. Unless we can use sharps and you would kill me.'

'That's women's talk, by your favour. You'd never say that again once you'd seen it done. Come. I'll not leave off till you do.'

A big, kindly man, some years older than herself, can usually persuade even a sad and sullen girl. In the end I rose and went in with him.

'That shield is too heavy,' he said. 'Here's the one for you. Slip it on, thus. And understand from the outset; your shield is a weapon, not a wall. You're fighting with it every bit as much as your sword. Watch me, now. You see the way I twist my shield – make it flicker like a butterfly. There'd be arrows and spears and sword points flying off it in every direction if we were in a hot engagement. Now: here's your sword. No, not like that. You want to grip it firm, but light. It's not a wild animal that's trying to run away from you. That's better. Now, your left foot forward. And don't look at my face, look at my sword. It isn't my face is going to fight you. And now, I'll show you a few guards.'

He kept me at it for a full half-hour. It was the hardest work I'd ever done, and, while it lasted, one could think of nothing else. I said not long before that work and weakness are comforters. But sweat is the kindest creature of the three; far better than philosophy, as a cure for ill thoughts.

'That's enough,' said Bardia. 'You shape very well. I'm sure now I can make a swordsman of you. You'll come again tomorrow? But your dress hampers you. It would be better if you could wear something that came only to your knee.'

I was in such a heat that I went across the passage into the dairy and drank a bowl of milk. It was the first food or drink that I had really relished ever since the bad times began. While I was in there, one of the other soldiers (I suppose he had had a sight of what we were doing) came into the passage and said something to Bardia. Bardia replied, I couldn't hear what. Then he spoke louder: 'Why, yes, it's a pity about her face. But she's a brave girl and honest. If a man was blind and she weren't the King's daughter, she'd make him a good wife.' And that is the nearest thing to a love-speech that was ever made me.

I had my lesson with Bardia every day after that. And I knew soon that he had been a good doctor to me. My grief remained, but the numbness was gone and time moved at its right pace again.

Soon I told Bardia how I wished to go to the Grey Mountain, and why.

'That's very well thought of, Lady,' he said. 'I'm ashamed I have not done it myself. We all owe the Blessed Princess that much at the least. But there's no need for you to go. I'll go for you.'

I said I would go.

'Then you must go with me,' he said. 'You'd never find the place by yourself. And you might meet a bear or wolves or a mountainy man, an outlaw, that'd be worse. Can you ride a horse, Lady?'

'No, I've never been taught.'

He wrinkled up his brow, thinking. 'One horse will do,' he said, 'I in the saddle and you behind me. And it won't take six hours getting up; there's a shorter way. But the work we have to do might take long enough. We'll need to sleep a night on the mountain.'

'Will the King let you be absent so long, Bardia?'

He chuckled. 'Oh, I'll spin the King a story easily enough. He isn't with us as he is with you, Lady. For all his hard words he's no bad master to soldiers, shepherds, huntsmen, and the like. He understands them and they him. You see him at his worst with women and priests and politic men. The truth is, he's half afraid of them.' This was very strange to me.

Six days after that, I and Bardia set out at the milking-time of the morning, the day being so cloudy that it was almost as dark as full night. No one in the palace knew of our going except the Fox and my own women. I had on a plain black cloak with a hood, and a veil over my face. Under the mantle I wore the short smock that I used for my fencing bouts, with a man's belt and a sword, this time a sharp one, at my side. 'Most likely we'll meet nothing worse than a wild cat or a fox,' Bardia had said. 'But no one, man or maid, ought to go weaponless up the hills.' I sat with both my legs on one side of the horse, and a hand on Bardia's girdle. With the other, I held on my knees an urn.

It was all silent in the city, but for the clatter of our own beast's hooves, though here and there you would see a light in a window. A sharp rain came on us from behind our backs as we went down from the city to the ford of the Shennit, but it ceased as we were crossing the water, and the clouds began to break. There was still no sign of dawn ahead, for it was in that direction the foul weather was packing off.

We passed the house of Ungit on our right. Its fashion is thus: great, ancient stones, twice the height of a man and four times the thickness of a man, set upright in an egg-shaped ring. These are very ancient, and no one knows who set them up or brought them into that place, or how. In between the stones it is filled up with brick to make the wall complete. The roof is thatched with rushes and not level but somewhat domed, so that the whole thing is a roundish hump, most like a huge slug lying on the field. This is a holy shape, and the priests say it resembles, or (in a mystery) that it really is, the egg from which the whole world was hatched or the womb in which the whole world once lay. Every spring the Priest is shut into it and fights, or makes believe to fight, his way out through the western door; and this means that the new year is born. There was smoke going up from it as we passed, for the fire before Ungit is always alight.

I found my mood changed as soon as we had left Ungit behind; partly because we were now going into country I had never known, and partly because I felt as if the air were sweeter as we got away from all that holiness. The Mountain, now bigger ahead of us, still shut out the brightening of the day; but when I looked back and saw, beyond the city, those hills where Psyche and I and the Fox used to wander, I perceived that it was already morning there. And further off still, the clouds in the western sky were beginning to turn pale rose.

We were going up and down little hills, but always more up than down, on a good enough road, with grass-lands on each side of us. There were dark woods on our left, and presently the road bent towards them. But here Bardia left the road and took to the grass.

'That's the Holy Road,' he said, pointing to the woods. 'That's the way they took the Blessed (peace be on her). Our way will be steeper and shorter.'

We now went for a long time over grass, gently but steadily upward, making for a ridge so high and so near that the true Mountain was quite out of sight. When we topped it, and stood for a while to let the horse breathe, everything was changed. And my struggle began.

We had come into the sunlight now, too bright to look into, and warm (I threw back my cloak). Heavy dew made the grass jewel-bright. The Mountain, far greater yet also far further off than I expected, seen with the sun hanging a hand-breath above its topmost crags, did not look like a solid thing. Between us and it was a vast tumble of valley and hill, woods and cliffs, more little lakes than I could count. To left and right, and behind us, the whole coloured world with all its hills was heaped up and up to the sky, with, far away, a gleam of what we call the sea (though it is not to be compared with the Great Sea of the Greeks). There was a lark singing; but for that, huge and ancient stillness.

And my struggle was this. You may well believe that I had set out sad enough; I came on a sad errand. Now, flung at me like frolic or insolence, there came as if it were a voice – no words, but if you made it into words it would be, 'Why should your heart not dance?' It's the measure of my folly that my heart almost answered, Why not? I had to tell myself over like a lesson the infinite reasons it had not to dance. My heart to dance? Mine whose love was taken from me, I, the ugly princess who must never look for other love, the drudge of the King, the jailer of hateful Redival, perhaps to be murdered or turned out as a beggar when my father died (for who knew what Glome would do then?). And yet, it was a lesson I could hardly keep in my mind. The sight of the huge world put mad ideas into me; as if I could wander away, wander for ever, see strange and beautiful things, one after the other to the world's end.

The freshness and wetness all about me (I had seen nothing but drought and withered things for many months before my sickness) made me feel that I had misjudged the world; it seemed kind, and laughing, as if its heart also danced. Even my ugliness I could not quite believe in. Who can *feel* ugly when the heart meets delight? It is as if, somewhere inside, within the hideous face and bony limbs, one is soft, fresh, lissom and desirable.

We had stood on the ridge only for a short time. But for hours later, while we went up and down, winding among great hills, often dismounting and leading the horse, sometimes on dangerous edges, the struggle went on.

Was I not right to struggle against this fool-happy mood? Mere seemliness, if nothing else, called for it. I would not go laughing to Psyche's burial. If I did, how should I ever again believe that I had loved her? Reason called for it. I knew the world too well to believe this sudden smiling. What woman can have patience with the man who can be yet again deceived by his doxy's fawning after he has thrice proved her false? I should be just like such a man if a mere burst of fair weather, and fresh grass after a long drought, and health after sickness, could make me friends again with this god-haunted, plague-breeding, decaying, tyrannous world. I had seen. I was not a fool. I did not know then, however, as I do now, the strongest reason for distrust. The gods never send us this invitation to delight so readily or so strongly as when they are preparing some new agony. We are their bubbles; they blow us big before they prick us.

But I held my own without that knowledge. I ruled myself. Did they think I was nothing but a pipe to be played on as their moment's fancy chose?

The struggle ended when we topped the last rise before the real Mountain. We were so high now that, though the sun was very strong, the wind blew bitterly cold. At our feet, between us and the Mountain, lay a cursed black valley: dark moss, dark peat-bogs, shingle, great boulders, and screes of stone sprawling down into it from the Mountain – as if the Mountain had sores and these were the stony issue from them. The great mass of it rose up (we tilted our heads back to look at it) into huge knobbles of stone against the sky, like an old giant's back teeth. The face it showed us was really no steeper than a roof, except for certain frightful cliffs on our left, but it looked as if it went up like a wall. It too was now black. Here the gods ceased trying to make me glad. There was nothing here that even the merriest heart could dance for.

Bardia pointed, ahead to our right. There the Mountain fell away in a smooth sweep to a saddle somewhat lower than the ground we stood on, but still with nothing behind it but the sky. Against the sky, on the saddle, stood a single leafless tree.

We went down into the black valley on our own feet, leading the horse, for the going was bad and stones slipped away from under us until, at the lowest place, we joined the sacred road (it came into the valley through the northern end, away to our left). We were so near now that we did not mount again. A few loops of the road led us up to the saddle and, once more, into the biting wind.

I was afraid, now that we were almost at the Tree. I can hardly say of what, but I know that to find the bones, or even the body, would have set my fear at rest. I believe I had a senseless child's fear that she might be neither living nor dead.

And now we were there. The iron girdle, and the chain that went from it about the gaunt trunk (there was no bark on the Tree) hung there and made a dull noise from time to time as they moved with the wind. There were no bones, nor rags of clothing, nor marks of blood, nor anything else.

'How do you read these signs, Bardia?' said I.

'The god's taken her,' said he, rather pale and speaking low (he was a god-fearing man). 'No natural beast would have licked his plate so clean. There'd be bones. A beast – any but the holy Shadow-brute itself – couldn't have got the whole body out of the irons. And it would have left the jewels. A man, now – but a man couldn't have freed her, unless he had tools with him.'

I had not thought of our journey's being so vain; nothing to do, nothing to gather. The emptiness of my life was to begin at once.

'We can search about a bit,' I said; foolishly, for I had no hope of finding anything.

'Yes, yes, Lady. We can search about,' said Bardia. I knew it was only his kindness that spoke.

And so we did; working round in circles, he one way and I the other, with our eyes on the ground; very cold, one's cloak flapping till leg and cheek smarted with the blows of it.

Bardia was ahead of me now, eastward and further across the saddle, when he called out. I had to thrust back the hair that was whipping about my face before I could see him. I rushed to him; half-flying, for the westwind made a sail of my cloak. He showed me what he had found – a ruby.

'I never saw her wear such a stone,' said I.

'She did though, Lady. On her last journey. They had put their own holy gear on her. The straps of the sandals were red with rubies.'

'Oh, Bardia! Then somebody – something – carried her thus far.'

'Or maybe carried only the sandals. A jackdaw'd do it.'

'We must go on; further on this line.'

'Carefully, Lady. If we must, I'll do it. You'd best stay behind.'

'Why, what's to fear? And anyway, I'll not stay behind.'

'I don't know that anyone's been over the saddle. At the Offering, even the priests come no further than the Tree. We are very near the bad part of the Mountain; I mean, the holy part. Beyond the Tree it's all gods' country, they say.'

'Then it is you must stay behind, Bardia. They can't do worse to me than they've done already.'

'I'll go where you go, Lady. But let's talk less of them, or not at all. And first, I must go back and get the horse.'

He went back (and for a moment out of sight – I stood alone on the edge of the perilous land) to where he had tied the horse to a little stunted bush. Then he rejoined me, leading it, very grave, and we went forward.

'Carefully,' he said again. 'We may find we're on the top of a cliff any moment.' And indeed it looked, for the next few paces, as if we were walking straight into the empty sky. Then suddenly we found we were on the brow of a steep slope; and at the same moment the sun – which had been overcast ever since we went down into the black valley – leaped out.

It was like looking down into a new world. At our feet, cradled amid a vast confusion of mountains, lay a small valley bright as a gem, but opening southward on our right. Through that opening there was a glimpse of warm, blue lands, hills and forests, far below us. The valley itself was like a cleft in the Mountain's southern chin. High though it was, the year seemed to have been kinder in it than down in Glome. I never saw greener turf. There was gorse in bloom, and wild vines, and many groves of flourishing trees; and plenty of bright water – pools, streams, and little cataracts. And when, after casting about a little to find where the slope would be easiest for the horse, we began descending, the air came up to us warmer and sweeter every minute. We were out of the wind now and could hear ourselves speak; soon we could hear the very chattering of the streams and the sound of bees.

'This may well be the secret valley of the god,' said Bardia, his voice hushed.

'It's secret enough,' said I.

Now we were at the bottom, and so warm that I had half a mind to dip my hands and face in the swift, amber water of the stream which still divided us from the main of the valley. I had already lifted my hand to put aside my veil when I heard two voices cry out; one, Bardia's. I looked. A quivering shock of feeling that has no name (but nearest terror) stabbed through me from head to foot. There, not six feet away, on the far side of the river, stood Psyche.

10

What I babbled, between tears and laughter, in the first wildness of my joy (the water still between us) I don't know. I was recalled by Bardia's voice.

'Careful, Lady. It may be her wraith. It may – ai! ai! – it is the bride of the god. It is a goddess.' He was deadly white, and bending down to throw earth on his forehead.

You could not blame him. She was so brightface, as we say in Greek. But I felt no holy fear. What? – I to fear the very Psyche whom I had carried in my arms and taught to speak and to walk? She was tanned by sun and wind, and clothed in rags; but laughing, her eyes like two stars, her limbs smooth and rounded, and (but for the rags) no sign of beggary or hardship about her.

'Welcome, welcome, welcome,' she was saying. 'Oh, Maia, I have longed for this. It was my only longing. I knew you would come. Oh, how happy I am! And good Bardia, too. It was he that brought you? Of course; I might have guessed it. Come, Orual, you must cross the stream. I'll show you where it's easiest. But, Bardia – I can't bid you across. Dear Bardia, it's not—'

'No, no, Blessed Istra,' said Bardia (and I thought he was very relieved). 'I'm only a soldier.' Then, in a lower voice, to me, 'Will you go, Lady? This is a very dreadful place. Perhaps—'

'Go?' said I. 'I'd go if the river flowed with fire instead of water.'

'Of course,' said he. 'It's not with you as with us. You have gods' blood in you. I'll stay here with the horse. We're out of the wind and there's good grass for him here.'

I was already on the edge of the river.

'A little further up, Orual,' Psyche was saying. 'Here's the best ford. Go straight ahead off that big stone. Gently! make your footing sure. No, not to your left. It's very deep in places. This way. Now, one step more. Reach out for my hand.'

I suppose the long bedridden and indoors time of my sickness had softened me. Anyhow, the coldness of that water shocked all the breath out of me; and the current was so strong that, but for Psyche's hand, I think it would have knocked me down and rolled me under. I even thought, momentarily amid a thousand other things, 'How strong she grows. She'll be a stronger woman than ever I was. She'll have that as well as her beauty.'

The next was all a confusion – trying to talk, to cry, to kiss, to get my breath back, all together. But she led me a few paces beyond the river and made me sit in the warm heather and sat beside me; our four hands joined in my lap, just as it had been that night in her prison.

'Why, Sister,' she said merrily, 'you have found my threshold cold and steep! You are breathless. But I'll refresh you.'

She jumped up, went a little way off, and came back, carrying something; the little cool, dark berries of the Mountain, in a green leaf. 'Eat,' she said. 'Is it not food fit for the gods?'

'Nothing sweeter,' said I. And indeed I was both hungry and thirsty enough by now, for it was noon or later. 'But oh, Psyche, tell me how—'

'Wait!' said she. 'After the banquet, the wine.' Close beside us a little silvery trickle came out from among stones mossed cushion-soft. She held her two hands under it till they were filled and raised them to my lips.

'Have you ever tasted a nobler wine?' she said. 'Or in a fairer cup?'

'It is indeed a good drink,' said I. 'But the cup is better. It is the cup I love best in the world.'

'Then it's yours, Sister.' She said it with such a pretty air of courtesy, like a queen and hostess giving gifts, that the tears came into my eyes again. It brought back so many of her plays in childhood.

'Thank you, child,' said I. 'I hope it is mine indeed. But, Psyche, we must be serious; yes, and busy too. How have you lived? How did you escape? And oh – we mustn't let the joy of the moment put it out of our minds – what are we to do now?'

'Do? Why, be merry, what else? Why should our hearts not dance?'

'They do dance. Do you not think – why, I could forgive the gods themselves. I'll shortly be able to forgive Redival; perhaps. But how can – it will be winter in a month or less. You can't – Psyche, how have you kept alive till now? I thought, I thought—' But to think of what I had thought overcame me.

'Hush, Maia, hush,' said Psyche (once more it was she who was comforting me). 'All those fears are over. All's well. I'll make it well for you too; I'll not rest till you're as happy as I. But you haven't yet even asked me my story. Weren't you surprised to find this fair dwelling-place, and me living here; like this? Have you no wonder?'

'Yes, Psyche, I am overwhelmed in it. Of course I want to hear your story. Unless we should make our plans first.'

'Solemn Orual,' said Psyche mockingly. 'You were always one for plans. And rightly too, Maia, with such a foolish child as me to bring up. And well you did it.' With one light kiss she put all those days, all of my life that I cared for, behind us, and began her story.

'I wasn't in my right mind when we left the palace. Before the two temple girls began painting and dressing me they gave me a sweet, sticky stuff to drink – a drug, as I guess, for soon after I had swallowed it everything went dreamlike, and more and more so for a long time. And I think, Sister, they must always give that to those whose blood is to be poured over Ungit, and that's why we see them die so patiently. And the painting on my face helped the dreaminess too. It made my face stiff till it didn't seem to be my own face. I couldn't feel it was I who was being sacrificed. And then the music and incense and the torches made it more so. I saw you, Orual, at the top of the stairway, but I couldn't lift even a hand to wave to you; my arms were as heavy as lead. And I thought it didn't matter much, because you too would wake up presently and find it was all a dream. And in a sense it was, wasn't it? And you are nearly awake now. What? still so grave? I must wake you more.

'You'd think the cold air would have given me my mind back when we came out of the great gates, but the drug must have been still coming to its full power. I had no fear; nor joy either. Sitting there on that litter, up above the heads of all that crowd, was a strange enough thing anyway ... and the horns and the rattles were going on all the time. I don't know whether the journey up the mountain was long or short. Each bit of it was long; I noticed every pebble on the road, I looked long, long at every tree as we passed it. Yet the whole journey seemed to take hardly any time. Yet long enough for me to get some of my wits back. I began to know that something dreadful was being done to me. Then for the first time I wanted to speak. I tried to cry out to them that there was some mistake, that I was only poor Istra and it couldn't be me they meant to kill. But nothing more than a kind of grunting or babbling came out of my mouth. Then a great bird-headed man, or a bird with a man's body—'

'That would be the Priest,' said I.

'Yes. If he is still the Priest when he puts on his mask; perhaps he becomes a god while he wears it. Anyway, it said, "Give her some more," and one of the younger priests got on someone else's shoulders and put the sweet sticky cup to my lips again. I didn't want to take it, but, you know, Maia, it all felt so like the time you had the barber to take that thorn out of my hand long ago – you remember, you holding me tight, and telling me to be good, and that it'd all be over in a moment. Well, it was like that, so I felt sure I'd better do whatever I was told.

'The next thing I knew – really knew – was that I was off the litter and on the hot earth, and they were fastening me to the Tree with iron round my waist. It was the sound of the iron that cleared the last of the drug out of my mind. And there was the King, shrieking and wailing and tearing his hair.

And do you know, Maia, he actually looked at me, really looked, and it seemed to me he was then seeing me for the first time. But all I wished was that he would stop it and then he and all the rest would go away and leave me alone to cry. I wanted to cry now. My mind was getting clearer and clearer and I was terribly afraid. I was trying to be like those girls in the Greek stories that the Fox is always telling us about, and I knew I could keep it up till they were gone, if only they would go quickly.'

'Oh, Psyche, you say all's well now. Forget that terrible time. Go on quickly and tell me how you were saved. We have so much to talk about and arrange. There's no time—'

'Orual! There's all the time there is. Don't you *want* to hear my story?'

'Of course I do. I want to hear every bit. When we're safe and—'

'Where shall we ever be safe if we're not safe here? This is my home, Maia. And you won't understand the wonder and glory of my adventure unless you listen to the bad part. It wasn't very bad, you know.'

'It's so bad I can hardly bear to listen to it.'

'Ah, but wait. Well, at last they were gone, and there I was alone under the glare of the sky with the great baked, parched mountain all round me, and not one noise to be heard. There wasn't a breath of wind even by the Tree; you remember what the last day of the drought was like. I was already thirsty – the sticky drink had done that. Then I noticed for the first time that they had so bound me that I couldn't sit down. That was when my heart really failed me. I did cry then; oh, Maia, how badly I wanted you and the Fox! And all I could do was to pray, pray, pray to the gods that whatever was going to happen to me might happen soon. But nothing happened, except that my tears made me thirstier. Then, a very long time after that, things began gathering round me.'

'Things?'

'Oh, nothing dreadful. Only the mountain cattle at first. Poor lean things they were. I was sorry for them, for I thought they were as thirsty as I. And they came nearer and nearer in a great circle, but never very near, and mooed at me. And after that there came a beast that I had never seen before, but I think it was a lynx. It came right up close. My hands were free and I wondered if I would be able to beat it off. But I had no need to. After advancing and drawing back I don't know how many times (I think it began by fearing me as much as I feared it) it came and sniffed at my feet, and then it stood up with its forepaws on me and sniffed again. Then it went away. I was sorry it had gone; it was a kind of company. And do you know what I was thinking all this time?'

'What?'

'At first I was trying to cheer myself with all that old dream of my gold and amber palace on the Mountain … and the god … trying to believe it. But

I couldn't believe in it at all. I couldn't understand how I ever had. All that, all my old longings, were clean gone.'

I pressed her hands and said nothing. But inwardly I rejoiced. It might have been good (I don't know) to encourage that fancy the night before the Offering, if it supported her. Now, I was glad she had got over it. It was a thing I could not like; unnatural and estranging. Perhaps this gladness of mine is one of the things the gods have against me. They never tell.

'The only thing that did me good,' she continued 'was quite different. It was hardly a thought, and very hard to put into words. There was a lot of the Fox's philosophy in it; things he says about gods or "the divine nature"; but mixed up with things the Priest said too, about the blood and the earth and how sacrifice makes the crops grow. I'm not explaining it well. It seemed to come from somewhere deep inside me; deeper than the part that sees pictures of gold and amber palaces, deeper than fears and tears. It was shapeless, but you could just hold on to it; or just let it hold on to you. Then the change came.'

'What change?' I didn't know well what she was talking about, but I saw she must have her way and tell the story in her own fashion.

'Oh, the weather of course. I couldn't see it, tied the way I was, but I could feel it. I was suddenly cool. Then I knew the sky must be filling with clouds, behind my back, over Glome, for all the colours on the Mountain went out and my own shadow vanished. And then – that was the first sweet moment – a sigh of wind – westwind – came at my back. Then more and more wind; you could hear and smell and feel the rain drawing near. So then I knew quite well that the gods really are, and that I was bringing the rain. And then the wind was roaring (but it's too soft a sound to call it a roar) all round me; and rain. The Tree kept some of it off me; I was holding out my hands all the time and licking the rain off them, I was so thirsty. The wind got wilder and wilder. It seemed to be lifting me off the ground so that, if it hadn't been for the iron round my waist, I'd have been blown right away, up in the air. And then – at last – for a moment – I saw him.'

'Saw whom?'

'The westwind.'

'*Saw* it?'

'Not it; him. The god of the wind: Westwind himself.'

'Were you awake, Psyche?'

'Oh, it was no dream. One can't dream things like that, because one's never seen things like that. He was in human shape. But you couldn't mistake him for a man. Oh, Sister, you'd understand if you'd seen. How can I make you understand? You've seen lepers?'

'Well, of course.'

'And you know how healthy people look beside a leper?'

'You mean – healthier, ruddier than ever?'

'Yes. Now we, beside the gods, are like lepers beside us.'

'Do you mean this god was so red?'

She laughed and clapped her hands. 'Oh, it's no use,' she said. 'I see I've not given you the idea at all. Never mind. You shall see gods for yourself, Orual. It must be so; I'll make it so. Somehow. There must be a way. Look, this may help you. When I saw Westwind I was neither glad nor afraid (at first). I felt ashamed.'

'But what of? Psyche, they hadn't stripped you naked or anything?'

'No, no, Maia. Ashamed of looking like a mortal; ashamed of being a mortal.'

'But how could you help that?'

'Don't you think the things people are most ashamed of are the things they can't help?'

I thought of my ugliness and said nothing.

'And he took me,' said Psyche, 'in his beautiful arms which seemed to burn me (though the burning didn't hurt) and pulled me right out of the iron girdle – and that didn't hurt either and I don't know how he did it – and carried me up into the air, far up above the ground, and whirled me away. Of course he was invisible again almost at once. I had seen him only as one sees a lightning flash. But that didn't matter. Now I knew it was he, not it, I wasn't in the least afraid of sailing along in the sky; even of turning head over heels in it.'

'Psyche, are you sure this happened? You must have been dreaming!'

'And if it was a dream, Sister, how do you think I came here? It's more likely everything that had happened to me before this was a dream. Why, Glome and the King and old Batta seem to me very like dreams now. But you hinder my tale, Maia. So he carried me through the air and set me down softly. At first I was all out of breath and too bewildered to see where I was; for Westwind is a merry, rough god. (Sister, do you think young gods have to be taught how to handle us? A hasty touch from hands like theirs and we'd fall to pieces.) But when I came to myself – ah, can you think what a moment that was! – and saw the House before me; I lying at the threshold. And it wasn't, you see, just the gold and amber House I used to imagine. If it had been just that, I might indeed have thought I was dreaming. But I saw it wasn't. And not quite like any house in this land, nor quite like those Greek houses the Fox describes to us. Something new, never conceived of – but, there, you can see for yourself; and I'll show you over every bit of it in a moment. Why need I try to show it in words?

'You could see it was a god's house at once. I don't mean a temple where a god is worshipped. A god's house, where he lives. I would not for any wealth have gone into it. But I had to, Orual. For there came a voice – sweet? oh, sweeter than any music, yet my hair rose at it too – and do you know, Orual, what it said? It said, "Enter your house" – yes, it called it *my* house – "Psyche, the bride of the god."

'I was ashamed again, ashamed of my mortality, and terribly afraid. But it would have been worse shame and worse fear to disobey. I went, cold, small, and shaking, up the steps and through the porch and into the courtyard. There was no one to be seen. But then the voices came. All round me, bidding me welcome.'

'What kind of voices?'

'Like women's voices – at least, as like women's voices as the wind-god was like a man. And they said, "Enter, Lady, enter, Mistress. Do not be afraid." And they were moving as the speakers moved, though I could see no one; and leading me by their movements. And so they brought me into a cool parlour with an arched roof, where there was a table set out with fruit and wine. Such fruits as never – but you shall see. They said, "Refresh yourself, Lady, before the bath; after it comes the feast." Oh, Orual, how can I tell you what it felt like? I knew they were all spirits and I wanted to fall at their feet. But I daren't; if they made me mistress of that house, mistress I should have to be. Yet all the time I was afraid there might be some bitter mockery in it and that at any moment terrible laughter might break out and—'

'Ah!' said I, with a long breath. How well I understood.

'Oh, but I was wrong, Sister. Utterly wrong. That's part of the mortal shame. They gave me fruit, they gave me wine—'

'The voices gave you?'

'The spirits gave them to me. I couldn't see their hands. Yet, you know, it never looked as if the plates or the cup were moving of themselves. You could see that hands were doing it. And, Orual' (her voice grew very low) 'When I took the cup, I – I – *felt* the other hands, touching my own. Again, that burning, though without pain. That was terrible.' She blushed suddenly and (I wondered why) laughed. 'It wouldn't be terrible now,' she said. 'Then they had me to the bath. You shall see it. It is in the delicatest pillared court, open to the sky, and the water is like crystal and smells as sweet as ... as sweet as this whole valley. I was terribly shy when it came to taking off my clothes, but—'

'You said they were all she-spirits.'

'Oh, Maia, you still don't understand. This shame has nothing to do with He or She. It's the being mortal; being, how shall I say it? ... insufficient. Don't you think a dream would feel shy if it were seen walking about in the waking world? And then' (she was speaking more and more quickly now) 'they dressed me again – in the most beautiful things – and then came the banquet – and the music – and then they had me to bed – and the night came – and then – he.'

'He?'

'The Bridegroom ... the god himself. Don't look at me like that, Sister. I'm your own true Psyche still. Nothing will change that.'

'Psyche,' said I, leaping up, 'I can't bear this any longer. You have told me so many wonders. If this is all true, I've been wrong all my life. Everything has to be begun over again. Psyche, it is true? You're not playing a game with me? Show me. Show me your palace.'

'Of course I will,' she said, rising. 'Let us go in. And don't be afraid whatever you see or hear.'

'Is it far?' said I.

She gave me a quick, astonished look. 'Far to where?' she said.

'To the palace, to this god's house.'

You have seen a lost child in a crowd run up to a woman whom it takes for its mother, and how the woman turns round and shows the face of a stranger, and then the look in the child's eyes, silent a moment before it begins to cry. Psyche's face was like that; checked, blank; happiest assurance suddenly dashed all to pieces.

'Orual,' she said, beginning to tremble, 'what do you mean?'

I too became frightened, though I had yet no notion of the truth. 'Mean?' said I. 'Where is the palace? How far have we to go to reach it?'

She gave one loud cry. Then, with white face, staring hard into my eyes, she said, 'But *this* is it, Orual! It is here! You are standing on the stairs of the great gate.'

11

If anyone could have seen us at that moment I believe he would have thought we were two enemies met for a battle to the death. I know we stood like that, a few feet apart, every nerve taut, each with eyes fixed on the other in a terrible watchfulness.

And now we are coming to that part of my history on which my charge against the gods chiefly rests; and therefore I must try at any cost to write what is wholly true. Yet it is hard to know perfectly what I was thinking while those huge, silent moments went past. By remembering it too often I have blurred the memory itself.

I suppose my first thought must have been, 'She's mad.' Anyway, my whole heart leaped to shut the door against something monstrously amiss; not to be endured. And to keep it shut. Perhaps I was fighting not to be mad myself.

But what I said when I got my breath (and I know my voice came out in a whisper) was simply, 'We must go away at once. This is a terrible place.'

Was I believing in her invisible palace? A Greek will laugh at the thought. But it's different in Glome. There the gods are too close to us. Up in the Mountain, in the very heart of the Mountain, where Bardia had been afraid and even the priests don't go, anything was possible. No door could be kept shut. Yes, that was it; not plain belief, but infinite misgiving – the whole world (Psyche with it) slipping out of my hands.

Whatever I meant, she misunderstood me horribly.

'So,' she said, 'you do see it after all.'

'See what?' I asked. A fool's question. I knew what.

'Why, this, this,' said Psyche. 'The gates, the shining walls—'

For some strange reason, fury – my father's own fury – fell upon me when she said that. I found myself screaming (I am sure I had not meant to scream), 'Stop it! Stop it at once! There's nothing there.'

Her face flushed. For once, and for the moment only, she too was angry. 'Well, feel it, feel it, if you can't see,' she cried. 'Touch it. Slap it. Beat your head against it. Here—' She made to grab my hands. I wrenched them free.

'Stop it, stop it, I tell you! There's no such thing. You're pretending. You're trying to make yourself believe it.' But I was lying. How did I know whether she really saw invisible things or spoke in madness? Either way, something hateful and strange had begun. As if I could thrust it back by brute force, I fell upon Psyche. Before I knew what I was doing I had her by the shoulders and was shaking her as one shakes a child.

She was too big for that now and far too strong (stronger than I ever dreamt she could be) and she flung my grip off in a moment. We fell apart, both breathing hard, now more like enemies than ever. All at once a look came into her face that I had never seen there; sharp, suspicious.

'But you tasted the wine. Where do you think I got it from?'

'Wine? What wine? What are you talking about?'

'Orual! The wine I gave you. And the cup. I gave you the cup. And where is it? Where have you hidden it?'

'Oh, have done with it, child. I'm in no mood for nonsense. There was no wine.'

'But I gave it to you. You drank it. And the fine honey-cakes. You said—'

'You gave me water, cupped in your hands.'

'But you praised the wine; and the cup. You said—'

'I praised your hands. You were playing a game (you know you were) and I fell in with it.'

She gaped open-mouthed, yet beautiful even then.

'So that was all,' she said slowly. 'You mean you saw no cup? tasted no wine?'

I wouldn't answer. She had heard well enough what I said.

Presently her throat moved as if she were swallowing something (oh, the beauty of her throat!). She pressed down a great storm of passion and her mood changed; it was now sober sadness, mixed with pity. She struck her breast with her clenched fist as mourners do.

'Aiai!' she mourned, 'so this is what he meant. You can't see it. You can't feel it. For you, it is not there at all. Oh, Maia ... I am very sorry.'

I came almost to a full belief. She was shaking and stirring me a dozen different ways. But I had not shaken her at all. She was as certain of her palace as of the plainest thing; as certain as the Priest had been of Ungit when my father's dagger was between his ribs. I was as weak beside her as the Fox beside the Priest. This valley was indeed a dreadful place; full of the divine, sacred, no place for mortals. There might be a hundred things in it that I could not see.

Can a Greek understand the horror of that thought? Years after, I dreamed, again and again, that I was in some well-known place – most often the Pillar Room – and everything I saw was different from what I touched. I would lay my hand on the table and feel warm hair instead of smooth wood, and the corner of the table would shoot out a hot, wet tongue and lick me. And I knew, by the mere taste of them that all those dreams came from that moment when I believed I was looking at Psyche's palace and did not see it. For the horror was the same; a sickening discord, a rasping together of two worlds, like the two bits of a broken bone.

But in the reality (not in the dreams), with the horror, came the inconsolable grief. For the world had broken in pieces and Psyche and I were not in the same piece. Seas, mountains, madness, death itself, could not have removed her from me to such a hopeless distance as this. Gods, and again gods, always gods ... they had stolen her. They would leave us nothing. A thought pierced up through the crust of my mind like a crocus coming up in the early year. Was she not worthy of the gods? Ought they not to have her? But instantly great, choking, blinding waves of sorrow swept it away and, 'Oh!' I cried. 'It's not right. It's not right. Oh, Psyche, come back! Where are you? Come back, come back.'

She had me in her arms at once. 'Maia – Sister,' she said. 'I'm here. Maia, don't. I can't bear it. I'll—'

'Yes ... oh, my child ... I do feel you ... I hold you. But oh ... it's only like holding you in a dream. You are leagues away. And I ...'

She led me a few paces further and made me sit down on a mossy bank and sat beside me. With words and touch she comforted me all she could. And as, in the centre of a storm or even of a battle, I have known sudden stillness for a moment, so now for a little I let her comfort me. Not that I took any heed of what she was saying. It was her voice, and her love in her voice, that counted. Her voice was very deep for a woman's. Sometimes even now the way she used to say this or that word comes back to me as warm and real as if she were beside me in the room; the softness of it, the richness as of corn grown from a deep soil.

What was she saying: '... and perhaps, Maia, you too will learn how to see. I will beg and implore him to make you able. He will understand. He warned me when I asked for this meeting that it might not turn out all as I hoped. I never thought ... I'm only simple Psyche, as he calls me ... never thought he meant you wouldn't even see it. So he must have known. He'll tell us ...'

He? I'd forgotten this *him*; or, if not forgotten, left him out of account ever since she first told me we were standing at his palace gates. And now she was saying *he* every moment, no other name but *he*, the way young wives talk. Something began to grow colder and harder inside me. And this also is like what I've known in wars; when that which was only *they* or *the enemy* all at once becomes the man, two feet away, who means to kill you.

'Who are you talking of?' I asked; but I meant, 'Why do you talk of him to me? What have I to do with him?'

'But, Maia,' she said, 'I've told you all my story. My god, of course. My lover. My husband. The master of my house.'

'Oh, I can't bear it,' said I, leaping up. Those last words of hers, spoken softly and with trembling, set me on fire. I could feel my rage coming back. Then (like a great light, a hope of deliverance, it came to me) I asked myself why I'd forgotten, and how long I'd forgotten, that first notion of her being mad. Madness; of course. The whole thing must be madness. I had been nearly as mad as she to think otherwise. At the very name *madness* the air of that valley seemed more breathable, seemed emptied of a little of its holiness and horror.

'Have done with it, Psyche,' I said sharply. 'Where is this god? Where the palace is? Nowhere – in your fancy. Where is he? Show him to me? What is he like?'

She looked a little aside and spoke, lower than ever but very clear, and as if all that had yet passed between us were of no account beside the gravity of what she was now saying. 'Oh, Orual,' she said, 'not even I have seen him ... yet. He comes to me only in the holy darkness. He says I mustn't ... not yet ... see his face or know his name. I'm forbidden to bring any light into his ... our ... chamber.'

Then she looked up, and as our eyes met for a moment I saw in hers unspeakable joy.

'There's no such thing,' I said, loud and stern. 'Never say these things again. Get up. It's time—'

'Orual,' said she, now at her queenliest, 'I have never told you a lie in my life.'

I tried to soften my manner. Yet the words came out cold and stern. 'No, you don't mean to lie. You're not in your right mind, Psyche. You have imagined things. It's the terror and the loneliness ... and that drug they gave you. We'll cure you.'

'Orual,' said she.

'What?'

'If it's all my fancy, how do you think I have lived these many days? Do I look as if I'd fed on berries and slept under the sky? Are my arms wasted? Or my cheeks fallen in?'

I would, I believe, have lied to her myself and said they were, but it was impossible. From the top of her head to her naked feet she was bathed in life and beauty and well-being. It was as if they flowed over her or from her. It was no wonder Bardia had worshipped her as a goddess. The very rags served only to show more of her beauty; all the honey-sweetness, all the rose-red and the ivory, the warm, breathing perfection of her. She even seemed ('But that's impossible,' I thought) taller than before. And as my lie died unspoken she looked at me with something like mockery in her face. Her mocking looks had always been some of her loveliest.

'You see?' she said. 'It's all true. And that – no, listen, Maia – that's why all will come right. We'll make – he will make you able to see, and then—'

'I don't want it!' I cried, putting my face close to hers, threatening her almost, till she drew back before my fierceness. 'I don't want it. I hate it. Hate it, hate it, hate it. Do you understand?'

'But ... Orual ... why? What do you hate?'

'Oh, the whole – what can I call it? You know very well. Or you used to. This, this—' And then something she had said about *him* (hardly noticed till now) began to work horribly in my mind. 'This thing that comes to you in the darkness ... and you're forbidden to see it. Holy darkness, you call it. What sort of thing? Faugh! it's like living in the house of Ungit. Everything's dark about the gods ... I think I can smell the very ...' The steadiness of her gaze, the beauty of her, so full of pity yet in a way so pitiless, made me dumb for a moment. Then my tears broke out again. 'Oh, Psyche,' I sobbed, 'you're so far away. Do you even hear me? I can't reach you. Oh, Psyche, Psyche ... you loved me once ... come back. What have we to do with gods and wonders and all these cruel, dark things? We're women, aren't we? Mortals. Oh, come back to the world. Leave all that alone. Come back where we were happy.'

'But Orual – think. How can I go back? This is my home. I am a wife.'

'Wife? Of what?' said I, shuddering.

'If you only knew him,' she said.

'You like it! Oh, Psyche!'

She would not answer me. Her face flushed. Her face, and her whole body, were the answer.

'Oh, you ought to have been one of Ungit's girls,' said I savagely. 'You ought to have lived in there – in the dark – all blood and incense and muttering and the reek of burnt fat. To like it ... living among things you can't see ... dark and holy and horrible. Is it nothing to you at all that you are leaving me ... going into all that ... turning your back on all our love?'

'No, no, Maia. I can't go back to you. How could I? But you must come to me.'

'Oh, it's madness,' said I.

Was it madness or not? Which was true? Which would be worse? I was at that very moment when, if they meant us well, the gods would speak. Mark what they did instead.

It began to rain. It was only a light rain, but it changed everything for me.

'Here, child,' said I, 'come under my cloak. Your poor rags! Quick. You'll be wet through.'

She gazed at me wonderingly. 'How should I get wet, Maia,' she said, 'when we are sitting indoors with a roof above us? And "rags"? – but I forgot. You can't see my robes either.' The rain shone on her cheeks as she spoke.

If that wise Greek who is to read this book doubts that this turned my mind right round, let him ask his mother or wife. The moment I saw her, my child whom I had cared for all her life, sitting there in the rain as if it meant no more to her than it does to cattle, the notion that her palace and her god could be anything but madness was at once unbelievable. All those wilder misgivings, all the fluttering to and fro between two opinions, was (for that time) quite over. I saw in a flash that I must choose one opinion or the other; and in the same flash knew which I had chosen.

'Psyche,' I said (and my voice had changed). 'This is sheer raving. You can't stay here. Winter'll be on us soon. It'll kill you.'

'I cannot leave my home, Maia.'

'Home! There's no home here. Get up. Here – under my cloak.'

She shook her head, a little wearily.

'It's no use, Maia,' she said. 'I see it and you don't. Who's to judge between us?'

'I'll call Bardia.'

'I'm not allowed to let him in. And he wouldn't come.'

That, I knew, was true.

'Get up, girl,' I said. 'Do you hear me? Do as you're told. Psyche, you never disobeyed me before.'

She looked up (wetter every moment) and said, very tender in voice but hard as a stone in her determination, 'Dear Maia, I am a wife now. It's no longer you that I must obey.'

I learned then how one can hate those one loves. My fingers were round her wrist in an instant, my other hand on her upper arm. We were struggling.

'You *shall* come,' I panted. 'We'll force you away – hide you somewhere – Bardia has a wife, I believe – lock you up – his house – bring you to your senses.'

It was useless. She was far stronger than I. ('Of course,' I thought, 'they say mad people have double strength.') We left marks on one another's skin. There was a thick, tangled sort of wrestling. Then we were apart again; she staring with reproach and wonder, I weeping (as I had wept at her prison door), utterly broken with shame and despair. The rain had stopped. It had, I suppose, done all the gods wanted.

And now there was nothing at all left that I could do.

Psyche, as always, recovered herself first. She laid her hand – there was a smear of blood on it; was it possible I could have scratched her? – across my shoulder.

'Dear Maia,' she said, 'you have very seldom been angry with me in all the years I can remember. Don't begin now. Look, the shadows have already crept nearly all the way across the courtyard. I had hoped that before this we should have feasted together and been merry. But, there – you would have tasted only berries and cold water. Bread and onions with Bardia will be more comfort to you. But I must send you away before the sun sets. I promised that I would.'

'Are you sending me away for ever, Psyche? And with nothing?'

'Nothing, Orual, but a bidding to come again as soon as you can. I'll work for you here. There must be some way. And then – oh, Maia – then we shall meet here again with no cloud between us. But now you must go.'

What could I do but obey her? In body she was stronger than I; her mind I could not reach. She was already leading me back to the river, back through the desolate valley she called her palace. The valley looked hideous to me now. There was a chill in the air. Sunset flamed up behind the black mass of the saddle.

She clung to me at the very edge of the water. 'You will come back soon, soon?' she said.

'If I can, Psyche. You know how it is in our house.'

'I think,' said she, 'the King will not be much hindrance to you in the next few days. Now, there's no more time. Kiss me again. Dear Maia. And now, lean on my hand. Feel for the flat stone with your foot.'

Again I endured the sword-cut of the icy water. From this side I looked back.

'Psyche, Psyche,' I broke out. 'There's still time. Come with me. Anywhere – I'll smuggle you out of Glome – we'll go for beggarwomen all over the world – or you can go to Bardia's house – anywhere, anything you like.'

She shook her head. 'How could I?' she said. 'I'm not my own. You forget, Sister, that I'm a wife. Yet always yours. Oh, if you knew, you'd be happy. Orual, don't look so sad. All will be well; all will be better than you can dream of. Come again soon. Farewell for a little.'

She went away from me into her terrible valley, and out of sight finally among the trees. It was already deep twilight on my side of the river, close in under the shadow of the saddle.

'Bardia,' I called. 'Bardia, where are you?'

12

Bardia, a grey shape in the twilight, came towards me.
'You have left the Blessed?' he said.

'Yes,' said I. I could not talk to him about it, I thought.

'Then we must speak of how to spend our night. We'd never find a way for the horse up to the saddle now, and if we did, we'd have to go down again beyond the Tree into the other valley. We couldn't sleep on the saddle itself; too much wind. It'll be cold enough here, where we're sheltered, in an hour or so. I fear we must lie here. Not where a man'd choose; too near the gods.

'What does it matter?' said I. 'It will do as well as anywhere else.'

'Then come with me, Lady. I've gathered a few sticks.'

I followed him; and in that silence (there was nothing now but the chattering of the stream, and it seemed louder than ever) we could hear, long before we came to the horse, the sound of the grass torn up by his teeth.

A man and a soldier is a wonderful creature. Bardia had chosen a place where the bank was steepest, and two rocks close together made the next best thing to a cave. The sticks were all laid and the fire alight, though still sputtering from the late rain. And he brought out of the saddle-bags things better than bread and onions; even a flask of wine. I was still a girl (which in many matters is the same thing as a fool) and it seemed to me shameful that, in all my sorrow and care, I was so eager for the food when it came. I never tasted better. And that meal in the firelight (which had made all the rest of the world a mere darkness as soon as it blazed up) seemed to me very sweet and homelike; mortal food and warmth for mortal limbs and bellies, no need (for a space) to think of gods and riddles and wonders.

When we had ended Bardia said, somewhat shamefacedly, 'Lady, you're not used to lying in the open and you might be cruelly chilled before day. So I'll make so free – for I'm no more to you, Lady, than one of your father's big dogs – as to say we'd best lie close, back to back, the way men do in the wars. And both cloaks over us.'

I said yes to that, and indeed no woman in the world has so little reason as I to be chary in such matters. Yet it surprised me that he should have said it; for I did not yet know that, if you are ugly enough, all men (unless they hate you deeply) soon give up thinking of you as a woman at all.

Bardia rested as soldiers do; dead asleep in two breaths but ready (I have seen him tested since) to be wide awake in one if need were. I think I never slept at all. First there was the hardness and slope of the ground, and after that the cold. And besides these, fast and whirling thoughts, wakeful as a madman's; about Psyche and my hard riddle, and also of another thing.

At last the cold grew so bitter that I slipped from under the cloak – its outer side was wet with dew by now – and began walking to and fro. And now, let that wise Greek whom I look to as my reader and the judge of my cause, mark well what followed.

It was already twilight and there was much mist in the valley. The pools of the river as I went down to it to drink (for I was thirsty as well as cold) seemed to be dark holes in the greyness. And I got my drink, ice-cold, and I thought it steadied my mind. But would a river flowing in the god's secret valley do that, or the clean contrary? This is another of the things to be guessed. For when I lifted my head and looked once more into the mist across the water, I saw that which brought my heart into my throat. There stood the palace; grey, as all things were grey in that hour and place, but solid and motionless, wall within wall, pillar and arch and architrave, acres of it, a labyrinthine beauty. As she had said, it was like no house ever seen in our land or age. Pinnacles and buttresses leaped up – no memories of mine, you would think, could help me to imagine them – unbelievably tall and slender, pointed and prickly as if stone were shooting out into branch and flower. No light showed from any window. It was a house asleep. And somewhere within it, asleep also, someone or something – how holy, or horrible, or beautiful or strange? – with Psyche in its arms. And I, what had I done and said? what would it do to me for my blasphemies and unbelievings? I never doubted that I must now cross the river, or try to cross it, even if it should drown me. I must lie on the steps at the great gate of that house and make my petition. I must ask forgiveness of Psyche as well as of the god. I had dared to scold her – dared, what was worse, to try to comfort her as a child – but all the time she was far above me; herself now hardly mortal, if what I saw was real. I was in great fear. Perhaps it was not real. I looked and looked to see if it would not fade or change. Then as I rose (for all this time I was still kneeling where I had drunk), almost before I stood on my feet, the whole thing had vanished. There was a tiny space of time in which I thought I could see how some swirlings of the mist had looked, for the moment, like towers and walls. But very soon, no likeness at all. I was staring simply into fog, and my eyes smarting with it.

And now, you who read, give judgement. That moment when I either saw or thought I saw the House – does it tell against the gods or against me? Would they (if they answered) make it a part of their defence? – say it was a sign, a hint, beckoning me to answer the riddle one way rather than the other? I'll not grant them that. What is the use of a sign which is itself only another riddle? It might – I'll allow so much – it might have been a true seeing; the cloud over my mortal eyes may have been lifted for a moment. It might not; what would be easier than for one distraught and not, maybe, so fully waking as she seemed, gazing at a mist, in a half-light, to fancy what had filled her thoughts for so many hours? What easier, even, than for the gods themselves to send the whole ferly for a mockery? Either way, there's divine mockery in it. They set the riddle and then allow a seeming that can't be tested and can only quicken and thicken the tormenting whirlpool of your guess-work. If they had an honest intention to guide us, why is their guidance not plain? Psyche could speak plain when she was three; do you tell me the gods have not yet come so far?

When I came back to Bardia he was just awake. I did not tell him what I had seen; until I wrote it in this book, I have never told it to anyone.

Our journey down was comfortless, for there was no sun and the wind was always in our faces, with scudding showers at times. I, sitting behind Bardia, got less of it than he.

We halted somewhere about noon, under the lee of a small wood, to eat what was left of our food. Of course my riddle had been working in my mind all morning, and it was there, out of the wind for a little and somewhat warmer (was Psyche warm? and worse weather soon to come) that I made up my mind to tell him the whole story; always excepting that moment when I looked into the mist. I knew he was an honest man, and secret, and (in his own way) wise.

He listened to it all very diligently but said nothing when I had ended. I had to draw his answer out of him.

'How do you read it all, Bardia?'

'Lady,' says he, 'it's not my way to say more than I can help of gods and divine matters. I'm not impious. I wouldn't eat with my left hand, or lie with my wife when the moon's full, or slit open a pigeon to clean it with an iron knife, or do anything else that's unchancy and profane, even if the King himself were to bid me. And as for sacrifices, I've always done all that can be expected of a man on my pay. But for anything more – I think the less Bardia meddles with the gods, the less they'll meddle with Bardia.'

But I was determined to have his counsel.

'Bardia,' I said, 'do you think my sister is mad?'

'Look, Lady,' he answered, 'there at your very first word you say what's better unsaid. Mad? the Blessed, mad? Moreover, we've seen her and anyone could tell she was in her right mind.'

'Then you think there really was a palace in the valley though I couldn't see it?'

'I don't well know what's *really*, when it comes to houses of gods.'

'And what of this lover who comes to her in the dark?'

'I say nothing about him.'

'Oh, Bardia – and among the spears men say you're the bravest! Are you afraid even to whisper your thought to me? I am in desperate need of counsel.'

'Counsel about what, Lady? What is there to do?'

'How do you read this riddle? Does anyone really come to her?'

'She says so, Lady. Who am I to give the Blessed One the lie?'

'Who is he?'

'She knows that best.'

'She knows nothing. She confesses she has never seen him. Bardia, what kind of a lover must this be who forbids his bride to see his face?'

Bardia was silent. He had a pebble between his thumb and forefinger and was drawing little scratches in the earth.

'Well?' said I.

'There doesn't seem to be much of a riddle about it,' he said at last.

'Then what's your answer?'

'I should say – speaking as mortal man, and likely enough the gods know better – I should say it was one whose face and form would give her little pleasure if she saw them.'

'Some frightful thing?'

'They called her the Bride of the Brute, Lady. But it's time we were riding again. We're not much better than half-way home.' He got up as he spoke.

His thought was not new to me; it was only the most horrible of the guesses which had been jostling and wrangling in my head. But the shock of hearing it from his lips lay in this, that I knew he had no doubt of it. I had come to know Bardia very well by now, and I could clearly see that all my difficulty in drawing out his answer came from his fear to say the thing and not from any uncertainty. As he had said, my riddle was no riddle to him. And it was as though all the people of Glome had spoken to me through him. As he thought, so, doubtless, every prudent, god-fearing man of our nation and our time would think too. My other guesses would not even come into their minds; here was the plain answer, clear as noonday. Why seek further? The god and the Shadowbrute were all one. She had been given to it. We had got our rain and water and (as seemed likely) peace with Phars. The gods, for their share, had her away into their secret places where something, so foul it would not show itself, some holy and sickening thing, ghostly or demonlike or bestial – or all three (there's no telling, with gods) – enjoyed her at its will.

I was so dashed that, as we continued our journey, nothing in me even fought against this answer of Bardia's. I felt as, I suppose, a tortured prisoner feels when they dash water in his face to rouse him from his faint, and the truth, worse than all his fantasies, becomes clear and hard and unmistakable again around him. It now seemed to me that all my other guesses had been only self-pleasing dreams spun out of my wishes, but now I was awake. There never had been any riddle; the worst was the truth, and truth as plain as the nose on a man's face. Only terror would have blinded me to it so long.

My hand stole to the sword-hilt under my cloak. Before my sickness, I had sworn that, if there were no other way, I would have killed Psyche rather than leave her to the heat or hunger of a monster. Now again I made a deep resolve. I was half frightened when I perceived what I was resolving. 'So it might come even to that,' my heart said; even to killing her (Bardia had already taught me the straight thrust, and where to strike). Then my tenderness came over me again, and I cried, never more bitterly, till I could not tell whether it was tears or rain that had most drenched my veil. (It was settling down to steadier rain as the day went on.) And in that tenderness I even asked myself why I should save her from the Brute, or warn her against the Brute, or meddle with the matter at all. 'She is happy,' said my heart. 'Whether it's madness or a god or a monster, or whatever it is, she is happy. You have seen that for yourself. She is ten times happier, there in the Mountain, than you could ever make her. Leave her alone. Don't spoil it. Don't mar what you've learnt you can't make.'

We were down in the foothills now, almost (if one could have seen through the rain) in sight of the house of Ungit. My heart did not conquer me. I perceived now that there is a love deeper than theirs who seek only the happiness of their beloved. Would a father see his daughter happy as a whore? Would a woman see her lover happy as a coward? My hand went back to the sword. 'She shall not,' I thought. Come what might, she should not. However things might go, whatever the price, by her death or mine or a thousand deaths, by fronting the gods 'beard to beard' as the soldiers say. Psyche should not – least of all, contentedly – make sport for a demon.

'We are king's daughters still,' I said.

I had hardly said it when I had good cause to remember, in a different fashion, that I was a king's daughter, and what king's. For now we were fording the Shennit again and Bardia (whose mind was ever on next things) was saying that when we had passed the city, and before we had reached the palace, I had best slip off the horse and go up that little lane – where Redival first saw Psyche being worshipped – and so through the gardens and into the women's quarters by the back way. For it was easy to guess how my father would take it if he found that I (supposed too sick to work with him in the Pillar Room) had journeyed to the Holy Tree.

13

It was nearly dark in the palace, and as I came to my chamber door a voice said in Greek, 'Well?' It was the Fox, who had been squatting there, as my women told me, like a cat at a mouse-hole.

'Alive, Grandfather,' said I, and kissed him. Then, 'Come back as soon as you can. I am wet as a fish and must wash and change and eat. I'll tell you all when you come.'

When I was re-clothed and finishing my supper, his knock came to the door. I made him come and sit with me at table and poured him drink. There was no one with us but little Poobi, my dark-skinned maid, who was faithful and loving and knew no Greek.

'You said *alive*,' the Fox began, raising his cup. 'See. I make a libation to Zeus the Saviour.' He did it Greek fashion with a clever twist of the cup that lets fall just one drop.

'Yes, Grandfather, alive and well and says she's happy.'

'I feel as if my heart would crack for joy, child,' said he. 'You tell me things almost beyond belief.'

'You've had the sweet, Grandfather. There's sour to follow.'

'Let me hear it. All is to be borne.'

Then I told him the whole story, always excepting that one glimpse in the fog. It was dreadful to me to see the light die out of his face as I went on, and to feel that I was darkening it. And I asked myself, 'If you can hardly bear to do this, how will you bear to wipe out Psyche's happiness?'

'Alas, alas, poor Psyche!' said the Fox. 'Our little child! And how she must have suffered! Hellebore's the right medicine; with rest, and peace, and loving care ... oh, we'd bring her into frame again, I don't doubt it, if we could nurse her well. But how are we to give her all or any of the things she needs? My wits are dry, daughter. We must think, though, contrive. I wish I were Odysseus, aye, or Hermes.'

'You think, then, she's mad, for certain?'

He darted a quick glance at me. 'Why, daughter, what then have you been thinking?'

'You'll call it folly, I suppose. But you weren't with her, Grandfather. She talked so calmly. There was nothing disordered in her speech. She could laugh merrily. Her glance wasn't wild. If I'd had my eyes shut, I would have believed her palace was as real as this.'

'But, your eyes being open, you saw no such thing.'

'You don't think – not possibly – not as a mere hundredth chance – there might be things that are real though we can't see them?'

'Certainly I do. Such things as Justice, Equality, the Soul, or musical notes.'

'Oh, Grandfather, I don't mean things like that. If there are souls, could there not be soul-houses?'

He ran his hands through his hair with an old, familiar gesture of teacher's dismay.

'Child,' he said, 'you make me believe that, after all these years, you have never even begun to understand what the word *soul* means.'

'I know well enough what you mean by it, Grandfather. But do you, even you, know all? Are there no things – I mean *things* – but what we see?'

'Plenty. Things behind our backs. Things too far away. And all things, if it's dark enough.' He leaned forward and put his hand on mine. 'I begin to think, daughter, that if I can get that hellebore, yours had better be the first dose,' he said.

I had had half a thought, at the outset, of telling him about the ferly, my glimpse of the palace. But I couldn't bring myself to it; he was the worst hearer in the world for such a story. Already he was making me ashamed of half the things I had been thinking. And now a more cheering thought came to me.

'Then, perhaps,' said I, 'this lover who comes to her in darkness is also part of the madness.'

'I wish I could believe it,' said the Fox.

'Why not, Grandfather?'

'You say she's plump and rosy? not starveling?'

'Never better.'

'Then who's fed her all this time?'

I was silenced.

'And who took her out of the irons?'

I had never thought of this question at all. 'Grandfather!' I said. 'What is in your mind? You – you of all men – are not hinting that it is the god. You'd laugh at me if I said so.'

'I'd be more likely to weep. Oh, child, child, child, when shall I have washed the nurse and the grandam and the priest and the soothsayer out of your soul? Do you think the Divine Nature – why, it's profane, ridiculous. You might as well say the universe itched or the Nature of Things sometimes tippled in the wine cellar.'

'I haven't said it was a god, Grandfather,' said I. 'I am asking who you think it was.'

'A man, a man, of course,' said the Fox, beating his hands on the table. 'What? Are you still a child? Didn't you know there were men on the Mountain?'

'Men!' I gasped.

'Yes. Vagabonds, broken men, outlaws, thieves. Where are your wits?'

Indignation came burning into my cheeks and I sprang up. For any daughter of our house to mix, even in lawful marriage, with those who have not (at least by one grandparent) divine descent, is an utter abomination. The Fox's thought was unendurable.

'What are you saying?' I asked him. 'Psyche would die on sharp stakes sooner than—'

'Peace, daughter,' said the Fox. 'Psyche doesn't know. As I read it, some robber or runaway has found the poor child, half-crazed with terror and loneliness, and with thirst too (likely enough), and got her out of her irons. And if she were not in her right mind, what would she most probably babble of in her ravings? Her gold and amber house on the Mountain, of course. She has had that fantasy from her childhood. The fellow would fall in with it. He'd be the god's messenger ... why, that's where her god of the westwind comes from. It would be the man himself. He'd take her to this valley. He'd whisper to her that the god, the bridegroom, would come to her that night. And after dark, he'd come back.'

'But the palace?'

'Her old fantasy, raised up by her madness and taken by her for reality. And whatever she tells the rascal about her fine house, he echoes it all. Perhaps adds more of his own. And so the delusion is built up stronger and stronger.'

For the second time that day I was utterly aghast. The Fox's explanation seemed too plain and evident to allow me any hope of doubt. While Bardia was speaking, his had seemed the same.

'It looks, Grandfather,' said I dully, 'as if you had read the riddle right.'

'It needs no Oedipus. But the real riddle's still to guess. What must we do? Oh, I'm barren, barren. I think your father has addled my brains with beating me about the ears. There must be some way ... yet we've so little time.'

'And so little freedom. I can't pretend to be on my sick-bed much longer. And once the King knows I'm whole, how shall I ever get to the Mountain again?'

'Oh, for that – but I'd forgotten. There's been news today. The lions have been seen again.'

'What?' I cried in terror. 'On the Mountain?'

'No, no, not so bad as that. Indeed, rather good than bad. Somewhere down south, and west of Ringal. The King will have a great lion-hunt.'

'The lions back ... so Ungit has played us false after all. Perhaps he'll sacrifice Redival this time. Is the King in a great rage?'

'Rage? No. Why, you'd think the loss of a herdsman and (what he values far more) some of the best dogs, and I don't know how many bullocks, was the best news he'd ever heard! I never saw him in better spirits. There's been nothing in his mouth all day but dogs and beaters and weather ... and such rummage and bustle – messages to this lord and that lord – deep talks with the huntsman – inspecting of kennels – shoeing of horses – beer flowing like water – even I have been slapped on the back in pure good-fellowship till my ribs ache with it. But what concerns us is that he'll be out at the hunting the next two days at least. With luck it might be five or six.'

'Then that's the time we have to work in.'

'No more than that. He goes at daybreak tomorrow. And anyway, we'd have little longer. She'll die if winter catches her on the Mountain. Living without a roof. And she'll be with child, no doubt, before we've time to look about us.'

It was as if I'd been hit about the heart. 'Leprosy and scabs on the man!' I gasped. 'Curse him, curse him! Psyche to carry a beggar's brat? We'll have him impaled if ever we catch him. He shall die for days. Oh, I could tear his body with my bare teeth.'

'You darken our counsels – and your own soul – with these passions,' said the Fox. 'If there were anywhere she could lie hidden (if we could get her)!'

'I had thought,' said I, 'we could hide her in Bardia's house.'

'Bardia! He'd never take one who's been sacrificed into his house. He's afraid of his own shadow where gods and old wives' tales are concerned. He's a fool.'

'That he is not,' said I; sharply enough, for the Fox often nettled me with his contempt for very brave and honest people if they had no tincture of his Greek wisdom.

'And if Bardia would,' the Fox added, 'that wife of his wouldn't let him. And everyone knows that Bardia's tied to his wife's apron-strings.'

'Bardia! And such a man. I couldn't have believed—'

'Pah! He's as amorous as Alcibiades. Why, the fellow married her undowered – for her beauty, if you please. The whole town knows of it. And she rules him like her slave.'

'She must be a very vile woman, Grandfather.'

'What does it matter to us whether she is or no? But you needn't think to find refuge for our darling in that house. I'll go further, daughter. There's nothing for it but to send her right out of Glome. If anyone in Glome knew that she had not died, they would seek her out and sacrifice her again. If we could get her to her mother's family ... but I see no way of doing it. Oh Zeus, Zeus, Zeus, if I had ten hoplites and a sane man to command them!'

'I can't see,' said I, 'even how to get her to leave the Mountain. She was obstinate, Grandfather. She obeys me no more. I think we must use force.'

'And we have no force. I am a slave and you are a woman. We can't lead a dozen spears up the Mountain. And if we could, the secret would never be kept.'

After that we sat silent for a long time; the fire flickering, Poobi sitting cross-legged by the hearth, feeding the logs into it, and playing a strange game of her own people's with beads (she once tried to teach it to me, but I could never learn). The Fox made as if to speak a dozen times but always checked himself. He was quick to devise plans, but no less quick to see the faults in them.

At last I said, 'It all comes to this, Grandfather. I must go back to Psyche. I must overrule her somehow. Once she is on our side, once she knows her shame and danger, then the three of us must devise as best we can. It may be that she and I must go out into the wide world together; wander like Oedipus.'

'And I with you,' said the Fox. 'You once bade me run away. This time I'll do it.'

'One thing's certain,' said I. 'She shall not be left to the felon who has abused her. I will choose any way – any way – rather than that. It rests on me. Her mother's dead (what mother but me has she ever known?). Her father's nothing; nothing for a father, and nothing for a king either. The honour of our house – the very being of Psyche – only I am left to care for them. She shall not be left. I'll – I'll—'

'What, child? You are pale! Are you fainting?'

'If there is no other way, I will kill her.'

'Babai!' said the Fox, so loud that Poobi stopped her game and stared at him. 'Daughter, daughter. You are transported beyond all reason and nature. Do you know what it is? There's one part love in your heart, and five parts anger, and seven parts pride. The gods know, I love Psyche too. And you know it; you know I love her as well as you do. It's a bitter grief that our child – our very Artemis and Aphrodite all in one – should live a beggar's life and lie in a beggar's arms. Yet even this ... it is not to be named beside such detested impieties as you speak of. Why, look at it squarely, as reason and nature have made it, not as passion would paint it. To be poor and in hardship, to be a poor man's wife—'

'Wife! You mean his trull, his drab, his whore, his slut.'

'Nature knows nothing of these names. What you call marriage is by law and custom, not nature. Nature's marriage is but the union of the man who persuades with the woman who consents. And so—'

'The man who persuades – or, more likely, forces or deceives – being some murderer, alien, traitor, runaway slave or other filth?'

'Filth? Perhaps I do not see it as you do. I am an alien and a slave myself; and ready to be a runaway – to risk the flogging and impaling – for your love and hers.'

'You are ten times my father,' said I, raising his hand to my lips. 'I meant no such thing. But, Grandfather, there are matters you don't understand. Psyche said so herself.'

'Sweet Psyche,' he said. 'I have often told her so. I am glad she has mastered the lesson. She was ever a good pupil.'

'You don't believe in the divine blood of our house,' I said.

'Oh yes. Of all houses. All men are of divine blood, for there is the god in every man. We are all one. Even the man who has taken Psyche. I have called him rascal and villain. Too likely he is. But it may not be. A good man might be an outlaw and a runaway.'

I was silent. All this meant nothing to me.

'Daughter,' said the Fox suddenly (I think no woman, at least no woman who loved you, would have done it). 'Sleep comes early to old men. I can hardly keep my eyes open. Let me go. Perhaps we shall see more clearly in the morning.'

What could I do but send him away? This is where men, even the trustiest, fail us. Their heart is never so wholly given to any matter but that some trifle of a meal, or a drink, or a sleep, or a joke, or a girl, may come in between them and it, and then (even if you are a queen) you'll get no more good out of them till they've had their way. In those days I had not yet understood this. Great desolation came over me.

'Everyone goes from me,' I said. 'None of them cares for Psyche. She lives at the very outskirts of their thoughts. She is less to them, far less, than Poobi is to me. They think of her a little and then get tired and go to something else; the Fox to his sleep, and Bardia to his doll or scold of a wife. You are alone, Orual. Whatever is to be done, you must devise and do it. No help will come. All gods and mortals have drawn away from you. You must guess the riddle. Not a word will come to you until you have guessed wrong and they all come crowding back to accuse and mock and punish you for it.'

I sent Poobi to bed. Then I did a thing which I think few have done. I spoke to the gods; myself, alone, in such words as came to me, not in a temple, without a sacrifice. I stretched myself face downward on the floor and called upon them with my whole heart. I took back every word I had said against them. I promised anything they might ask of me, if only they would send me a sign. They gave me none. When I began there was red firelight in the room and rain on the roof; when I rose up again the fire had sunk a little lower, and the rain drummed on as before.

Now, when I knew that I was left utterly to myself, I said, 'I must do it ... whatever I do ... tomorrow. I must, then, rest tonight.' I lay down on the bed. I was in that state when the body is so tired that sleep comes soon, but the mind is in such anguish that it will wake you the moment the body's sated. It woke me a few hours past midnight, with no least possibility of further sleep in me. The fire was out; the rain had stopped. I went to my window and stood looking out into the gusty blackness, twisting my hair in my fists and my knuckles against my temples, and thought.

My mind was much clearer. I now saw that I had, strangely, taken both Bardia's explanation and the Fox's (each while it lasted) for certain truth. Yet one must be false. And I could not find out which, for each was well rooted in its own soil. If the things believed in Glome were true, then what Bardia said stood; if the Fox's philosophy were true, what the Fox said stood. But I could not find out whether the doctrines of Glome or the wisdom of Greece were right. I was the child of Glome and the pupil of the Fox; I saw that for years my life had been lived in two halves, never fitted together.

I must give up, then, trying to judge between Bardia and my master. And as soon as I said that, I saw (and wondered I had not seen before) that it made no difference. For there was one point on which both agreed. Both thought that some evil or shameful thing had taken Psyche for its own. Murdering thief or spectral Shadowbrute – did it matter which? The one thing neither of them had believed was that anything good or fair came to her in the night. No one but myself had dallied with that thought even for a moment. Why should they? Only my desperate wishes could have made it seem possible. The thing came in darkness and forbade itself to be seen. What lover would shun his bride's eyes unless he had some terrible reason for it?

Even I had thought the opposite only for an instant, while I looked at that likeness of a house across the river.

'It shall not have her,' I said. 'She shall not lie in those detestable embraces. Tonight must be the last night of that.'

Suddenly there rose up before me the memory of Psyche in the mountain valley, brightface, brimming over with joy. My terrible temptation came back; to leave her to that fool-happy dream, whatever came of it, to spare her, not to bring her down from it into misery. Must I be to her an avenging fury, not a gentle mother? And part of my mind now was saying, 'Do not meddle. Anything might be true. You are among marvels that you do not understand. Carefully, carefully. Who knows what ruin you might pull down on her head and yours?' But with the other part of me I answered that I was indeed her mother and her father too (all she had of either), that my love must be grave and provident, not slipshod and indulgent, that there is a time for love to be stern. After all, what was she but a child? If the present case were beyond my understanding, how much more must it be beyond hers? Children must obey. It had hurt me, long ago, when I made the barber pull out the thorn. Had I not none the less done well?

I hardened my resolution. I knew now what (which of two things) I must do; and no later than the day which would soon be breaking. Provided only that Bardia were not going on the lion-hunt; and that I could get him clear of this wife of his. As a man, even in great pain or sorrow, can still be fretted by a fly that buzzes in his face, I was fretted by the thought of this wife, this petted thing, suddenly starting up to delay or to hinder.

I lay down on my bed to wait for morning; calmed and quiet in a way, now that I knew what I would do.

14

It seemed long to me before the palace was stirring, though it stirred early because of the King's hunting. I waited till that noise was well begun. Then I rose and dressed in such clothes as I had worn the day before; and took the same urn. This time I put in it a lamp and a little pitcher of oil and a long band of linen about a span and a half broad, such as bridesmaids wear in Glome, wrapped over and over round them. Mine had lain in my chest ever since the marriage night of Psyche's mother. Then I called up Poobi and had food brought to me, of which I ate some, and some I put in the urn under the band. When I knew by the horse-hooves and horns and shoutings that the King's party was gone, I put on my veil and a cloak and went down. I sent the first slave I met to find whether Bardia were gone to the hunting; and if he were in the palace, to send him to me. I waited for him in the Pillar Room. It was a strange freedom to be in there alone; and indeed, amid all my cares, I could not help perceiving how the house was, as it were, lightened and set at liberty by the absence of the King. I thought, from their looks, that all the family felt it.

Bardia came to me.

'Bardia,' said I, 'I must go again to the Mountain.'

'It's impossible you should go with me, Lady,' he said. 'I was left out of the hunting (ill luck for me) for one purpose only; to watch over the house. I must even lie here at nights till the King's back.'

This dashed me very much. 'Oh, Bardia,' said I, 'what shall we do? I am in great straits. It's on my sister's business.'

Bardia rubbed his forefinger across his upper lip in a way he had when he was gravelled. 'And you can't ride,' he said. 'I wonder now – but no, that's foolishness. There's no horse to be trusted with a rider that can't ride. And a few days hence won't serve? The best would be to give you another man.'

'But, Bardia, it must be you. No one else would be able ... it's a very secret errand.'

'I could let Gram off with you for two days and a night.'

'Who is Gram?'

'The small, dark one. He's a good man.'

'But can he hold his tongue?'

'It's more a question if he can ever loosen it. We get hardly ten words from him in as many days. But he's a true man; true to me, above all, for I once had the chance to do him a good turn.'

'It will not be like going with you, Bardia.'

'It's the best you can do, Lady, unless you can wait.'

But I said I could not wait, and Bardia had Gram called. He was a thin-faced man, very black-eyed, and (I thought) looked at me as if he feared me. Bardia told him to get his horse and await me where the little lane meets the road into the city.

As soon as he was gone, I said, 'Now, Bardia, get me a dagger.'

'A dagger, Lady? And for what?'

'To use as a dagger. Come Bardia, you know I mean no ill.'

He looked strangely at me, but got it. I put it on, at my belt, where the sword had hung yesterday. 'Farewell, Bardia,' said I.

'*Farewell*, Lady? Do you go for longer than a night?'

'I don't know, I don't know,' said I. Then, all in haste, and leaving him to wonder, I went out and went on foot, by the lane and joined Gram. He set me up on the horse (touching me, unless it was my fantasy, as one who touched a snake or a witch) and we began.

Nothing could be less like than that day's journey and the last. I never got more than 'Yes, Lady', or 'No, Lady', out of Gram all day. There was much rain and even between the showers the wind was wet. There was a grey, driving sky and the little hills and valleys, which had been so distinct with brightness and shade for Bardia and me the other day, were all sunk into one piece. We had started many hours later, and it was nearer evening than noon when we came down from the saddle into that secret valley. And there at last, as if by some trick of the gods (which perhaps it was), the weather cleared; so that it was hard not to think the valley had a sunlight of its own and the blustering rains merely ringed it about as the mountains did.

I brought Gram to the place where Bardia and I had passed the night and told him to await me there, and not to cross the river. 'I must go over it myself. It may be I shall re-cross it to your side by nightfall, or in the night. But I think that whatever time I spend on this side I will spend over yonder, near the ford. Do not come to me there unless I call you.'

He said, as always, 'Yes, Lady', and looked as if he liked this adventure very little.

I went to the ford; about a long bow-shot from Gram. My heart was still as ice, heavy as lead, cold as earth, but I was free now from all doubting and deliberating. I set my foot on the first stone of the crossing and called

Psyche's name. She must have been very close, for almost at once I saw her coming down to the bank. We might have been two images of love, the happy and the stern; she so young, so brightface, joy in her eyes and limbs; I, burdened and resolute, bringing pain in my hand.

'So I spoke truly, Maia,' she said as soon as I had crossed the water and we had embraced. 'The King has been no hindrance to you, has he? Salute me for a prophetess!'

This startled me for a moment, for I had forgotten her foretelling. But I put it aside to be thought of later. Now, I had my work to do; I must not, now of all times, begin doubting and pondering again.

She brought me a little way from the water – I don't know into what part of her phantom palace – and we sat down. I threw back my hood and put off my veil and set down the urn beside me.

'Oh, Orual,' said Psyche, 'what a storm-cloud in your face! That's how you looked when you were most angry with me as a child.'

'Was I ever angry? Ah, Psyche, do you think I ever scolded or denied you without grieving my heart ten times more than yours?'

'Sister, I meant to find no fault with you.'

'Then find no fault with me today either. For indeed we must talk very gravely. Now listen, Psyche. Our father is no father. Your mother (peace upon her!) is dead, and you have never seen her kindred. I have been – I have tried to be and still I must be – all the father and mother and kin you have. And all the King too.'

'Maia, you have been all this and more since the day I was born. You and the dear Fox are all I ever had.'

'Yes, the Fox. I'll have something to say of him too. And so, Psyche, if anyone is to care for you or counsel you or shield you, or if anyone is to tell you what belongs to the honour of our blood, it can be only I.'

'But why are you saying all this, Orual? You do not think I have left off loving you because I now have a husband to love as well? If you would understand it, that makes me love you – why, it makes me love everyone and everything – more.'

This made me shudder, but I hid it and went on. 'I know you love me, Psyche,' said I. 'And I think I should not live if you didn't. But you must trust me too.'

She said nothing. And now I was right on top of the terrible thing, and it almost struck me dumb. I cast about for ways to begin it.

'You spoke last time,' I said, 'of the day we got the thorn out of your hand. We hurt you that time, Psyche. But we did right. Those who love must hurt. I must hurt you again today. And, Psyche, you are still little more than a child. You cannot go your own way. You will let me rule and guide you.'

'Orual, I have a husband to guide me now.'

It was difficult not to be angered or terrified by her harping on it. I bit my lip; then said, 'Alas, child, it is about that very husband (as you call him) that I must grieve you.' I looked straight at her eyes and said sharply, 'Who is he? What is he?'

'A god,' she said, low and quivering. 'And I think, the god of the Mountain.'

'Alas, Psyche, you are deceived. If you knew the truth, you would die rather than lie in his bed.'

'The truth?'

'We must face it, child. Be very brave. Let me pull out this thorn. What sort of god would he be who dares not show his face?'

'*Dares not!* You come near to making me angry, Orual.'

'But think, Psyche. Nothing that's beautiful hides its face. Nothing that's honest hides its name. No, no, listen. In your heart you must see the truth, however you try to brazen it out with words. Think. Whose bride were you called? The Brute's. And think again. If it's not the Brute, who else dwells in these mountains? Thieves and murderers; men worse than brutes; and lecherous as goats, we may be sure. Are you a prize they'd let pass if you fell in their way? There's your lover, child. Either a monster – shadow and monster in one, maybe, a ghostly, un-dead thing – or a salt villain whose lips, even on your feet or the hem of your robe, would be a stain to our blood.'

She was silent a long time, her eyes on her lap.

'And so, Psyche,' I began at last, tenderly as I could – but she tossed away the hand that I had laid on hers.

'You mistake me, Orual. If I am pale, it is with anger. There, Sister; I have conquered it. I'll forgive you. You mean – I'll believe you mean – nothing but good. Yet how – or why – you can have blackened and tormented your soul with such thoughts ... but no more of that. If ever you loved me, put them away now.'

'Blackened my thoughts? They're not only mine. Tell me, Psyche, who are the two wisest men we know?'

'Why, the Fox for one. For the second – I know so few. I suppose Bardia is wise; in his own way.'

'You said yourself, that night in the five-walled room, that he was a prudent man. Now, Psyche, these two – so wise and so different – are both agreed with each other and with me concerning this love of yours. Agreed without doubt. All three of us are certain. Either Shadowbrute or felon.'

'You have told them my story, Orual? It was ill done. I gave you no leave. My lord gave no leave. Oh, Orual! It was more like Batta than you.'

I could not help it if my face reddened with anger, but I would not be turned aside. 'Doubtless,' I said. 'There is no end to the secrecy of this – this *husband* as you call him. Child, has his vile love so turned your brain that you can't see the plainest thing? A god? Yet on your own showing he hides and slinks and whispers "Mum", and "Keep counsel", and "Don't betray me", like a runaway slave.'

I am not certain that she had listened to this. What she said was, 'The Fox too! That is very strange. I never thought he would have believed in the Brute at all.'

I had not said he did. But if that was what she took out of my words, I thought it no part of my duty to set her right. It was an error helping her towards the main truth. I had need of all help to drive her thither.

'Neither he nor I nor Bardia,' said I, 'believes for one moment in your fancy that it is the god; no more than that this wild heath is a palace. And be sure, Psyche, that if we could ask every man and woman in Glome, all would say the same. The truth is too clear.'

'But what is all this to me? How should they know? I am his wife. I know.'

'How can you know if you have never seen him?'

'Orual, how can you be so simple? I – how could I not know?'

'But how, Psyche?'

'What am I to answer to such a question? It's not fitting ... it is ... and especially to you, Sister, who are a virgin.'

That matronly primness, from the child she was, went near to ending my patience. It was almost (but I think now she did not mean it so) as if she taunted me. Yet I ruled myself.

'Well, if you are so sure, Psyche, you will not refuse to put it to the test.'

'What test? Though I need none myself.'

'I have brought a lamp, and oil. See. Here they are.' (I set them down beside her.) 'Wait till he – or it – sleeps. Then look.'

'I cannot do that.'

'Ah! ... you see! You will abide no test. And why? Because you are not sure yourself. If you were, you'd be eager to do it. If he is, as you say, a god, one glimpse will set all our doubts at rest. What you call our dark thoughts will be put to flight. But you daren't.'

'Oh, Orual, what evil you think! The reason I cannot look at him – least of all by such trickery as you'd have me do – is that he has forbidden me.'

'I can think – Bardia and the Fox can think – of one reason only for such a forbidding. And of one only for your obeying it.'

'Then you know little of love.'

'You fling my virginity in my face again, do you? Better it than the stye you're in. So be it. Of what you now call love, I do know nothing. You can whisper about it to Redival better than to me – or to Ungit's girls, maybe, or the King's doxies. I know another sort of love. You shall find what it's like. You shall not—'

'Orual, Orual, you are raving,' said Psyche; herself unangered, gazing at me large-eyed, sorrowful, but nothing humble about her sorrow. You would have thought she was my mother, not I (almost) hers. I had known this long time that the old meek, biddable Psyche was gone for ever; yet it shocked me afresh.

'Yes,' I said. 'I was raving. You had made me angry. But I had thought (you will set me right, I don't doubt, if I am mistaken) that all loves alike were eager to clear the thing they loved of vile charges brought against it; if they could. Tell a mother her child is hideous. If it's beautiful she'll show it. No forbidding would stop her. If she keeps it hidden, the charge is true. You're afraid of the test, Psyche.'

'I am afraid – no, I am ashamed … to disobey him.'

'Then, even at the best, look what you make of him! Something worse than our father. Who that loved you could be angry at your breaking so unreasonable a command – and for so good a reason?'

'Foolishness, Orual,' she answered, shaking her head. 'He is a god. He has good grounds for what he does, be sure. How should I know of them? I am only his simple Psyche.'

'Then you will not do it? You think – you say you think – that you can prove him a god and set me free from the fears that sicken my heart. But you will not do it.'

'I would if I could, Orual.'

I looked about me. The sun was almost setting behind the saddle. In a little while she would send me away. I rose up.

'An end of this must be made,' I said. 'You shall do it. Psyche, I command you.'

'Dear Maia, my duty is no longer to you.'

'Then my life shall end with it,' said I. I flung back my cloak further, thrust out my bare left arm, and struck the dagger into it till the point pricked out on the other side. Pulling the iron back through the wound was the worse pain; but I can hardly believe now how little I felt it.

'Orual! Are you mad?' cried Psyche, leaping up.

'You'll find linen in that urn. Tie up my wound,' said I, sitting down and holding the arm out to let the blood fall on the heather.

I had thought she might scream and wring her hands or faint. But I was deceived. She was pale enough but had all her wits about her. She bound my arm. The blood came seeping through fold after fold, but she staunched it in the end. (My stroke had been lucky enough. If I had known as much then as I do now about the inside of an arm, I might not – who knows? – have had the resolution to do it.)

The bandaging could not be done in a moment. The sun was lower and the air colder when we were able to talk again.

'Maia,' said Psyche, 'what did you do that for?'

'To show you I'm in earnest, girl. Listen. You have driven me to desperate courses. I give you your choice. Swear on this edge, with my blood still wet on it, that you will this very night do as I have commanded you; or else I'll first kill you and then myself.'

'Orual,' says she, very queenlike, raising her head, 'you might have spared that threat of killing me. All your power over me lies in the other.'

'Then swear, girl. You never knew me break my word.'

The look in her face now was one I did not understand. I think a lover – I mean, a man who loved – might look so on a woman who had been false to him. And at last she said:

'You are indeed teaching me about kinds of love I did not know. It is like looking into a deep pit. I am not sure whether I like your kind better than hatred. Oh, Orual – to take my love for you, because you know it goes down to my very roots and cannot be diminished by any other, newer love, and then to make of it a tool, a weapon, a thing of policy and mastery, an instrument of torture ... I begin to think I never knew you. Whatever comes after, something that was between us dies here.'

'Enough of your subtleties,' said I. 'Both of us die here, in plainest truth and blood, unless you swear.'

'If I do,' said she hotly, 'it will not be for any doubt of my husband or his love. It will only be because I think better of him than of you. He cannot be cruel like you. I'll not believe it. He will know how I was tortured into my disobedience. He will forgive me.'

'He need never know,' said I.

The look of scorn she gave me flayed my soul. And yet, this very nobleness in her – had I not taught it to her? What was there in her that was not my work? And now she used it to look at me as if I were base beneath all baseness.

'You thought I would hide it? Thought I would not tell him?' she said; each word like the rubbing of a file across raw flesh. 'Well. It's all of a piece. Let us, as you say, make an end. You grow more and more a stranger to me at each word. And I had loved you so; loved, honoured, trusted, and (while it was fit) obeyed. And now; but I can't have your blood on my threshold. You chose your threat well. I'll swear. Where's your dagger?'

So I had won my victory and my heart was in torment. I had a terrible longing to unsay all my words and beg her forgiveness. But I held out the dagger. (The 'oath on edge', as we call it, is our strongest in Glome.)

'And even now,' said Psyche, 'I know what I do. I know that I am betraying the best of lovers and that perhaps, before sunrise, all my happiness may be destroyed for ever. This is the price you have put upon your life. Well, I must pay it.'

She took her oath. My tears burst out, and I tried to speak, but she turned her face away.

'The sun is almost down,' she said. 'Go. You have saved your life; go and live it as you can.'

I found I was becoming afraid of her. I made my way back to the stream; crossed it somehow. And the shadow of the saddle leaped across the whole valley as the sun set.

15

I think I must have fainted when I got to this side of the water, for there seems to be some gap in my memory between the fording and being fully aware again of three things: cold, and the pain in my arm, and thirst. I drank ravenously. Then I wanted food, and now first remembered that I had left it in the urn with the lamp. My soul rose up against calling Gram, who was very irksome to me. I felt (though I saw it to be folly even at the time) that if Bardia had come with me instead, all might have been different and better. And away my thoughts wandered to imagine all he would be doing and saying now if he had, till suddenly I remembered what business had brought me there. I was ashamed that I had thought, even for a moment, of anything else.

My purpose was to sit by the ford, watching till I should see a light (which would be Psyche lighting her lamp). It would vanish when she covered and hid it. Then, most likely far later, there would be a light again; she would be looking at her vile master in its sleep. And after that – very, very soon after it, I hoped – there would be Psyche creeping through the darkness and sending a sort of whispered call ('Maia, Maia') across the stream. And I would be half-way over it in an instant. This time it would be I who helped her at the ford. She would be all weeping and dismayed as I folded her in my arms and comforted her; for now she would know who were her true friends, and would love me again, and would thank me, shuddering, for saving her from the thing the lamp had shown. These were dear thoughts to me when they came and while they lasted.

But there were other thoughts too. Try as I would, I could not quite put out of my head the fear that I had been wrong. A real god ... was it impossible? But I could never dwell on that part of it. What came back and back to my mind was the thought of Psyche herself somehow (I never knew well how) ruined, lost, robbed of all joy, a wailing, wandering shape, for whom I had wrecked everything. More times than I could count, that night, I had the wish, tyrannously strong, to re-cross the cold water, to shout out that

I forgave her her promise, that she was not to light the lamp, that I had advised her wrongly. But I governed it.

Neither the one sort of thoughts nor the other were more than the surface of my mind. Beneath them, deep as the deep ocean-sea whereof the Fox spoke, was the cold, hopeless abyss of her scorn, her un-love, her very hatred.

How could she hate me, when my arm throbbed and burned with the wound I had given it for her love? 'Cruel Psyche, cruel Psyche,' I sobbed. But then I saw that I was falling back to the dreams of my sickness. So I set my wits against it and bestirred myself. Whatever happened I must watch and be sane.

The first light came soon enough; and vanished again. I said to myself – though indeed once I had her oath I never doubted her faith to it – 'So. All's well this far.' It made me wonder, as at a new question, what I meant by *well*. But the thought passed.

The cold grew bitter. My arm was a bar of fire, the rest of me an icicle, chained to that bar but never melted. I began to see that I was doing a perilous thing. I might die, thus wounded and fasting, or at least get such a chill as would bring my death soon after. And out of that seed there grew up, in one moment, a huge, foolish flower of fancies. For at once (leaping over all question of how it should come about) I saw myself laid on the pyre, and Psyche – she knew now, she loved me again now – beating her breast and weeping and repenting all her cruelties. The Fox and Bardia were there too; Bardia wept fast. Everyone loved me once I was dead. But I am ashamed to write all these follies.

What checked them was the next appearing of the light. To my eyes, long swilled with darkness, it seemed brighter than you would have thought possible. Bright and still, a homelike thing in that wild place. And for a time longer than I had expected, it shone and was still, and the whole world was still around it. Then the stillness broke.

The great voice, which rose up from somewhere close to the light, went through my whole body in such a swift wave of terror that it blotted out even the pain in my arm. It was no ugly sound; even in its implacable sternness it was golden. My terror was the salute that mortal flesh gives to immortal things. And after – barely after – the strong soaring of its incomprehensible speech, came the sound of weeping. I think (if those old words have a meaning) my heart broke then. But neither the immortal sound nor the tears of her who wept lasted for more than two heartbeats. Heartbeats, I say; but I think my heart did not beat till they were over.

A great flash laid the valley bare to my eyes. Then it thundered as if the sky broke in two straight above my head. Lightnings, thick-following one another, pricked the valley, left, right, near and far, everywhere. Each flash showed falling trees; the imagined pillars of Psyche's house were going down. They seemed to fall silently, for the thunder hid their crashing. But there was another noise it could not hide. Somewhere away on my left the walls of the Mountain itself were breaking. I saw (or I think I saw) fragments of rock hurled about and striking on other rocks and rising into the air again like a child's ball that bounces. The river rose, so quickly that I was overtaken by its rush before I could stumble back from it, wet to my middle; but that made little odds, for with the storm there had come a tyrannous pelting rain. Hair and clothes were already a mere sponge.

But, beaten and blinded though I was, I took these things for a good sign. They showed (so it seemed to me) that I was right. Psyche had roused some dreadful thing and these were its ragings. It had waked, she had not hidden her light soon enough; or else – yes, that was most likely – it had only feigned to be sleeping; it might be a thing that never needed sleep. It might, no doubt, destroy both her and me. But she would know. She would, at worst, die undeceived, disenchanted, reconciled to me. Even now, we might escape. Failing that, we could die together. I rose up, bent double under the battery of the rain, to cross the stream.

I believe I could never have crossed it – the deep, foaming death-race it had now become – even if I had been left free to try. I was not left free. There came as if it were a lightning that endured. That is, the look of it was the look of lightning, pale, dazzling, without warmth or comfort, showing each smallest thing with fierce distinctness, but it did not go away. This great light stood over me as still as a candle burning in a curtained and shuttered room. In the centre of the light was something like a man. It is strange that I cannot tell you its size. Its face was far above me, yet memory does not show the shape as a giant's. And I do not know whether it stood, or seemed to stand, on the far side of the water or on the water itself.

Though this light stood motionless, my glimpse of the face was as swift as a true flash of lightning. I could not bear it for longer. Not my eyes only, but my heart and blood and very brain were too weak for that. A monster – the Shadowbrute that I and all Glome had imagined – would have subdued me less than the beauty this face wore. And I think anger (what men call anger) would have been more supportable than the passionless and measureless rejection with which it looked upon me. Though my body crouched where I could almost have touched his feet, his eyes seemed to send me from him to an endless distance. He rejected, denied, answered, and (worst of all) he knew, all I had thought, done or been. A Greek verse says that even the gods cannot change the past. But is it true? He made it to be as if, from the beginning, I had known that Psyche's lover was a god, and as if all my doubtings, fears, guessings, debatings, questionings of Bardia, questionings of the Fox, all the rummage and business of it, had been trumped-up foolery, dust blown in my own eyes by myself. You, who read my book, judge. Was it so? Or, at least, had it been so in the very past, before this god changed the past? And if they can indeed change the past, why do they never do so in mercy?

The thunder had ceased, I think, the moment the still light came. There was great silence when the god spoke to me. And as there was no anger (what men call anger) in his face, so there was none in his voice. It was unmoved and sweet; like a bird singing on the branch above a hanged man.

'Now Psyche goes out in exile. Now she must hunger and thirst and tread hard roads. Those against whom I cannot fight must do their will upon her. You, woman, shall know yourself and your work. You also shall be Psyche.'

The voice and the light both ended together as if one knife had cut them short. Then, in the silence, I heard again the noise of the weeping.

I never heard weeping like that before or after; not from a child, nor a man wounded in the palm, nor a tortured man, nor a girl dragged off to slavery from a taken city. If you heard the woman you most hate in the world weep so, you would go to comfort her. You would fight your way through fire and spears to reach her. And I knew who wept, and what had been done to her, and who had done it.

I rose to go to her. But already the weeping was further away. She went wailing far off to my right, down to the end of the valley where I had never been, where doubtless it fell away, or dropped in sheer cliffs, towards the south. And I could not cross the stream. It would not even drown me. It would bruise and freeze and bemire me, but somehow whenever I grasped a rock – earth was no use now, for great slabs of the bank were slipping into the current every moment – I found I was still on this side. Sometimes I could not even find the river; I was so bewildered in the dark, and all the ground was now little better than a swamp, so that pools and new-formed brooks lured me now this way, now that.

I cannot remember more of that night. When day began to break, I could see what the god's anger had done to the valley. It was all bare rock, raw earth, and foul water; trees, bushes, sheep, and here and there a deer, floated in it. If I could have crossed the first river in the night it would not have profited me; I should have reached only the narrow bank of mud between it and the next. Even now I could not help calling out Psyche's name, calling till my voice was gone, but I knew it was foolishness. I had heard her leaving the valley. She had already gone into the exile which the god foretold. She had begun to wander, weeping, from land to land; weeping for her lover, not (I mustn't so cheat myself) for me.

I went and found Gram; a wet, shivering wretch he was, who gave one scared glance at my bandaged arm, and no more, and asked no questions. We ate food from the saddle-bags and began our journey. The weather was fair enough.

I looked on the things about me with a new eye. Now that I'd proved for certain that the gods are and that they hated me, it seemed that I had nothing to do but to wait for my punishment. I wondered on which dangerous edge the horse would slip and fling us down a few hundred feet into a gully; or what tree would drop a branch on my neck as we rode under it; or whether my wound would corrupt and I should die that way. Often, remembering that it is sometimes the god's way to turn us into beasts, I put my hand up under my veil to see if I could feel cat's fur, or dog's muzzle, or hog's tusks beginning to grow there. Yet with it all I was not afraid; never less. It is a strange, yet somehow a quiet and steady thing, to look round on earth and grass and the sky and say in one's heart to each, 'You are all my enemies now. None of you will ever do me good again. I see now only executioners.'

But I thought it most likely those words *You also shall be Psyche* meant that if she went into exile and wandering, I must do the same. And this, I had thought before, might very easily come about, if the men of Glome had no will to be ruled by a woman. But the god had been wide of the mark – so then they don't know all things? – if he thought he could grieve me most by making my punishment the same as Psyche's. If I could have borne hers as well as my own ... but next best was to share. And with this I felt a sort of hard and cheerless strength rising in me. I would make a good beggar-woman. I was ugly; and Bardia had taught me how to fight.

Bardia ... that set me thinking how much of my story I would tell him. Then, how much I would tell the Fox. I had not thought of this at all.

16

I crept in by the back parts of the palace and soon learned that my father had not yet come home from the hunting. But I went as soft and slinking to my place as if he had. When it became clear to my own mind (it did not at first) that I was hiding now not from the King but from the Fox, it was a trouble to me. Always before he had been my refuge and comforter.

Poobi cried over my wound and when she had the bandage off – that part was bad – laid good dressings on it. That was hardly done, and I was eating (hungrily enough) when the Fox came.

'Daughter, daughter,' he said. 'Praise the gods who have sent you back. I have been in pain for you all day. Where have you been?'

'To the Mountain, Grandfather,' said I, keeping my left arm out of sight. This was the first of my difficulties. I could not tell him of the self-wounding. I knew, now I saw him (I had not thought of it before), that he would rebuke me for putting that kind of force upon Psyche. One of his maxims was that if we cannot persuade our friends by reasons we must be content 'and not bring a mercenary army to our aid'. (He meant passions.)

'Oh, child, that was sudden,' he said. 'I thought we parted that night to talk it over again in the morning.'

'We parted to let you sleep,' said I. The words came fiercely, without my will and in my father's own voice. Then I was ashamed.

'So that's my sin,' said the Fox, smiling sadly. 'Well, Lady, you have punished it. But what's your news? Would Psyche hear you?'

I said nothing to that question but told him of the storm and the flood and how that mountain valley was now a mere swamp, and how I had tried to cross the stream and could not, and how I had heard Psyche go weeping away, on the south side of it, out of Glome altogether. There was no use in telling him about the god; he would have thought I had been mad or dreaming.

'Do you mean, child, you never came to speech with her at all?' said the Fox, looking very haggard.

'Yes,' I said. 'We did talk a little; earlier.'

'Child, what is wrong? Was there a quarrel? What passed between you?'

This was harder to answer. In the end, when he questioned me closely, I told him about my plan of the lamp.

'Daughter, daughter!' cried the Fox, 'what demon put such a device in your thoughts? What did you hope to do? Would not the villain by her side – he, a hunted man and an outlaw – be certain to wake? And what would he do then but snatch her up and drag her away to some other lair? Unless he stabbed her to the heart for fear she'd betray him to his pursuers. Why, the light alone would convince him she'd betrayed him already. How if it were a wound that made her weep? Oh, if you'd only taken counsel!'

I could say nothing. For now I wondered why indeed I had not thought of any of these things and whether I had ever at all believed her lover was a mountainy man.

The Fox stared at me, wondering more and more, I saw, at my silence. At last he said, 'Did you find it easy to make her do this?'

'No,' said I. I had taken off, while I ate, the veil I had worn all day; now I greatly wished I had it on.

'And how did you persuade her?' he asked.

This was the worst of all. I could not tell him what I had really done. Nor much of what I'd said. For when I told Psyche that he and Bardia were both agreed about her lover I meant what was very true; both agreed it was some shameful or dreadful thing. But if I said this to the Fox, he would say that Bardia's belief and his were sheer contraries, the one all old wives' tales and the other plain workaday probabilities. He would make it seem that I had lied. I could never make him understand how different it had looked on the Mountain.

'I – I spoke with her,' said I at last. 'I persuaded her.'

He looked long and searching at me, but never so tenderly since those old days when he used to sing *The Moon's gone down* ... I on his knee.

'Well. You have a secret from me,' he said in the end. 'No, don't turn away from me. Did you think I would try to press or conjure it out of you? Never that. Friends must be free. My tormenting you to find it would build a worse barrier between us than your hiding it. Some day – but you must obey the god within you, not the god within me. There, do not weep. I shall not cease to love you if you have a hundred secrets. I'm an old tree and my best branches were lopped off me the day I became a slave. You and Psyche were all that remained. Now – alas, poor Psyche! I see no way to her now. But I'll not lose you.'

He embraced me (I bit my lip not to scream when his arm touched the wound) and went away. I had hardly ever before been glad of his going. But I thought too how much kinder he was than Psyche.

I never told Bardia the story of that night at all.

I made one resolve before I slept, which, though it seems a small matter, made much difference to me in the years that followed. Hitherto, like all my countrywomen, I had gone bareface; on those two journeys up the Mountain I had worn a veil because I wished to be secret. I now determined that I would go always veiled. I have kept this rule, within doors and without, ever since. It is a sort of treaty made with my ugliness. There had been a time in childhood when I didn't yet know I was ugly. Then there was a time (for in this book I must hide none of my shames or follies) when I believed, as girls do – and as Batta was always telling me – that I could make it more tolerable by this or that done to my clothes or my hair. Now, I chose to be veiled. The Fox, that night, was the last man who ever saw my face; and not many women have seen it either.

My arm healed well (and so all wounds have done in my body) and when the King returned, about seven days later, I no longer pretended to be ill. He came home very drunk, for there'd been as much feasting as hunting on that party, and very out of humour, for they had killed only two lions and he'd killed neither and a favourite dog had been ripped up.

A few days later he sent for the Fox and me again to the Pillar Room. As soon as he saw me veiled, he shouted, 'Now, girl, what's this? Hung your curtains up, eh? Were you afraid we'd be dazzled by your beauty? Take off that frippery!'

It was then I first found what that night on the Mountain had done for me. No one who had seen and heard the god could much fear this roaring old King.

'It's hard if I'm to be scolded both for my face and for hiding it,' said I; putting no hand to the veil.

'Come here,' he said, not at all loud this time. I went up and stood so close to his chair that my knees almost touched his, still as a stone. To see his face while he could not see mine seemed to give me a kind of power. He was working himself into one of those white rages.

'Do you begin to set your wits against mine?' he said almost in a whisper.

'Yes,' said I, no louder than he, but very clearly. I had not known a moment before what I would do or say; that one little word came out of itself.

He stared at me while you could count seven and I half thought he might stab me dead. Then he shrugged, and snarled out, 'Oh, you're like all women. Talk, talk, talk ... you'd talk the moon out of the sky if a man'd listen to you. Here, Fox, are those lies you've been writing ready for her to copy?'

He never struck me, and I never feared him again. And from that day I never gave back an inch before him. Rather, I pressed on; so well that I told him not long after how impossible it was that I and the Fox should guard Redival if we were to work for him in the Pillar Room. He growled and cursed, yet henceforth he made Batta her jailer. Batta had grown very familiar with him of late and spent many hours in the Bedchamber. Not, I suppose, that he had her to his bed – even in the best of her days she had scarcely been what he called savoury – but she tattled and whispered and flattered him and stirred his possets; for he began to show his years. She was equally thick, for the most part, with Redival; but those were a pair who could be ready to scratch each other's eyes out one moment, and snuggling up for gossip and bawdy the next.

This, and all other things that were happening in the palace, mattered to me not at all. I was like a condemned man waiting for his executioner, for I believed that some sudden stroke of the gods would fall on me very soon. But as day came after day and nothing happened, I began to see, at first very unwillingly, that I might be doomed to live, and even to live an unchanged life, some while longer.

When I understood this I went to Psyche's room, alone, and put everything in it as it had been before all our sorrows began. I found some verses in Greek which seemed to be a hymn to the god of the Mountain. These I burned. I did not choose that any of that part of her should remain. Even the clothes that she had worn in the last year I burned also; but those she had worn earlier, and especially what were left of those she wore in childhood, and any jewels she had loved as a child, I hung in their proper places. I wished all to be so ordered that if she could come back she would find all as it had been when she was still happy, and still mine. Then I locked the door and put a seal on it. And, as well as I could, I locked a door in my mind. Unless I were to go mad I must put away all thoughts of her save those that went back to her first, happy years. I never spoke of her. If my women mentioned her name I bade them be silent. If the Fox mentioned it I was silent myself and led him to other things. There was less comfort than of old in being with the Fox.

Yet I questioned him much about what he called the physical parts of philosophy, about the seminal fire, and how soul arises from blood, and the periods of the universe; and also about plants and animals, and the positions, soils, airs, and governments of cities. I wanted hard things now, and to pile up knowledge.

As soon as my wound was well enough I returned very diligently to my fencing lessons with Bardia. I did it even before my left arm could bear a shield, for he said that fighting without shields was also a skill that ought to be learned. He said (and I now know it was true) that I made very good progress.

My aim was to build up more and more that strength, hard and joyless, which had come to me when I heard the god's sentence; by learning, fighting, and labouring, to drive all the woman out of me. Sometimes at night, if the wind howled or the rain fell, there would leap upon me, like water from a bursting dam, a great and anguished wonder; whether Psyche was alive, and where she was on such a night, and whether hard wives of peasants were turning her, cold and famished, from their door. But then, after an hour or so of weeping and writhing and calling out upon the gods, I would set to and re-build the dam.

Soon Bardia was teaching me to ride on horseback as well as to fence with the sword. He used me, and talked to me, more and more like a man. And this both grieved and pleased me.

So things went on till the Midwinter, which is a great feast in our country. On the day after it the King came home from some revels he had been at in a lord's house, about three hours after noon, and in mounting the steps that go up into the porch he fell. It was so cold that day that the water the house-boys had used for scouring the steps had frozen on them. He fell with his right leg under him across the edge of a step, and when men ran to help him he roared out with pain and was ready to set his teeth in the hands of anyone who touched him. Next minute he was cursing them for leaving him to lie there and freeze. As soon as I came I nodded to the slaves to lift him up and carry him in, whatever he said or did. We got him to his bed, with great agony, and had the barber to him; who said (as we all guessed) that his thigh was broken. 'But I've no skill to set it, Lady, even if the King would let my fingers near it.' I sent a messenger over to the house of Ungit to the Second Priest, who had the name of a good surgeon. Before he came the King had filled himself up with enough strong wine to throw a sound man into a fever, and as soon as the Second Priest got his clothes out of the way and began handling the leg, he started screaming like a beast and tried to pluck out his dagger. Then Bardia and I whispered to one another, and we got in six of the guards and held the King down. Between his screams he kept on pointing at me with his eyes (they had his hands fast) and crying out:

'Take her away! Take away that one with the veil. Don't let her torture me. I know who she is. I know.'

He had no sleep that night or the day and night after (on top of the pain from his leg, he coughed as if his chest would burst), and whenever our backs were turned Batta would be taking him in more wine. I was not much in the Bedchamber myself, for the sight of me made him frantic. He kept on saying he knew who I was for all my veil.

'Master,' said the Fox, 'it is only the Princess Orual, your daughter.'

'Aye, so she tells you,' the King would say. 'But I know better. Wasn't she using red-hot iron on my leg all night? I know who she is ... Aiai! Aiai! Guards! Bardia! Orual! Batta! Take her away!'

On the third night the Second Priest and Bardia and the Fox and I all stood just outside his door and talked in whispers. The Second Priest's name was Arnom; he was a dark man, no older than I, smooth-cheeked as a eunuch (which he cannot have been, for though Ungit has eunuchs, only a weaponed man can hold the full priesthood).

'It's likely,' said Arnom, 'that this will end in the King's death.'

'So,' thought I. 'This is how it will begin. There'll be a new world in Glome, and if I get off with my life, I shall be driven out. I too shall be a Psyche.'

'I think the same,' said the Fox. 'And it comes at a ticklish time. There's much business before us.'

'More than you think, Lysias,' said Arnom (I had never heard the Fox called by his real name before). 'The house of Ungit is in the very same plight as the King's house.'

'What do you mean, Arnom?' said Bardia.

'The Priest is dying at last. If I have any skill, he'll not last five days.'

'And you to succeed him?' said Bardia. The priest bowed his head.

'Unless the King forbids,' added the Fox. This was good law in Glome.

'It's very necessary,' said Bardia, 'that Ungit and the palace should be of one mind at such a moment. There are those who'd see their chance of setting Glome by the ears otherwise.'

'Yes, very necessary,' said Arnom. 'No one will rise against us both.'

'It's our good fortune,' said Bardia, 'that there's no cause of quarrel between the Queen and Ungit.'

'The Queen?' said Arnom.

'The Queen,' said Bardia and the Fox now both together.

'If only the Princess were married, now!' said Arnom, bowing very courteously. 'A woman cannot lead the armies of Glome in war.'

'This Queen can,' said Bardia; and the way he thrust out his lower jaw made him seem a whole army himself. I saw Arnom looking at me hard, and I think my veil served me better than the boldest countenance in the world; maybe better than beauty would have done.

'There is only one difference between Ungit and the King's house,' he said, 'and that concerns the Crumbles. But for the King's sickness and the Priest's I would have been here before now to speak of it.'

I knew all about this and saw now where we were. The Crumbles was good land on the far side of the river, and it had been a cat-and-dog quarrel ever since I started working for my father as to whether they belonged, or how much of them belonged, to the King or to Ungit. I had always thought (little cause as I had to love Ungit) that they should belong to her house; which was indeed poorly provided for the charge of continual sacrifices. And I thought too that if once Ungit were reasonably furnished with land, the priests could be stopped from wringing so much out of the common people by way of gifts.

'The King still lives,' said I; I had not spoken before, and my voice surprised them all. 'But because of his sickness I am now the King's mouth. It is his wish to give the Crumbles to Ungit, free and for ever, and the covenant to be cut in stone, upon one condition.'

Bardia and the Fox looked at me with wonder. But Arnom said, 'What is that, Lady?'

'That Ungit's guards be henceforward under the captain of the King's guard, and chosen by the King (or his successor), and under his obedience.'

'And paid by the King (or his successors) too?' says Arnom quick as lightning.

I had not thought of this stroke, but I judged any resolute answer better than the wisest pondering. 'That,' said I, 'must be according to the hours of duty they spend in Ungit's house and here.'

'You drive – that is, the King drives – a hard bargain, Lady,' said the priest. But I knew he would take it, for I knew that Ungit had more need of good land than of spears. Also, it would be hard for Arnom to succeed to the Priesthood if the palace was against him. Then my father began roaring out from within and the priest went back to him.

'Well done, daughter,' whispered the Fox.

'Long live the Queen,' whispered Bardia. Then they both followed Arnom.

I stood outside in the great hall, which was empty, and the fire low. It was as strange a moment as any in my life. To be a queen – that would not sweeten the bitter water against which I had been building the dam in my soul. It might strengthen the dam, though. Then, as a quite different thing, came the thought that my father would be dead. That struck me dizzy. The largeness of a world in which he was not ... the clear light of a sky in which that cloud would no longer hang ... freedom. I drew in a long breath; one way, the sweetest I had ever drawn. I came near to forgetting my great central sorrow.

But only for a moment. It was very still, and most of the household was in bed. I thought I heard a sound of weeping; a girl's weeping; the sound for which always, with or without my will, I was listening. It seemed to come from without, from behind the palace. Instantly crowns and policies and my father were a thousand leagues from my mind. In a torture of hope I went swiftly to the other end of the hall and then out by the little door between the dairy and the guard's quarters. The moon was shining, but the air was not so still as I thought. And where now was the weeping? Then I thought I heard it again. 'Psyche,' I called. 'Istra! Psyche!' I went to the sound. Now I was less sure what it was. I remembered that when the chains of the well swung a little (and there had been breeze enough to sway them just now) they could make a noise something like that. Oh, the cheat of it, the bitterness!

I stood and listened. There was no more weeping. But something was moving somewhere. Then I saw a cloaked form dart across a patch of moonlight and bury itself in some bushes. I was after it, quick as I could. Next moment I plunged my hand in among the branches. Another hand met it.

'Softly, sweetheart,' said a voice. 'Take me to the King's threshold.'

It was a wholly strange voice, and a man's.

17

'Who are you?' said I, wrenching my hand free and leaping back as if I had touched a snake. 'Come out and show yourself.' My thought was that it must be a lover of Redival's, and that Batta was playing bawd as well as jailer.

A slender, tall man stepped out. 'A suppliant,' he said, but with a merriment in his voice that did not sound like supplication. 'And one who never let a pretty girl go without a kiss.'

He'd have had an arm around my neck in a moment if I hadn't avoided him. Then he saw my dagger point twinkle in the moonlight; and laughed.

'You've good eyes if you can see beauty in this face,' said I, turning it on him to make sure he saw the blank wall of the veil.

'Only good ears, sister,' said he. 'I'll bet a girl with a voice like yours is beautiful.'

The whole adventure was, for such a woman as I, so unusual that I almost had a fool's wish to lengthen it. The very world was strange that night. But I came to my senses.

'Who are you?' I said. 'Tell me quick, or I'll call the guards.'

'I'm no thief, pretty one,' said he, 'though I confess you caught me slinking in a thief's fashion. I thought there might already be some kindred of my own in your garden whom I had no mind to meet. I am a suppliant to the King. Can you bring me to him?' He let me hear a couple of coins jingle in his hand.

'Unless the King's health mends suddenly, I am the Queen,' said I.

He gave a low whistle and laughed. 'If that's so, Queen,' he said, 'I've played the fool to admiration. Then it's your suppliant I am; suppliant for a few nights' – it might be only one – lodging and protection. I am Trunia of Phars.'

The news struck me almost stupid. I have written before how this prince was at war with his brother Argan and the old king their father.

'Defeated, then?' I said.

'Beaten in a cavalry skirmish,' he said, 'and had to ride for it, which would be little odds but that I missed my way and blundered into Glome. And then my horse went lame, not three miles back. The worst of it is, my brother's strength lies all along the border. If you can hide me for a day or so – his messengers will be at your door by daybreak, no doubt – so that I can get into Essur and so round to my main army in Phars, I'll soon show him and all the world whether I'm defeated.'

'This is all very well, Prince,' said I. 'But if we receive you as a suppliant we must, by all law, defend you. I'm not so young a queen as to think I can go to war with Phars at this time.'

'It's a cold night to lie out,' he said.

'You'd be very welcome if you were not a suppliant, Prince. But in that character you're too dangerous. I can give you lodging only as a prisoner.'

'Prisoner?' said he. 'Then, Queen, good night.'

He darted away as if he were not weary at all (though I had heard weariness in his voice) and ran as one who is used to it. But that flight was his undoing. I could have told him where the old millstone lay. He fell sprawling, made to leap up again with wonderful quickness, then gave a sharp hiss of pain, struggled, cursed, and was still.

'Sprained, if not broken,' he said. 'Plague on the god that invented man's ankle. Well, you may call your spears, Queen. Prisoner it is. And that prison leads to my brother's hangman?'

'We'll save you if we can,' said I. 'If we can do it any way without full war against Phars, we'll do it.'

The guards' quarters were on that side of the house, as I have said, and it was easy enough to go within calling distance of the men and yet keep my eye on the Prince. As soon as I heard them turning out I said, 'Pull your hood over your face. The fewer who know my prisoner's name, the freer my hands will be.'

They got him up and brought him hobbling into the hall and put him on the settle by the hearth, and I called for wine and victuals to be brought him, and for the barber to bind up his ankle. Then I went into the Bedchamber. Arnom had gone. The King was worse; his face a darker red, his breathing hoarse. It seemed he could not speak; but I wondered, as his eyes wandered from one to another of us three, what he thought and felt.

'Where have you been, daughter?' said the Fox. 'Here's terribly weighty news. A post has just ridden in to tell us that Argan of Phars with three – or maybe four – score of horse has crossed the border and now lies but ten miles away. He gives out that he is seeking his brother Trunia.'

How quickly we learn to queen or king it! Yesterday I should have cared little how many aliens in arms crossed our borders; tonight, it was as if someone had struck me in the face.

'And,' said Bardia, 'whether he really believes that we have Trunia here – or whether he's crossed the border of a crippled land only to make a cheap show of valour and mend his mouldy reputation – either way—'

'Trunia is here,' said I. Before their surprise let them speak, I made them come into the Pillar Room, for I found I could not bear my father's eyes on us. The others seemed to make no more account of him than of a dead man. I ordered lights and fire in the tower room, Psyche's old prison, and that the Prince should be taken there when he had eaten. Then we three went busily to our talking.

On three things we were all of one mind. First, that if Trunia weathered his present misfortune, he was likely enough to beat Argan in the end and rule Phars. The old king was in his dotage and counted for nothing. The longer the broils lasted, the more Trunia's party would probably increase, for Argan was false, cruel, and hated by many, and had, moreover, from his first battle (long before these troubles) an old slur of cowardice upon him which made him contemptible. Second, that Trunia as King of Phars would be a far better neighbour to us than Argan; especially if we had befriended him when he was lowest. But thirdly, that we were in no plight to take on a war with Phars, nor even with Argan's party in Phars; the pestilence had killed too many of our young men and we still had almost no corn.

Then a new thought, as if from nowhere, came scalding hot into my head.

'Bardia,' said I, 'what is Prince Argan worth as a swordsman?'

'There are two better at this table, Queen.'

'And he'd be very chary of doing anything that would revive the old story against his courage?'

'It's to be supposed so.'

'Then if we offered him a champion to fight against him for Trunia – pawned Trunia's head on the single combat – he'd be in a manner bound to take it up.'

Bardia thought for a time. 'Why,' he said, 'it sounds like something out of an old song. Yet, by the gods, the longer I look at it the better I like it. Weak though we are, he'll not want war with us while he has war at home. Not if we leave him any other choice. And his hope hangs on keeping or getting his people's favour. He has none of it to spare even now. And it's an odious thing to be pursuing his brother at our gates as if he were digging out a fox. That won't have made him more loved. If on top of it all he refuses the combat, his name will stink worse still. I think your plan has life in it, Queen.'

'This is very wise,' said the Fox. 'Even if our man's killed and we have to hand Trunia over, no man can say we've treated him ill. We save our good name and yet have no war with Phars.'

'And if our champion kills Argan,' said Bardia, 'then we've done the next thing to setting Trunia on the throne and earned a good friend; for all say Trunia's a right-minded man.'

'To make it surer still, friends,' said I, 'let our champion be one so contemptible that it would be shame beneath all shame for Argan to draw back.'

'That's too subtle, daughter,' said the Fox. 'And hard on Trunia. We don't want our man beaten.'

'What are you thinking of, Queen?' said Bardia, teasing his moustache in the old way. 'We can't ask him to fight a slave, if that's what you mean.'

'No. A woman,' said I.

The Fox stared in bewilderment. I had never told him of my exercises with the sword, partly because I had a tenderness about mentioning Bardia to him at all, for to hear Bardia called fool or barbarian angered me. (Bardia called the Fox Greekling and 'word-weaver' in return, but that never fretted me in the same way.)

'A woman?' said the Fox. 'Am I mad, or are you?'

And now a great smile that would do any heart good to see it broke over Bardia's face. But he shook his head.

'I've played chess too long to hazard my Queen,' he said.

'What, Bardia?' said I, steadying my voice as best I could. 'Were you only flattering when you said I was a better swordsman than Argan?'

'Not so. I'd lay my money on you if it came to a wager. But there's always luck as well as skill in these things.'

'And courage too, you'd say.'

'I've no fear of you for that, Queen.'

'I have no idea what you are both talking about,' said the Fox.

'The Queen wants to fight for Trunia herself, Fox,' said Bardia. 'And she could do it too. We've had scores of matches together. The gods never made anyone – man or woman – with a better natural gift for it. Oh, Lady, Lady, it's a thousand pities they didn't make you a man.' (He spoke it as kindly and heartily as could be; as if a man dashed a gallon of cold water in your broth and never doubted you'd like it all the better.)

'Monstrous – against all custom – and nature – and modesty,' said the Fox. On such matters he was a true Greek; he still thought it barbarous and scandalous that the women in our land go bareface. I had sometimes said to him when we were merry that I ought to call him not Grandfather but Grandam. That was another reason why I had never told him of the fencing.

'Nature's hand slipped when she made me anyway,' said I. 'If I'm to be hard-featured as a man, why shouldn't I fight like a man too?'

'Daughter, daughter,' said the Fox. 'In mercy to me, if for nothing else, put this horrible thought out of your head. The plan of a champion and a combat was good. How would this folly make it better?'

'It makes it far better,' said I. 'Do you think I'm so simple as to fancy I'm safe on my father's throne yet? Arnom is with me. Bardia is with me. But what of the nobles and the people? I know nothing of them nor they of me. If either of the King's wives had lived, I supposed I might have known the lords' wives and daughters. My father never let us see them; much less the lords themselves. I have no friends. Is this combat not the very thing to catch their fancy? Won't they like a woman for their ruler better if she has fought for Glome and killed her man?'

'Oh, for that,' said Bardia, 'it'd be incomparable. There'll be no one but you in their mouths and hearts for a twelvemonth.'

'Child, child,' said the Fox, his eyes full of tears, 'it's your life. Your life. First my home and freedom gone; then Psyche; now you. Will you not leave one leaf on this old tree?'

I could see right into his heart, for I knew he now implored me with the same anguish I had felt when I implored Psyche. The tears that stood in my eyes behind my veil were tears of pity for myself more than for him. I did not let them fall.

'My mind's made up,' I said. 'And none of you can think of a better way out of our dangers. Do we know where Argan lies, Bardia?'

'At the Red Ford, the post said.'

'Then let our herald be sent at once. The fields between the city and the Shennit to be the place of the combat. The time, the third day from now. The terms, these. If I fall, we deliver Trunia to him and condone his unlawful entering into our land. If he falls, Trunia is a free man and has a safe conduct to go over the border to his own people in Phars or where he will. Either way, all the aliens to be out of the land of Glome in two days.'

They both stared and said nothing.

'I'll go to bed now,' said I. 'See to the sending, Bardia, and then to bed yourself. A good night to you both.'

I knew from Bardia's face that he would obey, though he could not bring himself to assent in words. I turned quickly away and went to my own room.

To be alone there and in silence was like coming suddenly under the lee of a wall on a wild, windy day, so that one can breathe and collect oneself again. Ever since Arnom had said, hours ago, that the King was dying, there seemed to have been another woman acting and speaking in my place. Call her the Queen; but Orual was someone different and now I was Orual again. (I wondered if this was how all princes felt.) I looked back on the things the Queen had done and wondered at them. Did that Queen truly think she would kill Argan? I, Orual, as I now saw, did not believe it. I was not even sure that I could fight him. I had never used sharps before; nothing hung on my sham battles but the hope of pleasing my teacher (not that that was a small thing to me either). How would it be if, when the day came, and the trumpets had blown, and the swords were out, my courage failed me? I'd be the mockery of the whole world; I could see the shamed look on the Fox's face, on Bardia's. I could hear them saying, 'And yet how bravely her sister went to the offering! How strange that she, who was so meek and gentle, should have been the brave one after all!' And so she would be far above me in everything; in courage as well as in beauty and in those eyes which the gods favoured with sight of things invisible, and even in strength (I remembered her grip when we had wrestled). 'She shall not,' I said with my whole soul. 'Psyche? She's never had a sword in her hand in her life, never done man's work in the Pillar Room, never understood (hardly heard of) affairs of state ... a girl's life, a child's life ...'

I asked myself suddenly what I was thinking. 'Can it be my sickness coming back?' I thought. For it began to be like those vile dreams I had had in my ravings when the cruel gods put into my mind the horrible, mad fancy that it was Psyche who was my enemy. Psyche my enemy? – she, my child, the very heart of my heart, whom I had wronged and ruined, for whose sake the gods were right to kill me? And now I saw my challenge to the Prince quite differently. Of course he would kill me. He was the gods' executioner. And this would be the best thing in the world; far better than some of the dooms I had looked for. All my life must now be a sandy waste; who could have dared to hope it would be so short? And this accorded so well with all my daily thoughts since the god's sentence, that I now wondered how I could have forgotten that sandy waste for the past few hours.

It was queenship that had done it – all those decisions to make, coming pell-mell upon me without a breathing space, and so much hanging on each; all the speed, skill, peril, and dash of the game. I resolved that for the two days left to me I'd queen it with the best of them; and if by any chance Argan didn't kill me, I'd queen it as long as the gods let me. It was not pride – the glitter of the name – that moved me; or not much. I was taking to queenship as a stricken man takes to the wine-pot or as a stricken woman, if she had beauty, might take to lovers. It was an art that left you no time to mope. If Orual could vanish altogether into the Queen, the gods would almost be cheated.

But had Arnom said my father was dying? No; not quite that.

I rose up and went back to his Bedchamber; without a taper, feeling my way along the walls, for I would have been ashamed if anyone saw me. There were still lights in the Bedchamber. They had left Batta to be with him. She sat in his own chair, close to the fire, sleeping the noisy sleep of a sodden old woman. I went over to the bedside. He was seemingly wide awake. Whether the noises he was making were an attempt at speech, who knows? But the look in his eyes, when he saw me, was not to be mistaken.

It was terror. Did he know me and think I came to murder him? Did he think I was Psyche come back from the deadlands to bring him down there?

Some will say (perhaps the gods will say) that if I had murdered him indeed, I should have been no less impious than I was. For as he looked at me with fear, so I looked at him; but all my fear was lest he should live.

What do the gods expect of us? My deliverance was now so near. A prisoner may come to bear his dungeon with patience; but if he has almost escaped, tasted his first draught of the free air ... to be re-taken then, to go back to the clanking of that fetter, the smell of that straw?

I looked again at his face; terrified, idiotic, almost an animal's face. A thought of comfort came to me: 'Even if he lives, he will never have his mind again.'

I went back and slept soundly.

18

Next day I went as soon as I was risen to the Bedchamber to take my first look at the King; for indeed no lover nor doctor ever watched each change of a sick man's breath and pulse so closely as I. While I was still at his bedside (I could see no difference in him) in came Redival, all in a flurry and her face blubbered, and 'Oh, Orual,' she said, 'is the King dying? And what was going on all last night? And who's the young stranger? They say he's a wonderful, handsome man and looks as brave as a lion. Is he a prince? And oh, Sister, what will happen to us if the King dies?'

'I shall be Queen, Redival. Your treatment shall be according to your behaviour.'

Almost before the words were out of my mouth she was fawning upon me and kissing my hand and wishing me joy and saying she had always loved me better than anyone in the world. It sickened me. None of the slaves would cringe to me like that. Even when I was angry and they feared me, all knew better than to put on a beggar's whine; there's nothing moves my pity less.

'Don't be a fool, Redival,' said I, shoving her away from my hand. 'I'm not going to kill you. But if you put your nose out of the house without my leave, I'll have you whipped. Now be off.'

At the door she turned and said, 'But you'll get me a husband, Queen, won't you?'

'Yes; probably two,' said I. 'I've a dozen sons of kings hanging in my wardrobe. But go.'

Then came the Fox, who looked at the King, muttered, 'He might last for days yet,' and then said, 'Daughter, I did badly last night. I think this offer to fight the Prince yourself is foolish and, what's more, unseemly. But I was wrong to weep and beg and try to force you by your love. Love is not a thing to be so used.'

He broke off because just then Bardia came to the door. 'Here's a herald back from Argan already, Queen,' he said. 'Our man met the Prince (curse his insolence) a great deal nearer than ten miles.'

We went into the Pillar Room (my father's eyes followed me terribly) and had the herald in. He was a great, tall man, dressed as fine as a peacock. His message, stripped of many high words, was that his master accepted the combat. But he said his sword should not be stained with woman's blood, so he'd bring a rope with him to hang me when he'd disarmed me.

'That's a weapon in which I profess no skill,' said I. 'And therefore it's barely justice that your master should bring it. But then he's older than I (his first battle was, I think, long ago), so we'll concede it to make up for his years.'

'I can't say that to the Prince, Queen,' said the herald.

Then I thought I had done enough (I knew others would hear my gibe even if Argan didn't) and we went orderly to work on all the conditions of the fight and the hundred small things that had to be agreed on. It was the best part of an hour before the herald was gone. The Fox, I could see, was in great pain while all these provisions were being made; the thing growing more real and more irrevocable at each word. I was mostly the Queen now, but Orual would whisper a cold word in the Queen's ear at times.

After that came Arnom, and even before he spoke we knew the old Priest was dead and Arnom had succeeded him. He wore the skins and the bladders, the bird-mark hung at his chest. The sight of all that gave me a sudden shock, like a vile dream, forgotten on waking but suddenly remembered at noon. But my second glance braced me. He would never be terrible like the old Priest. He was only Arnom, with whom I had driven a very good bargain yesterday; there was no feeling that Ungit came into the room with him. And that started strange thoughts in my mind.

But I had no time to follow them. Arnom and the Fox went to the Bedchamber and fell into talk about the King's condition (those two seemed to understand each other well) and Bardia beckoned me out of the room. We went out by the little eastern door, where the Fox and I had gone on the morning Psyche was born, and there paced up and down between the herb-beds while we talked.

'Now, Queen,' said he, 'this is your first battle.'

'And you doubt my courage?'

'Not your courage to be killed, Queen. But you've never killed; and this must be a killing matter.'

'What then?'

'Why, just this. Women and boys talk easily about killing a man. Yet, believe me, it's a hard thing to do; I mean, the first time. There's something in a man that goes against it.'

'You think I'd pity him?'

'I don't know if it's pity. But the first time I did it – it was the hardest thing in the world to make my own hand plunge the sword into all that live flesh.'

'But you did.'

'Yes; my enemy was a bungler. But how if he'd been quick? That's the danger, you see. There's a moment when one pause – the fifth part of the time it takes to wink your eye – may lose a chance. And it might be your only chance, and then you'd have lost the battle.'

'I don't think my hand would delay, Bardia,' said I. I was trying to test it in my mind. I pictured my father, well again, and coming at me in one of his old rages; I felt sure my hand would not fail me to stab him. It had not failed when I stabbed myself.

'We'll hope not,' said Bardia. 'But you must go through the exercise. I make all the recruits do it.'

'The exercise?'

'Yes. You know they're to kill a pig this morning. You must be the butcher, Queen.'

I saw in a flash that if I shrank from this there would at once be less Queen and more Orual in me.

'I am ready,' said I. I understood the work pretty well, for of course we had seen the slaughtering of beasts ever since we were children. Redival had always watched and always screamed; I had watched less often and held my tongue. So now I went and killed my pig. (We kill pigs without sacrifice, for these beasts are an abomination to Ungit; there is a sacred story that explains why.) And I swore that if I came back alive from the combat Bardia and the Fox and Trunia and I should eat the choicest parts of it for our supper. Then, when I had taken off my butcher's apron and washed, I went back to the Pillar Room; for I had thought of something that must be done, now that my life might be only two days. The Fox was already there; I called Bardia and Arnom for witnesses and declared the Fox free.

Next moment I was plunged in despair. I cannot now understand how I had been so blind as not to foresee it. My only thought had been to save him from being mocked and neglected and perhaps sold by Redival if I were dead. But now, as soon as the other two were done wishing him joy and kissing him on the cheeks, it all broke on me. 'You'll be a loss to our councils—' 'There are many in Glome who'll be sorry to see you go—' 'Don't make your journey in winter—' What were they saying?

'Grandfather!' I cried, no Queen now; all Orual, even all child. 'Do they mean you'll leave me? Go away?'

The Fox raised towards me a face full of infinite trouble, twitching. 'Free?' he muttered. 'You mean I could ... I can ... it wouldn't matter much even if I died on the way. Not if I could get down to the sea. There'd be tunnies; olives. No, it'd be too early in the year for olives. But the smell of the harbours. And walking about the market talking; real talk. But you don't know, this is all foolishness, none of you know. I should be thanking you, daughter. But if ever you loved me, don't speak to me now. Tomorrow. Let me go.' He pulled his cloak over his head and groped his way out of the room.

And now this game of queenship, which had buoyed me up and kept me busy ever since I woke that morning, failed me utterly. We had made all our preparations for the combat. There was the rest of the day, and the whole of the next, to wait; and hanging over it, this new desolation, that if I lived I might have to live without the Fox.

I went out into the gardens. I would not go up to that plot behind the pear trees; that was where he, and Psyche, and I had often been happiest. I wandered, miserably, out on the other side, on the west of the apple orchard, till the cold drove me in; it was a bitter, black frost that day, with no sun. I am both ashamed and afraid to revive, by writing of them, the thoughts I had. In my ignorance I could not understand the strength of the desire which must be drawing my old master to his own land. I had lived in one place all my life; everything in Glome was to me stale, common, and taken for granted, even filled with memories of dread, sorrow, and humiliation. I had no notion how the remembered home looks to an exile. It embittered me that the Fox should even desire to leave me. He had been the central pillar of my whole life, something (I thought) as sure and established, and indeed as little thanked, as sunrise and the mere earth. In my folly I had thought I was to him as he was to me. 'Fool!' said I to myself. 'Have you not yet learned that you are that to no one? What are you to Bardia? as much perhaps as the old king was. His heart lies at home with his wife and her brats. If you mattered to him he'd never have let you fight. What are you to the Fox? His heart was always in the Greeklands. You were, maybe, the solace of his captivity. They say a prisoner will tame a rat. He comes to love the rat; after a fashion. But throw the door open, strike off his fetters, and how much'll he care for the rat then?' And yet, how could he leave us, after so much love? I saw him again with Psyche on his knees. 'Prettier than Aphrodite,' he had said. 'Yes, but that was Psyche,' said my heart. 'If she were still with us, he would stay. It was Psyche he loved. Never me.' I knew while I said it that it was false, yet I would not, or could not, put it out of my head.

But the Fox sought me out before I slept; his face very grey, and his manner very quiet. But that he did not limp, you would have thought he had been in the hands of the torturers. 'Wish me well, daughter,' he said. 'For I have won a battle. What's best for his fellows must be best for a man. I am but a limb of the whole and must work in the socket where I'm put. I'll stay, and—'

'Oh, Grandfather!' said I, and wept.

'Peace, peace,' he said, embracing me. 'What would I have done in Greece? My father is dead. My sons have, no doubt, forgotten me. My daughter ... should I not be only a trouble – *a dream strayed into daylight* as the verse says? Anyhow, it's a long journey and beset with dangers. I might never have reached the sea.'

And so he went on, making little of his deed, as if he feared I would dissuade him from it. But I, with my face on his breast, felt only the joy.

I went to look at my father many times that day, but could see no change in him.

That night I slept ill. It was not fear of the combat, but a restlessness that came from the manifold changes which the gods were sending upon me. The old Priest's death, by itself, would have been matter for a week's thought. I had hoped it before (and then, if he had died, it might have saved Psyche) but never really reckoned to see him go more than to wake one morning and find the Grey Mountain gone. The freeing of the Fox, though I had done it myself, felt to me like another impossible change. It was as if my father's sickness had drawn away some prop and the whole world – all the world I knew – had fallen to pieces. I was journeying into a strange, new land. It was so new and strange that I could not, that night, even feel my great sorrow. This astonished me. One part of me made to snatch that sorrow back; it said, 'Orual dies if she ceases to love Psyche.' But the other said, 'Let Orual die. She would never have made a queen.'

The last day, the eve of the battle, shows like a dream. Every hour made it more unbelievable. The noise and fame of my combat had got abroad (it was no part of our policy to be secret) and there were crowds of the common people at the palace gates. Though I valued their favour no more than it deserved – I remembered how they had turned against Psyche – yet, willy-nilly, their cheering quickened my pulse and sent a kind of madness into my brain. Some of the better sort, lords and elders, came to wait upon me. They all accepted me for Queen, and I spoke little but, I think, well – Bardia and the Fox praised it – and watched their eyes staring at my veil and manifestly wondering what it hid. Then I went to Prince Trunia in the tower room and told him we had found a champion (I did not say whom) to fight for him and how he would be brought in honourable custody to see the fight. Though this must have been uneasy news for him, he was too just a man not to see that we were using him as well as our weakness would bear. Then I called for wine that we might drink together. But when the door opened – this angered me for the moment – instead of my father's butler it was Redival who came in bearing the flagon and the cup. I was a fool not to have foreseen it. I knew her well enough to guess that once there was a strange man in the house she'd eat her way through stone walls in order to be seen. Yet even I was astonished to see what a meek, shy, modest, dutiful younger sister (perhaps even a somewhat downtrodden and spirit-broken sister) she could make of herself carrying that wine; with her downcast eyes (which missed nothing from Trunia's bandaged foot to the hair of his head) and her child's gravity.

'Who's that beauty?' said Trunia as soon as she was gone.

'That's my sister, the Princess Redival,' said I.

'Glome is a rose garden; even in winter,' said he. 'But why, cruel Queen, do you hide your own face?'

'If you become better known to my sister, she'll doubtless tell you,' said I; more sharply than I had intended.

'Why, that might be,' said the Prince. 'If your champion wins tomorrow; otherwise death's my wife. But if I live, Queen, I wouldn't let this friendship between our houses die away. Why should I not marry into your line? Perhaps yourself, Queen?'

'There's no room for two on my throne, Prince.'

'Your sister then?'

It was of course an offer to be seized. Yet for a moment, saying yes to it irked me; most likely because I thought this prince twenty times too good for her.

'For all I can see,' said I, 'this marriage can be made. I must speak to my wise men first. For my own part, I like it well.'

The day ended more strangely than it began. Bardia had had me into the quarters for my last practice. 'There's that old fault of yours, Queen,' he said, 'in the feint reverse. I think we've conquered it; but I must see you perfect.' We went at it for half an hour and when we stopped to breathe he said, 'That's as perfect as skill can go. It's my belief that if you and I were to fight with sharps you'd kill me. But there are two things more to say. This first. If it should happen, Queen – and most likely it won't happen to you, because of your divine blood – but if it should happen that when your cloak's off and the crowd's hushed and you're walking out into the empty space to meet your man – if you should then feel fear, never heed it. We've all felt it at our first fight. I feel it myself before every fight. And the second's this. That hauberk you've been wearing is excellent for weight and fit. But it's a poor thing to look at. A trace of gilding would suit a queen and a champion better. Let's see what the Bedchamber has.'

I have said before that the King kept all manner of arms and armours in there. So in we went. The Fox was sitting by the bedside; why, or with what thoughts, I don't know. It was not possible he should love his old master. 'Still no change,' he said. Bardia and I fell to rummaging among the mail, and soon to disputing; for I thought I'd be safer and more limber in the chain-shirt which I knew than in any other, and he kept on saying, 'But wait – wait – now here's a better.' And it was when we were most busied that the Fox's voice from behind said, 'It's finished.' We turned and looked. The thing on the bed which had been half-alive for so long was dead; had died (if he understood it) seeing a girl ransacking his armoury.

'Peace be upon him,' said Bardia. 'We'll be done here very shortly. Then the women can come and wash the body.' And we turned again at once to settle the matter of the hauberks.

And so the thing that I had thought of for so many years at last slipped by in a huddle of business which was, at that moment, of more consequence. An hour later, when I looked back, it astonished me. Yet I have often noticed since how much less stir nearly everyone's death makes than you might expect. Men better loved and more worth loving than my father go down making only a small eddy.

I kept to my old hauberk, but we told the armourer to scour it well, so that it might pass for silver.

19

On a great day the thing that makes it great may fill the least part of it, as a meal takes little time to eat, but the killing, baking and dressing, and the swilling and scraping after it, take long enough. My fight with the Prince took about the sixth part of an hour; yet the business about it, more than twelve.

First of all, now that the Fox was a freeman and the Queen's Lantern (so we call it, though my father had let the office sleep) I would have him at the fight and splendidly dressed. But you never had more trouble with a peevish girl going to her first feast. He said all barbarians' clothes were barbarous and the finer the worse. He would go in his old moth-eaten gown. And when we had brought him into some kind of order, then Bardia wanted me to fight without my veil. He thought it would blind me and did not see how it could well be worn either over or under my helmet. But I refused altogether to fight bareface. In the end I had Poobi to stitch me up a hood or mask of fine stuff, but such as could not be seen through; it had two eyeholes and covered the whole helmet. All this was needless, for I had fought Bardia himself in my old veil a dozen times; but the mask made me look very dreadful, as a ghost might look. 'If he's the coward they'd make him,' said Bardia, 'that'll cool his stomach.' And then we had to start very early, it seemed, for the crowd in the streets would make us ride slowly. So we had Trunia down and were all presently on horseback. There was some talk of dressing him fine too, but he refused this.

'Whether your champion kills or is killed,' he said, 'I'll fare no better in purple than in my old battle order. But where is your champion, Queen?'

'You shall see when we come to the field, Prince,' said I.

Trunia had started when he first saw me shrouded like a ghost; neither throat nor helmet to be seen, but two eyeholes in a white hummock; scarecrow or leper. I thought his starting boded well how it would taste to Argan.

Several lords and elders waited for us at the gate to bring us through the city. It's easy to guess what I was thinking. So Psyche had gone out that day to heal the people; and so she had gone out that other day to be offered to the Brute. Perhaps, thought I, this is what the god meant when he said *You also shall be Psyche*. I also might be an offering. That was a good, firm thought to lay hold of. But the thing was so near now that I could think very little of my own death or life. With all those eyes upon me, my only care was to make a brave show both now and in the fight. I'd have given ten talents to any prophet who could have foretold me that I'd fight well for five minutes and then be killed.

The lords who rode nearest me were very grave. I supposed (and indeed one or two confessed as much to me afterwards when I came to know them) they thought Argan would soon have me disarmed, but that my mad challenge was as good a way as any of getting him and Trunia both out of our country. But if the lords were glum, the common people in the streets were huzzaing and throwing caps in the air. It would have puffed me up if I had not looked in their faces. There, I could read their mind easily enough. Neither I nor Glome was in their thoughts. Any fight was a free show for them; and a fight of a woman with a man better still because an oddity; as those who can't tell one tune from another will crowd to hear the harp if a man plays it with his toes.

When at last we got down to the open field by the river there had to be more delays. Arnom was there, in his bird-mask, and there was a bull to be sacrificed; so well the gods have wound themselves into our affairs that nothing can be done but they have their bit. And opposite us, on the far side of the field, were the horsemen of Phars, and Argan sitting on his horse in the midst of them. It was the strangest thing in the world to look upon him, a man like any other man, and think that one of us presently would kill the other. *Kill*; it seemed like a word I'd never spoken before. He was a man with straw-coloured hair and beard, thin, yet somehow bloated, with pouting lips; a very unpleasing person. Then he and I dismounted and came close and each had to taste a tiny morsel of the bull's flesh, and take oaths on behalf of our peoples that all the agreements would be kept. And now, I thought, surely now they'll let us begin. (There was a pale white sun in a grey sky that day, and a biting wind; 'Do they want us to freeze before we fight?' I thought.) But now the people had to be pressed back with the buttends of spears, and the field cleared, and Bardia must go across and whisper something to Argan's chief man, and both of them must go and whisper to Arnom, and Argan's trumpeter and mine must be placed side by side.

'Now, Queen,' said Bardia suddenly, when I had half despaired of ever getting to the end of the preparations, 'the gods guard you.'

The Fox was standing with his face set like iron; he would have wept if he had tried to speak. I saw a great shock of surprise come over Trunia (and I never blamed him for turning pale) when I flung off my cloak, drew my sword, and stepped out on to the open grass.

The men from Phars roared with laughter. Our mob cheered. Argan was within ten paces of me, then five; then, we were at it.

I know he began despising me; there was a lazy insolence in his first passes. But I took the skin off his knuckles with one lucky stroke (and maybe numbed his hand a little) and that brought him to his senses. Though my eye never left his sword, yet I somehow saw his face as well. 'Crosspatch,' thought I. He had a puckered brow and a sort of blackguardly fretfulness about his lip, which perhaps already masked some fear. For my part, I felt no fear because, now that we were really at it, I did not believe in the combat at all. It was so like all my sham fights with Bardia; the same strokes, feints, deadlocks. Even the blood on his knuckles made no difference; a blunt sword, or the flat of a sword, could have done as much.

You, the Greek for whom I write, may never have fought; or if you did you fought, most likely, as a hoplite. Unless I were with you and had a sword, or at least a stick, in my hand I could not make you understand the course of it. I soon felt sure he could not kill me. But I was less sure I could kill him. I was very afraid lest the thing should last too long and his greater strength would grind me down. What I shall remember for ever is the change that presently came over his face. It was to me an utter astonishment. I did not understand it. I should now. I have since seen the faces of other men as they began to believe, 'This is death.' You will know it if you have seen it; life more alive than ever, a raging, tortured intensity of life. Then he made his first bad mistake, and I missed my chance. It seemed a long time (it was a few minutes really) before he made it again. That time I was ready for it. I gave the straight thrust and then, all in one motion, wheeled my sword round and cut him deeply in the inner leg, where no surgery will stop the bleeding. I jumped back of course, lest his fall should bear me down with him; so my first man-killing bespattered me less than my first pig-killing.

People ran to him, but there was no possibility of saving his life. The shouting of the mob dinned in my ears, sounding strange as all things sound when you're in your helmet. I was scarcely out of breath even; most of my bouts with Bardia had been far longer. Yet I felt of a sudden very weak and my legs were shaking; and I felt myself changed too, as if something had been taken away from me. I have often wondered if women feel like that when they lose their virginity.

Bardia (the Fox close behind him) came running up to me, with tears in his eyes and joy all over his face. 'Blessed! Blessed!' he cried. 'Queen! Warrior! My best scholar! Gods, how prettily you did it! A stroke to remember all one's days.' And he raised my left hand to his lips. I wept hard and kept my head well down so that he should not see the tears dropping from under the mask. But long before I had my voice back they were all about me (Trunia still on horseback because he could not walk) with praises and thanks, till I was almost pestered with it, though a little sweet-sharp prickle of pride thrust up inside me. There was no peace. I must speak to the people, and to the men of Phars. I must, it seemed, do a score of things. And I thought, 'Oh, for that bowl of milk, drunk alone in the cool dairy, the first day I ever used a sword!'

As soon as I had my voice I called for my horse, mounted, brought it alongside Trunia's, and held out my hand to him. Thus we rode forward a few paces and faced the horsemen of Phars.

'Strangers,' said I, 'you have seen Prince Argan killed in clean combat. Is there any more debate concerning the succession of Phars?'

About half a dozen of them, who had, no doubt, been Argan's chief partisans, made no other answer than to wheel about and gallop off. The rest all raised their helmets on their spears and shouted for Trunia and peace. Then I let go his hand, and he rode forward and in among them and was soon talking with their captains.

'Now, Queen,' said Bardia in my ear, 'it's an absolute necessity that you should bid some of our notables and some of those from Phars (the Prince will tell us which) to a feast in the palace. And Arnom too.'

'A feast, Bardia? Of bean-bread? You know we've bare larders in Glome.'

'There's the pig, Queen. And Ungit must let us have a share of the bull; I'll speak to Arnom of it. You must let the King's cellar blood to some purpose tonight, and then the bread will be less noticed.' Thus my fancy of a snug supper with Bardia and the Fox was dashed, and my sword not yet wiped from the blood of my first battle before I found myself all woman again and caught up in housewife's cares. If only I could have ridden away from them all and got to the butler before they reached the palace and learned what wine we really had! My father (and doubtless Batta) had had enough to swim in during his last few days.

In the end there were five-and-twenty of us (counting in myself) who rode back from that field to the palace. The Prince was at my side, saying all manner of fine things about me (as indeed he had some reason) and always begging me to let him see my face. It was only a kind of courteous banter and would have been nothing to any other woman. To me it was so new and (I must confess this also) so sweet that I could not choose but keep the sport up a little. I had been happy, far happier than I could hope to be again, with Psyche and the Fox, long ago, before our troubles. Now, for the first time in all my life (and the last), I was gay. A new world, very bright, seemed to be opening all round me.

It was of course the gods' old trick; blow the bubble up big before you prick it.

They pricked it a moment after I had crossed the threshold of my house. A little girl whom I'd never seen before, a slave, came out from some corner where she'd been lurking and whispered in Bardia's ear. He had been very merry up till now; the sunlight went out of his face. Then he came up to me, and said, half shamefacedly, 'Queen, the day's work is over. You'll not need me now. I'd take it very kindly if you'll let me go home. My wife's taken with her pains. We had thought it could not be so soon. I'd be glad to be with her tonight.'

I understood in that moment all my father's rages. I put terrible constraint on myself and said, 'Why, Bardia, it is very fit you should. Commend me to your wife. And offer this ring to Ungit for her safe delivery.' The ring which I took off my finger was the choicest I had.

His thanks were hearty; yet he had hardly time to utter them before he was speeding away. I suppose he never dreamed what he had done to me with those words *the day's work is over*. Yes, that was it; the day's work. I was his work; he earned his bread by being my soldier. When his tale of work for the day was done, he went home, like other hired men, and took up his true life.

That night's banquet was the first I had ever been at and the last I ever sat through (we do not lie at table like Greeks but sit on chairs or benches). After this, though I gave many feasts, I never did more than to come in three times and pledge the most notable guests and speak to all and then out again; always with two of my women attending me. This has saved me much weariness, besides putting about a great notion either of my pride or my modesty which has been useful enough. That night I sat nearly to the end, the only woman in the whole mob of them. Three parts of me was a shamed and frightened Orual who looked forward to a scolding from the Fox for being there at all, and was bitterly lonely; the fourth part was Queen, proud (though dazed too) amid the heat and clamour, sometimes dreaming she could laugh loud and drink deep like a man and a warrior, next moment, more madly, answering to Trunia's daffing, as if her veil hid the face of a pretty woman.

When I got away and up into the cold and stillness of the gallery my head reeled and ached. And 'Faugh!' I thought. 'What vile things men are!' They were all drunk by now (except the Fox, who had gone early), but their drinking had sickened me less than their eating. I had never seen men at their pleasures before: the gobbling, snatching, belching, hiccuping, the greasiness of it all, the bones thrown on the floor, the dogs quarrelling under our feet. Were all men such? Would Bardia—? then back came my loneliness. My double loneliness, for Bardia, for Psyche. Not separable. The picture, the impossible fool's dream, was that all should have been different from the very beginning and he would have been my husband and Psyche our daughter. Then I would have been in labour ... with Psyche ... and to me he would have been coming home. But now I discovered the wonderful power of wine. I understand why men become drunkards. For the way it worked on me was not at all that it blotted out these sorrows, but that it made them seem glorious and noble, like sad music, and I somehow great and reverend for feeling them. I was a great, sad queen in a song. I did not check the big tears that rose in my eyes. I enjoyed them. To say all, I was drunk; I played the fool.

And so, to my fool's bed. What was that? No, no, not a girl crying in the garden. No one, cold, hungry, and banished, was shivering there, longing and not daring to come in. It was the chains swinging at the well. It would be folly to get up and go out and call again; Psyche, Psyche, my only love. I am a great queen. I have killed a man. I am drunk like a man. All warriors drink deep after the battle. Bardia's lips on my hand were like the touch of lightning. All great princes have mistresses or lovers. There's the crying again. No, it's only the buckets at the well. Shut the window, Poobi. To your bed, child. Do you love me, Poobi? Kiss me good night. Good night. The King's dead. He'll never pull my hair again. A straight thrust and then a cut in the leg. That would have killed him. I am the Queen; I'll kill Orual too.

20

On the next day we burnt the old King; on the day after that we betrothed Redival to Trunia (and the wedding was made a month later); the third day all the strangers rode off and we had the house to ourselves. My real reign began.

I must now pass quickly over many years (though they made up the longest part of my life) during which the Queen of Glome had more and more part in me and Orual had less and less. I locked her up or laid her asleep as best I could somewhere deep down inside me; she lay curled there. It was like being with child, but reversed; the thing I carried in me grew slowly smaller and less alive.

It may happen that someone who reads this book will have heard tales and songs about my reign and my wars and great deeds. Let him be sure that most of it is false, for I know already that the common talk, and especially in neighbouring lands, has doubled and trebled the truth, and my deeds, such as they were, have been mixed up with those of some great fighting queen who lived long ago and (I think) further north, and a fine patchwork of wonders and impossibilities made out of both. But the truth is that after my battle with Argan there were only three wars that I fought, and one of them, the last, against the Wagon Men who live beyond the Grey Mountain, was a very slight thing. And though I rode out with my men in all these wars, I was never such a fool as to think myself a great captain. All that part of it was Bardia's and Penuan's. (I met him first the night after I fought Argan, and he became the trustiest of my nobles.) I will also say this: I was never yet at any battle but that, when the lines were drawn up and the first enemy arrows came flashing in among us, and the grass and trees about you suddenly became a place, a Field, a thing to be put in chronicles, I wished very heartily that I had stayed at home. Nor did I ever do any notable deed with my own arm but once. That was in the war with Essur, when some of their horse came out of an ambush and Bardia, riding to his position, was surrounded all in a moment. Then I galloped in and hardly knew what I was doing till the matter was over, and they say I had killed seven men with my own strokes. (I was wounded that day.) But to hear the common rumour you would think I had planned every war and every battle and killed more enemies than all the rest of our army put together.

My real strength lay in two things. The first was that I had, and especially for the first years, two very good counsellors. You couldn't have had better yokefellows, for the Fox understood what Bardia did not, and neither cared a straw for his own dignity or advancement when my needs were in question. And I came to understand (what my girl's ignorance had once hidden from me) that their girding and mocking at one another was little more than a sort of game. They were no flatterers either. In this way I had some profit of my ugliness; they did not think of me as a woman. If they had, it is impossible that we three, alone, by the hearth in the Pillar Room (as we were often) should have talked with such freedom. I learned from them a thousand things about men.

My second strength lay in my veil. I could never have believed, till I had proof of it, what it would do for me. From the very first (it began that night in the garden with Trunia) as soon as my face was invisible, people began to discover all manner of beauties in my voice. At first it was 'deep as a man's, but nothing in the world less mannish'; later, and until it grew cracked with age, it was the voice of a spirit, a Siren, Orpheus, what you will. And as years passed and there were fewer in the city (and none beyond it) who remembered my face, the wildest stories got about as to what that veil hid. No one believed it was anything so common as the face of an ugly woman. Some said (nearly all the younger women said) that it was frightful beyond endurance; a pig's, bear's, cat's, or elephant's face. The best story was that I had no face at all; if you stripped off my veil you'd find emptiness. But another sort (there were more of the men among these) said that I wore a veil because I was of a beauty so dazzling that if I let it be seen all men in the world would run mad; or else that Ungit was jealous of my beauty and had promised to blast me if I went bareface. The upshot of all this nonsense was that I became something very mysterious and awful. I have seen ambassadors, who were brave men in battle, turn white like scared children in my Pillar Room when I turned and looked at them (and they couldn't see whether I was looking or not) and was silent. I have made the most seasoned liars turn red and blurt out the truth with the same weapon.

The first thing I did was to shift my own quarters over to the north side of the palace, in order to be out of that sound the chains made in the well. For though, by daylight, I knew well enough what made it, at night nothing I could do would cure me of taking it for the weeping of a girl. But the change of my quarters, and later changes (for I tried every side of the house) did no good. I discovered that there was no part of the palace from which the swinging of those chains could not be heard; at night, I mean, when the silence grows deep. It is a thing no one would have found out who was not always afraid of hearing one sound; and at the same time (that was Orual, Orual refusing to die) terribly afraid of not hearing it if for once – if possibly, at last, after ten thousand mockeries – it should be real, if Psyche had come back. But I knew this was foolishness. If Psyche were alive and able to come back, and wanted to come back, she would have done it long ago. She must be dead by now; or caught by someone and sold into slavery ... When that thought came, my only resource was to rise, however late and cold it was, and go to my Pillar Room and find some work. I have read and written there till I could hardly see out of my eyes; my head on fire, my feet aching with cold.

Of course I had my bidders in every slave market, and my seekers in every land that I could reach, and listened to every traveller's tale that might put us on Psyche's track. I did these things for years, but they were infinitely irksome to me for I knew it was all hopeless.

Before I had reigned for a year (I remember the time well, for the men were picking the figs) I had Batta hanged. Following up a chance word which one of the horseboys said in my hearing, I found that she had long been the pest of the whole palace. No trifle could be given to any of the other slaves, and hardly a good bit could come on their trenchers, but Batta must have her share of it; otherwise she'd tell such tales of them as would lead to the whipping-post or the mines. And after Batta was hanged I went on and reduced the household to better order. There were far too many slaves. Some thieves and sluts I sold. Many of the good ones, both men and women, if they were sturdy and prudent (for otherwise to free a slave is but to have a new beggar at your door), I set free, and gave them land and cottages for their livelihood. I coupled them off in pairs and married them. Sometimes I even let them choose their own wives or husbands, which is a strange, unusual way of making even slaves' marriages, and yet it often turned out well enough. Though it was a great loss to me I set Poobi free, and she chose a very good man. Some of my happiest hours have been beside the fire in her cottage. And most of these freed people have become very thriving husbandmen, all living near the palace, and very faithful to me. It was like having a second body of guards.

I set the mines (they are silver mines) on a better footing. My father had never, it seems, thought of them save as a punishment. 'Take him to the mines!' he'd say. 'I'll teach him. Work him to death.' But there was more death than work in the mines, and the yield was light. As soon as I could get an honest overseer (Bardia was incomparable for finding out such men) I bought strong, young slaves for the mines, saw that they had dry lodging and good feeding, and let every man know that he should go free when he had, adding day by day, dug so much ore. The tale was such that a steady man could hope for his freedom in ten years; later, we brought it down to seven. This lowered the yield for the first year, but had raised it by a tenth in the third; now, it is half as great again as in my father's day. Ours is the best silver in all this part of the world, and a great root of our wealth.

I took the Fox out of the wretched dog-hole in which he had slept all these years and gave him noble apartments on the south side of the palace; and land for his living, so that he should not seem to hang by my bounties. I also put money into his hands for the buying (if it should prove possible) of books. It took a long time for traders, perhaps twenty kingdoms away, to learn that there was a vent for books in Glome, and longer still for the books to come up, changing hands many times and often delayed for a year or more on the journey. The Fox tore his hair at the cost of them. 'An obol's worth for a talent,' he said. We had to take what we could get, not what we chose. In this way we built up what was, for a barbarous land, a noble library: eighteen works in all. We had Homer's poetry about Troy, imperfect, coming down to that place where he brings in Patroclus weeping. We had two tragedies of Euripides, one about Andromeda and another where Dionysus says the prologue and the chorus is the wild women. Also a very good, useful book (without metre) about the breeding and drenching of horses and cattle, the worming of dogs, and such matters. Also, some of the conversations of Socrates; a poem in honour of Helen by Hesias Stesichorus; a book of Heraclitus; and a very long, hard book (without metre) which begins *All men by nature desire knowledge.* As soon as the books began to come in, Arnom would often be with the Fox, learning to read in them; and presently other men, mostly younger sons of nobles, came too.

And now I began to live as a Queen should, and to know my own nobles, and to show courtesies to the great ladies of the land. In this way, of necessity, I came to meet Bardia's wife, Ansit. I had thought she would be of dazzling beauty; but the truth is she was very short, and now, having borne eight children, very fat and unshapely. All the women of Glome splay out like that, pretty early in their lives. (That was one thing, perhaps, which helped the fantasy that I had a lovely face behind my veil. Being a virgin, I had kept my shape, and that – if you didn't see my face – was for a long time very tolerable.) I put great force upon myself to be courteous to Ansit; more than courteous, even loving. More than that, I would have loved her indeed, for Bardia's sake, if I could have done it. But she was mute as a mouse in my presence; afraid of me, I thought. When we tried to talk together, her eyes would wander round the room as if she were asking, 'Who will deliver me from this?' In a sudden flash, not without joy in it, the thought came to me, 'Can she be jealous?' And so it was, through all those years, whenever we met. Sometimes I would say to myself, 'She has lain in his bed, and that's bad. She has borne his children, and that's worse. But, has she ever crouched beside him in the ambush? Ever ridden knee to knee with him in the charge? Or shared a stinking water-bottle with him at the thirsty day's end? For all the dove's eyes they've made at one another, was there ever such a glance between them as well-proved comrades exchange in farewell when they ride different ways and both into desperate danger? I have known, I have had, so much of him that she could never dream of. She's his toy, his recreation, his leisure, his solace. I'm in his man's life.'

It's strange to think how Bardia went to and fro daily between Queen and wife, well assured he did his duty by both (as he did) and without thought, doubtless, of the pother he made between them. This is what it is to be a man. The one sin the gods never forgive us is that of being born women.

The duty of queenship that irked me most was going often to the house of Ungit and sacrificing. It would have been worse but that Ungit herself (or my pride made me think so) was now weakened. Arnom had opened new windows in the walls and her house was not so dark. He also kept it differently, scouring away the blood after each slaughter and sprinkling fresh water; it smelled cleaner and less holy. And Arnom was learning from the Fox to talk like a philosopher about the gods. The great change came when he proposed to set up an image of her – a woman-shaped image in the Greek fashion – in front of the old shapeless stone. I think he would like to have got rid of the stone altogether, but it is, in a manner, Ungit herself and the people would have gone mad if she were moved. It was a prodigious charge to get such an image as he wanted, for no one in Glome could make it; it had to be brought, not indeed from the Greeklands themselves, but from lands where men had learned of the Greeks. I was rich now and helped him with silver. I was not quite certain why I did this; I think I felt that an image of this sort would be somehow a defeat for the old, hungry, faceless Ungit whose terror had been over me in childhood. The new image, when at last it came, seemed to us barbarians wonderfully beautiful and lifelike, even when we brought her white and naked into her house; and when we had painted her and put her robes on, she was a marvel to all the lands about and pilgrims came to see her. The Fox, who had seen greater and more beautiful works at home, laughed at her.

I gave up trying to find a room where I should not hear that noise which was sometimes chains swinging in the wind and sometimes lost and beggared Psyche weeping at my door. Instead, I built stone walls round the well and put a thatched roof over it and added a door. The walls were very thick; my mason told me they were madly thick. 'You're wasting enough good stone, Queen,' he said, 'to have made ten new pigsties.' For a while after that an ugly fancy used to come to me in my dreams, or between sleeping and waking, that I had walled up, gagged with stone, not a well but Psyche (or

Orual) herself. But that also passed. I heard Psyche weeping no more. The year after that I defeated Essur.

The Fox was growing old now and needed rest; we had him less and less in my Pillar Room. He was very busy writing a history of Glome. He wrote it twice, in Greek and in our own tongue, which, he said, he now saw was capable of eloquence. It was strange for me to see our own speech written out in the Greek letters. I never told the Fox that he knew less of it than he believed, so that what he wrote in it was often laughable and most so where he thought it most eloquent. As he grew older he seemed to be ever less and less a philosopher, and to talk more of eloquence, and figures, and poetry. His voice grew always shriller and he talked more and more. He often mistook me for Psyche now; sometimes he called me Crethis, and sometimes even by boys' names like Charmides or Glaucon.

But I was too busy to be with him much. What did I not do? I had all the laws revised and cut in stone in the centre of the city. I narrowed and deepened the Shennit till barges could come up to our gates. I made a bridge where the old ford had been. I made cisterns so that we should not go thirsty whenever there was a dry year. I became wise about stock and bought in good bulls and rams and bettered our breeds. I did and I did and I did – and what does it matter what I did? I cared for all these things only as a man cares for a hunt or a game, which fills the mind and seems of some moment while it lasts, but then the beast's killed or the king's mated, and now who cares? It was so with me almost every evening of my life; one little stairway led me from feast or council, all the bustle and skill and glory of queenship, to my own chamber, to be alone with myself; that is, with a nothingness. Going to bed and waking in the morning (I woke, most often, too early) were bad times – so many hundreds of evenings and mornings. Sometimes I wondered who or what sends us this senseless repetition of days and nights and seasons and years; is it not like hearing a stupid boy whistle the same tune over and over, till you wonder how he can bear it himself?

The Fox died and I gave him a kingly funeral and made four Greek verses which were cut on his tomb; I will not write them here lest a true Greek should laugh at them. This happened about the end of harvest. The tomb is up behind the pear trees where he used to teach Psyche and me in summer. Then the days and months and years went on again as before, round and round like a wheel, till there came a day when I looked about me at the gardens and the palace and the ridge of the Grey Mountain out eastward, and thought I could no longer endure to see these same things every day till I died. The very blisters of the pitch on the wooden walls of the byres seemed to be the same ones I had seen before the Fox himself came to Glome. I resolved to go on a progress and travel in other lands. We were at peace with everyone. Bardia and Penuan and Arnom could do all that was needed while I was away; for indeed Glome had now been nursed and trained till it almost ruled itself.

I took with me Bardia's son Ilerdia, and Poobi's daughter Alit, and two of my women and a plump of spears (all honest men), and a cook and a groom with pack animals for the tents and victuals, and rode out of Glome three days later.

21

The thing for whose sake I tell of this journey happened at the very end of it; and even when I had thought it was finished. We had gone first into Phars, where they harvest later than we, so that it was like having that piece of the year twice over; we found what we had just left at home – the sound of the whetting, the singing of the reapers, the flats of stubble widening and the squares of standing corn diminishing, the piled wagons in the lanes, all the sweat and sunburn and merriment. We had lain ten nights or more in Trunia's palace, where I was astonished to see how Redival had grown fat and lost her beauty. She talked, as of old, everlastingly, but all about her children, and asked after no one in Glome except Batta. Trunia never listened to a word she said, but he and I had much talk together. I had already settled with my council that his second son, Daaran, was to be King of Glome after my day. This Daaran was (for the son of so silly a mother) a right-minded boy. I could have loved him if I had let myself and if Redival had been out of the way. But I would never give my heart again to any young creature.

Out of Phars we had turned westward into Essur by deep passes through the mountains. This was a country of forests greater than I had yet seen, and rushing rivers, with plenty of birds, deer, and other game. The people I had with me were all young and took great pleasure in their travels, and the journey itself had by now linked us all together; all burned brown, and with a world of hopes, cares, jests, and knowledge, all sprung up since we left home, and shared among us. At first they had been in awe of me and had ridden in silence; now we were good friends. My own heart lifted. The eagles wheeled above us and the waterfalls roared.

From the mountains we came down into Essur and lay three nights in the King's house. He was, I think, not a bad sort of man, but too slavish-courteous to me; for Glome and Phars in alliance had made Essur change her tune. His queen was manifestly terrified by my veil and by the stories she had heard of me. And from that house I had meant to turn homewards, but we were told of a natural hot spring fifteen miles further to the west. I knew Ilerdia longed to see it; and I thought (between sadness and smiling) how the Fox would have scolded me if I had been so near any curious work of nature and not examined it. So I said we would go the day's journey further and turn then.

It was the calmest day; pure autumn; very hot, yet the sunlight on the stubble looked aged and gentle, not fierce like the summer heats. You would think the year was resting, its work done. And I whispered to myself that I too would begin to rest. When I was back at Glome I would no longer pile task on task. I would let Bardia rest too (I had often thought he began to look tired) and we would let younger heads be busy, while we sat in the sun and talked of our old battles. What more was there for me to do? Why should I not be at peace? I thought this was the wisdom of old age beginning.

The hot spring (like all such rarities) was only food for stupid wonder. When we had seen it we went further down the warm, green valley in which it rose and found a good camping place between a stream and a wood. While my people were busied with the tents and the horses, I went a little way into the wood and sat there in the coolness. Before long I heard the ringing of a temple bell (all temples, nearly, have bells in Essur) from somewhere behind me. Thinking it would be pleasant to walk a little after so many hours on horseback, I rose and went slowly through the trees to find the temple; very idly, not caring whether I found it or not. But in a few minutes I came out into a mossy place free of trees, and there it was; no bigger than a peasant's hut but built of pure white stone, with fluted pillars in the Greek style. Behind it I could see a small thatched house where, no doubt, the priest lived.

The place itself was quiet enough, but inside the temple there was a far deeper silence and it was very cool. It was clean and empty and there were none of the common temple smells about it, so that I thought it must belong to one of those small, peaceful gods who are content with flowers and fruit for sacrifice. Then I saw it must be a goddess, for there was on the altar the image of a woman, about two feet high, carved in wood; not badly done and all the fairer (to my mind) because there was no painting or gilding but only the natural pale colour of the wood. The thing that marred it was a band or scarf of some black stuff tied round the head of the image so as to hide its face – much like my own veil, but that mine was white.

I thought how much better all this was than the house of Ungit, and how unlike. Then I heard a step behind me and, turning, saw that a man in a black robe had come in. He was an old man with quiet eyes; perhaps a little simple.

'Does the Stranger want to make an offering to the goddess?' he asked.

I slipped a couple of coins into his hand and asked what goddess she was.

'Istra,' he said.

The name is not so uncommon in Glome and the neighbouring lands that I had much cause to be startled; but I said I had never heard of a goddess called that.

'Oh, that is because she is a very young goddess. She has only just begun to be a goddess. For you must know that, like many other gods, she began by being a mortal.'

'And how was she godded?'

'She is so lately godded that she is still a rather poor goddess, Stranger. Yet for one little silver piece I will tell you the sacred story. Thank you, kind Stranger, thank you. Istra will be your friend for this. Now I tell you the sacred story. Once upon a time in a certain land there lived a king and a queen who had three daughters, and the youngest was the most beautiful princess in the whole world ...'

And so he went on, as such priests do, all in a singsong voice, and using words which he clearly knew by heart. And to me it was as if the old man's voice, and the temple, and I myself and my journey, were all things in such a story; for he was telling the very history of our Istra, of Psyche herself – how Talapal (that's the Essurian Ungit) was jealous of her beauty and made her to be offered to a brute on a mountain, and how Talapal's son Ialim, the most beautiful of the gods, loved her and took her away to his secret palace. He even knew that Ialim had there visited her only in darkness and had forbidden her to see his face. But he had a childish reason for that: 'You see, Stranger, he had to be very secret because of his mother Talapal. She would have been very angry with him if she had known he had married the woman she most hated in the world.'

I thought to myself, 'It's well for me I didn't hear this story fifteen years ago; yes, or even ten. It would have reawakened all my sleeping miseries. Now, it moves me hardly at all.' Then, suddenly struck afresh with the queerness of the thing, I asked him, 'Where did you learn all this?'

He stared at me as if he didn't well understand such a question. 'It's the sacred story,' he said. I saw that he was rather silly than cunning and that it would be useless to question him. As soon as I was silent he went on.

But now all the dreamlike feeling in me suddenly vanished. I was wide awake and I felt the blood rush into my face. He was telling it wrong; hideously and stupidly wrong. First of all, he made it that both Psyche's sisters had visited her in the secret palace of the god (to think of Redival going there!). 'And so,' he said, 'when her two sisters had seen the beautiful palace and been feasted and given gifts, they—'

'They *saw* the palace?'

'Stranger, you are hindering the sacred story. Of course they saw the palace. They weren't blind. And then—'

It was as if the gods themselves had first laughed, and then spat, in my face. So this was the shape the story had taken. You may say, the shape the gods had given it. For it must be they who had put it into the old fool's mind or into the mind of some other dreamer from whom he'd learned it. How could any mortal have known of that palace at all? That much of the truth they had dropped into someone's mind, in a dream, or an oracle, or however they do such things. That much; and wiped clean out the very meaning, the pith, the central knot, of the whole tale. Do I not do well to write a book against them, telling what they have kept hidden? Never, sitting on my judgement seat, had I caught a false witness in a more cunning half-truth. For if the true story had been like their story, no riddle would have been set me; there would have been no guessing and no guessing wrong. More than that; it's a story belonging to a different world, a world in which the gods show themselves clearly and don't torment men with glimpses, nor unveil to one what they hide from another, nor ask you to believe what contradicts your eyes and ears and nose and tongue and fingers. In such a world (is there such? it's not ours, for certain) I would have walked aright. The gods themselves would have been able to find no fault in me. And now to tell my story as if I had had the very sight they had denied me ... is it not as if you told a cripple's story and never said he was lame, or told how a man betrayed a secret but never said it was after twenty hours of torture? And I saw all in a moment how the false story would grow and spread and be told all over the earth; and I wondered how many of the other sacred stories are just such twisted falsities as this.

'And so,' the priest was saying, 'when these two wicked sisters had made their plan to ruin Istra, they brought her the lamp and—'

'But why did she – they – want to separate her from the god, if they had seen the palace?'

'They wanted to destroy her *because* they had seen her palace.'

'But why?'

'Oh, because they were jealous. Her husband and her house were so much finer than theirs.'

That moment I resolved to write this book. For years now my old quarrel with the gods had slept. I had come into Bardia's way of thinking; I no longer meddled with them. Often, though I had seen a god myself, I was near to believing that there are no such things. The memory of his voice and face was kept in one of those rooms of my soul that I didn't lightly unlock. Now, instantly, I knew I was facing them; I with no strength and they with all; I visible to them, they invisible to me; I easily wounded (already so wounded all my life had been but a hiding and staunching of the wound), they invulnerable; I one, they many. In all these years they had only let me run away from them as far as the cat lets the mouse run; now, snatch! and the claw on me again. Well; I could speak. I could set down the truth. What had never perhaps been done in the world before should be done now. The case against them should be written.

Jealousy! I jealous of Psyche? I sickened not only at the vileness of the lie but at its flatness. It seemed as if the gods had minds just like the lowest of the people. What came easiest to them, what seemed the likeliest and simplest reason to put in a story, was the dull, narrow passion of the beggars' streets, the temple brothels, the slave, the child, the dog. Could they not lie, if lie they must, better than that?

'... and wanders over the earth, weeping, weeping, always weeping.' How long had the old man been going on? That one word rang in my ears as if he had repeated it a thousand times. I set my teeth and my soul stood on guard. A moment more and I should have begun to hear the sound myself again. She would have been weeping in that little wood outside the temple door.

'That's enough,' I shouted. 'Do you think I don't know a girl cries when her heart breaks? Go on, go on.'

'Wanders, weeping, weeping, always weeping,' he said. 'And falls under the power of Talapal, who hates her. And of course Ialim can't protect her because Talapal is his mother and he's afraid of her. So Talapal torments Istra and sets her to all manner of hard labours, things that seem impossible. But when Istra has done them all, then at last Talapal releases her, and she is reunited to Ialim and becomes a goddess. Then we take off her black veil, and I change my black robe for a white one, and we offer—'

'You mean she will some day be reunited to the god; and you will take off her veil then? When is this to happen?'

'We take off the veil and I change my robe in the spring.'

'Do you think I care what you do? Has the thing itself happened yet or not? Is Istra now wandering over the earth or has she already become a goddess?'

'But, Stranger, the sacred story is about the sacred things; the things we do in the temple. In spring, and all summer, she is a goddess. Then when harvest comes we bring a lamp into the temple in the night and the god flies away. Then we veil her. And all winter she is wandering and suffering; weeping, always weeping ...'

He knew nothing. The story and the worship were all one in his mind. He could not understand what I was asking.

'I've heard your story told otherwise, old man,' said I. 'I think the sister – or the sisters – might have more to say for themselves than you know.'

'You may be sure that they would have plenty to say for themselves,' he replied. 'The jealous always have. Why, my own wife now—'

I saluted him and went out of that cold place into the warmth of the wood. I could see through the trees the red light of the fire my people had already kindled. The sun had set.

I hid all the things I was feeling – and indeed I did not know what they were, except that all the peace of that autumnal journey was shattered – so as not to spoil the pleasure of my people. Next day I understood more clearly. I could never be at peace again till I had written my charge against the gods. It burned me from within. It quickened; I was with book, as a woman is with child.

And so it comes about that I can tell nothing of our journey back to Glome. There were seven or eight days of it, and we passed many notable places in Essur; and in Glome, after we had crossed the border, we saw everywhere such good peace and plenty and such duty and, I think, love towards myself as ought to have gladdened me. But my eyes and ears were shut up. All day, and often all night too, I was recalling every passage of the true story, dragging up terrors, humiliations, struggles, and anguish that I had not thought of for years, letting Orual wake and speak, digging her almost out of a grave, out of the walled well. The more I remembered, the more still I could remember; often weeping beneath my veil as if I had never been Queen, yet never in so much sorrow that my burning indignation did not rise above it. I was in haste too. I must write it all quickly before the gods found some way to silence me. Whenever, towards evening, Ilerdia pointed and said, 'There, Queen, would be a good place for the tents,' I said (before I had thought what I would say), 'No, no. We can make three more miles tonight; or five.' Every morning I woke earlier. At first I endured the waiting; fretting myself in the cold mist, listening to the deep-breathed sleep of those young sleepers. But soon my patience would serve me no longer. I took to waking them. I woke them earlier each morning. In the end we were travelling like those who fly from a victorious enemy. I became silent, and this struck the others silent too. I could see they were bewildered and all the comfort of their travels was gone. I suppose they whispered together about the Queen's moods.

When I reached home, even then I could not set about it so suddenly as I had hoped. All manner of petty work had piled up. And now, when I most needed help, word was sent me that Bardia was a little sick and kept his bed. I asked Arnom about Bardia's sickness, and Arnom said, 'It's neither poison nor fever, Queen; a small matter for a strong man. But he'd best not rise. He's ageing, you know.' It would have given me a thrust of fear but that I already knew (and had seen growing signs of it lately) how that wife of his cockered and cosseted him, like a hen with one chicken; not, I'd swear, through any true fears, but to keep him at home and away from the palace.

Yet at last, after infinite hindrances, I made my book and here it stands. Now, you who read, judge between the gods and me. They gave me nothing in the world to love but Psyche and then took her from me. But that was not enough. They then brought me to her at such a place and time that it hung on my word whether she should continue in bliss or be cast out into misery. They would not tell me whether she was the bride of a god, or mad, or a brute's or villain's spoil. They would give no clear sign, though I begged for it. I had to guess. And because I guessed wrong they punished me; what's worse, punished me through her. And even that was not enough; they have now sent out a lying story in which I was given no riddle to guess, but knew and saw that she was the god's bride, and of my own will destroyed her, and that for jealousy. As if I were another Redival. I say the gods deal very unrightly with us. For they will neither (which would be best of all) go away and leave us to live our own short days to ourselves, nor will they show themselves openly and tell us what they would have us do. For that too would be endurable. But to hint and hover, to draw near us in dreams and oracles, or in a waking vision that vanishes as soon as seen, to be dead silent when we question them and then glide back and whisper (words we cannot understand) in our ears when we most wish to be free of them, and to show to one what they hide from another; what is all this but cat-and-mouse play, blindman's buff, and mere jugglery? Why must holy places be dark places?

I say, therefore, that there is no creature (toad, scorpion, or serpent) so noxious to man as the gods. Let them answer my charge if they can. It may well be that, instead of answering, they'll strike me mad or leprous or turn me into beast, bird, or tree. But will not all the world then know (and the gods will know it knows) that this is because they have no answer?

PART 2

I

Not many days have passed since I wrote those words *No answer*, but I must unroll my book again. It would be better to re-write it from the beginning, but I think there's no time for that. Weakness comes on me fast, and Arnom shakes his head and tells me I must rest. They think I don't know they have sent a message to Daaran.

Since I cannot mend the book, I must add to it. To leave it as it was would be to die perjured; I know so much more than I did about the woman who wrote it. What began the change was the very writing itself. Let no one lightly set about such a work. Memory, once waked, will play the tyrant. I found I must set down (for I was speaking as before judges and must not lie) passions and thoughts of my own which I had clean forgotten. The past which I wrote down was not the past that I thought I had (all these years) been remembering. I did not, even when I had finished the book, see clearly many things that I see now. The change which the writing wrought in me (and of which I did not write) was only a beginning; only to prepare me for the gods' surgery. They used my own pen to probe my wound.

Very early in the writing there came also a stroke from without. While I related my first years, when I wrote how Redival and I built mud houses in the garden, a thousand other things came back into my mind, all about those days when there was no Psyche and no Fox; only I and Redival. Catching tadpoles in the brook, hiding from Batta in the hay, waiting at the door of the hall when our father gave a feast and wheedling titbits out of the slaves as they went in and out. And I thought, how terribly she changed. This, all within my own mind. But then the stroke from without. On top of many other hindrances came word of an embassy from the Great King who lives to the South and East.

'Another plague,' said I. And when the strangers came (and there must be hours of talk, and a feast for them afterwards) I liked them none the better for finding that their chief man was a eunuch. Eunuchs are very great men at that court. This one was the fattest man I ever saw, so fat his eyes could hardly see over his cheeks, all shining and reeking with oil, and tricked out with as much doll-finery as one of Ungit's girls. But as he talked and talked I began to think there was a faint likeness in him to someone I had seen long ago. And, as we do, I chased it and gave it up, and chased it and gave it up again, till suddenly, when I least thought of it, the truth started into my mind and I shouted out, 'Tarin!'

'Oh yes, Queen, oh yes,' said he, spiteful-pleased (I thought) and leering. 'Oh yes, I was him you called Tarin. Your father did not love me, Queen, did he? But ... te-hee, te-hee ... he made my fortune. Oh yes, he set me on the right road. With two cuts of a razor. But for him I should not have been the great man I am now.'

I wished him joy of his advancement.

'Thank you, Queen, thank you. It is very good. And to think (te-hee) that but for your father's temper I might have gone on carrying a shield in the guard of a little barbarous king whose whole kingdom could be put into one corner of my master's hunting park and never be noticed! You will not be angry, no?'

I said I had always heard that the Great King had an admirable park.

'And your sister, Queen?' said the eunuch. 'Ah, she was a pretty little girl ... though, te-hee, te-hee, I've had finer women through my hands since ... is she still alive?'

'She is the Queen of Phars,' said I.

'Ah, so. Phars. I remember. One forgets the names of all these little countries. Yes ... a pretty little girl. I took pity on her. She was lonely.'

'Lonely?' said I.

'Oh yes, yes, very lonely. After the other princess, the baby, came. She used to say, "First of all Orual loved me much; then the Fox came and she loved me little; then the baby came and she loved me not at all." So she was lonely. I was sorry for her ... te-hee-hee ... Oh, I was a fine young fellow then. Half the girls in Glome were in love with me.' I led him back to our affairs of state.

This was only the first stroke, a light one; the first snowflake of the winter that I was entering, regarded only because it tells us what's to come. I was by no means sure that Tarin spoke truly. I am sure still that Redival was false and a fool. And for her folly the gods themselves cannot blame me; she had that from her father. But one thing was certain; I had never thought at all how it might be with her when I turned first to the Fox and then to Psyche. For it had been somehow settled in my mind from the very beginning that I was the pitiable and ill-used one. She had her gold curls, hadn't she?

So back to my writing. And the continual labour of mind to which it put me began to overflow into my sleep. It was a labour of sifting and sorting, separating motive from motive and both from pretext; and this same sorting went on every night in my dreams, but in a changed fashion. I thought I had before me a huge, hopeless pile of seeds, wheat, barley, poppy, rye, millet, what not? and I must sort them out and make separate piles, each all of one kind. Why I must do it, I did not know; but infinite punishment would fall upon me if I rested a moment from my labour or if, when all was done, a single seed were in the wrong pile. In waking life a man would know the task impossible. The torment of the dream was that, there, it could conceivably be done. There was one chance in ten thousand of finishing the labour in time, and one in a hundred thousand of making no mistake. It was all but certain I should fail, and be punished; but not certain. And so to it: searching, peering, picking up each seed between finger and thumb. Yet not always finger and thumb. For in some dreams, more madly still, I became a little ant, and the seeds were as big as millstones; and labouring with all my might, till my six legs cracked, I carried them to their places; holding them in front of me as ants do, loads bigger than myself.

One thing that shows how wholly the gods kept me to my two labours, the day's and the night's, is that all this time I hardly gave Bardia a thought, save to grumble at his absence because it meant that I was more hindered in my writing. While the rage of it lasted nothing seemed to matter a straw except finishing my book. Of Bardia I only said (once and again), 'Does he mean to slug abed for the rest of his life?' or, 'It's that wife of his.'

Then there came a day when that last line of the book (*they have no answer*) was still wet, and I found myself listening to Arnom and understanding, as if for the first time, what his looks and voice meant. 'Do you mean,' I cried, 'that the Lord Bardia is in danger?'

'He's very weak, Queen,' said the priest. 'I wish the Fox were with us. We are bunglers, we of Glome. It seems to me that Bardia has no strength or spirit to fight the sickness.'

'Good gods,' said I, 'why did you not make me understand this before? Ho! Slave! My horse. I will go and see him.'

Arnom was an old and trusted counsellor now. He laid his hand on my arm. 'Queen,' he said gently and very gravely, 'it would make him the less likely to recover if you now went to him.'

'Do I carry such an infection about me?' said I. 'Is there death in my aspect, even through a veil?'

'Bardia is your loyalest and most loving subject,' said Arnom. 'To see you would call up all his powers; perhaps crack them. He'd rouse himself to his duty and courtesy. A hundred affairs of state on which he meant to speak to you would crowd into his mind. He'd rack his brains to remember things he has forgotten for these last nine days. It might kill him. Leave him to drowse and dream. It's his best chance now.'

It was as bitter a truth as I'd ever tasted, but I drank it. Would I not have crouched silent in my own dungeons as long as Arnom bade me if it would add one featherweight to Bardia's chance of life? Three days I bore it (I, the old fool, with hanging dugs and shrivelled flanks). On the fourth I said, 'I can bear it no longer.' On the fifth Arnom came to me, himself weeping, and I knew his tidings without words. And this is a strange folly, that what seemed to me worst of all was that Bardia had died without ever hearing what it would have shamed him to hear. It seemed to me that all would be bearable if, once only, I could have gone to him and whispered in his ear, 'Bardia, I loved you.'

When they laid him on the pyre I could only stand by to honour him. Because I was neither his wife nor kin, I might not wail nor beat the breast for him. Ah, if I could have beaten the breast, I would have put on steel gloves or hedgehog skins to do it.

I waited three days, as the custom is, and then went to comfort (so they call it) his widow. It was not only duty and usage that drove me. Because he had loved her she was, in a way, surely enough, the enemy; yet who else in the whole world could now talk to me?

They brought me into the upper room in her house where she sat at her spinning; very pale, but very calm. Calmer than I. Once I had been surprised that she was so much less beautiful than report had made her. Now, in her later years, she had won a new kind of beauty; it was a proud, still sort of face.

'Lady – Ansit,' I said, taking both her hands (she had not time to get them away from me), 'what shall I say to you? How can I speak of him and not say that your loss is indeed without measure? And that's no comfort. Unless you can think even now that it is better to have had and lost such a husband than to enjoy any man else in the world for ever.'

'The Queen does me great honour,' said Ansit, pulling her hands out of mine so as to stand with them crossed on her breast, her eyes cast down, in the court fashion.

'Oh, dear Lady, un-queen me a little, I beseech you. Is it as if you and I had never met till yesterday? After yours (never think I'd compare them) my loss is greatest. I pray you, your seat again. And your distaff; we shall talk better to that movement. And you will let me sit here beside you?'

She sat down and resumed her spinning; her face at rest and her lips a little pursed, very housewifely. She would give me no help.

'It was very unlooked for,' said I. 'Did you at first see any danger in this sickness?'

'Yes.'

'Did you so? To me Arnom said it ought to have been a light matter.'

'He said that to me, Queen. He said it would be a light matter for a man who had all his strength to fight it.'

'Strength? But the Lord Bardia was a strong man.'

'Yes; as a tree that is eaten away within.'

'Eaten away? And with what? I never knew this.'

'I suppose not, Queen. He was tired. He had worked himself out; or been worked. Ten years ago he should have given over and lived as old men do. He was not made of iron or brass, but flesh.'

'He never looked nor spoke like an old man.'

'Perhaps you never saw him, Queen, at the times when a man shows his weariness. You never saw his haggard face in early morning. Nor heard his groan when you (because you had sworn to do it) must shake him and force him to rise. You never saw him come home late from the palace, hungry, yet too tired to eat. How should you, Queen? I was only his wife. He was too well-mannered, you know, to nod and yawn in a Queen's house.'

'You mean that his work—?'

'Five wars, thirty-one battles, nineteen embassies, taking thought for this and thought for that, speaking a word in one ear, and another, and another, soothing this man and scaring that and flattering a third, devising, consulting, remembering, guessing, forecasting ... and the Pillar Room and the Pillar Room. The mines are not the only place where a man can be worked to death.'

This was worse than the worst I had looked for. A flash of anger passed through me, then a horror of misgiving; could it (but that was fantastical) be true? But the misery of that mere suspicion made my own voice almost humble.

'You speak in your sorrow, Lady. But (forgive me) this is mere fantasy. I never spared myself more than him. Do you tell me a strong man'd break under the burden a woman's bearing still?'

'Who that knows men would doubt it? They're harder, but we're tougher. They do not live longer than we. They do not weather a sickness better. Men are brittle. And you, Queen, were the younger.'

My heart shrivelled up cold and abject within me. 'If this is true,' said I, 'I've been deceived. If he had dropped but a word of it, I'd have taken every burden from him; sent him home for ever, loaded with every honour I could give.'

'You know him little, Queen, if you think he'd ever have spoken that word. Oh, you have been a fortunate queen; no prince ever had more loving servants.'

'I know I have had loving servants. Do you grudge me that? Even now in your grief, will your heart serve you to grudge me that? Do you mock me because that is the only sort of love I ever had or could have? No husband; no child. And you – you who have had all—'

'All you left me, Queen.'

'Left you, fool? What mad thought is in your mind?'

'Oh, I know well enough that you were not lovers. You left me that. The divine blood will not mix with subjects', they say. You left me my share. When you had used him, you would let him steal home to me; until you needed him again. After weeks and months at the wars – you and he night and day together, sharing the councils, the dangers, the victories, the soldiers' bread, the very jokes – he could come back to me, each time a little thinner and greyer and with a few more scars; and fall asleep before his supper was down; and cry out in his dream, "Quick, on the right there. The Queen's in danger." And next morning – the Queen's a wonderful early riser in Glome – the Pillar Room again. I'll not deny it; I had what you left of him.'

Her look and voice now were such as no woman could mistake.

'What?' I cried. 'Is it possible you're jealous?'

She said nothing.

I sprang to my feet and pulled aside my veil. 'Look, look, you fool!' I cried. 'Are you jealous of this?'

She started back from me, gazing, so that for a moment I wondered if my face were a terror to her. But it was not fear that moved her. For the first time that prim mouth of hers twitched. The tears began to gather in her eyes. 'Oh,' she gasped, 'oh. I never knew ... you also ...?'

'What?'

'You loved him. You've suffered too. We both ...'

She was weeping; and I. Next moment we were in each other's arms. It was the strangest thing that our hatred should die out at the very moment she first knew her husband was the man I loved. It would have been far otherwise if he were still alive; but on that desolate island (our blank, un-Bardia'd life) we were the only two castaways. We spoke a language, so to call it, which no one else in the huge heedless world could understand. Yet it was a language only of sobs. We could not even begin to speak of him in words; that would have unsheathed both daggers at once.

The softness did not last. I have seen something like this happen in a battle. A man was coming at me, I at him, to kill. Then came a sudden great gust of wind that wrapped our cloaks over our swords and almost over our eyes, so that we could do nothing to one another but must fight the wind itself. And that ridiculous contention, so foreign to the business we were on, set us both laughing, face to face; friends for a moment, and then at once enemies again and for ever. So here.

Presently (I have no memory how it came about) we were apart again; I now resuming my veil; her face hard and cold.

'Well!' I was saying. 'You have made me little better than the Lord Bardia's murderer. It was your aim to torture me. And you chose your torture well. Be content; you are avenged. But tell me this. Did you speak only to wound, or did you believe what you said?'

'Believe? I do not believe. I know, that your queenship drank up his blood year by year and ate out his life.'

'Then why did you not tell me? A word from you would have sufficed. Or are you like the gods who will speak only when it is too late?'

'Tell you?' she said, looking at me with a sort of proud wonder. 'Tell you? And so take away from him his work, which was his life (for what's any woman to a man and a soldier in the end?) and all his glory and his great deeds? Make a child and a dotard of him? Keep him to myself at that cost? Make him so mine that he was no longer his?'

'And yet – he would have been yours.'

'But I would be his. I was his wife, not his doxy. He was my husband, not my house-dog. He was to live the life he thought best and fittest for a great man; not that which would most pleasure me. You have taken Ilerdia now too. He will turn his back on his mother's house more and more; he will seek strange lands, and be occupied with matters I don't understand, and go where I can't follow, and be daily less mine; more his own and the world's. Do you think I'd lift up my little finger if lifting it would stop it?'

'And you could – and you can – bear that?'

'You ask that? Oh, Queen Orual, I begin to think you know nothing of love. Or no; I'll not say that. Yours is Queen's love, not commoners'. Perhaps you who spring from the gods love like the gods. Like the Shadowbrute. They say the loving and the devouring are all one, don't they?'

'Woman,' said I, 'I saved his life. Thankless fool! You'd have been widowed many a year sooner if I'd not been there one day on the field of Ingarn – and got that wound which still aches at every change of weather. Where are *your* scars?'

'Where a woman's are when she has borne eight children. Yes. Saved his life. Why, you had use for it. Thrift, Queen Orual. Too good a sword to throw away. Faugh! You're full fed. Gorged with other men's lives; women's too. Bardia's; mine; the Fox's; your sister's; both your sisters'.'

'It's enough,' I cried. The air in her room was shot with crimson. It came horribly in my mind that if I ordered her to torture and death no one could save her. Arnom would murmur. Ilerdia would turn rebel. But she'd be twisting (cockchafer-like) on a sharp stake before anyone could help her.

Something (if it was the gods, I bless their name) made me unable to do this. I got somehow to the door. Then I turned and said to her:

'If you had spoken thus to my father, he'd have had your tongue cut out.'

'What? Afraid of it?' said she.

As I rode homeward I said to myself, 'She shall have her Ilerdia back. He can go and live on his lands. Turn oaf. Grow fat and mumble between his belches about the price of bullocks. I would have made him a great man. Now he shall be nothing. He may thank his mother. She'll not have need to say again that I devour her men-folk.'

But I did none of these things to Ilerdia.

And now those divine Surgeons had me tied down and were at work. My anger protected me only for a short time; anger wearies itself out and truth comes in. For it was all true; truer than Ansit could know. I had rejoiced when there was a press of work, had heaped up needless work, to keep him late at the palace; plied him with questions for the mere pleasure of hearing his voice. Anything to put off the moment when he would go and leave me to my emptiness. And I had hated him for going. Punished him too. Men have a hundred ways of mocking a man who's thought to love his wife too well, and Bardia was defenceless; everyone knew he'd married an undowered girl, and Ansit boasted that she'd no need (like most) to seek out the ugliest girls in the slave market for her household. I never mocked him myself; but I had endless sleights and contrivances (behind my veil) for pushing the talk in such directions as, I knew, would make others mock him. I hated them for doing it, but I had a bittersweet pleasure at his clouded face. Did I hate him, then? Indeed, I believe so. A love can grow to be nine-tenths hatred and still call itself love. One thing's certain; in my mad midnight fantasies (Ansit dead, or, better still, proved whore, witch, or traitress) when he was at last to be seeking my love, I always had him begin by imploring my forgiveness. Sometimes he had hard work to get it. I would bring him within an ace of killing himself first.

But the result, when all those bitter hours were over, was a strange one. The craving for Bardia was ended. No one will believe this who has not lived long and looked hard, so that he knows how suddenly a passion which has for years been wrapped round the whole heart will dry up and wither. Perhaps in the soul, as in the soil, those growths that show the brightest colours and put forth the most overpowering smell have not always the deepest root. Or perhaps it's age that does it. But most of all, I think, it was this. My love for Bardia (not Bardia himself) had become to me a sickening thing. I had been dragged up and out on to such heights and precipices of truth, that I came into an air where it could not live. It stank; a gnawing greed for one to whom I could give nothing, of whom I craved all. Heaven knows how we had tormented him, Ansit and I. For it needs no Oedipus to guess that, many and many a night, her jealousy of me had welcomed him home, late from the palace, to a bitter hearth.

But when the craving went, nearly all that I called myself went with it. It was as if my whole soul had been one tooth and now that tooth was drawn. I was a gap. And now I thought I had come to the very bottom and that the gods could tell me no worse.

2

A few days after I had been with Ansit came the rite of the Year's birth. This is when the Priest is shut up in the house of Ungit from sunset, and on the following noon fights his way out and is said to be born. But of course, like all these sacred matters, it is and it is not (so that it was easy for the Fox to show its manifold contradictions). For the fight is with wooden swords, and instead of blood wine is poured over the combatants, and though they say he is shut into the house, it's only the great door to the city and the west that is shut, and the two smaller doors at the other end are open and common worshippers go in and out at will.

When there is a King in Glome he has to go in with the Priest at sunset and remain in the house till the Birth. But it is unlawful for a virgin to be present at the things which are done in the house that night; so I go in, by the north door, only an hour before the Birth. (The others who have to be there are one of the nobles, and one of the elders, and one of the people; chosen in a sacred manner of which I am not allowed to write.)

That year it was a fresh morning, very sweet, with a light wind from the south; and because of that freshness out of doors, I felt it, more than ever, a horrible thing to go into the dark holiness of Ungit's house. I have (I think) said before that Arnom had made it a little lighter and cleaner. But it was still an imprisoning, smothering sort of place; and especially on the morning of the Birth, when there had been censing and slaughtering, and pouring of wine and pouring of blood, and dancing and feasting and towsing of girls, and burning of fat, all night long. There was as much taint of sweat and foul air as (in a mortal's house) would have set the laziest slut to opening windows, scouring, and sweeping.

I came and sat on the flat stone which is my place, opposite the sacred stone which is Ungit herself; the new, woman-shaped image a little on my left. Arnom's seat was on my right. He was in his mask, of course, nodding with weariness. They were beating the drums, but not loud, and otherwise there was silence.

I saw the terrible girls sitting in rows down both sides of the house, each cross-legged at the door of her cell. Thus they sat year after year (and usually barren after a few seasons) till they turned into the toothless crones who were hobbling about the floor, tending fires and sweeping – sometimes, after a swift glance round, stooping as suddenly as a bird to pick up a coin or a half-gnawed bone and hide it in their gowns. And I thought how the seed of men that might have gone to make hardy boys and fruitful girls was drained into that house, and nothing given back; and how the silver that men had earned hard and needed was also drained in there, and nothing given back; and how the girls themselves were devoured and were given nothing back.

Then I looked at Ungit herself. She had not, like most sacred stones, fallen from the sky. The story was that, at the very beginning, she had pushed her way up out of the earth; a foretaste of, or an ambassador from, whatever things may live and work down there, one below the other, all the way down, under the dark and weight and heat. I have said she had no face; but that meant she had a thousand faces. For she was very uneven, lumpy and furrowed, so that, as when we gaze into a fire, you could always see some face or other. She was now more rugged than ever because of all the blood they had poured over her in the night. In the little clots and chains of it I made out a face; a fancy at one moment, but then, once you had seen it, not to be evaded. A face such as you might see in a loaf, swollen, brooding, infinitely female. It was a little like Batta as I remembered her in certain of her moods. Batta, when we were very small, had her loving moods, even to me. I have run out into the garden to get free – and to get, as it were, freshened and cleansed – from her huge, hot, strong yet flabby-soft embraces, the smothering engulfing tenacity of her.

'Yes,' I thought, 'Ungit is very like Batta today.'

'Arnom,' said I, whispering, 'who is Ungit?'

'I think, Queen,' said he (his voice strange out of the mask), 'she signifies the earth, which is the womb and mother of all living things.' This was the new way of talking about the gods which Arnom, and others, had learned from the Fox.

'If she is the mother of all things,' said I, 'in what way more is she the mother of the god of the Mountain?'

'He is the air and the sky; for we see the clouds coming up from the earth in mists and exhalations.'

'Then why do the stories sometimes say he's her husband too?'

'That means that the sky by its showers makes the earth fruitful.'

'If that's all they mean, why do they wrap it up in so strange a fashion?'

'Doubtless,' said Arnom (and I could tell that he was yawning inside the mask, being worn out with his vigil), 'doubtless to hide it from the vulgar.'

I would torment him no more, but I said to myself, 'It's very strange that our fathers should first think it worth telling us that rain falls out of the sky, and then, for fear such a notable secret should get out (why not hold their tongues?) wrap it up in a filthy tale so that no one could understand the telling.'

The drums went on. My back began to ache. Presently the little door on my right opened and a woman, a peasant, came in. You could see she had not come for the Birth feast, but on some more pressing matter of her own. She had done nothing (as even the poorest contrive for that feast) to make herself gay, and the tears were wet on her cheeks. She looked as if she had cried all night, and in her hands she held a live pigeon. One of the lesser priests came forward at once, took the tiny offering from her, slit it open with his stone knife, splashed the little shower of blood over Ungit (where it became like dribble from the mouth of the face I saw in her) and gave the body to one of the temple slaves. The peasant woman sank down on her face at Ungit's feet. She lay there a very long time, so shaking that anyone could tell how bitterly she wept. But the weeping ceased. She rose up on her knees and put back her hair from her face and took a long breath. Then she rose to go, and as she turned I could look straight into her eyes. She was grave enough; and yet (I was very close to her and could not doubt it) it was as if a sponge had been passed over her. The trouble was soothed. She was calm, patient, able for whatever she had to do.

'Has Ungit comforted you, child?' I asked.

'Oh yes, Queen,' said the woman, her face almost brightening, 'oh yes. Ungit has given me great comfort. There's no goddess like Ungit.'

'Do you always pray to *that* Ungit,' said I (nodding toward the shapeless stone), 'and not to *that*?' Here I nodded towards our new image, standing tall and straight in her robes and (whatever the Fox might say of it) the loveliest thing our land has ever seen.

'Oh, always this, Queen,' said she. 'That other, the Greek Ungit, she wouldn't understand my speech. She's only for nobles and learned men. There's no comfort in her.'

Soon after that it was noon and the sham fight at the western door had to be done and we all came out into the daylight, after Arnom. I had seen often enough before what met us there; the great mob, shouting, 'He is born! He is born!' and whirling their rattles, and throwing wheat-seed into the air; all sweaty and struggling and climbing on one another's backs to get a sight of Arnom and the rest of us. Today it struck me in a new way. It was the joy of the people that amazed me. There they stood, where they had waited for hours, so pressed together they could hardly breathe, each doubtless with a dozen cares and sorrows upon him (who has not?), yet every man and woman and the very children looking as if all the world was well because a man dressed up as a bird had walked out of a door after striking a few blows with a wooden sword. Even those who were knocked down in the press to see us made light of it and indeed laughed louder than the others. I saw two farmers whom I well knew for bitterest enemies (they'd wasted more of my time when I sat in judgement than half the remainder of my people put together) clap hands and cry, 'He's born!', brothers for the moment.

I went home and into my own chamber to rest, for now that I am old that sitting on the flat stone wearies me cruelly. I sank into deep thought.

'Get up, girl,' said a voice. I opened my eyes. My father stood beside me. And instantly all the long years of my queenship shrank up small like a dream. How could I have believed in them? How could I ever have thought I should escape from the King? I got up from my bed obediently and stood before him. When I made to put on my veil, he said, 'None of that folly, do you hear?' and I laid it obediently aside.

'Come with me to the Pillar Room,' he said.

I followed him down the stair (the whole palace was empty) and we went into the Pillar Room. He looked all round him, and I became very afraid because I felt sure he was looking for that mirror of his. But I had given it to Redival when she became Queen of Phars; and what would he do to me when he learned that I had stolen his favourite treasure? But he went to one corner of the room and found there (which were strange things to find in such a place) two pickaxes and a crowbar. 'To your work, goblin,' he said, and made me take one of the picks. He began to break up the paved floor in the centre of the room, and I helped him. It was very hard labour because of the pain in my back. When we had lifted four or five of the big stone flags we found a dark hole, like a wide well, beneath them.

'Throw yourself down,' said the King, seizing me by the hand. And however I struggled, I could not free myself, and we both jumped together. When we had fallen a long way we alighted on our feet, nothing hurt by our fall. It was warmer down here and the air was hard to breathe, but it was not so dark that I could not see the place we were in. It was another Pillar Room, exactly like the one we had left, except that it was smaller and all made (floor, walls, and pillars) of raw earth. And here also my father looked about him, and once again I was afraid he would ask what I had done with his mirror. But instead, he went into a corner of the earthen room and there found two spades and put one into my hand and said, 'Now, work. Do you mean to slug abed all your life?' So then we had to dig a hole in the centre of the room. And this time the labour was worse than before, for what we dug was all tough, clinging clay, so that you had rather to cut it out in squares with the spade than to dig it. And the place was stifling. But at last we had done so much that another black hole opened beneath us. This time I knew what he meant to do to me, so I tried to keep my hand from his. But he caught it and said:

'Do you begin to set your wits against mine? Throw yourself down.'

'Oh no, no, no; no further down; mercy!' said I.

'There's no Fox to help you here,' said my father. 'We're far below any dens that foxes can dig. There's hundreds of tons of earth between you and the deepest of them.' Then we leaped down into the hole, and fell further than before, but again alighted unhurt. It was far darker here, yet I could see that we were in yet another Pillar Room; but this was of living rock, and water trickled down the walls of it. Though it was so like the two shallower rooms, this was far the smallest. And as I looked I could see that it was getting smaller still. The roof was closing in on us. I tried to cry out to him, 'If you're not quick, we shall be buried,' but I was smothering and no voice came from me. Then I thought, 'He doesn't care. It's nothing for him to be buried, for he's dead already.'

'Who is Ungit?' said he, still holding my hand.

Then he led me across the floor; and, a long way off before we came to it, I saw that mirror on the wall, just where it always had been. At the sight of it my terror increased, and I fought with all my strength not to go on. But his hand had grown very big now and it was as soft and clinging as Batta's arms, or as the tough clay we had been digging, or as the dough of a huge loaf. I was not so much dragged as sucked along till we stood right in front of the mirror. And in it I saw him, looking as he had looked that other day when he led me to the mirror long ago.

But my face was the face of Ungit as I had seen it that day in her house.

'Who is Ungit?' asked the King.

'I am Ungit.' My voice came wailing out of me and I found that I was in the cool daylight and in my own chamber. So it had been what we call a dream. But I must give warning that from this time onward they so drenched me with seeings that I cannot well discern dream from waking nor tell which is the truer. This vision, anyway, allowed no denial. Without question it was true. It was I who was Ungit. That ruinous face was mine. I was that Batta-thing, that all-devouring, womblike, yet barren, thing. Glome was a web; I the swollen spider, squat at its centre, gorged with men's stolen lives.

'I will not be Ungit,' said I. I got up, shivering as with fever, from my bed, and bolted the door. I took down my old sword, the very same that Bardia had taught me to use, and drew it. It looked such a happy thing (and it was indeed a most true, perfect, fortunate blade) that tears came into my eyes. 'Sword,' said I, 'you have had a happy life. You killed Argan. You saved Bardia. Now, for your masterpiece.'

It was all foolishness, though. The sword was too heavy for me now. My grip – think of a veined, claw-like hand, skinny knuckles – was childish. I would never be able to strike home; and I had seen enough of wars to know what a feeble thrust would do. This way of ceasing to be Ungit was now too hard for me. I sat down, the cold, small, helpless thing I was, on the edge of my bed, and thought again.

There must, whether the gods see it or not, be something great in the mortal soul. For suffering, it seems, is infinite, and our capacity without limit.

Of the things that followed I cannot at all say whether they were what men call real or what men call dream. And for all I can tell, the only difference is that what many see we call a real thing, and what one only sees we call a dream. But things that many see may have no taste or moment in them at all, and things that are shown only to one may be spears and waterspouts of truth from the very depth of truth.

The day passed somehow. All days pass, and that's great comfort; unless there should be some terrible region in the deadlands where the day never passes. But when the house slept I wrapped myself in a dark cloak and took a stick to lean on; for I think the bodily weakness, which I die of now, must have begun about that time. Then a new thought came to me. My veil was no longer a means to be unknown. It revealed me; all men knew the veiled Queen. My disguise now would be to go bareface; there was hardly anyone who had seen me unveiled. So, for the first time in many years, I went out bareface; showed that face which many had said, more truly than they could know, was too dreadful to be seen. It would have shamed me no more to go buff-naked. For I thought I would look as like Ungit to them as I had seen myself to be in that mirror beneath the earth. As like Ungit? I *was* Ungit; I in her and she in me. Perhaps if any saw me, they would worship me. I had become what the people, and the old Priest, called holy.

I went out, as often before, by the little eastern doorway that opens on the herb-garden. And thence, with endless weariness, through the sleeping city. I thought they would not sleep so sound if they knew what dark thing hobbled past their windows. Once I heard a child cry; perhaps it had dreamed of me. 'If the Shadowbrute begins coming down into the city, the people will be greatly afraid,' said the old Priest. If I were Ungit, I might be the Shadowbrute also. For the gods work in and out of one another as of us.

So at last, fainting with weariness, out beyond the city and down to the river; I myself had made it deep. The old Shennit, as she was before my works, would not, save in spate, have drowned even a crone.

I had to go a little way along the river to a place where I knew that the bank was high, so that I could fling myself down; for I doubted my courage to wade in and feel death first up to my knee, and then to my belly, and then to my neck, and still to go on. When I came to the high bank I took my girdle and tied my ankles together with it, lest, even in my old age, I might save my life, or lengthen my death, by swimming. Then I straightened myself, panting from the labour, and stood footfast, like a prisoner.

I hopped (what blending of misery and buffoonery it would have looked if I could have seen it!) – hopped with my strapped feet a little nearer to the edge.

A voice came from beyond the river: 'Do not do it.'

Instantly – I had been freezing cold till now – a wave of fire passed over me; even down to my numb feet. It was the voice of a god. Who should know better than I? A god's voice had once shattered my whole life. They are not to be mistaken. It may well be that, by trickery of priests, men have sometimes taken a mortal's voice for a god's. But it will not work the other way. No one who hears a god's voice takes it for a mortal's.

'Lord, who are you?' said I.

'Do not do it,' said the god. 'You cannot escape Ungit by going to the deadlands, for she is there also. Die before you die. There is no chance after.'

'Lord, I am Ungit.'

But there was no answer. And that is another thing about the voices of the gods; when once they have ceased, though it is only a heartbeat ago and the bright, hard syllables, the heavy bars or mighty obelisks of sound, are still master in your ears, it is as if they had ceased a thousand years before, and to expect further utterance is like asking for an apple from a tree that fruited the day the world was made.

The voice of the god had not changed in all those years, but I had. There was no rebel in me now. I must not drown and doubtless should not be able to.

I crawled home, troubling the quiet city once more with my dark witch-shape and my tapping stick. And when I laid my head on my pillow it seemed but a moment before my women came to wake me; whether because the whole journey had been a dream or because my weariness (which would be no wonder) threw me into a very fast sleep.

3

Then the gods left me for some days to chew the strange bread they had given me. I was Ungit. What did it mean? Do the gods flow in and out of us as they flow in and out of each other? And again, they would not let me die till I had died. I knew there were certain initiations, far away at Eleusis in the Greeklands, whereby a man was said to die and live again before the soul left the body. But how could I go there? Then I remembered that conversation which his friends had with Socrates before he drank the hemlock, and how he said that true wisdom is the skill and practice of death. And I thought Socrates understood such matters better than the Fox, for in the same book he has said how the soul 'is dragged back through the fear of the invisible'; so that I even wondered if he had not himself tasted this horror as I had tasted it in Psyche's valley. But by the death which is wisdom I supposed he meant the death of our passions and desires and vain opinions. And immediately (it is terrible to be a fool) I thought I saw my way clear and not impossible. To say that I was Ungit meant that I was as ugly in soul as she; greedy, blood-gorged. But if I practised true philosophy, as Socrates meant it, I should change my ugly soul into a fair one. And this, the gods helping me, I would do. I would set about it at once.

The gods helping ... but would they help? Nevertheless I must begin. And it seemed to me they would not help. I would set out boldly each morning to be just and calm and wise in all my thoughts and acts; but before they had finished dressing me I would find that I was back (and knew not how long I had been back) in some old rage, resentment, gnawing fantasy, or sullen bitterness. I could not hold out half an hour. And a horrible memory crept into my mind of those days when I had tried to mend the ugliness of my body with new devices in the way I did my hair or the colours I wore. I'd a cold fear that I was at the same work again. I could mend my soul no more than my face. Unless the gods helped. And why did the gods not help?

Babai! A terrible, sheer thought, huge as a cliff, towered up before me; infinitely likely to be true. No man will love you, though you gave your life for him, unless you have a pretty face. So (might it not be?) the gods will not love you (however you try to pleasure them, and whatever you suffer) unless you have that beauty of soul. In either race, for the love of men or the love of a god, the winners and losers are marked out from birth. We bring our ugliness, in both kinds, with us into the world; with it our destiny. How bitter this was, every ill-favoured woman will know. We have all had our dream of some other land, some other world, some other way of giving the prizes, which would bring us in as the conquerors; leave the smooth, rounded limbs, and the little pink and white faces, and the hair like burnished gold, far behind; their day ended, and ours come. But how if it's not so at all? How if we were made to be dregs and refuse everywhere and everyway?

About this time there came (if you call it so) another dream. But it was not like a dream, for I went into my chamber an hour after noon (none of my women being there) and without lying down, or even sitting down, walked straight into the vision by merely opening the door. I found myself standing on the bank of a bright and great river. And on the further bank I saw a flock; of sheep, I thought. Then I considered them more closely, and I saw that they were all rams, high as horses, mightily horned, and their fleeces such bright gold that I could not look steadily at them. (There was deep, blue sky above them, and the grass was a luminous green like emerald, and there was a pool of very dark shadow, clear-edged, under every tree. The air of that country was sweet as music.) 'Now those,' thought I, 'are the rams of the gods. If I can steal but one golden flock off their sides, I shall have beauty. Redival's ringlets were nothing to that wool.' And in my vision I was able to do what I had feared to do at the Shennit; for I went into the cold water, up to my knee, up to my belly, up to my neck, and then lost the bottom and swam and found the bottom again and came up out of the river into the pastures of the gods. And I walked forward over that holy turf with a good and glad heart. But all the golden rams came at me. They drew closer to one another as their onrush brought them closer to me, till it was a solid wall of living gold. And with terrible force their curled horns struck me and knocked me flat and their hooves trampled me. They were not doing it in anger. They rushed over me in their joy; perhaps they did not see me; certainly I was nothing in their minds. I understood it well. They butted and trampled me because their gladness led them on; the Divine Nature wounds and perhaps destroys us merely by being what it is. We call it the wrath of the gods; as if the great cataract in Phars were angry with every fly it sweeps down in its green thunder.

Yet they did not kill me. When they had gone over me, I lived and knew myself, and presently could stand on my feet. Then I saw that there was another mortal woman with me in the field. She did not seem to see me. She was walking slowly, carefully, along the hedge which bordered that grassland, scanning it like a gleaner, picking something out of it. Then I saw what. Bright gold hung in flecks upon the thorns. Of course! The rams had left some of their golden wool on them as they raced past. This she was gleaning, handful after handful, a rich harvest. What I had sought in vain by meeting the joyous and terrible brutes, she took at her leisure. She won without effort what utmost effort would not win for me.

I now despaired of ever ceasing to be Ungit. Though it was spring without, in me a winter which, I thought, must be everlasting, locked up all my powers. It was as if I were dead already, but not as the god, or Socrates, bade me die. Yet all the time I was able to go about my work, doing and saying whatever was needful, and no one knew that there was anything amiss. Indeed the dooms I gave, sitting on my judgement seat, about this time, were thought to be even wiser and more just than before; it was work on which I spent much pains and I know I did it well. But the prisoners and plaintiffs and witnesses and the rest now seemed to me more like shadows than real men. I did not care a straw (though I still laboured to discern) who had a right to the little field or who had stolen the cheeses.

I had only one comfort left me. However I might have devoured Bardia, I had at least loved Psyche truly. There, if nowhere else, I had the right of it and the gods were in the wrong. And as a prisoner in a dungeon or a sick man on his bed makes much of any little shred of pleasure he still has, so I made much of this. And one day, when my work had been very wearisome, I took this book, as soon as I was free, and went out into the garden to comfort myself, and gorge myself with comfort, by reading over how I had cared for Psyche and taught her and tried to save her and wounded myself for her sake.

What followed was certainly vision and no dream. For it came upon me before I had sat down or unrolled the book. I walked into the vision with my bodily eyes wide open.

I was walking over burning sands, carrying an empty bowl. I knew well what I had to do. I must find the spring that rises from the river that flows in the deadlands, and fill it with the water of death and bring it back without spilling a drop and give it to Ungit. For in this vision it was not I who was Ungit; I was Ungit's slave or prisoner, and if I did all the tasks she set me perhaps she would let me go free. So I walked in the dry sand up to my ankles, white with sand to my middle, my throat rough with sand; unmitigated noon above me, and the sun so high that I had no shadow. And I longed for the water of death; for however bitter it was, it must surely be cold, coming from the sunless country. I walked for a hundred years. But at last the desert ended at the foot of some great mountains; crags and pinnacles and rotting cliffs that no one could climb. Rocks were loosened and fell from the heights all the time; their booming and clanging, as they bounced from one jag to another, and the thud when they fell on the sand, were the only sounds there. Looking at the waste of rock, I first thought it empty, and that what flickered over its hot surface were the shadows of clouds. But there were no clouds. Then I saw what it really was. Those mountains were alive with innumerable serpents and scorpions that scuttled and slithered over them continually. The place was a huge torture chamber, but the instruments were all living. And I knew that the well I was looking for rose in the very heart of these mountains.

'I can never get up,' said I.

I sat upon the sand gazing up at them, till I felt as if the flesh would be burned off my bones. Then at last there came a shadow. Oh, mercy of the gods, could it be a cloud? I looked up at the sky and was nearly blinded, for the sun was still straight above my head; I had come, it seemed, into that country where the day never passes. Yet at last, though the terrible light seemed to bore through my eyeballs into my brain, I saw something; black against the blue, but far too small for a cloud. Then by its circlings I knew it to be a bird. Then it wheeled and came lower and at last was plainly an eagle; but an eagle from the gods, far greater than those of the highlands in Phars. It lighted on the sand and looked at me. Its face was a little like the old Priest's, but it was not he; it was a divine creature.

'Woman,' it said, 'who are you?'

'Orual, Queen of Glome,' said I.

'Then it is not you that I was sent to help. What is that roll you carry in your hands?'

I now saw, with great dismay, that what I had been carrying all this time was not a bowl but a book. This ruined everything.

'It is my complaint against the gods,' said I.

The eagle clapped his wings and lifted his head and cried out with a loud voice, 'She's come at last. Here is the woman who has a complaint against the gods.'

Immediately a hundred echoes roared from the face of the mountain, 'Here is the woman ... a complaint against the gods ... plaint against the gods.'

'Come,' said the eagle.

'Where?' said I.

'Come into court. Your case is to be heard.' And he called aloud once more, 'She's come. She's come.' Then from every crack and hole in the mountains there came out dark things like men, so that there was a crowd of them all round me before I could fly. They seized on me and hustled me and passed me on from one to another, each shouting, towards the mountain-face, 'Here she comes. Here is the woman'; and voices (as it seemed) from within the mountain answered them, 'Bring her in. Bring her into court. Her case is to be heard.' I was dragged and pushed and sometimes lifted, up among the rocks, till at last a great black hole yawned before me. 'Bring her in. The court waits,' came the voices. And with a sudden shock of cold I was hurried in out of the burning sunlight into the dark inwards of the mountain, and then further and further in, always in haste, always passed from hand to hand, and always with that din of shouts: 'Here she is. She's come at last. To the judge, to the judge.' Then the voices changed and grew quieter; and now it was, 'Let her go. Make her stand up. Silence in the court. Silence for her complaint.'

I was free now from all their hands, alone (as I thought) in silent darkness. Then a sort of grey light came. I stood on a platform or pillar of rock in a cave so great that I could see neither the sides nor the roof of it. All round me, below me, up to the very edges of the stone I stood on, there surged a sort of unquiet darkness. But soon my eyes grew able to see things in that half-light. The darkness was alive. It was a great assembly, all staring upon me, and I uplifted on my perch above their heads. Never in peace or war have I seen so vast a concourse. There were tens of thousands of them, all silent; every face watching me. Among them I saw Batta, and the King my father, and the Fox, and Argan. They were all ghosts. In my foolishness I had not thought before how many dead there must be. The faces, one above the other (for the place was shaped that way) rose and rose and receded in the greyness till the very thought of counting – not the faces, that would be madness – but the mere ranks of them, was tormenting. The endless place was packed full as it could hold. The court had met.

But on the same level with me, though far away, sat the judge. Male or female, would could say? Its face was veiled. It was covered from crown to toe in sweepy black.

'Uncover her,' said the judge.

Hands came from behind me and tore off my veil; after it, every rag I had on. The old crone with her Ungit face stood naked before those countless gazers. No thread to cover me, no bowl in my hand to hold the water of death; only my book.

'Read your complaint,' said the judge.

I looked at the roll in my hand and saw at once that it was not the book I had written. It couldn't be; it was far too small. And too old – a little, shabby, crumpled thing, nothing like my great book that I had worked on all day, day after day, while Bardia was dying. I thought I would fling it down and trample on it. I'd tell them someone had stolen my complaint and slipped this thing into my hand instead. Yet I found myself unrolling it. It was written all over inside, but the hand was not like mine. It was all a vile scribble; each stroke mean and yet savage, like the snarl of my father's voice, like the ruinous faces one could make out in the Ungit stone. A great terror and loathing came over me. I said to myself, 'Whatever they do to me, I will never read out this stuff. Give me back my Book.' But already I heard myself reading it. And what I read out was like this:

'I know what you'll say. You will say the real gods are not at all like Ungit, and that I was shown a real god and the house of a real god and ought to know it. Hypocrites! I do know it. As if that would heal my wounds! I could have endured it if you were things like Ungit and the Shadowbrute. You know well that I never really began to hate you until Psyche began talking of her palace and her lover and her husband. Why did you lie to me? You said a brute would devour her. Well, why didn't it? I'd have wept for her and buried what was left and built her a tomb and ... and ... But to steal her love from me! Can it be that you really don't understand? Do you think we mortals will find you gods easier to bear if you're beautiful? I tell you that if that's true we'll find you a thousand times worse. For then (I know what beauty does) you'll lure and entice. You'll leave us nothing; nothing that's worth our keeping or your taking. Those we love best – whoever's most worth loving – those are the very ones you'll pick out. Oh, I can see it happening, age after age, and growing worse and worse the more you reveal your beauty; the son turning his back on the mother and the bride on her groom, stolen away by this everlasting calling, calling, calling of the gods. Taken where we can't follow. It would be far better for us if you were foul and ravening. We'd rather you drank their blood than stole their hearts. We'd rather they were ours and dead than yours and made immortal. But to steal her love from me, to make her see things I couldn't see ... oh, you'll say (you've been whispering it to me these forty years) that I'd signs enough her palace was real; could have known the truth if I'd wanted. But how could I want to know it? Tell me that. The girl was mine. What right had you to steal her away into your dreadful heights? You'll say I was jealous. Jealous of Psyche? Not while she was mine. If you'd gone the other way to work – if it was my eyes you had opened – you'd soon have seen how I would have shown her and told her and taught her and led her up to my level. But to hear a chit of a girl who had (or ought to have had) no thought in her head that I'd not put there, setting up for a seer and a prophetess and next thing to a goddess ... how could anyone endure it? That's why I say it makes no difference whether you're fair or foul. That there should be gods at all, there's our misery and bitter wrong. There's no room for you and us in the same world. You're a tree in whose shadow we can't thrive. We want to be our own. I was my own and Psyche was mine and no one else had any right to her. Oh, you'll say you took her away into bliss and joy such as I could never have given her, and I ought to have been glad of it for her sake. Why? What should I care for some horrible, new happiness which I hadn't given her and which separated her from me? Do you think I wanted her to be happy, that way? It would have been better if I'd seen the Brute tear her in pieces before my eyes. You stole her to make her happy, did you? Why, every wheedling, smiling, catfoot rogue who lures away another man's wife or slave or dog might say the same. Dog, now. That's very much to the purpose. I'll thank you to let me feed my own; it needed no titbits from your table. Did you ever remember whose the girl was? She was mine. *Mine*; do you not know what the word means? Mine! You're thieves, seducers. That's my wrong. I'll not complain (not now) that you're blood-drinkers and man-eaters. I'm past that...'

'Enough,' said the judge.

There was utter silence all round me. And now for the first time I knew what I had been doing. While I was reading, it had, once and again, seemed strange to me that the reading took so long; for the book was a small one. Now I knew that I had been reading it over and over; perhaps a dozen times. I would have read it for ever, quick as I could, starting the first word again almost before the last was out of my mouth, if the judge had not stopped me. And the voice I read it in was strange to my ears. There was given to me a certainty that this, at last, was my real voice.

There was silence in the dark assembly long enough for me to have read my book out yet again. At last the judge spoke.

'Are you answered?' he said.

'Yes,' said I.

4

The complaint was the answer. To have heard myself making it was to be answered. Lightly men talk of saying what they mean. Often when he was teaching me to write in Greek the Fox would say, 'Child, to say the very thing you really mean, the whole of it, nothing more or less or other than what you really mean; that's the whole art and joy of words.' A glib saying. When the time comes to you at which you will be forced at last to utter the speech which has lain at the centre of your soul for years, which you have, all that time, idiot-like, been saying over and over, you'll not talk about joy of words. I saw well why the gods do not speak to us openly, nor let us answer. Till that word can be dug out of us, why should they hear the babble that we think we mean? How can they meet us face to face till we have faces?

'Best leave the girl to me,' said a well-known voice. 'I'll lesson her.' It was the spectre which had been my father.

Then a new voice spoke from beneath me. It was the Fox's. I thought he too was going to give some terrible evidence against me. But he said, 'Oh Minos, or Rhadamanthus, or Persephone, or by whatever name you are called, I am to blame for most of this, and I should bear the punishment. I taught her, as men teach a parrot, to say "Lies of poets", and "Ungit's a false image". I made her think that ended the question. I never said, too true an image of the demon within. And then the other face of Ungit (she has a thousand) ... something live anyway. And the real gods more alive. Neither they nor Ungit mere thoughts or words. I never told her why the old Priest got something from the dark House that I never got from my trim sentences. She never asked me (I was content she shouldn't ask) why the people got something from the shapeless stone which no one every got from that painted doll of Arnom's. Of course, I didn't know; but I never told her I didn't know. I don't know now. Only that the way to the true gods is more like the House of Ungit ... oh, it's unlike too, more unlike than we yet dream, but that's the easy knowledge, the first lesson; only a fool would stay there, posturing and repeating it. The Priest knew at least that there must be sacrifices. They will have sacrifice; will have man. Yes, and the very heart, centre, ground, roots of a man; dark and strong and costly as blood. Send me away, Minos, even to Tartarus, if Tartarus can cure glibness. I made her think that a prattle of maxims would do, all thin and clear as water. For of course water's good; and it didn't cost much, not where I grew up. So I fed her on words.'

I wanted to cry out that it was false, that he had fed me not on words but on love, that he had given, if not to the gods, yet to me, all that was costliest. But I had not time. The trial, it seemed, was over.

'Peace,' said the judge. 'The woman is a plaintiff, not a prisoner. It is the gods who have been accused. They have answered her. If they in turn accuse her, a greater judge and a more excellent court must try the case. Let her go.'

Which way should I turn, set up on that pillar of rock? I looked on every side. Then, to end it, I flung myself down into the black sea of spectres. But before I reached the floor of the cavern one rushed forward and caught me in strong arms. It was the Fox.

'Grandfather!' I cried. 'But you're real and warm. Homer said one could not embrace the dead ... they were only shadows.'

'My child, my beloved,' said the Fox, kissing my eyes and head in the old way. 'One thing that I told you was true. The poets are often wrong. But for all the rest – ah, you'll forgive me?'

'I to forgive you, Grandfather? No, no, I must speak. I knew at the time that all those good reasons you gave for staying in Glome after you were a freeman were only disguises for your love. I knew you stayed only in pity and love for me. I knew you were breaking your heart for the Greeklands. I ought to have sent you away. I lapped up all you gave me like a thirsty animal. Oh, Grandfather, Ansit's right. I've battened on the lives of men. It's true. Isn't it true?'

'Why, child, it is. I could almost be glad; it gives me something to forgive. But I'm not your judge. We must go to your true judges now. I am to bring you there.'

'My judges?'

'Why, yes, child. The gods have been accused by you. Now's their turn.'

'I cannot hope for mercy.'

'Infinite hopes – and fears – may both be yours. Be sure that, whatever else you get, you will not get justice.'

'Are the gods not just?'

'Oh no, child. What would become of us if they were? But come and see.'

He was leading me somewhere and the light was strengthening as we went. It was a greenish, summery light. In the end it was sunshine falling through vine leaves. We were in a cool chamber, walls on three sides of us, but on the fourth side only pillars and arches with a vine growing over them on the outside. Beyond, and between, the light pillars and the soft leaves I saw level grass and shining water.

'We must wait here till you are sent for,' said the Fox. 'But there is plenty here that's worth studying.'

I now saw that the walls of the place were all painted with stories. We have little skill with painting in Glome, so that it's small praise to say they seemed wonderful to me. But I think all mortals would have wondered at these.

'They begin here,' said the Fox, taking me by the hand and leading me to part of the wall. For an instant I was afraid that he was leading me to a mirror as my father had twice done. But before we came near enough to the picture to understand it, the mere beauty of the coloured wall put that out of my head.

Now we were before it and I could see the story it told. I saw a woman coming to the river bank. I mean that by her painted posture I could see it was a picture of one walking. That at first. But no sooner had I understood this than it became alive, and the ripples of the water were moving and the reeds stirred with the water and the grass stirred with the breeze, and the woman moved on and came to the river's edge. There she stood and stooped down and seemed to be doing something – I could not at first tell what – with her feet. She was tying her ankles together with her girdle. I looked closer at her. She was not I. She was Psyche.

I am too old, and I have no time, to begin to write all over again of her beauty. But nothing less would serve, and no words I have would serve even then, to tell you how beautiful she was. It was as though I had never seen her before. Or had I forgotten ... no, I could never have forgotten her beauty, by day or by night, for one heartbeat. But all this was a flash of thought, swallowed up at once in my horror of the thing she had come to that river to do.

'Do not do it. Do not do it,' I cried out; madly, as if she could hear me. Nevertheless she stopped, and untied her ankles and went away. The Fox led me to the next picture. And it too came alive, and there in some dark place, cavern or dungeon, when I looked hard into the murk I could see that what was moving in it was Psyche; Psyche in rags and iron fetters, sorting out the seeds into their proper heaps. But the strangest thing was that I saw in her face no such anguish as I looked for. She was grave; her brow knitted as I have seen it knitted over a hard lesson when she was a child (and that look became her well; what look did not?). Yet I thought there was no despair in it. Then of course I saw why. Ants were helping her. The floor was black with them.

'Grandfather,' said I, 'did—'

'Hush,' said the Fox, laying his thick old finger (the very feel of that finger again, after so many years!) on my lips. He led me to the next.

Here we were back in the pasture of the gods. I saw Psyche creeping, cautious as a cat, along the hedgerow; then standing, her finger at her lip, wondering how she could ever get one curl of their golden wool. Yet now again, only more than last time, I marvelled at her face. For though she looked puzzled, it was only as if she were puzzled at some game; as she and I had both been puzzled over the game Poobi used to play with her beads. It was even as if she laughed inwardly a little at her own bewilderment. (And that too I'd seen in her before, when she blundered over her tasks as a child; she was never out of patience with herself, no more than with her teacher.) But she did not puzzle long. For the rams scented some intruder and turned their tails to Psyche and all lifted their terrible heads, and then lowered them again for battle, and all charged away together to the other end of the meadow, drawing nearer to their enemy, so that an unbroken wave or wall of gold overwhelmed her. Then Psyche laughed and clapped her hands and gathered her bright harvest off the hedge at ease.

In the next picture I saw both Psyche and myself; but I was only a shadow. We toiled together over those burning sands, she with her empty bowl, I with the book full of my poison. She did not see me. And though her face was pale with the heat and her lips cracked with thirst, she was no more pitiable than when I have seen her, often pale with heat and thirsty, come back with the Fox and me from a summer day's ramble on the old hills. She was merry and in good heart. I believe, from the way her lips moved, she was singing. When she came to the foot of the precipices I vanished away. But the eagle came to her, and took her bowl, and brought it back to her brim-full of the water of death.

We had now travelled round two of the three walls and the third remained.

'Child,' said the Fox, 'have you understood?'

'But are these pictures true?'

'All here's true.'

'But how could she – did she really – do such things and go to such places – and not ...? Grandfather, she was all but unscathed. She was almost happy.'

'Another bore nearly all the anguish.'

'I? Is it possible?'

'That was one of the true things I used to say to you. Don't you remember? We're all limbs and parts of one Whole. Hence, of each other. Men, and gods, flow in and out and mingle.'

'Oh, I give thanks. I bless the gods. Then it was really I—'

'Who bore the anguish. But she achieved the tasks. Would you rather have had justice?'

'Would you mock me, Grandfather? Justice? Oh, I've been a queen and I know the people's cry for justice must be heard. But not my cry. A Batta's muttering, a Redival's whining: "Why can't I?" "Why should she?" "It's not fair." And over and over. Faugh!'

'That's well, daughter. But now, be strong and look upon the third wall.'

We looked and saw Psyche walking alone in a wide way under the earth; a gentle slope, but downwards, always downwards.

'This is the last of the tasks that Ungit has set her. She must—'

'Then there is a real Ungit?'

'All, even Psyche, are born into the house of Ungit. And all must get free from her. Or say that Ungit in each must bear Ungit's son and die in childbed – or change. And now Psyche must go down into the deadlands to get beauty in a casket from the Queen of the Deadlands, from death herself; and bring it back to give it to Ungit so that Ungit will become beautiful. But this is the law for her journey. If, for any fear or favour or love or pity, she speaks to anyone on the way, then she will never come back to the sunlit lands again. She must keep straight on, in silence, till she stands before the throne of the Queen of Shadows. All's at stake. Now watch.'

He needed not to tell me that. We both watched. Psyche went on and on, deeper into the earth; colder, deeper, darker. But at last there came a chilly light on one side of her way, and there (I think) the great tunnel or gallery in which she journeyed opened out. For there, in that cold light, stood a great crowd of rabble. Their speech and clothes showed me at once that they were people of Glome. I saw the faces of some I knew.

'Istra! Princess! Ungit!' they called out, stretching their hands towards her. 'Stay with us. Be our goddess. Rule us. Speak oracles to us. Receive our sacrifices. Be our goddess.'

Psyche walked on and never looked at them.

'Whoever the enemy is,' said I, 'he's not very clever if he thinks she would falter for that.'

'Wait,' said the Fox.

Psyche, her eyes fixed straight ahead, went further on and further down, and again, on the left side of her road, there came a light. One figure rose up in it. I was startled at this one, and looked to my side. The Fox was with me still; but he who rose up in the cold light to meet Psyche by the wayside was also the Fox – but older, greyer, paler than the Fox who was with me.

'Oh Psyche, Psyche,' said the Fox in the picture (say, in that other world; it was no painted thing), 'what folly is this? What are you doing, wandering through a tunnel beneath the earth? What? You think it is the way to the Deadlands? You think the gods have sent you there? All lies of priests and poets, child. It is only a cave or a disused mine. There are no deadlands such as you dream of, and no such gods. Has all my teaching taught you no more than this? The god within you is the god you should obey; reason, calmness, self-discipline. Fie, child, do you want to be a barbarian all your days?

I would have given you a clear, Greek, full-grown soul. But there's still time. Come to me and I'll lead you out of all this darkness; back to the grass plot behind the pear trees, where all was clear, hard, limited, and simple.

But Psyche walked on and never looked at him. And presently she came to a third place where there was a little light on the left of the dark road. Amid that light something like a woman rose up; its face was unknown to me. When I looked at it I felt a pity that nearly killed my heart. It was not weeping, but you could see from its eyes that it had already wept them dry. Despair, humiliation, entreaty, endless reproach: all these were in it. And now I trembled for Psyche. I knew the thing was there only to entrap her and turn her from her path. But did she know it? And if she did, could she, so loving and so full of pity, pass it by? It was too hard a test. Her eyes looked straight forward; but of course she had seen it out of the corner of her eye. A quiver ran through her. Her lip twitched, threatened with sobbing. She set her teeth in the lip to keep it straight. 'O great gods, defend her,' I said to myself. 'Hurry, hurry her past.'

The woman held out her hands to Psyche, and I saw that her left arm dripped with blood. Then came her voice, and what a voice it was! So deep, yet so womanlike, so full of passion, it would have moved you even if it spoke happy or careless things. But now (who could resist it?) it would have broken a heart of iron.

'Oh, Psyche,' it wailed. 'Oh, my own child, my only love. Come back. Come back. Back to the old world where we were happy together. Come back to Maia.'

Psyche bit her lip till the blood came and wept bitterly. I thought she felt more grief than that wailing Orual. But that Orual had only to suffer; Psyche had to keep on her way as well. She kept on; went on out of sight, journeying always further into death. That was the last of the pictures.

The Fox and I were alone again.

'Did we really do these things to her?' I asked.

'Yes. All here's true.'

'And we said we loved her.'

'And we did. She had no more dangerous enemies than us. And in that far distant day when the gods become wholly beautiful, or we at last are shown how beautiful they always were, this will happen more and more. For mortals, as you said, will become more and more jealous. And mother and wife and child and friend will all be in league to keep a soul from being united with the Divine Nature.'

'And Psyche, in that old terrible time when I thought her cruel ... she suffered more than I, perhaps?'

'She bore much for you then. You have borne something for her since.'

'And will the gods one day grow thus beautiful, Grandfather?'

'They say ... but even I, who am dead, do not understand more than a few broken words of their language. Only this I know. This age of ours will one day be the distant past. And the Divine Nature can change the past. Nothing is yet in its true form.'

But as he said this many voices from without, sweet and to be feared, took up the cry, 'She comes. Our lady returns to her house; the goddess Psyche, back from the lands of the dead, bringing the casket of beauty from the Queen of Shadows.'

'Come,' said the Fox. I think I had no will in me at all. He took my hand and led me out between the pillars (the vine leaves brushed my hair) into the warm sunlight. We stood in a fair, grassy court, with blue, fresh sky above us; mountain sky. In the centre of the court was a bath of clear water in which many could have swum and sported together. Then there was a moving and rustling of invisible people, and more voices (now somewhat hushed). Next moment I was flat on my face; for Psyche had come and I was kissing her feet.

'Oh, Psyche, oh, goddess,' I said. 'Never again will I call you mine; but all there is of me shall be yours. Alas, you know now what it's worth. I never wished you well, never had one selfless thought of you. I was a craver.'

She bent over me to lift me up. Then, when I would not rise, she said, 'But Maia, dear Maia, you must stand up. I have not given you the casket. You know I went a long journey to fetch the beauty that will make Ungit beautiful.'

I stood up then; all wet in a kind of tears that do not flow in this country. She stood before me, holding out something for me to take. Now I knew that she was a goddess indeed. Her hands burned me (a painless burning) when they met mine. The air that came from her clothes and limbs and hair was wild and sweet; youth seemed to come into my breast as I breathed it. And yet (this is hard to say) with all this, even because of all this, she was the old Psyche still; a thousand times more her very self than she had been before the Offering. For all that had then but flashed out in a glance or a gesture, all that one meant most when one spoke her name, was now wholly present, not to be gathered up from hints nor in shreds, not some of it in one moment and some in another. Goddess? I had never seen a real woman before.

'Did I not tell you, Maia,' she said, 'that a day was coming when you and I would meet in my house and no cloud between us?'

Joy silenced me. And I thought I had now come to the highest, and to the utmost fullness of being which the human soul can contain. But now, what was this? You have seen the torches grow pale when men open the shutters and broad summer morning shines in on the feasting-hall? So now. Suddenly, from a strange look in Psyche's face (I could see she knew something she had not spoken of), or from a glorious and awful deepening of the blue sky above us, or from a deep breath like a sigh uttered all round us by invisible lips, or from a deep, doubtful, quaking and surmise in my own heart, I knew that all this had been only a preparation. Some far greater matter was upon us. The voices spoke again; but not loud this time. They were awed and trembled. 'He is coming,' they said. 'The god is coming into his house. The god comes to judge Orual.'

If Psyche had not held me by the hand I should have sunk down. She had brought me now to the very edge of the pool. The air was growing brighter and brighter about us; as if something had set it on fire. Each breath I drew let into me new terror, joy, overpowering sweetness. I was pierced through and through with the arrows of it. I was being unmade. I was no one. But that's little to say; rather, Psyche herself was, in a manner, no one. I loved her as I would once have thought it impossible to love; would have died any death for her. And yet, it was not, not now, she that really counted. Or if she counted (and oh, gloriously she did) it was for another's sake. The earth and stars and sun, all that was or will be, existed for his sake. And he was coming. The most dreadful, the most beautiful, the only dread and beauty there is, was coming. The pillars on the far side of the pool flushed with his approach. I cast down my eyes.

Two figures, reflections, their feet to Psyche's feet and mine, stood head downward in the water. But whose were they? Two Psyches, the one clothed, the other naked? Yes, both Psyches, both beautiful (if that mattered now) beyond all imagining, yet not exactly the same.

'You also are Psyche,' came a great voice. I looked up then, and it's strange that I dared. But I saw no god, no pillared court. I was in the palace gardens, my foolish book in my hand. The vision to the eye had, I think, faded one moment before the oracle to the ear. For the words were still sounding.

That was four days ago. They found me lying on the grass, and I had no speech for many hours. The old body will not stand many more such seeings; perhaps (but who can tell?) the soul will not need them. I have got the truth out of Arnom; he thinks I am very near my death now. It's strange he should weep; and my women too. What have I ever done to please them? I ought to have had Daaran here and learned to love him and taught him, if I could, to love them.

I ended my first book with the words *No answer*. I know now, Lord, why you utter no answer. You are yourself the answer. Before your face questions die away. What other answer would suffice? Only words, words; to be led out to battle against other words. Long did I hate you, long did I fear you. I might—

(I, Arnom, priest of Aphrodite, saved this roll and put it in the temple. From the other markings after the word *might*, we think the Queen's head must have fallen forward on them as she died and we cannot read them. This book was all written by Queen Orual of Glome, who was the most wise, just, valiant, fortunate, and merciful of all the princes known in our parts of the world. If any stranger who intends the journey to Greece finds this book let him take it to Greece with him, for that is what she seems mostly to have desired. The Priest who comes after me has it in charge to give up the book to any stranger who will take an oath to bring it into Greece.)